Portrait of India

To Martha,
   With much love and
many happy returns of the day,
         Ved and Lin
         March, 2004

Books by Ved Mehta

PORTRAIT OF

INDIA

BY VED MEHTA

Yale University Press

NEW HAVEN & LONDON

Originally published 1970 by Farrar, Straus and Giroux.
Paperbound edition published 1993 by Yale University Press.

Printed in the United States of America.

Library of Congress Catalog Card Number: 92–83817
International Standard Book Number: 0–300–05538–2

Most of the contents of this book appeared originally in *The New Yorker*.

The paper in this book meets the guidelines for permanence and durability
of the Committee on Production Guidelines for Book Longevity of the
Council on Library Resources.

10 9 8 7 6 5 4 3 2

To

L. K.

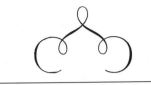

Preface to the Paperbound Edition

IN DECEMBER OF 1965, AT THE AGE OF THIRTY-ONE, I returned to India from my home in New York after an absence of seventeen years—not counting one brief visit in 1959. I spent six months travelling all over the country. My heart was Indian—I had but to speak Punjabi or Hindi, in which I had remained fluent, to feel a tug. Yet my head was Western—all my formal education had been in America and in England. Despite the fact that one out of every six persons in the world was an Indian, that India was the world's most populous democracy, and that it had one of the world's oldest and richest cultures, India had been little studied in the West. The purpose of my visit was to collect material for a general book about India, in the hope of understanding the country of my birth—of explaining it to myself and, in the process, to others.

I crisscrossed the land in airplanes, in trains, in jeeps, in bullock carts, on elephants, on bicycles, and on foot. I had no itinerary or system for my journey, and since, for the most part, I travelled alone, I was free to go anywhere I chose. I was guided only by whom I happened to meet, what caught my interest, what stories were in the news, what appointments or government permissions I was able to obtain. In those days, many troubled areas in the Himalayas were off-limits to tourists and foreign correspondents, but, because I held an Indian passport, had published several books, and happened to know some people in the government, I was eventually allowed to go anywhere I liked—luckily, for without special government arrangements I could not have penetrated the more remote areas. Wherever I was during the day, I talked with everyone: peasants, politicians, and soldiers; engineers, officers, and government planners; priests and maharajas; economists, workers, farmers, teachers, and students; musicians, dancers, and film makers; philosophers and poets. I listened and observed, but, so as not to interfere with the spontaneity of the moment, made no on-the-spot record of my conversations; what I wanted to remember I set down each night—no matter how late it was or how tired I felt.

The following June, I returned to New York with several suitcases full of notes, and for the next three or four years I meditated on my experiences, deepened my impressions by reading, and shaped my material. Employing the journal form, I composed reports on, among other things, India's early experiences with the industrial revolution and the scientific revolution (introducing the spirit of free inquiry into a caste-ridden society), the abortive invasion of India by China, India's war with Pakistan, India's Five-Year Plans, and the abrupt, belated arrival of the twentieth century in India's villages; on Hinduism, Islam, Sikhism; on Calcutta, Bombay, Goa, the Ganges, the Himalayas, the Communist state of Kerala; on the film director Satyajit Ray, Jayaprakash Narayan (the latter-day disciple of Mahatma Gandhi), the Prime Minister Indira Gandhi. My approach was not that of the social scientist, the political economist, the encyclopedist, or the statistician; what I sought to do was to construct an artistic mosaic to suggest the spirit of India. Throughout, my model was the panoramic and poetic accounts of India by British writers of the nineteenth century, who described in minutest detail the land, its climate, its leaders, it rebels, its holy men, and, above all, its common people— their customs, their manners, their beliefs, and their daily concerns and pursuits. What made those accounts memorable was that, though they were set in a particular time and place, they never seemed to date; rather, they had the enduring quality of literature. Seeking to emulate those British authors presented one immediate difficulty, however: they had plenty of leisure in which to collect their impressions and write them down, because they were well off or were stationed in India as government officers. In contrast, I was in New York, was supporting myself entirely by writing, and, as a young writer, was constantly bedevilled by doubts about my abilities. But I had the good fortune to have an association with *The New Yorker* and was blessed with a great editor in William Shawn. Indeed, without his receptivity and encouragement I would not have been able to pay the rent—to say nothing of bringing this project to fruition.

Perhaps in closing I should mention that a few readers who had read my first book, a youthful autobiography, and knew I had been blind since the age of four, and who then read the first edition of this book, were puzzled at how I had managed to write as though I could see. The answer is simply that I wanted no concessions, no quarter for my disability. I was determined to prove that I could write like anyone else, and so strained my four senses to the utmost in the effort to piece together the world of five. I was helped in this endeavor possibly by subconscious visual memories from my early childhood, together with the casual remarks of friends and strangers, and certainly by the fact that I lived and functioned among people who could see and whose talk was full of visual details. I have not felt compelled to explain this in any of my dozen non-autobiographical books, because I feel that such personal information is distracting; it is bound to have the effect of shifting the focus from the subject to the method. My style of reporting in these books is a lifelong experiment, and, although it may have succeeded in that most readers seem to have accepted it, I feel that I myself cannot fully know its outcome until the end of my life. If occasionally I become discouraged with my experiment, I can always seek inspiration in the poetry of Milton when he was blind and the music of Beethoven when he was deaf.

V. M.

New York
January, 1993

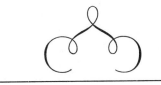

Acknowledgments

I AM MORE GRATEFUL THAN I CAN SAY HERE for the secretarial and editorial help of Rhoda Brandes, Gwyneth Cravens, Ann D. Kindred, and Marcia Knittle over the years in preparing this manuscript for publication. I am also more grateful than I can say to the late William Shawn for his unwavering support.

I wish to thank Aziz Ahmad (Professor of Islamic History and Islam in South Asia, University of Toronto), Sarvepalli Gopal (Reader in South Asian History, Oxford University), Daniel H. H. Ingalls (Professor of Sanskrit and Indian Studies, Harvard University), Stanley Insler (Assistant Professor of Sanskrit, Yale University), Alastair Lamb (Senior Fellow in the Institute of Advanced Studies, Australian National University), and Amartya Sen (Professor of Economics, Delhi School of Economics) for reading portions of this book in proofs. I also wish to thank all the others —far too many to mention here by name—who showed me kindness and courtesy while I was working on this book.

V. M.

New York
October, 1969

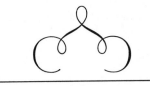

CONTENTS

Contents   [*xv*

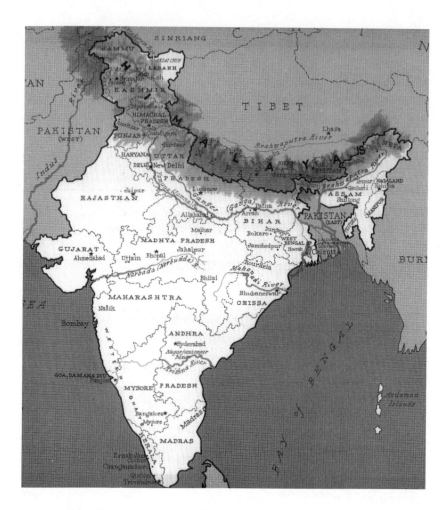

BOOK ONE

I

Forbidden to Come

to the Shore

_____

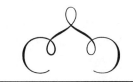

The Guide

TODAY, IN THE COURSE OF A PROLONGED VISIT I am paying to my native country in late 1965 and 1966, I go on a tour of New Delhi. Since I was here last, on another visit, in 1959—I have spent nearly all my adult life in Britain and the United States—the city has fanned out in all directions. Where once there were waste tracts, there are now little self-contained suburbs, each busily searching for an exclusive identity. (There is Defense Colony, Diplomatic Enclave, Golf Links, and one that is called simply Friends' Colony.) An index to the status of the denizens of a particular suburb is the size of their houses, and an index to their snobbery, perhaps, is their system of naming, numbering, and lettering these dwellings—which are, however, no easier to tell apart than the streets. The general plan seems to be to confound the interloper from the next suburb—and, certainly, the stranger to the city, who is additionally burdened with the necessity of remembering English street names from the days of the British raj along with new Indian street names (for instance, King Edward Road, named after Edward VII, has become Maulana Azad Road, named after the late Indian leader), for the two sets of names appear to be used interchangeably. Nor is there any limit to the burgeoning of oppressive suburbs (which now also have English and Indian names; for instance, Diplomatic Enclave is called Chanakya Puri)—the Indian version of the nightmare that is Los Angeles, and with, even for the well-off, nothing more advanced than a bicycle or a tonga or a scooter-driven rickshaw to cover the distances that go with them.

I present myself at nine o'clock at the Imperial Hotel, an embarkation point for city tours. I notice that foreigners, for the most part, head for big private cars with their own private guides, but I wait by two public buses, amid tourists from other parts of India, who show a curiosity about things Indian that would have been inconceivable when I was here last. In the babel of Indian languages, I can distinguish Bengali, Gujarati, Tamil, Telugu, Malayalam, and Kannada; most of my fellow-tourists, I gather, are from south India. I take a seat in the front of the first bus, near the guide, who is an elderly Sikh with a long beard. He is clad in a dingy beige turban, a patched beige tweed coat, loose gray flannels, and brown sandals, with a white drip-dry shirt, which is the only immaculate part of his dress; the shirt is open at the neck, showing a bit of maroon neckcloth. He talks through a microphone over the deafening noise of the bus's motor: "Gentlemen and ladies, I am your friendly guide, and perhaps I ought to begin by giving you a tour of myself."

I brace myself for anything.

He goes on, "Gentlemen and ladies, I have three daughters and they are all well married, thank God. One of my sons-in-law is a successful veterinarian. One of my sons-in-law is a horticulturalist in London, and if you go to London he will be pleased to meet you. One of my sons-in-law, without asking me, applied for the Air Force and was accepted as one of the few; I wanted to encourage him to prospect in Canada or America. I have officiated as a personal secretary to a celebrated maharaja; I still have a telephone, even though I have retired from the maharaja's service."

A voice directly behind me asks, "What do you mean, 'officiated'? "

"Officiating from leave vacancy," the guide says, clarifying little.

A voice, this time from the back of the bus, shouts, "Sirdarji, I cannot hear you! I shall have to write a letter of complaint to the Government of India Tourist Office!" The voice belongs to an old man who is, if anything, more rumpled than the guide. He is obviously ready for a good verbal joust.

But the guide, raising his voice until it almost cracks, says to the bus in general, with perfect good humor, "I suggest, gentlemen and ladies, all of you write letters of complaint to the Government of India Tourist Office. You must state in the letter (a) that the microphone should be more up-to-date and that instead of being placed here in front it should be planted in the middle of the bus, and (b) that the motor should be well oiled, so that you can all hear my words and be rewarded for your pains and money." The roar of the motor diminishes a little as the driver changes gears, and the guide continues, "Gentlemen and ladies, I want you to know that I have done my share of the work well. I went to the classes held by the Government of India Tourist Office. I attended them for two or three months and I qualified with a license. Now I get three or four requests a month to lead bus tours. This trade has been increasing, but it is not so good this year, owing to the war with Pakistan. From nine to twelve-forty-five I give the tour of New Delhi, and from two-fifteen to six I give the tour of Old Delhi, the ancient seat of power on the banks of the sacred river Yamuna. For one day's service, I get twenty-two rupees—four dollars. Other days, I call around at a dozen or so travel agencies here in the hope of finding an American tourist who will want a private guide. But there are more than forty of us licensed, about a dozen of whom are lady guides, and they are the most popular. Some of them are very highly connected—wives of Deputy Secretaries—and they are very good at taking the American tourists to shop, and they get good commissions from the tourists as well as the shopkeepers. Some of the men guides may only be able to get American tourists to send them Terylene shirts from abroad."

The pugnacious old man, who turns out to be a Delhi-wallah, moves up to the front and, pencil and pad of paper in hand, settles himself on the right, practically under the guide's nose. "Get to the business of the day," he says menacingly, writing something on his pad. "The bus has been moving through New Delhi, and I have heard you talk only about your family and—"

"On your right, sir," the guide breaks in smartly, "is the Indian Institute of Technology, which is one of the five such institutes in India; the others are in Bombay, Calcutta, Madras, and Kanpur. It gives education in mechanical, civil . . . The admission here is very difficult; a candidate must be a first divisioner in the intermediate and then take a competition which itself is very difficult. But once you are admitted your future is secure."

Lapsing into his earlier, relaxed manner, the guide goes on, "Gentlemen and ladies, we are now on the first lap of a sightseeing tour of New Delhi. Delhi remains the center of power and culture, a city that offers a stimulant to the present and future, and is always interesting to all mankind. This city has grown beyond recognition during the last few decades, owing to many developments and improvements, and the new colonies are on your either side. Gentlemen and ladies, the population of Delhi was eight hundred thousand, but after Independence Delhi cannot be recognized. Delhi has a checkered and eternal history, like the city of Rome. Bombay, Calcutta, and Madras were not cities five hundred years ago, but Delhi was even then the capital of India, and Bombay, Calcutta, and Madras were only cities of mud. Delhi was also the capital of the Pandya during the Mahabharata days—B.C.—and during the Rajput rule. The Rajputs were a very brave people, always ready to die for a national cause, always ready to die in wars, and their wives burnt themselves alive on the funeral pyres of their husbands. This was known as *sati,* which was banned by Regulation No. 17 of 1829." This fact, right or wrong, brings me up short, for it fits in oddly with the guide's vague, rambling discourse. But then I remember that Indians, who delight in generalities, will often drop in a fact as if the raison d'être of facts were to clinch a vague argument.

The bus stops, and we follow the guide out into the gentle winter sun of Delhi and stand in front of a sort of yard cluttered with large, strangely shaped stone structures painted a bright orange-red, which suggest that Brobdingnagian children have been at work here with Plasticine. "Gentlemen and ladies, here we are at last at Jantar Mantar," the guide says. " 'Jantar' comes from *'yantra,'* which is Sanskrit for 'instruments,' and *'mantar'* is Sanskrit for 'functions'—of astronomy. Jantar Mantar was built by the Maharaja Jai Singh. In the eighteenth century, he ruled the Jaipur state, once known as Amber. Maharaja Jai Singh was a great astrological astronomer of his time." The guide turns to a Brobdingnagian sundial and says, "This measures time by shadows. We can see the time of any part of the world, provided we know the latitude. This is the International Timing Clock. By this International Timing Clock, gentlemen and ladies, we can see time for England, Switzerland, Japan, and the Pacific islands. In Delhi it is now ten hours twelve minutes thirty seconds and one-tenth. All of you may please set right your watches. If the sun is not visible, we have got to keep a pot of sand and watch the sand coming out of it, and then it is called 'sand time.' "

Next, the guide leads us to a circular cavity with markings dividing it into twelve parts, and proclaims, "I can read your whole life from this clock, if you tell me the time, date, and exact longitude of the place of your birth." And he is now an astrologer, collecting from the tourists the places, dates, and hours of their births, and making predictions that are as bright as his disposition.

More cavities, more sundials. Other stone structures, with columns and windows. There is nothing about them that is peculiar to Delhi, but the tourists trail the guide dutifully. Only the Delhi-wallah protests. He complains that the narration is lacking in factual detail. The guide obliges the man—whom I look upon as merely a boring heckler—as best he can, with muddled technical disquisitions. The more abstruse the explanation, the more strongly the guide seems to be impressed by his own words.

At length, the guide says it is getting late, and, indeed, he is noticeably

less expansive on our next two stops—at India Gate, which commemorates
the dead of the First World War, and the Humayun Tomb, which is
encircled by an enormous, geometrically laid-out garden—though he still
manages to be eloquent. ("This Humayun's mausoleum was built by the
widow of the Mogul emperor who lived in the sixteenth century. It is a
precursor to the Taj; I feel it is my duty to tell a little about this mausoleum. It is for a hundred and seventy members of the royal family of
Humayun. So you may also call it the Westminster Abbey of the Mogul
Empire.")

Back in the bus, the guide breathlessly names stores, buildings, and even
stretches of road as we bounce along, and fills in with whatever comments
time allows. He points out the statue of the late Deputy Minister Sardar
Vallabhbhai Patel, the Reserve Bank of India, the Broadcasting House of
All India Radio, the Indian Red Cross, the Ministry of Food and Agriculture, Air Headquarters, Rajpath, the Chelmsford Club, the statue of
George V, the National Stadium, Jaipur House, the Old Fort, the Oberoi
Intercontinental Hotel, the Methodist Church, the Golf Course, Diplomatic Enclave, the Lodhi Gardens, Safdarjung Airport, the All India Institute of Medical Sciences, Safdarjung Hospital. At the next-to-the-last
stop, in front of a seven-hundred-year-old tower of carved red sandstone
and white marble, Qutab Minar, which was built by the Muslims—the
guide calls it a combination of the Tower of Pisa, the Eiffel Tower, and
the Empire State Building—I detach myself from the crowd of tourists
and, welcoming a few minutes of silence, drink a Coca-Cola at the monument's outdoor coffee shop.

I clamber aboard the bus as it is pulling out, and, this time, take a seat
far in the back. I am enchanted with the guide, but the stones of Delhi are
weighing me down, and I look forward to an early release—all the more
when I discover that our last stop is a temple of garish appearance and
recent origin, full of stone idols. The tourists having all dutifully shed
their shoes and gone in, I find myself standing alone out front with the
guide and the pugnacious old man.

"Sirdarji, you know Mr. S. N. Chib?" the old man asks. "He is a friend
of mine."

The guide adjusts his neckcloth under his beard. "He is the director
general of tourism, with the rank of Joint Secretary," he says warily.
"But, of course, I am too lowly in the department for him to know me."

"I have drafted my letter of complaint at your suggestion," the heckler
goes on, obviously enjoying the effect of his words, and, to my horror, he
reads aloud a long letter of accusation, as though, instead of having set

eyes on the guide for the first time this morning, he harbored an ancestral vendetta against him. The heckler charges that the guide has been deceitful, in that he has covered up his lack of knowledge about Delhi with high-flown words; mendacious, in that he has dubbed Qutab Minar "an Empire State Building without lifts;" corrupt, in that he has invited tips from the tourists by calling their attention to the American tourists' custom of showering gifts like drip-dry shirts upon their guides; subversive, in that he has dwelt on a practice like *sati;* and generally smug, supercilious, insulting, and heaven knows what else. At first, the guide tries to interrupt, but as one charge follows another, proclaimed always in a serious, threatening voice, his face takes on a bewildered look, and eventually he drops to his knees, touches the feet of his accuser, and begs for mercy, saying over and over that he has no pension from the maharaja, and the tours are his only source of income.

I am at a loss to understand why this merely boring heckler should have suddenly turned into a threat to the livelihood of the guide, nor can I understand the guide's complete loss of dignity. It is all like a scene out of cheap melodrama, and for a time I find it impossible even to be moved by it. But finally I do convince myself that it is real, and intervene; my pleadings to the heckler take on the abject tone of the guide's, and have no greater effect. A hint of an explanation appears in a remark his accuser makes to me, but this, again, is so bizarre that it is hard to give it any credence. Back in the bus, he sanctimoniously repeats the remark for the benefit of all the tourists. "This guide has been a quack and, from beginning to finish, a charlatan," he says. "I could have overlooked everything else, but I can't ignore his falsehoods about the science of astrology." The accuser, it seems, is a Brahman who fancies himself an astrologer. One or two fellow-tourists who are also Brahmans now mollify him, and by the time we get back to the Imperial Hotel the potential destroyer of our guide's livelihood has become once more—and just as inexplicably—a mere heckler.

"So, gentlemen and ladies," the guide says, having rapidly regained his composure, "this is the end of the first lap of our sightseeing tour. Have a good lunch and rest your minds, and come back at two-fifteen exactly for the second lap of our tour—to Old Delhi."

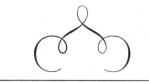

Son et Lumière

TODAY, I TAKE NOTE OF THE ADVERTISEMENTS for the *son et lumière*. It seems that this medium is being used, for the first time in India, to reënact the history of an ancient citadel, the Red Fort of Delhi, just as it is used elsewhere in the world to tell the histories of Hampton Court Palace, Versailles, the Acropolis, and the Pyramids. The *son et lumière* of the Red Fort, which is performed alternately in Hindi and in English, is billed as the cultural event of the year. A friend of my family's who has seen it is, if anything, more enthusiastic than the notices. He says, "Centuries of history are miraculously telescoped, and the spectacle is as accurate in its details as it is thrilling." I find that in saying this he has done no more than echo the program of the event, which he shows me, and which also says, "Unlike an historical play, a *son et lumière* spectacle does not deviate from the facts of history. The scope for dramatic licence is, therefore, considerably limited. This principle has been strictly adhered to in telling the story of the Red Fort."

With high expectations, I take a taxi ride this evening to Old Delhi and the fort's enormous red sandstone wall; then, inside the wall, I stroll through a long, covered market that once sold bangles to Mogul princesses and now sells everything from antiques to Coca-Cola to the public. Next, I walk across a lovely lawn, passing fountains, beds of flowers, and Mogul buildings, and enter the grandstand, becoming a member of a huge crowd, with a view of the harem quarters of the fort, its audience hall, its royal baths, and its Pearl Mosque.

The English performance begins with the sounds of a musical fanfare and hubbub—now of another, recorded crowd—and then come the howls, hoots, and croaks of jackals, owls, and frogs while waves of light play across the walls and domes of the buildings, until the mind begins to reel and the imagination to boggle. A narrator's voice, whose cadences recall Churchillian oratory, takes possession of the audience, ricocheting from loudspeaker to loudspeaker. The contours of the narrative are simple: Once upon a time, there was a wilderness by the bank of the sacred river Yamuna, where we now sit. Shah Jehan, the fifth Mogul emperor, who built the Taj Mahal, chose the wilderness as the site for the Red Fort. The year was 1638. When the fort was completed, its battlements, which were octagonal, rose sixty feet high and measured a mile and a half around. The Palace of Colors, the Hall of Private Audience, the Prayer Room, the Royal Baths (colored lights play over the buildings) were as impressive as the gigantic walls guarding them. Around this fort there came to life the Delhi of the Moguls as the members of the royal household and the seraglio built, within a second, outer wall, their own palaces and mosques— replicas of Shah Jehan's dream in red sandstone. The fort, with its Peacock Throne in the Hall of Private Audience, became "the center of the universe." One of its rooms carries the inscription "If on earth be an Eden of bliss/It is this, it is this, it is this." As emperors came and went—the magnificent Shah Jehan, the fanatical Aurangzeb, the fratricidal and insane Bahadur Shah, the fratricidal and foolish Jahandar Shah, and, still later, a consumptive and a dope addict—the country was racked by wars and religious massacres, and finally it was invaded by Nadir Shah, King of Persia, who, among other things, stripped the fort of its Peacock Throne.

The lurid narrative progresses, to the sounds of bath water splashing, peddlers hawking their wares, women making merry, soldiers shouting, mahouts crying imprecations, swords clanging, flesh ripping, horses neighing, tigers roaring, and throngs cheering—the chronicler consistently dotting his "i"s and crossing his "t"s, and swelling his jabberwocky with little historical playlets. In one, Aurangzeb, the scourge of beauty, shouts, "What impious sounds assault our ears? Chamberlain, go and put a stop to this noise!" His shout interrupts the airy tintinnabulation of dancers' anklets, this being replaced by the piercing ululations of mourners. The emperor, puzzled by the screams, asks, "What means this wailing and lamentation?" He is answered, "Shadow of God, music is dead. We are carrying its corpse for burial." But this only elicits from Aurangzeb the command "Bury it so deep that no sound or cry is again heard from it."

So the *son et lumière,* with its unnerving cacophony of moans and giggles and the rest, turns the fort into an amusement park. One historical explanation follows another, each on the level of "For the want of a nail . . ." But my fellow-spectators, even though they are English-speaking, educated Indians, and mostly middle-aged or elderly, seem completely unaware that, contrary to the promises, dramatic license has done away with the past. The play is a circus, the history is fable, yet it goes down with them as though they were in a university lecture hall listening to an eminent pedagogue.

Then I remember that India turns children into adults very early, thrusting not only upon the poor but also upon the well-off a constant preoccupation with mere subsistence, for the poverty that haunts every corner of the country is, however submerged, an ever-present threat to all. This premature adulthood is one of the saddest things about India, but here, at the cultural event of the year (as so often in my stay), I seem to detect that actual adulthood in India has a compensatory touching innocence about it.

Birth Control

TODAY, EVERY AVAILABLE TREE OR LAMPPOST is abloom with posters proclaiming Family Planning Week. (Since I first left India, in 1949, the population, according to one estimate, has increased by a number almost equal to the present population of the United States.) Most of the posters, which are huge and gaudy, show an expressionless woman doctor holding up an intra-uterine contraceptive device for the benefit of a woman patient, under a caption that counsels "USE LOOP." Press releases elaborate on the theme, and the President of India, Sarvepalli Radhakrishnan, speaks out from a flyer: "With the lowering of infantile mortality, raising of the expectation of life, and the conquest of communicable diseases, there is no need to assume that only half the children will survive. . . . I hope this week will make us think of the meaning of Family Planning." The Prime Minister of India, Lal Bahadur Shastri, speaks from another flyer: "On account of the urgent need to find resources for development of our defenses and industries, and the shortage of food grains, it is essential to control increase in consumption. . . . I send my best wishes for the success of the Family Planning Week."

Family-planning centers everywhere are holding political rallies to promote birth control, and I look in on one of a hundred or so centers in the Delhi district—a one-room shack set in one of the countless slums of the city that are washed by open drains. The rally is heralded by the setting up of a *shamiana,* or cloth canopy, behind the shack and by the monotonous thudding of a drum, but there is no sign of a crowd when I arrive, though it is past the announced time for the rally to begin. In the shack, on a straight-backed metal chair behind a small metal table, a woman in a white cotton sari sits facing the door; behind her is a half curtained-off bed. She is the doctor in charge of the center. Though she has a workmanlike air about her, she is clearly bedevilled by troubles. "Fifteen years, twenty-six billion rupees, and the efforts of three Five-Year Plans have all achieved nothing," she tells me. "Sterilization, we were told, would be the answer, but in the past eleven years we have been able to operate on only a million fathers. There are not enough doctors; even the best surgeons can't do more than a few operations a day. Everything else is in short supply, too. Anyway, villagers associate sterilization with castration, so most of them won't hear of the operation. Now it is the intra-uterine contraceptive device that we are told is the answer. In the past five months—since the program was started, in July—three hundred thousand insertions have been made, at government expense. I have done ninety-two myself. In every case, there has been bleeding. Just today, I have had a total of five patients, and I have had to remove the I.U.C.D.s from three of them, because of the bleeding. In other countries, bleeding has been reported in less than five per cent of the cases."

"How do you explain the discrepancy?" I ask.

"Our women bleed because they are anemic, and they are anemic because they have nothing to eat, and they have nothing to eat because they have too many children. It is a vicious circle. What can be done?" (Later, I discover that another woman doctor, Usha Dey, who is in charge of an urban family-planning clinic in another part of India, regards bleeding as nothing more than a passing occurrence. Reporting in the *Journal of the Indian Medical Association,* she writes that her clinical experience disclosed that bleeding—minor, moderate, or severe—was "the common symptom for which patients sought advice" but that "such symptoms were not serious and were relieved with treatment." She simply advises iron for the anemic patients and says that "heavy doses of vitamins C and K and 'styptovit' often control the bleeding" in others. Of course, the problem of paying for these medicines remains. In any event, Dr. Dey's optimism is not shared by many of her colleagues, who declare that the I.U.C.D. cannot begin to solve India's population problem. They point out that Indian women will not submit to gynecological examinations by male doctors, that there are only ten thousand women doctors in all India, and that of these only one thousand are actively engaged in birth-control work. They point out what the proportions of the problem are: simply in order to reduce the yearly population increase, the government must annually prevent nine million children from being born, and there are now ninety million couples of childbearing age.)

Now the doctor facing me, as though she were a housewife who had just been discussing a laundry list instead of the enormous difficulties of birth control in India, shouts across to a girl who is sweeping the drain in front of the shack, "I gave the time for the rally as eleven o'clock! It's now past noon! Where are all the mothers?"

"They are just coming, Mistress, just coming," the girl replies.

When I follow the doctor out to the yard behind the shack, it is thronged with children, who dodge in under the canopy and out again, as if the rally were just another *tamasha,* or spectacle.

The doctor, all hustle and bustle, shoos them away. Self-appointed barkers appear and form a ring around the canopy. They yell for the mothers to come, and also serve as a cordon against the milling children. The doctor has now cleared a space for some women who are approaching. At last, the drumbeat having become frenetic, the canopied area is filled with women—all with impassive faces, and all given to explosions of coughing—sitting cross-legged on the bare ground with babies in their laps.

The doctor has stationed herself behind a display table set up at one end of the area and flanked by multicolored streamers and by bright posters, with Hindi or Urdu captions, that have the simplicity of Dick-and-Jane books; for instance, there is a poster that shows two hemp *charpoys,* one sagging under the weight of a family of eight, and the other, as taut as a tennis racket, holding a family of four. On the table in front of the doctor are pamphlets, but these are all in English, as if they were intended for the educated inhabitants of a middle-class suburb; their gimmickry, though, is clearly aimed at another public. (One offers the mnemonic aid " 'G'—Go and visit government-sponsored family-planning centers." Another uses what might be called the "if-only-they-could-speak" formula, showing a child who says, "I am one of your five children—how I wish I had remained the second and last child of the family!") But what is most prominent on the table in front of the doctor is a garish display of a plastic torso with detachable parts, which is hedged in by shiny brass trays, some piled with samples of contraceptive devices—including I.U.C.D.s of half a dozen types—and others with model meals offering substitutes for the fruits and meats that contain necessary vitamins and proteins but are beyond the reach of most Indians.

The doctor claps her hands for silence, but she does not say anything. Both she and the crowd remain mute. One of the barkers, practically trumpeting, clears a path, carrying the doctor's metal chair ahead of him.

He is followed by a bespectacled gentleman—an officer of the Health Ministry—who sits down in it, on the doctor's right, and begins speaking immediately. "Sisters," he says, in Hindi, "you know why we are all here. This exhibition has been arranged by my department, which cares for your health, to tell you that there are ways of having small families. I have heard it said that only the poor have many children and the rich have few children. But, sisters, you, too, now, thanks to modern science, can be richer than you are by having fewer children. In recent times, I have also heard the argument that our enemies, Pakistan and China, together have eight hundred million people, while India has only four hundred and eighty million; how can four hundred and eighty million people defeat eight hundred million? This is the numbers argument. But wars, sisters, as you should know, are not won only by numbers of people; they are won also by the number of weapons a nation has, the size of the weapons, the way they are used, and the health of the soldiers. So when you get back to the streets where you live, tell your other sisters that today you went to an exhibition and saw many different ways of having few children, and that it is not necessary to have many children to fight our enemies. Now your doctor will demonstrate different ways to have smaller, happier families."

The officer of the Health Ministry leaves as unexpectedly and hurriedly as he arrived—with the barker trumpeting as before. Evidently, this was one of a series of appearances the officer was making at rallies about the city.

The doctor holds up one contraceptive device after another and describes at some length the advantages and disadvantages of each. Her remarks seem to leave her audience far behind. "If you want a double-check system," she says, "you can do two of thirteen different things." Here she outlines just about all the possible combinations of the various alternative methods, most of them quite unfeasible for the impoverished women, who, however, watch her with awe. At the end, she explains that she realizes that probably the best thing for Indian women is the use of I.U.C.D.s or their husbands' sterilization; it is a matter of principle with her to acquaint them with all the other methods. "We are a democracy," she explains, "and I want you to be aware of all the choices open to you, even if you cannot avail yourself of them."

Now the doctor moves through the crowd, passing the articles around and giving further explanations to the speechless women. While this is going on, I hear strange sounds from the direction of the shack, and, going inside to investigate, discover that a troupe made up of teen-age relatives of the doctor is busy rehearsing a skit called "Happy Home." I am informed that it will wind up the rally, but not for some time, because the officer was only the first of several itinerant politicians and Ministry officials who are expected to put in an appearance. One teen-ager proclaims, his voice breaking as he essays the sonorous tone of a radio announcer, "Yes, thanks to the doctor and what he calls *family planning*. We do not want any more children. We would like to feed, educate, and clothe our children well. Frequent pregnancies are the cause of misery in our village homes."

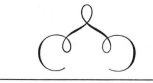

College Girls

TODAY, I CONTINUE MAKING THE ROUNDS of a university that is an air hop from Delhi. I have been spending a few days here, mostly in the company of two delightful girls, Nina and Chuni. As the most fashionable and most widely admired young ladies at their college, they have been asked by a professor to take me in tow. Like many educated Indian girls, Nina and Chuni, who are both Hindus, received their early schooling at convents; the Catholic Church was the pioneer of women's education in India and remains in its vanguard today. The two girls and their friends consider themselves emancipated women and their college a modern institution, every bit the equal of the best men's college of the university, to which the majority of the boys come from private boarding schools that were originally modelled on that substantial Victorian institution the British public school. As it happened, though, this kind of school, in its transplantation to India, went through mutations in which the intellectual part of the cricket-and-classics curriculum became recessive, with the result that a hybrid form of education, at once English and Indian, is now dominant. This means that professors in these modern colleges more often than not read out their lectures sentence by sentence in an English that does no more than meet the unexacting standards of present-day India (to understand a Madrasi or a Maharashtrian lecturing in English, one almost has to know his native Tamil or Marathi), and that the students take down the lectures word for word. Yet perhaps this is as it should be, for now that the British-born teachers have gone home, English is on its way to becoming a native language—or, rather, native languages. (One native language has already been given the name Hinglish. It uses English parts of speech for more complicated functions and Hindi parts of speech for simpler functions, as in this Hinglish sentence: "Dekho great democratic institutions kaise India main develop ho rahi hain," which in English is "See how the great democratic institutions are developing here in India.") In any event, the contemporary *gurus* and *chelas,* or teachers and disciples, give the impression in their classes of running through a dictation session at a secretarial school, mindful only of the spectre of the final examination —as faceless as its markers—waiting to sort the students out, when they leave the university, as if they were eggs of different sizes.

Chuni, Nina, and I are now sitting in a coffee shop near the university, and the girls are looking at the matrimonial advertisements in the Sunday *Hindustan Times,* a leading English-language daily. The advertisements in the *Hindustan Times* are probably the best in the field, and the field is a large one, for such notices appear regularly in most Indian papers and, along with a constant canvassing of relatives and friends, serve as match-makers and marriage brokers for the majority of the young people who live in the cities—the cities being a sort of no man's land between, on the one hand, hundreds and thousands of villages, with their almost pre-destined caste and community marriages, and, on the other, the promised land of titillating Hollywood and Bombay screen romances. In either case, love, as it is portrayed in "Romeo and Juliet," is inconceivable, the romantic tradition of the West being for the most part still alien to India.

"Listen to this," Chuni says, with a giggle. " 'Wanted, Sikh/Hindu match for beautiful Convent educated graduate Sikh girl, 21, daughter of highly placed Class 1 Officer of well connected family. Young men with Public School education from Class 1 Central Services Foreign or highly qualified engineers and covenanted executives with status, family background need correspond. Box 22404-CH. Hindustan Times, New Delhi-1.' Gosh, Nina, she doesn't want to miss by a hair. 'Well-placed match for Hindu, legally divorced virgin girl, aged 27. . . .' How dare *she* advertise? She is ultra-modern if she has had a divorce. And here is a fabulous bachelor, who should at least be modern, with *his* background. 'Medico, Vaish girl for bachelor, running 23, appearing Medical Final, belonging million-aire, educated, reputed Jain family. Father Surgeon. Medical College Professor. . . .' Dash it, even Christians advertise—'Protestant Christian . . . Varsity Lecturer, invites offers from parents of accomplished girls. . . .' And how about this! 'Orthodontia U.S.A., practicing in Canada. Early marriage. Detailed information at first instance.' Dash it, even someone in

Canada!" She puts down the paper in disgust at the very idea of matrimonial advertisements.

Nina picks it up and reads some other advertisements, in an antiphonal response. Both girls speak English with a singsong Punjabi accent, which makes the ads sound like Chaucer read aloud. " 'Match for educated Jat girl, of 19, early marriage. Dowry seekers please excuse. . . .' Poor girl, she probably won't get anyone if she can't afford a dowry. And listen to this: 'Settled bachelor, issueless widower for beautiful, homely W/V in H/H' and 'Matric Khatri Virgin of 28 with bit slow gait, due typhoid. . . .' Poor thing!"

In reply to a question from me, she explains some of the jargon of the matrimonial advertisements. "W/V" is well-versed; "H/H" is household. Other terms, like "matric" (the school-leaving examination) and "homely" (accomplished at housekeeping), I can interpret for myself, just as I can recognize the religions, like Jain, and the castes, like Khatri and Vaish.

"Oh, gosh, here are some really sad cases!" Nina exclaims. " 'Suitable match for Sikh boy, clean shaven with deformity spine. . . .' And 'Suitable match for an Agrawal girl, beautiful. . . . The girl had one extra finger in each hand which have been removed by operation.' "

Chuni seems chastened. Soon, over coffee, she and Nina are talking about how strange it is that in an advancing society like India's the advertisement should still be, for shopkeepers and millionaires alike, one of the common ways of arranging marriages. The girls' views have a modern ring, in keeping with the furnishings of the coffee shop. The chic students congregate here. At first glance, it seems indistinguishable from any coffee bar in London or Paris, for it has a jukebox, several *espresso* machines, and a generally seedy air. However, there are differences. The jukebox plays one sentimental love song after another, all from the cinema—the inexhaustible reservoir of treacle in India. Boys and girls sit at separate tables, in groups of two, three, or four, elaborately ignoring each other or, very occasionally, from the safety of their tables, exchanging remarks about professors and reading.

In the buzz of conversation I catch an occasional "dashed," always in a feminine voice, or "ruddy," always in a masculine—slang that was current in England several generations ago. There are furtive glances at our table, and at one other table that does not follow the pattern of sexual segregation. At that table a couple are sitting. The girl has a pile of books in front of her. She is constantly fidgeting with them, or else patting her hair, while the boy talks earnestly, sometimes with the wistful expression of one recalling his childhood. They have a surreptitious air about them, such as I have noticed in other young couples here, who somehow all give the impression of making their first tryst.

Nina and Chuni, who are just nineteen and are studying for M.A.s, seem happy, and so do the rest of the students in the coffee shop. Everybody is eating, with an air of frank enjoyment, from a plate of potato or of fish or of chicken patties dripping with tomato sauce. Now Chuni begins telling me about "the assault"—a scandal that has set the whole university talking, and especially the M.A. classes, in which girls and boys sit together. Nina, the victim, is for the most part quiet, as though she were still numbed by the incident, which took place almost a month ago.

"It started off with these dashed insulting poems," Chuni says, speaking in a quick, nervous manner. "We used to get hundreds of them, but mostly we threw them out without reading them—"

"I remember one addressed to Chuni," Nina breaks in. " 'Boys call Thy Chuni/Girls name Thy Funny/I call Thee Honey/Won't you give me Any?' "

"And I remember one addressed to *you*," Chuni says sharply. " 'Some used Patton/Some used Gun/If you are one/Forgive me then!—I am?' "

"I don't get that, Chuni," I say.

She explains that the admiring bard is comparing Nina to a Patton tank; since the recent second Indo-Pakistan war, in which the Indians captured many such tanks, given to the Pakistanis by the Americans only for use against the Chinese, "the Patton," thought to be a very modern piece of equipment, has become something of a joke term among the Indians for the "backwoods mentality" of Muslim soldiery.

Both girls are pretty, with dark eyes and long, shiny black braids, and it is bizarre to think of either one of them in connection with forty-five tons of murderous steel. They are dressed, like twin sisters, in orange-trimmed white pajama-style trousers, orange veils, and orange shirts trimmed with sequins and buttoned up to the neck with silver bells—typical Punjabi clothes.

"But, after the poems, Red Flag started writing us letters," Chuni says. "We named him Red Flag because he always wears this revolting red sweater. It has this thick cable stitching. I know one of his letters by heart." And, to my surprise, Chuni actually recites the letter. " 'Hallo both of you,' " she begins, not so much in a student's monotone as in an actress's soulful voice. " 'How was the first one—the Patton? No appreciation. Surprising. I think I defined you two rather well. You are two ultra-modern domesticated creatures of the twentieth century, both basking in the glory of each other's love. Please keep up my confidence in you two. I know you two have a soft corner for me. You think I am crazy! Well, I am not. I think by now you must be curious to know who I am. My name is in the dictionary, anywhere from A to Z. You think it is "Jawahar" [Urdu for "jewel"]. Well, it is not. If you guess my name, I will treat you anywhere to a gala party. So get busy. Ask Sheila to help you. She is very intelligent. We are both alike. I have written my names in this letter in a twisted form. You can't guess them. Please, Sheila, help them. My name is in a name which is not my name. That is all for now. See you again.'"

I smile to myself, and ask the girls, who had in fact known his identity all along, to tell me a little about him. But they are obsessed by his red sweater, which seems to sum him up for them. I can picture him only in the most general terms—reticent, gauche, and possibly desperate.

"What did he actually do?" I ask.

"We girls were standing under a tree, five of us—we usually go in our group—and a group of boys was standing not very far away," Chuni says. "Red Flag was one of the group of boys. Suddenly he walked over to us. He always makes a nuisance of himself like that. He begged to shake Nina's hand. We all, of course, put our hands behind our backs. But he had the *nerve* to reach back and seize Nina's hand and shake it *forcibly* as the boys looked on and clapped. They must have put him up to it with a bet. Nina started crying. I looked daggers at them. Later, when I looked at my hands, there was blood on them. I must have had my fists clenched very tight, I was so mad. And Nina couldn't stop crying."

"Is that all that happened?" I ask. "Is that what you call 'the assault'?"

Both girls appear shocked at the question. They still seem so affected by the incident that, ridiculous though it is in itself, I find I am feeling sympathy for them.

"Have you made your peace with him now?" I ask.

"Certainly not!" Chuni says. "We complained to Dr. Lal, our favorite professor, and he made Red Flag apologize to us in front of the whole class; he didn't want to, but Dr. Lal forced him to. But Red Flag still hasn't learned his lesson. Just today, we have got another anonymous letter, and we are sure that it's from him. I have a good mind to turn this one over to Dr. Lal."

Chuni passes me a long letter. I read it over, and I am charmed by its touching innocence, by its special Indian English. "Lovely Friends," the salutation reads. And what follows is in the same ingenuous vein:

It is really very sad that, due to certain unfortunate and involuntary circumstances, a wide gulf of misunderstanding has cropped up amongst you two and me. Maybe we are ourselves to be blamed for it all. Anyhow, let me not go into full details in this letter.

I also feel, on my part, that my behavior has at times been most unreasonable and unjustifiable—it may look so, to you—but I haste to assure you, dear ladies, especially Miss Nina in particular, that I have slapped back sharply, only when I was provoked in the most blatant manner.

The best thing for us all to do will be not to dig up old memories, even if we all live by memories alone, and forget the malice and start a friendship based on the fairest of all ideals.

Please take care to note that this letter is neither a letter begging your pardon nor flattering you at the same time. It is a letter bringing to you my warm hand of great expectations.

As to signify your rising to my expectations, please put on a white dress—from Dupatta [Urdu for "veil"] to shoes—all white—on Friday, 29th of this month. If in case it is not sunny on that day, then I expect you to put on the dress of peace on the next sunny day.

I am posting this letter with a lovely hope, which is, that "a woman is like a reed, it bends to every breeze but the tempest breaks it not."

I beg to remain Yours Forever, the one you know so well, or the one you know as GUMNAAM [Urdu for "nameless"].

P.S. If your answer is in affirmative, I would like to contact you there in the campus, but for the sake of man and God, remain aloof for a few days, after the day of peace—till I meet you—from your group of Five Girls. I am, in fact, a bit shy by nature or perhaps it is something else, I don't know what.

So long then, with many best wishes, The Same Unchangeable ME.

"But the letter is well meant," I say. I am astonished that Chuni and Nina regard it as another insult.

"Rubbish," Chuni says. "You don't understand."

"After all, he only shook your hand, Nina."

"He touched me," Nina says.

"He touched her *forcibly!*" Chuni adds.

"Will you ever make peace with him?" I ask.

"Never," Chuni says.

In the few days I have spent in the company of Chuni and Nina, I have come to like them very much. They have an overwhelming disposition for affection; spontaneous in everything, they are always either scornful or adulatory; they never have any doubt about what is right and what is wrong; and once they have made up their minds they are immovable. So, after a halfhearted attempt to plead the cause of the boy whose poems and letters have been so disdainfully spurned, I give up.

Around us in the coffee shop, the students are still eating and the mixed couple are still talking. Then both talking and eating nearly come to a stop as the jukebox plays the first few bars of a particularly melancholy song. I recognize it as being from a picture called "Zeenat" (Urdu for "decoration"), which I went to as a child of eleven. At that time, the picture was wildly popular in India. No one, young or old, could sit through it with dry eyes, and practically everyone sobbed when the heroine—played by Nur Jehan, the most passionately adored actress in India at the time—sang this song. The reaction to Nur Jehan's singing is not very different today, I notice as she moans, on the record:

> "Nightingales don't cry here,
> Overflowing tears are forbidden here.
> Even you, the prisoners of these cages, are forbidden to wail here.
> I am the cry whose listener is dead;
> I am that tear, forbidden to fall even into a veil.
> I am left in the middle of the storm,
> And the boatman has gone, saying,
> 'Drown yourself in the whirlpool;
> You are forbidden to come to the shore.' "

When, at the end of the song, I say goodbye to the two girls, kohl-tinged tears have gathered in their eyes.

Native Wood-Notes

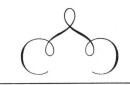

All India Radio Music Festival

WILLARD RHODES, DIRECTOR OF THE Center for Studies in Ethnomusicology at Columbia University, who is at present spending a sabbatical year in Madras studying Indian classical music, said recently, in a lecture, "Music is . . . as universal as language, and there are as many musics as languages. . . . The Westerner is ofttimes perplexed by the strangeness of Oriental music, and the Asian is apt to have difficulty in understanding the music of the West. An unprejudiced ear, a receptive mind, and a little knowledge will go a long way toward the understanding and enjoyment of a foreign musical culture. If people can be bilingual and multilingual, they can be bimusical and multimusical." I consider myself multimusical. While I was growing up, in India, I spent many years learning classical Indian music, with a view to taking it up as a vocation, and later, in the United States, I studied a little violin, accordion, and piano. In any case, I feel completely at ease with the music that Narayana Menon is now picking out on his *vina*. I also feel a little nostalgic, reminded of the summer of 1959, when the poet Dom Moraes and I first met Narayana, here in Delhi, and found his home a refuge from the lacerating world outside. In "Gone Away," a book in which Moraes told about some of our travels together in India, he recounted:

Narayana Menon lives in a cool second-floor flat with a . . . drawing room . . . the walls palisaded with paintings by modern Indian painters. He waved his long hand toward one and said in his light and gentle voice: "Do you like that? Hussein's latest. He painted it only the other day. I think it's good, don't you? Come and sit down. . . ." The servant brought in gin-and-limes, and a pretty little girl came in behind him. "My daughter, Mala," Narayana said, and his face grew gentler than ever. . . . "She likes to hear me practice. . . ." We said, "Why don't you? We'd love to hear it."

"Would you really?" Narayana smiled. "Mala, fetch the *vina.*" Narayana twiddled a few keys, tightening the strings, then bent over the instrument and began to play it. The long, very flexible fingers of his left hand [actually, his right hand] struck the strings slowly, and a long-drawn-out succession of notes, like the calls of a mechanical bird, filled the room. Each faded out and was imperceptibly replaced by another, or overlapped and sung at different ends of the same golden bough.

On this winter day in 1965, as I sit in Narayana's drawing room again, with some of those paintings still about me, I reflect that the intervening years have only mellowed the calls. Mala, now in her teens, is doing her homework in the next room. Twiddling the keys, Narayana talks about our fortuitous meeting the other day, after so many years. We ran into one another at the Paris airport, of all places, while I was on my way to India and Narayana was returning home from an international conference, which he had attended in the capacity of acting director general of the All India Radio. "It had to do with satellites," he explained. "Several of us—leaders in our fields from different countries—were invited to Paris to discuss the problems connected with communications satellites. The day is at hand when you will take your letter to the post office and it will be photostated there and, a minute later, transmitted ten thousand miles by satellite. The airlines have already started to worry for fear that business executives will find it easier to send such instantaneous letters than to travel themselves."

Narayana seemed almost giddy at the prospect of the brave tomorrow, and since I thought of him primarily as a musician, his enthusiasm struck me as a bit bizarre. Now, in Delhi, he talks about the way the bureaucracy is wearing him down; the confirmation of his appointment as director general has become a political issue, because he is a Malayalam-speaking Keralan from the south, the home of the Carnatic system of music, and many north Indians want a Hindi-speaking northerner who is familiar with the Hindustani system of music—the two systems being the two branches of Indian classical music. Narayana says he wishes to escape from India and settle down in London or New York. At the moment, however, he is grateful for the refuge provided by the All India Radio Sangeet Sammelan, or music festival, which he has organized and has invited me to attend.

"A full week of planned concerts, and the President of India will open it!" Narayana says, again speaking with enthusiasm. "Bismillah Khan and Manik Varma and Ali Akbar Khan and Kumar Gandharva and Begum Akhtar and Bhimsen Joshi will all be performing. The program is not as good as some programs we have had in the past—I wish we had Vilayat Khan on the *sitar*—but it's still splendid for the money available. We have got, playing the *sarod,* Ali Akbar Khan, whom I personally consider the finest Indian musician performing today. In sheer depth and musical feeling I would put him above Ravi Shankar. And Bismillah Khan is the outstanding exponent of the *shahnai,* which he has converted from a band instrument into a highly refined and sensitive chamber-music instrument. He's one of the half-dozen musicians in India who are most in demand and get the highest fees. Kumar Gandharva is an extraordinary character. He had a meteoric rise as a musician. By the age of fifteen or sixteen, he was established as one of the more impressive bright young singers. Though he is a classicist, he is also very much of an innovator—the orthodox would say too much of an innovator. Begum Akhtar sings that light-classical form of love lyric, the *thumri,* with wonderful elegance and charm. Though she may have passed her peak as a singer, she, too, is an extraordinary character. As the wife of a barrister of Lucknow, she is a tremendously energetic society lady. Manik Varma is a good singer, although not easy to enjoy the first time you hear her, because she does go on a bit long. If I take Mala, she says, 'Daddy, let's go out and have a Coca-Cola now.' Incidentally, how about having a whiskey on the rocks? Everyone drowns whiskey here, and in summer I like it drowned myself, but in this cold weather I like to taste my whiskey."

I accept.

The Sangeet Sammelan concerts are held in a broadcasting-studio auditorium amid the paraphernalia necessary for live broadcasting, and most of them are of Hindustani music, which is said to derive from the Vedic chants written over three thousand years ago; so closely does it resemble this ancient form, in fact, that in the view of some musicians the two are fundamentally alike. The Hindustani system of music, which does not employ harmony or counterpoint, is built around some thousands of *ragas,* or melodic scale patterns, each *raga* having its own particular traditional combination of notes—chosen from among the twelve possible tones of the octave, with the tonic and sometimes the dominant fixed—and each *raga* being based upon one of seventy-two *melas,* generic scale patterns that have their own ascending and descending structures. Each *raga* has its own texture and character, and, because it celebrates either a time of day or a season of the year or a specific occasion, is essentially atmospheric. There is practically no notation, and everything is left to the ability to improvise imaginatively—to wring new combinations from the given structure of the *raga*. A typical *raga* played on an instrument—a *sarod* or a *sitar*, perhaps— has two or three distinct phases. It may open with a slow, exploratory invocation (*alap*), which gives way to a melodic variation together with a rhythmic passage (*jor*), which, in turn, moves into a rapid flourish of runs (*jhala*). But this may be only an introduction to the second phase (*gath*), which is governed by one of a hundred and seventy-five *talas*, or rhythmic cycles; these range from units of three to units of two hundred and sixty-one beats, or pulsations, in various traditional combinations of stressed and unstressed beats. Since the *talas* and beats are a matter of tradition, there is considerable difference of opinion on their numbers, one authority maintaining that there are three hundred and sixty *talas*, which range from units of three to units of a hundred and eight beats. In any case, the musicians tend to use the same few *talas* again and again. The *talas* are drummed out on a pair of *tablas*, or hand drums, in accompaniment to the instrument during the *gath* and the *jor*, so that alongside the melodic structure is established another, rhythmic structure. Tensions between the melodic instrument and the rhythmic instrument develop and increase, the two being held together only by the coincidence of the fixed notes of the *raga* and the principal stresses of the *tala* as runs, variations, and recapitulations build up in a crescendo.

The festival concerts are likely to begin at the awkward hour of 6:30 P.M. and last only an hour and a half, which includes an interval, and, besides being tantalizingly brief, they are uneven. But I attend them all, for the music and the musicians create in my imagination the atmosphere of some elfin royal court, recalling my childhood as nothing else can.

At the first concert, Bismillah Khan, a man of about fifty, wearing one earring and a neat little mustache, presides, with his *shahnai*—an instrument resembling an oboe—over a troupe of half a dozen. The *shahnai* that takes possession of the auditorium is as shrill and piercing as a child's pipe, but its wailing, nasal sound is somehow transformed into music by Bismillah Khan's playing. As he plays, another *shahnai* serves as a drone, a couple more start echoing and answering Bismillah Khan's phrases, and, throughout, a drummer, working in deep concentration, flicks, raps, and cuffs the *tablas* in a rapid pitter-patter. Bismillah Khan settles down to a progression of lilting runs—singling out a phrase, toying with it, embellishing it—and the listeners, who are mostly government officers and their wives invited to the concerts as guests, nod gently and tap their feet lightly on the floor. Bismillah Khan now holds a note on the *shahnai* for a pain-fully long time, and the listeners hold their breath in sympathy until the note trails off into a barely audible squeak. Then, having taken a long breath, Bismillah Khan suddenly fills the hall with a burst of thin bagpipe-like notes, and the hall explodes with cheers: *"Wahwah!"* and *"Bohut acche!"*

Another day, Ali Akbar Khan takes the stage, and he sets me to think-ing about how well the *sarod* would do for jazz. The instrument consists of an unfretted metal bar with about a score of strings, some constantly resonating in the background, some serving as percussive drones, and some tuned to the tones of the *raga* to be played. Its muted twang can be compared to the sound of a banjo, but in the hands of Ali Akbar Khan the *sarod* is as expressive as a complete jazz combo. Whether Ali Akbar Khan tunes the instrument—as he often does—in the middle of a *raga,* or snaps a string, or suddenly launches into what sounds like the refrain of "Lemon Tree," or clicks his nails against the bar as his left hand moves swiftly up and down, or subdues his playing in deference to the stir caused by a distinguished late arrival, all is somehow gathered into the accommodat-ing *raga,* which he plays much of the time in an almost impenetrable trance, his eyes closed.

The concerts of Manik Varma and Begum Akhtar send my thoughts in a different direction. (Begum Akhtar sits on the floor of the stage, decked out in emeralds and diamonds—including a nose ring—and with a green shawl to match the emeralds thrown carelessly about her shoulders. She sings love lyrics with abandon, a coquettish smile on her lined face, sending the audience, young and old, into raptures.) They start a multi-musical discussion in my head about the limitation that Indian singers have imposed on themselves from ancient times by singing mostly from the throat, and often closing off the enormous range of chest tones and head tones, so that their voices have the light quality of childhood. It is clear, though, that this in no way disturbs the enjoyment of the listeners, who exuberantly nod to the rhythm until they seem to be physically con-trolled by the performer. Their musical experience, limited to unharmo-nized melodies, is more akin to that of medieval Christian monks, limited to plainsong, than to that of a modern Western audience, whose apprecia-tion encompasses the vast body of complex music that includes Monte-verdi, Wagner, and Webern. The music reviews published in the Indian newspapers seem appropriately pre-Baconian. One, in the English-language *Times of India,* is headlined "UNFORGETTABLE RECITAL BY K. GANDHARVA," with the by-line "By Our Music Critic," and reads, in part:

A figure of despair in a dark dungeon with not a ray of hope from any quarter, wailing and whimpering—this image seemed to dance in many a tearful eye as Kumar Gandharva sang. . . . Kumar Gandharva is among the most imaginative musicians, ignited by a divine spark. . . . The artiste [the plain word "artist" is seldom used in India] has carved out a style, an utterance of his own—a style consisting of short and pithy phrases which become an ideal vehicle to convey the pain and privation of his heart. The pithy utterance, coming out with a vocal outburst, acts like a dagger dealing a deep stab at every step. In the slow movement . . . for how long did he suspend the use of an ornamental flourish which came at last like rain on parched, unslaked earth? How many in the audience averred their appreciation? There was not a syllable not suffused with the deepest emotion. To this was added the soft muffled beauty of his voice and a clean and incisive attack on the intonations.

But saying that the music of Bismillah Khan, Ali Akbar Khan, and the rest is uncultivated may be rather like Milton's saying "If . . . sweetest Shakespeare, Fancy's child,/Warble his native wood-notes wild." In some ways, the music appears wholly contemporary. Sometimes the absence of a determinable key makes it resemble that of the atonal school. At other times, the engrossing inventiveness, the vast room for improvisation, variation, and embellishment, makes it seem akin to jazz—not all jazz but some. Moreover, many of the instruments, which at first may grate on Western ears, open up a new world of sound, in which the seeming dissolution of half tones into quarter tones, eighth tones, and so on—the result of endless elisions—endows the squeaks, peeps, drones, and twangs with unexpected lyrical qualities. The very delicacy of their music commands attention. Similarly, the vocalists, given their laryngeal limitations, perform marvels. By the end of the series of concerts, therefore, I find myself sharing in the exuberant enjoyment of the listeners around me.

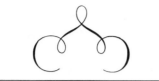

The Two Systems
and Subbulakshmi's Voice

MOSTLY, SUBBULAKSHMI SINGS the Carnatic music of the south, yet she thrills audiences brought up on the Hindustani system of the north, to whom her music is, as it were, Greek. Although the Carnatic system shares *ragas* and *talas,* and its origins and basic concepts, with the Hindustani system, and also has no harmony, the systems have developed in regional isolation over so many centuries that some practitioners have not been aware of the common ancestry of the two, and this is still true, despite the fact that some of the minor distinctions between them—for instance, the difference in instruments, such as the use of the *mridangam,* a single barrel-shaped drum, in the Carnatic system instead of the *tablas* of the Hindustani system; the varying degrees of emphasis of instrument and voice in the two systems; and the use of two different names for the same *raga,* or, conversely, the use of the same name for two different *ragas*— have lately been melting under the heat of nationalism. The reason the practitioners of the two systems at times still appear hostile, like nationals of warring countries, is that the systems do, in a sense, differ in fundamentals. Carnatic music, because it has some notation and a body of compositions—a succession of pupils having noted down the performances of their masters—is likely to be intricate, rigid, mathematical, and intellectual, whereas Hindustani music is likely to be simple, flexible, charming, and elegant. The voice of Subbulakshmi is the closest thing to an Indian lingua franca. The music she sings is not easy for the uninitiated to comprehend, yet the Indian populace, which as a rule enjoys only sentimental love songs, is overcome by her performances, especially when her songs are devotional—and they generally are. Narayana Menon, who, like many other enthusiastic Indians, tries to enhance home-grown talent with the magic of foreign associations, has written, "Subbulakshmi's reputation today is not unlike Galli-Curci's or Melba's. . . . More aptly, her following can be compared with that of Om Kulsum's in the Middle East. Neither has a world reputation like Pablo Casals or Yehudi Menuhin, but in their own spheres both have left perhaps stronger imprints. And the spheres are by no means constricted geographically or in terms of population."

Today, I am in Madras—an open, neatly laid-out city on the Bay of Bengal—in the house of Subbulakshmi, which breathes an atmosphere of politics, journalism, and, above all, religion. It is evening, and I am talking with Subbulakshmi's husband, T. Sadasivam—renowned as her "guide, philosopher, and friend"—in his offices, which take up the ground floor of the house. He is a tall man, wearing a *dhoti,* a *kurta,* or loose shirt, and eyeglasses. In the manner of orthodox Hindus, his head is shaven except for a *bodi*—a tuft of hair at the back of the head. And, in the manner of the ultra-orthodox, his forehead is smeared with even stripes of white ash. He tells me that his wife helped to found his periodicals—the popular weekly *Kalki,* in Tamil, and the weekly *Swarajya,* in English—both of which today specialize in advancing the fighting views of C. Rajagopalacharya, who was once a leader of the ruling Congress Party but is now the tutelary of the anti-Congress, rightist Swatantra Party. After our talk, Sadasivam takes me up a wooden staircase, which leads to a huge veranda and a crowd of people. He introduces to me a woman in her thirties named Radha, who is his daughter by a previous marriage; Mr. K. S. Narayanaswami, a *vina* player; Mr. V. V. Subramaniam, a violinist; Mr. T. K. Murti, a *mridangam* player; a dozen other people, identified simply as family members; and, finally, Subbulakshmi. She stands in the background, with her hands pressed together in the Hindu greeting. She is petite and plump, with almond eyes and a cupid's-bow mouth that breaks easily into a smile. Her hair is drawn tightly back into a chignon surrounded by flowers. Besides diamond earrings, she has a diamond on either nostril, in the fashion of a south Indian lady of means. She is dressed in a dazzling, luxurious sari of heavy green silk shot through with purple and bordered in black and gold, but she shows no signs of discomfort, though the heat is suffocating. (It is said that autumn, winter, and spring in Madras are hot and summer is hotter still, but, whatever the season, the ladies of means here wear the same heavy silks.)

All of us follow Sadasivam in a sort of procession into a living room with pink walls, on which hang several pictures showing Subbulakshmi and Sadasivam with other famous people. Sadasivam gives a signal, and everyone sits down on green straw matting on the floor facing Sadasivam, who himself sits on a divan, asking me to sit beside him. "Our Carnatic music is old," he says to me, in the manner of one beginning a lecture. The musicians are tuning their instruments and warming up with little runs and snatches of *ragas*. Subbulakshmi and Radha—who is also wearing a chignon with flowers and a silk sari with a black-and-gold border—quietly arrange themselves on the floor, as if in a tableau. "We owe most of our Carnatic music to three great composers—Tyagaraja, Muthuswami Dikshitar, and Syama Sastri," Sadasivam goes on. "They were all three contemporaries of Beethoven, and they were all born in Tiruvarur, a village in Tanjore, but Dikshitar composed almost all his songs in Sanskrit and Tyagaraja and Sastri composed theirs in Telugu. These composers are known as the trinity of Carnatic music." As if in that household private concerts were a daily occurrence, Sadasivam reels off a program of songs for Subbulakshmi to sing. Every one of them is religious. He tells her to start with a hymn in praise of the goddess Kamakshi, to go on to hymns addressed to Shiva and to Vishnu and his incarnation, Lord Krishna, and to conclude with a couple of hymns from "Meera." In one period of her life, Subbulakshmi acted and sang in a number of Indian films, the most successful of which, perhaps, was "Meera." For a serious religious film—it was built around the life of Princess Meera, who was a saintly poetess and a love of Lord Krishna—it became extraordinarily well known throughout India.

The drummer and the violinist leave off their exercises, and then the *vina* player also falls silent, and Subbulakshmi, without so much as clearing her throat, starts to sing. Her voice, easy, with a fine resonance, has the hypnotic quality of the Pied Piper's flute, or of the *shahnai,* and the violinist, the *vina* player, and the drummer, when they begin playing, seem to follow slightly behind her, note by note, rather than to accompany her. Radha sings along with Subbulakshmi, also note by note. (Traditionally, in Carnatic music, a star pupil learns by imitating his teacher, in concerts as well as in practice sessions.) Sometimes Radha's singing clouds the voice of Subbulakshmi, making her sound as if she were singing with tissue paper over her mouth. At other times, the supporting voice serves as a sounding board for Subbulakshmi's stronger one, and one forgets that she is being accompanied. The words of Subbulakshmi's songs are always simple. What gives the singing its power is the cadenzas, each more intricate than the last. As she sings, almost in *samadhi,* or trance, she taps the floor in front of her with her left hand.

When Subbulakshmi begins singing the hymns from "Meera," everyone in the room seems to be caught up in her *samadhi,* and the sweetness of the hymns makes me remember the remarks of a critic who, in a spoken introduction on the sound track of the film, said, "The story of Meera is the story of India, the story of Indian faith, devotion, and ecstasy. Meera . . . has no equal—no sequel, rather—in any part of the world . . . [though] Santa Theresa, Saint`Cecilia were great lovers of the mystic and had communion with Christ. . . . I am sure that whoever hears this wonderful voice [of Subbulakshmi], whoever comes under the enchantment of her great gifts, will agree with me that she is not an interpreter of Meera but Meera herself."

Subbulakshmi finishes the hymns.

"Now the encore," Sadasivam says, breaking the spell. And Subbulakshmi at once resumes singing. This time, it is "Shambu Mahadev": "O Lord, whatever sins I may have committed, either by word of mouth or by thought or by act, let me take the blame for them."

"This is a *raga* with the peaceful atmosphere of the dawn," Sadasivam whispers to me. "She sang it recently at the Edinburgh Festival, and the man in the next seat said to me, 'Her song makes me feel I am melting away into nothingness.' "

"O Lord, whatever sins I may have committed, either by word of mouth or by thought or by act, let me take the blame for them," Subbulakshmi repeats again and again.

After the private concert, Sadasivam ushers us all into a large dining room, with paintings of Hindu deities and princely personages looking down on high-backed carved chairs and a long table set with brass bowls and banana leaves. The charm of the room is heightened by a swing, made of polished wood, and larger than a bed, that hangs from strong metal cords off to one side. Sadasivam stands at the head of the table, and Subbulakshmi goes to the foot. The rest of us line up along its sides as Sadasivam directs. As soon as we take our seats, servants start heaping the banana leaves and brass bowls with one kind of food after another, mostly combinations of rice, curd, and lentils with *ghi,* or clarified butter, spices, and coconut chutneys. Each dish has its own name. I count nineteen names and then give up as my banana leaf continues to be heaped with new foods, until it almost overflows. Everyone eats, and what little conversation there is has to do with the food.

By and by, though, I try to draw Subbulakshmi out on the subject of her training as a musician and her life before her marriage to Sadasivam (all such facts about her have been obscured by myth), but she seems to have left matters of this sort far behind. She lets Sadasivam do all the talking, even though he is at the opposite end of the table. She appears happiest when he talks about their life together and their religious devotion.

"Subbulakshmi has a very simple nature," Sadasivam says, his voice filling the room. "There is nothing in the world for her except her music and her devotion to God. I first saw her in 1933, at the All India Spinners' Exhibition. We were married in 1940. Subbulakshmi, who has since given hundreds of concerts for charity, began her charity at home. She has absolutely no conception of money, but when I decided to start a paper, she helped me by making films. With the money from one picture, I was able to start *Kalki*. In 1954, when Subbulakshmi was awarded the title Padma Bhushan, at a public gathering, she became tearful and said, 'How am I to deserve all this honor?' Then she somehow got the courage to speak up, and she said, 'My husband has been advising me throughout my career. He is my *guru,* so all the honor must go to him.' That is Subbulakshmi. She is a good Hindu wife. Now her mind is removed from all mundane things; she has given up everything for a life of religion, because in 1956 she had the great good fortune to meet the holy *jagadguru* [universal teacher] Sankaracharya, of Sri Kanchi Kamakoti Peetam, in Kanchipuram, on a propitious day. Kanchipuram is where the first *jagadguru*— some say he lived three hundred years ago, some say twelve hundred—became one with the Lord. Subbulakshmi had a weak back, but she wouldn't wear a brace. The doctors couldn't cure her, but our *jagadguru* cured her, with sacred ash. Since Subbulakshmi met the *jagadguru,* she has been going to Kanchipuram every year to sing for twelve hours during the Durgapuja. And she spends a great deal of her time in the *puja* [Sanskrit for "worship"] room in this house."

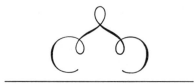

Pupil

I DECIDE TO ASCEND TO THE MUSICAL HEIGHTS by seeking out the legendary, versatile Alauddin Khan, who is known simply as Baba (Urdu for "old man"). He is Hindustani music's unrivalled *ustad* (Urdu for "master"). Actually, *"ustad"* is a sort of Muslim counterpart of *"guru,"* and since Baba, unlike *ustads* traditionally, has had many Hindu pupils, he is considered to be both *ustad* and *guru*. Ustad Alauddin Khan—Khan is a common Muslim name—has not only taught but adopted, along with a few pupils of promise, many students with no talent at all, because, orphaned or unwanted, they were desperate for some means of subsistence. He has tried to give them a trade that could also offer them solace, though many of his fellow-musicians feel he has set himself the thankless task of extracting, as they say, "music from stones." He has made his real son Ali Akbar Khan his heir apparent by revealing to him all the secrets of the art (even today the techniques of music are passed down only by word of mouth, as they have been for centuries), and has further insured the continuation of the musical dynasty by marrying one of his real daughters to another of his pupils, Ravi Shankar. On different occasions, I talk with both the heirs about Baba. They give confused and somewhat conflicting versions of his life, but they agree that, except for Baba himself, His Highness Maharaja Sir Brijnath Singh Ju Deo Bahadur, K.C.I.E., is the best authority on it. He was Baba's first *chela*—or, rather, *shagird* (Urdu for "pupil"), *"shagird"* being a sort of Muslim counterpart of *"chela"*—and for much of his life has been Baba's patron. As Maharaja of Maihar, one of the some six hundred autonomous princely states that were integrated into India after Independence, he once wrote about his master:

No lover of music is unfamiliar with Baba, whose lifelong devotion to music and whose perseverance—a veritable penance—in enriching it add a glorious chapter to the history of Indian music. . . . I, his first student and the recipient of many an act of kindness and love, have also enjoyed the privilege of being consulted by him on many personal matters. . . . It is our devout wish and prayer that to Ustad Alauddin Khan, who is not only a truly great musician but, with his simple way of life, a virtual saint, and his wife, who is one of the finest examples of a dutiful, devoted wife, and highly respected for her nobility and grace, may be granted the complete span (a hundred and twenty years) of healthful life.

The Maharaja, who is seventy, has, since the loss of Maihar, lived a retired life about a hundred miles away in the town of Jabalpur—both are in the state of Madhya Pradesh—and, having been asked to lunch, I am today waiting on the veranda of his house. A slim, sprightly man of medium height, dressed in a gray suit and looking no more than middle-aged, strolls up the drive with a newspaper under his arm, followed at a discreet distance by a couple of servants, and they by a car. He is the Maharaja, returning from a preprandial constitutional. He greets me like an old friend and takes me into a large drawing room containing ornate pieces of furniture, a big picture almost hidden by ropes of marigolds—His Highness identifies this as a picture of Baba—and many smaller pictures, which make up a sort of family album on the walls. Every now and then, a dozen or more children dressed up in bright-colored clothes dart in and out of the room, shrieking with laughter. The Maharaja ignores the children, and, as we sit on a capacious sofa, says, with a deep laugh, "The man in that picture of a tiger shoot over there is me. I did a lot of shooting in my day. My total score must be over two hundred tigers." From an adjacent room come sounds of women fervently chanting prayers and singing hymns in chorus. The prayers are accompanied by the ringing of bells and the clanking of fire tongs and the clashing of cymbals, and also by the sputtering and crackling of *ghi* and incense thrown on a fire—all of it sending into the drawing room aromas and reverberations such as have been associated time out of mind with Hindus worshipping around a brazier. *"Om jai jagdish hare,"* the women intone. The idea of such prayers in the middle of the day anywhere except at a temple seems strange to me, and I say as much to my host. "I like to live my life—pass the day—to the sound of prayers," he explains affably. "The praying goes on from morning to night. All the women in the house pray, for at least an hour at a time."

Throughout lunch, which is served to us at a table in the drawing room, and which consists of fried fish, *tanduri* chicken, and pea pilaf, the Maharaja talks serenely over the bedlam. He dwells on the sad times on which he has fallen, mentioning the burden of supporting upward of forty members of his immediate family, and also his servants, who are equally numerous; the difficulty that his older children, brought up in the palace in Maihar, face in adjusting to their new situation; and other problems associated with the cut in his income. He supplements the privy purse allotted him by the government of India—it is calculated at ten per cent of his former income—with money he receives from two cinemas he now owns in Jabalpur, but he finds his present income inadequate. He is in a reminiscent mood, and I am in no hurry to press him on the subject of Baba. After all, I am sitting with a maharaja, and I am curious about the changes that have been visited upon the dispossessed potentates, who as recently as twenty years ago were absolute rulers, enjoying feudal powers of life and death over their subjects, and who still have their titles in perpetuity; their privy purses; their tax-free lands; immunity, in large measure, from arrest or suit; and the rights to fly their own flags over their residences and cars, to have special armed guards for their residences and special license plates for their cars, to fish and hunt without licenses, to have free medical and telegraphic services, and to have their birthdays celebrated as public holidays. Besides, my host, who often caps his remarks with an apt *shloka*—a verse from Sanskrit scriptures—has a touch of the scholar about him, and is very congenial company, whatever the topic.

"In my time, I was the Secretary to the Chamber of Princes, and I have known practically every maharaja who ruled an Indian state in this century," he says nostalgically. "Under the British, the highest prince got a twenty-one-gun salute, the lowest a nine-gun salute. For some reason, the salute was traditionally an odd number. One of my closest friends got twenty-one guns, but he's no better off today than I am, and I was only an eleven-gun maharaja. We all sleep under our beds instead of on them, and with cotton in our ears, we are so frightened of the government. They are talking about cutting off our privy purses and taking away our rights. I came to Jabalpur because the only alternative I had was to stay with my people and weep. When the British departed, the Viceroy, Lord Mountbatten, said that we maharajas could choose whether or not to join independent India. But did we actually have such a choice? Had any of us not joined, we would have been dealt with as the Nizam of Hyderabad was. When he made trouble about acceding to India, Hyderabad was integrated through a "police action" by Sardar Vallabhbhai Patel, the strong-arm Minister in Nehru's government. V. P. Menon, who helped engineer the accession of the princely states, was a good civil servant—he did what he was told. Toward the end of his life, he came to live here in Jabalpur and I got to know him very well. He said to me that if he could do it over again, he would form a federation consisting of Pakistan, India, and all the princely states, in which each of the three units would have the same weight. He thought that the integration of the princely states into the Indian Union had killed their individual character."

At several points, I think of taking issue with the Maharaja on his rather partisan view of events. Maybe the people of Maihar do regret the departure of their ruler, but I imagine few of them would vote today to reinstate a monarchy. Maybe the kind of federation that the Maharaja speaks of would have been ideal, but could it ever have come about? And, if it had, would it—being made up of, among other things, hundreds of feudal states—have survived long in times like these? But such objections, like some of the questions the Maharaja raises, belong to the "if"s and "can"s of history. In any event, as I listen to him I haven't the heart to tamper with any of his memories or opinions—particularly when he goes on to say, "I am seventy now. I can't have much longer to live. I can't even play polo or go on a *shikar* anymore, because of a bad knee. The world I knew has passed. All the friends I had have either died or been left behind in Maihar. I go to Maihar only twice a year now, to see Baba and to pray at the temple of Sharda Devi. Before I die, I would like to sell my palace in Maihar. Death duties are so heavy that it is better to dispose of it while I'm still alive. The rooms are too vast for it to be converted into a hotel, so I will probably have to sell it to the government. They could perhaps open a military academy there."

After lunch, the Maharaja suggests iced coffee and orders a servant to bring two tumblers of it, with lots of ice. "Incidentally," the Maharaja then says in a booming voice, his earlier sadness giving way to a little rakishness, "I am looking for a wife for one of my sons. I would like him to have a wife so pretty he would never look at another girl. In fact, I want the prettiest girl there is—preferably a Rajasthani girl from Jaisalmer. Those girls have the best complexion and carriage, and are very spirited. If, in your travels, you hear of such a girl, will you let me know? I have arranged for my son to have an income of sixteen thousand rupees a month for the rest of his life." Although I very much doubt whether I will come across a girl who would fit his specifications, I say I will keep his request in mind.

From the adjacent room comes the diminuendo of the closing benediction: *"Om shanti, shanti, shanti. Shan-ti, shan-ti, sha-a-an-ti."* But if this marks the end of one group's devotions and the beginning of another's, the change is scarcely apparent, for the prayers start anew without a pause: *"Om jai jagdish hare."*

"Would you like to hear me sing?" the Maharaja asks, adding, "I have given up singing for palmistry, which I now find all-engrossing. Some time ago, I had a heart attack, and I realized that in old age the voice cannot remain the same."

I am a little mystified, but the Maharaja calls for a record of his singing to be put on a phonograph. A servant obeys immediately. To the general din a loudspeaker now adds, at almost full volume, the lusty voice of the Maharaja singing a hymn in praise of Lord Krishna. The rendition is passionate but blurred, partly because a note-for-note accompaniment by a harmonium threatens to drown out the voice. "The beauty of Indian music is that it expresses the deepest emotions of man and therefore has the power to give him inner tranquillity," the Maharaja says, leaning toward me. "Western music is too chaotic—it only adds to one's tensions and confusion."

When the record ends, I at last raise the subject of Baba, asking the Maharaja what he regards as Baba's most lasting achievement.

"His greatest contribution was the band," he says. "Its history is unique. After the First World War, there was an influenza epidemic, which left many children orphaned in Maihar. I got some *ayahs* for the children, and when the children were a little older, I put them in Baba's care. He started teaching them instrumental music, and made them into a band."

I ask whether he wouldn't rank Baba's own music just as high.

"The heavenly music of Baba I have not encountered in any other musician in the world," the Maharaja says. "He used to accompany the birds on his *sarod* and talk to them with his flute, and you couldn't tell the birds' song from his music."

I am curious to know how a protégé who was a non-princely Bengali Muslim happened to make a *chela* of his patron, a Hindi-speaking Hindu prince. When I ask the Maharaja about that, he says, "I was his *chela* for thirty-five years. Every day from two o'clock in the afternoon on, Baba was at the court teaching music—to Ministers and servants alike. He would stay for dinner, and in the evening he would teach. At the end of the evening, I would give him *pan*, spices, and scents. I gave his children Ali Akbar and Annapurna their names. Annapurna is a Hindu name. As a Hindu, I always wished that Annapurna might marry a Hindu, so when Uday Shankar came to me and asked my permission for Baba to accompany his troupe of Indian actors, dancers, and musicians on a European tour, I gave it on condition that after the tour Ravi Shankar, Uday Shankar's brother, should come to Maihar, become Baba's *chela,* and, in the traditional manner, marry Annapurna."

"How did you and Baba meet?"

"I was in Gwalior in 1918 to celebrate the Maharaja of Gwalior's birthday," he replies. "About eight hundred musicians were in attendance. After we had heard them all perform, Gwalior asked me which of them I liked best. I said I didn't like any of them. He dispatched one of his aides-de-camp as a scout to the great *ustad* Wazir Khan, in the princely state of Rampur. Wazir Khan introduced the A.D.C. to Alauddin Khan, and the A.D.C. brought him to Maihar. At the time, I was celebrating my twenty-first birthday and my receipt of a colonelship from Sandhurst. The British had to work for their colonelships, but we maharajas were given them. Baba played at the celebration, and I was charmed by his sweet hand at the flute. I offered myself to him as a *chela,* and he tied a sacred thread around my wrist. Once, when he was teaching me, he hit me with a book. Then he realized he had struck his own monarch and benefactor, and he fell down at my feet and began to cry. I picked him up and said, 'Baba, after all, you are my *guru.'*"

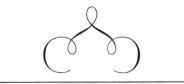

Master

Nowadays, I have been told, Alauddin Khan makes no appointments but simply welcomes friends and strangers alike at his cottage in Maihar in the late mornings and late afternoons. All the same, it is with trepidation that today, late in the morning, I go unannounced to his cottage, which is known as the House of Peace. I feel that the designation could easily apply to the whole of Maihar—a drowsy place that seems isolated by its three surrounding hills, for the inroads of modern civilization amount to hardly more than a few bicycle rickshaws. On one of the hills is perched a diminutive shrine to Sharda Devi, who is renowned among the neighboring villages for her healing powers. At the gate of the cottage, I am greeted by an elderly man who looks very much like a little white bear. He has bright eyes, a full face, and a white mustache and goatee. With a *kurta* he wears a sort of sarong—both are ash-colored—and an ash-colored cap and tennis shoes. This is Baba.

I introduce myself, and immediately Baba takes me by the shoulder and begins showing me around his cottage. There is a small garden planted with roses, rhododendrons, and queen of the night; beyond the garden is a well, and beyond that is a sizable cowshed.

"I think of the cows as my mothers," Baba says while we are in the shed. "They have given me milk. Until recently, I used to mow the grass and feed them with my own hands." Patting the rumps of a couple of calves, he adds, "I wouldn't mind being reincarnated as Silver or January here, but in my next incarnation I want to carry on all I have learned in this one. I am a hundred and twenty-six."

The fantastic figure does not take me by surprise. Many of Baba's well-wishers have said publicly that he is a hundred and twenty-six years old, though it is a matter of common knowledge that some of the same well-wishers were among the celebrants of his hundredth birthday in 1962, and that some of these 1962 celebrants, even as they fêted him in their centennial tributes, put his age at a few years short of a hundred. (In an essay in the centennial collection—one of whose entries is entitled "A Hundred Years of Dedicated Effort"—His Highness Brijnath Singh confidently gives Baba's birth date as 1869.) In India, of course, this sort of confusion cannot be cleared up by anything as simple as recourse to a birth certificate; such records were unheard of here until quite recently. Anyway, one of the centennial well-wishers has told me, "The point of a centennial is not to count years but to honor a great man, and great men are legends. Baba is such a legend. Everything about his life is grist for the mill. Just as Baba improvises on an ancient *raga,* so everyone, including Baba, improvises on Baba's life. For all anyone cares, Baba could be a hundred and fifty. What difference does it make?" Now, as I talk on with Baba, I come to feel the force of these remarks, hearing in them overtones of the fate of Esmiss Esmoor, whose deification obliterated all earthly distinctions in one eternal *"boum."*

"A hundred and twenty-six," Baba repeats, as if to impress his age upon me, and then, walking with quick, jaunty steps, he takes me inside his cottage and into his bedroom, a corner room with green walls, on which hang pictures of Beethoven, Yehudi Menuhin, and Ali Akbar Khan, along with snapshots of Baba's three daughters and a framed certificate naming him Padma Bhushan. Beside the pillow of a wooden single bed stand, side by side on a shelf, a Koran, a Ramayana, and a few books of Bengali music. Baba insists that I take the only armchair in the room, and he himself sits on the bed.

I remark that I have just seen His Highness Brijnath Singh.

"His Highness is constantly after news of me," Baba says happily. "Whenever he comes to Maihar, he makes his obeisance to Sharda Devi and pays his respects to me; we are both devotees of Sharda Devi. Sharda Devi sometimes blesses me by visiting me in my dreams. Though I am a Muslim and she is a goddess of Hindus, I worship her just as I do Allah. When I was younger, I used to climb the five hundred and sixty steps up the hill to her temple seven times a day. When I was young, I used to get up at four o'clock in the morning and, fearless of the stalking lions, begin my first climb."

"What stalking lions?"

"The lions who used to roar under my window. When I first came to Maihar, this whole place was a jungle. I had never heard of Maihar—in those days no one had. But then a delegation of Ministers arrived in Calcutta with His Highness of Maihar's compliments."

"I thought the Ministers came from Gwalior and found you in Rampur," I say, recalling the Maharaja's account.

"They came from Maihar and I was in Calcutta," Baba says, in the manner of a man who is not accustomed to being contradicted. (Apparently, just where and by whom Baba was summoned is more grist for that mill.) "I came to Maihar with the delegation and was established in a small house near the palace. One day, His Highness asked me to play for him. It was five-thirty in the evening. I sat down with my *sarod* for an evening's playing, but I had hardly begun the *alap* when His Highness stopped me. I thought: What is the point of playing for a man who lacks the patience to listen to me even for five minutes? But when, as a matter of protocol, I stood up, His Highness said, 'I have recognized what a great *ustad* you are. Music is true wealth, and I would like you to add to my wealth. I would like you to be my *guru.'* I tied a thread around his wrist and His Highness presented me with a woollen *sherwani,* woollen shawls, gold coins, and a basket of sweetmeats. His Highness started paying me about two hundred rupees a month, and in those days I could buy forty pounds of flour and sixteen pounds of *ghi* for two rupees. Their Highnesses of Kashmir, Patiala, and Jodhpur asked me to come to their states, at much bigger salaries, but I refused to go, because I had eaten the salt of the Maharaja of Maihar."

Baba continues, talking a sonorous language of his own, made up of Hindi and Urdu, with occasional Bengali words, "And just the other day His Highness was here in my house, sitting right where you are and crying over our separation. Once, when I was teaching His Highness, I struck him with a hammer and broke his thumb."

"A book," I murmur.

"A sledgehammer," Baba says imperiously. "I hold with the old idea that beating and teaching go together."

Baba's wife comes in to serve us tea. She is a lady of short stature and serene maternal expression, and is dressed in a simple white homespun cotton sari. The tea is spiced, and Baba takes his with lots of milk and sugar. Soon after Baba's wife leaves, I ask Baba when and how he first discovered music. According to one account, he was playing practically from birth; according to another, he became a musician through a series of miraculous incidents, like running away from home at the age of four and being adopted by a succession of benevolent *ustads*. Such contradictions are common in the plethora of stories about Baba.

"In the little village of Shivpuri, in the princely state of Tripura, near Bengal," he begins, like a storyteller, "I was born. Almost the whole village belonged to one landlord. He was called Guru Singh Chaudhari, but our village was called Shivpuri, after its temple of Lord Shiva. My father was called Sadhu Khan. I had an elder brother and sister and many younger brothers and sisters. My father and my elder brother both played the *sitar,* and so from the beginning I was inclined toward music. I used to sit in my mother's lap and clap in time to the *sitar* when I was a month old. And my elder brother took lessons from Ustad Qasim Ali Khan, the court musician of the King of Tripura. I was admitted to a school called Nab Kishore Chaudhari, whose headmaster was named Mohadev Chandra Bhattacharya. But I did not like to go to school. On my way there, I would stop at the Shiva temple instead and listen to the *ķirtana* [Hindi for "chanted hymns"], or I would go behind the temple to look at the carvings of serpents on the well. One day, Mohadev Chandra Bhattacharya complained to my mother, and I told my mother that I would never go back to school. My mother was beside herself with anger. She beat me and tied me to a lamppost and left me there without food for two days. But I was firm. Finally, my elder sister came and released me and took me to her home. I was very happy with my elder sister and decided not to return to my mother. But my mother was unable to sleep for worry. So I gave in and went home. But she now made me sleep in her bed."

His voice quavers, and I remark that perhaps he should rest. He insists that his voice will return. He takes some tea, and, indeed, soon he is talking in his earlier strong tone.

"One night, when my mother was sleeping, I undid the little knot at the corner of her sari where she always kept her keys and money," he resumes. "I took a handful of rupees and left home in search of my destiny. I was six years old. I walked for the whole night. I was cold and hungry. I had nothing on except a thin *dhoti*. At eight o'clock in the morning, I arrived by the side of a steamer. I had never seen or heard of a steamer, but I got aboard. I was a stowaway. I didn't mind being hungry anymore; I was drunk with my adventure. Two days later, the steamer put me down in Calcutta. I walked along Harrison Road until I came to the bank of the Hooghly, the tributary of Mother Ganga, where I found some men from

Orissa cooking *puris* [wheat cakes] and potatoes. I gave four annas to the *puri*-wallahs, and, for the first time in days, I had something to eat. I bent down and drank some water. It was muddy and tasted bad, but it was the water of Mother Ganga. I lay down on a nearby bench—for a year sidewalks and benches were to be my beds in Calcutta—and fell asleep. When I woke the next morning, I discovered that all my money was gone. I had been robbed in the night. I bathed in the water of Mother Ganga and walked along, and I came to Nimtala Ghat, where the dead were being cremated. A holy man stopped me and asked me why I was crying. I told him my troubles. He gave me a pinch of ashes and told me to bathe in Mother Ganga and then eat them. I did, and, for good measure, drank five handfuls of the sacred water. Then I walked along and I came to a temple where a Brahman was feeding little children. He took pity on me. I ate out of his hand every day for six days. It was while I was at that temple that I first heard the sound of a *sitar* in Calcutta. I followed the *sitar* to a window of a house. From then on, nights I would sleep by Mother Ganga and days I would stand at the window to catch every last note of the *sitar*. After a while, I made the acquaintance of Vireshawar Babu, whose sweet hand at the *sitar* I had come to know so well, and of the chemist Vaise Chandra Chatterji, who recognized me as a fellow-Tripurian and gave me shelter in his shop, and I got to know Habul Dutt, the brother of Swami Vivekananda. But Western music I learned first from Robert Memsahib and then from Robert Sahib himself."

Names are coming thick and fast, as if Baba were reciting a calendar of saints. Earlier in his reminiscences, I was struck by the improbability of the age of the fugitive and some other circumstances of his flight, but now I want to interrupt for complete hagiographies of Vireshawar Babu, Vaise Chandra Chatterji, Habul Dutt. I do not, for I am in the presence of an extraordinary storyteller. I sometimes think I detect in Baba, in addition to the vanity of the members of that brotherhood, an old man's fear of losing the thread of his narrative. Then I am afraid that any interruption at all, like his wife's return to collect the tea things, or a knock at the door by some other visitor, will distract him and cut the story short, leaving me to cherish, as it were, a few tantalizing pages of a book never really to be read. Sometimes even the rustling of the leaves outside the bedroom windows makes me start. But now I am reassured by the determined voice of Baba as, full of emotion, he continues to recount his experiences in Calcutta.

"Every morning, I used to leave the shop of Vaise Chandra Chatterji and go for my rounds of lessons. Habul Dutt would teach me to play

Hindustani *ragas* on the clarinet, and Amrit Lal Dutt would teach me violin. It was through my violin that I met Robert Sahib and his mem-sahib, which is a heartrending story in itself. I was at the Eden Gardens, begging at the roadside by playing a little violin, when I heard the beauti-ful sounds of a piano. I followed them to a window. The person at the piano was a memsahib, Robert Memsahib. She noticed me at the window and asked me to come in and play the violin for her. I did, and when I finished, she complimented me on my sweet hand. That day, she taught me how to play Western music and also how to read notation. She used to give me lessons in the morning, when Robert Sahib was out practicing with his brass band—he was a bandmaster. One day, he caught us at a lesson. He was beside himself with anger. He scolded his memsahib for teaching a 'blackie.' Yet Robert Sahib himself was a Negro, though the memsahib was white. But then I played a little for Robert Sahib and he was beside himself with joy. For four happy years, both Robert Memsahib and Robert Sahib taught me Western music. Time passed, and I felt my-self to be an *ustad*. Jagat Kishore Maharaj, the landlord of Meman Singh, used to hold music competitions. I decided to enter a competition. When I called on Jagat Kishore Maharaj, I had a clarinet case in one hand and a violin case in the other, but he asked me what I wanted. I told him that I was an *ustad* and wanted an opportunity to play for him. He laughed and asked me to come back the next day. When I did, I found myself at a great musical conference, for his house was filled with hundreds and thousands of people, and Ustad Ahmad Ali Khan, of the princely state of Rampur, was playing a *raga* on the *sarod*. When I had heard only a few notes, I was dumfounded. The *raga* lasted for four hours—from seven o'clock in the morning to eleven. For all that time, I could not check the flow of my tears. I cried and cried with joy. I was delirious. When Ustad Ahmad Ali Khan finished, I fell down at his feet and told him that, compared to him, I was an ignoramus. I pleaded with him to let me be his servant, be his slave for life. He agreed, and how I learned from him is a heartrending story in itself. He lived in Guj-Danga Mohalla, under the patronage of Puri Chand Marwari. Daily I massaged the Ustad's arms and legs, daily I cooked for him, and daily I tried to emulate his sweet hand at the *sarod* by practicing secretly while he was out of the house. He was out of the house every morning until lunch, visiting two renowned courtesans, Goharbai and Malkabai. While he was out, I was supposed to prepare his lunch, which I did speedily, so that I would have plenty of time to practice. I always knew when he was returning, because he always hired a coach and eight horses to pay his calls upon Goharbai and Malkabai. When I heard the thunder of the returning coach, I immediately wrapped the *sarod* up in its cloth and stood it in the corner where the Ustad kept it, and busied myself in the kitchen. Six years passed in this way. But one day he heard me at the *sarod,* because he had returned early and on foot. He was beside himself—like one possessed. He cried out that I had undone him, that I had stolen his music, that I was a demon who had charmed his knowledge out of him, that I was now an *ustad* equal to him. He bound me hand and foot and dragged me through the streets to his parents' house. His father, Abid Ali Khan, asked me to play for him. When I had finished, he embraced me and called me *ustad*. He said I was a second Ahmad Ali Khan. He told his son to be grateful and to praise Allah. At this moment, I presented Ahmad Ali Khan with ten thousand rupees. Now, when I started serving Ahmad Ali Khan, I was as poor as a mouse. Since he was too much taken up with the courtesans to go to the bazaar himself, he used to give me the money to buy his vegetables and *ghi*. I saved the change. Over the years, it added up to ten thousand rupees. Abid Ali Khan embraced me again and said he had never seen or heard of a more honest boy. I was now sixteen and as good as Ustad Ahmad Ali Khan. Ten years had passed since I had arrived at Calcutta, and no one from my family had been able to find me. But now my brother Aftab Uddin, who had been looking for me for all those ten years, at last found me, and he took me back to Shivpuri and my mother, who had been crying for ten years without ceasing. She decided to have me married immediately, so that I would feel tied down and stay in Shivpuri. One day, my mother came up to me, put some red coloring on my hands, and sat me down in a palanquin. She put a veiled bundle next to me and told the bearers to take the palanquin to the house of a relative. Then my mother told me that the bundle was my wife. I unveiled her face. She was a pretty little girl, eight years old; in those days, after the ceremony the girl returned to her parents' home until she was grown up. I had got used to my free life of grandeur, so as soon as everyone was asleep that night, I ran away from home a second time."

Baba's voice again seems on the verge of giving out. I stand up to take leave of him. He asks me to visit him the next day, before I depart from Maihar—an invitation I readily accept, since the saga of the runaway *ustad* has brought its hero only to the age of sixteen.

Alauddin Khan has said, "My last wish is that my school and my band should survive as long as there are stars in the sky." Early on my second morning in Maihar, I go to see his school, and I discover that it consists of three dilapidated rest houses that once, as part of the network of British law and order, quartered civil servants on tours of duty. The school is deserted at this hour, except for a ghost of a man who is sweeping the road in front of the bungalows with a long bundle of twigs. It is a familiar Indian landscape. To repeated inquiries from me about the hours of the school, he mutters, without looking up, something about my checking at the hostel nearby.

As I approach the hostel, which resembles the school bungalows, a young man in pajamas and undershirt is brushing his teeth on the veranda. He greets me, and I call to him, "When does the school open?"

"The men are just getting up," he says. "They have gone to get water. It can sometimes take an hour to get water."

"The well must be very far," I say.

He chuckles and says something indistinct through his toothbrush. A few minutes later, he dons a *kurta,* identifies himself as one of Baba's students, and walks back with me to the school. On the way, he tells me a little bit about himself.

"I did nothing before I came to Baba's school," he says. "I used to just roam about the village—roam about with one or two friends and act out the verses from the Ramayana. Baba gave me shelter after seeing my act. I lived with Baba for many years. He really is the head of the school still, and if he makes me a master here, then I will get a salary of a hundred and sixty-five rupees a month." He goes on to tell me that the school follows traditional Indian lines, and that the students, the masters, and the peons attached to the school are all housed either in the hostel, which has eight rooms, or in the school, its few rooms being used to absorb any overflow from the hostel. Each resident, however, must make his own arrangements for food and water. This has turned out to be a blessing since the outbreak of the second Indo-Pakistan war, when, as a part of the emergency, which still continues, government rationing was instituted. The lack of communal eating arrangements has allowed each resident to make what he considers the best use of his small ration, which sometimes amounts to no more than one good meal a day. For some students, even this meal is in jeopardy, because a monthly stipend of twenty-five rupees allotted by the government to each student was suspended at the beginning of the emergency and has not been resumed. Their future looks bleak, particularly since the full course for even those students who have come to the school after completing their secondary education covers a five-year period—three years for an intermediate degree in music, and two more years for a bachelor's degree in music.

We arrive at the school, and my companion goes into one of the classrooms. Other students are beginning to straggle in, and soon each class-room, its door ajar, is humming with the sound of a different instrument, the sounds echoing and clashing all around the school. I pause in the doorway of the violin class. The master plays a phrase, and a couple of students repeat the phrase after him, copying exactly not only his intonation but also his bowing. The fragments, it soon becomes clear, are from a *raga* with a sombre, devotional atmosphere. No words are ever exchanged, and the violin class gives the impression of a Zen pantomime. So do the other classes I visit. In the *tabla* class, the master is teaching half a dozen students rhythm by imitating the sound of the instrument. He demonstrates a phrase orally, his voice now ascending, "Ggi ggi ggi ggi *ggi*" (the students, in chorus, repeat after him, "Ggi ggi ggi ggi *ggi*"), and now descending, *"Ggi* ggi ggi ggi ggi" (*"Ggi* ggi ggi ggi ggi").

I walk back to the hostel to visit Baba's band, which nowadays is a dozen strong. All the members are sitting cross-legged on the floor of a small, shabby room that serves them as practice room, stage, and hall—it being understood that if there should be an audience, people will listen to the band from the outside—and in this room they are continuing the tradition established when Baba formed and led his original, forty-piece band at court. The Maharaja and Baba have wrung out of the government another kind of small stipend for the band members, to earn which they must assemble for a few hours a day six days a week—Friday, the Muslim sabbath, being excepted, out of deference to Baba's origins. This income in no case exceeds thirty rupees a month. The band is apt to convene late and adjourn early, probably because almost all the members hold full-time jobs —they are flower sellers, *pan* sellers, or farmhands. The fact that they play gives pleasure to Baba, for Baba and his wife have been foster parents to most of the members almost from their birth.

The band is playing frenetically, filling the room with the music of a vocalist, harmoniums, *tablas,* a *shahnai,* a clarinet, a *sarangi,* a mouth organ, and two instruments of Baba's invention, one of which is a cross between a *sitar* and a *sarod,* and the other—the noisiest part of the band—a contraption of gun barrels of different sizes struck like a xylophone. In accordance with the dictates of Indian music, every *raga* is played in unison, a melody at a time. Because all the instruments have identical musical parts, and some, by the nature of things, are louder than others, the more delicate instruments try to make up for their inherent weakness with a little cheating, starting ahead of or trailing behind the others during the rests, as if to remind the listener that playing in ensemble is almost as new in India as Baba's gun-barrel xylophone. But this musical Darwinian struggle does not extend to the three harmonium players, two of whom pump their instruments gently in order to set off the harmonium playing of Jamuna Prasad Chauriha, the "in-charge" of the band. (Chauriha, who is addressed respectfully by one and all as "Maharaj," works at two jobs— as a farmhand and as a laborer in a limestone quarry—and supports a wife and five children, his father, and, in part, a brother and the brother's family, with all of whom he shares a small house.) The band begins by playing the *raga* "Tilak Kamod," worked out and named by Baba. Then it plays a sort of hybrid *raga*, combining Indian and English motifs, and then an indeterminate *raga*, performed at such a brisk tempo and with such sound and fury that one thinks it should be called "Prestissimo Fortissimo." Now the group is in the middle of a slow, traditional *raga* called "Bhairavi," with the single, bleak repeated refrain "I have abused my love for nothing. I have abused my love for nothing." (And I have to think twice to get the meaning.) Throughout the session, Chauriha continually shifts his glance from the band to the open door, as if haunted by a private phantom. "Baba!" he suddenly shouts over the music. All the members look to their instruments, and the gun-barrel player engulfs with his thunder even the sound of Chauriha's harmonium. But soon the storm abates. The sounds become scattered and desultory, and then the music comes to a halt. Chauriha explains to me that these days Baba hardly ever stops by at the sessions but that the mere invocation of Baba's name serves to help him, Chauriha, run a taut ship.

Late on my second morning in Maihar, when I pay my second call on Baba, he receives me in his living room, which is larger than his bedroom but equally bare. He pauses before a picture of a suited and booted gentleman. "This is a picture of me," he says proudly. "It was taken when I went abroad with Uday Shankar's troupe." He goes on to catalogue the countries he visited and the highlights of his travels—apparently at different times—as if monologue were his natural way of speech. "I have seen the pyramids of Egypt," Baba declaims. "I have met the Jews of Palestine. I have been to France and Italy and Yugoslavia and Switzerland and Belgium. I have been to Kabul and complained to the King about the food. When I met the King of Afghanistan, he gave me dried fruits and fresh grapes and said, 'I hope you like our food.' I said, 'I like everything in Afghanistan except the food,' and since I take no meat and that was all they served in the hotel, I asked him if he would arrange for boiled eggs, boiled potatoes, and boiled milk for me. I made the *hadj;* Nehruji, who had great regard for me, had written to the Badshah of Saudi Arabia, and when I arrived, the Badshah declared me a state guest. I met the Kaiser in Germany, and I told him that I considered the entire world to be one. He introduced me to *Kuchen*. In Germany, I bought *Kuchen* with abandon and fed them to the whole troupe. His Majesty King Edward of Britain asked me if I was comfortable, when we met in London. And on the tour, whenever I played, the halls were so silent that you could hear a pin drop. Whenever I finished a program, I heard"—here he speaks English—" 'Once more! Once more!' "

Baba leads the way to the bedroom, which opens off the living room. Once again he proffers me the armchair. Once again he sits on the bed.

"I stay in Maihar because of Sharda Devi," he says. "I have the greatest respect for her, because all my prosperity has come from her, although, like a good Muslim, I recite the prayers of the Koran five times a day. I take twenty-one thousand six hundred breaths in saying them—one breath for every word. If you say these prayers every day, mind and body stay well. My *guru* Ustad Wazir Khan was a Shia Muslim, but I have the greatest respect for him, though I was born a Suni and think of myself as a Muslim-Hindu."

I ask him to tell me something about Wazir Khan, and, to my delight, this launches him on the story of his turning fugitive for the second time, at the age of sixteen. It is as though he had never left off the saga—as though the saga were one long *raga*.

"From my birthplace in Shivpuri, in the princely state of Tripura, I ran away a second time," he says. "I ran away from my marriage to meet Ustad Wazir Khan. Ustad Wazir Khan lived in Rampur. Rampur had five hundred musicians, but the *ustad* of *ustads* was Wazir Khan. When I reached Rampur, I discovered that Ustad Wazir Khan was too grand for someone like me to meet. I tried to see him by meeting the Nawab of Rampur. The Nawab of Rampur, as patron of the arts in his princely state, was the employer of Wazir Khan, but it was impossible to get past the Nawab's bodyguards. So I started taking lessons from another *ustad*—not so great a one as Ustad Wazir Khan, of course, but greater than Ahmad Ali Khan. This *ustad's* name was Mohammed Hussein Khan. To pay Ustad Mohammed Hussein Khan, I got a job in the Rampur band. At first, the bandmaster didn't want to grant me an audition, but after I played for him he was beside himself with joy. He admitted me to his band at the high salary of twelve rupees a month. I gave half my salary to Ustad Mohammed Hussein Khan; I lived on the rest. I practiced on the *sarod* far into the night. Some Pathans who lived across the road would throw stones through my window to make me stop—yes, I have seen days when people threw stones at great *ustads*. But, undeterred by the stones, I practiced night after night; in six months I had learned all that Ustad Mohammed Hussein Khan could teach me. I had become a second Ustad Mohammed Hussein Khan. I was more desperate now than ever to prove worthy, one day, of the turban of the great Ustad Wazir Khan. But I had lost all hope of seeing him. I bought two rupees' worth of morphine to put an end to my misery. I went to the mosque to say the *namaz* for the last time. The mullah asked me why I looked so crestfallen. I told him. The mullah counselled perseverance. The mullah told me that Allah helps those who help themselves. The next morning, inspired by the mullah, I made my last attempt to see the Nawab. Every morning, the Nawab used to take the air in his huge carriage, drawn by more than a dozen powerful horses. I threw myself in front of the carriage. The horses reared and the carriage lurched to a stop. Several of the Nawab's bodyguards jumped out to pick me up. They had no choice but to present me to the Nawab. I told the Nawab that if he wouldn't arrange for me to meet Ustad Wazir Khan I would die. The Nawab thereupon took me in the carriage to Hamid Manzil, where Ustad Wazir Khan lived, and summoned the Ustad. Ustad Wazir Khan came running up to the carriage, and I was presented to him as his new *shagird*. The Nawab also made arrangements for my board and lodging, and gave me clothes, ornaments, and sweetmeats such as became my high station now. For thirty-three years, I studied with the great Wazir Khan. At the age of forty-nine, I went to Calcutta for the greatest music conference of the century. Ustad Karamat Ullah Khan and Ustad Imdad Khan were in attendance. They dismissed me as just another Bengali who ate fish and wore a *dhoti*. But when I played the Puriah *raga,* which lasted for four hours, on the *sarod,* Karamat Ullah Khan, Imdad Khan, and everyone else were beside themselves. The hands of those who were fitting *pans* into their mouths were paralyzed. The hands of those who were smoking cigarettes froze in midair—at the end of the Puriah *raga,* they discovered that their fingers were burnt. Listeners fell unconscious. The president of the music conference was Manind Nandi, of Qasim Bazaar. Manind Nandi declared me to be the best *ustad* at the conference. The newspaper reports of the music conference gave my family the first news they had had of me since I ran away from my marriage thirty-three years before. Once again, I was taken to Shivpuri, where I found my first wife patiently waiting for me. I learned that after my flight her parents had tried to get her remarried but that she had defied them by a fast of eight days. Her parents never broached the subject again. We consummated our marriage. It was then that I came to Maihar."

For some time, I have been aware of the hushed sounds of guests arriving and paying their respects to Baba's wife. Baba now jumps up and rushes into the living room. I follow. The band members, the school staff, the students—all those I've met in Maihar, it seems—are gathered in the room. A dark-skinned, black-bearded man of unfathomable age, wearing a saffron-colored *dhoti,* spots me as a stranger and comes over with Chauriha. Chauriha introduces him to me. "This is One-oh-eight Raj Raj Shri, Naga Deo Anand Giri, Badri ka Ashram," Chauriha says.

This sounds to me more like an address than a name, and I inquire about it.

Chauriha explains that our bearded companion, who is looking on with the happy expression of a man in a Buddhist drawing, has taken the path of Nirvana and done away with such ordinary human frailties as a name. Instead, he goes merely by the address of his monastery. "One-oh-eight Raj Raj Shri, Naga Deo Anand Giri, Badri ka Ashram has been in Maihar now for about a month," Chauriha continues. "He is going to Allahabad, on a pilgrimage to the Kumbha *mela* [the greatest of the Hindu festivals], and he has been holding a nightly *kirtana* for all of us. Baba has heard him and has accepted him as a *chela.*"

"Wherever I go, I shall repeat the name of my new *guru,*" the ascetic says.

Baba claps once, and everyone sits down on the floor. Baba's wife fetches a basket of sweetmeats. The ascetic intones a few words over the sweetmeats. Chauriha hands Baba a piece of thread. Baba ties the thread around the wrist of the ascetic, who immediately sets about dabbing everyone's forehead with vermilion paste. Baba's wife passes the blessed sweetmeats around. Baba, raising his hand for attention, says, "One-oh-eight Raj Raj Shri, Naga Deo Anand Giri, Badri ka Ashram, I am very grateful to you for enlarging the circle of my *chelas.*"

"I am very grateful to you, Baba, for accepting me," the *chela* responds.

Chauriha hands Baba a *sarod,* and everyone begins coaxing Baba to play.

"I haven't touched a *sarod* in six years," Baba says reticently.

The entreaties multiply, and Baba, sitting down, starts picking the strings with his left hand. (He is left-handed.) He plays a few measures of something resembling a Victorian music-hall song, says, "Robert Sahib taught me that," and lays down the *sarod,* to a burst of applause. Everyone deferentially gets up to go, and Baba escorts his guests as far as the garden. During the leave-taking, Baba breaks into a song, his voice supple and perfectly pitched. It is an invocation: "O Sharda Devi, Giver of Knowledge, Giver of Pleasure, give us now blessings. Goddess who plays the *vina,* please put your hands on us and give us your blessings."

"Please put your hands on us and give us your blessings," the guests respond, in chorus.

"O Sharda Devi, Giver of Knowledge . . ." Baba and the chorus sing together, repeating the invocation.

"Victory to Sharda Devi!" the *chela* cries out, and everyone takes up the cry.

Baba turns majestically and goes into his cottage.

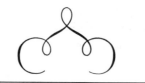

The Sacred Handbook of the Arts

"Natya Sastra," a handbook of the arts, whose origin is uncertain, regards dance—not music—as the consummation of all the arts. (Seven chapters out of thirty-six in the handbook deal with the subject of the dance.) The dance is given this exalted place because, according to "Natya Sastra," the dancer must, among other things, respond to rhythm and melody like a musician, to drama like an actor, to form like a sculptor, and to line like a painter. According to the handbook, Indra, the god of the sky and storms, complained to Brahma, the Creator, that the four Vedas, which sum up all existing knowledge, were not really comprehensible to common men. Indra pleaded for the creation of a fifth, easily accessible Veda, and Brahma created the Natya Veda ("natya" is Sanskrit for "dance"), which he resolved would illustrate the principles of art and morality and bring together the teaching of all the holy books. In fact, the account goes on, Brahma wrought the Natya Veda out of the contents of the Rig, Atharva, Sama, and Yajur Vedas, which are, respectively, intellectual, emotional, musical, and what might be called expressive, and did so by epitomizing all the Vedas in the dance. To impart the dance to mortals, Brahma taught it to a minion called Bharata, and at one point, for the benefit of Bharata, expatiated, if in a rather haphazard fashion, upon the new art, saying that it depicted virtue, play, profit, peace, laughter, battle, love, and slaughter; that it yielded to the obedient the fruits of righteousness, discipline, and pleasure, and served as a restraint to the unruly; that it endowed the weak with vigor, the warrior with zeal, the ignorant with wisdom, the scholar with learning, kings with sport, sufferers with endurance, the ambitious with profit; that, in fact, the dance represented, through its varied moods and situations, the deeds of mankind. In Brahma's words in "Natya Sastra":

This drama [of dance] shall be the source of all counsel. . . .
It shall serve as a timely resting place for those who are grieved, weary, unhappy, or engaged in an arduous discipline—bestowing righteousness, renown, long life, fortune, increase of reason. . . .
That which is not found herein is not knowledge, nor craft, nor wisdom, nor any art, nor application, nor deeds.

Narayana Menon, in an extravagant essay on "Natya Sastra," remarks that this celestial dialogue catches exactly the intellectual, philosophical, and moral view of the dance in India, where, religion and art being identical, the dance is a way of realizing God, and the spectator's capacity for delight does not depend primarily on the accomplishment of the dancer, because both are seeking religious fulfillment, and in that search the dancer's gestures, steps, and songs and the spectator's knowledge of the dance are both irrelevant, for dancer and spectator are ultimately incapable of attaining religious fulfillment for each other. Menon quotes a medieval theoretician's definition of religious fulfillment as "intellectual ecstasy devoid of conceptual contacts . . . [the] summit of being . . . impossible to analyze and yet in the likeness of our very being." According to Menon, these high ideals, having withstood the profanation of time (because, one supposes, they are too fine to be violated by the mortal world), are considered to govern the various present-day schools of dancing: the Kathakali, of Kerala; the Kuchipudi, of Andhra Pradesh; the Odissi, of Orissa; the Manipuri, of the northeast; and the more widely practiced northern Kathak and southern Bharatanatyam, the last school being perhaps the purest expression of the ageless tradition. In a companion essay—this time photographic—Menon offers evidence to prove that Balasaraswati, a woman who was born in 1918 and who lives in Madras, is today the purest exponent of the purest school of dance. Even aside from the philosophical ramifications, I ask myself, what can dance in India, performed mostly solo, without costumes, on a bare stage, and consisting of minute gestures, many of them improvised, have in common with balletic choreography, presented with the help of sets and costumes—that is, with classical dance as it is understood in Europe?

Today, to meet Balasaraswati, I am back in Madras, where it is so hot that the sun seems to be falling down with the sky. "There are only two good months here, when the climate is bearable—December and January," a Madrasi tells me. "We Hindus say that the universe has a *pralaya*, a death—a period of withdrawal for rest. We Madrasis have our *pralaya* all the time."

Balasaraswati turns out to live in a big two-story house, which is so new that some of the windowpanes are still not in. A workman shows me into a living room, whose total furnishings are a small red carpet, a sofa and two matching armchairs, a cuckoo clock, a couple of instruments swathed in their cloths and leaning against a wall, and a tall, elaborately carved glass-fronted cabinet in which is an old *vina* and over which hangs a delicate painting of a woman playing the *vina*. The room, like the outside of the house, suggests a place that has not yet been lived in.

Balasaraswati comes in shyly, her hands pressed together. Belying the notion of a south Indian lady of means, she wears a plain white sari with a little embroidery, a white *choli*, or blouse, no jewelry, and, except for the inevitable kohl on the eyelids and a red mark on her forehead, no makeup. Her figure is full and her manner matronly, but her firm, supple body identifies her as a dancer. She sits down in one armchair and I in the other.

I ask her how she happened to take up dancing.

"My family have all been dancers and musicians," she replies, speaking a mixture of Hindi and Tamil. "On my mother's side, we have been musicians and dancers for seven generations, and"—she turns toward the *vina* case and the painting—"we always called my grandmother Dhanam 'Vina Dhanam,' she was so famous for her playing of the *vina*."

I ask her about the present state of dancing in India.

"That is a delicate question," she replies, a little uneasily. "I am still a professional, and the matter is a very delicate one to talk about. Whoever gets involved in dancing puts much work into it. It is not easy to pass judgment. Dancers are like venders; they specialize in different things. Some dancers specialize in Kuchipudi and some dancers in Odissi; some dancers mix everything up and get an adulterated dance form. The techniques have become well known, but their quality I am doubtful about. The point is that nowadays when you announce you are going to dance, people expect a film star. Since I started dancing, so many dancers have come and so many dancers have gone—I am like a milestone. Dancers have their ups and downs, but I myself have had mostly ups. I love the art and have always been happy with what acclaim I received. Kamala Laxman, Vyjanthimala, Yamini Krishnamurthi, Rukmini Devi, Indrani Rehman—all at one time or another have received good hands from their audiences. Uday Shankar may be the best known of all. He is a very imaginative artist and has very good taste, but Uday Shankar is a Kathakali dancer. That is a masculine dance form. There are some gestures that are common to Kathakali and Bharatanatyam, a feminine dance, but Kathakali is too vigorous for women. Bharatanatyam is more ladylike."

"You've always specialized in Bharatanatyam?"

"Yes. Bharatanatyam is the true dance of India, though it is south Indian. Some people say it comes from the second century B.C., and some say from the fourth century A.D. It may date from sometime in between. Some people say it was created by Bharata. Others say there never was a Bharata. But it is all set down in "Natya Sastra," by Bharata—or whoever he was. I've read only a little of the treatise, in Tamil translation—the treatise is a very big volume—because I started dancing when I was four, and I knew nothing about the treatise then. I learned by imitation. Bharatanatyam is a solo dance, and its theme is usually love. We Hindus always exalt love into love of the gods, so in Bharatanatyam my lover may be Lord Krishna, or Lord Shiva, or his son, whom we Madrasis call Subramaniam. The songs that accompany a dance indicate his identity. The big love-affair songs last for ten minutes. Short love-affair songs may last for only five minutes. The songs are interpreted through facial expression and gesture. The movements of the dance are angular, and it relies mostly on mime. I don't think one comes across such miming in any other dance culture. Of course, the program of the dance includes many things besides love songs."

"What kinds of things does the program include?"

"It begins with *alarippu,* which is a purely rhythmic, non-verbal invocation. It is a drum item, without music. The dance begins with that, and goes on to *jatiswaram*. This adds melody to the rhythm, but it is a song without a text to illustrate. Then comes *shabdam,* which adds mime to rhythm and melody. *Shabdam* has a text, and the theme, when it is not about a love affair with the gods, may concern honorable maharajas, or wise men described in the ancient books. But *alarippu, jatiswaram,* and *shabdam* are all only an introduction to the *varnam,* which combines all the elements of the others, and lasts for an hour or an hour and a half, depending on the mood of the artist and the response of the audience. The buildup is gradual, but the *varnam* is very strenuous, so the program calls for an interval, after which there are the *padams*—those love songs—plus *javalis* and a *tillanam."*

"Doesn't the program ever change?"

"A Bharatanatyam dancer always sticks to this program, but different performers give different interpretations. *Shabdam* may have a line about the dancer's falling in love with Shiva. The text may say, 'You have fallen in love with Shiva, the Great Lord.' But a dancer may conjure up Shiva destroying demons, Shiva with ashes smeared all over his body, Shiva holding up a trident, Shiva with a half-moon over his head, Shiva with a necklace of snakes. Or a dancer may conjure up Shiva wearing Mother Ganga on his head—like this." Still seated, passive and reverent, she extends one hand over her head and parallel to the ground, and moves her arm in a wide arc with a wavy, rippling gesture, her hand rolling gently back and forth. "There are so many ways of re-creating Shiva," she goes on. "I have been learning them since childhood."

She now tells me how as a child she danced and sang from six in the morning until bedtime, and she talks about her first public performance, at the age of seven; about her dance teacher Kandappan, who taught her from the time she was four until she was twenty-three; about his son, who, after Kandappan's death, in 1941, started working with her and her troupe of musicians. She talks about her only child, a daughter named Lakshmi, who has never shown any interest in dancing, and who has just taken a degree in history at a university; about her own mother, Jayammal, who was noted as a singer; and about her several brothers, who are employed in such disparate occupations as building construction, music teaching, and airline work, and how they all live together in the new house. "I still keep a clarinettist in my troupe of musicians," she remarks. "In ancient days, in Bharatanatyam, they had male singers in the first half of the program and female singers in the second half. The *vina* has always been the favorite instrument for Bharatanatyam, but it did not project well enough to accompany the males, so they used bagpipes and clarinets. In the old days, they did not have microphones."

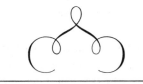

Jazz in Bombay

I HAVE BECOME GOOD FRIENDS WITH Asha Puthli and Vivan Sundaram, whom I recognize as spiritual kin to some of my friends in London and New York, though neither Asha nor Vivan has been abroad. Asha is a beautiful, mercurial girl, just out of the university, who has applied for a job as a B.O.A.C. air hostess simply in order to go to London and hear a real jazz vocalist, and perhaps become one herself. Vivan, who was educated at the Doon School, the most expensive public school in India, with a reputation for turning out very self-assured young men, nevertheless has a gentle, unassuming manner. I first met them when I went with a friend to a party that Vivan gave to celebrate his having been granted a finalist's interview for a Commonwealth Fellowship to study painting in London. The party was in New Delhi, at his parents' house, which was full of paintings by his aunt, the late Amrita Shergil, and also held some of Vivan's own. One of Vivan's paintings—a very large Pop affair, hanging over the mantel—was made up of patches of Indian costumes and masks thickly daubed with paint. Vivan's paintings have something of the naturalness and simplicity of nursery sketches, and connoisseurs agree that they show much originality, though Vivan himself acknowledges the influence of Robert Rauschenberg. Asha, Vivan, and I have now all met again in Bombay, where Asha is studying classical Indian music with a *pandit* while she awaits the outcome of her job application, where Vivan is trying to arrange an exhibition while *he* awaits the verdict on his Commonwealth Fellowship, and where I have happened to stop over in the course of my peregrinations.

Today, we go to their favorite haunt, a restaurant called the Venice, in the run-down Hotel Astoria, to listen to jazz, which is having its first stirrings in India—of course, in this avant-garde city, which, psychologically and geographically, lies closer to Europe than any other Indian city does, and, together with nearby Goa, which was a Portuguese colony for over four hundred years, is the chief remaining bastion of Western influence in the country.

For what might be called formal relaxation, city people here in India seem to do one of three things: they go to cultural events, on the order of the Sangeet Sammelan; they go to clubs, which, with their swimming tanks and tennis courts, resemble the typical country club elsewhere; or they go to Western-style restaurants, such as the Gaylord and the Volga in Delhi, the Blue Fox in Calcutta, and, in lesser cities, the local Kwality. Following the custom of British days, most of these restaurants have small dance floors, with bands playing Western music almost continuously from morning to night, whether or not anyone is dancing, or even listening. They play such old standbys as "Greensleeves" and "Green Eyes" and such current favorites as "Lemon Tree." At the moment, the rage is a number called "Mamma Loves Papa, Papa Loves Mamma." These Western-style restaurants, unlike most of their Indian-style counterparts—and also unlike most offices and private houses—are air-conditioned in the summer. They provide a refuge for students, housewives, government officers, and businessmen alike, though the groups seem to patronize them at different times of day—housewives coming for elevenses, government officers and businessmen for lunch, and the student crowd for tea and a little dancing. In the evenings, there is a similar cycle of attendance, beginning with husbands bringing their wives—or wives their husbands—for dinner, and ending with students in mixed groups, who arrive later in the evening for coffee. At their best, these restaurants give one the illusion of being in Europe; at their worst, they suggest a barricade set up against the sights, sounds, and smells of the India outside.

Some of the owners of Western-style restaurants in Bombay are now permitting their old-time bands to play jazz, and without question the best of the jazz combos is a quintet made up of piano, alto saxophone, tenor saxophone, bass, and drums that holds forth at the Venice. The jazz here is as pure as any—though the restaurant tries to capture the atmosphere of its namesake city with a tacky décor of gondolas and canals, and the bearers serve "sahib-and-memsahib" food, such as roast mutton and boiled vegetables, with the hauteur usually found in aspirants to metropolitan Indian chic. Starting at six-thirty, the quintet first plays, in shirtsleeves, for the student crowd, then, in lounge suits, for the business and cover-charge set, then for the visiting Indian tourists, who are in and out almost with the two ten-minute cabaret shows (these feature a belly dancer, a little on the heavy side, dressed in silver tassels and black gloves), and, finally, around eleven-thirty, for a few serious-looking stragglers and friends—the music modulating, as the evening progresses, from brilliant jazz, with echoes of Miles Davis, to overstuffed old melodies, complete with crooner, to a frenetic, sleazy beat, and, ultimately, to unpredictable experimentation and fun. It is this last period that Asha, Vivan, and I have been looking forward to this evening.

The quintet plays "The Dove," "The Pond," and "Karim Blues" (Karim was the owner of a Bombay speakeasy), all composed by Braz Gonzalves, the quintet's leader and alto saxophonist. As the musicians play, they throw glances at Asha, who blows kisses to them. Presently, the professional crooner having just departed, Gonzalves calls out to Asha to take the stage and sing. She goes up without fuss but stands facing the musicians, with her back to the tables. "She always sings with her back to the audience," Vivan tells me. "I suppose, like other jazz musicians here, she just doesn't feel comfortable with people. The state of jazz in India is such that when musicians really play and sing, it is only for themselves."

The quintet swings into the opening bars of "My Funny Valentine" with a huge bang, and then subsides as Asha's voice, at first muffled and distant, takes over. Soon Asha is belting out her song in a very un-Indian way. "My funny valentine. Sweet comic valentine. You make me smile with my heart. Your looks are laughable"—her voice suddenly slurs up through an octave—"unphotographable. Yet you're my favorite work of art." Her voice slurs up a couple of octaves, as if she were struggling to break out of the Indian mode of singing that imprisons the voice mostly in the larynx. The words give way to scatting, and the melody shifts into another key, into another tune, and back again. Asha and the quintet take turns improvising and embellishing, as if they had been working together for years. Bearers look on, puzzled but admiring.

Asha returns to the table, followed closely by Casmiro Lobo, the tenor saxophone player; Wancy de Souza, the drummer; and Dinshaw Balsara, the bass player. (Gonzalves and the piano player, Xavier Fernandes, have stepped out for some air.) They surround Asha at the table.

"Whew, Asha! Boy, that was good!" Balsara says.

Asha says apologetically, "All my singing is copied from records. I've never heard the real thing." Then she compliments herself by adding, "But I'm the most advanced singer in India."

"You should record it and send it to the United States," Balsara says. "A voice like that—where wouldn't it reach? You are the best crooner in India." Balsara—or Balsi, as he is nicknamed—is a short, stoutish Parsi, and, like the other members of the quintet, is showily dressed, down to his pearl cufflinks. He talks to Asha with impressive emphasis while Wancy, who is a little taller, and Casmiro look on with awe.

Asha listens, and then, a little embarrassed, remarks, "I've never been taught to sing jazz. I just sing because I like it." She goes on, "Anyway, Balsi, this is the best jazz place in India—the only place where jazz is played seriously at all."

"Good crooners are impossible to find in India," Balsi says. "But, Asha, I would never let you sing professionally here in Bombay. I would rather die than have you sing where there is no respect for music."

A serious Parsi girl whom I met once or twice in Cambridge, Massachusetts, when I was studying at Harvard is at the Venice, I discover. She spots me, comes over to our table, and soon embarks on a lecture that makes me nostalgic for the cafeterias around Harvard Square. "So nice that you've discovered the Venice," she says to me, and then informs the table judicially, "Bombay is a bourgeois intellectual desert. I haven't found anybody in this country who is thinking. Middle-class Indians today are more grossly Philistine than any other people. They are three times as materialistic as any American, and they are twenty times as guilty as any American. If I were sentencing an American for being materialistic and grossly Philistine and living in a bourgeois intellectual desert, I would give him one year, because he had no chance to learn better, but if I were judging an Indian, I would give him twenty years, because he has the culture and philosophy of the Vedas and the Upanishads and the *puranas.*"

"It *is* a desert," Casmiro says.

"Now that they have good jazz at the Venice, they should do away with the food and with a cover charge, and just have an *espresso* bar," Vivan says. "Then people could buy a cup of coffee for a few annas and simply sit and listen to jazz. We are trying to ape the Americans in every other respect, so we should have a place like the Village Gate."

"You know about the Village Gate?" I ask.

"All the Village places are very well known here in Bombay," he replies.

"*Down Beat* now has the largest circulation of any American little magazine in Bombay."

"*Down Beat* once mentioned Braz," Balsi tells me. "A customer walked in and showed Braz the magazine and said, 'See, Braz, you are in *Down Beat.*' Braz had never heard of *Down Beat,* but he played beautifully that night. Do you read Nat Hentoff or Barbara Gardner?"

"Sometimes," I say.

"Braz is the greatest musician anywhere," Balsi continues excitedly. "He's the best. He's terrific. No one in the world is better. If he went to New York and had a good promoter, he would be more famous than Miles Davis."

"Braz *is* the best," Wancy says. "He's the best."

"He's terrific," Casmiro puts in.

"Balsi, you're the best bass player in Bombay, and I mean it," Wancy goes on, patting Balsi on the arm.

Balsi returns the compliment: "And you, Wancy, are the best drummer now in Bombay." Then, changing the subject, he complains, "But every bearer, every hanger-on at the Venice thinks *he* is our manager."

"I tell Braz, 'Stick up for us. You are the leader,' " Wancy says. "But he's gentle and never gets angry unless he's had a drink or two."

"And then—whew!" Balsi exclaims.

"You are right, Wancy," Casmiro puts in.

"We all have other jobs during the day," Balsi tells me. "From nine-thirty to five-thirty I work as a commercial artist, and at six-thirty I have to start playing at the Venice. We get some rest at seven-thirty, though, when our interval for dinner starts. We begin playing again at nine-thirty and play on till one. I don't mind playing late, but no one—no one—understands the music at all. There is no respect for music here."

"You are right," Casmiro repeats.

"And, Balsi, you get only four hundred rupees a month, so unimportant is the bass considered to be," Wancy complains. "For my drums I get twice as much."

"A cabaret dancer gets two thousand rupees a month," Balsi continues. "And cabaret dancers who bill themselves as Egyptian or Persian are usually just Bombay suburbanites. Most people come to the Venice only for the cabaret. There is no respect for musicians in this country, no respect."

"Absolutely no respect," Casmiro echoes.

The three musicians invite all of us upstairs to their room for a drink. Bombay, the stronghold of Indian prohibition and prohibitionists, has many rules—more often transgressed than observed—about who may serve drinks to whom. In any case, there are no drinks to be had in the Venice, and Asha, Vivan, and I immediately accept the invitation. The serious girl declines and goes back to her table.

Balsi leads the way—through the restaurant, up countless flights of stairs, down a hallway, and into the room, which, being near a pantry, is thick with the smell of stale curry. It seems little larger than a train compartment. The impression is reinforced by clothes that, hanging from pegs, jut out into the room from all sides, half concealing the wooden beds under them. The furniture of the room consists entirely of four beds, which have somehow been fitted in at right angles to each other, leaving a narrow passage to the door. The floor space between the beds is taken up by a pillow and a large bath towel. On one of the beds a man is sound asleep. "This is the Venice telephone operator," Balsi says nonchalantly, pointing to the sleeping figure. "Edward, the Venice steward, also lives here." After telling me that Braz and Xavier do not live in the hotel, he continues, "Edward used to sleep on the towel, but one night a rat woke him up by jumping over him, and he couldn't sleep for the rest of the night. I gave him my bed, and now I sleep on the towel."

We all sit down on a couple of the beds, pushing against the clothes hanging at our backs to make ourselves comfortable. From under a bed Balsi brings out two quarter-pint-size whiskey bottles filled with Goan moonshine. He explains that the whiskey empties are picked up at the thieves' bazaar in Bombay, taken to Goa, filled with moonshine called Cashew or Phani, and smuggled back into Bombay for sale. (The point of the whiskey bottles, apparently, is to add a touch of class to the illicit trade.) He pours us each a thimbleful of Cashew and says, "Bottoms up! Cheerio!"

We drink. Cashew, made out of the fruit of the cashew tree, smells to me like vanilla extract but tastes a little gluey and sour, like milk that has been kept too long. After that, I'm content not to sniff or taste Phani, a coconut extract, but simply hold my breath and toss it down. Drink follows drink, and, to help Asha, Vivan, and me make a pretense of keeping up with the three musicians, Coca-Colas are produced from under the bed. (In spite of our noisy drinking and talking, the Venice telephone operator sleeps on, perhaps taking us for figures in a dream.)

"I may be leaving for America soon," Balsi says, settling down with another round of Phani. "I have a motorbike. It is my only worldly possession, and I hope to sell it for ten thousand rupees. I would then use five thousand rupees to buy a plane ticket to New York. The other five thousand I would give to a man I know. He is the father of a friend of mine who has already emigrated to America. I would try to get my friend in America to give me the equivalent of five thousand rupees in dollars when I got there. In New York, I'd work as a commercial artist during the day and play bass at a place like the Village Vanguard in the evening. In America, they appreciate good music."

Balsi quizzes me about jazz in New York. Asha and Vivan talk about what they will do once they reach England. Wancy—with nods of approval from Casmiro—talks about Goa as if it were a Riviera, dwelling on its singular history, which allowed the Portuguese settlers and the Goan natives to intermarry freely and adopt each other's customs, and describing its resortlike beaches, its climate, and its festive atmosphere of constant drinking, partying, and musicmaking.

When we come downstairs, there isn't a bearer in evidence. The restaurant seems all but closed for the night. Braz is sitting alone on the stage working out something on his sax, and while Asha, Vivan, and I take a table, and Wancy goes in search of coffee, Casmiro and Balsi join Braz. The three men are soon playing together, two accompanying the third as he strikes out on a little improvised jag of his own. The music comes through fuddled and wild.

Wancy returns with the coffee and stays at the table with us. Asha coquettishly snuggles up to him and says, "Wancy, darling, you're the best-looking member of the quintet." As though nothing were happening on the stage, she starts serenading him in a small, whispery voice with "My Funny Valentine," which she sings in a manner that exaggerates the song's mawkishness: "My funny, handsome valentine. Sweet, comic, handsome valentine . . ."

While Vivan looks on, amused, Wancy and Asha leave the table and start dancing a few steps. Asha continues her song. The music onstage comes to an abrupt halt. The couple continue to move around the tables, not so much dancing as doing a sort of vaudeville act.

"He's my drummer! He's my drummer!" Braz cries out, his voice cracking with anger. "Asha, I'm sacking Wancy! I'm giving him the sack! He will never play drums at the Venice as long as I am playing here. I will never play with him. You have no respect for the musician if you dance with him. Is it right? Is it right? Is it right that she should dance with my drummer? That she should dance with a musician? Do musicians have no respect? Should respectable musicians dance?"

Asha bursts into tears. Vivan takes her hand. Her crying subsides like a summer storm. Wancy remains fixed in one spot, and makes no effort to defend himself. Balsi tries to pacify Braz, but Braz continues his harangue.

He sounds like a betrayed man seeking full revenge. Balsi motions to us to go. I don't understand any of it.

In the taxi, Vivan says to me, "Don't worry. Asha's tears are just one of her nightly routines. It helps soothe her to sleep."

"Has Wancy really been given the sack?" I ask. "What happened to Braz? Every night, he plays for the belly dancer—"

"But a belly dancer's not a musician," Vivan interjects. "Braz just doesn't like the idea of a musician, who should know the value of music, dancing to jazz." He shifts his ground. "Braz's point is that if Wancy is on duty he should not be dancing. If he sacks Wancy tonight, he may be too proud to take him back tomorrow—and Wancy may be too proud to come back." Carefully avoiding any mention of Asha, Vivan goes on to analyze everyone else's conduct. "Since Braz has no opportunity to listen to any other good musicians, he only knows his own little world," he says at one point. "He thinks he is the best, and in that little world he may be the best. But he has therefore got bigheaded. They are all bigheaded."

When Vivan and Asha and I pull up in front of the Venice the following evening, Braz is standing outside smoking a cigarette. Asha, who has not eaten all day, sits quite still in the taxi. She conspicuously shuts her eyes, as if making a wish, and then slips out and runs up to Braz.

"Sorry, Asha," Braz says quickly. "I have sacked Wancy, and Balsi has quit with him. I gave Wancy the sack. He will never play at the Venice as long as I'm playing here. I will never play with him."

"Dave Brubeck is always quarrelling with Paul Desmond and making up with him," Vivan says lightly.

Braz starts to say something but stops, takes a drag on his cigarette, and walks away.

Inside, we ask the bearer who shows us to a table about Balsi and Wancy.

"They have moved on," he remarks casually. "Musicians are like that nowadays. You'll soon be able to hear them again. They'll be playing somewhere else."

The musicians take the stage. In appearance, the quintet seems unchanged; in the dark restaurant, two Goans manning the drums and bass could easily pass for Wancy and Balsi.

Asha, with a show of spirit, calls out to the two new musicians to ask whether they can sing. The drummer says he can croon, and Asha persuades him to sing. He does—with the slurred accents of a rock-and-roll star. I can make out only one protracted, repeated line: "I wanna pla-aace in your hea-art." When he finishes, Asha goes up and sweetly sings several songs, each more imaginatively than the last, with her large eyes full upon Braz, as if she were a *pujari* before a graven image.

The end of the evening finds Asha, Vivan, and me plying Casmiro, Xavier, and Braz with drinks in a speakeasy renowned for its undiluted Scotch—at undiluted prices—and the conversation skittishly roaming over every possible subject.

Finally, in the small hours of the morning, Vivan says, "How about it, Braz?"

"I don't like Wancy," Braz says. "He's not a good drummer. He's a no-good drummer. I've never liked him. For a year and a half I have worked with him and I haven't liked him. I am the greatest, and Xavier is next-greatest, and Casmiro—"

"Braz and Wancy have been at each other's throat for a year and a half," Xavier breaks in. "It had to come to a head sooner or later, and his dancing brought it to a head. Wancy was probably just high. Braz, you're very nice, but you have come in high yourself, and I've always said there should be a certain amount of give-and-take. If only I'd been there last night, perhaps I might have made peace."

"Xavier has made peace dozens of times before," Braz says. "He's the best peacemaker in the world. But this is a question of *respect*."

On subsequent evenings, we return to the Venice and we canvass other night spots, but there is no trace of Balsi or Wancy anywhere. "They may be in Calcutta or Philadelphia," a bearer at the Venice observes. "They may be vacationing in Goa. Who can say? This is Bombay." Another evening, when we drop by the Venice, the same bearer talks in nearly the same vein about Braz and Xavier, who are inexplicably absent from their places. "Xavier? I think he's playing the piano at the Sun 'n Sand, that new hotel a few miles from here, at Juhu Beach. Braz went to Delhi to the Gaylord—or is it the Volga? He has a job there." It isn't important to know which, I think as we wave to Casmiro and leave. At either the Gaylord or the Volga, Braz would be playing "Lemon Tree" or "Mamma Loves Papa, Papa Loves Mamma"—not jazz.

Asha gets her job, and she flies away to London for her training. Vivan gets his Commonwealth Fellowship and is to follow Asha to London, but not until the beginning of the academic year, in the autumn. Meanwhile, he plans to travel around India and paint.

III

The Sacred River

of the Hindus

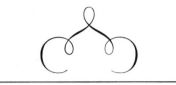

The Ageless Festival

IF RIVERS ARE RANKED ACCORDING TO LENGTH, the Nile, the Amazon, the Mississippi-Missouri-Red Rock, the Yangtze, the Ob, the Irtish, the Huang, the Congo, the Amur, the Lena, the Mackenzie-Peace, the Mekong, the Niger, the Parana, the Murray-Darling, and the Volga all take precedence over the Ganges—or the Ganga, as the Indians call it—and so do the two other major Indian rivers, the Indus and the Brahmaputra. However, for Hindus the Ganga has long had a unique importance. Hindus have gone for centuries to the banks of the Ganga to chant the names of the river, along with the names of the gods. In ancient times, Hindus called the Ganga the Surasarit, or the River of the Gods, and since then they have addressed the river by a hundred or a thousand different names. (The names of the Ganga, usually Sanskrit compound words, defy translation, but they may be rendered into English as Daughter of the Lord of Himalaya, Born from the Lotuslike Foot of Vishnu, Dwelling in the Matted Locks of Shiva, Taking Pride in the Broken Egg of Brahma, Having the Appearance of the Sacred Syllable Om, Resort of the Eminent, Flowing like a Staircase to Heaven, Leaping Over Mountains in Sport, Radiant like the Autumnal Moon, Light Amid the Darkness of Ignorance, Mother of the World, Protector of the Sick and Suffering Who Come for Refuge, Cow That Gives Much Milk, Making a Noise like a Conch Shell and Drum, Adorned with a Net of Water, Affording Delight to the Eye, Ever Moving, Having a Pure Body, Triple-Braided, Stimulator, and so on.) The Ganga, which rises as a snow pool from an ice cave in the Himalayas and, flowing swiftly through tortuous mountain valleys, follows a south-easterly course of about fifteen hundred miles to the Bay of Bengal, goes through some of the hottest plains in the world, but it has always been a river of great concentrations of people, and today nearly a third of India's population inhabits the Gangetic plains, living in some of the few great cities in the country (Benares, Allahabad, and Calcutta) and in some of the largest states (Uttar Pradesh, Bihar, and West Bengal). As a river, the Ganga is distinctive for sudden and frequent changes in its riverbed (the Ganga is always eroding its banks and then leaving them, to reappear as a new stream somewhere else), for severe floods (Ganga floods have been known to last as long as forty days), and for being generally capricious (the ruins of ancient cities and villages on its banks, or former banks, testify to the perpetual physical changes of the river). But the Ganga is perhaps most renowned for the extraordinary properties of its water. Although the river is used by the Hindus for ritual bathings and for ritual immersion of the bones and ashes of the dead, and for the disposal of diseased human corpses and the carcasses of animals, and although at numerous points the river receives sewage from open drains—conditions that continually introduce into the Ganga dangerous bacteria like the cholera vibrio—Ganga water is nevertheless considered to be quite pure. It is said that not only do most bacteria die in the water in a matter of hours but the bones of the dead dissolve in it with astonishing speed. (There is reported to be a tank of Ganga water at Soron, a town on the right bank of the river, in Uttar Pradesh, in which the bones of the dead dissolve in three days.) It is also said that, because of the special properties of the water, sailors used to prefer a supply of it to a supply of any other drinking water for long voyages. Now, as in the past, Hindu pilgrims to the river wash in the water, cook with it, and drink it. Indeed, to the Hindus the Ganga is so sacred that if once in his life a Hindu bathes in the Ganga—ideally, at one of the ancient sacred places, like Prayaga (the modern name is Allahabad), Benares, or Hardwar, and on one of the prescribed days during a *mela* (imperfectly translated by the English word "festival"), but also at any place or time—he is vouchsafed a more certain salvation than if he should devote himself to prayer and meditation from infancy to death, for in Hinduism the ritual of bathing enables a man to cross the ocean of life and transcend his mortal existence.

The time for a *mela* may be determined by an astrological event, like the conjunction of the sun and the moon, or by a legendary religious event, like the epic battle fought at Kurukshetra and described in the Bhagavad-Gita, or, of course, by the coincidence of an astrological event with a leg-

endary one, like the occurrence of the famous Kurukshetra *mela* during a
solar eclipse in 1962. The greatest *mela* of all is the Kumbha *mela* at
Prayaga. This *mela,* which is attended by hundreds of thousands, sometimes millions, of pilgrims from every part of India, all of them united in
the wish to take part in the bathing rites, is perhaps the largest religious
assemblage on earth. In recent years, the Institute of Indian Culture, in
Bombay, has been publishing, in English, under the general title of the
Book University, a series of a hundred books that are intended to provide
"higher education" and to disseminate "such literature as reveals the
deeper impulsions of India;" one book in this series is a paperback volume
of a hundred and ninety-nine pages, published in 1955, that is called
"Kumbha: India's Ageless Festival." Dilip Kumar Roy and Indira Devi
are the co-authors of "Kumbha," which has been commended by Indian
pandits for showing the central place of a *mela* in the life of a Hindu and
also for serving in itself as an illustration of the ancient spirit of the *mela.*

"Kumbha" has half a dozen prefaces. Among them is an invocation that
is a long poem from the pen of a friend of Roy's and Miss Devi's named
Richard Miller, to whom, in turn, the book is dedicated, with these lines:

> Who showed us once again that, East or West,
>> Wherever one calls for Light
> In simple faith—to him His Gleaming Grace
>> Will come her troth to plight.
>>>> With love,
>>>> DADA
>>>> INDIRA

("*Dada,*" which is Hindi for either "elder brother" or "grandfather," is
what Miss Devi calls Roy, both in the text and in life, as a footnote indicates; although she is not related to him by blood, she is identified in the
book as his "daughter disciple.")

The invocation by Miller is in harmony with Roy's and Miss Devi's
general approach:

> O Flame of Love and Truth,
> Burning flickerless in the storm-winds' throng!
> Herald Lord Krishna, playing the Marvel Flute.
>
> Lo, at the confluence of the twin hoary rivers,
> He beckons in endless Grace to all who yearn!
> Hark, hark, He calls to the waylost pilgrim souls:
> "Come, come, my children! Fret no more for phantoms.
> Float on my gleaming ocean of loveliness,

> Sent in streams of ambrosia over India's mountains:
> Ganga and Yamuna flowing."

(The Yamuna, or Jumna, River rises, like the Ganga, in the north, but flows first south and then southeast; because of its association with Lord Krishna, it is the second most sacred river to Hindus.) The poem, itself an "ambrosial" abstraction, continues for forty-four more lines.

In the body of the book, Roy and Miss Devi, to suggest the origin of the Kumbha *mela,* retell one of the many delightful Hindu stories of the creation. Before the creation of Heaven and earth, there was a primeval ocean, on which Brahma, the God of gods, floated in a trance. He awoke, and, wishing to manifest himself in multiplicity, created the cosmos. Lesser gods and demons, not satisfied with the creation, took the mountain Mandar and the python Ananta Naga and, making of them a paddle and a rope, set about churning the primeval ocean. The waters heaved evil gases, but Lord Shiva drained the gases away in a long draught. Then the cow and the flying horse and the lyre and the siren came out of the ocean, followed by Dhanvantari, the physician of the gods, who carried in his arms a pitcher filled with nectar that had the power to bestow immortality. The lesser gods and demons fought for possession of the pitcher. The demons won it, but Dhanvantari turned himself into a rook, snatched the pitcher from the demons, and started flying toward Paradise. In the course of his flight, which took him twelve days, he rested and refreshed himself at four places on the earth—Prayaga, Hardwar, Nasik, and Ujjain. (Sayana, the fourteenth-century Vedic commentator, interprets this creation story as an allegory in which the nectar is actually the God of gods, the lesser gods are the forces of good, the demons are the forces of evil, and the pitcher is man. The more the forces of evil prevail in man, the more he is hidden from the God of gods by *maya,* and the more the forces of good prevail in him, the closer he is brought to the God of gods.)

This creation story varies from account to account (in another version the pitcher broke during the struggle, spilling the nectar on Prayaga, Hardwar, Nasik, and Ujjain), but, in whatever version, the story is regarded as a basis for the Kumbha *melas* ("*kumbha*" is the Sanskrit word for "pitcher"), which are usually held in a twelve-year cycle so that every three years there can be a Kumbha *mela* at one of the four consecrated places. Among the four Kumbha *melas,* the one at Prayaga is preëminent, because it takes place by the *sangam* (from "*samgama,*" Sanskrit for "union")—the spot where the right bank of the Ganga meets the left bank of the Yamuna, just below Prayaga, and the waters of the two rivers flow together. (It is popularly believed that the *sangam* also receives the waters of a third sacred river, a mythical underground stream called the Sarasvati.) The duodecennial cycle of Kumbha *melas* is probably recent, but it happens that the Kumbha *mela* at Prayaġa is observed in Magha (a month in the Hindu lunar calendar corresponding to parts of January and February), and the Magha *melas* at Prayaga are probably the oldest in the country. The first detailed account of attending a *mela* was set down by Hsuan-tsang, a seventh-century Chinese Buddhist who made a pilgrimage to India, the birthplace of Buddha, in search of religious instruction. (The record of his travels, along with accounts of other Chinese pilgrims in the early Buddhist period, was preserved in China as part of the sacred writings of Buddhism.) For a time, Hsuan-tsang was a guest of Siladitya-Raja, also known as King Harsha, whose dominion extended over most of northern India. According to Hsuan-tsang, King Harsha put up thousands of *stupas* on the banks of the Ganga, built hospices in all the towns and villages for the care of the sick, the poor, and the homeless, and forbade the killing of animals on pain of death. Hsuan-tsang writes that King Harsha "sought to plant the tree of religious merit to such an extent that he forgot to sleep or to eat," and goes on to report on some of King Harsha's more spectacular religious activities, describing a religious convocation in Kanauj, the capital of Harsha's empire:

> It was now the second month of springtime. . . . All along . . . there were highly decorated pavilions, and places where musicians were stationed. . . . The king . . . made them bring forth on a gorgeously caparisoned great elephant a golden statue of Buddha about three feet high, and raised aloft. On the left went the king, Siladitya . . . whilst Kumara-Raja [the prince regent] . . . went on the right. Each of them had as an escort five hundred war elephants clad in armor; in front and behind the statue of Buddha went one hundred great elephants, carrying musicians, who sounded their drums and raised their music. The king, Siladitya, as he went, scattered on every side pearls and various precious substances, with gold and silver flowers. . . . Having first washed the image in scented water at the altar, the King then himself bore it on his shoulder to . . . a tower, where he offered to it tens, hundreds, and thousands of silken garments, decorated with precious gems. . . . After the feast, they assembled the different men of learning, who discussed in elegant language the most abstruse subjects.

Many of these celebrants escorted King Harsha from Kanauj to Prayaga for his quinquennial ritual of almsgiving. At the Prayaga ceremony, which was attended by throngs of monks and mendicants from all parts of Harsha's empire, Harsha occupied himself for seventy-five days with a public renunciation of his treasuries.

> Between the two confluents of the river [Hsuan-tsang writes], for the space of ten li or so, the ground is pleasant upland. The whole is covered with a fine sand. From old times till now, the kings and noble families, whenever they had occasion to distribute their gifts in charity, ever came to this place, and here gave away their goods. . . . At the present time, Si-laditya-Raja, after the example of his ancestors, distributes here . . . the accumulated wealth of five years.

Harsha heaped on this ground all his gold and jewels, making gifts first to the statue of Buddha, then to statues of Hindu gods, then to ten thousand monks, then to Brahmans, then to Jains, and then to beggars, widows, and orphans. When he had renounced everything, including his raiment, his vassal rajas went from beneficiary to beneficiary, using their own money to buy back the gifts, which they later restored to the King, so that he was as rich as he had been before coming to Prayaga. The vassal rajas apparently felt that this ransoming of King Harsha's property was a way of doing him homage; Harsha, for his part, felt that the act of renunciation had earned him merit. Commenting on this extraordinary ritual, Arthur Waley writes of Harsha, "He said that if he did not from time to time get rid of all his possessions his 'merit' (*punya*) would not grow and his run of luck might be broken; to which he added that safeguarding one's property involved a lot of worry and anxiety. As he knew that he was shortly to get his property all back and once more have the worry of looking after it, the second argument seems to fall completely to the ground; and one would have supposed that if 'luck' is acquired by giving away it must surely be 'broken' by taking back one's gifts."

But not all the offerings that Hsuan-tsang witnessed at Prayaga and the *sangam* were merely symbolic. He records that other pilgrims held these places so sacred that in the hope of attaining immortality they came there to drown themselves or mortify their flesh:

> At the confluence of the two rivers, every day there are many hundreds of men who bathe themselves and die. The people of this country consider that whoever wished to be born in Heaven ought to fast to a grain of rice, and then drown himself in the waters. By bathing in this water (they say) all the pollution of sin is washed away and destroyed; therefore from various quarters and distant regions people come here together and rest. During seven days they abstain from food, and afterward end their lives. . . .
> The heretics [to the Buddhists, Hindus were heretics] who practice ascet-

icism have raised a high column in the middle of the river; when the sun is about to go down they immediately climb up the pillar; then, clinging on to the pillar with one hand and one foot, they wonderfully hold themselves out with one foot and one arm; and so they keep themselves stretched out in the air with their eyes fixed on the sun, and their heads turning with it to the right as it sets. When the evening has darkened, then they come down. . . . They hope by these means to escape from birth and death, and many continue to practice this ordeal through several decades of years.

Two centuries before Hsuan-tsang's Indian pilgrimage, Kalidasa, one of the greatest Sanskrit poets, described, in his epic "Raghuvamsa," the beauty of the *sangam* in similes that contrast the traditional whiteness of the Ganga with the blueness of the Yamuna, Ganga's sister stream:

> See where Ganga's stream meets the waves of Yamuna
> Like a necklace of spaced pearls
> On which alternating sapphires cast their light,
> Or like a garland of white lotuses
> Interwoven with dark waterlilies;
> Here like a flight of wild geese
> Flying from Lake Manasa against the thunderclouds,
> There like a design upon the cheek of Lady Earth,
> Painted with black aloe over sandalpaste;
> Like moonlight speckled with spots of darkness in the shade of trees,
> Or like white clouds of autumn opening on patches of blue sky;
> Like the very body of Lord Shiva,
> Covered with holy ash and wearing cobras for his ornaments.

Roy and Miss Devi follow the long literary and religious tradition of celebrating the sacred rivers.

A poor pilgrim in Hardwar [Roy reports] once admonished me when, inadvertently, I had spat into the Ganga while bathing. "You, a *pilgrim*, must never spit into the Ganga," he said. "For, others may deny, but *you* must accept that the Ganga *is* a Devi, a Divine Mother, who has been sent to us from Heaven to absolve us from our earthliness." I was startled to realize how living and deep-rooted was our veneration for the Ganga. Millions of men and women who believe in symbols and in their power to turn our consciousness Godward cherish the Ganga as a super-conscient Mother, an emblem of purity—a Mother who is at once human and divine. In the one aspect she gives us physical purity, washing away our dust and sweat; in the other, that inner purity, which purges us of our wrong desires. It is to teach this that our saints and sages have all along enjoined on us to look upon her as the "molten compassion" of the Supreme.

Not only in devotional works like "Kumbha" but also in the epics, the Ganga is often exalted as a divine mother, and whenever the river is so exalted, the *sadhus* (Sanskrit for "pious man") and sages are described again and again as if they were the Mother's male counterpart.

The main purpose of Roy and Miss Devi is to elevate the mystical at the expense of the rational. (Their book is full of inspired sources.) The authors go as pilgrims to the Kumbha *mela* at Prayaga in 1954, the first in independent India, and describe at length and with rapture the many mystical experiences they had there. A fourth of the book is an imaginary dialogue between a Western rationalist and an Indian yogi.

PRAYAGA, the holy town—Allahabad, India [the playlet opens]. In a small but charming hut on the bank of the immemorial Ganga, two men are discovered conversing on the . . . Kumbha day. The younger of the two, an Englishman and an Orientalist, is in his early thirties. Dressed in a blue lounge suit, he looks distinguished and virile, if not aggressive. We will call him WEST. The other is a Yogi in his middle sixties—radiant, tranquil, and extremely handsome. He is reputed to be a God-realized saint, which is the reason, perhaps, why he looks at once humble and confident, keen-eyed and sympathetic. His eyes are the most remarkable part of him, penetrating and alert and yet radiating kindliness like twin stars. He often smiles, though somewhat abstractedly. He is dressed in the traditional ochre-colored robe— *gerua*—of the Indian mystic, with a *tulsi* garland round his shining neck. We will call him EAST. "Oh, but he is a Vaishnava of the traditional type!"— say his detractors, the ultra-moderns. "But he can deliver the goods," counter his admirers, not to mention his disciples. Time—afternoon.

WEST: I have a few questions to ask you, sir—that is, if you have time.

EAST (*smiling*): We live in eternity, my friend, haven't they told you?

WEST (*smiling back reassured*): We Westerners are—I warn you, sir— somewhat—er—critical, though not irreverent, I hope.

EAST: What made you come to me? Are you a reporter of a paper?

WEST (*deprecating*): No, not nearly as bad as that. I am, well, a—student of philosophy. . . . You see, I saw you, in the morning, bathing at the confluence with your eyes fixed on the sun. It impressed me, for you looked for a long time at the sun without blinking. . . . There was a light on your face which—er—shall we say, spoke to me. . . . I felt—er—strangely drawn to you. (*Pause*) I cannot accept hearsay, either, but—er—I assure you I— well, I am open to conviction.

EAST (*with a faint smile*): But on your own terms, is that it?

WEST (*coloring*): I don't get you, sir—

EAST: What I mean is: you came to me to be convinced, but only through mental reasonings. Am I not right? But in that case—I warn you, in my turn —you have come to the wrong shop. For the One who is beyond philosophy happens to be too strong and elusive to be grasped by so weak a net as can be woven by the mind, with its arguments.

WEST: Alas, sir, but it's the only net we have!

EAST: What about the other—that of the *Atman?*

WEST (*pulling a long face*): You don't mean—the Soul?

Roy's and Miss Devi's script continues for forty-four more pages, and just prior to the curtain it reads:

EAST . . . (*closes his eyes. . . . Two tears slowly trickle down his cheeks, as he sings abstractedly in a low voice*):

> *Esha devo Vishwakarma Mahatma*
> *Sada jananam hridaye sannivishtah:*
> *Hrida manisha manasa 'bhiklipto*
> *Ya etad vidur amritas te bhavanti.*

The quotation, which is from the Svetsvatara Upanishad, may be translated as "The great-souled god, responsible for all acts, is ever present in the hearts of men, appearing as feeling, intelligence, and understanding. Those who know this to be so become immortal."

Being in India in 1966, I prepare to go as a pilgrim to independent India's second Kumbha *mela* at Prayaga. As a first step, I get hold of a state guidebook to Uttar Pradesh—a guidebook that, from its opening sentences, sets a grandiose, if apologetic, tone:

It would not be inappropriate to describe Uttar Pradesh as the centre of the stage on which the drama of Indian history has been played. . . . Uttar Pradesh has reflected and interpreted the significance of the most important events in the country's history, though it has not actually staged many.

As a second step, I tackle the special Kumbha number of the Uttar Pradesh *Panchayati Raj Gazette,* which is represented by the state government as an indispensable guide for pilgrims, and which, I discover, brings up to date and amplifies Roy's and Miss Devi's book. (Because Uttar Pradesh is in the vanguard of the movement to eliminate all traces of Westernization in India and to rediscover the Golden Age of Hinduism, the *Gazette* has an aura of sanctity about it, but because it is written in heavily Sanskritized Hindi, it is beyond the reach of most of even those pilgrims who can read and write.) According to the *Gazette,* the duodecennial cycle of Kumbha *melas* derives its significance not only from Dhanvantari's twelve-day flight but from the fact that a student of Sanskrit grammar, "the chief of all sciences," must traditionally study twelve years before he can attain the title either of *pandit* or of *shastri*. Further, the mystical significance of the twelve-year study perhaps derives from the recognition in Hindu philosophy of twelve instincts in man—five associated with sense organs, five with motor organs, and two, perception and reason, with the mind—all of which must be mastered if one is to rise above attachments and aversions, pleasures and pains, and achieve inner happiness. The *Gazette* dwells on the great boons of the *sangam,* stating that a bath in the *sangam* any time in Magha of any year is a thousand times as beneficial as a bath anywhere in the Ganga any time in Ashwina (parts of September and October) or any time in Kartika (parts of October and November), and ten million times as beneficial as a bath in any other sacred river any time in Chaitra (parts of March and April) or any time in Vaishakha (parts of April and May), and is even more beneficial than giving away millions of cows as alms. The boons of a bath in the *sangam* in Magha during a Kumbha *mela* are so numerous that not even Brahma can hope to count them, the *Gazette* says. It goes on to praise both the temporal preëminence of Prayaga ("Prayaga's leading role in the social, religious, political, and economic fields has existed for thousands of years. . . . Both Nehru and Shastri came from Prayaga. One can no more dismiss this as an accident of history—as something unconnected with Prayaga's long religious traditions—than fail to detect the hand of some inscrutable power behind these developments") and its divine preëminence ("The loins of the earth are betwixt the Ganga and the Yamuna. . . . Besides the Trinity of Brahma, Vishnu, and Shiva, all gods and goddesses, sages and *sadhus* . . . and celestial nymphs dwell here. . . . Taking, in the right spirit, even a single step in the direction of Prayaga is an expiation of one's sins").

According to the *Gazette,* several million Hindus were expected to attend the 1966 Kumbha *mela* at Prayaga. Arrangements for the gathering, which would help to bind the country together on the political level as well as in other ways, were being made in accordance with the 1938 Uttar Pradesh Mela Act, which had standardized the existing methods of controlling the business transactions of the *mela.* The Act had empowered the local district magistrate to form a committee of legislators, prominent citizens, and representatives of participating religious and voluntary groups, and, in consultation with this committee, to fix any tolls, registration fees, and license fees and to levy taxes on animals, vehicles, persons, and processions at the *mela;* also, at his own discretion, to frame rules about the movement of goods, the health of persons, and the extent of photographing, hunting, and fishing, to oversee the size, type, allotment, re-allotment, and rental of all plots and dwellings, to inspect premises, to confiscate goods, and to search out and punish offenders. Further arrangements for the 1966 Kumbha *mela* called for subdividing the whole area into sectors, each with its own additional magistrate or, in the case of the larger sectors, with two additional magistrates; for constructing new roads, broadening old roads, mapping out routes for vehicles, pedestrians, and river craft, and floating pontoon bridges; for opening money-changing booths and a branch of the State Bank of India; for organizing thousands of volunteer attendants; for installing electric lighting, and erecting watch, control, and direction towers equipped with radio, television, telephones, and flood-lights; and for setting up rest stations, inquiry counters, government exhibitions, fair-price shops, fire stations, police stations, first-aid posts, and hospitals. Addenda to the *Gazette* gave these statistics: two crores of rupees would be spent by the Uttar Pradesh government alone; sixty-two special trains would be coming to the *mela* each week; sixty thousand pilgrims would be able to bathe in the *sangam* at one time; seven thousand policemen would be on duty; forty-two hundred sweepers would be employed; and in the *mela* area there would be eight post offices, thirteen tube wells, a thousand taps, sixty miles of water pipes, and three hundred and thirty-six thousand trench latrines. Among an enumeration of "do"s and "don't"s in the *Gazette* was the counsel "Do not travel on the footboards, roofs, and buffers of trains. . . . Getting on top of any train is dangerous —particularly in the case of trains running between Allahabad-Mughal Sarai and Allahabad-Kanpur, because electric wires of 25,000 kilowatts pass over them."

Naturally, the difficulty inherent in planning for any *mela* is stupendous, and in the *Gazette's* discussion of the arrangements one detected an over-zealous tone, as if the *Gazette* were haunted by the memory of the 1954 Kumbha *mela* at Prayaga, the most important *mela* of the century. It seems that from the ancient period Hindus have believed that auspicious times for religious ceremonies like bathing are governed by the movements of the sun (the lord of the soul), the moon (the lord of perception), and the planet Jupiter (the lord of reason). The most auspicious part of the year for bathing is between the winter solstice, when the sun appears to begin moving northward, and the summer solstice, when the sun appears to reverse its direction—events set by Hindu astrologers on the 14th of January and the 14th of July, respectively, or some three weeks later than the dates used in the West. In this auspicious period, which is called Uttarayana (Sanskrit for "northward course"), the most auspicious time for bathing is in Magha—or, rather, in the part of it that falls between the beginning of Makara Rashi, the sign of Capricorn, and the beginning of Kumbha Rashi, the sign of Aquarius. In Magha (or, strictly, under Makara Rashi), the most auspicious day for bathing is Amavasya, the New Moon Day, which is the last day of the dark half of a lunar month, when the sun and the moon, at the time of their conjunction, appear to be of the same degree. (Although the sun stays for about a month in each house of the zodiac, and the moon for two and a quarter days, they appear to be of the same degree for only a day.) Every twelfth year—or, very rarely, every eleventh or thirteenth year—the appearance of the sun in Capricorn coincides with the appearance of Jupiter in Aries. This astrological event is the occasion for the Kumbha *mela* at Prayaga, because bathing then is even more auspicious than during any other Magha (or, again, strictly, under any other Makara Rashi). Every hundred and eight years, however (some Hindu astrologers reckon every hundred and forty-four years), there are still other astrological phenomena in Makara Rashi during the time of the Kumbha *mela* at Prayaga, such as a lunar eclipse; this is the occasion for a Purna (Sanskrit for "perfect" or "full") Kumbha, and bathing then is incomparably auspicious. The astrologers and *pandits* in all parts of the country were unanimous in ranking the 1954 *mela* as a Purna Kumbha.

Because of technological progress since the nineteenth-century Purna Kumbha, Prayaga had become a junction of several main railway lines and also of several main roads, including the Grand Trunk Road, and, partly for this reason, more pilgrims than ever before were expected to attend the twentieth-century Purna Kumbha. Yet at any one time no more than sixty thousand pilgrims could bathe in the *sangam*. The *sangam* is a few miles down the Ganga from Prayaga, which lies between the two rivers. All pilgrims had to enter the *sangam* from a small wedge of land— only a hundred and sixty feet across at its narrowest point—lying between the two rivers and beside a great Mogul fort. Emperor Akbar had built the fort in the sixteenth century, on the right, or west, bank of the Ganga, in view of the *sangam,* and had called the fort Ilahabas (Urdu for "abode of God")—a name that his grandson, the Emperor Shah Jehan, altered to Allahabad, which in British times replaced Prayaga as the name of the city. A high embankment extending from Akbar's fort to the city was built to protect the foundations of the fort from being eroded away by the changes in the Ganga's channel—in this area the changes were so frequent that new bridges had to be put up practically every year—but an additional effect of the barrier formed by the embankment was that whenever the Ganga cut its channel close to Akbar's fort the wedge of land that constituted the *mela* bathing area was drastically reduced. (Between 1942 and 1954, for instance, the bathing area had been reduced from five hundred and twenty-one acres to a mere seventy-five acres.) At the *melas,* this bathing area was often further reduced by a sort of shantytown that materialized around the *sangam* and Akbar's fort. The makeshift dwellings were inhabited by Brahmans, who were connected with the bathing rites; by *sadhus,* who came to bathe; and by barbers, whose presence was explained by the belief that any Hindu who had his head shaved above the *sangam* was promised as many years in Heaven as the number of his hairs that fell into the water. In 1954, the authorities were able to uproot some of these campers and resettle them in Jhusi, a village that lies on the east bank of the Ganga, across from the wedge of land, thereby enlarging the entire *mela* area to about fifteen hundred acres, but other campers proved too well entrenched by custom to be moved. Moreover, the layout of the local roads from Allahabad was such that most pilgrims going to and from the bathing area had to use one or the other of two ramps descending the side of the embankment near the fort; the layout of the bridges across the Ganga from Jhusi was such that most campers going to and from the bathing area had to pass the foot of the ramps; and all three of the approaches to the bathing area—the Mahabirji Temple Road, the Sangam Road, and the Gangapati Road—were narrow, sandwiched between the embankment and the Ganga.

The chances of dangerous congestion on the ramps, on the bridges, and on the three crucial approaches were increased because a number of *akharas,* or sectarian organizations, of *sadhus* who regularly attended the Kumbha *melas* paraded on important *mela* days to the *sangam,* where members of each *akhara* bathed en masse. Altogether there were eight such *akharas*—the Mahanirvani Akhara, the Niranjani-*cum*-Juna Akharas, the Nirvani Akhara, the Digambar Akhara, the Nirmohi Akhara, the Chhota Panchayati Akhara, the Bara Panchayati Akhara, and the Nirmala-*cum*-Vrindavani Akharas. The *sadhus* in each of these *akharas* had certain bonds, like the worship of Shiva, the trade of banking, or the practice of mendicancy or of nudism. Each *akhara* was fierce and militant about its practices, and each was extremely jealous of its own *akhara;* considering its procession a demonstration of its status, each wanted its own to be grander than the next. The militancy of these *sadhus* dated from the fifteenth and sixteenth centuries, when *sadhus* had first organized themselves into paramilitary *akharas* to resist Mogul interference with Hindu bathing rites. Upon the advent of the British, who, as a matter of policy, did not interfere with the religious practices of their subjects, the *akharas,* while losing their original raison d'être, had kept up their military traditions. Although, according to Hindu sacred writings, a *sadhu* ought to exemplify *nirasa, visada,* and *gunamaya* (Sanskrit for "freedom from emotional attachments," "freedom from ignorance," and "goodness"), the *sadhus* of these *akharas* valued physical prowess as much as spiritual attainment. Although other groups of *sadhus* went naked as a symbolic gesture of renunciation, these *akharas,* in recent times, had vaingloriously hired men to march naked in their processions. Although other *sadhus* at the *melas* went from their camps to the *sangam* individually or in loosely organized groups, singing hymns and reciting *mantras* (Sanskrit for "prayers"), these *akharas* still marched to the *sangam* in military formation, as if they were going to an aboriginal war, many of the *sadhus* (or their hired entourage) in each procession marching naked, and waving flags or beating fire tongs or brandishing swords, lances, or tridents; the processions being accompanied by drums, gongs, bugles, and conchs; and some *sadhus* proceeding on elephants with elaborately painted howdahs, on decorated camels or horses, in gold or silver palanquins, or, lately, in jeeps or cars. The *akharas* were so much a part of a Kumbha *mela* that their processions and their bathing had become its greatest public event.

In 1954, because of bureaucratic confusion, some of the precious space around Akbar's fort was given over to a *sangam* railway station for special shuttle trains from Allahabad; shopkeepers, *sadhus,* pilgrims, and at least ten thousand beggars were allowed to set up their camps around the railway station, not only above and below the ramps but along the three approaches to the *sangam*—areas that should all have been left free for the movement of the crowds. Moreover, for all those entering Allahabad and its outlying areas, arrangements had originally been made for compulsory inoculation against cholera (in spite of the special properties of Ganga water, outbreaks of cholera were common at bathing *melas*), but, as a result of protests against the delay and harassment that the inoculations entailed, the authorities had, about a week before Amavasya, abandoned this health requirement and, with it, most of their control over the movement of the crowds to the *sangam.*

On Amavasya, a million pilgrims bathed between midnight and sunrise. After sunrise, when the processions of the *akharas* were due to start from their camps in Jhusi, the crowds were without precedent. The authorities had so staggered the order of the processions that the Mahanirvanis, who were to form the first procession, were to leave their camp at six o'clock in the morning, and the Nirmala-*cum*-Vrindavanis, who were to form the last, were to return to their camp by four-thirty in the afternoon. The official timetable called for the Mahanirvanis to travel from their camp to the *sangam*—across the Ganga and over the Sangam Road—by seven; bathe; start on the return journey, by the Mahabirji Temple Road, at seven-forty-five, passing the first ramp, designated for ingress, at eight-five and reaching the Ganga's Bridge No. 3 (one of half a dozen newly constructed bridges over the Ganga) at eight-twelve; cross the bridge; and continue to their camp, reaching it at eight-thirty. The Niranjani-*cum*-Junas, whose procession was second, were to follow the identical route exactly an hour later. The Mahanirvanis left on schedule, and their magnificent procession was viewed by dense crowds all along the way to the *sangam*. Some pilgrims jostled forward to see the *tamasha,* some to receive their *darshana* (Sanskrit for "holy audience"), some to touch the feet of the *sadhus,* some to pick up dust from the ground that the *sadhus* had trodden on, and some to get a glimpse of the *nagas,* or naked *sadhus,* for it was popularly believed that women who were barren would be made fertile by seeing a *naga.* In spite of the crowds, the Mahanirvanis were able to keep to the timetable until their arrival at the ingress ramp on their return journey. Then their procession stopped. All night pilgrims, as many as a hundred abreast, had been arriving at the *mela* area on foot from Allahabad; all night other pilgrims, many of them carrying loads and bundles on their heads, had been pouring out of the *sangam* railway station; and all night both crowds of pilgrims had been moving steadily down the ingress ramp. Many of the pilgrims were in a state of exhaustion from the journey, but there was no way to rest, or even to turn back, for a pilgrim, once caught in the *mela* crowd, could only move forward in the direction of the *sangam.* By the time the Mahanirvanis reached the ingress ramp, the crowd was surging, pushing, stumbling toward the *sangam,* and the pressure from behind was relentless.

The only reliable account of what happened next—or, indeed, of the entire 1954 *mela*—is contained in a volume bearing the official title "Report of the Committee Appointed by the Uttar Pradesh Government to Enquire Into the Mishap Which Occurred in the Kumbha Mela at Prayaga on the 3rd February, 1954." From the report, it seems that about a dozen cars and a couple of elephants at the head of the Mahanirvani procession remained stationary immediately across the foot of the ramp for at least an hour, partly because several of the cars, which were forced to advance almost at a crawl, got overheated and stalled. Such police as had been assigned to control the crowd became lost in it. Yet more and more pilgrims were joining the crowd from the *sangam* railway station, where trains were still arriving, adding to the pressure on the crowd now trapped on the ramp. The congestion, already suffocating, worsened when the Niranjani-*cum*-Junas, in accordance with their timetable, arrived in the area on their way to the *sangam*. A couple of pilgrims tried to escape from the crush by slipping through a gap between the two lead elephants in the Mahanirvani procession. Other pilgrims followed. Several *nagas,* incensed by the violation of their procession line, stabbed at the pilgrims with their tridents in order to force them back. At this, the crowd, becoming panic-stricken, surged in the one direction it could take—to one side of the ramp, toward a big ditch partly filled with water, near which about a hundred beggars squatted, and near·which, also, a group of *sadhus* who were not part of any *akhara* had set up their camp—only to be attacked with long iron fire tongs by these *sadhus*. It had rained during the night, and the ground was swampy. Pilgrims were struck down by other pilgrims, who carried sticks and staffs. Pilgrims fell over bundles that had been dropped, over one another, and over the beggars on the ground. All were caught in the stampede. The Mahanirvani procession, lurching forward, somehow rammed its way through the crowd and across Bridge No. 3 to Jhusi. Fifty or sixty *nagas* at the end of the procession were left behind, however, and they set about clearing a path for themselves with their weapons. Some pilgrims tried to reach safety in Jhusi by clambering onto the bridges, but the bridges were small and unstable; one pontoon bridge collapsed under the weight of the people who rushed onto it, and plunged them all into the Ganga, which was crowded with boats, many of which now capsized. Everywhere, people died. They were trampled to death, swept into the ditch, or drowned in the river.

The authorities were helpless. Dr. Rajendra Prasad and Nehru (the President and Prime Minister of India) and K. M. Munshi and Govind Vallabh Pant (the Governor and Chief Minister of Uttar Pradesh) were at the *mela* with their families or with official parties, but they could do nothing except look on, from their boats or launches, from the banks of the rivers, or from the terraces of Akbar's fort. When the authorities were finally able to assert control, they stopped the special trains bound for the *mela,* cordoned off the bathing area for the remainder of the day, and made what use they could of the police. The casualties nevertheless continued to grow. Official estimates put the number of dead—who included pilgrims so disfigured that they could not be identified—at five hundred, and the number of injured at twice that. Unofficial estimates put the numbers of dead and injured much higher—in the thousands. The dead were cremated on the banks of the rivers and their ashes immersed in the sacred waters, as is the Hindu practice.

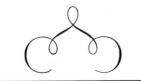

The Loins of the Earth Are
Betwixt the Ganga and the Yamuna

TODAY, I AM IN ALLAHABAD, which, like the other Indian cities, is a jumble of British, Muslim, and Hindu influences. The British Allahabad, which now exists only for the benefit of a few educated Indians, takes in the military and civil cantonments, the race course, the clubs, and the university. The Muslim Ilahabas is well represented by Akbar's great fort, which lies three miles to the east of the city, but the wedge of land has by now been so eroded that the water flows very close to the embankment, leaving a correspondingly larger sandbank at Jhusi, across the Ganga. The ancient Hindu Prayaga can be observed in the parched, dusty, but joyful faces of tens of thousands of pilgrims coming to the city on the Grand Trunk Road—some in buses, tongas, ekkas, and bullock carts, some on bicycles, horses, and even elephants, but most on foot, patiently trudging, with loads on their head, as if they had been walking for years.

The country is in mourning for the death of Prime Minister Shastri, at Tashkent, but the *mela* goes on, and at one point on the day before Amavasya I find myself resting in a tent—pitched near the *sangam*—which I have reserved in advance, and composing a letter to Roy and Miss Devi, who print in "Kumbha" a letter to a friend relating some of their experiences at the Purna Kumbha *mela* of 1954:

I have heard from you such a lot about the *sadhus* you have met [their letter says] that I may as well return the compliment by telling you about a few *we* have had the good fortune to contact here—at the Kumbha *mela*.

What we have seen at this great congregation of *sadhus* and pilgrims has moved us to our depths. We were given, as it were, a glimpse into the heart of Reality, the Great Reality that *is* India—where dreams come true and the dynasty of the holy still abides! We may well be proud. But to begin . . .

And my letter, never sent, begins, "Once, in your book, you resorted to a letter, as though that perfunctory but intimate form were the best you had at your disposal for conveying an impression of the *mela*. I have just spent some time at Jhusi, which is one vast stretch of saffron tents interrupted by straw huts, by sheds roofed with sheets of corrugated iron, by bamboo towers, and by bamboo poles flying the flags or signs of every imaginable sect of *sadhus*. And though I am not clear yet about what those dreams are that come true here, at times I did feel as though I were sleepwalking through some celestial bazaar. Or was it a medieval battlefield with hordes of Saracens in disarray? No, perhaps it was an ancient camp of Hannibal. Every man or beast was covered with dust. In front of the tents, which seemed to extend nearly to the horizon, camp fires burned. By the camp fires, beneath the open sky, were huddles of squatting *sadhus* and milling or motionless crowds of pilgrims. Now and again, I passed an elephant, festooned with flower garlands and embroidered rugs. All along the way, beggars held out their bowls, into which pilgrims dropped coins or grain. There were naked *sadhus* and *sadhus* opulently robed. There were *sadhus* wearing *dhotis* and marigolds, with horizontal stripes of ash on their foreheads. There were *sadhus* with ash-smeared naked bodies, offering *ghi, jaggery,* and *sesamum* to a sacrificial fire that crackled in a brazier, and chanting 'Hare Ram. Hare Krishna. Hare Om.' Elsewhere, *sadhus* were shaking bells or clapping tongs or cymbals, or were singing or haranguing crowds over loudspeakers, or were leaping up and down, or were hanging by their feet from trees. Here was a *sadhu* reclining on a bed of thorns; there was a *sadhu* waist-deep in mud; nearby, a *sadhu* stood on one foot, and opposite him another balanced himself on one arm; farther along were *sadhus* fixed in still other yogic contortions. Beyond, a man wearing a skimpy loincloth was in the middle of a ritualistic dance to the music of a harmonium. Then, there was a group of seated men, each with a finger pressed to his lips. Opposite them sat other men, each with his forefingers in his ears. The names of the sects of *sadhus* were as endless as the ways they conceived of God: for the Vedantists, it was as the One; for the Vaishnavas, as all things; for the Shankarites, as the self; for the Tantriks, as the doctrines in their sacred books; for the Shaktas, as Kali; for the Shaivas and Avadhutas, as Mother Ganga—all, of course, overlapping even as they asserted their contradictions."

Since at the *mela* anyone can go anywhere and talk to anyone, I visit a number of the *sadhus'* camps at Jhusi. On a *gaddi* (Hindi for "cushion") of straw in one tent, pitched a little apart from the others, a man sits silent and withdrawn, like a *guru*. Near him sits a fast-talking man who is answering questions addressed to the silent man by an Indian filmmaker.

"Looking at your face, I get the impression you have achieved great peace," the filmmaker is saying, in Urdu. "In your eyes there is this wonderful glow of happiness. How do you achieve this peace?" He adds, "This question may seem very foolish to you, but I would like to know if you encounter any difficulty in keeping your vow of celibacy."

"How do I know you're not a spy?" the fast-talking man asks.

"Spy for what?" the filmmaker cries.

The man on the *gaddi* seems about to say something, but the fast-talking man speaks up again. "You could be a spy for another *akhara,* or a spy for the government," he says.

The filmmaker courteously identifies himself as Habib Tanvir and explains that he is shooting a documentary on the Kumbha *mela,* which he hopes to sell to the B.B.C.

The fast-talking man listens warily, and then says, "The question you ask about peace would take months to answer, because the answer is very difficult, and I would have to go through many highways and byways. As for the other matter, if you have had that experience, it's much more difficult. It's not at all difficult for us, because we have never had that experience."

One large colony of tents is marked by a sign that reads, "Spiritual Regeneration Movement Foundation of India." This is the headquarters of Maharishi Mahesh Yogi. I know of him, or know the few available facts about him (all uncorroborated): that he was born around 1910; that his father was a revenue inspector; that he attended Allahabad University; that he worked in a factory for a time; that for some years he studied in the Himalayas with the *jagadguru* Shankaracharya of Badri ka Ashram; and that, unlike most Indian sages, who use one religious title, he prefers to use two—Maharishi, which is Sanskrit for "great seer," and Yogi, which is from the Sanskrit *"yoga,"* meaning "effort." Inside the first tent, which is packed with such items as tomato sauce, cornflakes, soap, toothpaste, and chewing gum—all imports, to judge from the labels—a man in a brown lounge suit and with a vermilion mark on his forehead comes up to me. He tells me his name and continues, in English, "I am America-returned. I am M.A. and Ph.D. in public administration from the States. Guruji has fifty-four *chelas* from distant foreign lands here at Kumbha. I myself am going to be initiated on this Amavasya, when Guruji will recite some *mantras* to me by the side of Mother Ganga, and I will recite them back. I met the Guruji only a month ago. After I set my eyes on Guruji, I left my five children to follow him."

He takes me to an open area among the tents, where many Westerners, some in Indian dress, are standing around a serving table finishing a meal of macaroni and custard. I accept a small dish of custard from a girl in Western dress. She has very long eyelashes and the slightly bored expression of a fashion model.

"Where are you from?" I ask her.

"From Canada," the girl replies. "Guruji is a fact, and, like a fact, he manifested himself to me in Canada."

When I ask her to tell me something about the Spiritual Regeneration Movement, she says tersely, "You must address any questions you have to Guruji himself."

An Englishwoman joins us. "Guruji has been around the world six times, and now we have a half-dozen Spiritual Regeneration Movement centers in Britain," she says. "They teach Guruji's simple technique of meditation."

The members of the group start moving into a tent. They arrange themselves as best they can on the floor in front of Maharishi Mahesh Yogi, a merry-looking little man with smooth skin, blunt features, and long, well-oiled hair. He is dressed in a flowing cream-colored silk robe. Three tape recorders stand near him on the floor, as sacred books might surround another *guru*.

Maharishi Mahesh Yogi urges the audience to ask questions, and I ask a general question about the nature of his movement.

He asks me to identify myself, and when I do, he says, in English, in a soft, rich, bemused voice, "All I teach is a simple method of meditation. We are all conscious on a mundane level, but beneath that consciousness, in each one of us, there is an ocean vaster than any in the world. It's there that most new thoughts originate. The bridge between the mundane level of consciousness and the ocean is meditation—not reading, because if you read you can have only second-hand thoughts. Meditation expands the consciousness and leads to the greatest production of goods and services. The ultimate test of my method of meditation is therefore its utility—the measure of the usefulness of people to society. Through my method of meditation, the poor can become as rich as the rich, and the rich can become richer. I taught my simple method of meditation to a German cement manufacturer. He taught the method to all his employees and thereby quadrupled the production of cement. As I said when addressing a meeting in the Albert Hall, in London, my technique does not involve withdrawal from normal material life. It enhances the material values of life by the inner spiritual light. My method is, in my London example, 'like the inner juice of the orange, which can be enjoyed without destroying the outer beauty of the fruit. This is done simply by pricking the orange with a pin again and again, and extracting the juice little by little, so that the inner juice is drawn out on the surface, and both are enjoyed simultaneously.' "

During the rest of the session, which goes on for a few hours, with the tape recorders running, Maharishi Mahesh Yogi expounds on his simple method of meditation. He has a way of dismissing everything. Not only does he rule out at the start all questions concerning morality, theology, and philosophy—implying at one point that men are free to do anything in their personal lives, to themselves or to others, as long as, by the technique of meditation, they experience the bliss that is within themselves—but he seems to remove himself from the whole process of intellectual discourse by giggling at every question put to him and then at his own answer to the question, so one feels that no matter how long one talked to him one would come away with, at worst, chagrin at having been ridiculed and, at best, vague excitement at having been tantalized. He does not satisfactorily answer any question. (If by a few minutes of meditation a day the poor can become rich, why do they continue to be poor? Maharishi Mahesh Yogi's answer is that they are too indolent to master his simple method of meditation.)

The literature of the movement is equally unsatisfactory. One of its newsletters carries an excerpt from a B.B.C. television interview that Robert Kee, the B.B.C.'s star interviewer, had with Maharishi Mahesh Yogi:

KEE: Maharishi Mahesh Yogi brings with him an allegedly very simple technique of meditation which enables man to do away with all his inner conflicts and tensions both individually and in society as a whole. This technique of meditation, it appears from Maharishi's published sayings, doesn't involve any sort of abandonment of worldly desires or any monkish withdrawal from life at all. Nor are any physical exercises involved in it or any sort of self-deprivation or abstinence.

Now in America, this teaching of Maharishi has been hailed as a non-medicinal tranquillizer, and an improvement on sleeping pills. It's been noted there that people who practice it look younger, and even get on better with their relatives. But Maharishi contends that these are but ordinary side effects or by-products of his teaching, and that the important thing about his teaching is that it enables the ordinary man to get in touch with that Kingdom of God which Christianity teaches is within everyone.

Now, first, Maharishi, could you tell me just how you arrived at this technique. . . . Can anyone learn it?

MAHARISHI: Everyone can do it, because it doesn't need doing, it only needs allowing the mind to fathom more joyful regions of one's own inner personality. . . . The nervous system should be intact, a disabled nervous system won't do, the inner Being of man is blissful, the mind coming into that blissful Being which is the Kingdom of Heaven within. . . . So that process of going within is very simple and anyone can do it.

By one of the tents, a number of *nagas,* all quite rotund, sit around a smoky fire. Most of them have mischievous expressions, though their eyes appear glazed. "Join in! Join in!" they call out to me, in Hindi, as I approach. Every one of them is ebulliently puffing a hookah or a cheroot, and the atmosphere is a little dizzying. "Come and sit awhile," one of them says. He wears a bracelet made of hippopotamus hide, as a talisman against illness, and by nodding frequently he jangles three silver chains around his neck, from one of which hangs a flaming-red stone. He is called Bhola Nath, he tells me.

"How did you travel to the Kumbha?" I ask these men, sitting down among them. Their nakedness, I know, must have prevented them from using public transport.

Some of them nudge each other with familial camaraderie. Bhola Nath breaks into a grin, and asks, "How did *you* come to the Kumbha?"

"By train," I say. The reply arouses general mirth.

"We came on the power of *ganja, bhang,* and *charas,*" Bhola Nath says, referring to three narcotics made from the hemp plant and commonly eaten or smoked. "Would you like a dream smoke?"

I decline, with thanks.

"Then we came on the backs of elephants and horses," Bhola Nath continues.

"Where do you make your home?" I ask.

"On the backs of elephants and horses," Bhola Nath says. He adds, becoming a little more serious, "The villagers along the way always give all the *sadhus* lodging and food. They know we are coming when they hear our conchs and gongs."

"You spend all your time travelling?" I ask.

"We sleep on the backs of elephants and horses," Bhola Nath says. "We must travel all the time, because we go to every Kumbha—Hardwar Kumbha, Nasik Kumbha, Ujjain Kumbha, and Prayaga Kumbha."

"But the *mela* comes only once in three years," I say. "The distances between these places could be covered in a few weeks."

"But *we* take three years to get from one Kumbha to another," Bhola Nath says emphatically. "We travel very slowly. You know how elephants travel? We travel like them." All the *nagas* around the fire laugh.

"Why do you go naked? What is the theory behind it?" I ask the assembly.

"As a baby, you have no shame," Bhola Nath says affably. "You snuggle happily in your mother's lap. That is the age when you are most loving and affectionate. You love your mother and father without self-consciousness, and you instinctively know the oneness of life. You grow up, you start giving yourself airs, and you reject your mother, who brought you into the world. You start wearing pantaloons and shoes, and you think there is something sinful about sitting in your mother's lap. You are no longer innocent. You have shame, because you've become guilty. You can't love your mother any longer. Now, take you. You've become a *babu*. No doubt you wear fancy suits, you have a lot of education, but you are full of shame and guilt. We are not full of shame and guilt, because we go naked." He buttresses his argument with a bit of verse:

> "You move from fifth standard to sixth standard,
> You go from more awareness to less awareness.
> You move from sixth standard to seventh standard,
> You go from less ignorance to more ignorance."

I am now in a tent filled with serene-looking women. They are sitting at the feet of another woman, who looks to be in her seventies. She is bundled up in a coarsely woven black blanket, which is faded, dirty, and patched. Her face is fine and bright, with the sweet expression that elderly ladies in India seem to acquire like gray hair. Everyone addresses her as "Mataji" (Hindi for "mother"). When I am presented to her, she invites me to sit down.

"Ask Mataji something," the women in the tent say, almost in unison.

"I have been living abroad, and the question I want to ask you may sound a little strange." I say hesitantly. "But all the while I've been walking through Jhusi, the question that has been going through my head—"

"Ask your question," the chorus cuts in.

"Well, I've been wondering how one gets *chelas*—how one becomes a *guru*," I say. "I would like to know how your sect got started."

"Our sect is called Kali Kumbli Vali, child," Mataji says. She speaks rustic Punjabi. "And Kali Kumbli Vali, as you know, means 'the lady of

the black blanket.' I am the Kali Kumbli Vali. I was born into a very good
family in Rawalpindi. Some of my relatives were doctors and lawyers, and
one of my close relatives was a judge. I was married into a very good
family, too, and my husband also had relatives who were doctors and lawyers, but my husband died when I was ten years old. And, child, as you
should know, in our country marriage can be entered into only once, so, a
widow of ten without education but with much life before me, I had
nothing to do. I started sitting with some ladies who were my neighbors
and who knew about godly matters. So I came to know about godly matters, too, and some other widows and such ladies started coming and sitting with me. And so I fell into the godly way. Now Kali Kumbli Vali is
known in the four corners as a refuge for widows, and when mothers lose
their husbands and want to follow the godly path, they ask their way to
my abode, in Hardwar. Many know about me, and they direct the good
widows to me."

"She has *shakti,*" the chorus says. (*"Shakti"* is Sanskrit for "capability,"
but sometimes also means "female essence.")

A demure young disciple adds, "She has *shakti,* so people follow her.
We don't have *shakti,* and no one follows us. But everyone follows and
obeys Mataji."

Another disciple, who is toothless and seems to be the oldest member of
the congregation, says, "You see, most people are born upside down, and
they haven't any *shakti.* A few people are born with their feet first, and
they have *shakti,* and they show the way. Most people are so unfortunate
that they can't even find someone who was born feet first to follow. Mataji
is one with *shakti,* for she was born feet first."

In the village of Arail, which lies on the right bank of the Yamuna, and
which is being used this year, for the first time, to enlarge the *mela* area to
two thousand acres, there is, instead of the Jhusi crowds, the eerie, abandoned feeling of a ghost town. It is peopled with dust devils, which dance
down the lanes and across the sand dunes to the temple of Satyababa
(Hindi for "old man of truth"). Near one of the temple walls is Satyababa
himself, lying on a lion's skin under a beach umbrella, as if to leave no
room for doubt that even though he is alone, he is one of the leading *gurus*
in residence at Arail. He is a bulky man, naked to the waist, and he has an
impressive beard. He bestirs himself to greet me in Hindi.

"How did you get your name?" I ask.

"I gave myself the name, because I am the truthful father, and all people are my children!" he says, in a shout, as if he were born to sing hymns of praise.

Satyababa acquired his reputation as a *guru* in 1962. On February 5th of that year, the moon's eclipse of the sun coincided with the conjunction of Mercury, Venus, Mars, Jupiter, Saturn, and the earth. Many Hindus and Buddhists all over India were persuaded that the eclipse—interpreted as the serpent Rahu swallowing up the sun—signified the end of the world. (An identical phenomenon occurring some millennia earlier had caused the earth-shaking war of the Mahabharata, it was believed.) To placate the wrath of the gods, public prayer meetings were held around *havans* (Hindi for "sacrificial fire") in many cities in India. One leader of such prayer meetings was Satyababa, who had collected considerable sums to buy *ghi* in order to feed his *havan* in Allahabad.

I ask him now about his particular role.

"I have not yet quite saved the world!" he shouts. "But I lighted the *havan* in 1960 and kept it going for two years in order to avert the influences of the conjunction. Although the faithless world doesn't know it, I've averted the disaster only temporarily. People think the evil conjunction is past, but the curse is still upon us. I had this temple erected with some gifts from openhanded landlords, and my disciples are keeping up uninterrupted twenty-four-hour prayers. We shall see what we shall see."

Ananda, who is camped with the *sadhus* in Jhusi, is regarded as one of the most important Hindu religious leaders in India. She has a large following throughout the country. She has been taken seriously by Hindu intellectuals brought up in the skeptical tradition of the West, among them Nehru, and some of her devotees, sequestered in a score of *ashrams* (Hindi for "hermitage") founded by her congregation, believe that she has been sent to this world to spread divine light, and even that she is an incarnation of Kali, the wife of Shiva and the goddess of destruction (some images show Kali garlanded with serpents and dancing on the supine body of Shiva), or else an incarnation of Sarasvati, a river goddess for whom both the legendary river in the *sangam* and a high-caste sect of Brahmans is named; in fact, Sarasvati, because she is the goddess of speech, is, in some myths, the mother of the Vedas and also the goddess of wisdom, science, and music, the inventor of the Devanagari alphabet, and the wife of Brahma Himself (some images show Sarasvati riding on a swan or a peacock and holding a lute and a manuscript). Ananda, like many other present-day Hindu religious leaders, relies on her exemplary

life and on her presence to inspire followers, but, unlike many of the
others, she is the subject of a written gospel, which was set down by Jyo-
tish Chandra Ray, one of her main disciples. Ray first came in contact with
Ananda in 1924, when he was forty-four years old. When he died, thirteen
years later, he had just completed a record of his feverish, intense relationship with Ananda. This record, which was written in Bengali (both
Ananda and Ray came from the eastern part of Bengal), was published in
Bengali in 1937, in Hindi, by Ananda's *sangha* (Sanskrit for "association"
or "congregation"), in 1951, and in English, in a translation by G. Das
Gupta, in 1952. The book has enjoyed wide acclaim; indeed, some readers
in the West as well as in the East place it among the contemporary religious classics of the world.

According to Ray's book, which is titled "Mother As Revealed to Me"—
devotees address Ananda as "Mother"—Ananda was born Nirmala Devi
Bhattacharji, a high-caste Brahman, in 1896, in a small village in the district of Tippera. Her parents were simple, poor, pious people, natives of
the district. As a child, Nirmala did not receive any formal education. She
neither opened a book nor learned to write. She was not entrusted to any
guru for spiritual instruction. She was regarded by the other people in the
village, who themselves could neither read nor write, as mentally retarded,
apparently because she was moody and distracted, talked and gesticulated
to plants and trees, and was forgetful to the extent of becoming unaware
of her surroundings and of being unable to recall things that she had been
told only a few minutes before. When she was twelve, she was given in
marriage to Srijut Ramani Mohan Chakravarty, who was engaged in
some form of social work. For the next few years, husband and wife,
sometimes together, sometimes separately, lived with relatives in various
cities in Bengal. While Mrs. Chakravarty was still in her teens, she became
a vehicle for certain supernatural phenomena.

> Many *mantras* spontaneously came from her lips [Ray reports] and many
> images of Gods and Goddesses flashed out of her body. Her limbs spontane-
> ously formed into various yogic poses. . . . The currents of the outer and
> inner worlds ceased to affect her altogether. She looked like one reposing in
> the absolute calm of the Self.

Such manifestations recurred—Mrs. Chakravarty once lost the power of
speech for three years—and her husband, afraid that she might be possessed, sought the help of exorcists, who found their craft useless and, daz-
zled by what they saw, retreated in awe. In 1923, the Chakravartys were
invited to take up residence in Dacca—in the Shah-Bagh, the private gar-

dens belonging to the Nawab of Dacca. Ray, as it happened, had been living in Dacca since 1918. After completing his education in Chittagong,
where he was born, and working for the government in Calcutta, he had
come to Dacca as a government servant. In spite of his proximity to Mrs.
Chakravarty, he did not hear of her until she had been there for a year.
By then, she was leading a few devotees in *kirtana* and was being called the
Mother of Shah-Bagh. Ray had been looking for a spiritual mother since
his childhood.

> I lost my mother when I was but a small boy [Ray recalls]. I have heard
> my relations say that my eyes used to swim in tears whenever I heard in-
> fants babbling out "Ma, Ma;" and that I would soothe my heart by lying on
> the floor and weeping silently.
>   My father was a saintly person. During my very childhood the deep reli-
> gious spirit of his life implanted in me seeds of divine aspiration. In 1908,
> I had my initiation in *shakti mantra* from our family *guru*. On that account
> I had to worship the Mother Divine. When I could pour out all my devo-
> tional fervour with "Ma, Ma," during my prayer time, I found great relief
> and happiness. Even then I could hardly realize that Mother is the fountain-
> head of supreme joy and happiness for all living beings. There was an over-
> powering desire in me to find such a Living Mother who, by her loving
> glances, could transform my storm-tossed soul. I approached many saintly
> persons and was desperate enough even to consult astrologers for an answer
> to my query: "Shall I have the good fortune to meet such a Mother?" All
> held out high hopes.
>   With that object in view, I visited many holy places and had the oppor-
> tunity of meeting numerous spiritual personalities; but none could satisfy
> my desire.

Ray went to Shah-Bagh, met Chakravarty—who by now was addressed
as "Pitaji" (Hindi for "father")—and was introduced to his wife. "It sent
a thrill into my heart to see her serene yogic posture along with all the
modesty and grace of a newly married girl," Ray writes. "My whole
being was flooded with joy and every fibre of my body danced with
ecstasy." The two sat near each other, both shy of speech. Ray longed to
touch her feet (a Hindu gesture of homage), but something about her
stopped him, and when she finally spoke, it was to rebuke him for his lack
of spiritual appetite. He returned home unsatisfied and in a sulky mood.
He felt slighted; she had not embraced him, like a mother. He felt he
could not go to her again, and yet the wish to be with her would not let
him rest. He discovered that from the garden wall, at a spot near a temple,
he could, hidden from the world, feast his eyes on the object of his devo-

tion whenever he chose. After seven agonizing months, he arranged to entertain her in his house. Once more, he was filled with intense joy by her presence. Once more, he tried to touch her feet. Once more, she stopped him—this time by withdrawing her feet out of his reach. But now, instead of sulking, he set about reading religious books, and even went to the length of writing one himself and dispatching it to her. She sent for him, and at their third meeting, during which Chakravarty was present, Ray felt like a little child reunited with his parents. Afterward, he sent his wife (in "Mother As Revealed to Me" Ray scarcely mentions his wife and son) to the Mother of Shah-Bagh with an offering of a diamond nose ring, a silver platter, flowers, sandalwood paste, and curds, and she ate from the silver platter. Ray explains that she had previously eaten off the bare floor, and that subsequently, for a period of a couple of years, she gave up eating with her fingers, because, though there appeared to be nothing wrong with them, whenever she raised food to her mouth, the food would slip through them. Devotees were given the task of feeding her, according to a strict regimen she had set up for herself. It consisted of a total of six grains of boiled rice—three grains in the course of the day and three grains in the course of the night—and two or three fruits that had fallen ripe from the tree. After several months, she relaxed the regimen, changing it to a daily ration of two ounces of boiled rice and lentils. As if this diet were not strict enough, there were days when she would not accept any food at all. After two years, she gave up this regimen, and then she would either eat a child's ration or, alternatively, gorge herself on food enough for a dozen people; once, she demanded more food after she had finished off a helping of rice pudding that had been made with five gallons of milk. On or off a regimen, she was like a little girl. She would lie down on the ground and go into a tantrum at the sight of nothing more than a dog eating a portion of food a little larger than her own for that day, and she would pass into ecstasy when she was presented with an offering of sweetmeats.

The late Babu Tarak Bandhu Chakravarty [no relation of Ananda's husband] came walking about five miles with some pure sweets prepared at his house from his own cow's milk [Ray recalls]. It was not yet dawn when he arrived. Mother was still in bed. Like an impatient child, the old man called out: "Ma, Ma, I have brought you some sweets prepared with special care; won't you eat them?" Mother sat up on her bed and without having washed her face, mouth, or hands, she at once began to eat the sweets from the hands of the old man. She clapped her hands with joy. Tears of gratitude for Mother's childlike love and affection rolled down Tarak Babu's cheeks.

The style of the gospel is partly epical ("We have seen Mother become as stern as a thunderbolt, although she is by nature as soft and tender as a flower") and partly biblical ("She will take the brunt of all your responsibilities from your shoulders and give you strength to bear the cross"); in essence, the writing is that of someone describing a succession of supernatural events. At one point, Ray relates that his own image unaccountably appeared in the background of a photograph of Ananda. Skeptics have explained this mystery as a photographer's trick (superimposing a picture of Ananda over one of Ray), but Ray preferred to think of it as a supernatural event—a sign of their spiritual union. Throughout his book, there are accounts of Ananda's powers of telekinesis, telepathy, and healing, and miracles like this one, which calls to mind the episode of the loaves and the fishes in the New Testament:

> There was a *kirtana* party. . . . Food for about fifty to sixty people was prepared, but the number of guests swelled to about a hundred and twenty. Mother noticed it and till the end of the serving stood in a corner of the room where the food was kept. When all had eaten, it was found that some food was left over even then.

All these supernatural deeds are surrounded by a romantic aura. Ray dwells on Ananda's radiance, which enveloped everything around her; on her "gentle smile or loud laughter," which stopped quarrels among her devotees; and on the intense heat that emanated from any place where she happened to sit or lie down. Ballads and hymns praising her came to him spontaneously. Hymns came spontaneously to her, too. (The hymns were in the Vedic tradition, celebrating the light of the universe.) She sang his hymns in a voice "as sharp and piercing as a sword" or "as soothing as the evening zephyr." He collected his paeans in a book for her, titling one ballad "The Song of a Crazy Fellow." (She frequently told him, "I am only a crazy little daughter of yours.")

In the middle of the night, as in the middle of the day, Ray would be seized with a desire to see her. He would walk alone on his balcony, which was bathed in moonlight, and her image would float before his eyes. She would say to him, "You called me, and I have come." Always, she would uplift him with her love.

> Whoever has watched Mother's bright face ever radiant with a smile [he writes], her childlike simplicity, her playful jokes flowing from a heart brimming over with joy, must have been charmed beyond measure. . . . A divine fragrance always emanates from her body, from her every breath, and from her clothes and bedding.

But he could not stop tormenting himself about his senses, which demanded other kinds of satisfaction. He had read in a treatise, "The man who hankers after the material objects of sense for the indulgence of the tongue, stomach, and sex cannot find Lord Krishna" (though Krishna was originally a voluptuary deity of the Hindus, they have come to think of him in connection with abnegation of the senses), and yet this was precisely his condition, almost to the point of madness. Once, Ananda accidentally killed a fly, and then lovingly held it in her closed hand for several hours. When she let it go, she asked Ray, who had been with her all the while, if he could aid the poor fly. He immediately swallowed it. On another occasion, she placed a glowing coal on her foot to test whether she could do this without feeling pain. (She learned that she could.) For a month, the burn would not heal. Finally, Ray licked the burn, and it began to heal.

The book is full of references to his *guru's* "holy feet." Though he probably touched her no more than three times in his life, and, when he was with her, hardly ever sat down, preferring always to stand respectfully a little to one side of her, people gossiped about them, and this gossip only multiplied Ray's doubts about his sensual appetites, but whenever he gave in to his doubts and resisted going to her, even for a few days, it seemed to him that she mocked him, and that her hold on him became tighter still; his attempts to exercise his will left him "dumb and inert." Ordinarily, he tried to be the first person to see her every day, arriving at her house by the light of dawn. Sometimes he would find her "sitting idly on one side of her bed with all the languor of sleep still over her eyelids." Together they would spend five, six, or seven hours taking walks in the fields. "Mother, how are you today?" he asked her once, in the course of a ramble. The account continues:

> She responded with such an emphasis: "I am very, very well," that my whole being from head to foot throbbed and danced with the vibration of her words, and I halted on the way suddenly, almost losing myself.

Once, on the way to an *ashram,* Ananda sat down in a hollow in the ground. Ray recalls, "Her face was beaming with a smile, breathing radiant joy." He was moved to say, "From today we shall call Mother by the name of Anandamayi." She raised no objection, and from that moment she became Anandamayi. Ananda, Sanskrit for "joy," is a masculine name; Mayi is a variation of Mataji. She was soon addressed as "Sri Sri Anandamayi Ma," which in English would be "Venerable Venerable Joy Mother Mummy." It can be conjectured with a fair degree of certainty that the new name was meant to convey that the *guru* united in her person the male and female principles, especially since Ray reports that a lingam was later set up in the hollow. Perhaps it should be mentioned that among the Hindus it is the custom to give a woman an entirely new name upon her marriage.

The number of Ananda's devotees in the locality grew day by day, and so did the popularity of certain religious practices whose purpose was to channel the egoistical impulses into contemplation of God—to lose the self in "the Eternal Thou." Because the most elemental impulse of man was expressed in the sound "Ma" ("The first cry of a child as he emerges from the womb of his mother is 'Om-Ma' which is the same as 'Om,'" Ray writes; he probably means to suggest that the elemental sound "Ma" was as sacred as *"Om"*), devotees incessantly murmured "Ma" to themselves, hoping to make the sound as regular and as constant as their breathing. For them, "Ma" summed up the relationship between child and mother, man and God—all sacred books being ultimately a gloss on "Ma," and all names and forms being reducible to "Ma." Their particular Ma was at once more human and more godlike than anyone else they knew. If she laughed while she was playing with children, she would continue to laugh long after the games were over; if she cried at parting with her devotees, she would continue to cry long after they had ceased to cry; and if, as the rites of her cult dictated, a goat was sacrificed, she would take upon herself the blood of the goat by going through the motions of sacrifice with herself as the goat, even to the point of tapping the knife on her neck. (When the goat was eventually killed, it was invariably found to be bloodless.) She would allow herself to be fondled like a bride, letting her devotees take turns brushing her teeth, washing her face, bathing her, changing her saris, combing her hair, and adorning her. She would give in to their whims, as when she permitted them to clothe her as a boy Krishna for photographs. In fact, she was greedy for every token of their tenderness, and sometimes seemed to them to be an animated doll, but, they felt, this simply happened to be the way God had chosen to manifest Himself in a world of illusion. Had she not revealed to them that she was God incarnate when, during a Kali *puja,* instead of anointing the image of the goddess with sandalwood paste, as was the custom, she anointed herself and permitted herself to be worshipped? Combining in her person all the attributes of the universal mother, she had the capacity for winning, with one *darshana,* devotees for life, for comforting them with overpowering love, and for making them tingle with religious fervor.

The most important religious observance was the daily *kirtana,* which might go on well into the evening. These *kirtanas* (they sometimes included goats and dogs, which pressed against Ananda or nestled in her lap) were built around the repetition of the central sound symbol of the cult. To the accompaniment of a harmonium and bells, the devotees would raise their voices in resounding hymns of their faith:

> In joy and sorrow, in happiness and misery
> Call out Ma, Ma, Ma, Ma, Ma,
> Ma, Ma, Ma, Ma, Ma, Ma, Ma, Ma,
> Ma, Ma, Ma, Ma.

Or:

> Ma, Ma, Ma, Ma, Ma, Ma, Ma,
> Call Ma, Ma, Ma, Ma,
> Say Ma, Ma, Ma, Ma,
> Sing Ma, Ma, Ma, Ma,
> Worship Ma, Ma, Ma, Ma,
> Repeat Ma, Ma, Ma, Ma,
> Call, say, sing, worship, pray
> Ma, Ma, Ma.

As the devotees serenaded Ananda, her eyes would at times become fixed in a vacant stare, her limbs would relax, and her body would seem to melt down to the floor, or shrink away, leaving only her sari visible. At other times, she would dance lightly, for hours, to the rhythm of the music —her clothes trailing about her—and then collapse on the ground. She might remain prostrate with her body still writhing and undulating in the motion of the dance. She would breathe and twist in time to the hymns, sending "wavelike thrills" through the worshippers, who, transported though they were, might leave off singing in order to revive her. These "abnormal symptoms," as Ray calls them, are described at great length. The following passage is typical:

Her breath became deep and prolonged; her whole body would twist right or left with an expression of languor and fatigue. She would then lie down on the floor or roll up like a bundle. . . . When any question was put to her, she would respond with one or two words in a very faint, soft voice. . . . She would feel a fine threadlike upward current of life flowing from the lower end of the spinal cord right up to the topmost centre in the brain, and along with it a thrill of joy would run through every fibre of her body and even through the pores of her hair. She would feel at that time that every particle of her physical frame danced, as it were, with infinite ripples of bliss. Whatever she touched or saw appeared to her to be a vital part of herself.

. . . At that time, if her backbone was massaged or the joints of her body were rubbed for a long time, she would remain quiet for a while and recover her normal condition. It was at this stage that she was found to be brimming over with heavenly joy.

Once, Ray, who was Ananda's "favorite child," and whom the other devotees called Bhaiji, or "elder brother," remarked to her that perhaps he would be a celibate and live in her *ashram* in his next life, and she said she wondered why he felt he had to wait. Though he did not give her the reason, it was, he notes, his wife. But some time later Ananda took a gold chain from her neck and fastened it around his, and pronounced him reborn, and with that it was all but settled that he would abandon his wife and son to follow her. Soon afterward, she left Dacca to travel around the country, and he accompanied her.

In 1937, according to a preface to Ray's book which was written after his death, Ray went with Ananda on a pilgrimage to Mount Kailas, held sacred because of its association with Shiva. In spite of the bitter-cold Himalayan weather and the fact that toward the end of his stay in Dacca tuberculosis had kept him in bed for two years, when he arrived at Lake Manasa—held sacred because of its association with Brahma—he threw off his clothes and, in an act of total renunciation, plunged into the icy water, resolving as he did so to pass the rest of his days wandering naked in the Himalayas. However, Ananda, who reached the lake shortly after he did, persuaded him to return to the plains with her, and she pronounced him a *guru* by reciting some *mantras* over his head. By that time, though, he had taken a chill, and, back in the plains, he developed a fever. Some days later, he died, chanting, "Ma-*Om, Ma, Ma*."

Arthur Koestler, in his book "The Lotus and the Robot," chooses Ananda as one of the "contemporary 'saints,'" and although he dismisses Ray as "a kind of saintly, tragic clown to Ananda," he takes Ray's book seriously as an objective record of Ananda's mystical life, writing, "Though none of it can be regarded as evidence, I must confess that I found Bhaiji's narrative in most parts convincing, partly because the whole story reflects a very humble, saintly, and simpleminded person." Koestler argues, "There are two ways of looking at Anandamayi Ma, the psychiatrist's and the mystic's, and the two need not be mutually exclusive." But, not surprisingly, Koestler's own attempt to analyze Ananda and Ray fails.

In "Words of Sri Anandamayi Ma," a collection of Ananda's utterances, it is said, "She has the right word, at the right time, in the right manner, for every seeker after Truth, be he a believer in any faith or an agnostic, an intellectual or an artist, a scholar or an illiterate, a beginner or highly advanced on the path." I am standing near a saffron-colored tent, Ananda's, in Jhusi. The air is pungent with the scent of guavas and bananas, and from the sanctum come gay sounds of women chattering and laughing, the clatter of a dipper against a bucket, and the splashing of water, as if someone were bathing. "Is it possible to have a discussion with Anandamayi Ma?" I ask a man who seems to be in charge of the tent and also of several men standing about the camp in the manner of sepoys protecting a maharani.

The man replies, "Sri Sri Anandamayi Ma has no time at Kumbha to teach." He continues, "She is getting dressed. She will come out in a little while and show herself to the public. You may wait for the meeting and have your *darshana,* too."

I persist, saying, "I would like a chance to talk with her."

Impulsively, he says, "You can never tell about Ma. If you wish, you can call out 'Ma!' and see if she'll ask you in. Maybe you will be let in and maybe not."

I hesitate, for I find the idea of following this strange procedure distasteful. But then I take a couple of steps forward and call out "Ma!"

The flap of the saffron tent is raised by a young man, and I am let in. Inside, it is cozy and neat. Ananda, looking freshly bathed, her head half covered with a white veil, sits cross-legged on a bed, massaging her toes. She is surrounded by baskets heaped with opulent *prasad* (Hindi for "blessed food")—guavas, bananas, apples, oranges, pomegranates. A yard or so above her head hangs a large umbrella. (Umbrellas are used in some parts of India as shields against falling insects and detritus.) She is half turned away from me, talking excitedly in Bengali to a couple of pleasant-looking middle-aged women sitting opposite her. Finally, she turns to me. Her face is flushed, and she looks more like a fiery tribal queen than like a saint.

"Come here," she says.

I go up to her, and she takes a banana and a guava and thrusts them into my hand.

"Prasad," she says. *"Prasad."* Then she turns away.

I realize that the *darshana* is over, but, with some trepidation, I stay on.

"Ma is very angry," one of the ladies says to me in Hindi. "Go! Go!"

"Don't you know that when you get your *prasad, darshana* is over?" Ananda says to me, in a mixture of Hindi and Bengali, but her voice is more scolding than angry. Then she relents and asks me to sit down, indicating a spot quite far away from her, near a water bucket.

In answer to a couple of random questions from me about her ascetic life, she dwells on the virtues of vegetarianism. She advocates an abstinence from onions, however. "I used to eat onions, but I found out they heat up the nerves and make the heart go faster," she says.

I mention that I have read Ray, and ask her what she thinks of the book.

"When he came to me, I thought of him the way I think of you now," she says.

She seems too imperious to be asked to explain herself. "What about Ray's book?" I ask.

"Just the same," she says.

Some Hindu theologians, using the phenomenon of Ananda as a paradigm, have lately been engaged in abstruse speculation about whether, in a religious tradition where *gurus* are the means of spiritual instruction, there could be such a phenomenon as a *guru*less *guru*. I now ask her about this problem.

She says, "You are my *guru.*"

"Hardly," I say.

"Whatever you say," she says, undaunted.

"What would be your counsel to a skeptic—or, for that matter, to a religious person—for finding God?" I ask.

"You are God," she says. "You are my God." She adds, as an afterthought, "God is in you. God is like a harmonium. Whatever you play on it is what you will hear."

"Then what is the point of having any *guru?*" I ask.

"No point," she says moodily.

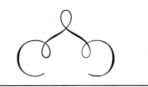

From the Sindhu

THE VARIETY OF RELIGIOUS MEN AND WOMEN camped at the *mela,* who seem
sometimes to agree on nothing except the importance of bathing in the
rivers, reminds one that, in a sense, the Hindu religion can be defined only
in terms of a region and its rivers. The word "Hindu" was first used by
Persians who invaded northwestern India in the sixth century B.C., and
they applied it to the Sanskrit-speaking people they found living by the
Indus River, which in Sanskrit is called the Sindhu and which the Persians called the Hindu. These people, who called themselves Aryans (Sanskrit for "noble"), were of the same stock as the Persian invaders but had
migrated to India about a thousand years earlier. The first Aryan settlements had, in fact, been along the Indus, or, rather, on the alluvial plain of
the Punjab, in northwestern India, which was watered by the Indus and
its five tributaries—the Jhelum, the Chenab, the Ravi, the Sutlej, and the
Beas. By the sixth century B.C., however, the Aryans had extended their
settlements eastward and southward from the Punjab—first to the valleys
of the upper and middle stretches of the Ganga and the Yamuna, then to
the entire Gangetic plain, which came to have the greatest concentration
of Aryans and to be called Hindustan (Persian for "abode of the Hindus"), and, finally, to the area south of the Nerbudda River called the
Deccan (from *"dakshina,"* Sanskrit for "south")—and had become the
dominant people in the Indian peninsula. The Aryans, in the course of
their advance, had encountered and overwhelmed the Dravidians and
numerous other indigenous peoples, assimilating the local customs and

religious practices into the Aryan civilization, and the word Hindu eventually came to describe the entire admixture.

The religion of the early Hindus is preserved in several Sanskrit compilations of sacred writings, or Vedas, and their ancillary literature—the Brahmanas, the Aranyakas, and the Upanishads—which were composed over a period of eight or nine hundred years from sometime before the first millennium B.C. to sometime between the seventh and the fourth centuries B.C. From much of this literature, it appears that at the center of at least the later Vedic religion was the performance of elaborate magical *yajnas,* or sacrifices; in fact, the Brahmanas are, for the most part, a catalogue of sacrificial formulas, *mantras,* and prescribed ritual acts, like presenting rice and *ghi* to fire, which, as a medium for sacrificial offering, was deified. The Vedic Hindus, who were herdsmen and husbandmen, also venerated water from the earliest times, as is clear from the Rig-Veda, the oldest collection of Hindu sacred writings. (Archeological excavations at Mohenjo-Daro, in Sind, and Harappa, in the Punjab, suggest that water may have been venerated even before the time of the Vedic Hindus.) Originally, the Vedic Hindus may have revered water for its physical functions, but in time they came to associate with it spiritual functions. Certainly the early sacred writings praise the special merits of *yajnas* performed at rivers. There is abundant evidence to indicate that the rituals of the *yajnas,* which were performed over a period of weeks or months, included—in addition to *mantras*—*snana* (bathing), *dana* (almsgiving), and *tapasya* (austere meditation). The Vedic *rishis,* or seers, seem to have considered a confluence of rivers especially propitious for their *yajnas.* In the Vedic period, the rise of a sort of sacerdotal caste, the Brahmans, made the *yajnas* more intricate than ever, despite the fact that the Brahmans' concept of deity was more elevated. Even when philosophical mysticism and abstruse speculation about the nature of man and the universe entered Vedic literature, they did not diminish the power of sacrificial practices in the religion. Because *snanas* and *yajnas* performed in the most sacred places were thought to be the most efficacious, and perhaps also because the Ganga and, to some degree, the Yamuna in time became the main rivers of the Aryan settlements, the Ganga came to be regarded as the most sacred of the sacred rivers, and the Yamuna as the second most sacred river, and their confluence as the most sacred place of all. (Later, it was believed that even the gods had performed their sacrifices at this confluence.) A settlement of *rishis* and pilgrims eventually grew up around the confluence and came to be called Prayaga (*"pra"* is a Sanskrit prefix denoting excellence, and *"yaga"* is related to *"yajna"*), or Tirtharaj (Sanskrit for

"king among bathing places"). One commentator, explaining the theological implications of *"tirtha,"* writes, "The word *'tirtha'* means 'that which
enables one to go across.' It is applied to the place, the thing, or the person
—a *guru* or preceptor—which or who enables one to go across. It thus
conveys the idea of a place or a thing or a person which or who enables
human beings to cross *bhavasaghara*—the ocean of existence—and thus to
achieve *moksha*—salvation."

The idea of sacrifices at prescribed times as well as in propitious places
also seems to have developed in the Vedic period, probably as a result of
the study of astronomy. Later, the idea of sacrifice at a prescribed time and
place assumed such importance that it was extended to include suicide.
Indeed, some Hindu kings, *sadhus,* and sages committed suicide either by
immolating themselves at Prayaga or by drowning themselves in the *sangam.* These ultimate sacrifices may have been prompted by several beliefs.
One was that the sacred writings counselled shedding the body at Prayaga.
Numerous passages in post-Vedic Sanskrit literature of various periods—in
the Mahabharata, the *puranas,* the Dharmashastra Nibandhas, and separate religious treatises on Prayaga—as well as in the Vedas themselves, if
they are read literally, can be taken to extoll suicide at Prayaga. At least
one famous student of the Vedas immolated himself at Prayaga, apparently as a direct result of this verse from the apocrypha of the Rig-Veda:
"Where the two rivers, clear and turbid, commingle, bathing there, people
go up to Heaven and those wise ones who shed their bodies there attain to
immortality." Another belief that perhaps influenced the suicides was that
any death in Prayaga brought immediate *moksha,* for committing suicide
in Prayaga was a good way to insure that one died in Prayaga; Hindus
have traditionally gone to the sacred rivers not only to immerse the ashes
of their dead but also to wait for their own deaths. A third belief was that
the greater the value of a sacrificial offering, the more merit its sacrifice
bestowed; after all, nothing was more valuable than one's body. Most
Hindus, however, have been satisfied with undertaking pilgrimages to the
sacred places, bathing in the sacred rivers, and making private or public
offerings there.

Although the idea of *snana* and *yajna* happens to be the basis not only of
the *mela* at Prayaga but also of many other *melas,* and although most
Hindus today believe in going on pilgrimages, in bathing in the sacred
rivers, in leading an ascetic life, and in learning from a personal *guru,* and
also believe in the concepts of reincarnation, universal salvation, and a
personal God, whom they call, variously, Bhagavan, Paramesvara, Ishvara,

Brahma, and Narayana—still, as in the past, to be a Hindu one does not have to practice any particular set of observances, adhere to any particular beliefs, accept any particular metaphysic or any particular prophet, or believe in any particular god, or, indeed, in any god. Hinduism depends neither on any particular historical event, comparable to the birth of Christ or the hegira of Mohammed, nor on any revealed truth, comparable to the Gospels or the Koran; it has neither a founder nor a sacred book, neither an established institution nor, ultimately, any vested authority. In fact, Hinduism has always been a religion of such eclectic beliefs and practices that a belief or a practice that is followed by some Hindus may be shunned by others. Since its Vedic origins, the religion has grown to encompass more and more philosophical and theological schools (Sankhya, Yoga, Vedanta) and more and more independent sects (Vaishnavas, Shaivas, Shaktas), and, in addition, has branched out into the separate religions of Buddhism, Jainism, and Sikhism. These schools, sects, and religions propound, accept, reject, and reinterpret a multiplicity of doctrines (*dharma, karma, avatar, samsara, trimurti, bhakti, maya*) and attach varying degrees of importance to their own literature or a common body of literature (the Vedas, the Mahabharata, the Ramayana, the *puranas,* the Pitakas, the Granth). All gradations of beliefs, from the crudest to the most highly refined, have coexisted in Hinduism from the earliest times, making it the most syncretic religion in the world—what one of its students has called "a tapestry of almost endless diversity of hues." Hindus today worship animals, ancestors, sages, spirits, natural forces, divine incarnations, or the absolute itself, finding God in snake or lingam, in stone or wood, in water or fire, in planets or stars, in the heart or the mind, in Rama or Krishna or Buddha.

With its traditions of periodically repeated incarnations of the deity in the most diverse forms [the late Professor Clement Webb, of Oxford, once wrote], its ready acceptance of any and every local divinity or founder of a sect or ascetic devotee as a manifestation of God, its tolerance of symbols and legends of all kinds, however repulsive or obscene, by the side of the most exalted flights of world-renouncing mysticism, it could perhaps more easily than any other faith develop, without loss of continuity with its past, into a universal religion which would see in every creed a form suited to some particular group or individual, or the universal aspiration after one Eternal Reality.

Because manifestations of Hinduism have varied from age to age, from community to community, and from person to person, because the Hindu sees every man as receiving a form and a degree of enlightenment corresponding to his particular circumstances and capacity, and because there is little in the requirements of Hinduism to set it off from any other creed, some students of Hinduism have gone as far as to claim that all religions and all cults, everywhere in the world, can be regarded simply as further manifestations of Hinduism.

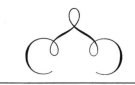

The Commingling Streams

It is midnight, and Amavasya has arrived. Through the night, the loud-speakers continue to bellow information about pilgrims lost and pilgrims found, the din robbing those of us secure in our tents of all hope of sleep. All night, it seems, I've been trying to put myself to sleep by counting sheep, only to have my lambs sacrificed to the electrical god who commands, "Would Mahesh Lal of Patnabagh of Bihar please report to the information officer in the information booth of Sector Seven." Just as I feel that I'm finally dropping off to sleep, the unearthly loudspeaker seems to float into my tent and clap itself onto my ear, the disembodied voice of the announcer taking the avatar of a Brahman government officer whose acquaintance I have made at the *mela*. "It's Amavasya, and you've overslept," he thunders. "You've missed the most colorful processions. There's still some auspicious time left for bathing. I'm going for another dip in the *sangam*. You can come with me. I have requisitioned a boat."

To be at Prayaga at Kumbha on Amavasya, in a tent pitched almost at the top of the *sangam,* with a Brahman for an escort, and to miss bathing! I leap out of my cot and follow my friend.

"This *mela* is beautifully organized," he says. "Millions are expected to bathe today, but the flow of the crowd is very well regulated by strategically placed barriers. The crowd can be stopped, turned back, or diverted if it starts a stampede anywhere. The Governors of Bihar and Uttar Pradesh have already had a wonderful dip. If it weren't for the tragic death of Shastriji right in the middle of this Kumbha, he might be here, too. As it is, tragically, only his ashes will be immersed in the *sangam* today. Have you heard that a hundred thousand *sadhus* are fasting here in order to stop all cow slaughter?"

We pass booths of Pandas (a subcaste of Brahmans charged with keeping the genealogies of other castes and subcastes) poring over records and registers; then a stall of barbers reverently collecting for their clients all the shaven hair; then a group of beggars raising paralyzed faces or withered limbs to us; then a colony of lepers; then a camp of *sadhus* where a dwarf strolls up and down like a king of fairyland, receiving homage from pilgrims, who bend down and touch his feet. We are being swept along in the thick of the crowds, our feet scarcely touching ground. Finally, we are on a quay, at the site, according to legend, of Buddha's first penance, the Triveni Ghat—"*triveni,*" Sanskrit for "triple-braided," and "*ghat,*" Hindi, from Sanskrit "*ghatta,*" for "bathing place," "*triveni*" being an alternative name not only for the *sangam* at Prayaga but for the Ganga and for other Indian rivers, which, like the braids of Indian women, twist and plait their dark courses through the land. Everything is confusion: the sounds of gongs, conchs, bells, drums, loudspeakers, distant trains; pilgrims, with ashes or sandalwood paste on their foreheads, launching marigolds in half coconut shells, tossing offerings of fruit, milk, flowers, and their own hair into the sacred rivers, drinking water from their cupped hands, scrambling to get into the water, walking away with brass pots of the water on their heads, shouting from one end of the quay to the other, "Victory to Mother Ganga!" In the *sangam* are countless country boats with white canopies, and, bobbing among them, countless heads. Wherever the boats or the crowds part, the two distinct streams of the Ganga and the Yamuna are revealed, running side by side—one dark ochre, the other greenish blue.

My Brahman companion resolutely elbows his way along the quay, which creaks and sags as if it were about to buckle. He spots a boy standing in the stern of a boat and waving his Gandhi cap. With extraordinary agility, the boy pushes and shoves his boat up to the quay, and we step into it. The Brahman somehow manages to make himself heard above the roar of voices, which sounds like a dozen ship turbines going full throttle: "Keep your balance. . . . Shift left. . . . No. . . . A little to the right. . . . Forward now. . . . Easy. That's it." The boat jolts us as it bangs and crashes ahead through the jam. At last, we are in a patch of open water.

"You go in first," the Brahman says.

I lower myself into the water, which here is barely six inches deep, and think of Chaucer: "And pilgrimes were they alle."

"No! You are just sitting!" the Brahman shouts. "You have to be wet all over! Lie down!"

I do—and sink into a quagmire of sand and bits of fruit, flowers, and hair.

"You are still not all wet! Roll over!" the Brahman shouts.

I do—and immediately try to raise myself.

"Your hair isn't wet!" the Brahman shouts. "Take some water and put it over your head!"

I do.

The Brahman chants, *"Hari Om. Hari Om. Hari Om."*

IV

The Holy Hair of the Muslims

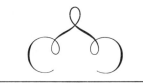

The Vale of Kashmir

SRINAGAR. CLEAR WATER, SOFT SUN in a late-afternoon sky, mountains that seem close, steep. I am being rowed to dinner on a houseboat that is in Claremont Colony, Nagin Lake, some hours away from Gagribal Point, Dal Lake, where I've just hired a *shikara*—a kind of gondola. I prefer floating through the network of Srinagar's waterways to taking the ordinary roads. I lie back in the *shikara* and allow myself to be lulled by the gentle rocking motion. Along one shore is a boulevard on which there is an occasional rickshaw or bicycle. Along the opposite shore are moored houseboats with little painted signboards: "Highland Queen: Sanitary Fitted," "Cutty Sark Enterprise," "Zam-Zam," "Pride of Kashmir Super Deluxe."

"Sahib like full tour Dal Lake?" the *shikara*-wallah asks, in pidgin English. He propels the *shikara* with little, toylike, heart-shaped oars. When we get snarled in undergrowth, he frees the *shikara* with a pole and then punts until we are in the clear. "Sahib is first tourist this year. Tourists staying away from Kashmir these days. Very troubled times. Sahib will give Kashmir happy fortune." He has left off his rowing and edged around to the stern, where he prepares tea over open coals. He serves it to me from an urn. "We reach Nagin Lake in two hours. If Sahib is lucky, Sahib will meet flower-wallah Bulbul. If Sahib likes, he'll sing native Kashmiri song telling of the affair of the bumblebee and the tulip. Every day he rending heart singing song on Nagin Lake."

We drift past "Princess Margret," "White House: With Sanitation,"

"Cherry Stone," "Lucky Kashmir." Among the houseboats, on thick float-ing mats of roots and weeds, are gardens of cucumbers, tomatoes, melons, and watermelons. All along the shores are stark poplars and weeping wil-lows, fresh green and silver, and then we pass banks full of flowers—nar-cissi and tulips, apple blossoms and cherry blossoms.

A merchant rows up in a *shikara* with "Galloping Snail" lettered on the prow. The *shikara* is laden with filigree necklaces, bracelets, and earrings, painted papier-mâché boxes and vases, and embroidered woollen shawls. "Would Sahib like a charm bracelet of Kashmiri wonders for his girl friend?" he asks, hooking my *shikara* with his oar. "Here is the first won-der—a genuine likeness of a native Kashmiri flat shoe worn by a Kashmiri-village native wallah." Descriptions of the other wonders are lost among the voices of children in *shikaras* hawking vegetables from houseboat to houseboat.

"Sahib is not shopping on Dal Lake," my *shikara*-wallah informs other waterborne merchants who paddle up. He adds, to me, "Suffering Moses is the very best shop in Kashmir. Sahib should shop at Suffering Moses." (Some English names and phrases here suggest local misadventures with the language.)

"Churchill," "King's Panama," "Martians," "Pim Tail." On a deck veranda, an elderly English lady wearing a lace fichu is sunning herself, drinking tea, watching swans and kingfishers dive and paddle around her houseboat. Silver service, crumpets, scones. A memsahib to her toes. I imagine she came here sometime after the First World War, loved the place, and settled down with a retinue of houseboys. I imagine her think-ing, Yes, some things have changed, but in things that count all is as it used to be. Slightly fewer friends, perhaps.

"Titwillow," "Pandora," "Lucifer: Special Class," "Snipe: Special Class," "New Golden Fleece," "Fairy Land: Sanitary Fitted." It is one of those unpredictable Kashmiri days, and now there is rain, hill-station rain—a steady shower that can go on for days. At Claremont Colony, I clamber aboard a houseboat. Everyone is in the dining room: enormous log fire reflected in the panes of the bay window on the starboard side; unpolished furniture, all of it intricately carved with Oriental plane leaves. At dinner are some houseboat holidayers I've met in Kashmir: Jasleen Dhamija, a handicraft expert; her husband, Ram Dhamija, a keen amateur photog-rapher; a correspondent from the London *Sunday Mirror;* and a few of the Dhamijas' other friends.

The talk is about the hardships of travelling to Kashmir. In winter, the Vale of Kashmir is completely cut off from the outside world for two or three weeks at a time. Sudden and treacherous landslides make hazardous, and sometimes impassable, the single motorable road, which was built a few years back to connect Kashmir with the Indian plains. Because of storms, airplanes can't reach Kashmir, and telephone wires go dead. A local textile designer, who was introduced to me simply as Jawad Sahib, tells a story. It seems that a while ago some scientists representing foreign governments arrived in Delhi to attend a conference. They were a day or two early and got talked into flying to Kashmir to catch a glimpse of "the Switzerland of India." There was a blizzard and they were stranded here. In the meantime, the conference in Delhi met and disbanded. After days (or was it weeks?), the embarrassed scientists returned to their several countries to face the reproaches of their governments.

We drink contraband red wine and eat a Kashmiri delicacy—mutton that has been soaked in curds for days and then simmered in milk.

"The three of us went to Gulmarg on a picnic yesterday," Jasleen tells the guests. "It was still covered with snow."

Jasleen, Ram, and I went on the picnic. To get to the snowy meadows of Gulmarg, a resort high up in the mountains, we first had a long ride in a taxi from Srinagar to the village of Tangmarg. Then we rode mountain ponies up a narrow trail—frightening, because ponies have a tendency to skirt the very edge of precipices. Then came a halting and bumpy climb up a snow-crusted trail on sleds. My sled, like the others, was attended by four hunched men in makeshift straw shoes. Three men pulled the sled from the front, like huskies, while the fourth gripped my shoulders from behind and steered. The snow track was a series of abrupt turns, sharp inclines, and sheer gullies. The sled skidded and knocked from side to side, swerving and tilting, sometimes at an incredible angle. The man who held me by the shoulders also ran from side to side, but if the rear of the sled skidded right he veered left, always shifting to keep the sled on course. The sled-wallahs were racked with coughs. They panted, and spat on the clean snow, and perpetually roused themselves with yells, like "Whom do you remember?" "God we remember!"

The man steering the sled would shout, *"Yad kar!"*

The others would reply, *"Nad kar!"*

"La illah!"

"Il illah!"

"Shahi madda!"

"Sherai khuda!"

"Sher jwana!"

"Gardhi vahana!"

"Yad kar!"

"Nad kar!"

When they stopped to catch their breath, they filled the air with a cacophony of complaints. Since the British left, things had been getting worse and worse. The trouble between India and Pakistan over Kashmir that reached a climax in the war last year had just about killed the tourist trade. There were always at least two hundred sled-wallahs in Tangmarg waiting for business. During the off season, weeks went by without a single tourist, and during the season, when a few persistent tourists did come, they paid the sled-wallahs only the fixed government rate of three rupees for going up to Gulmarg and coming back. Now that sled-wallahs were organized into a union, part of the fare went into the common pool. And no tourist gave *baksheesh* anymore.

"Sahib, we have nothing to eat."

"No money for tea."

"When does Sahib think things will get better?"

"Yad kar!"

"Nad kar!"

"Yad kar!"

In Gulmarg, hill cottages and pine trees were half buried in snow, which brilliantly reflected the noonday sun. The boiled eggs and chapatties of the picnic were bitter in my mouth.

Now, at the dinner table, there is confused talk about the tranquillity and religious harmony in the Kashmir of the raj, and about the explosive mixture of religion and politics in the Kashmir of independent India. "Kashmir is still a romantic place for a holiday, but somehow the fun has gone out of the place," a journalist from a national Indian paper says. "The people one meets here are jittery. They always act as if they were being watched. Even in the cafés—even at the bar at Nedou's Hotel, where I'm staying—whenever people talk to one another, they look over their shoulders to see if anybody is watching, as if the police were listening to each word, just waiting to clap them into jail. Sometimes I think that India can remain here only because our government has turned this place into a virtual police state."

Others agree that Kashmir indeed seems to have taken on the atmosphere of an occupied territory. General talk follows about the sad history of the state of Jammu and Kashmir. (Jammu, a Hindu area south of the Vale of Kashmir, is part of the official state of Jammu and Kashmir, but the heart of the state is the Vale of Kashmir—also called just Kashmir, or the Valley—which is formed by the Jhelum River and surrounded by mountains of the Karakoram and Himalayan ranges.) In 1947, when the partition of India brought the separate, Islamic nation of Pakistan into being, and when the princely states had to decide whether to join Pakistan or India, in most cases Hindu states acceded to India and Muslim ones to Pakistan. But the state of Jammu and Kashmir, which was preponderantly Muslim, was ruled by a hereditary Hindu maharaja, Sir Hari Singh. Pakistani infiltrators tried to take the Vale of Kashmir by force for Pakistan, and the maharaja appealed to India for military help and acceded to the Indian Union. This started the first war between India and Pakistan— the war of 1947—which was ended by a United Nations cease-fire agreement that left the northwestern third of the state, designated Azad Kashmir (Urdu for "free Kashmir"), with Pakistan and the rest of the state with India.

"It's all religion and politics now," the Indian journalist says. "Things have really deteriorated since the second war with Pakistan. If we Indians would only learn the lesson of the upheaval over the hair from Mohammed's head, there might be peace today."

From what I know of Kashmir, I can understand what he means about the lesson. In any case, his words are borne out by what I learn during subsequent days in the Valley, for my researches into present-day Kashmir always lead me back, one way or another, to a single, sacred strand of the prophet Mohammed's hair, and to its sanctuary in Srinagar—Hazratbal, Kashmir's most important mosque.

The Theft of Mohammed's Hair

AT MIDNIGHT ON THE EVE OF FRIDAY, December 27, 1963, Hadji Mohammed Khalil Ghanai, Khwaja Ghulam Hassan Bhatt, and Khwaja Mahadju, who were worshippers at the Hazratbal Mosque, arose from their fifth, and last, daily prayer in its main hall and retired for the night. To look at, the mosque was just another Kashmiri-Mogul monument, its solid construction, of brick masonry on a foundation of dressed stone, being distinctively Indian Mogul, and its roof, in three tiers, distinctively Kashmiri. For the three Muslim worshippers, however, and for all their Kashmiri brethren, everything about the mosque was special and specially consecrated: it had been erected by Emperor Shah Jehan, who also erected the Taj Mahal; it was situated on the western shore of Dal Lake, one of the natural marvels of the world; and, above all, it had been the repository of a strand of Mohammed's hair since the beginning of the eighteenth century, when the strand was brought to Kashmir. Because of this sacred possession, Srinagar was, in the eyes of Kashmiri Muslims, a second Medina.

At four-forty-five in the morning, Mohammed Khalil Ghanai, after sleeping for some four hours and then bathing in the *hammam* of the mosque, returned to the main hall for his first daily prayer. When he entered the hall, he looked to the right, toward the *hujra-e-khas* (Urdu for "special chamber") where the relic was kept, and saw that the chamber's outer doors, of engraved silver, were open. Yet the chamber was supposed to be entered only ten times a year, on such holy days as Bakar Id (commemorating Abraham's willingness to sacrifice his son) and Akhiri-Chahar Shamba (commemorating Mohammed's last ablution). On those ten holy days, a locked cupboard in the *hujra-e-khas* was opened and, from a precious box inside, a silver-capped glass vial, an inch in diameter, containing a silver pendulum to which the strand of Mohammed's hair was attached, was removed for a few minutes and carried from the *hujra-e-khas* across the main hall to a balcony overlooking the expanse of the lake. Here the relic was ceremonially raised before crowds gathered below on the shore of the lake for its *deedar,* or exhibition. Now Mohammed Khalil Ghanai found that the engraved silver outer doors of the *hujra-e-khas* were hanging on broken hinges. The inner doors, of wood and glass, which had three locks (the three keys were kept by three trustees), had been sawed through from the bottom. Inside these wooden doors, in the chamber, the doors of the cupboard stood ajar, and the box in which the vial was kept lay open on the floor. The vial was gone.

Mohammed Khalil Ghanai rushed down the street to the house of Abdul Rahim Bande, who was chief trustee of the mosque, and whose ancestors were the first custodians of the holy hair after it reached Kashmir. Upon hearing the news of the theft, Abdul Rahim Bande moaned, tore at his clothes, and fell into a swoon. The news swept through Srinagar. All offices and shops, schools and colleges were closed. The streets were cleared of all buses, taxis, tongas, rickshaws, and bicycles, and the waterways of all boats. In every house and every hut the hearth fire was extinguished, as at a death in the family. Everywhere, men, women, and children ran about barefoot, oblivious of the snow on the ground and the wind from the mountains. Some came out of the lanes and byways marching in processions with black flags (signs of bereavement) and wailing and beating their chests like mourners. The processions converged on squares and shrines for general meetings and for prayers. At the Hazratbal Mosque, thirty thousand mourners were told by one leader that the theft was "a deep intrigue to injure Muslim sensibilities and foment communal trouble for nefarious political ends." All kinds of rumors were soon abroad. It was a people's plot to overthrow the puppet government of Jammu and Kashmir, which was made up of opportunistic Kashmiri Muslims working for India. It was a plot of Indian politicians to end the *de-facto* division of the state of Jammu and Kashmir between India and Pakistan. It was a plot of Pakistani politicians to conquer India's two-thirds of the state by starting a religious war between the Kashmiri Muslims and the Sikh and Hindu infidels. It was a plot of the Hindus and Sikhs—who together were overwhelmingly outnumbered in the Valley, and who themselves overwhelmingly outnumbered Muslims in India—to

destroy the Islamic religion. No, it was the work of Bakshi Ghulam Mohammed, who, though a Muslim, had stolen the hair in order to come
back into power by restoring it. Bakshi Ghulam Mohammed, president of
the Jammu and Kashmir National Conference Party, had been Prime
Minister of Jammu and Kashmir from 1953 to 1963. He had first arranged
for the dismissal of his predecessor, Sheikh Mohammed Abdullah—popularly called the Lion of Kashmir—who had been the leading political figure
in the state, and then, after coming to power, had arrested him. (Sheikh
Abdullah, who had originally supported the accession of Kashmir to India
and had gone on to become Prime Minister in 1948, had fallen out with
India over, among other things, the question of self-determination for
Kashmir.) In the autumn of 1963, Bakshi Ghulam Mohammed had reluctantly resigned, going along with a plan of the Congress Party—with
which his National Conference was allied—for certain political leaders to
renounce power and work disinterestedly for the good of party and country. At the time of the theft, the Prime Minister of Jammu and Kashmir
was Khwaja Shamsuddin, a protégé of Bakshi Ghulam Mohammed and a
member of the National Conference.

The day after the theft was discovered, a mob was on the move. It set
fire to cars, shops, cinemas, office buildings—most of them the property of
Bakshi Ghulam Mohammed and his powerful family. It set fire to a police
station where brutal methods were reputed to have been applied during
Bakshi's regime. It tried to burn alive the Additional District Magistrate
and the Superintendent of Police. It mauled firefighters, and then, when it
was about to destroy the local radio station, which in the minds of the
people was identified with the detested state government, it was finally
subdued by tear gas, *lathis* (heavy bamboo sticks bound with iron), and
bullets. For the next eleven days, there was a *hartal,* or an organized cessa-
tion of work and business. All shops remained shuttered and all offices
locked. Such local Urdu papers as were able to publish (they caught the
mood of the people better than the English-language national papers)
were full of the black news of the theft. On Sunday, the twenty-ninth of
December, under the heading "This Tragic Incident," *Aftab* (Urdu for
"sun") printed an editorial that read, in part:

> The night between 26th and 27th December will be known for all time as
> a very ominous night. . . . Long mourning processions are being taken out
> in which the only demand voiced is that this extremely shocking and ex-
> tremely serious incident should be immediately inquired into. The incident
> is not an·ordinary one. . . . Such a thing has not been heard of in the last
> four and a half centuries. The entire population of Kashmir is the very pic-

ture of grief, and this tragedy will never be tolerated by the Kashmiri Muslims. . . .

The dearest treasure of the people has been snatched. . . . The entire population is restless, and everybody is looking to the government and waiting for the moment when the holy hair will be traced and the restlessness that has gripped the total Valley will be over. . . . The feelings of the people are deep, and the entire population is agitated, but not a single individual has so far given up hope or patience. . . . Even patience has a limit, and we feel it our duty to warn the government, so that fruitful steps may be taken quickly, before the situation gets out of control.

Two days later, the editorial was repeated word for word. By then, every dwelling in Srinagar was marked by a black flag. No food was cooked in any home, and people sought such consolation as they could find in the companionship of the streets. They bought tea and rice from specially set-up ration depots, took their provisions to hastily constructed clay fire pits in the open air, and there, by the roadside, cooked and ate together, sharing whatever they had. Every day, people walked in procession, raising their voices in threnodies, chanting *"Allah O Akbar"* and *"Ya Rasul Allah"* ("God is great" and "O Messenger of God") and interspersing these wails with shouts of "Let us have our holy hair back!" and "Expose the plot!" At the main intersections, on the main streets, and at important mosques, people prayed and lamented their loss, the women tearing their hair and their veils and the men striking their foreheads against a wall until they bled. Through most of the villages and hamlets of the Valley— Islamabad, Pulwama, Kulgam, Pampore, Sopore, Bandipore, Baramula, Handwara—similar spontaneous demonstrations of grief and anger broke out, and continued for eleven days. Soon after the theft, a number of political and religious leaders of Kashmir—among them Maulana Mohammed Sayid Masoodi, Mufti Jalaluddin, Mufti Bashiruddin, Ghulam Mohammed Mir, Maulana Saifuddin Kari, and Maulvi Mirwaiz Mohammed Faruq (*"maulana," "sayid,"* and *"maulvi"* are religious or inherited titles) —banded together as the Holy Relic Action Committee and took charge of the demonstrations. They set the period of mourning. They represented the people before the government. They collected donations of money and goods, mustered volunteers to man the ration depots and outdoor kitchens, and, to support their cause, mobilized political and religious organizations. The Holy Relic Action Committee, voicing the public resentment against state-government institutions like the police, who they said were "past-masters in converting truth into untruth, and vice versa," demanded that the central government take over from the state the direction of the search for the relic, that a judge from outside the state try the case, and that the people be told the details of the investigation, whatever the political consequences. After a group of political leaders—Ghulam Mohiuddin Kara, Khwaja Sadruddin Mujahid, Ghulam Mohammed Shah, Hadji Mohammed Isaq, Sheikh Abdul Rashid, and others—were arrested, the Holy Relic Action Committee demanded their immediate release. These demands were expressions of a revolutionary movement that was continually threatening to pass into more violent hands. Gangs of thugs, thought to be in the pay of politicians, roamed the streets terrorizing Hindus. Local papers called for primitive justice, as when an editorial printed in *Hamdard* (Urdu for "sympathizer") advocated lynching: "The accursed person who has committed this reprehensible act . . . is not only an enemy of the state but an enemy of the whole country and the enemy of humanity. Such . . . an accursed person deserves to be pelted to death." In the meantime, inflammatory reports were finding their way into the Valley from Pakistan, where the news of the disappearance of the hair had set off sympathy demonstrations, and where the secretary general of the Kashmir Liberation Movement, echoing a popular belief, hinted that India was behind the theft by calling it "the latest attack on Muslim culture by the enemies of the people of Kashmir." There were riots in East Bengal—East Pakistan—in which many Hindus died; order was restored only after hundreds of rioters had been arrested.

In Kashmir, all attempts of the Shamsuddin government to limit the expressions of grief, to check the revolution, and, by constant recourse to the Indian Army, to restore some measure of order were confounded by general and complete disobedience. The government, invoking Section 144 of the Criminal Procedures Code, banned all meetings and processions for which specific permission had not been obtained, and it imposed curfews, censored press reports, tapped telephones, arrested more leaders, restricted the freedom of movement of others, and threatened with dismissal anyone in government service who took part in the agitation, but all these measures proved ineffective. It was no secret that for many years most Kashmiris had been discontented with their accession to India, with the *de-facto* division of their state, and with the government imposed upon them, and that if they were given a choice they would prefer either integration with Pakistan or independence. And now a sense of religious outrage, combined with the smoldering political grievances, threatened to turn the Valley yet again into a battleground between India and Pakistan. Shamsuddin made desperate pleas to the people. He would, if it were any use, sacrifice his eyes for the recovery of the hair, he assured them, and he declared:

It is the belief of a Muslim that as long as he does not entertain more love for God's Prophet (may peace be on him) than he has for his children and for his property, his faith is not complete. I am a Muslim by religion, and I have the same belief. Thus, the removal of the holy hair of the Holy Prophet (may peace be on him) has injured our spiritual sentiments. It has actually injured the heart of humanity. I share in equal measure the grief that is being expressed by the common people. . . . I can offer my very life for recovery of the holy hair. If my transitory life be of any use toward this end, I will not hesitate to offer it. It is indeed a miracle of the holy hair itself that today Hindus, Muslims, and Sikhs are all mourning alike.

The Hindus and Buddhists to the east of the Valley, in Ladakh (part of Kashmir), did indeed offer prayers of sympathy, and the Hindus and Sikhs who formed the majority in Jammu, and who actually wanted complete and final integration with India, nevertheless now made common cause with the Kashmiri Muslims, thereby preventing new outbreaks of religious rioting. And so the life of Shamsuddin's government was prolonged. Non-Muslims marched in procession with their Islamic brethren, red Hindu flags embroidered with *"Om"* alongside green Muslim flags embroidered with verses from the Koran. Such a display of unity had not been seen in Kashmir since its division, and the unity persisted even when two bronze statues were stolen from a Hindu temple in Jammu—supposedly in a Muslim act of retaliation. However, the Shamsuddin government could not have survived without the intervention of the central government; in fact, the central government had assumed the powers of the Shamsuddin government in all but name, and considered invoking a provision of the Constitution called President's Rule, which authorized the President of India to take over the administration of any state if its own government proved unable to exercise authority. Travel plans of Ministers in the central government were postponed, messages of condolence were dispatched, and Prime Minister Jawaharlal Nehru went on the air to calm the nearly fifty million Muslims living in India, many of whom feared a repetition of the Hindu-Muslim riots that had accompanied Partition. In Delhi, there were frantic meetings between Nehru and Karan Singh, the son of Maharaja Sir Hari Singh and the nominal head of the state of Jammu and Kashmir; between Nehru and Sarvepalli Radhakrishnan, the President; between Nehru and Lal Bahadur Shastri, the former Home Affairs Minister (within the next few months he acquired a sort of portfolio in the Kashmir problem); between Nehru and Gulzarilal Nanda, the Home Affairs Minister; between Nanda and B. N. Mullick, the director of the Central Intelligence Bureau, who was dispatched to Srinagar with a staff of detectives; and between Nanda and his Home Secretary, V. Viswanathan, who was also sent to Srinagar. Yet, intense though the activity was in the central government and in the government of Jammu and Kashmir, it was all futile in the eyes of Kashmiri Muslims as long as the hair was missing and possibly destroyed—never to be seen again. Sheikh Abdullah, who had been in prison for virtually a decade (he had had a few weeks of freedom in 1958), wrote in a letter to the President:

> You are aware that this holy hair was brought to Kashmir about three hundred years ago, during the Mogul regime, and that it was installed by the Mogul rulers at Hazratbal, in a specially built chamber. These rulers had attached extensive estates to the shrine for keeping it provided with expenses for maintenance, et cetera. This shrine has been considered the greatest one and is a sacred spiritual center for Muslims. Throughout the centuries it has been respected as such. Since the people deeply love the Prophet of Islam (may peace be on him), they throng to this place on different religious occasions for spiritual benefits and blessings. . . . I think a conspiracy is at the root of what has happened. My eyes and the eyes of my friends are concentrated on you in this hour of darkness. We are sure that behind this theft there are intricate political aims. It is very clear that the accursed person who is responsible for this theft will do everything in his power to keep himself untouched and hidden. . . . I hope you will excuse my audacity, but the tragedy is so great and so painful that I have been forced to gather the courage to address you directly.

After pleading with the President to "take a bold step to save the people of Kashmir," he stated that the sacrilege was a logical outcome of corrupt Indian practices in Kashmir:

> Of late Kashmir has been going through a process of dehumanization, which was actually initiated in August, 1953, when the murder of the democracy was committed in the state. . . . Crores of rupees of the Indian exchequer have been used to corrupt the people of Kashmir and almost kill their very souls, so as to drug them against any possible resistance to the onslaught on their basic human rights. . . . I ask for early action in the direction of revising the Kashmir policy. It is the root cause of all evils.

> A life burnt and scorched
> If Kashmir it would enter,
> Be it even a roasted bird,
> It would surely grow wing and feather.

So the Persian poet Urfi Sherazi celebrates the home of the relic. And other bards of Islam tell of pilgrims through the centuries who, coming to see the relic, have so fallen under the enchantment of the beauty of Kashmir that they have been prepared to surrender their lives after being vouchsafed a mere glimpse of the place. So the poets sing, but always they return to the theme of the relic, saying that, compared to the constant, undiminished light that it sheds on the soul, all things—even the marvels of Kashmir—are ephemeral.

Attempting to establish the authenticity of the relic, the author of an Urdu pamphlet called "The Second Medina," Mohammed Husam-ud-Din, whose nom de plume is Johar, and who is a relative of Abdul Rahim Bande, records that the prophet Mohammed, on the night of his ascent to Paradise, was told by Allah, "With each of your sacred hairs, I will deliver thousands of the sinful among your followers from the burning fires of Hell." There are, says Johar, two ways of authenticating such episodes—the revealed way and the empirical way—and both are sanctioned by the Sunna. Johar cites instances of the two ways. In a revelation, the prophet Mohammed appeared to a Kashmiri named Hazrat-e-Khwaja-e-Khwajgan Khwaja Ahmed Yasvee and told him that the relic was his own "fragrant hair" and that it was from the tresses of his "right lock." Wishing an empirical basis for faith in the hair, another believer, Abdul Muzzafar Alamgir, tested it successively in fire, sun, and honey. He placed the hair in fire, and the hair did not burn; he placed the hair in the sun, and the hair did not cast a shadow; he placed the hair in honey, and the hair did not thereafter attract a single fly. According to Johar, the hair was originally in the custody of the descendants of Mohammed in Arabia, who were the hereditary attendants of his mosque in Medina. The hair remained in Medina until 1634, when its custodian, Sayid Abdullah, incurred the displeasure of the ruling caliph. The caliph confiscated Sayid Abdullah's property and banished him. Sayid Abdullah managed to take the hair into exile with him, and also two other relics—the saddle and the turban of Ali, the fourth caliph of Islam and the son-in-law of the prophet Mohammed. Sayid Abdullah reached India two years later, where, probably because of his possession of the three relics, an estate in Bijapur, in the Deccan, was settled on him by Emperor Shah Jehan. Sayid Abdullah and his family, who had come with him, lived in comfort in Bijapur for the next twenty-three years. Then Sayid Abdullah died and the relics passed to his son Sayid Hamid. (Sayid Abdullah's benefactor, Shah Jehan, was ill at the time, and his sons were fighting over his throne.) Thereafter, the fortunes of Sayid Abdullah's house declined, and Sayid Hamid was left destitute. Toward the end of the century, Sayid Hamid confided his financial difficulties to a Kashmiri trader named Khwaja Nuruddin Ashawari. "How

could a true lover of the Prophet (may peace be on him) bear it?" Johar
asks, in his account. He continues:

> Khwaja presented a sum to him in the garb of a loan. . . .
> Khwaja also had the chance of being blessed with a sight of the sacred
> relics. . . . He . . . abandoned all his other desires and hopes for the sake
> of his love for the hair of the Prophet (may peace be on him). [Probably
> because Johar is primarily interested in the hair, the saddle and the turban
> of Ali get little attention at this point in the narrative.] The flame of love in
> him became more intense every day, and at last there came a day when he
> presented himself in a state of spiritual intoxication and prayed:

> > "With thy benevolence grasp my needy hand
> > And grace me with one out of these gifts."

> The great Sayid did not relish this request. He said, "O Khwaja, take care
> of your lost senses and steady yourself. . . . Is it your plan to deprive me of
> this everlasting treasure?"
> When the distraught lover of the Prophet (may peace be on him) ap-
> pears to be sinking in the whirlpool of disappointment, the Loved One him-
> self turns into a favorable wind and extricates the distressed lover from the
> whirlpool. . . . During the same night, the exalted Sayid had a vision in
> which he saw the Prophet himself. In his own dignified speech he addressed
> Sayid and gave him instructions with regard to Khwaja's desire:

> > "Don't disappoint the trader.
> > Grace him with the everlasting treasure."

In the Islamic tradition of Urdu literature, influenced by the Koran,
Johar uses appropriate verse in his text—in his case, verse taken mostly
from the Kashmiri poet and scholar Hazrat Mirza Qalandar Beg, whom
Johar compares to the great Persian poet Firdausi.

Khwaja Nuruddin Ashawari, having thus obtained the hair, set out
with it for his native Kashmir. He broke his journey in Lahore, in the
Punjab, where he was besieged by crowds eager to have a glimpse of the
hair. Emperor Aurangzeb, the son of Shah Jehan who had won the
throne, and who happened to be in Lahore, summoned Khwaja and ap-
propriated the hair, saying, "This supreme blessing ranks higher than all
my domain, my throne, my crown, my faith, and my world." Emperor
Aurangzeb decreed that the hair be taken to a famous shrine in Ajmer, a
city some distance south of Lahore. When the people of Lahore heard that
the hair was to be taken from them, they were inconsolable. They wept;
they held funeral processions. There were meetings of viziers and amirs,
who chose a delegation to plead the cause of Lahore with Emperor Au-

rangzeb. Meanwhile, Khwaja Nuruddin Ashawari, after begging a friend, Medanish, to devote his life to the recovery of the hair and its preservation in Kashmir, died of a broken heart. Khwaja's last wish was that his remains be buried near the hair. The Emperor, of course, was not likely to be swayed by the entreaties of such a humble man as Medanish if the petitions of the powerful viziers and amirs had no effect, but when the hair had been in Ajmer for nine days, Mohammed appeared to the Emperor in a dream and announced:

> "You have grieved the heart of Khwaja.
> He was mad with love for me.
> I have appeared before you only to tell you that
> You must aid the fulfillment of his desire."

Wonderful! Wonderful! All this was wonderful! [So Johar exclaims.] This is exactly what ought to have happened, otherwise the hearts of the helpless and the friendless would have been trampled.

With the Emperor's blessing, the hair was now placed in a fragrant sandalwood box, and the sandalwood box placed beside the body of Khwaja Nuruddin Ashawari in an ornate palanquin. The palanquin was borne by believers to Kashmir—being hailed along the way by cheering throngs—and when it arrived, believers there were waiting to receive the hair, the prophet Mohammed having told their spiritual leaders in a vision that they should make themselves ready to receive his gift. The hair was installed in a mosque called Bagh Sadiq Khan, whose name was soon changed to Hazratbal (Urdu for "hair of the Prophet"). Khwaja Nuruddin Ashawari was buried in the garden of the mosque, through the efforts of his daughter Inayet Begum. Her husband, Khwaja Balagi Bande, presently arranged for a ceremonial *deedar* of the hair. The descendants of the couple inherited the functions of giving *deedars* and managing the mosque, the future of which was secured by revenue from estates donated by the government. It is these same functions that Abdul Rahim Bande and his several brothers and Mohammed Husam-ud-Din (Johar) performed.

Johar's highly embellished narrative, on which the preceding account primarily relies, is confused, but not any more so than other narratives, which differ on such points as when, if at all, the hair was submitted to empirical tests, why Sayid Abdullah was exiled from Medina, whether Sayid Abdullah smuggled the relics out of Medina or took them out with the blessing of the caliph, whether Sayid Abdullah journeyed to India on foot or by ship, whether the hair reached India in 1634 or 1636, why the

relic was relatively unknown in India before Khwaja Nuruddin Ashawari
inherited it, whether the hair was ever taken to Ajmer, whether Khwaja
died of a broken heart or of tuberculosis, whether it was a revelation or an
advance party that informed the Kashmiris about the coming of the gift,
whether the turban and the saddle were lost or are still extant—in fact, on
practically every point. But then it has to be kept in mind that the history
of the relic is based on a combination of legend, hearsay, and inspiration.

On the evening of Saturday, January 4, 1964, a little over a week after
the theft of the hair, members of the Holy Relic Action Committee—
among them Maulvi Mirwaiz Mohammed Faruq, who was its president,
although he was only in his teens (his family had been prominent in the
religious and political affairs of Kashmir), and Maulana Mohammed
Sayid Masoodi, who was fast becoming the head of the revolution—were
called to a house from which Mullick, the director of the Central Intelligence Bureau, was conducting an investigation. They arrived at exactly
7 P.M., the appointed time. By then, they had heard an All India Radio bulletin announcing that the relic had been recovered. The bulletin had first
been broadcast over All India Radio at five-thirty that evening, and it had
been regularly repeated, in English, Urdu, and Kashmiri, along with self-
congratulatory messages from Indian leaders. On their way to Mullick's
quarters, the members of the committee had passed through snowy streets
crowded with women throwing off their veils and men tossing their caps
and turbans in the air and shouting, "Long live the Central Intelligence
Bureau!" The committee members, however, had remained very much on
their guard. The bulletin had been suspiciously terse. It had not given a
single detail about the circumstances of the recovery, about the present
whereabouts of the hair, about the identity of the thieves, or about any
steps to bring them to justice. Nor had there been any mention of who, if
anyone, had vouched for the authenticity of the hair. For a decade, ever
since Sheikh Abdullah's arrest, the state government had been derided for
obvious corruption, for rigged elections, and for attempts to whitewash its
failures, but until the sacrilege strong police measures had succeeded in
suppressing the opposition. Now, with the complete breakdown of law
and order, might not the government go to any lengths to restore its authority? Might it not even simulate a holy hair? Indeed, the lack of detail
about the recovery of the stolen relic augured ill. True, the bulletin origi-
nated with the central government, which was considered more reliable
than the state government, but, after all, the central government had
been behind the arrest of Sheikh Abdullah, and had kept in power the

state governments of Bakshi Ghulam Mohammed and Shamsuddin. Now that the theft threatened India with the loss of Kashmir, the central government might stop at nothing. The members of the committee, who wanted to examine the hair for themselves and have their religious elders verify it, knew that it was in their interest to prolong the agitation over the theft of the relic and use the incident to rid Kashmir once and for all of an unpopular government. It had already been suggested that the loss of the hair might be the prophet Mohammed's way of leading the Kashmiris at long last to a successful revolution. The momentum had to be sustained.

Mullick kept the members of the committee waiting for eight hours. His intention may have been to prevent them from airing their doubts among the people celebrating in the streets, but the long wait had the effect of deepening those doubts. When the members of the committee were finally ushered into his presence, at 3 A.M., his manner with them was rather offhand. He congratulated them on the recovery of the relic and said that now they could go about their everyday business. They tried to elicit details from him. How had the hair been found? Just as it had been taken away, they were told—in mysterious circumstances. Mullick said that his investigation had made things so hot for the thieves that they had expeditiously returned the relic to the Hazratbal Mosque. Had anyone been apprehended? No. How was it that the thieves returning the hair had gone unnoticed by the crowd of mourners holding a twenty-four-hour vigil at the mosque? The government had its way of knowing things before anyone else; the fact was that the relic was returned. Mullick told them that the moment he was informed of the return of the relic he had gone over to the mosque himself and retrieved it. Was the hair now going to be reinstalled, with due respect and honor, in the *hujra-e-khas* at Hazratbal, where at least the elders could view it? Mullick said that for a time it would remain in the custody of the central government and no one would be allowed to see it. There were legal difficulties in the way of its verification and installation; any precipitate action would be ill-advised. Could the members of the committee perhaps see the hair now and satisfy themselves? No.

The members of the committee did not press the point further. Though they were not fearful men, they knew that under the Defense of India Rules they were liable to arrest without any such legal remedy as habeas corpus. (The Defense of India Rules, instituted by presidential proclamation during the Chinese advance on the Himalayas in 1962, were a set of regulations that empowered the central government to suspend fundamental constitutional rights in national emergencies. Although the regulations were extremely unpopular, they had been kept in force and had been invoked in the arrest of, among others, friends of the committee members.) The committee members left Mullick's presence convinced that the central government, like the state government, was out of touch with the realities of the revolution. The people in the streets, after a few hours of uncertain jubilation, had gone back to mourning. *Hamdard* expressed some of the doubts of the public: "Some ask how it could be possible for anybody to take back the holy hair to its place while the whole area was being watched by government detectives and other officers. How could anybody get such an opportunity? Some are heard asking why the person could not be caught red-handed while he was trying to put it back. There are other questions like these which are raised in the light of these statements and are asked in various circles." (The editors of the local newspapers were also well acquainted with the Defense of India Rules.)

Processions and public meetings soon adopted the slogans "Get the holy hair identified by the elders" and "Expose the conspiracy" and "Hang the conspirators." Almost every day, there were skirmishes between crowds and the police. The crowds would assault the police with brickbats and *kangris* (pots of burning coals that individuals carry around for warmth), and the police would open fire with rifles. Since the government's announcement of the recovery, the newspapers could no longer overtly praise popular agitation, so they cunningly ran stories about the heroic conduct of the people in the interval between the theft of the hair and its supposed recovery. One such story read:

> It is the miracle of the greatness of the Prophet (may peace be on him) that none dared sell anything in the black market, nor did anybody think of profiteering. As a matter of fact, milk and vegetables became cheaper than usual, differences ended, people were recharged with feelings of love and affection, fresh sentiments of fellowship and brotherhood could be noticed all round, a new atmosphere came into being, and a new life emerged from noble feelings.

Perhaps because the agitation showed no signs of subsiding, the authorities declared the eleventh of January a public holiday and on the eve of that day escorted the supposed relic to Hazratbal and, without any attempt to get it verified as Mohammed's hair, had it ostentatiously locked in an iron safe that had previously been installed in the *hujra-e-khas;* took charge of the keys; assigned a twenty-four-hour guard to the mosque; for further security, set up a permanent police post near the mosque; announced that the Department of Public Works had been instructed to reinforce the walls and doors of the *hujra-e-khas;* and stated that thenceforward the relic would be handled and exhibited only by written order of the District Magistrate. The authorities explained that the government had decided to return the relic to the *hujra-e-khas* now because an investigation and trial would take time and meanwhile the government did not wish to deny the people the satisfaction of praying in a mosque once again blessed by the presence of the relic. Around nine o'clock that evening, many of the Ministers of the state government (all with bodyguards), the Inspector General of Police, the District Magistrate, Mullick, and the Home Secretary, Viswanathan, gathered in the mosque with the reluctant members of the committee. They all sang and prayed and offered thanks for the return of the relic to the *hujra-e-khas.*

In the days following, however, commerce remained paralyzed. The members of the committee and other leaders of the revolution harangued excited crowds about the consequences of a failure to have the hair verified and the real conspirators brought to justice. The old demands and slogans were repeated day after day: "Let the elders identify the hair," "Let Sheikh Abdullah and Maulana Masoodi identify the hair," "Tell us the results of the investigation," "Stop covering up for the accursed criminals," "Produce those accursed criminals," "Release prisoners," "All Kashmiri politics are corrupt," "Give us honest police from the central government," "Give us an honest judge from the central government," and "Call *hartal.*" Parties that had been regarded as subversive—among them the Plebiscite Front, which, taking its lead from Sheikh Abdullah, stood for a free ballot to settle the future of Kashmir—had been muzzled for years, but now they presented their programs publicly. The Holy Relic Action Committee openly proclaimed that the struggle over the hair had all along had political as well as religious aims.

The central government conducted itself with aplomb, as at a press conference given by Viswanathan in Srinagar:

Q: You have said anybody who doubts the integrity of the recovered holy hair is speaking with the voice of Pakistan. But on last Sunday [January 12th] people repeated this demand in a public meeting at Jama Masjid [an important mosque in Srinagar]. What have you to say about that?

A: I do not want to indulge in discussion about this. I can say only that the holy hair which has been recovered is absolutely genuine and there should be no doubt about it.

Q: You have said that no black flags in a public meeting will be tolerated.

But following that warning black flags have continued to appear on jeeps and other vehicles and they were hoisted also on the stage of the public meeting at Jama Masjid. What have you to say about this?

A: The officers on the spot have complete freedom to act in such a situation.

Q: The holy hair . . . was not shown to any member of the Holy Relic Recovery Committee [another name for the Holy Relic Action Committee]. This was not shown to them even when they came to meet you.

A: I cannot show the holy hair to all the people who visit me.

Q: Will you show it to the people whenever they demand it?

A: It depends upon circumstances. . . .

Q: The Holy Relic Recovery Committee complains that the ruling party has reappeared and is harassing people. Does your warning against the disturbance of the peace apply to these people also?

A: The warning that I have issued will apply . . . to everybody in the same measure.

Q: Are you satisfied with this warning?

A: Yes.

Perhaps because Prime Minister Nehru was ill (he never quite regained his health afterward), the official statements from Delhi, for the most part, reiterated that the central government would not allow itself to be coerced by a mob, that the relic was authentic, and that all the agitation had been inspired by Pakistan, and stipulated that resumption of normal life was a precondition of any political reform in Kashmir. In private conversations, the authorities admitted that they were in a dilemma: if they gave in to the demand for verification, the relic might be repudiated, yet if they tried to suppress the demand—for instance, by arresting all the leaders of the revolution—they ran the risk that the revolution might turn violent and uncontrollable. It was thought that the Shamsuddin government was too weak, and the case for the presence of India in Kashmir too attenuated, for the central government to take any strong action. The authorities vacillated and followed a policy of compromise. For instance, they allowed the fundamental liberties of free speech and free association to flourish in practice, although in theory these had been all but abolished. The compromises were useless. On the twenty-fifth of January, mobs—one of them numbered at least nine hundred—attacked small parties of policemen in three different parts of Srinagar. The police tried to repulse them first with *lathis,* then with tear gas, and finally with rifles. Four demonstrators, it was said, were killed in the clashes, and eight demonstrators and a dozen constables were injured. All this was the official version of the day's events. The popular version put the number of dead at eighteen and the number of wounded at sixty-one, and had it that for that entire day the whole of Srinagar had risen up in arms and had taken over the rule of the city because trigger-happy policemen had massacred innocent Kashmiris, some of whom were doing nothing more provocative than sitting on their verandas. In the month since the upheaval began, Maulana Mohammed Sayid Masoodi had emerged as the most important leader of the people. In the Holy Relic Action Committee, he had all along been an advocate of restraint and patience. On the twenty-fifth, he was ill in bed, but as soon as he received word of the riots, he sprang up and rushed over to Jama Masjid and declared in a speech to the throngs assembled there that the police, by shooting innocent Kashmiris, had destroyed the last vestige of the people's confidence in the government, that the dead had not shed their blood in vain, that the people of Kashmir would one day be rewarded for their sacrifices, and that the people would never rest until the authenticity of the relic was established beyond all doubt. The dead were given a martyrs' burial, and the trouble quickly spread from Srinagar all over the Valley. For the next three days, in protest against the "government of hooligans" (a term that had been applied to the state government for years), there was a complete *hartal*. Even after the three days were up, the situation in the Valley did not improve. On the strength of a mere rumor that Maulana Masoodi and Maulvi Mirwaiz Mohammed Faruq had been imprisoned, *hartal* began all over again in Srinagar. It was repeatedly charged in public meetings that the same political bosses who had stolen the hair so that they could later come to power by taking credit for restoring it had, upon failing in their initial design, hired "hooligans" to instigate riots and disorder, so that anarchy might give them an excuse to make another effort to seize power. An editorial in *Rehnuma* (Urdu for "leader") read:

The movement that was conducted in the Vale of Kashmir for the relic's recovery has brought the history of the state to a turning point. . . . The truth is that the movement was peaceful and non-political. But certain hooligans have given it a violent character and succeeded in disrupting the peace of the Valley. The local administration, police and judiciary have become almost helpless against them. . . . The state government should have suppressed these hooligans and satisfied the people. . . . Even the tragedy of the theft was turned into a medium for power politics. Under the circumstances, certain demands are made, and fulfilling them would in any case be advantageous for the state. It is a pity that power-seekers, instead of sharing the troubles of the people, are busy demanding a termination of the present constitutional government and a promulgation of President's Rule in the state. They are aware that even this would not succeed in controlling the present situation in the state. On the other hand, this would render conditions less settled. Such people are not worried about the results. They want to come to power. . . . It is these people who are responsible for giving birth to hooliganism in Kashmir. It is these people who never uttered a word in favor of protecting the life and property of the common people and saving their honor. If they had raised their voices against steps that gave rise to hooliganism, conditions would not be as bad as they are now. . . . If the people demand anything at all from the Kashmir government, it is that the state be liberated from hooliganism, hooligans, monopolists, and power-seekers. These evils have taken root in the state. Peace will not be established in the state by merely bringing in big officers from other states, by importing a police force from outside, or even by establishing President's Rule in the state. The best and the only remedy is that hooliganism, corruption, nepotism, and inefficiency should be terminated. The government should also terminate the means and methods that were introduced to feed hooliganism.

At the time of the theft, there were about ten million Hindus living in officially Islamic Pakistan (primarily in East Bengal, Pakistan having been created mostly by the separation of East Bengal and West Punjab from India) and about fifty million Muslims in predominantly Hindu India. The original news of the theft touched off violence about a thousand miles away from Kashmir—against both Hindus in East Bengal and Muslims in West Bengal, with each side accusing the other of starting the riots. Thousands of refugees crossed from West Bengal into East Bengal and thousands more from East Bengal into West Bengal, each group bringing stories of arson and looting, and prompting further reprisals. The attacks and counterattacks may have had causes other than the theft itself. (Some of the Hindu refugees were merchants who had managed to prosper in certain Muslim villages and towns in East Bengal, and, as a consequence, had stored up ill will in these communities. Some of the Muslim refugees were impoverished residents of Calcutta slum tenements owned by Hindu landlords, and there was evidence to suggest that these landlords had hired arsonists to burn down the tenements so that they might later put the land to more profitable use.) However that may have been, in each country the police and the local authorities seemed to lose control of the riot-stricken areas, and authority passed to the Army. There had been some disturbances and a flow of refugees ever since the creation of Pakistan, but the present disorders were the most violent since those of 1950, which themselves had a precedent only in the disorders of Partition, when tens of thousands of people were killed and millions were displaced from their homes. In a sense, the Muslims in India and the Hindus in Pakistan were all hostages.

Sarvepalli Radhakrishnan and the President of Pakistan, Field Marshal Ayub Khan, both made appeals for religious toleration, but any coöperation between the governments of the two countries was impossible, because of the strong feelings about the question of Kashmir. Pakistani officials now claimed that India was using the disturbance over the theft as a cover for moves to settle the Kashmir question unilaterally. By their account, the Indian Constitution, which was adopted nearly two years after the 1948 United Nations cease-fire in Kashmir, had tacitly acknowledged Kashmir's special, disputed status, in that the state of Jammu and Kashmir had a prime minister and a head of state, like the central government itself, whereas every other state in the Indian Union had a chief minister and a governor; recently, however, India had announced that Kashmir, too, would have a chief minister and a governor. The contemplated change may have been more semantic than political (so Thomas F. Brady, writing in the New York *Times,* maintained), but the government of Pakistan, perhaps to call world attention to the uprising in Kashmir over the theft, denounced it as "a violation of India's commitments to the United Nations." Pakistan said that any move to integrate Kashmir further into India was a violation of Security Council resolutions to hold a plebiscite in Kashmir under United Nations supervision. Both countries considered the outcome of a plebiscite a foregone conclusion: because Muslims made up over ninety per cent of the Valley's population, most of the votes would go to Pakistan. India claimed that such a vote along religious lines would compromise the principle of secularism and religious toleration on which she was trying to build her society, and thus would put the Muslim minority within her borders in jeopardy. Pakistan dismissed this claim as a pretext for an Indian occupation of Kashmir. On February 3rd, the Security Council met for its hundred-and-tenth debate on the issue of Kashmir, this time as a result of the disorders touched off by the theft. The Pakistani Minister of External Affairs, Zulfikar Ali Bhutto, warned the assembled powers that the theft had mobilized an oppressed people, saying, "The people of Kashmir have unmistakably risen in open rebellion. . . . We can no longer doubt that they are unreconciled to Indian occupation." He insisted that because India's "colonial hold" had now been loosened, India was employing police-state tactics in Kashmir, with the result that Pakistan and India were heading toward a second war over Kashmir. But the hope that the United Nations would take any decisive action on Kashmir which was acceptable to Pakistan had been dissipated two years earlier, when Russia used her veto to side with India; debate in New York could do nothing to dispel the threat of a holy war of a kind that the West had not known since the seventeenth century. The Calcutta correspondent of the London *Observer* wrote:

> In most of India—and Pakistan—the tension between the two communities [Hindu and Muslim] has never abated, even when it has been kept within tolerable bounds. The tiniest spark can always set fire to the powder barrel and it is not really surprising that the theft of the sacred hair of the Prophet Mohammed in a Srinagar mosque should have started the chain reaction that ended in the bloodbath of Calcutta.
>
> In West Bengal the situation is particularly explosive because of the tens of thousands of refugees from Paskistan who are crowding the camps and the slums. When anti-Hindu rioting started on the other side of the nearby border, these refugees saw friends and parents whom they had left behind [arrive in] Calcutta with highly coloured stories of wholesale murder in East Pakistan. . . . Nobody accepts the official figure, which sets the number of dead at no more than 100, and the usual estimate is around 500 killed, while tens of thousands have lost their homes through fire, or dare not return to a place where they feel insecure.

The riots in East Bengal and West Bengal continued well into 1964, displacing hundreds of thousands of people. Meanwhile, toward the end of January, Lal Bahadur Shastri, who was now virtually acting as Prime Minister, flew to Srinagar to take charge. He heard out officials and politicians of all shades of opinion on the subject of the crisis over the relic. Some counselled him not to yield under any circumstances to the demand for verification of the relic, because even to entertain a question as to its authenticity, especially after the central government had vouched for it, could set off popular agitation on such a scale that India might well lose Kashmir to Pakistan; others advised him to yield to that demand at any cost, because as long as the slightest doubt remained about the authenticity of the relic, popular agitation would not subside, nor would India be able to feel secure in her control over Kashmir. Shastri soon realized what had been apparent to Kashmiris for weeks. In the words of *Hamdard,* "Without a proper identification, the Muslims would not have believed that the hair was genuine even if all the governments of the world combined in declaring that it was." Shastri therefore committed the Indian government to the cause of "proper identification," but not before he had conducted long secret talks with all the religious leaders who might be called upon to verify the relic and had satisfied himself that they were honest men, and would not repudiate it simply for political ends.

The third of February was the day settled upon for the verification of the relic. The weather that day was exceptionally bleak. As the climax of a week-long cold wave, parts of Dal Lake were frozen over, many streets were impassable, and the water in some wells had turned to solid ice. At the appointed time of 3 P.M., thousands of believers gathered on the terraced lawns around Hazratbal Mosque and in the streets, and inside the mosque were the same officials, the same political dignitaries, and the same members of the Holy Relic Action Committee who had been present for the installation ceremony, but prominent among those assembled this time were—besides Shastri—fifteen divines led by Fakir Mirak Shah, the most venerated ascetic in Kashmir. Maulana Masoodi recited, "All of you are in the house of God and the Holy Koran is before you. Whatever you will say will be only the truth." From the iron safe in the *hujra-e-khas,* a silver-capped vial containing a silver pendulum to which a strand of hair was attached was brought out. While the other divines recited verses from the Koran, the vial was ceremoniously raised to the face of Fakir Mirak Shah. Because his eyesight was failing, the vial was held close to his eyes. He peered at the hair and cried out, "The Garden is bright with the light of Mohammed. The light of Mohammed is reflected in every flower and every plant." The congregation sobbed with joy, people embraced and gave thanks, and many of the leaders made offerings and congratulated one another on the restoration of the hair.

Later that afternoon, the officials and dignitaries, even while commenting to the press on the verification of the relic, reverted to their old postures and themes, indicating that the events in the mosque had settled nothing. "The authorities and the officers who helped in the recovery of the holy relic were sure about the genuineness of the recovered holy hair, since they had taken all the necessary steps before concluding that it was genuine," Shamsuddin said, in a statement that seemed to dismiss the tidings of the divines as gratuitous. Bakshi Ghulam Mohammed, for his part, seemed to dismiss the political importance of the relic. "Although I have had the rare luck of repeatedly seeing the holy hair for about thirty years, I did not present my name as one of those who might finally identify it, because I consider it to be a purely religious matter," he said. Shastri's comments were a warning both to the Kashmiris, who might mistake India's about-face over verification of the relic for a sign of weakness, and to the Pakistanis, who had hopes of a United Nations intervention in the uprising over the hair in Kashmir. "India's stand on the Kashmir issue is clear," he said. "We cannot budge an inch from it. The relic is our domestic question. I do not know how Pakistan comes into the picture." As for the members of the Holy Relic Action Committee, they went over to Jama Masjid the following day to give the tidings to believers assembled there. On that occasion, Maulana Masoodi repeated many of the old charges and demands. He reviled the party of Shamsuddin and derided the authorities for trying to discredit the revolution over the hair by charging that it was the work of a handful of Pakistani agents. He demanded that the leaders of Azad Kashmir have free access to the Indian-held part of Kashmir. He asserted that the government was continuing to shield the real conspirators and to persecute innocent men. (Abdul Rahim Bande had been held in prison as a suspect since the morning of the theft.) Maulana Masoodi raised the slogans "Produce the real culprit," "Send an honest judge from outside for the investigation of the case," and "Terminate hooliganism." Asking the Kashmiris to make themselves ready for further sacrifices, he announced that the *hartals* and the public meetings would continue, and that the Holy Relic Action Committee would remain in existence. One part of Maulana Masoodi's speech, however, was completely new. In a surprise move, he asked for the release of Sheikh Abdullah and for his reinstatement as the leader of the Kashmiris. The Holy Relic Action Committee, as a matter of prudence, had avoided asking for the release of Sheikh Abdullah; it had not agitated publicly for his leadership. Maulana Masoodi, in now bringing this explosive political issue officially into the open, seemed to be declaring that the uprising was in fact revolutionary in character—a point immediately grasped by the crowd at the mosque, who shouted, "Long live the Lion of Kashmir!" (The *Hindustan Times* conjectured, "It appears that today's reference to Abdullah's release by Maulana Masoodi has been done at the instance of the pro-Abdullah wing of the Action Committee. . . . A feeling within the committee seems to be that the present controversy could be utilized to strengthen opposition to the government.")

After the meeting, Maulana Masoodi partly retracted his words about Sheikh Abdullah, but now it was clear that the feelings released by the theft of the hair and unassuaged by its restoration would not subside with its verification. Tension rose as the sixth of February neared, for this date, the anniversary of the death of Ali, the fourth caliph, was one of the ten days of the year on which there was a *deedar*. Police armed with rifles and *lathis* were stationed everywhere that day. But Kashmiris who had walked for miles in the cold to reach Hazratbal now patiently squatted for hours

in the snow waiting for their *deedar.* Finally, they saw an unfamiliar figure—it was Khwaja Nuruddin Bande, a relative of the imprisoned Abdul
Rahim Bande—walk out on the balcony in the traditional green robes and
raise the vial high. The people cried out and recited the Darood, the
Salam, and Naats in praise of the prophet Mohammed. But although
there was no violence that day, and, on the surface, things had returned to
normal, the basic conditions were thought to be unchanged. The political
correspondent of the Calcutta English-language daily, the *Statesman,* who
visited Kashmir a few days after the *deedar,* analyzed some of the deeper
causes of the revolution.

> The winter of Kashmir's discontent [he wrote, in part] is unlikely to end
> until the promises of drastic political and administrative reforms lately
> emanating from New Delhi are translated into action. . . . To imagine that
> with the recovery, verification, and peaceful *deedar* of the holy relic the mass
> upsurge in Kashmir is over would be a grave error. The only thing graver
> than this would be the belief that all the trouble in Kashmir, past, present,
> or potential, is caused only by Pakistan agents or pro-Pakistan elements. . . .
> Interestingly, the greatest exaggeration of Pakistan influence over the mass
> movement has been directed by the Kashmir government, which, for all
> practical purposes, continues to mean Bakshi Ghulam Mohammed and a few
> co-sharers in power. That they are wide of the mark in magnifying Pakistan
> influence is a matter not so much of opinion as of facts which speak for them-
> selves. First, nothing would have suited Pakistan's purpose more than giving
> the agitation in Kashmir a communal turn. Yet there has not been a single
> communal incident in the Valley even during the days when the Srinagar
> administration simply did not exist and when neither Bakshi Ghulam Mo-
> hammed nor any functionary of the government cared or dared to face the
> people. Curiously, the former Prime Minister [Bakshi Ghulam Mohammed]
> is unable or unwilling to move about in Srinagar even today without heavy
> police protection, and his house is among the most heavily guarded build-
> ings in Srinagar. Secondly, the arson during the lawlessness in Srinagar was
> highly selective, directed against the property of Bakshi Ghulam Moham-
> med's family and against a police station which had acquired notoriety as a
> centre of strong-arm methods on behalf of the Bakshi regime. Thirdly, in
> sharp contrast to Bakshi Ghulam Mohammed, the dissident leaders of the
> National Conference, Mr. G. M. Sadiq and Mir Qasim, whose love for, and
> identification with, India is no less pronounced than Bakshi's, were able to
> move about freely among the mob. . . . Having thus established the ap-
> proximate proportions of the undoubted Pakistan element in the recent mass
> upsurge, and with the religious sentiment now out of the way, one comes to
> the heart of the matter, which is, beyond reasonable doubt, the widespread
> and deep-seated discontent against Bakshi Ghulam Mohammed's rule. This

discontent has been building up over a period of ten years, getting more and more pronounced as time went by, until the Hazratbal incident proved to be a flash point of the repressed feelings of resentment and anger. The reasons for this discontent . . . can be broadly summed up as widespread corruption and strong-arm tactics often described by observers as "political gangsterism." These resentments are further fanned by the evidence of the sudden affluence acquired by some of those who wield power, and suspicion about the methods by which support is secured. Little wonder, therefore, that both the National Conference party and the party organization have been effectively stultified and made subservient by a judicious use of the spoils system and unabashed intimidation. If Bakshi Ghulam Mohammed had gone only thus far, he would have done practically the same thing which some other Chief Ministers have done elsewhere, more noticeably in the neighboring Punjab. But things in Bakshi Ghulam Mohammed's Kashmir went much farther . . . because Kashmir has always been treated as a "special case" and therefore immune from checks and balances operative in the rest of India. The judiciary can be left out of this discussion, but to talk of an independent civil service in Srinagar would be an invitation to ridicule. Indeed, the extent to which the Kashmir administration is dependent on Bakshi Ghulam Mohammed, even after he has technically ceased to be Prime Minister, is horrifying. The worst thing to happen in Kashmir, however, was the systematic and ruthless suppression of any attempt to organize a democratic opposition. The instrument of destruction invariably was a paramilitary organization paradoxically called the "Peace Brigade," or the strong-arm gentlemen within the National Conference itself, whose tribe has steadily increased during Bakshi Ghulam Mohammed's ascendancy. In fairness, it must be recorded that the authoritarian and other objectionable developments in Kashmir would not have reached the proportions they did if only the Centre [that is, the central government] had done its elementary duty. But there has been a strange mystique in Delhi that nothing unsavory about internal affairs should be brought to light lest Pakistan should make unscrupulous use of the disclosure—a logic which should have led to a suppression of the news of recent riots in Calcutta. Far from being a brake on Bakshi Ghulam Mohammed's authoritarianism, Mr. Nehru took the extraordinary step of destroying the only worthwhile opposition Mr. Sadiq, Mir Qasim, and Mr. D. P. Dhar had organized, ordering these leaders to go back to the National Conference fold. Under the circumstances, it should be no surprise to anybody that the people of Kashmir want a clean break with the past. They want Bakshi Ghulam Mohammed to be removed from the scene, for as long as he is there it would not be possible to free the administration from his stranglehold, "assiduously and ruthlessly" built up over a decade. . . . Mr. Shamsuddin, the new Prime Minister, is a nice and well-meaning gentleman. In a long interview, he tried hard to explain that he had a mind of his own and that he intended to allow no extraneous interference in the administration. But he hastened to add that he would not pick a quarrel with Bakshi Ghulam Mohammed just to convince his critics. Unfortunately, however, not even Mr. Shamsuddin's friends take this statement seriously, not to speak of his critics, who attack him merely on the ground that he is Bakshi Ghulam Mohammed's "shadow." From this it should follow that any arrangement under which Mr. Shamsuddin continues to be the head of the government would be unpopular. . . . A National Conference government headed by Mr. Sadiq would certainly be more popular than the present one. But judging from the present mood of the Kashmiri people, the change would not be considered adequate. . . . First, Mr. Sadiq and his associates have neither a hold on the National Conference nor a tremendous mass appeal. They are honest and honorable men, and in their hope of displacing Bakshi Ghulam Mohammed they depend entirely on New Delhi and Mr. Nehru. Secondly, they had been members of the Bakshi regime for long periods, not once but twice. . . . At any rate, in all fairness, Mr. Sadiq and his friends cannot claim credit for all the good things that happened during the Bakshi Ghulam Mohammed regime, and many good things have happened, including an impressive economic advance, and disclaim responsibility for all the bad things. All this brings one back to the "clean sweep" and the "complete break with the past." . . . But it is recognized that the time and opportunity for such a drastic step has passed.

In the absence of any freely elected representatives of the people of Kashmir, Sadiq, Mir Qasim, and a few other leaders of the National Conference were the only men whom the central government could trust to form another government in Kashmir that would be loyal to India. And so, on the twenty-eighth of February, Shamsuddin was replaced by Sadiq. Kashmiris saw the advent of Sadiq and his new government as a mere changing of the guard. *Aftab* commented in an editorial:

> More or less the same people will come back who have been in power for a number of years. For this reason the people do not show interest in this Ministerial change. . . . The main trouble is that the democracy is talked about by the ruling party and their yes-men. If anybody else talks about it he is painted black and dubbed an enemy of the country.

Maulana Masoodi and the other members of the Holy Relic Action Committee still did not succeed in obtaining satisfaction for many of their demands. For instance, the authorities had at first made no attempt to investigate the police shootings on the twenty-fifth of January, which came to be known as "Martyrs' Day." *Aftab* had noted, "Whenever firing is resorted to in any other part of the country, the central government takes steps so as to give satisfaction to the people. What sins have Kashmiris committed that all their legitimate and constitutional demands are being treated lightly?" Then, when the authorities appointed a commission to investigate the shootings, it consisted of only one man, a sub-magistrate of Jammu named Ghulam Mohammed Taq. Within a week, *Aftab* was complaining:

> But people, so far, know neither where the Magistrate is nor whether any inquiries have taken place anywhere. . . . Are we to understand that this announcement was only a political stunt? . . . People had not expressed any satisfaction or joy at this announcement because nobody was certain that this inquiry would be held according to the principles of justice. . . . It was expected that they would invite all the people who had any knowledge of the facts. It is a pity, however, that the people know nothing about it so far.

A more important demand was the apprehension and trial of the "real thieves." On the nineteenth of January, Gulzarilal Nanda, who, as Home Affairs Minister, was chiefly responsible for the maintenance of law and order, promised Parliament in Delhi that the thieves would be tried in "a week or two." On the twelfth of February, he assured Parliament that he would give the names of the accused the very next day. But on the thirteenth of February he changed his mind and, pleading "the public interest," postponed disclosure of any of the names. Finally, on the seventeenth of February, he named, of all people, Abdul Rahim Bande, along with two other Kashmiris—Abdul Rashid, whom Nanda identified as a man caught running away from the shrine about the time the relic was returned, and Kadir Butt, of whom Nanda said that he "has been coming and going from and into Pakistan-held territory and therefore it cannot be ruled out that there has been some kind of inspiration [*sic*] of complicity." Nanda's announcement touched off more disturbances in Kashmir. Maulana Masoodi declared, "Muslims of the state are convinced that the real culprit has not been arrested and that they have been hoodwinked."

A few weeks later, Maulana Masoodi expressed the general discontent of the leaders of the revolution over their unsatisfied demands by saying, "The mass upsurge all over Jammu and Kashmir is the melting of snow that has been collecting for ten years. It is now up to us to channel these floodwaters to better our lives, or let them destroy us." But in the subsequent months, under Sadiq's government, the leaders of the revolution were not so much destroyed as made impotent by a combination of token concessions and delays. In March, Sadiq's government restored to office civil servants who had been dismissed for their part in the agitation, and released most of the political prisoners taken during the uprising. In April, almost as a direct result of the uprising, even Sheikh Abdullah himself was released, and was allowed to make a triumphant return to Srinagar and, as a spokesman for the Kashmiris, to hold discussions both with leaders in Pakistan and with leaders in India. These gestures toward Sheikh Abdullah were interpreted as signs that Nehru was finally moving in the direction of an accommodation with Pakistan over Kashmir. In May, Nehru died, but the hopes for this accommodation did not diminish, for Shastri was credited with bringing about the change in Nehru's position on Kashmir, and Shastri was Nehru's successor. And that autumn, on a vague charge of corrupt practices, Bakshi Ghulam Mohammed was arrested. After eleven weeks, however, Bakshi Ghulam Mohammed was released. December 27th, the first anniversary of the theft of Mohammed's hair, came and went with no progress made toward a trial of the accused thieves; instead, the central government turned the case over to the state government, and it was rumored that the state was only waiting for a politically opportune moment to drop the charges. Gradually, as the months passed, the force of the Holy Relic Action Committee was spent and the urgent need that had been felt in India for a political settlement of Kashmir diminished. Sheikh Abdullah was put back in prison—for, among other things, holding a private meeting with Chou En-lai in Algeria. Kashmir's special status under the Indian Constitution was gradually abolished, and the state was fully integrated into India. August, 1965, marked the beginning of a second war between India and Pakistan over Kashmir, which soon spread to a second front, in the Punjab. The war, though it was short and, for the most part, inconclusive, had bitter religious overtones, and whatever its causes—India's failure to grasp the full meaning of the theft of Mohammed's hair; waning hope in Pakistan over Kashmir; India's uneasiness at the new friendship between Pakistan and China; the appearance of large numbers of Pakistani infiltrators in Indian-held Kashmir—it was generally agreed that after such a war a permanent settlement between India and Pakistan over Kashmir and other questions would be a long time in coming, if it ever came at all.

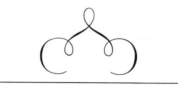

Believers at the Gate

IN KASHMIR, I AM SURPRISED TO FIND that even now a mention anywhere of Mohammed's hair stirs up emotions as strong as if it were still missing and the conspiracy were still to be investigated. (A university professor in Srinagar solemnly assures me that the real relic has been auctioned in the international market and bought by a devout Muslim who lives in the Middle East, where he gives private *deedars*.) Some of the members of the Holy Relic Action Committee, including Maulana Masoodi, are behind bars and incommunicado, but in Srinagar I am able to meet Khwaja Sadruddin Mujahid, a leader of the Plebiscite Front, and Abdul Rahim Bande, who is still the government's prime suspect. I also talk with Abdul Rahim Bande's successor at Hazratbal, Khwaja Nuruddin Bande, and the ascetic Fakir Mirak Shah.

Khwaja Mujahid is out on parole, granted because he is in poor health. Indeed, when I call on him, in a tenement house, where he lives with relatives, he seems to be near physical collapse. He is stretched out on a pallet on the floor, and, with an effort, raises himself to greet me, only to sink back onto the pallet. I mention to him my research into the events connected with the theft of Mohammed's hair. Although I have received advance personal assurances from the authorities, including Chief Minister Sadiq himself, that they no longer have any interest in the activities and views of Khwaja Mujahid, I nevertheless ask him if he thinks our conversation could in any way jeopardize his parole.

"I don't care what the conditions of parole are," he replies, in vigorous

Urdu. He sounds as if he had always talked through a megaphone at street-corner rallies. "I was exiled from Kashmir when I was ten and a half for violating the law of the state—I had joined a movement against the despotic rule of the Maharaja. That was in 1931, and I've been making trouble ever since."

In reply to a couple of questions, he tells me that in 1932 he returned to Kashmir from his exile, which he spent in Lahore, and that in the next thirty-odd years he was repeatedly tried and imprisoned for sedition—first for agitating against the absolutism of Maharaja Sir Hari Singh, and later for agitating against the undemocratic state governments of Bakshi Ghulam Mohammed and Shamsuddin. (Sometimes the ground for his arrest was trade-union activities—organizing the tonga-wallahs, for instance—and sometimes it was journalistic activities; he was managing an Urdu weekly at the age of eighteen.) He announces that between 1932 and 1965 he spent, all told, sixteen years in jail. "This time, they released me only because of my asthma, my ulcers, and my heart condition," he says. "In my last few months in jail, my weight dropped from a hundred and twenty-five pounds to eighty pounds. You must understand that I've always considered it my only duty to follow Sheikh Mohammed Abdullah's lead. It is his aim to obtain for the people of Kashmir the right of self-determination. Any deviation from the path laid down by him has given me a sense of unfulfillment. In 1953, when Sheikh Abdullah was unconstitutionally dismissed, I happened to be in a government job, and I resigned at once in protest."

I ask Khwaja Mujahid about his reactions to the first news of the theft.

He seems so weak that one would scarcely imagine he could sit up, but at this he leaps to his feet and starts marching excitedly around the room. "The theft was nothing but a conspiracy to destroy this Muslim center!" he cries out. "All Kashmiri Muslims regard the Hazratbal Mosque as the second Kaaba. Thousands go there every Friday to pray. We Muslims have the same regard for the holy hair that we have for the Prophet (may peace be on him) himself, since the hair is a part of his sacred body, and when we see it we have a feeling that we are seeing the Prophet (may peace be on him) himself."

I ask about what, actually, he did when he heard about the theft.

"The rumor was impossible for me to believe," he says. "But more and more people came to my house with the same report, so I went out to learn the truth myself. The streets were full of people—barefooted, bareheaded, beating their chests. They were rushing toward Hazratbal. In truth, the holy hair had been stolen. Maulana Atta Ullah Suhrawardy, a leader of the

Plebiscite Front, went with me over to Lal Chowk, one of our main intersections. Thousands of people were already there. Maulana Atta Ullah
Suhrawardy, Maulvi Faruq, and I addressed them. We appealed to them to
maintain communal harmony. We demanded that the tragedy be immediately investigated, and so we were arrested, but our work was continued
by the Holy Relic Action Committee. Sheikh Abdullah sent a message
from jail urging the people to maintain communal harmony at any cost, so
all his relatives, friends, and associates were arrested, on one pretext or
another. One of these relatives—a businessman not at all interested in politics—was not only arrested but, it has been acknowledged, tortured for days.
The theft of the holy hair was the result of a deep-laid conspiracy." He
is off again. "Everyone knows that the thievery was part of a planned
attempt to keep a certain political clique of hooligans in power. The clique
had controlled the government for ten years. The clique engineered the
theft because it was tottering and wanted to strengthen its position in any
way that it could. When it was rumored that the clique was behind the
theft, the hooligans didn't have a word to say about it. Some of them just
disappeared, and later it was learned that they had taken up residence in
Delhi. They returned to Srinagar months afterward, and they could travel
to their houses from the airport only by lying down in the back seats of
their cars, hidden under bedsheets, and some of them haven't dared to
show their faces in the streets since. The hooligans had banked on the fact
that the theft would create widespread disorder in Kashmir—communal
riots, and murder and arson—and that they could then stabilize their
power by ruthlessly suppressing the riots, but there were no communal
riots. The clique had always ruled the state by means of the Army—a
reign of terror. People had been detained, implicated in trumped-up cases,
or released—at the whim of the clique. People had tried to draw Mr.
Nehru's attention to the clique, but he had taken no action, and the hooligans had been rampant for a decade."

Like Khwaja Mujahid, Abdul Rahim Bande has been released for reasons of health, and he is back at his home—a small, modest house in the
shadow of the mosque. He has a round face, with friendly eyes, and, perhaps because he has a white beard, he looks older than his age, which is
sixty-eight. When I call on him, he is wearing a white turban, a long green
robe, and a shawl—the same color as his robe—which he continually pulls
and folds around him, like a man afraid of catching cold. I put only one
question to Mr. Bande: What is the present state of the case against him?
"I am often summoned to court," he says absently, in Kashmiri. "I go

there and am kept waiting for hours, and then I'm told to come back another day. They say the case will be resumed on another date. The case has already been going on for several years, and the judges have been changed again and again. A judge used to preside over hearings at the Central Jail, where I was locked up. He retired, and another judge took over. He has also retired. And now the case is with still another judge. I hear that the charges against the two others accused have been dropped, and that the charges against me will be dropped, too, when the government can safely do it. In the meantime, I must go to court, and in the meantime, too, I must not be allowed a *deedar* of the holy hair."

Mr. Bande starts at a sound from the street. He listens for a few moments, and then, pulling his shawl more tightly around him, goes on, "I exhibited the holy hair for thirty-eight years, and now I'm not even allowed to see it. The holy hair has been a source of livelihood and honor for my family, all of whom have served at the Hazratbal Mosque over hundreds of years. How could anyone believe that I would lift a finger against the very source of our livelihood and honor? It was because of the holy hair that we occupied a position of honor in the courts of Maharaja Gulab Singh, Maharaja Ranbir Singh, Maharaja Pratap Singh, and Maharaja Hari Singh—all the Dogra rulers of Kashmir. All those Hindu kings used to award robes of honor to us Sayids. We have been held in high esteem by many of the tourists who visit Kashmir. How could anyone be made to believe the charge that I committed the theft? I have been implicated in the case on political grounds, because I never sided with the embezzling politicians—the hooligans."

Almost as soon as I walk into the Hazratbal Mosque, Khwaja Nuruddin Bande appears out of the *hammam,* on the far side of the main hall. He has an expansive air. "Sahib, Sahib, Sahib," he says, raising his palm to his forehead and bowing in salaam. He continues, in Urdu, "I know exactly who you are. It is to friends like you that we look in promoting the welfare of this shrine and the hair. You're a big sahib from All India Radio—yes?" Over a black *kurta* and black pajamas Mr. Bande sports a handsome black *achkan,* or tunic. He wears the traditional skullcap, and his beard is neatly trimmed according to the specifications for a Muslim divine.

Overwhelmed by his greeting, I rather reluctantly explain that he has taken me for someone else.

"Then it is a simple case of mistaken identity," he says, with a deep, full laugh.

Mr. Bande sets about showing me around Hazratbal. It is like many other small mosques, but Mr. Bande regards the twelve ceiling fans in the main hall, its many hanging lamps, its three wall clocks (they do not show the correct time, or even the same time), its red, yellow, and black patterned carpet—everything in the hall, in the mosque—as a part of the heritage of the relic.

I ask if the hair in Hazratbal is the only relic of its kind.

Mr. Bande takes a long breath and says, "There are many holy hairs in Kashmir. There is a holy hair in Kalashpur, there is a holy hair in Saoora, there is a holy hair in Andarwara, there is a holy hair in Islamabad, and Mr. Ansari, former president of the Anti-Corruption Board, also possesses a holy hair, all his own, which I have seen myself. He will not show it to many people."

"Is there, then, some special quality associated with the hair at this mosque?" I ask.

"We have *deedars* for the public," he says proudly.

When I take leave of him, he is standing near the engraved silver doors of the *hujra-e-khas,* which are just then being guarded by an elderly man with a long, flowing beard. The guard is softly intoning the Kalmá: *"La ilaha illal 'lah, Muhammed Rasul Allah"* ("Allah is the one God, and Mohammed his greatest prophet").

"A glimpse of Fakir Mirak Shah, for believers, is like a *deedar* of the holy hair," says a Kashmiri friend who is a Muslim. "You can see him any time, any day, in his house in Shalimar. He has been sitting on the same *gaddi,* in the same spot, in the same room, in the same house, for at least forty years, and maybe longer."

The entrance to Fakir Mirak Shah's house, a two-story structure near a mosque, resembles a cobbler's stall: dozens of pairs of slippers, leather sandals, clogs, mountain boots, pumps, and high-heeled shoes are lined up on the floor. All the way to the top of a narrow, dilapidated stairway, people sit, nursing babies or tidying up children or eating out of newspapers or tiffin-carriers while they wait for their audience. At the top of the stairway is a large, bare hall. Here there are more people, all sitting on the floor cross-legged. At the far end of the hall is Fakir Mirak Shah, in a white turban and a loose wheat-colored robe. He is old and small and bearded, and his expression is stern. He is sitting upright on a *gaddi*. In one hand he holds a cardboard box of incense sticks, which he nervously waves about like a wand. Men, women, and children, a few at a time, move across the floor to his *gaddi*. They receive blessings, make offerings, and then move away. Eventually, I am one of the circle around his *gaddi.* "I do not distribute any charms," he is saying, in Urdu. "I offer prayers, which are as a pinch of dust. This place where I am squatting is the seat of my spiritual preceptors. I have sat on this *gaddi* since childhood. My ancestors migrated from Kashan. The first to come over and settle here was Sayid Habib Ullah Kashan. I belong to the family of Sayids and am a descendant of the Prophet. Listen to my *silsillah* [Urdu for "genealogy"]: Fakir Sayid Mirak Shah Talib II, Abdul Qadus Shah Talib Sheikh II, Abdul Qadir Talib, Lal Shah Sahib Talib, Rasul Sahib Ludhianvi Talib, Sheikh Mohammed Ganai Talib, Shah Mohammed Faruq Qalandar, Mir Sayid Ali Hamdani, Hazrat Ali, Hazrat Mohammed . . ." The names of his ancestors now come so fast that sometimes it is difficult to catch more than a syllable and other times a name is simply a breath, but the people within hearing distance listen throughout with full attention.

He breaks off and turns to me. I tell him that I am not a Muslim, but that I had wanted to meet him, because he had verified the hair.

"It was not at all difficult for me to recognize the holy hair," he says. "I had seen it many times before. I knew the exact color of the hair. I knew it to be brownish. I remembered even the smallest details about the vial and knew that one side of it looked very clean and the other side not so clean. I found the vial in absolutely the same condition. But even before I saw the holy hair I had an inner vision that testified to the genuineness of the hair. My soul had spoken that the holy hair was real. I had a premonition that the real hair had been restored to its sanctuary even before I saw it. I had a premonition even before the theft was committed that the hair would be disturbed, but only temporarily. But the subject is closed, and no one should talk about it."

Fakir Mirak Shah thrusts a cup of *qahwa,* or Kashmiri tea, at me, along with handfuls of almonds, sweetmeats, and roasted grams—first blessing them. I am not able to take more than a swallow of the Kashmiri tea, for it is as sweet and heavy as molasses. Descending Fakir Mirak Shah's stairway, crowded with expectant children in the faith patiently waiting to see him, I think of "Ash Wednesday," and of another stairway, and of other "children at the gate who will not go away and cannot pray."

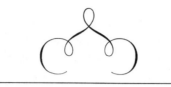

May Peace Be on Them

"EDWARD GIBBON ONCE WROTE THAT IF THE Moslem warriors had not been defeated at Tours in 732 A.D., the Koran instead of the Bible would be taught at Oxford and Cambridge," the New York *Times* noted in 1964 in an editorial on the troubles over Mohammed's hair. The editorial went on to say:

At that point in history, the Moslems were embarked on holy war. They were not the first or last to do so: other religions before and after Mohammedanism have gone to war against "infidels." Today we do not think of the doctrine of Jihad in terms of the sword; more peaceful forms of religious persuasion have come into practice. Religious war, in common with war for other causes, is now considered obsolete.

There are echoes of the past, and portents for the present, in the demonstrations reported from Srinagar. . . .

Of course, the Kashmir question itself, and the rivalry between India and Pakistan, looms in the background of the religious demonstrations.

By 1965, India and Pakistan were fighting an actual, if perhaps obsolete, war, not only in Kashmir but in the Punjab—a war that threatened to spread throughout the subcontinent. And yet Kashmir had enjoyed a long tradition—maintained even during the worst days of the demonstrations over the hair—of exemplary religious tolerance. In 1895, Sir Walter Lawrence, in his famous work "The Valley of Kashmir," wrote of this tolerance:

Kashmiri Sunnis are only Musalmans in name. In their hearts they are Hindus, and the religion of Islam is too abstract to satisfy their superstitious cravings, and they turn from the mean priest and the mean mosque to the pretty shrines of carved wood and roof bright with iris flowers where the saints of past time lie buried. They like to gaze on the saint's old clothes and turban, and to examine the cave in which he spent his ascetic life. In connection with the suggestion that the Kashmiris are at heart Hindus, it may be mentioned that certain places are held in reverence by Hindus and Musalmans alike. As an instance, at Fattehpura in the Vernag Ilaka, and at Waripura in the Magam Ilaka, I have seen the imprint of a foot in a stone worshipped by the Musalmans as Kadam-i-Rasul (the Prophet's footprint), and by the Hindus as Vishna pad (Vishnu's foot). . . . It was only natural that the Musalmans, when they were converted to Islam, should cling with tenderness to the old religious places, and should adopt sacred spots already familiar to the countryside. . . . Certain ideas are common to the Hindus and Musalmans of Kashmir, but I attribute much of the delightful tolerance which exists between the followers of the two religions chiefly to the fact that the Kashmiri Musalmans never really gave up the old Hindu religion of the country. There are two reasons for this tolerance which should be mentioned. In the first place, the strict prohibition of kine-killing removes one of the principal causes of ill feeling, and, in the second place, the strong rule under which the people have lived for generations would not brook any quarrelling between Hindus and Musalmans. A government which maintained State Mullahs to celebrate marriages and farmed out the right of celebration was not likely to allow any signs of intolerance or fanaticism, and a revivalist in the old days would have met with short shrift.

Today, however, in divided Kashmir, most of the "delightful tolerance" has gone. Through the years of religious and political turmoil, many people, here and elsewhere, have believed that a solution to the problem of Kashmir would take India and Pakistan a long way toward peace. Proposed solutions include administrative reform, cession of Kashmir to Pakistan, independence for Kashmir, maintenance of the status quo, dilution of the Muslim majority by resettling Hindu refugees in the Valley, and accommodation with Sheikh Abdullah. As I make my way around Kashmir, I keep hearing more about each of these proposals, and I set them down here in turn.

Administrative reform: Karan Singh would have the Indian government integrate the predominantly Hindu Jammu with the adjacent territory of Himachal Pradesh (a weak sister in the Indian Union) and make the predominantly Muslim Valley a separate Indian state. Karan Singh explains that this is only an interim solution (he says he does not know what the ultimate solution should be), but he argues that it would at least put an end to the present unwieldy state administration, which, to please both Hindus and Muslims, is ruled in the winter from Jammu and in the summer from Srinagar, though Kashmir lacks even the convenience of an all-weather road between the two capitals. The proposal has come under attack from a great many Indians. "If Karan Singh's plan were to go into effect," one critic tells me, "it would mean that the population of the new state of Kashmir Valley would be over ninety per cent Muslim. Such a communal solution would be the thin edge of the wedge that would eventually sunder the Valley from India. As for administrative problems, the road connecting the winter and summer capitals should soon be functional all year round."

Cession to Pakistan: One Kashmiri Muslim who would have the Valley join Pakistan says, "The argument is made that there would be political and religious chaos in India if Kashmir were allowed to join Pakistan, or even if it were given independence. It is said that Hindus would retaliate against Muslims in India and that parts of India would fight to secede. Maybe so, but why should we Kashmiris care what happens to India? Why should we care about chaos in India? We have chaos here now. By geography and by religion, we are connected with the Islamic people who inhabit all the area from Kashmir to Morocco. One day, these Islamic people as a nation are going to rule the world."

Independence for Kashmir: A Kashmiri Muslim in favor of this course explains, "We Kashmiri Muslims are very different from both Indians and Pakistanis. The Muslims who originally came to Kashmir came from Central Asia through Ladakh. Our culture today still bears distinct marks of Central Asian influence. The domes and arches in our architecture are like those to be found in Tashkent and Samarkand. Kashmiri Muslims have more in common with the Buddhists of Ladakh and Tibet than they have with the Muslims of India or Pakistan. Buddhists put a great deal of emphasis on relics. They revere Buddha's teeth, his nails, his hair. We worship the relics of our Prophet (may peace be on him). They say since the second Indo-Pakistan war that no Indian government could give us independence and remain in power, and also that even if we somehow got our independence we would not be independent for long—we would vote to join with Pakistan. This may be true, but the Indian government might be able to test us by giving us independence in stages and then we would grow so used to being independent that we wouldn't take any vote to join Pakistan."

Maintenance of the status quo: Arguing this view, a central-government

officer on loan to the Sadiq government says, "The status quo, the division
of Kashmir at the present cease-fire line, will be accepted in time, as division has been accepted in Korea and Germany. In fact, there is a question
in my mind whether Pakistan really wants a change in the status quo. Already, East Pakistan, which is separated from West Pakistan and Kashmir
by about a thousand miles of Indian territory, resents the wealth and power
of West Pakistan, and some people believe that East Pakistan would rather
be with India. Annexation of Kashmir to Pakistan could have the effect of
pushing East Pakistan into India's arms. You might well ask, then, why
Pakistan has kept the Kashmir question alive all these years. Because Pakistan hoped to break up the Indian Union by fanning the fires of commu-
nalism. On our side, we made a mistake in continuing here the anachro-
nistic British policy of gold and guns for all border areas; India poured
money into Kashmir and then sent in the Army, which helped keep bad
state governments in power. Even if we grant that there is mass discontent
in Kashmir today, it has always been there, and we still have time to deal
with certain basic grievances. In any event, what alternative do we have to
the status quo? If we ever let go of Kashmir, we might as well give all of
Ladakh to the Chinese. The best access to Ladakh is through the Valley,
and though India could, at great expense, build a road to Ladakh that
would not go through the Valley, Ladakh could never be militarily secure
without Kashmir. You might say, 'Then give up Ladakh, too.' But a nation doesn't go about giving up territory just like that. In any case, the
majority of the Ladakhis want to stay with India, and they count on us.
Are they just to be sacrificed?"

Dilution of the Muslim majority: A proponent of this policy says,
"Nehru always had moral qualms about Kashmir, and in spite of all his
talk about Kashmir's being part of India, he kept Kashmir cordoned off.
The only Hindus whom Kashmiris ever got to know were government
officers and soldiers. He should have resettled the Hindu and Sikh refugees from Pakistan here; they would have solved the problem once and for
all. Then you could have held ten plebiscites in Kashmir and the state
would have voted for India every time. But Nehru was a victim of his
scruples. He sat on the problem, and, being a great man, he *could* sit on a
problem. There is still time for us to outnumber the Muslims."

Accommodation with Sheikh Abdullah: One of the small minority of
Indians who have all along considered the Indian position in Kashmir
immoral and indefensible says, "Since the second Indo-Pakistan war, the
idea of giving Kashmir independence has been out of the question. The
only solution possible now is somehow to win over Sheikh Abdullah. We

should tell him, 'Look, independence for Kashmir is now out. If you don't reach some sort of understanding with us, you're going to die in prison, forgotten. We will give you and your people anything short of complete independence. You may, like Sikkim, have the status of an associated state, with authority over everything except your external affairs, defense, and communications. Eventually, a time may come when the government of India will let you control even your own external affairs, defense, and communications. Of course, it may be too late now for any such understanding between India and Kashmir, and you, in advocating it, may be destroyed as the leader of your people, but the alternative may be to have your people destroyed in another war between India and Pakistan.' If Sheikh Abdullah were thus asked to choose between gambling on his own destruction and gambling on the destruction of his people, he might well choose to risk himself—though a friend of mine at the Home Affairs Ministry says that if *he* were Sheikh Abdullah, he would not take any such risk, since, after all, Abdullah has suffered years of imprisonment at the hands of India. My friend also contends that if Sheikh Abdullah did agree to coöperate with India, he would simply lose face with his people and would be out of power before the ink was dry on any agreement to that effect. Maybe my friend at the Home Affairs Ministry is right. Maybe time has run out for India. Maybe Kashmir will always be here to prevent any hope for peace between India and Pakistan. Maybe India and Pakistan will have to continue spending money for defense and preparing for war, and, whether there is eventual war or not, maybe the chance to bring either India or Pakistan out of poverty will be forfeited. Maybe Kashmir will take India and Pakistan down with it in a war."

An outsider's view: A foreigner says, "Perhaps ultimately there is no solution for Kashmir other than to choose the least of many evils—U.N.-guaranteed independence—even if that does mean a risk of eventual integration with Pakistan."

The Himalayas:

Toward the Forest of Arden

and the Dead Land

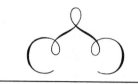

Chini Hindi Bye-Bye

TODAY, I DECIDE TO JOURNEY TO SOME of the isolated principalities and regions in the Himalayas along the Sino-Indian border, but I soon learn that reaching them is not easy. To go as a civilian to some of them, one must, among other things, receive clearance from several Ministries and give assurances that the identities of all officers, civilian and military, and the exact positions of any military posts there will not be revealed. I complete the tortuous formalities and get ready to go.

The Himalayas are the highest mountains in the world. Formed in the same geological period as the Caucasus Mountains and the Alps, they extend in a broad curve for fifteen hundred miles from southeast to northwest, bordering the Indian subcontinent, lying between the arms of the Indus and Brahmaputra Rivers, and climbing from the northern Indian plain in three intricate parallel chains—the Outer Himalayas, the Lesser Himalayas, and the Greater Himalayas—which become successively higher, until the mountains buttress the southern face of the Tibetan plateau. The Outer Himalayas are no more than three or four thousand feet high, but the peaks of the Greater Himalayas reach nearly thirty thousand feet. Because of monsoon winds from the Indian Ocean, parts of the Outer and Lesser Himalayas are drenched in as much as a hundred and twenty inches of rain a year, and because of cold winds from Central Asia parts of the Greater Himalayas are frozen in perpetual snow. (The word *"hima-laya"* is Sanskrit for "abode of snow.") In the Himalayas, glaciers descend as low as eleven thousand feet, and earthquakes and avalanches are fre-

quent. Most of the major Indian rivers—the Jhelum, the Chenab, the Ravi,
the Sutlej, the Beas, the Yamuna, the Ganga, the Sarda, the Gogra, the
Gandak, the Kosi, the Tista, and the Subansiri, as well as the Indus and
the Brahmaputra—have their sources in the Himalayas, where, together
with smaller rivers, they irrigate valleys inhabited mostly by tribal people
who, shut away from the outside world, have preserved their ancient customs and traditions. For the Hindus, who have always worshipped rivers
and mountains, the Himalayas are more than mountains; they figure in
the Hindu sacred writings not only as the source of the Ganga but also
as the home of the old gods. Most Westerners who have travelled to the
Himalayas have fallen under their spell. W. Crooke, an Englishman who
lived in India in the nineteenth century, described with rapture the dramatic spectacle of the Himalayas seen from different places and at different times and seasons, and viewed in the light of Hindu religious my-
thology:

We have a scene which only a poet or painter could depict—a chaotic
mass of mountains, thickly wooded hillsides seamed with deep ravines, dark
blue ranges piled one beyond another; and, as a background to the landscape,
the immense snowy peaks, never trodden by the foot of man; the evening
falls and they fade slowly into the darkening sky, peopled by innumerable
stars. . . . As the mists dissolve from the lowlands, we have an unrivalled
panorama of wood and silver streams encircled by rocky or forest-covered
hills, now glowing with the amber tints that accompany the fall of the leaf,
now at night lit by the fierce glare of a jungle fire, and here and there in the
distance the emerald green of rice or wheatfields. Grander still is the first
burst of the monsoon, when the water-laden clouds from the ocean impinge
on the mountain barrier and pour a deluge over the lower hills, setting every
rivulet in flood, and sometimes bearing down the wooded hillsides in a chaos
of ruin. By and by the damp billows of fog roll up from the valley and shroud
the landscape in an impenetrable pall of vapour.

All this, to the Hindu of the Plain, is the land of myth and mystery, associated with the most ancient and sacred traditions of his race. Here live his
deities, each in a paradise of his own, on the summits of the trackless peaks.
Here the Pandavas [a legendary family of heroes and demigods] sought a
way to heaven amidst the eternal snows, and in dark caves and secluded
hermitages the sages of the old world puzzled out the secrets of life and
time. In sequestered valleys, deep amid the bosom of the hills, were shrines,
like Kedarnath and Badarinath, which were far beyond the range of the
Pathan and Mughal who raided and ravished in the Plain below. . . . Every
rock and spring and stream is the home of some legend told by the forefathers of the people.

The Himalayas have always served India as a natural barrier against invasion from the north. The kingdoms of Nepal and Bhutan and the Protectorate of Sikkim, lying within these mountains, have, with Tibet, the "forbidden land" of fable, provided an additional shield. The conquerors of India—Aryans, Macedonians, Moguls, Persians—came not through the Himalayas but through a corridor in the northwest leading from Central Asia, and after the partition of India the defense of this corridor became the concern of Pakistan.

The dominion over Tibet, at first military and then political, established by the People's Republic of China within several years of its founding, in 1949, made parts of the Himalayas a common frontier between India and China, and through the fifties and the early sixties the two powers were engaged in a continuing quarrel over territories along the Sino-Indian border: over the North East Frontier Agency, or NEFA, in the Assam Himalayas; over Ladakh, in the Punjab Himalayas; and over the so-called Middle Sector, in the Kumaun Himalayas. Topographically, the curve of the Himalayas is divided into four sections—from east to west, the Assam Himalayas, the Nepal Himalayas, the Kumaun Himalayas, and the Punjab Himalayas. NEFA is the northeast frontier of India, and Ladakh, which is the easternmost district of the state of Jammu and Kashmir, constitutes part of the northwest frontier. Both China and India tried to establish their claims to these two territories by appealing to place names, to old maps, to old treaties, and, more generally, to religious and racial affinities. Various arguments were marshalled in official letters and diplomatic notes and in extensive reports, some of which covered the history of Sino-Indo-Tibetan relations for two thousand years. The Sino-Indian discussions that began in the fifties were so vague in their early stages that it was difficult even to grasp exactly what areas were being disputed. In any event, neither side pressed its claims decisively, partly because at this time the Chinese were still busy extending their dominion over Tibet, and partly because the Indians did not as yet attach any great importance to NEFA and Ladakh, which, even during the expansionist period of the raj, were considered so primitive and remote that most of the time they were left alone, being visited only by occasional parties of explorers, climbers, or surveyors. Then, in 1954, China consolidated her political hold on Tibet and concluded with India a treaty known as the Agreement for Trade and Cultural Intercourse. The spirit of this treaty was embodied in the preamble, which set forth the so-called Panch Shila, or Five Principles, whereby the two powers agreed to refrain from interfering in each other's internal affairs, to respect each other's territory and sovereignty, to work toward each other's benefit, to forswear aggression, and to adhere to the ideal of peaceful coexistence. Soon after the treaty was signed, however, the Indian government received reports that a Chinese patrol was camped in Barahoti —a barren area two miles square and sixteen thousand feet high, for which the Chinese name was Wuje—in the Middle Sector. India dismissed this violation of the Panch Shila as of no importance and accepted a Chinese suggestion for a discussion about the Indo-Tibetan border. Prime Minister Chou En-lai thereupon began a series of visits to India to take up with Prime Minister Nehru the Chinese claims not only to Barahoti but also to a total of over fifty thousand square miles of territory in NEFA and Ladakh. Chou En-lai, as part of China's claim to NEFA, challenged the validity of the McMahon Line, the eastern Indo-Tibetan border from Bhutan to Burma; this had been designated by Sir Henry McMahon, who had led the British delegation at the 1913-14 Simla Conference—a meeting that was held to determine Indo-Tibetan and Sino-Tibetan boundaries and was attended by all three interested powers. While the discussions between Nehru and Chou En-lai were in progress, India, which had only scant forces in the disputed areas, was startled to discover that the Chinese had clandestinely built a motorable road across the Aksai Chin, a plateau in Ladakh. This road gave the Chinese a relatively convenient overland approach to Tibet from Sinkiang, *de-facto* control of twelve thousand square miles of Indian-claimed territory in Ladakh, and an excellent base for military operations in the rest of Ladakh. The Indians belatedly set up military and administrative posts of their own in Ladakh, and in 1959, around the time when the Chinese completed their absorption of Tibet, and when the Dalai Lama, the spiritual and political ruler of Tibet, sought and received asylum in India, there were serious clashes between Chinese and Indian troops. The Indian troops got the worst of it, and Nehru was roundly attacked in the Indian Parliament for allowing himself to be duped by the Chinese for five years into a one-sided observance of the Panch Shila. He wrote to Chou En-lai, "Reports have reached us that some Chinese officers in Tibet have repeatedly proclaimed that the Chinese authorities will before long take possession of Sikkim, Bhutan, Ladakh, and our North East Frontier Agency. I do not know what authority they had to make these remarks, but I would like to draw Your Excellency's attention to them, as those remarks have naturally added to the tension on the frontier." Tibetan refugees had started arriving in India and were saying that China regarded NEFA, Bhutan, Sikkim, Nepal, and Ladakh as her own, referring to them as "the five fingers of her Tibetan hand." Despite the 1959 military clashes, and many more in the next three years, Nehru remained publicly unconcerned about the Chinese claims, and so did V. K. Krishna Menon, who was India's Defense Minister from 1957 to 1962. (Menon was also India's representative at the United Nations from 1952 to 1962.) When, in the summer of 1962, the Chinese made their strongest border incursions thus far, Menon dismissed them as nothing more than a little jostling, and said that all was well on the Sino-Indian border. Nehru said that India would not on any account engage in a war with China, that nothing would be allowed to disturb the historic peace existing between India and China, that he would rather India "sank and died" than that she should become a "camp follower of a military bloc," and that if China and India ever found themselves at war Pakistan would take the opportunity to invade India. It was said that Nehru and Menon had thought from the beginning of the controversy that India's main enemy was Pakistan, and had believed that if China and India ever did find themselves at war the Soviet Union would come to India's rescue, as a reward for India's neutrality in the Cold War.

On September 8th of that same year, the Army of the People's Republic of China crossed the McMahon Line at Thag La Ridge (*"la,"* which is sometimes used as a suffix, means "pass"), and on October 20th it invaded India, moving down through the passes and over the trails that led out of Tibet. The Chinese not only attacked NEFA but also overwhelmed and captured several military outposts in Ladakh and breached the border of the Middle Sector in and around Barahoti. During the first few days of the invasion, the Chinese took possession of strategic passes at both the eastern and the western ends of NEFA, putting themselves in a position to encompass the whole of it. In Ladakh, coming, guerrilla-fashion, westward from Tibet and southward over the Karakoram ranges from the province of Sinkiang, Chinese troops took possession of the trails running along the important Indus and Shyok Rivers, and thus gained control of Chip Chap Valley, the Lake Pangong area, and the village of Demchok—which is to say, the whole of eastern Ladakh, from north to south. The capture of this territory put them within reach of Leh, the capital of Ladakh and the key to the Indian defense of eastern Kashmir. India, fearing for her survival, resisted as well as she could, and the two countries, which together represented a third of the world's population, and which since the Chinese absorption of Tibet had shared a twenty-two-hundred-mile frontier, were at war, in a confusion of irregular slopes and sheer ridges anywhere from fourteen thousand to twenty-one thousand feet high and perpetually subject to sudden landslips and avalanches.

The Indian Army, thanks to the many Gurkha, Sikh, and Jat regiments that had fought in the Second World War, had an illustrious reputation, but since Independence it had been weakened by the loss of its British officers, by the difficulty of finding and training successors to them, and by bureaucratic, political, and financial problems, and it had also become a victim of the religious, racial, regional, and linguistic schisms besetting the country at large. The Army had a total strength of four hundred and fifty thousand men, and a substantial portion of them were deployed along the West Pakistan border; if it had not been for the enmity with Pakistan, it was said, the Army might well have disintegrated by that time. India did not feel that she could safely divert her troops to the fronts opened up by the Chinese, and the beginning of the invasion found the Indian Army with just one division, of between twelve and fifteen thousand men, in Ladakh; two or three divisions in the plains of the state of Assam; only a semi-military police force in NEFA; token defenses in Sikkim; and not so much as a platoon in Bhutan, which, though it had hundreds of miles of common frontier with Tibet, had consistently refused Indian offers of military aid. As for Nepal, it had been flirting with China for some time now, and, in spite of an Indian warning that political and military penetration follows economic help, its king, Mahendra Bir Bikram Shah Deva, had arranged for a highway to be built, with the aid of Chinese money and technicians, connecting Katmandu, the capital of Nepal, and Lhasa, the capital of Tibet. Moreover, India, having spurned military alliances and possessing scarcely the rudiments of an armaments industry, could not equip such troops as she had been able to mobilize against the Chinese; the soldiers had to make do with single-shot rifles of a type used in the Boer War. And the lack of troops and weapons was just part of the difficulty. Because the fighting was going on across an area of hundreds of square miles, where posts might be as much as a week's march apart, the Army groupings of brigades and battalions were futile. Despite an absence of good, or all-weather, roads in the mountains, all those supplies which were not airlifted had to be taken up by motor convoys. Owing to the sub-zero cold and the rough terrain, all types of vehicles stalled, and airplanes taking off and landing at such high altitudes could carry only small loads. This meant that a man fighting in the mountains required upward of twenty coolies to maintain him; even troops that had become acclimated to Ladakh by long service there could carry no more than a third or a quarter of the weight that they could carry in the plains, and such troops were few. Most of the soldiers were from the parched flatlands and had never seen a snowflake, and they had been rushed to the Sino-Indian frontier in their summer clothes, sometimes without blankets. Then, when snow clothes and blankets and other provisions were air-dropped to them, the equipment was more often than not lost among the ravines and precipices, and the soldiers, already suffering the paralyzing effects of altitude sickness, were left at the mercy of frostbite.

The Chinese faced some of the same difficulties of mountain warfare, but their Army, whose total strength was estimated at two and a half million, was said to have in Tibet seven hundred airworthy planes and fourteen divisions composed of warmly clad and well-armed troops who either had originally come from mountain areas, like the province of Sinkiang, or had been acclimating themselves for years to the altitudes of Tibet, much of which lies above sixteen thousand feet. It was also said of the Chinese Army that its men had gained considerable experience of guerrilla warfare in the mountains of Korea as well as on the Tibetan plateau, and that it had in Tibet a network of phenomenal roads going over theretofore impassable terrain, along with a system of forced labor whereby the entire populations of villages were conscripted into a sort of ancillary army of coolies, who were now believed to be getting supplies to the invading Chinese troops with unflagging efficiency. Certainly the Chinese Army had at its disposal a superior armaments industry, which had been developed with the assistance of Soviet technology.

Analysts everywhere debated the motives of the Chinese. Had they been preparing for such an invasion all along, and had they used the many years of discussion as a smoke screen for their preparations? A few analysts argued that the Chinese invasion was not premeditated—that the Chinese had resorted to force only after years of pointless discussion, during which they had asked for nothing more than Indian recognition of their control of Aksai Chin, and that even now they had attacked NEFA only to barter it later for possession of Ladakh. (In any event, it was true, as the Chinese asserted, that both Ladakh and NEFA had strong racial and historical links with Tibet.) But most analysts argued that the Chinese invasion had been long in the planning, and that its purpose was multiple: to pull into China's orbit, or to annex outright, Sikkim, Bhutan, and Nepal; to replace India as the leader of the Afro-Asian world; to use this international position to purvey Communist ideology; to inflict on India a humiliating defeat; and to undermine the Indian Union by weakening India's democratic system, discrediting India's leadership, and subverting the loyalties of the tribal people who lived in India's borderlands. According to the Chinese themselves, the invasion, like all previous military provocations, had been the work of the other side. The official Chinese Communist press agency, Hsin Hua, declared:

In the last two years, first in the western and then in the eastern sector of the Chinese-Indian border, Indian troops crossed the line of actual control [presumably where Chinese or Indians had set up military posts in order to back up their claims to the disputed territory] . . . nibbled Chinese territory, set up strong points for aggression, and provoked a number of border clashes.

Relying on the advantageous military positions they had occupied, and having made full preparations, the Indian troops eventually launched massive armed attacks all along the line on the Chinese frontier guards on October 20, 1962. . . .

The Chinese Government served repeated warnings in regard to the increasingly serious Indian encroachments and provocations, and pointed out the gravity of their consequences. The Chinese frontier guards all along maintained maximum self-restraint and forbearance in order to avert any border conflict.

However, all these efforts by China proved of no avail and the Indian acts of aggression steadily increased.

Pressed beyond the limits of endurance and left with no room for retreat, the Chinese frontier guards finally had no choice but to strike back resolutely in self-defense. After the present large-scale border conflict broke out, the Chinese Government quickly took initiative measures in an effort to extinguish the flames of conflict that had been kindled.

The Chinese "initiative measures" to "extinguish the flames of conflict" took the form of proposing, on the twenty-fourth of October, terms for a cease-fire which called for new talks between Chou En-lai and Nehru, and, pending demarcation of the border through these talks, the withdrawal of Indian and Chinese troops twenty kilometres (a little over twelve miles) behind "the line of actual control" as it existed before the outbreak of the fighting. The Chinese had more than once proposed a similar withdrawal during the military clashes of previous months, but until the invasion India had insisted, as a minimum condition, that the forces of both sides withdraw to "the line of actual control" as it existed in 1959, when, the Indians contended, the Chinese had started openly extending their "line of actual control" by means of military operations. (The Chinese had, of course, been surreptitiously extending their "line of actual control" since 1954.) India now rejected the cease-fire proposals, but the Chinese, after a week of straight successes and of a rapid advance that met with little resistance, unilaterally stopped fighting. From military posts on the various fronts came reports that the Chinese were regrouping and were extending their supply roads to their newly established forward positions. The Indians used the lull to send supplies and reinforcements to

NEFA and Ladakh. For most of the year, Ladakh, because of its altitude, was accessible only by air, and airplanes could fly in and out of its valleys during only a few hours of the day. Some parts of NEFA could be reached by road, but to supply even such military posts as were situated on the best road meant that a convoy of trucks and jeeps leaving the corps headquarters of the Eastern Command, in Tezpur (a town on the north bank of the Brahmaputra River, in the plains of Assam), had to go to the foothills and then lumber up the main hill road, mostly unpaved and climbing almost vertically to Bomdila, which, at nine thousand feet, was one of the highest administrative posts in the country; from there to Se La, at fourteen thousand feet, which was India's main defense post in NEFA; and, finally, to the village of Tawang, which lay in the shadow of Bum La, a pass sixteen thousand feet high—and Bum La was already in the hands of the Chinese. This was a mountain journey of two hundred miles, which under good conditions might take three days but under bad conditions could take as long as two or three weeks. From Tawang, supplies were taken up to outlying military posts by coolies.

The reprieve from the Chinese onslaught lasted three weeks. Then the Chinese Army struck again, moving down, where the terrain permitted, in seemingly unending columns, flanked by hosts of coolies bearing ammunition. In Ladakh, the Chinese employed the tactics of the pincers movement to take many posts and villages, and to encircle and shell the airstrip of Chushul—one of just three airstrips in the whole of Ladakh. In NEFA, they employed the same tactics: at the eastern end, near the Burmese border, they captured the village of Walong and started moving south on the trails leading to Tezpur; at the western end, marching down from Bum La, they quickly captured first Tawang and then Jang, a village near the border of Bhutan, and after that they concentrated four brigades with heavy artillery on Se La. The Indian high command, considering this pass unassailable, had decided that the Army should make its main stand there, and had in readiness at Se La the 4th (Kitehawk) Division, which had proved itself in the Second World War at El Alamein and at Monte Cassino, and also in battles in Burma, and which had just been armed with modern weapons, supplied for the emergency by Britain and the United States. The battle, when it came, was fierce, but the Chinese could not be stopped. A reporter for the *Christian Science Monitor* later interviewed some of the Indians who had taken part in the Se La battle, and wrote:

A corporal gleefully related to this correspondent the following story: . . . Firing into wave after wave of Chinese—the second wave trampling the casualties of the first wave underfoot—the ammunition became exhausted.

Seeing the position was well nigh hopeless, the corporal then jumped out of his defensive position—he is a famous Indian army wrestler—and advanced unarmed toward the enemy, calling out that he was prepared to fight, man to man.

The Chinese, puzzled by this seeming madness, halted. The corporal was followed by all his remaining Indian colleagues, who also offered to fight and wrestle the enemy into submission. The Chinese Communists are automatons, unused to anything unusual, the Indian claimed. They suspected a trap. They retreated. The corporal lives to tell the tale and get his hand warmly shaken by the visitor to his Himalayan hideout.

The Chinese "retreat" described by the corporal was temporary. After encircling and trapping the 4th Division and capturing Se La, the Chinese troops took Bomdila. This put them only eighty miles from Tezpur, with the road to Tezpur lying below—undefended, for the most part. Indeed, within a day a Chinese contingent had come down into the foothills to an Indian checkpoint at the edge of the Assam plains. The entire north bank of the Brahmaputra River was in turmoil. That same day, two thousand Americans and British were evacuated from Tezpur in a period of two hours. Throughout the day, NEFA refugees and soldiers were fleeing to the plains. According to a *Newsweek* correspondent in Tezpur:

> Just a few days ago I watched a World War I army headed north for battle armed only with outmoded Lee-Enfield single-action rifles and a few antique Sten guns. . . .
>
> The morale of the front-bound troops was high despite their shoddy and deficient equipment. Then, as the news of the defeat in the north poured in, the first traces of panic appeared. They were exacerbated by the arrival of thousands of refugees from NEFA. . . .
>
> Then the ranks of the refugees were swollen by stragglers whose units had been crushed or overrun by the Chinese. U.S. and British officials began the evacuation of their nationals from missions and tea estates on the north bank of the Brahmaputra. [Assam, besides being India's main source of oil, produces tea in quantities sufficient to earn India sixty per cent of her foreign exchange.] . . . Still the bad news poured in. The Chinese had cut the Indian defense line south of Bomdila. . . . Truckloads of refugee children rolled off toward the Brahmaputra ferry. The children wept. Buddhist monks, refugees from the monastery at Tawang . . . conducted prayer services in the front yard of a bungalow.

In just thirty-two days, which included a three-week lull in the fighting, the Chinese in Ladakh and NEFA had routed three or four Indian divisions with a strategy that was as brilliant as it was weird. Elisabeth Partridge, writing from India, described part of the strategy in the *Nation:*

The Himalayan campaign was masterly in conception and audacity. . . . It was reportedly under the over-all direction of General Lin Piao, the Korean Fourth Field Army veteran. . . . [The Chinese in NEFA] regrouped by night, appearing out of the morning mist in different positions. They disguised themselves as local tribals; then, once within range, pulled submachine guns from under their long robes. Using several Indian languages, they called on the outposts to surrender, explaining that the Indians were their brothers, only the "imperialist-aided Indian government" was their enemy. They also advanced with banshee shrieks and firing wildly (ten Indians were wounded to one killed) to create the maximum confusion. Indian Army veterans have said that the Chinese, man to man, were not such formidable fighters as the Japanese, but that "they seemed to be everywhere at once, charging like screaming madmen."

The military advances in NEFA put the Chinese in a position to cut off the plains of Assam. Owing to an accident of political geography, the plains and hills of Assam were all but isolated from the rest of India by East Pakistan. A very narrow gap, called Siliguri, between the northeast tip of East Pakistan and the wall of the Himalayas was the only way to reach Assam from India. The Chinese had fairly direct access to Siliguri, thanks to a road system that came down from Lhasa, passing through Chumbi Valley (a wedge of land between Bhutan and Sikkim) and through Sikkim, and it was reported that they were massing troops at the head of Chumbi Valley—an activity suggesting that their next move was in fact to be against Siliguri. The Indians had strong forces in the Siliguri area; this was now the only place on the entire eastern frontier where Indian troops were in a position to give any sort of account of themselves. In Ladakh, the danger from the Chinese was even greater. Ladakh was a point of contention in the general quarrel between Pakistan and India over Kashmir; the cease-fire line of the first Indo-Pakistan war in Kashmir, in 1947–48, had given Pakistan the subdistrict of Skardu, or Baltistan, in northern Ladakh, which was traditionally Muslim, and had left India the two other subdistricts, Leh and Kargil, in southern Ladakh, which were traditionally Buddhist. (The second Indo-Pakistan war in Kashmir did not notably affect either country's position in Ladakh.) The situation was complicated further by the fact that Pakistan and China did not agree on *their* common border in Ladakh any more than India and China did on theirs. For some time before China's invasion of India, however, Pakistan had been holding secret talks with China. In India, some people thought that Pakistan was merely trying to reach a border settlement with China and was using China to blackmail the United States into supplying more arms, but most people believed that, having failed to get the Vale of Kashmir either by war or through the help of the Western powers, she had turned to China, and had planned an invasion of Kashmir to coincide with the Chinese invasion. The subscribers to the conspiracy theory could draw upon abundant volatile comment by journalists and politicians in Pakistan. This comment included, among other things, demands that Pakistan seize the opportunity afforded by India's reverses at the hands of the Chinese to conquer the Vale of Kashmir; that Pakistan forthwith pull out of the Southeast Asia Treaty Organization and the Central Treaty Organization, the two Western military alliances to which she belonged; and that Pakistan condemn the West for its failure to help her gain the Vale of Kashmir peacefully in the past, and for rushing military aid to India now to defend spurious Indian claims to NEFA and Ladakh, and, as a consequence, abetting "Hindu imperialism." In India, it was realized that an attack from Pakistan just then would be disastrous, but at the same time it was felt that India was in no position to make any concessions to Pakistan; aside from the fact that to lose the Vale of Kashmir would render Ladakh indefensible, what choice could there be between losing an area that Nehru had often characterized, with only a little exaggeration, as a desert "where not a blade of grass grows" and losing what was renowned throughout the world as a rich, romantic paradise? India therefore tried to present the Chinese invasion as a threat to Pakistan as well. Nehru said, "There are all kinds of bizarre rumors [about Pakistan]. They have been promised large chunks of India. . . . But it surely is obvious that any threat from outside, as this is, to us, is bound to be a threat to them." India, like the Western powers, looked to Ayub Khan to restrain the warmongers among his countrymen, as he had done in the past, but, in the words of a correspondent for the London *Observer* writing from Lahore:

> President Ayub Khan of Pakistan is not prepared to take the entire responsibility for shaping his country's attitude and policy toward the undeclared war between China and India. . . .
>
> In the absence of representative institutions, the Press in Pakistan has assumed a crucial and powerful role. It was made crystal clear . . . that the Press had no sympathy for India's troubles with China and that it regarded the Western demand on Pakistan to assure a peaceful posture as an "impertinence." . . .
>
> It was always understood that the West did not wish to go against India. But the headlong manner in which the Anglo-Americans have taken up Delhi's cause has created the worst possible impression about their motives. . . .

The Western leaders have held out no hope of a Kashmir solution precisely at a time when they are believed to have the greatest influence with Delhi. This is regarded as pure and simple betrayal.

In spite of the "betrayal," the Western powers were able to get Ayub Khan and Nehru to agree to hold talks about Kashmir, thereby averting any immediate threat of a Pakistani invasion of India.

In the meantime, India prepared for a long war with China. Nehru asserted, "We are not going to tolerate this kind of invasion of India by any foreign country. This is the first war of independent India to maintain her independence, and India is not going to lose this war, however long it lasts and whatever harm it may do us." In the Indian capital, the municipal authorities awarded contracts for the digging of trenches; householders taped up their windowpanes against air raids, much as they had done in the Second World War; and families laid in supplies of food and water. All the major cities held rallies to raise a volunteer force of a million men to fight the Chinese; instead of the old slogan *"Chini Hindi, Bhai Bhai,"* meaning "Chinese Indian, Brother Brother," the meetings sent up the cry *"Chini Hindi* Bye-Bye." Throughout the country, known Communists and Chinese residents were interned. In Assam and West Bengal, seventeen hundred Chinese residents were jailed, in accordance with the Defense of India Rules, and suspected Communists and aliens were assaulted. (Japanese, Vietnamese, and Koreans wore identifying badges stating "We're Your Friends, Not Your Chinese Enemies.") A National Defense Fund was started, for which the poorest village tried to raise a rupee and to which rich citizens contributed their jewels and other valuables. (The Chief Minister of one state was so successful at collecting for the Defense Fund that he was able to make a presentation to Nehru of twice Nehru's weight in gold.) In spite of the upsurge of patriotism, however, Nehru's government was blamed for the entire military and political debacle, some analysts saying that the generals had given battle to the Chinese indiscriminately when they should have retreated in good order and entrenched themselves in positions more favorable to defense. Nehru changed his corps commanders and his chiefs of staff, and tried to explain why the Indian Army did not have even such essentials as automatic weapons. "Well, there are many reasons," he told a foreign television interviewer. "Our whole thinking was directed to peaceful progress—not that we ignored the military side, but we didn't prepare for war, you might say—and we thought that even from the military point of view the development of our industrial base was important, although it doesn't bring results immediately; from the military point, ultimately, it strengthens the military position. So we laid stress on that. Well, before we could properly get the results from that this attack came. . . . We were mistaken in thinking that such an attack in modern conditions is unlikely. A regular— I would say it's not a frontier conflict—it is a regular, massive attack on India. And certainly we thought that this kind of thing was unlikely. . . . As a matter of fact, even after they had started hitting us, or, rather, just before, we still—maybe we're foolish—we did not expect them to hit us in a massive way." Some military experts were unconvinced by Nehru's statement that the emphasis on economic development was largely responsible for India's rout; they insisted that thirty thousand troops, or just one-fifteenth of India's standing army, could have held the line in NEFA if they had been armed with automatic weapons and acclimated to the mountains. Menon was the first target of the critics. Frank Moraes wrote in an editorial in the *Indian Express*, "Mr. Menon is now left with no alibi for inaction. He is . . . left naked to his friends and enemies. The future of peace, socialism, and democracy, he now asserts, depends upon good will between the Chinese and ourselves. But it is no longer a question of peace, socialism, and democracy. It is a question of India's survival." Nehru was forced to demote Menon to a minor portfolio and then to drop him from the Cabinet altogether, thereby, in the opinion of some, saving his government. (Miss Partridge wrote in the *Nation*, "Most observers here believe that a military coup was averted only because Mr. Nehru gave way to popular demand; he sacked Krishna Menon and put India on a war footing. Even now, if Mr. Nehru shows any weakness, there could still be a military takeover." Pakistan and Burma, like a number of underdeveloped countries on other continents, had already succumbed to military control.) But when Nehru's critics pressed him to make a formal declaration of war, and also to take India's case to the United Nations, he refused to do either, saying that he did not wish to activate any Sino-Soviet alliance. (A formal declaration could have put into effect the provisions of the Sino-Soviet mutual-defense pact of 1950.) And when his critics pressed him to recognize the Dalai Lama as head of the government-in-exile of Tibet and to pledge military assistance for the return of the Dalai Lama to Tibet one day, Nehru again refused, saying that India was not now, and never had been, in any position to fight in Tibet; he argued that in Tibet all the logistics favored China, so that even if India diverted most of her resources to the Tibetan cause she could not hope to assist Tibet. Still, there was no hiding the fact that many of the views and policies long cherished by Nehru, who was now seventy-three and ill much of the time, were in ruins, including his dream of India's economic betterment. The Chinese had attacked at a moment when most of the economic indicators in India were pointing downward. For instance, in 1959–60, the last year of India's Second Five-Year Plan, her national income had increased by 7.1 per cent, her industrial output by 10.5 per cent, and her agricultural production by 8.1 per cent, but in 1961–62, the first year of her Third Five-Year Plan— partly because of power, fuel, and transport shortages created by the industrial expansion of the previous years—her national income had increased by only 2.2 per cent, her industrial output by only 4.3 per cent, and her agricultural production by only 1.6 per cent. To quote Miss Partridge's article again:

> Thus what China invaded, in fact, was India's Five-Year Plan—at a critical moment of economic imbalance. . . . As a result of the military reverses, India's planners are now suggesting a defense budget amounting to the astronomical total of sixteen billion dollars in order to create a 2.5 million-man military force to equal China's (the largest in the world).

On November 21st, when the attack was just four weeks old and the Chinese stood almost on the plains of Assam, China again unilaterally declared a cease-fire. The organ of the Central Committee of the Chinese Communist Party, *Jen Min Jih Pao,* asserted, "The growth of the Sino-Indian border dispute into a massive military conflict is the last thing the Chinese Government and people want. . . . We always hope to live in friendship with our neighbor India and are absolutely unwilling to see the two countries crossing swords. . . . To resolve the dispute amicably, China is ready to exercise forbearance and make concessions." The cease-fire was as sudden and surprising as the war's original onset, and the New York *Times* reflected the mystification of analysts everywhere when it commented, "The decision of the Chinese Communists to call a halt to their border war with India is startling and puzzling in the extreme. . . . It is hard to believe that anything could have stopped them from moving down to the plains of Assam if they had pressed forward. Until some satisfactory explanation is forthcoming, there can only be wild speculation on the reasons for Peking's decision." It was felt that the least wild speculation came from military men, some of whom had thought all along that the Chinese equipment and tactics, so successful in the mountains, could not be adapted to the plains. In any case, they pointed out, the Himalayan winter was fast approaching. The *Christian Science Monitor* noted, "By the time the Himalayan winter freezes the fronts, Chinese Communist aggression may well have 'paid off' by ousting India from its natural defense lines along mountain ranges and incorporating them instead in a

new great wall of China. India would then be faced in the spring with a
choice between starting an all-out campaign to oust the Chinese or accepting the new frontiers." But once again the Chinese surprised everyone.
They voluntarily started pulling back. Their forces in NEFA abandoned
Bomdila on December 13th, Walong on December 20th, and Tawang
just after the New Year, and by the middle of January they were north of
the McMahon Line. However, military men, and many members of
Nehru's government as well, continued to believe that the halt in fighting
was temporary—that sooner or later, perhaps one spring, the Chinese
would return.

But the Chinese, who, in a sense, had already won the political war, did
not return—not even when the Indians reoccupied some of their old positions in NEFA and Ladakh. India, for her part, put aside any such impractical idea as raising a standing army of two and a half million, but to this
day she has continued to fear another attack, and to spend—with mixed
results—vast sums on defense (in 1966 and 1967 she spent somewhere between a billion three hundred million dollars and a billion and a half, or
three and a half per cent of her gross national product) and on the development of Ladakh, Nepal, Sikkim, Bhutan, NEFA, and Nagaland, a small
Indian tribal state in the Assam Himalayas. On the one hand, India's
northern frontier remains vulnerable at many points: in Assam, NEFA, and
Nagaland some of the tribes seem to be showing secessionist tendencies,
and a few, with the active assistance of Pakistan and China, have actually
taken up arms against India; in Bhutan there are only twenty thousand
troops, most of them with rudimentary training, and although the mountains and the absence of roads make it unlikely that the Chinese will pour
into the kingdom in great numbers, Bhutan remains particularly vulnerable; in Nepal the government's position of neutrality, combined with a
ruthless suppression of political opposition, has led some people to fear
that Nepal may be the first buffer state to fall to the Chinese. On the other
hand, that northern frontier has been built up at many points: in addition
to the work of economic development, there are, according to one estimate,
nearly thirty thousand troops in NEFA, Sikkim, and Ladakh, with large
back-up forces stationed in the plains of Assam and of the Punjab (in fact,
twenty divisions, or half of the total standing army, which now numbers
seven hundred and fifty thousand men, are committed in one way or another to the Chinese front); to supply the frontier troops, and also to open
up the tribal areas, five thousand miles of roads have been blasted out in
the Himalayas, and these make a considerable difference to the troops
manning concrete blockhouses and sandbagged trenches on the frontier,

though it is true that landslips and avalanches can still cut them off for weeks at a time. Because of China's recent nuclear tests, the situation on the border is as tense as ever. Harrison Salisbury, travelling in Asia for the New York *Times,* recently began a story out of India, "The Indian spoke with deliberate precision: 'For us in Asia, there have been two epochal events in this century. The first was Japan's defeat of Russia in 1905. The second was China's atom bomb,'" and ended it by pointing out that without a strong India there could be neither Asian security nor Asian stability, and that it was in the interests of many powers, including the Soviet Union, to wish India well in the Himalayas.

NEFA

THE NORTH EAST FRONTIER AGENCY, which forms a horseshoe north of the Brahmaputra Valley of Assam and south of Tibet, touching Burma on the east and Bhutan on the west, is a tract of bare, craggy hills, huge tropical and alpine forests, steep, rugged valleys, and great, cascading rivers. The region is so wild that even today much of it can be traversed only on foot, and some people have spent a year journeying from one end of it to the other. It has an area of 31,438 square miles and a population of some four hundred thousand. The land is inhabited by the Indo-Mongoloid tribes of Monpas, Sherdukpens, Mijis, Akas, Khowas, Sulungs, Apatanis, Daflas, Adis, Mishmis, Khamptis, Singphos, Wanchos, Noctes, Tangsas; by the sub-tribes of Thongs, Ghaos, Nyubbus, Nyullus, Bogums, Bomis, Khambas, Membas, Tagins, Idus, Mijus, Dagarus, Lungchangs, Moklongs, Yuglis, Lungris, Havis, Moshangs, Rundras, Tikhaks, Ponthais, and Longphis; and by the sub-sub-tribes of Minyongs, Kharkos, Shimongs, Bomdo-Janbos, Panggis, Palibos, Karkangs, Boris, Mayuns, Thangams, Padams, Milangs, Dalbings, Gallongs, Paktus, Riba-Basars, Tai-Padias, Nalobags, Tatar-Tenis, Bokars, Ramos, Mihis, Milhus, Miemras, Midris, Mihuis, Mitanongs, Matuns, and Mathuns. The people of these tribes, sub-tribes, and sub-sub-tribes may be distinguished, anthropologically, by their religions (ranging from animism to Buddhism), by the bases of their economies (farming, husbandry, slavery, barter, handicrafts), by their systems of government (ranging from absolute rule by village or clan headmen to democratic management by village councils), by their types of social organization (some have complicated caste and class structures, and others do not), by their family organization (extended family or clan systems, which may be, in various degrees, patriarchal, patrilineal, or patrilocal), by their marriage customs (there are polyandry, polygamy, and many other forms of conjugal relationships, and there may be use of marriage brokers and bride money), by their physical appearance (skins olive, yellow, or brown; stature short or tall; faces narrow or round), and by their style of dress and physical adornment (skirts, blouses, blankets, body cloths, leaves; armbands, beads, earplugs, and cloth, bamboo, or yak-hair headdresses; hair knotted, plaited, matted, or shaved, in a variety of prescribed ways; bodies painted or tattooed). Some tribes (and sub-tribes and sub-sub-tribes) continue to be known for their practices of raiding and feuding, kidnapping and ransoming, and hunting animal and human heads—though of late the headhunters have, for the most part, been satisfied to collect wooden heads.

Before and during the raj, these hills were scarcely administered, or even explored. In 1873, the British formally quarantined the hills by introducing what were called the Inner Line Regulations, which forbade all traffic and intercourse between the tribal people and other Indians, and from then on, except when a punitive expedition was mounted to control any tribal disturbance that threatened to spread to the plains, the hills were visited only by a few officers and travellers. After Independence, India began a serious attempt to develop the hills. In 1950, the President became constitutionally responsible for the administration of the area, which was now called the North East Frontier Agency and was divided into five districts—Kameng, Subansiri, Siang, Lohit, and Tirap. The actual work of development and administration was entrusted to the Ministry of External Affairs and, because of the border problem with China, was conducted—by the Governor of Assam and, in the field, by a handful of deputy commissioners with small staffs of civilian officers—on a "top-secret" basis. The policy of the Inner Line was continued, now on the ground that while the government was helping the people of NEFA to relinquish their barbarous customs and achieve a better standard of living it wished them to be protected from an invasion of such elements of the plains as usurers, profiteers, land speculators, and land-hungry peasants. The government declared that once the tribal people had reached a sufficiently high level of development the Inner Line would be abolished and NEFA would be made a part of Assam. Following the Chinese attack, the government speeded up the building of schools, hospitals, roads, and garrisons.

Today, after a flight from Calcutta to Gauhati, a town in the plains of

Assam, and a sixty-four-mile automobile ride up a treacherous hill road, I have come to Shillong, which, as the capital of Assam, is the administrative center for NEFA, though separated from it by the valley of the Brahmaputra. Shillong, which is set on a hilltop, is one of the hill stations that the British created as a refuge for their officers, who wanted to escape the heat and dust of the plains in summer and sought temporary refuge from "the real India." Unlike most other hill stations, which are small resorts with bridle paths and cottages, Shillong is a year-round seat of government, with streets, cars, and large bungalows. One of the government officers who live here tells me, "Once you get used to Shillong, you never even want to go near the plains. They're full of mosquitoes and things like that. Even if you go down, you don't spend the night there. You always rush back to Shillong as fast as you can."

I am here for a briefing on NEFA, so I talk with the Chief Minister and the Governor of Assam, and also attend a session of the Legislative Assembly, in the hope that it will throw some light on the tribal question. (It is my first brush with an Indian state legislative assembly, and not an altogether encouraging one. To follow the proceedings here, one has to know Assamese, Bengali, Hindi, and English. This particular morning, the quadrilingual debate appears to be about a civil servant who has tendered his resignation because he was not addressed with the respect due him. The Minister for Industrial Affairs is now lecturing the members of the Legislative Assembly on the uses of *"tum"* and *"aap"*—Hindi for the familiar "thou" and the polite "you": "The whole difficulty arose out of the word *'tum.'* You will appreciate that this word is used in various ways. It would have been better to use the word *'aap.'* As you know, sir, in administration many people use *'tum.'* I am not justifying the use of the word *'tum,'* but I am just interpreting that for the use of this word he should not have resigned, and if he thought that the word *'tum'* was derogatory, his duty should have been to report to the managing director, but instead of that he resigned." And so on.) I talk with a number of the officers concerned with NEFA. One of them, who is in charge of mapping out my program, says, "You could spend a lifetime going around NEFA, but if you want to see something of the tribal life and what we are doing in the way of tribal development, I would recommend your going to the Siang district. Economically, it's a representative tribal area, and, as far as the fun the tribes are famous for goes, it's second to none. If you like, you can go to the Kameng district, too. The scene of most of the fighting with the Chinese was the road in Kameng that goes up to Tawang. On the road, you can spend some time talking with engineers and Army officers

and civil officers. They all have their camps along the way. You'll get a
pretty good idea of what we're doing in the way of defenses there. You
may want to go on to Nagaland, where we've already had a dress rehearsal for what may happen in NEFA."

He hands me a formidable-looking document headed:

ITINERARY FOR THE VISIT OF
SHRI VED MEHTA TO NEFA

and signed

M D TYAGI
Deputy Secretary (Pol.)
NEFA Administration
U/O No. PLA. 1180–NDA . . . 1966

He also hands me a stapled sheaf of papers headed "NEFA: The Land
and the People." The paragraphs on Siang contain, along with straight
information (area, 8,196 square miles; population, 84,000), such random
remarks as:

> One of the most fascinating and exciting parts of NEFA. . . . It is a coun-
> try of song and dance, of hard, eager work, of fine spinning and weaving.
> . . . The northern part is full of high mountains and wild valleys with diffi-
> cult communications. The mountains in the south running northeast to south-
> west stand as a solid wall shutting out the Brahmaputra Valley in the plains
> of Assam.

Today, I have reached Siang, most of which is jungle. By land the journey could have taken five days, but, thanks to an air sortie for supplying
rations to Along, the district headquarters, I hopped the wall of mountains
in twenty-five minutes. I have just arrived by jeep in a village called Bagra,
inhabited by the Gallong tribe. It lies sixteen miles south of Along, and it
is a member of a group of Gallong villages called Pusi Bango, which is one
of nine groups of villages that make up Siang. It is dusk, and I am standing in a terraced mountain field overlooking a river. Everyone in Pusi
Bango seems to be here, celebrating the opening of a new lower primary
school, which is the event of the year.

"Now has come Ved Mehta, a great friend from Delhi," chants a boy,
dressed in girls' clothes, who is walking slowly around inside a huge,
slowly moving circle made up of all the people on the festival grounds. At
every second step, he pauses before a man, woman, or child and brandishes, with a flourish worthy of an ancient warrior, a long, blunt sword,

shaking it so that iron discs set in the pommel clash like prayer tongs. "Now has come Ved Mehta, a great friend from Delhi," the boy repeats.

"Friend from Delhi," chirps the circle, in chorus.

"He's come from America, on the other side of the stars. Our friend from Delhi."

"Friend from Delhi."

"He's come to see the life on this side of the stars. Friend from Delhi."

"Friend from Delhi."

"His mother is Hindu, his father is Hindu, but he lives on the other side of the stars. Friend from Delhi."

"Friend from Delhi."

The chant of welcome, which goes on like a minor saga, is rather baffling until I remember how widespread the custom of governmental briefing is in India. One of the serenaders, who is singing in a charmingly haphazard way, takes me in a bear hug, balancing a bamboo beaker full of drink on my shoulder. When the greeting is done, my private serenader draws me to a nearby bonfire, which has been blazing away throughout the ceremony. A man of medium height, a little on the heavy side, he is dressed in an old homespun tie, an old, patched woollen coat, old corduroy trousers, and very old suède boots. He has an Indian face, and looks to be in his late thirties. He is the Deputy Commissioner of Along, which is to say that he is virtually the king of Siang.

"Sorry I couldn't meet your plane," he says. "It's not often that a plane comes to Along. But I had to be here early to open the celebrations for the lower primary school. I hope your jeep ride to Bagra wasn't too rough."

A small girl who has the clear complexion of a hill girl and whom the Deputy Commissioner identifies for me as Yapi Loya hands me a bamboo beaker, a duplicate of the D.C.'s. It contains *apong,* or rice beer, which smells like incense and tastes a bit like molasses. *"Apong* is very good for your health," the D.C. says. "I have a touch of diabetes, and the doctors have forbidden me to drink. I don't keep anything in my house. But I'm always open to persuasion. When in Bagra, do as the Gallongs do." Around the bonfire there are members of the D.C.'s staff—assistant commissioners, and other regional and research officers—all of them young Indians. Though the weather is only a little chilly, they can't seem to get close enough to the fire. Each of them is handed a bamboo beaker, and, under the D.C.'s eye, they drink.

"Come on, Yapi, Yandra, Yayum, Yade, Yabom, Yaken, Yaniyak—you girls—let's have the *ponung!*" the D.C. shouts, clapping his hands. "Dance —the *ponung!*"

The people in the field look at him happily. They all have high cheekbones, slanting eyes, and flat-bridged noses. Most of the men are wearing
white *dhotis* and buttonless black coats, swords in bamboo scabbards, and
conch-shell-studded leather belts. Most of the women are wearing green
blouses and ankle-length cotton skirts geometrically patterned in black
and white.

The D.C., fixing red, tigerish eyes on a few girls who are now fluttering
and hovering around him, continues, "Come on! Quick, quick, quick!
Yapi, Yade, Yandra, Yayum, Yabom, Yaniyak, Yaken, you are fined five
rupees each for disobedience." There is general laughter. "Ten rupees."
He takes a draught from his beaker. "You chaps, get in there and start
doing the *ponung*. Get those girls. Twenty rupees—"

"Sir, it's time for the variety show," one of the officers breaks in.

"All right. There's all night for the *ponung*," the D.C. says, and, as if he
were opening the variety show then and there, he starts singing in ringing
tones in a language that, from a short time I once spent in Nepal, I recognize as Gurkhali:

> "O lads, O lasses, where is the road to Bakloh?
> O lads, O lasses, show me the road to Bakloh!
> O lads, O lasses, where is the road to Bakloh?
> O lads, O lasses, show me the road to Bakloh!"

He repeats the refrain again and again, to expressions of pleasure from
his audience.

Soon an improvised stage is ready, the officers and I are seated on folding chairs, and the Gallongs have ranged themselves on the ground. The
D.C., however, paces back and forth between the chair-wallahs and the
ground-wallahs.

"We people of the jungle beseech you to sit down," says the boy in girls'
clothes, coming up to the D.C.

"I am more jungly than all of you put together," the D.C. says, but he
takes a chair.

The variety show begins with a bamboo-stick dance, which is followed
by a physical-training act with dumbbells. The next act is a duckbill dance,
in which a group of boys wearing rimless bamboo hats with long brick-red
yak-hair tassels and long duckbills that stick out of the top bend over and
shake their torsos gracefully so that the duckbills dart, bob, and peck.
Among the other acts is a skit centering on bloodthirsty Chinese and the
heroic role of the NEFA tribesmen during the Chinese invasion. For me,
the high point of the show is a song crooned in English by one of the
duckbill dancers, making fun of the modern, emancipated woman:

"Fashion! Fashion! But you have no knowledge to do.
Gazing! Gazing! I couldn't locate a good quality in you.
Without knowledge, to indulge in fashion
Is a matter to evoke laughter.
Donyi Yanya, you sport long hair and think it your fashion,
But the sport is a matter to evoke laughter.
You look fore and hind—
Sometimes you halt and then go.
What you gaze at down and above,
That is a matter to evoke laughter.

Fashion! Fashion!
You are haughty in appearance.
You take your seat in such a way
That you give inconvenience to all—
You sit before all.
For no one will you stand.
You do not accept the precedence
Of the elders or the young.
Fashion!"

As a final item on the program, a newsreel is projected on a makeshift screen, and after a couple of minutes the D.C. says to me, "Let's go to the *hawaghar.*"

The *hawaghar* ("air house") is a *basha,* or hut constructed entirely of bamboo, which is the most accessible building material in the jungle. It is decorated with bamboo shavings. It has been put up as a dining room for the officers and is complete with a long table and folding chairs, but instead of shelter it seems to provide little more than vents for the wind.

"Have some whiskey," the D.C. says. "It will warm you up. I've given orders that as long as I am in Bagra, peons, drivers—one and all—should be given as much rum as they can hold."

I accept the whiskey, and we drink, to the accompaniment of distant voices on a sound track ("The President of India . . . The Food Minister of India . . . Mrs. Indira Gandhi said today . . . Mont Blanc . . . Plane crash"). At last, there is the steely rumble of the national anthem, and girls, among them Yapi Loya, rush into the *hawaghar* and busy themselves arranging huge banana leaves on the table. In an instant, the leaves disappear under mountains of rice, mutton, and vegetables. Even though all the government officers eat with gusto, they only make dents in the peaks. Nonetheless, the girls, who have taken up stations behind the folding chairs, continually heap up more food, as if failure to maintain the moun-

tains at their original elevation might be a sign of disrespect to the assembled dignitaries. The D.C. eats little and keeps up a stream of banter with
the girls.

When we return to the field after dinner, the D.C. shouts, "Let there be
ponung!" and the Gallongs, who have been eating in other *bashas,* start
arriving. The D.C. says to me, "Last time I stayed up all night for a *ponung* was when I went to a village to stop an epidemic of cholera. The
village was dank and congested, and a doctor I took along told me that the
only hope was to abandon the place. The village council told me that the
evil spirits were behind the fever and that the only hope of appeasing them
lay in my taking part in an all-night *ponung.* I said I would dance all night
if they would move out of the village in the morning. They said they
would if the morning was clear, for that would be a sign that the evil
spirits had been appeased. We did the *ponung* all night, and, fortunately,
the sun came out for fifteen minutes in the morning. I was able to evacuate
the village."

"Did you have any trouble resettling the people?" I ask.

"No. We just moved them to another ridge. It doesn't take long for
them to put up *bashas,* and *bashas* have to be rebuilt about every three
years anyway."

The field is crowded now. Under brilliant starlight, everyone falls into a
winding line and begins a sort of strolling dance, going counterclockwise.
At the head of the line is the boy in girls' clothes, shaking the sword. As
before, he sings, but this time in Adi, the language of the Gallongs. The
D.C. softly intones the translation for me.

The boy calls, "*Aipe alangka, go goi.*" ("Welcome," whispers the D.C.
" '*Go goi*' is for rhythm.")

"*Go goi,*" chants the chorus.

"*Tebo ne ajar, go go goi . . .*" ("To you people we will entertain . . .")
"*Go goi.*"

"*Jarmene gelaju, go goi . . .*" ("We, all the hosts, will entertain
you . . .")

"*Go goi.*"

"*Ane so Higi so, go goi . . .*" ("Here, this motherland, Higi . . .")
"*Go goi.*"

"*Higi so diri so, go goi . . .*" ("More beloved land than the heart . . .")
"*Go goi.*"

Throughout the dance, the jangling of the sword is echoed by jangles
from all sides, as if the dancers were shaking invisible swords. I ask the
D.C. about the mysteriously echoing sounds.

"We don't talk about such things now," the D.C. says, with a laugh. "The government doesn't even want to admit that such things exist. Until recently, some tribal people went naked. Sometimes a Gallong man wore a leaf, and a Gallong woman, until she had her first baby, wore a belt of brass discs—heart-shaped discs—around her hips. Some women still wear the belt, under their clothes." To the dancers he shouts, *"Ulta, ulta!"* Then he says, "No matter how often I shout *'Ulta'* at them, I can never get them to *ponung* clockwise."

The dance continues into the night. Sometimes a step is added or omitted, sometimes the caller is a girl or an old man, sometimes the dancers move in a circle, sometimes they go snakelike across the field, sometimes the chorus chants *"Go go go goi"* instead of *"Go go goi"* or *"Go goi"*—nonsense syllables either way—but the sound of the melodic call and the response, always in the tonic key, and the rhythm and the pace do not change at all. The dance is as soothing and hypnotic as a lullaby.

Yapi, detaching herself from the *ponung,* comes up to the fire, where I've been standing. Putting her hand over her mouth and squinting slightly, she invites me to join the *ponung.* But we stand talking for a time while she warms herself. She tells me in pidgin Hindi that she is from a village called Kabu, near Along; that she is fifteen; and that if schooling opportunities had existed when she was five she would now be in the tenth standard. As it is, she is in the fifth standard in the secondary school in Along. The Gallong girls are very free with their own people, but with outsiders they tend either to become a little giggly or to assume the manner of silent petitioners at court. Not so Yapi.

When Yapi and I join the *ponung*—the D.C. and Yade take places beside us in the circle—it has settled down to the song of genealogy.

The leader calls, *"Jajine tone, tone, ja jin ja . . ."*
"Ja jin ja," the chorus responds.
"Melore ogo, ogo, ja jin ja . . ."
"Ja jin ja."
"Topolo Puyi, puyi, ja jin ja . . ."
"Ja jin ja."
"Maboge duke, duke, ja jin ja . . ."
"Ja jin ja."
"Pagbogge duke, duke, ja jin ja . . ."
"Ja jin ja."
"Rilikla dula, dula, ja jin ja . . ."
"Ja jin ja."
"Ketiba ruba, ruba, ja jin ja . . ."

"*Ja jin ja.*"
"*Tiji ba ruba, ruba, ja jin ja . . .*"
"*Ja jin ja.*"
"*Mabo pagbo gadge, gadge, ja jin ja . . .*"
"*Ja jin ja.*"
"*Duḵube lele, lele, ja jin ja . . .*"
"*Ja jin ja.*"
"*Gipenba ruba, ruba, ja jin ja . . .*"
"*Ja jin ja.*"

(The call translation: "In the ancient times,/In the place Topo Puyi by name,/In the plains,/The human residents/All assembled,/All together./An assembly was held./After the assembly,/The human residents,/Separately, into the forests,/Here and there, dispersed.")

The caller, who is a gaunt old man, perhaps the eldest in this assembly, now recites one string of names after another, tracing the history of the human residents from the beginning, which must have been very far in the past indeed. The call, in its lengthy catalogue of ancestors, resembles the Old Testament "begat"s, but, whether because the names are so familiar to the progeny that the caller is lax in his enunciation or because the names are unwieldy and have to be recited fast to fit them into the Procrustean bed of the *ponung* metre, I cannot make out any of them. I have no trouble, however, catching the call of "*Ja jin ja*"—more of those rhythmic nonsense syllables—which seems to come each time the leader needs to pause for breath, and I repeat it with the rest of the dancers. After a couple of hours of going around and about the field, I drop out of the *ponung* and return to the fire.

"The song of genealogy will probably go on for the rest of the night," the D.C. says, coming up to me. "They can do the *ponung* for nights and days, and afterward go out in the fields or the jungle and do hard work, and after that they may start the *ponung* all over again. They have extraordinary energy."

An officer who has been dancing throughout comes up and tries to say good night to the D.C.

"No good nights," the D.C. says. "The lower primary school is opening tomorrow. How can any of us go to sleep? We must go on doing the *ponung.*"

The D.C., probably remembering that I have been travelling, orders me to bed, and I am shown into a nearby *basha* perched on high stilts. As I walk on the floor, which is of bamboo matting, I feel I'm walking on a trampoline. As I consider the walls and the ceiling, which are of split bamboo tied with cane, I feel I'm back in the *hawaghar*. And as I lie down on the bed, which is of poles of bamboo laid across a bamboo trestle, I feel I'm lying down on a table. Tonight, I think, I'm going to sleep Gallong style. Yet, though the euphonious *"Ja jin ja"*s are showered upon me like a thousand and one good-night kisses, I cannot sleep. I cannot push out of my mind a glimpse I had of Gallong life outside the special atmosphere of the festival.

I was on my way from Along to Bagra. The government officer who was escorting me had to drop off some medicine for a newborn baby in a village along the way. The village was on a hillside, and, leaving the jeep below, we walked up a rough slope lined with *bashas*. All the *bashas* were on stilts about ten feet high, and all of them were hooded with slanting thatched roofs. Each *basha* had a sty attached to it, and the "oink-oink" of the pigs seemed to come from everywhere.

"Why does each house have a pigsty?" I asked.

The officer cleared his throat and waved a hand. "You know—well, there are no proper drains in these areas. You know—well, most of the tribes live on the spurs and ridges, for health and other reasons, like security. Well, then, don't you know why they have the need for scavengers? Most of the hill tribes use pigs for the purpose."

In front of the *basha* with the newborn baby, the officer hesitated, as though he were afraid to show anyone who was not an officer assigned to the tribal areas the inside of a Gallong house without first clearing the matter with higher-ups and perhaps receiving a permit. "There's not much to a *basha*," he said evasively. "It's just one square room with a fire in the middle. I'm just going to go up, leave the medicine, and come straight down. Of course, if you want to come up . . ."

"I'd like to," I said, but it was now my turn to hesitate. A typical *basha*, it could be entered by either of two bamboo ladders—one at the front and one at the side. From my reading, I knew that complicated rites were associated with the use of the ladders. ("The Gallongs," by L. R. N. Srivastava, notes, "Women enter the house by the side ladder and men by the front one. Women are never allowed to go in or come out of the house by the ladder meant for men. If, by a mistake, which is rarely committed, a woman uses the men's ladder, she faces a shower of rebukes and scoldings from the elders of the family. There will be no game, the Gallongs believe, in the hunt, nor fish in the river, if any woman uses the men's ladder.") I also knew from "The Gallongs" that the hearth was the focal point of the house, and that complicated rites were associated with it. ("The side of the fireplace facing the entrance is *bago,* to be occupied by the guests. The side opposite to it is *nyosi,* where the slaves of the family and the old men and women sleep; on the left hand side is *nyode,* and on the right hand side is *udu.* The former is meant for the eldest son and his wife. The second son also may sleep here with his wife, if he has one, while the latter is to be occupied by the unmarried children.") I asked the officer, "Which ladder are we supposed to use? And do you know if we must confine ourselves to the *bago?"*

He laughed, and was somehow no longer the officer. "You would have to bother about *bago* only if you were a Gallong and were going to spend the night here," he told me. He led the way up the front ladder.

As he had said, the *basha* consisted of one square room. There was an open veranda all around it, but the room itself was dark and filled with smoke. More than twenty people were there, including some young children, and all of them seemed to be part of the household. At one side of the room, a wizened man was chopping wood and a woman of about seventy was sitting and winnowing rice, her short fingers rapidly sifting the grains. The rest were sitting or standing in the middle of the room, around a huge fire burning in a pit made of stone slabs. Though the woman did not leave off her winnowing or the man his chopping when we arrived, all of them seemed a little taken aback, like schoolchildren surprised by the headmaster. The officer and I stood about awkwardly. There were no cots, no furniture of any kind in the room. There were only baskets of rice and other grain, pots, winnowing pans, and mortars and pestles, and the only decorations were wooden heads and animals' jawbones. The young mother served us tea. We downed it quickly and left.

For a long time after I lie down in my *basha,* I hear the distant *"Ja jin ja"* of the *ponung.*

In the morning, the *ponung* stops in order to shift from the festival grounds to the site of the lower primary school, a few hundred yards away, for the dedication ceremony. The schoolhouse, which is surrounded by a bamboo cattle guard, is a small wooden structure with a roof of corrugated galvanized iron. It stands between the river and the road to Along, and on the road, which the school faces, an immense crowd has gathered, the men and boys standing to one side of the road, and the women and girls to the other. At the approach of the Deputy Commissioner and his party of officers, everyone cries out *"Jai Hind!"* ("Victory to India!") The D.C., waving to the crowd, which looks fresh and relaxed in spite of the night-long *ponung*, walks rapidly up to the schoolhouse, accepts a sword from a village headman, and cuts a bamboo ribbon that has been stretched across the doorway.

The D.C. brandishes the sword and sings out, "It's a good thing that the school has opened."

All the men fall in line behind him and start the *ponung*.

"It's a good thing we have opened the lower primary school," continues the D.C.

"Lower primary school," chants the chorus.

"It's a good thing we don't have a *basha* anymore for a lower primary school."

"Lower primary school."

"We've had a *basha* in Pusi Bango since 1950 for a lower primary school."

"Lower primary school."

"We've had a *basha* in Bagra since 1953 for a lower primary school."

"Lower primary school."

"It's a good thing we now have a *pukka* [permanent] lower primary school."

"Lower primary school."

The D.C. leads the line of men into and through and around the three bare rooms of the schoolhouse, the newness of which is accentuated by the fact that its windows have not yet been fitted with panes. Boys, women, and girls, in that order, dance behind the men, following them into and through and around the school, and each of the four sections of the *ponung* does its own steps and raises its voices in a separate chorus to proclaim the "good thing." The old man who led the song of genealogy has relieved the D.C. of the sword and has taken his place at the head of the line.

"This motherland, Higi, *ho delo* . . ." he calls, in Adi.

"*Ho delo.*"

"More beloved land than the heart, *ho delo* . . ."

"*Ho delo.*"

"You people have come, *ho delo* . . ."

"*Ho delo.*"

"From you, it is hoped, *ho delo* . . ."

"*Ho delo.*"

"With bountiful heart, *ho delo* . . ."

"*Ho delo.*"

"Way toward little learning, *ho delo* . . ."

"*Ho delo.*"
"Light of some knowledge, *ho delo* . . ."
"*Ho delo.*"
"We hope to receive from you, *ho delo* . . ."
"*Ho delo.*"

Call follows call, praising the gods, the spirits, and the Indian government. When the last girl has danced through the school, the D.C., his party of officers, and the village headmen approach a table and some folding chairs that have been set up in front of the school, and the rest of the dancers settle down on the bare ground. The officers take their seats at the table, but the village headmen remain standing in a huddle for some time. They engage in a heated altercation in Adi. Now and again one of them addresses a remark to a small, tense boy with pencil and paper who is standing at their elbow, and he immediately writes something down. The sun is out strong, and it is very hot. For the first time, the people show signs of discomfort.

"Come on, let's get the *kebang* going," the D.C. says to the huddle of village headmen. "Do take your seats. I'm ready for your bombshell."

"What's the delay?" I ask the D.C.

"The headmen are making some last-minute changes in a petition. They think it's going to be a bombshell for me. Probably they're also waiting for a progress report on the cooking of the *mithun*, which has to be done exactly when the *kebang* finishes." The *mithun*, a straight-horned bison of the species *Bos frontalis*, is the most valued possession of many of the hill tribesmen, and I am surprised that this occasion calls for such a sacrifice, but the D.C. adds, "A feast can't be grand without *mithun*, and the opening of a *pukka* school requires a grand feast."

Eventually, the headmen take their seats, and the *kebang* is called to order. The first speaker turns out to be the boy with the paper and pencil, and he reads his speech, which is in English, in a soft, halting voice: "Honorable Deputy Commissioner, Siang District, Along, Camp Bagra. The *gams* [village leaders] and public of Pusi Bango welcome you and the other officers. Really we deem it a great pleasure to welcome you on this auspicious occasion in this remote and backward area of NEFA, and your visit will give us an inspiration in the way of development of our school to the fullest extent. We solemnly affirm that the great impediments which are the crucial factors in the way of our development will be removed and brought to light by your visit. We the children of Pusi Bango are highly inspired by your visit. The innocent children of this backward *bango* are quite ignorant about the modern civilization of the world, as we are the inhabitants of a most remote corner of India. Please help us to get ourselves duly qualified to serve our motherland. Our *bango* is one of the big *bangos* in the district of Siang, and our lower primary school was established in the year 1950. At the time, it was in an early venture state, but in 1953 the government undertook some of the responsibilities of the school, and since then it has been remaining in the same state. The aims and object of the *bango* people are those that your august visit will enlighten in the functioning of our school into a new status, and this visit will remain in the minds of the young generation to time immemorial. We the people of Pusi Bango are highly pleased to welcome you and with these few words we conclude and convey our best regards and wishes to you all. *Jai Hind!* Yours faithfully, *gams* and public of Pusi Bango."

Other speeches in this vein follow, but they are in Adi, so to the voice of each speaker the voice of a Hindi interpreter is now added. The D.C. listens patiently for perhaps an hour, and then cries out, "What is the point of welcoming us now? We have been eating and drinking and dancing together since yesterday afternoon! Let's have the bombshell!"

An old man, who is introduced as the secretary to the leaders of Pusi Bango, stands up. "Your Honor, I want to state some blunt facts," he says, in Adi. "And, Your Honor, I want to make a request. We would like our school to be upgraded—"

"This is the bombshell," the D.C. whispers to me.

"—and we would like a compounder for Pusi Bango. When our people get sick, they have to walk sixteen miles to Along to get a pill. We in Pusi Bango are many people. We are enough people to have a compounder for ourselves here in Pusi Bango, and we are enough people to have our lower primary school go up to middle English level. We, the *gams* of Ango, Doje, and Bagra, all the villages of Pusi Bango, would like to submit to you this letter, hoping that the same will be sent to the Director of Education, NEFA, in faraway Shillong for favor of information, Your Honor requesting him earnestly to pay his kind attention to this matter."

He now reads the petition: " 'To the Deputy Commissioner, Siang District, Along, Camp Bagra. Respected Sir, I on behalf of the leaders of Pusi Bango beg most humbly and respectfully to approach Your Honor with the following facts and prayers and hopes. We have full confidence in our popular government in respect to the upliftment of our undeveloped and underdeveloped areas, but we are extremely sorry to state that it has paid no attention to the upgrading of our school until now. Several other schools which are junior to our own have been upgraded, but our school is so unfortunate that it has not got that favor from our benevolent government to date. We do believe that our school is in no respect inferior to any other school that has been upgraded. That, since Your Honor has kindly visited our school on this happy occasion, we fervently hope and are sure to see a much better and brighter future for our school due to Your Honor's kindness. Our *bango* is one of the biggest *bangos* of this district and the enrollment of our school is also not less. Should not, therefore, the huge number of our poor children get the benefits of a middle English school?' *Jai Hind!*" (At first, the demand strikes me as reasonable, but then I recall that the first schools were started in Siang only in 1947, and that the *pukka* school in Bagra is part of the government's plan to raise the student population of Siang this year to twenty-three hundred, enrolled in sixty-two schools, counting the district's single secondary school, in Along, which graduated its first class, of six students, in 1965. That school, which I have visited, so far has *pukka* buildings only for the older students, and even these buildings, equipped with insubstantial desks holding a few worn textbooks in Assamese, cheap calendars, and Boy Scout jamboree albums, give the impression of being *kutcha,* or temporary, accommodations.)

"Without your having asked for a middle English school, I had thought on my own, and the government had thought on their own, of giving you a middle English school," the D.C. is saying now. "You will have the school within five years. The compounder is another matter. Compounders are very difficult to get, all over India, and we need seventeen more in Siang district alone. At least, you in Pusi Bango can walk to Along, but there are people in upper Siang who can't even walk for a pill. They are completely cut off from receiving any pills. So the first compounders we get will have to go to upper Siang. You must remember that India has very limited resources and many demands. No right of reply," he finishes good-humoredly. "The meeting is adjourned."

Haversacks made of banana leaves and filled with rice and *mithun* appear, and everyone is served generously. The table in front of the school is piled with huge quantities of food. The D.C. attacks the *mithun* vigorously, but some of the other officers ask for mutton.

"*Mithun* is technically not beef," the D.C. says to the officers. "You should learn to eat *mithun.*" Soon afterward, he stands up and announces, "The D.C.'s party is going."

Everyone rises.

"Farewell, *go goi* . . ." chants the old man, in Adi.

"*Go goi.*"

"Hey, respected officers, *go goi* . . ."

"Go goi."
"While crossing the hills, *go goi . . ."*
"Go goi."
"Having crossed, *go goi . . ."*
"Go goi."
"Do not put your heart, *go goi . . ."*
"Go goi."
"To feelings of anxiety, *go goi . . ."*
"Go goi."
"Do not put your heart, *go goi . . ."*
"Go goi."
"To feelings of evil, *go goi . . ."*
"Go goi."

The D.C. has invited me to ride back to Along with him in his jeep. In the jeep, which he drives fast, careering around the curves, holding the steering wheel tight, and honking the horn—which is a special one, extra loud—with his wrist or elbow, so that everyone within hearing distance will be aware that the D.C. is travelling, he says to me, "The officers were very tired, and the people will enjoy themselves more without us. The feast will probably go on for another day or two. It cost them thousands of rupees, and they have to get full enjoyment out of it."

At Along (and, later on, at other administrative posts in the interior), many officers tell me that they are uncertain what they should do about detribalization. On the one hand, the government they serve has charged them with the task of overseeing development, one phase of which is to make modern education available eventually to every tribal child; on the other, the government has charged them with the task of preserving the tribal culture as far as possible, one phase of which is to foster the tribal traditions. The purpose of this dual policy is to extend to the tribal people the scientific benefits of modern society without cutting off the tribal people from their roots, and its author was an Englishman named Verrier Elwin. There were other pioneers, in one sense or another, in NEFA— among them J. P. Mills, a Colonel Betts, and, above all, Christoph von Fürer-Haimendorf, at present Professor of Asian Anthropology at the University of London—but Elwin, who died in 1964, at the age of sixty-one, was one of the first to become widely known for his penetration of the tribal areas and for his acceptance by the tribesmen. Although he was born of English parents, he took Indian citizenship. Although he was the son of a missionary bishop, was himself ordained, and for a time belonged to a missionary society, he early retired to lay life. Although he was clearly at home in the scholarly world of Oxford, where he took Firsts in English literature and theology, he chose to live much of his adult life in central India with the aboriginal tribesmen, and he married one of the tribal girls. Although he was only an amateur ethnologist, his ideas acquired an authority seldom enjoyed by professionals. Although he wrote many books devoted exclusively to his researches among the tribes, his writings at times seem like religious, philosophical, or literary diaries, or like polemics against the modern world penned by a Victorian who romanticized the bucolic life. But, whatever the ambiguities in the life and thought of Elwin, the government, being confronted after Independence by tribal problems and needing an adviser, turned to him, and his writings have become the basis of the government's paternalistic policy toward the tribal people.

Among the several books Elwin wrote on NEFA, the most important is "A Philosophy for NEFA," which embodies his dream for the development of an ideal tribal society. In a chapter headed "The Fundamental Problem," he writes:

> The problem of the best way of administering so-called "primitive," "aboriginal," or "tribal" populations has been debated for hundreds of years, and those people who even today so unfailingly remind us, whenever there is a proposal for a scientific approach to the subject, that we must not keep them as "museum specimens," are in fact only intervening in a very old controversy.
>
> It is an interesting controversy, for it is linked up with several allied questions. Is mankind really progressing? Is civilization any good? Is the country better than the town? Is Man better in a state of Nature or of Art? Is the untutored "savage" happier, more moral, in a word better than the sophisticated and urban product of the modern world?

In the next dozen pages he discusses the views on primitives held by, among others, Hesiod, Horace, Vergil, Cato, Columella, Montaigne, Spenser, Drayton, Beaumont, Fletcher, Shakespeare, Cowley, Vaughan, Waller Marvell, Milton, Dryden, Mrs. Aphra Behn, Dr. Johnson, Boswell, Diderot, Rousseau, Captain Cook, Bishop Heber, Darwin, Dickens, Matthew Arnold, William Morris, Ruskin, Tolstoy, C. M. Sarbiewski, A. O. Lovejoy, Franz Boas, Margaret Fitzgerald, R. W. Frantz, Walter Hammond, Gandhi, Vivekananda, Gauguin, Picasso, Aldous Huxley, George Orwell, Rebecca West, and Frank Kermode. He then continues:

The invention of the hydrogen bomb, the establishment over a large part of the earth of totalitarian governments, the ever-increasing power of the bureaucracy in the most democratic nations has made people of today rethink their whole attitude to civilization and progress.

It is impossible to consider the fundamental problem of the tribal people without bearing in mind the context of contemporary society. Is it worthwhile making them part of a way of life whose standards we ourselves are beginning to doubt?

But after all perhaps our doubts are wrong. For the bombs, the secret police, the tortures in hidden prison cells, the taxation, the corruptions, the intrigues are not the last word about the modern world. There is a great fund of goodness; there are executions, but there is also mercy; there are countries curtained off with iron, but there are other lands where the winds of thought blow freely and men can speak their minds. There is art, beauty, comfort, health, and the ideal of freedom from want and fear.

The difference in our outlook on the future of the tribal people today is this. Formerly, the artists and poets said: "Because these people are noble and good, there is no need to do anything for them." The reformers, the uplifters, the clergy said: "Because these people are ignoble, superstitious and miserable, we must do something for them."

We say: "It is just because we believe them to be noble and good that we want to do all we can for them. We do not do this because we pity them, we do it because we respect them. We do it because we believe that we can bring them the best things of our world without destroying the nobility and the goodness of theirs, and that one day in their turn they will help us."

Thus, the administrators who are now left to reconcile "the best things of our world" and "the nobility and the goodness of theirs" find Elwin and the Forest of Arden (the tribes in their primitive state) on one side and themselves and progress (gradual but certain advancement, with all its psychological, social, and political consequences) on the other. A Gallong child who graduates from secondary school and perhaps attends a university is likely to shun the communal life of the one-room *basha,* which has its own kinds of sexual arrangements, and also to shun the obligations of kinship, the customary occupations of farming, hunting, and fishing, the magic rites associated with these, and the collective ceremonial expressions, like the *ponung.* Instead, he is likely to want the privacy of a multiple-room dwelling in town, and a white-collar job. Officers can try to see to it that the school instills in the child respect for his culture; that, once he has been educated, he returns to his tribe and participates in the work of developing it; and that he remains free from the pernicious influences of outsiders. The result of such paternalism is often distrust, resentment, and unrest. And the urgency of finding a workable policy for NEFA is accentuated by the fact that NEFA is only one small part of the general tribal picture, and that political troubles just dawning in NEFA have reached their noon elsewhere.

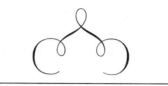

Nagaland

THERE ARE ABOUT TWENTY MILLION TRIBAL PEOPLE in India. Because many of these people live on India's borders, it was thought after the British departed that if India did not court them and win their allegiance, China or Pakistan would, and that such subversion of the tribal people would compromise India's security; it was also thought that the loss of any tribal area might be a first step in the Balkanization of India, already beset by schisms. However, the government's attempt to assimilate the tribal people has been a notable failure, for some of the people have risen up in arms to protest being assimilated, and the government has shown itself (and continues to show itself) uncertain about the best measures to adopt in its dealings with them and with the others. Is there a single policy that can work for all the tribal people? If so, does it perhaps include resettling people from other parts of India in the disturbed areas, or else resettling people from the disturbed areas in other parts of India, and thereby diluting the tribes until they will have practically no separate political identity left? This course has been seriously advocated in some quarters, but it has been rejected by the government on the ground that it might lead to genocide. Is the policy, then, to be one of rapid economic development? Of strategic political concessions? Of ruthless military suppression? Economic development, at any speed, means a risk of detribalization, and yet the alternative seems to be to treat the tribes as anthropological curiosities. Political concessions may simply invite demands for further concessions, and yet the alternative seems to be to ignore the stirrings of political consciousness among the tribes. A military solution, even if it could succeed, would be only an admission of economic and political failure, and yet the alternative seems to be to leave the insurgent tendencies of many of the tribes unchecked. In the absence of a single clear policy, the government has settled for a combination of *ad-hoc* economic, political, and military measures, only to be attacked by critics who predict that its vacillation and delay will eventually lose India the allegiance of all the tribal people, and who declare that her administrators in the field show contempt for the tribal people, remaining ignorant of tribal ways and languages, and conducting themselves like gentlemen sent to carve out an empire from the bush. These critics maintain that the government has never seriously tried to make the tribal people feel that they are a real part of India; that its work of economic development has so far amounted to little more than broadening a few arterial mule trails into military supply roads and disseminating ineffective political propaganda; that it has tended to think of the tribal people primarily in terms of a problem of "law and order;" that in some tribal areas it goes on trying a military solution, with disastrous results, and has been guilty of military atrocities in these areas; and that it has one policy toward warring tribes and another toward peaceful ones— sometimes negotiating with the first almost on terms of equality while saying to the second, "There can be no negotiating with our own people." As things stand, the government is confronted by brush-fire wars for independence in some tribal areas, like Nagaland, and by the possibility that these wars will spread and multiply.

Nagaland, which lies southeast of NEFA along the south bank of the Brahmaputra, is a narrow strip of hills. This strip, which is mostly jungle, has an area of 6,366 square miles and is inhabited by some four hundred thousand Nagas, almost half of whom, as a result of the work of American Baptist missionaries in the nineteenth century, are Christians. Actually, the name Naga designates a collection of tribes that, like the other tribes in the northern and northeastern hills and plains of India, are believed to belong to the Indo-Mongoloid race, which is itself an omnibus term used by Indians for tribal people who speak any language of the Sino-Tibetan family—which the late George A. Grierson, perhaps the greatest student of Indian languages, described as a "formless evermoving ant-horde of dialects"—and who have ever, in the words of the Indian scholar S. K. Chatterji, "entered into or touched the fringe of the cultural entity that is India." But exactly what it is that distinguishes the Naga tribes from other Indo-Mongoloid tribes, what the Naga tribes have in common, and, indeed, why they are called Nagas in the first place are by no means settled issues. The popular belief used to be that because *"naga"* meant "naked," all the tribal people who, as a matter of practice, did not wear clothes were Nagas. Although no scholar today subscribes to this belief, the subject of the tribal areas is so sensitive and the state of research into it so elementary that anyone who ventures an opinion even on why the Nagas are Nagas finds himself bearding a host of adversaries. And the Nagas themselves have not helped matters. Elwin, in his book "Nagaland," wrote, "There is a legend told by many of the hill tribes against themselves, that in the very early days God gave men skins of deer on which he told them to write their traditions. The people of the plains obeyed his command, but the hillmen, hungry and omnivorous, cooked and ate their writing materials, with the result that they were unable to leave any records of their past." It is, however, a matter of record that during the raj some of these Naga tribes lived in Tuensang, which was part of NEFA, and the rest in what was called the Naga Hills district, which, like NEFA, was designated an Excluded Area under the Inner Line Regulations. After Independence, there was a revolt against the government of India. The Naga insurgents announced that they represented all the Naga tribes, which formed a separate nation, and that they were the Naga Federal Government of the Naga Federal Republic, and they started waging a guerrilla war against Indian troops. (In due course, the insurgent Naga Federal Government had a president, a vice-president, a prime minister, a home minister, a foreign secretary, a corps of tax collectors, and a parliament, or Tatar Hoho.) In 1957, the Indian government, as a concession to the Naga underground, made the Tuensang area and the Naga Hills district one administrative unit, and in 1960, as another concession, it made this administrative unit a separate state, calling it Nagaland and giving it greater autonomy than was enjoyed by any other state in the Indian Union. All the same, the Naga underground continued its war for the better part of fifteen years, with the help of ammunition stores left over from the Second World War, when Japanese troops occupied parts of the Tuensang area and the Naga Hills district, and also with the help of arms from Pakistan and China. Then, in the autumn of 1964, the Nagas agreed to stop fighting and negotiate, but only for a limited period. The truce, however, has been extended again and again, though sometimes for no more than a month. The Indian government has used the truce to dwell on its good will toward the Nagas, publishing literature like a brochure entitled "Nehru and Nagaland." (Page 3: "His [Nehru's] kinship with Nagas was so great that he always came to their defence whenever something the people have been doing here in these border areas came in for adverse comments. Challenged about the head-hunting practice prevailing in some parts of the country [Nagaland], he replied, 'It is often better to cut off a hand or head than to crush and trample on the heart!' ") The Naga underground has used the truce to dwell on past Indian military atrocities, publishing compilations like "Indian Atrocities in Nagaland." (Page 9: "March 9, 1957, Marumi. Mr. Khehoto of Marumi, aged 52 years, was fried alive with *ghi* and mustard oil by Indian Army troops." Page 14: "February, 1957, Sukomi. Mr. Zhemithi of Sukomi, aged 45, his legs were tied together, hands tied backward and knocked down to the ground. A big log was placed over him in the fashion of a see-saw, six soldiers were seated on each side and rolled for hours.") In spite of the truce, many Indian politicians have urged that the government give the military a free hand in dealing with the Naga insurgents. Such pressures suggest to some critics that time is running out for the Indian government, and that if it cannot persuade the Naga underground to accept anything less than independence, Nagaland will become a test case for the military solution. Also in spite of the truce, railway carriages have been blown up, trains derailed, and Indian troops ambushed in Nagaland and surrounding areas. Such incidents, which are thought to be the work of the Naga underground, suggest to some critics that either the underground leaders in charge of negotiations are employing calculated acts of terrorism to reinforce their threat to resume the war or these leaders have lost control and their ranks are splitting up into factions. But the talks continue, and in Nagaland there is at least a semblance of peace.

This is not the situation in all the tribal areas. For instance, just a step behind the Naga insurgents in militancy are the Lushai tribes. They are two hundred thousand strong and inhabit the Mizo Hills district, a narrow, densely wooded strip of hills that has an area of 8,134 square miles and lies southwest of Nagaland, on the border between Assam and East Pakistan. The Lushais (sometimes called Mizos) have started a guerrilla war of their own, also demanding independence. The Indian government has sent in the military with planes and bombs. (The military were given a free hand in the Mizo Hills in early 1967 and started in earnest the task of "pacification," which consisted of the evacuation of some nine hundred villages in which the Lushais lived, the resettlement of the villagers in refugee camps, and the bombing of the village sites in the hope of flushing out the guerrillas.) There are other tribes in revolt (several of them have asked why, if the Maldive Islands, which have a population of ninety-

208]   THE HIMALAYAS

seven thousand, can be a nation, with membership in the United Nations, they cannot exist as separate nations, too), but they pose less of a peril, because, unlike the Nagas and the Lushais (and, more recently, the tribes in Naxalbari, in West Bengal), they have as yet nothing more modern in their arsenals than bows and arrows.

Throughout the uneasy truce in Nagaland, there has been a steady verbal crossfire between the champions of Naga independence and the champions of the Naga status quo, and the heaviest barrage, as it happens, has taken place in Fleet Street, a forum for controversies. Witness this round, concerning the recent history of the Nagas, in the correspondence pages of the London *Times*. A. Z. Phizo, a leader of the Naga underground, writes:

It should perhaps be more widely known that Nagaland consists of two parts: Free Nagaland in the North [Tuensang] which the British never sought to conquer or administer, and the "Naga Hills Excluded Areas" which from 1879 to 1947 were to a limited extent administered by the British Governor of Assam as the Agent of the Crown, but the civilian and criminal administration over the people has always been under the control of the Naga national assembly and the British never interfered. . . . In 1947, in their haste to leave India, the British failed to secure for the Nagas the independence which they sought. . . . On August 14, 1947, before the British left, the Nagas declared their independence and confirmed it by a referendum in May 1951, and reunited with Free Nagaland on March 22, 1956, as the Federal Republic of Nagaland. Of all these events the Indian Government was kept fully informed. . . . Unless India intends to liquidate the Nagas— (and not less than 100,000 Nagas have perished since 1955 out of a population of at most one million)—would not a secure frontier be better guaranteed by having a friendly neighbour than a people kept in subjection by force of arms?

J. H. Hutton, an authority on the British administration of Nagaland, replies:

The civil and criminal control of the Naga Hills was exercised by the Deputy Commissioner appointed by the Governor of Assam. No Naga national assembly, nor anything like one, existed before 1947, nor was there even any common language spoken among the Naga tribes. . . . Except in cases of serious crime, which were dealt with under the Indian penal code, the Nagas were administered by the Deputy Commissioner and his assistants according to their own customs, which varied from tribe to tribe and even from village to village; but to write of a Naga national assembly with which from 1879 to 1947 the British never interfered is more completely nonsense than I could have expected to read from anyone literate enough to write a letter to you, Sir.

Or, concerning what, in the light of present Naga-Indian relations, may be expected in the future, witness this exchange—this time in the news pages of the London *Times.* The Reverend Dr. Michael Scott, a clergyman of the Church of England and British member of the Indian Peace Mission for Nagaland, states:

After spending more than two years in Nagaland, with four visits to Delhi, and having maintained silence during that time in the hope of being able to help to bring about a peace [Scott wrote this dispatch soon after he was expelled by India from both India and Nagaland for allegedly becoming a partisan of the Naga underground and so losing the trust of the Indian government, which had accepted his good offices as a conciliator in 1964], I now feel bound to warn that I see no hope of a massacre being avoided in Nagaland, unless Delhi is large enough to invite a third-party mediation of some kind, as the Nagas have proposed. I see no sign of this happening. If there is a further massacre in Nagaland, a bell will toll for more than the death of the Naga people. . . . It has been the "integrity of the Indian Constitution" and the "Sovereignty of the Indian Union" which have been advanced as the grounds of India's claim that the Naga territory is part of the Indian Union. . . . I have been slowly and reluctantly driven to the conclusion that the Government of India has never taken seriously the problem of negotiating a political settlement with the Nagas. . . . It is a certainty that if no generous political proposals are made, and if the terms of a durable peace are not agreed, then another bloodbath in Nagaland is inevitable. . . . If all negotiations break down and the fighting is resumed . . . disaffection could easily spread into the other hill areas of Assam and the North East Frontier Agency.

Dr. J. N. Mehta, the Indian High Commissioner in London, replies:

The Reverend Michael Scott . . . has threatened a "bloodbath" . . . unless a settlement entirely favourable to the Naga hostiles . . . is made immediately by the Government of India. He has further threatened an extension of the present conflict. . . . One is entitled to expect from a pastor of a church, who seeks to present his credentials as an non-partisan cc ıciliator . . . to talk at least the language of peace and conciliation. . . . If ıe Reverend Michael Scott is interested in quenching the flames of conflict and not stoking them, he should join his fellow Christians in India in the appeal which they recently issued to the Nagas and the Mizos through the all-India Christian Conference on "Peace with Justice and Charity" organized by all the Christian denominations representing eleven million Christians in India. . . . Article 371-A of the Constitution lays down that no Act of the Indian Parliament will apply to Nagaland in respect of:—(i) religious or social practices of the Nagas; (ii) Naga customary law and procedure; (iii) administration of civil and criminal justice involving decisions according to Naga customary law; (iv) ownership and transfer of land and its resources. . . . Thus, in two main fields, namely, economic and political, the Nagas have been guaranteed autonomy and freedom of an order not known in the other states of India.

Making a detour from NEFA, I spend some time in Nagaland. On my first evening there—in Kohima, a forlorn, spread-out town in the south of Nagaland which serves as the state capital—I visit a Naga Christian household for dinner. The house is cozy. The drawing room is filled with Naga guests, all wearing Western-style clothes—suits and frocks—and all very friendly. There are sofas and easy chairs in the room, a log fire in the fireplace, whiskey in the glasses, Mozart on the gramophone, a Bible on a side table. Some children in pajamas and dressing gowns have just filed away after singing, in four-part harmony, a song in Angami—the language of the local tribe, which is also called Angami—set to the tune of "O Come All Ye Faithful." The guests are now serving themselves from a buffet that consists of various meat dishes, including one of venison and one of *mithun*.

I enter into conversation with an old Naga gentleman standing next to me. He is tall and of martial bearing—as many Angamis are. "You must go to Tuensang," the old gentleman says. "In some parts of Tuensang there are still Nagas going naked. And why not? When you chase an animal through a thicket, clothes only get in the way. Anyhow, in some parts of Tuensang, near the Burmese border, a family of eight may still have only two pieces of cloth; when the father of the family goes out, he will take one piece of cloth. But in Tuensang headhunting is mostly gone."

From a room across a corridor come the drowsy voices of the children: "Now I lay me down to sleep . . ."

"The last reported raid was in 1965," the old gentleman continues. "That time, because of some misunderstanding, one village went on a raid and took the heads of some people in another village. But, as we Naga Christians say, anything that grows out of violence can never really be considered a victory. When you accept Christ, you accept not a religion but a person, a living Christ. When the first missionary brought Christ to my part of Nagaland, it is said, the villagers threw spears and javelins at him. A javelin hit him and tore his shoe off. The rest of the javelins and all the spears fell by the wayside. The missionary collected the spears and javelins, and, with a smile, handed them to the villagers, saying, 'Take them. These can't harm me.' Christianity was the beginning of civilization in Naga-land."

I make some remark about the kind hospitality here, and the old Naga gentleman tells me about another Indian who was impressed by Naga hospitality. He was an officer in the Indian government, and he went to a festival in a village near Kohima, where he had become friends with a Naga family. When he reached their house, he realized that he had forgotten to bring sweetmeats for the children of the household. The children clamored for sweetmeats, and he bundled eight or nine of them—some were neighbors' children—into his little jeep and set off to look for sweetmeats. He had to drive some distance before he found a sweet shop that was open. On the way back, part of the steering mechanism failed and the jeep began a plunge into what seemed like a bottomless gorge. Fortunately, the jeep was halted by a tree, and he and the children escaped with nothing more serious than bruises. But almost before he was able to get the children out of the jeep a mob set upon him and began beating him, calling him "murderer of Naga children." He was saved by an Indian military patrol that happened to be passing by. They escorted him back to the home of his Naga friend, and left. But soon the Indian officer was set upon all over again—this time by his Naga friend and a crowd of neighbors who had gathered at his house. Once again he was mauled, and once again he was just saved by the military patrol, which, luckily, was still in the village. "He had been writing to a friend in London about how nice the Nagas were to Indians," the old gentleman says. "Then, when he wrote about how he had been nearly killed by the Nagas, and how he was scarred all over, the friend wrote back, 'I thought you said the Nagas were nice.' He had no answer for his friend, and yet when he was offered a transfer from Nagaland he refused it. He should go. Nagas and Indians can never live together."

On subsequent days, I am treated to discourses by Indian and Naga officers on such subjects as how much support the Naga underground can count on from the Chinese if there is a resumption of Naga-Indian hostilities and whether Nagaland is an internal, Indian issue or an external, international issue. I listen to the Prime Minister of the Naga Federal Government ("If the Indian government doesn't recognize Nagaland to be a separate nation, we will fight. Every Naga. We don't care about the Indian Union. We care only about our Naga nation. We are not the Naga hostiles, we are the Nagas. The state government of Nagaland is a stooge of

the Indian government"), to the Chief Minister of Nagaland ("I say
to Naga hostiles, 'Now that you have got a state, why ask for trouble?
Let's have peace.' The majority of the Nagas are not with the Naga hostiles, but you don't need many for guerrilla warfare. I was ambushed six or
seven times by Naga hostiles. Once, I just escaped death"), to a leader of
the Naga Baptist Christian Convention, the association of all Naga
churches ("We don't want any part of heathen India. Nagaland is for
Christ. We are intellectually and spiritually a part of the West, not of
India at all"). I also listen to an Indian military leader who is a hard-liner
("I was here at the time we were asked to solve the problem of Nagaland.
We had started a program of regrouping all the people in Nagaland from
three thousand villages into two hundred villages with stockades around
them. We had told the people that anyone seen outside the stockades at
night would be shot. The women were happy because they had their husbands home in the evening, and the men were happy because we provided
them with work in the fields. In time, we would have made them happier
by converting the regrouped villages into modern villages with schools
and hospitals. For some months, they might have disliked living in regrouped villages, but then they would have got used to it. But just when
we were getting somewhere, our politicians stopped us. The military solution has never really had a fair trial in Nagaland"), to an Indian military
leader who is a soft-liner ("The Naga hostiles are always using Indian
military atrocities as propaganda. Some are imagined and some are real.
But how do these real military atrocities come about? Once, the guerrillas
not only killed some recruits but mutilated them in order to steal their
guns—the guns were chained to the recruits' bodies. The comrades of the
recruits couldn't trace the murderers, so they simply razed all the villages
where they thought the murderers might be hiding. If their superiors had
tried to prevent the retaliation, they would have had mutiny. But we
know now that the guerrillas can never be defeated, because the conditions
in all these tribal areas are such that the guerrillas can strike and vanish
and live in the jungles indefinitely. The tribal problem requires a political
solution"), to an Indian senior civil servant who is a pessimist ("Everything here is mad and impossible. Some of these Nagas are so Westernized
that they think we Indians are backward. Others are more backward than
any other savages in the world. If we had done certain things in Nagaland
—for instance, given the Nagas statehood in the Union in 1948, when they
first asked for it—maybe they would have accepted the idea of staying
with India, or enough of them would have done so to deprive the guerrillas of means of support. Our relations with the Nagas have always been a

story of our missing the bus"), to an Indian senior civil servant who is an optimist ("I know that from the outside this still looks like a boiling pot. But, perhaps because we are in the middle of it, we don't feel that it is a boiling pot. A general of the Army of the Naga Federal Republic who used to march forty-five miles a day in the jungle—he married a girl who used to be my office assistant; it was a love marriage, and now they lead a very bourgeois town life—recently came and asked me to help him to get a priority for a Fiat. I am responsible for giving priorities for cars. Well, when you get a guerrilla general coming and asking for a Fiat—and he's only one of many from the Naga Federal Government who are constantly asking me for cars and petrol—I think something has changed"), and, finally, to a visiting Indian politician ("Suppose we agree to give the Nagas independence. It might not be a great loss to us. You could cut off Nagaland from India without creating any geographical anomaly. But then what are you going to do about the Lushais, who, as it happens, look like Europeans? Maybe we could let them make a separate nation out of the Mizo Hills; this would mean only cutting off the tail of Assam. But then how are you going to stop other tribes—other regional and linguistic groups—from seceding? Ultimately, everything is going to depend on our ability to deal with the guerrillas in Nagaland and the Mizo Hills").

Mao Tse-tung once compared guerrillas to fish and the people who sup- port the guerrillas to water, and asked, "How can it be said that these two cannot exist together?" To find out how the people in Nagaland regard their fish, I go east, deep into the interior, across the scattered ridges and gorges. I am confounded by the number and diversity of the Naga tribes (there are fifty distinct tribes and sub-tribes), speaking tongues and dia- lects so numerous that they differ not only from village to village but almost from household to household—apparently because until recently inter-village feuds and the absence of land communication limited social contacts. According to the latest census, the Naga languages are, in the order of their official importance, Angami, Sema, Rengma, Khezha, Ao, Monsang (or Mongsen), Lotha, Tableng, Chang Naga, Kacha Naga, Kabui, Khoirao, Mao, Maram, Tangkhul, Maring, Konyak, Chakru, Meluri-Rengma, Poma, Nokpu, Lemei, Liangmei, Upama Naga, Urima Naga, Zemi Naga, Rongmei, Paomata, Shamnyuyangan, Tabu, Phelungre, Pochury, Sangtam, Orangkong, Phom, Tikhir, Yimchungre, Khiemnun- gam, Pangsha, Nocte, Wancho, Makware, Tangsa, Tikhak, Chakesang, and Zeliang. But I think there must be others, waiting to be discovered by the next set of census-takers. In fact, I feel as if I had been transported to the plain of Shinar just after the confounding of the language of all the earth. Everywhere I go, I find unalloyed tribal gaiety, which is sometimes shattered by a sudden act of violence or by an extraordinary display of sophistication, sometimes made bathetic by a remark of primitive naïveté. Even the most learned, Westernized Nagas remind me of those archetypal child prodigies who turn up at universities with their copies of "Phänomenologie des Geistes" and their air guns. Perhaps this is as it should be. After all, the majority of the population is pagan, with a primitive strain. The strength of this paganism is to be seen in a passage from Elwin's "Nagaland":

> The practice of head-hunting is found all over the world and has attracted great attention. . . . The Nagas say that originally they did not know how to make war but one day a bird dropped a berry from a tree, and a lizard and a red ant fought for it. Someone saw the ant cut off the lizard's head and thus men learnt to take heads. . . . The reasons for head-hunting are complicated and interesting. The practice is probably based on a belief in a soul-matter of a vital essence of great power which resides in the human head. By taking a head from another village, therefore, it was believed that a new injection of vital and creative energy would come to the aggressor's village when he brought the head home. This was valuable for human and animal fertility. It stimulated the crops to grow better, especially when the head was that of a woman with long hair. Moreover, the Nagas have always been a warlike race, and the warrior, especially the young warrior, who had taken a head held a great advantage over his fellows in attracting the most beautiful girl of his village for marriage. Indeed, it is said that a youth who had not taken a head found considerable difficulty in obtaining a wife at all. Head-hunting was something more than war. It inspired wonderful dances. It stimulated artistic production, for the most elaborate textiles could only be worn by a successful head-hunter or his relations. Small replicas of heads were carved to be worn almost like medals. Wooden pipes, with their bowls fashioned as heads, were made. Strong and vigorous human figures were carved and attached to baskets and the warrior's grave was the most splendid of all.

And yet a significant minority of the population is now Baptist, with a strong fundamentalist strain. The strength of this fundamentalism is to be seen in the following passage, also taken from Elwin's "Nagaland," which describes the kinds of demands that the missionaries made of their Naga converts:

> They insisted on a convert becoming a teetotaller; he had to restrict himself to one wife; at one time he was not even allowed to eat the flesh of the *mithun* since this animal was associated with sacrifices at "heathen" festivals.

The missionaries stopped the great Feasts of Merit. They forbade boys to attend the Morungs (men's domitories). They often stopped dancing, and even the art of weaving suffered since generally the convert adopted European mill-made dress.

Thus, elaborate hand-woven Naga textiles and plain machine-woven European cloth have been sewn together in a slapdash manner, and so far the result appears to be nothing more than patchwork. Take this discussion of Naga Christianity in an up-to-date history produced by the Naga underground:

The blessings which Christianity brought to the Nagas are not altogether unmixed, although this is not the fault of Christianity as such but of the people themselves. . . . It cannot be gainsaid that in many cases conversion into Christianity only brings into the life of a man a break with the past coupled with the development of a taste for everything Western with no change of the heart. Many a Christian gets the notion that after becoming a Christian he should disdain the singing of the native song and such other things. J. P. Mills said of the Naga Christians, "They take themselves very seriously and are apt to go about with long faces." This is a sweeping generalization and may rather be the vision of a prejudiced eye. True, the Christians take their faith seriously and do not go about in indecent hilarious, drunken spears [*sic*]. . . . However, every person has his little prejudices, and indeed opinions widely differ on this question. Visiting missionaries claim that the faces of those "who walk with the inner light" are easily distinguishable from those of others. But there are some things to be said against the Christians. The communal life of the Nagas is a very happy one. There are many communal utility services, but owing to their obvious association with the pagan faith the Christians tend to dissociate themselves from taking part in such activities of communal life. Christianity is not a religion of faith, and where it does not involve a compromise with their faith or moral code it is not easily understandable why they should not join in the native dances and community sing-songs in real national spirit and also serve to improve communal life.

The trouble is, the Naga underground must prove that the confusion that is Nagaland, of which the Naga Christian confusion is only a part, constitutes the separate nation it wants, and the Indian government must prove that the Naga confusion is Indian confusion in order to preserve the Indian Union.

One source of confusion, which worries the Naga underground and the Indian government, the state governments of Nagaland and Assam, and the local government of Manipur (Manipur consists of a series of hill ranges lying between Nagaland and the Mizo Hills district and is, like NEFA, a Union territory), is Gaidilu, the queen of a Zeliang-speaking Naga tribal group called Zeliangs, who at the latest count numbered 9,460. Also according to that count, 5,250 Zeliangs live in the hills of southern Nagaland and 4,210 in the hills of eastern Assam and northern Manipur. For some years, all the governments concerned have been struggling with what they have come to consider an intractable problem, which is that Gaidilu has irrevocably made up her mind that her Zeliang-speaking tribal group must have a separate polity, made up of the Zeliang-speaking parts of Nagaland, Assam, and Manipur; that though this polity must be separate, it must also be firmly within the Indian Union; and that this Union polity must be called Zeliang Rong (*"rong"* is Zeliang for "district"). The Naga underground maintains that Gaidilu's proposed polity is a Naga splinter movement, which, if the Indian government should have a chance to exploit it, would infect the Naga national movement with factionalism, setting Naga against Naga and breaking up the Naga homeland. The governments of Nagaland, Assam, and Manipur maintain that if they are partitioned in order to create Gaidilu's polity, they will not be able to control other centrifugal forces, with which they are also contending. The Indian government maintains that if Gaidilu's proposed polity should be allowed to take hold in India, the effect would be the same as if the Indian government yielded to the Naga underground's demand for Naga independence: India would soon be pockmarked with hundreds or thousands of separate states, kingdoms, and fiefdoms.

Gaidilu, who was born sometime before the First World War (no one seems to be certain of the date) in the village of Langklao, in Manipur, first came to public notice during the early thirties, when the British authorities apprehended and hanged her brother Jadunam for leading a Zeliang uprising against the British Empire, whereupon Gaidilu took over the leadership of the Zeliangs. Soon afterward, the British, claiming that Gaidilu was the priestess of a heinous cult that worshipped the Devil, practiced human sacrifice, and held blood feasts, put her in prison, where she remained until Independence. From the moment of her arrest, however, the Indians fighting for independence had regarded her as a queen, and she therefore passed into the folklore of the struggle for Indian freedom as Rani Gaidilu. Since her release, she has lived mostly in the hills and jungles of the Zeliang country. Recently, she made a visit to the outside world —an infrequent occurrence—during which she met Mrs. Gandhi in New Delhi and held talks with her on the question of Zeliang Rong. Around this time, the leaders of the Naga underground were making one of *their* infrequent visits outside Nagaland to meet Mrs. Gandhi in New Delhi and hold talks on the question of Naga independence. The leaders of the Naga underground considered their talks with the Indian Prime Minister to be talks between two sovereign powers, and Mrs. Gandhi's talks with Rani Gaidilu to be talks between India and a malcontent subversive of the Naga nation—or, at least, so they told me, pointing to the timing of the Naga-Indian talks and the Zeliang-Indian talks and calling it a typical imperialist plot of the Indian government to debase the Naga question to the level of the Zeliang question.

Rani Gaidilu is in Kohima while I am here, and, to hear her views on the Naga nation and Zeliang Rong, I seek her out in the house where she is staying. There, in a stark little room, are a number of people, all in elaborate tribal costumes and arranged as if for a group photograph. A woman sits in the foreground on a low stool, and directly behind the stool stands a girl in her teens. Flanking the stool are half a dozen men, two of them elderly, the rest quite young. The woman wears two elaborate multicolored shawls, which are heavily bordered and fringed with beads and shells. One shawl—much the larger of the two—is wrapped around her hips; the other is thrown around her shoulders. Under the shawls she wears a man's shirt, which is loose and frayed. Her hands are folded in her lap, and on each wrist is a man's stainless-steel wristwatch. She is plumpish and appears to be advanced in years, but she sits proudly upright. Something of the weary sweetness in her expression is reflected in the face of the girl behind her, who might be the woman as a girl. There are no introductions, but clearly the woman is Rani Gaidilu.

I ask the Rani, in Hindi, how she regards the Naga-underground talks being held in New Delhi.

The men flanking her stiffen perceptibly. They talk among themselves, in a language I take to be Zeliang. They talk for some time, and, having nothing else to do, I find myself listening to their speech as if I were a linguist. I conclude that Zeliang must be a very difficult language for an outsider to master. In Zeliang, as in other languages I have heard in NEFA and Nagaland, all vowels seem to be indistinct and all liquid sounds aspirated. The language is tonal, and it seems to specialize in glottal stops. From an occasional Hindi or English word I gather that all the men hold the rank of general.

The youngest-looking general presently says to me, rather self-consciously, in halting English, "She come Kohima dentist get new teeth, but you repeating question—" He stops.

I repeat my question, this time in English. There is another conference among the generals, and then the one I take to be the senior speaks to the Rani.

The Rani raises a hand and peremptorily motions toward her back. The girl immediately rearranges the shawl and, putting her hands under the collar of the shirt, begins vigorously massaging the Rani's shoulders. The Rani starts speaking in a slow stream of clenched bilabials. When she has finished, a third general interprets for me, in Hindi: "The Rani party and the Naga Federal party should try for a bright future for Nagaland. But the Rani party does not know about the views of the Naga Federal party. It is not true that there is fighting between the Rani party and the Naga Federal party. Some people who do not like the Rani party views say that the Naga Federal party and the Rani party quarrel. This is not true. But why should Nagas want to be separate from Mother India, as we are all brothers and sisters? Nagaland will remain with India forever."

The Rani raises her hand again and motions toward the small of her back. The girl kneels, pulls out the Rani's shirttail, and begins vigorously massaging the small of the Rani's back. The Rani speaks again, and the third general interprets again: "People say all sorts of things. Some people who do not like the Rani party say that Rani Gaidilu did some terrible things to nine Nagas last year with *jadu* [magic]. If she could use *jadu*, would she go all the way to New Delhi and ask Mrs. Gandhi for Zeliang Rong? If she knew *jadu*, would she come all the way to Kohima for new teeth? Zeliangs do not follow the Rani because she has *jadu*. They follow her because of her big fight for Zeliang welfare and Zeliang uplift."

The details of the Rani's life are obscure, and I ask the Rani a couple of questions about them.

More conferences, and then I am given this single answer: "Ever since the Rani was born, she has been working for the Zeliangs. The Rani had no school education, but learned everything from her Zeliang elders. Her whole life, the Rani has fought for the Zeliangs. Zeliang Rong will come about."

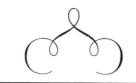

The McMahon Line

BACK IN NEFA, A GOVERNMENT OFFICER TELLS ME, "Though here in NEFA we don't have any Naga-type guerrillas to contend with yet, we do have the Chinese." The greatest concentration of Chinese soldiers in NEFA is probably at the head of the Tawang tract, and to get an idea of the Indian preparations for the defense of the tract I make a journey through it. My journey takes me from the leech-infested swamps of Tezpur all the way up to Tawang, one of the last Indian administrative outposts below the McMahon Line. For three days, as weather and daylight permit, my jeep jolts and bounces up the road, winding ahead like an interminable spiral. As the jeep negotiates one vertiginous hairpin curve after another, the wheels seem to spin off the edge of the road, which in some sections is nothing more than a broadened mule trail. The road is so high up that planes flying past sometimes seem level with it.

A neat, well-appointed bungalow stands at the foot of an enormous kitchen garden. It is the residence of the military commander responsible for the defense of NEFA and the road. He has a solitary air about him; in far-flung posts, top Army officers, barred by their rank from the camaraderie of the junior officers, seem more aloof than ever. Over tea, the commander solicits my opinion of his garden-grown lettuce, cucumbers, and tomatoes in the sandwiches we are eating. When I express wonder at the crispness and succulence of the vegetables, he expands with pride, and his reserve gives way to what proves to be a natural gregariousness.

I ask him if his officers and men encounter any special problems here.

"The main complaint of the recruits—the *jawans*—is absence-of-women sickness," he says. "We have to keep the *jawans* under the tightest possible discipline, because the tribal women are very free in their ways, and if our *jawans* were allowed to indulge themselves it could embitter our relations with the tribesmen. We caught a couple of Sikhs womanizing once, and we gave it to them in the neck. We said to them that they had to take the ruddy consequences. We make sure, however, that all *jawans* in NEFA get two months' leave a year, and they can also get ten to fifteen days' casual leave. We officers have family-separation sickness. My daughter once asked me, when I was posted in Delhi, 'Where are we going to be transferred next?' I said, 'My dear, you're going to stay put. I'm the one who's going to be transferred.' The officers' wives are always saying to me, 'What good is it having my husband in my old age? I want him in my youth!' I always reply, 'But can you find better husbands than our officers?'"

I ask him about the measures that have been taken to bolster India's defenses here.

"In 1962, such troops as we had in NEFA were scattered in penny packets," he says. "Now, provided the Chinese stick to conventional arms, we have sufficient troops—for security reasons, I can't tell you how many—to beat the socks off them. The big question now is whether they will give us the opportunity. In the evening, I read as many Chinese history books as I can. I read until my eyes give out, which means two pegs of whiskey and ten o'clock."

At one of many traffic checkpoints, a military guard is inspecting a jeep ahead of ours. My driver waits, his permit in hand ("Willys jeep conveying Mr. Mehta will be permitted to go against convoy timings . . . while proceeding to Tawang and on the return journey"). The guard walks back to our jeep, barely glances at the permit, and says, "I see you have my good friend for your driver. He's excellent. Just now you need good drivers for this road. It is terrorized by a rogue elephant."

"There was this very foolish driver, Sahib," my driver says, shifting gears and pulling out of the post. "The sahib and he were driving in the evening. It was getting dark when they saw this rogue elephant. This foolish driver thought he could frighten the elephant away by blowing the horn. The sahib shouted at the foolish driver, 'Put on your lights! Put on your lights!' By the time the foolish driver got around to putting on his lights, the elephant was too close for them to do any good. He was so close that if he had reared up he could have come down on the jeep and crushed the sahib. Thank Ram, the foolish driver finally had enough sense to put the jeep in reverse. When the headlights finally shone in the eyes of the elephant, the sahib told me that the elephant did an about-face and leaped away at at least forty miles an hour. The sahib told me he'd never seen an elephant run like that before."

In a roadside hut, a woman is serving tea to an officer in the uniform of a *havildar*. "My husband has gone for training in the militia," she tells him. "He will be gone fifteen days. Even when he's here, he's working all the time on the construction of the road. He's paid three rupees a day. The work is all out in the cold."

"I get chilblains all the time, and I'm in a vehicle most of the day," the *havildar* says.

At the rest bungalow in Bomdila, where I spend a night, the only other guests are an elderly Indian couple—a police bigwig from a tribal area and his wife. They sit in the yard, surrounded by huge supplies of tinned foodstuffs, and tell me about jungles and *shikars* in NEFA. "All the jungles here are alive with leeches," the police officer says. "I am very good game for them. The other day, I was on a *shikar,* and when I came out of the jungle, in spite of all the precautions I had taken against the leeches, thirty of them the size of your thumb were hanging from my leg and I was bleeding like a goat. My tracker, whom I had left behind to follow the *shikar,* took one look at my leg and fainted. And he was from the area!"

"What did you do about the leeches?" I ask.

"I pulled them off," he replies. "They just want blood, that's all. You can get an infection if the leech comes from an animal with a festering wound, but my leeches so far have always been clean. Did you come across any rogue elephants on the way?"

"No. The only elephants on the road were tame ones, and were being used for road construction," I say.

"There are at least four rogue elephants roaming the road now, and I'm going to get them all," he says. "Elephant is my favorite *shikar.*"

"Is it difficult to hunt down an elephant?"

"Not really. Elephants have good hearing but very bad eyesight. So you stay quiet when the elephant is still and move when the elephant moves. The spot to aim at is near the ear. I always take a couple of trackers with me, but I'm the only one with a gun."

"What do you do with an elephant once you've killed it?"

"I take the tusks and the feet and leave the rest, but in some of these tribal areas the carcass isn't there more than half an hour. Before I've even collected my trophies, every man, woman, and child will be hacking away at the meat. The other day, I killed a sleeping elephant that was half buried in mud. It was gone within an hour. Elephant meat is as tough as a tire, but the people in these parts think it the greatest delicacy. Of course, they smoke the meat for months before they eat it."

A few miles up from Bomdila, I have lunch at a road-construction camp, where my host is an engineer with the rank of colonel. He expatiates on the virtues of his organization, which is paramilitary, and which has the task of building the border roads. "What the Public Works Department, with its bureaucratic procedures, would take six months to do we can do in a week, because we have military discipline," he tells me. "The Army may do the blasting for our roads, but it's our job to widen them and blacktop them and maintain them. In many of these border areas, we have only single-road systems, and one landslide can cut off our troops in the forward areas. Landslides are so common on this particular road that everyone who works or travels on it risks his life. I hope you get through to Tawang. There's blasting going on ahead. I've known people to take two or three weeks to get to Tawang from Bomdila, and that's a distance of only a hundred miles."

Up ahead, where the blasting echoes like cannon fire, the driver pulls up at an Army encampment. He indicates a wind-swept tent flapping and swaying on its pegs, and says, "That's the junior officers' mess of the unit. Sahib can wait in there in comfort until the blasting is over." Inside, a young man with a flushed face, who looks no more than fifteen, tells me, straining to be heard over the tumult, "I am only the doctor of the unit, and I have a temperature of a hundred and one, but I have been left in charge here. All the other officers are up the road supervising the blasting. We've been given orders to surface a long stretch of the road so it can take seven-tonners. Our orders are to do it in ten days. It's a task and we have to do it. We have to work day and night to do it."

We drive on. It is getting dark, and the road is fast disappearing under billows of fog. A group of high-ranking officers who are camped down in a muddy, slushy ravine have a vacant bunk and give me shelter for the night. They wine and dine me in their mess as if I had crossed the seven seas just to call on them. Throughout the dinner, as an added courtesy to me, they talk about writing—primarily about the merits of one particular book, in honor of which they have named their camp. The camp is called Shangri La.

Next morning, the driver maneuvers to pass a convoy loaded with wooden planks, and the left back wheel of our jeep spins off the edge of the road, tilting us over a several-thousand-foot drop. We sit paralyzed for an instant, and then shift our weight away from the drop, as if we had the power to rock the jeep back onto the road. People from the convoy rush over to our jeep and seize it. The driver and I ease ourselves out. Everyone helps to heave our jeep back onto the road. After much turning and moving backward and forward by the convoy vehicles, our jeep is finally climbing the road again.

Se La has a lake with a snow-covered ridge on either side. The driver refuses to budge until I have put a stone on a cairn to placate the evil spirits of the pass.

At a village called Jang, a goatherd alternately attends to his goats and sees to the brewing of tea, which he serves me with ginger biscuits.

The Tawang Monastery, which used to be a daughter house of Drebung, one of the great monasteries of Lhasa, is more than three hundred and fifty years old, and remains one of the leading Buddhist centers in Asia. Built on a hillside, it looks from the outside like a fortress, and from the inside, because of its narrow streets and low buildings, it has the atmosphere of a little medieval European town. For a guide to the monastery I have a lama, who unceasingly murmurs the *mantra "Om Mani Padme Hum"* ("O God, Jewel in the Lotus Flower"). He belongs to the local tribe of Monpas, who are known for a gentleness verging on docility. Certainly he is placid. He conducts me upstairs and downstairs. First, we go through the monastery's school. This is a little room serving both as a dormitory and as a classroom. Nine boy lamas are reciting something in high, piercing voices for three adult lamas. It seems that the boy lamas have a set routine of prayer and recitation from four o'clock in the morning, when they wake up, until nine in the evening, when they go to sleep, and that ear-pulling, knuckle-rapping, and thrashing are integral parts of the routine. Next, I am shown the library, a room containing hundreds of long, narrow volumes with thick wooden boards for covers. Many of the books are carefully swaddled in cloth. On the floor there are mattresses and squat lecternlike tables for reading. Then I go through a temple, a large room dominated by a towering figure of Buddha; throwing a scarf full of rice up at him is said to bring blessings. Finally, my guide presents me to the abbot, who sits in a room among likenesses of Buddha during different stages of his life. The abbot gives me a cup of salted and buttered tea, and while I am slowly swallowing it he downs about a dozen cups. He tells me about the old days when the Tawang Monastery was a government unto itself, levying and collecting taxes; about the Dalai Lama, who rested there during his flight in 1959; and about the fall of Tawang to Chinese troops in 1962, concluding, "Most of

the lamas fled, but a few of the older ones stayed back and were treated
with respect by the Chinese, who lavished presents on them. The Chinese
are very good for the first year or two. They were so in Tibet, too, but
after that they become very difficult. The Indians are now here, and next
time they will be able to defend us."

At Tawang (and at other military posts in the interior), military officers
tell me they are convinced that India should fight for NEFA, even if it
means directing the whole Indian economy toward guns instead of *ghi*
and sacrificing all hope of economic progress. They are convinced that
India should fight for NEFA even if it means risking the lasting enmity of
China, which, acting with the other enemy, Pakistan, might one day destroy India in a multiple-front war. They insist that NEFA belongs to India, and that even if India's claims were not valid it would make little difference, since, just as in the case of Ladakh, no country ever voluntarily
cedes territory.

The Indian case for the existing Indo-Tibetan boundary, as Nehru and
his Ministers developed it, was that the natural northern boundary of
India was the Himalayan watershed; that this natural boundary had been
accepted by tradition for at least twelve centuries; that part of it, the Mc-
Mahon Line, had been formally accepted by China and Tibet in the Simla
Conference of 1913–14, as a result of the diplomatic efforts of Sir Henry
McMahon; and that NEFA lay on the Indian side of the McMahon Line.
But according to the recent researches of Alastair Lamb, a Cambridge-
trained historian who is a Senior Fellow of the Institute of Advanced
Studies of the Australian National University, India's case for her presence
in NEFA leaves much to be desired. In a brilliantly researched but rather
controversial two-volume work entitled "The McMahon Line: A Study
in the Relations Between India, China and Tibet, 1904 to 1914," he writes:

> Since the deterioration in Sino-Indian relations in the 1950's, Indian offi-
> cials have maintained that the McMahon Line notes [exchanged by McMahon
> and the Lönchen Shatra, the Tibetan delegate at the Simla Conference]
> merely "formalized the natural, traditional, ethnic and administrative bound-
> ary in the area." The tribal tracts in the Assam Himalayas, it has been stated,
> were already under Indian administration in the eighth century A.D. . . .
> and have been continuously so from that date to the present time. . . . Un-
> fortunately, it cannot be said that this picture of the administrative history
> of the Assam Himalayas, however much it might suit the demands of modern
> Indian diplomacy, is a true one. . . . The McMahon Line . . . was not an
> ancient Indian border. It was a new frontier alignment. . . . [In reality,

Lamb argues, the internationally accepted Indo-Tibetan boundary at the time ran along the foothills of the Assam Himalayas.] It was not based on traditions of great age. . . .

The obvious principle upon which to base the new frontier alignment was, as many Indian observers have pointed out during the course of the Sino-Indian dispute, the watershed between rivers flowing into Assam and those flowing into Tibet. Unfortunately, the Assam Himalayas do not lend themselves particularly well to a uniform application of the watershed concept of boundary making. The range is cut through by the Tsangpo-Brahmaputra, one of the great rivers of Asia flowing through thousands of miles of undoubted Tibetan territory from its source not far from the sources of the Indus. The true watershed between the Indian plains and Central Asia would lie north of the Tsangpo and its tributaries; and a boundary following this line would include Lhasa, Shigatse and Gyantse and most of the towns of Central Tibet within India. . . . It was clear, therefore, that, unless the new boundary was going to result in the British annexation of a great deal of Tibet, it would have to run across at least six major rivers. The McMahon Line, the final form of this boundary, therefore, did not, in fact, follow the main India-Central Asia watershed. Rather, it was drawn along a series of watersheds between the valleys of the major rivers which had their sources to the north of the line of the highest peaks of the Himalayan range.

There can be no doubt that McMahon was being less than straightforward in his scheme for obtaining Chinese approval for his Line. Had the Chinese actually signed the Convention, they would certainly have found it hard to deny some degree of validity to the definition of the Indo-Tibetan boundary in the Assam Himalayas. However, the Chinese did not sign, and by 1929, when the Anglo-Tibetan notes of 24/25 March [the reference is to that exchange between McMahon and the Lönchen Shatra] were first published—if not much earlier—they surely perceived that they had been the intended victims of a British trick, which would go far to explain the Chinese loathing for the "illegal" McMahon Line.

Lamb acknowledges that the Chinese delegate at Simla initialled the Convention, but he does not attach any legal importance to this act. Even if the Indians reject Lamb's conclusions—and they do—recent researches have cast India's claims, at least to some parts of NEFA, into the limbo of doubt. Certainly some of the agents of the Indian presence in NEFA feel at times that they are living in limbo. I recall an evening at the house of the Deputy Commissioner of Tawang. He had all the government officers in Tawang seated around a couple of card tables in his parlor, which was heated by a large stove called a *bukhari*. They were playing bridge and drinking rum toddies. At a point when the D.C., a tall, handsome Kashmiri, was the dummy, he sat back and said to me, "I want to go on leave next month, because my niece is getting married, but I have no idea whether my leave will be sanctioned. We would all like to get down to the plains once in a while to have a good bath and eat some green vegetables and fresh fruit. But we civilian officers can't be spared, and it's very diffi-cult to get leave. Some of us have been stuck up here for three or four years. If the Chinese make any trouble again, we may be stuck here for-ever. In 1962, the officers packed up and left. Now our orders are to stay here and fight, regardless. But life in Tawang is not all bad. Take me. I have a rent allowance, a cost-of-living allowance, a hardship allowance. I have a six-room house with three servants. This style of living would cost a good deal in Delhi." He added, with a smile, "Of course, I live in only one room of the house, because one can hardly think of bringing one's wife and children up here, but at least one has the consolation of knowing the rooms are there."

"Life is terrible up at Bum La, though," his partner said, taking a trick. "I was posted in Bum La for a year. It's two days' ordinary march up from here or one day's tough march. It was so cold up there that none of us could look out of our tents—we couldn't even get out of our sleeping bags. Yet our job was to spy on the Chinese, and that meant patrolling a frontier that was two thousand feet higher still. Once, I did venture out of my tent and carry out the patrol. I saw a couple of Chinese, and I informed them that they weren't supposed to be there. They said, 'Who are you? Go away.'"

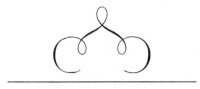

Bhutan

To OUTSIDERS, UNTIL RECENTLY, the Kingdom of Bhutan, which has a population of about seven hundred thousand and an area of about eighteen thousand square miles, was little more than a mysterious rectangle on the map in the Assam Himalayas, between NEFA and Sikkim. Bhutan, which the Bhutanese call Drukyul ("land of the thunder dragon"), was autonomous and had a closed-door policy, and in historical times no more than a score of Europeans had managed to enter it. Moreover, it had no towns, no post offices, no shops, and no law courts or other instruments of public administration. Its government was feudal and autocratic, and its economy was based on serfdom and barter. A well-known article on Bhutan, written for the Encyclopaedia Britannica around 1900 by the Superintendent of Frontier Surveys of India, Sir Thomas Hungerford Holdich, noted:

Subordinate officers and rapacious governors of forts wield all the power of the state, and tyranny, oppression, and anarchy reign over the whole country. The Dharm raja [the spiritual ruler] succeeds as an incarnation of the deity. On the death of a Dharm raja a year or two elapses, and the new incarnation then reappears in the shape of a child who generally happens to be born in the family of a principal officer. The child establishes his identity by recognizing the cooking utensils, &c., of the late Dharm raja; he is then trained in a monastery, and on attaining his majority is recognized as raja, though he exercises no more real authority in his majority than he did in his infancy. The Deb raja [the temporal ruler] . . . in practice . . . is merely the nominee of whichever of the two governors of East and West Bhutan happens for the time to be the more powerful. . . . The people are oppressed and poor. "Nothing that a Bhutia [Bhutanese] possesses is his own," wrote the British envoy in 1864: "he is at all times liable to lose it if it attracts the cupidity of any one more powerful than himself. . . . There never was, I fancy, a country in which the doctrine of 'might is right' formed more completely the whole and sole law and custom of the land than it does in Bhutan."

In 1907, however, the reigning Dharm raja having died and the reigning Deb raja retired to a life of contemplation, political and ecclesiastical forces chose the strongest feudal lord, Ugyen Wangchuk, as hereditary maharaja —the first man to be so named in Bhutan. Nonetheless, for a time the effective government continued to reside, as it had for centuries, with numerous feudal lords, each of whom maintained order and wielded the power of life and death over the people living in the vicinity of his *dzong,* or fortress. Today, although the *dzongs* are still the centers of administration, the present heir of Ugyen Wangchuk, Maharaja Jigme Dorji Wangchuk, who is in his late thirties, enjoys dominion over all of Bhutan. He has the nucleus of a government, with a Secretary-General, who looks after economic development, and a Chief Secretary, who looks after civil administration.

Bhutan has always been a stronghold of black magic, and to this day the practice of witchcraft is common everywhere. Bon, a form of shamanism, is the main religion, though the Bhutanese do observe Buddhism or Hinduism to some degree. The benefits of technology—white magic, in a manner of speaking—first became known in Bhutan in the late fifties, when, with the help of the Indian government, Bhutan cleared a space in the forest and established a new township named Phuntsholing ("beginning of everything") in the foothills on the Indo-Bhutanese border, just inside the Bhutan Gate. (There actually is a gate—a high wooden one.) Soon afterward, again with the help of the Indian government (between 1960 and 1966 India gave Bhutan technical and financial assistance to the amount of a hundred and twenty million rupees, or sixteen million dollars), work was begun on the first road. For this project, and for others like it, every man and woman in Bhutan was required to work for one month out of every year on construction, under a system of more or less forced labor. That first road, which today can be traversed by jeep, goes up from Phuntsholing to Thimbu, the capital under construction, and to Paro, the interim capital.

About three miles up from Phuntsholing on the Thimbu-Paro road is the new Don Bosco Technical School. I first learned about the school while it was still in the planning stage, from "New Frontier for Christianity at the Top of the World," a pamphlet distributed in the United States by the Salesian Society of the Catholic Church. After noting that the Bhutanese government had donated forty acres of land, and that boys over the age of twelve would receive instruction at the school in reading, writing, and arithmetic, and also in the elements of carpentry, mechanics, and agriculture, the pamphlet stated, "With God's help . . . school buildings will rise in Bhutan. . . . The first Catholic church will be built and the work of spreading the Faith will begin." The reader was invited to "adopt" a Bhutanese boy, and a picture of a smiling boy was reproduced, with the caption "Just $5.00 will support a boy for one full month. Just $60.00 will support a boy for one full year." The text explained, "If you wish to adopt a Bhutanese boy, his photograph, name, and all particulars will be sent to you. In addition, you will receive letters from your adopted son translated from Bhutanese and, later, in English as he learns the language." The reader was also invited to dedicate a building or buy equipment, with the list of needs and costs going like this:

8 CLASSROOMS:	$250 ea. to dedicate
Desks for two (100)	$150 each set
Crucifixes (8)	$200 each
Blackboards (8)	$100 each
2 DORMITORIES:	$500 ea. to dedicate
Beds (200)	$100
Chairs (200)	$100
Crucifixes (2)	$400
1 DINING ROOM:	$500 to dedicate
Tables (21)	$120
Benches (42)	$100
LIBRARY	$400 to dedicate
STUDY HALL	$400 to dedicate
GYMNASIUM	$400 to dedicate
ROOMS FOR FATHERS AND BROTHERS (8)	$400 each
WORKSHOPS:	
Lathes (10)	$120 each
Vises (50)	$120 each
Planing Machine (1)	$250
CARPENTRY:	
Sets of tools (50)	$140 each set

I visit the Don Bosco Technical School, which stands a little off the road, in a large clearing, with heavily forested mountains in the background. So far, it consists only of four Quonset huts—the familiar long aluminum sheds with arched roofs and rows of vents for windows. The huts form a quadrangle. From one of them come the halting, languorous voices of boys reciting: "Don Bosco, Apostle of Youth, we beg you to intercede for all the youth of the world and especially for the youth of the mission to Bhutan, that they may be inspired by the ideals of Christian love, labor, and modesty, and thus obtain the grace to join you and Our Lady in Paradise." Pacing in front of another of the huts is a tall, lean, youngish man, who has blue eyes and blond hair and is dressed in a white cassock. He is the principal, the Reverend Philip Giraudo. After an exchange of greetings, he takes me into his office, a small room that contains no decoration, no books, no papers, no filing cases—only a couple of wooden chairs, a plain wooden table, and, on the table, a figurine of Christ with one hand pressed over His heart, the other raised in an attitude of benediction.

"Pick him up," Father Philip says.

I do. A thin, tinny sound issues from the figurine. It is music, played at an extremely slow tempo and a little off key. I recognize the melody —Schubert's "Ave Maria." Father Philip remains silent until the music has come to a halt. Then he takes the figurine and sets about winding it up.

"Are the boys encouraged to become Christians?" I ask.

"We don't try to convert any of the boys, but we will be very happy if any of them should decide to become Christians," Father Philip says.

I ask him about Don Bosco, for whom the school is named, and Father Philip tells me that he was an Italian saint—Giovanni Bosco, who was born in the Piedmont in 1815, just after the Battle of Waterloo, and grew up in the confusion of the industrial revolution. At the age of nine, he had the first of a series of prophetic dreams that determined the course of his life. In the dream he saw savage animals becoming gentle and unruly children becoming obedient. The dream decided his vocation for him: to work among poor boys as a priest and teacher. He did this work until his death, in 1880, founding in Turin the Oratory of St. Francis of Sales, a hostel for apprentices and schoolboys that in time became a trade school, and eventually establishing the Salesian Congregation—later Society— which spread to Spain and France, and sent its first mission to work among the Indians of Patagonia. At last count, the Society had twenty-five thousand priests working in seventy-five countries.

"I was the prefect of the Salesian school in Shillong," Father Philip says, setting the figurine down. Shillong lies a hundred and seventy-five miles southeast of Bhutan. "Some of the first Bhutanese children to be educated came to us there a few years ago. Because of those children, His Majesty Jigme Dorji Wangchuk invited us to open a school here. We have fine students. They're optimistic, and they have a lot of enthusiasm for anything new. Our motto is 'Learn and Produce.' "

An Indian priest looks in. Father Philip introduces him as the school bursar, the Reverend Thomas Arackal, from the state of Kerala. "He has written an article about the school," Father Philip says. "He can tell you all about it."

"Father Philip is a very good linguist," Father Thomas says. "He speaks Hindi, Assamese, Bengali, Nepalese, Garo, and, now, perfect Bhutanese."

"I'm just learning Bhutanese," Father Philip says.

"This is the only technical school in Bhutan, but it is probably also the best general school," Father Thomas goes on. "The boys come here on foot from all over the country. The journey can take days."

"They come here after attending primary schools, and they learn very quickly," Father Philip says.

"How long has the school been going?" I ask.

"Since May, 1965, but we already have sixty boys, ten of them Tibetan," Father Thomas says. "This place was all jungle, which was cut down for us by the Bhutan Engineering Service. And then these Quonset huts were put up. It is so different from Calcutta, where I was before. I have not had much time to travel in Bhutan—we've been so busy. I have never been to Thimbu or Paro, or anywhere, but then I like it here. The students are so good."

Father Thomas and Father Philip show me through the school— through the few classrooms, through the carpentry shop, and through the machine shop. As yet, there is no electricity in the school, and everything in the workshops is hand-driven and handmade, including the wrenches, the pliers, the hinges, and the nuts and bolts in the machine shop.

"We hope to add a motor-repair shop," Father Philip says. "It will take some time. You must remember that until a few years ago the Bhutanese had never seen a nail or a wheel."

Today, I am riding in a jeep up the Thimbu-Paro road. It runs along beside the turbulent Thimbu River, which flows out of Tibet and empties into the Brahmaputra. The river loops around the hills and mountains, and so does the road. The road, however, shoots up hundreds of feet and then drops down hundreds of feet, and it crisscrosses the river over an

endless series of insubstantial-looking bridges. Sometimes it snakes
through oppressive rain forests, where the hills are of loose mud and look
as if they might slide down and bury the road—as, indeed, they do during
heavy rains—and eventually it reaches the open, rocky plateaus of the
higher ranges. Along the way, swarms of laborers, many of them Nepalese
or Sikkimese migrant workers or Tibetan refugees, are clearing forests,
blasting mountainsides, and breaking and hauling stones. They occupy
roadside camps that are collections of little wooden shacks, thatched *bashas,* and canvas shelters.

Thimbu is in the river valley, whose slopes, scattered with stunted trees,
rise and dissolve into dark mountains, which, in turn, disappear in snow
and fog; it is dusk. My driver speaks only Bhutanese, and all I can gather
is that his name is Lengo. First, he drives to a sort of compound at the
head of the valley, where he stops and talks with a couple of sentries
posted at the gates. Then he drives into the compound and stops in front
of a small, elegant house, daintily carved, like a jewel box. The house is
shuttered, and Lengo drives on to a second, smaller house in the compound; this house is also shuttered. He then drives all around the
compound, stopping to talk with several sentries.

After that, Lengo drives out of the compound and down the valley to a
huge edifice with clay walls so high and thick that they might conceal a
city. He stops and gets out. I make a move to follow, but he indicates that
I should remain in the jeep. Lengo disappears through a gateway, and
soon returns, climbs into the jeep, and starts back toward the compound.
On the way, he stops in front of a big, solid-looking house, built of raw
pine and with a slanted roof, that resembles a Swiss chalet. The house is
on stilts and is entered by a tall ladder. Lengo goes up the ladder and into
the house. After some time, he comes down and indicates that I should go
up. I do. The door at the top of the ladder is open. It is a planklike affair
ingeniously hung on wooden swivels, with a high wooden slat for a door-
sill. I put one foot over the sill and into the house. As I do so, I barely clear
a wooden beam that suddenly looms overhead. A powerfully built man
with an enormous head is standing just inside, and he grips my hand. We
are in a large room, the walls of which are covered with coarse, heavy
cloth painted with flower designs in bright primary colors. About the
room are squat divans, and these are covered with lush carpets, also in
bright primary colors. In the middle of the room there is a stove with a fire
in it, and around this are gathered several men and one young girl. All of
them are stocky, have broad faces with high cheekbones and almond-
shaped eyes, and resemble many of the other Indo-Mongoloid people who

live in the Himalayas. The girl can speak a little English. She says she will interpret.

I ask many questions, about Thimbu and the Maharaja, about the government, and about the people, but I don't get coherent answers. Although the girl speaks English with a charming accent, which, surprisingly, is reminiscent of Charles Boyer's, her knowledge of the language is so fragmentary and unidiomatic that it is hard to get even the drift of her remarks. Eventually, though, I gather that I am in the house of the Chief Secretary and that he is the man who received me at the door.

I ask the Chief Secretary if it will be possible for me to meet the Maharaja.

As best I can make out, the answer is that the Maharaja is camping somewhere near Punakha, and Punakha is a long march from Thimbu. If I like, I can march there, but because of a recent snowfall the trails, never good, are especially bad. The Maharaja himself would have been very happy to march to see me in Thimbu, but he is not very well just now.

Before long, I reconcile myself to the fact that my impressions of Bhutan are bound to be sketchy.

Jewel box in compound is palace. Huge edifice is new *dzong*. When completed, will contain monastery offices with filing cabinets, bathrooms with plumbing, an eating place with waiters, and an electric lift.

Military unit parading in Thimbu with matchlock guns.

Paro. Another river valley. Beautiful. Improvement of agriculture and animal husbandry. Introduction of small-scale industries and modern medicine. (For all diseases, the Bhutanese seem to use the word *"dha,"* which actually means "gonorrhea.")

Houses made of mud blocks five feet thick. Ingenious system of joins.

Bakkhu, baggy robe with all-purpose pouch in front above waist.

Monastery. Butter lamps. Bodhisattvas—thirty-foot figures of unbaked clay. Last for years because of cold climate. Everywhere, in strong reds, yellows, and blues, painted demons, lucky symbols, Trees of Life, Heavens and Hells.

Ritualistic dances. Death's-heads. Masks of clay and wood depicting grim faces from nether worlds.

Royal family and a few members of government beginning to use wheels and nails—the new system of magic.

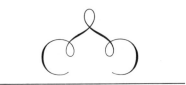

Sikkim

THE PROTECTORATE OF SIKKIM, which the Sikkimese also call Denjong ("land of rice"), which has a population of about a hundred and seventy thousand and an area of about twenty-six hundred square miles, and which is stuck between Bhutan and Nepal like a postage stamp, is my next port of call. I'm travelling in a jeep up a hill road—a thirty-five-mile-long zig-zag that goes past hamlets, forests, waterfalls, lakes, scrub, and moss-grown rock, and that rises from Gangtok, the capital of Sikkim, which is about six thousand feet above sea level, to the most strategically important pass of the entire Himalayan rampart, Natu La, fourteen thousand four hundred feet above sea level. The hill road is part of a road system—once an ancient caravan route for trade in tea, salt, incense, spices, and silks—that, starting in Lhasa and passing through the Chumbi Valley, over Natu La, and through Sikkim, descends to the Siliguri Gap; if the Siliguri Gap were ever to fall to the Chinese, Bhutan, NEFA, Assam, and Nagaland would be cut off from India. Natu La, where today Tibet ends and Sikkim begins, and where Indian and Chinese troops confront each other, is the point at which India hopes to stop any Chinese advance toward Siliguri. In the jeep with me, besides the driver, is a major from the Indian Army's public-relations office. He's a Punjabi with a matter-of-fact manner. "We must hurry back from Natu La," he is saying, in a flat voice. "It has been snowing at Natu La for nearly twenty days non-stop; the snow let up only yesterday, and fog is a routine feature on this road. It's as bright as any-thing now, but thick fog and darkness often cover this road by four in the afternoon. To navigate in that kind of pea soup you need a driver who knows every twist and turn by heart. Even then it takes two to navigate— one to look out the window, the other to drive. And just the other day I had to walk in front of my jeep for miles to guide the driver down the road."

Our driver is now repeatedly racing the motor, but the front wheels have disappeared into a huge snowdrift and our jeep is stuck. Fortunately, Natu La is only a thousand yards away. The major and I put on snow boots, take up walking sticks, and, leaving the driver to dig the jeep out, begin trekking up to the pass. Winds lash us and throw us back. With every step, we gasp for air. The drifts are so deep that our walking sticks are of little help.

"Routine features," the major remarks.

We trudge on, bracing each other. We come upon some *jawans* urging a train of mules laden with tins of kerosene up toward the pass. The mules can't budge for the snow, which is almost up to their flanks.

"You want to break their legs?" the major shouts.

The *jawans* turn around and salute. Then they set about hoisting the tins onto their own backs.

"It's a matter of honor with the officers to see that the best stuff is sent straight up to the *jawans* at Natu La," the major says as we gasp along. "It's a matter of honor to send up fresh rations each day as long as the road is open. The *jawans* get meat three times a week, and water and fuel for two baths a week. It's a routine feature to give the *jawans* holiday time in Gangtok, where they can get a haircut and go to the cinema."

Now an abandoned bulldozer with snow still heaped on the blade obstructs the path. Now there is a black rock face on one side, a black abyss on the other, and a formation of ravens overhead. Now all is white. We traverse a tortuous gully of snow and a ledge scarcely a foot wide. A couple of stones roll down the rock face and crash at our feet. More stones pitch down and come to rest in a bank of snow a little ahead, where they balance precariously, as if lying in wait for us to draw abreast. Heads down, we continue to pick our way, testing the snow underfoot with each step, even though we know that there is no protection against slick patches. Finally, a snowfield with high, jutting, jagged ridges in the background comes into view. It is Natu La. On the ridges to our right are bunkers, and a few *jawans* with guns and field glasses are standing on guard outside them. The ridges on the left and in front seem completely desolate. Suddenly, from behind a rock on the far left, a Chinese soldier bobs up. In one hand he holds a rifle with a bayonet, in the other a camera.

"We are in excellent firing range," the major says. "It's a routine feature. But wait a minute." The Chinese soldier tucks the rifle under his arm and raises the camera. "He's taking our picture for their intelligence service. Say 'Birdie.'"

I say "Cheese."

The Chinese soldier ducks out of sight.

"It's very frustrating for our *jawans* not to know when the enemy may start something," the major says. "Recently, the Chinese gave us an ultimatum—we must remove our fortifications here. But there were no fortifications—only some old piles of stones. They were probably left here by Tibetan travellers for good luck. I brought up a number of correspondents and showed them the stones."

"And the stones were removed?" I ask.

"Oh, eventually somebody removed them."

The Chinese soldier returns with half a dozen other soldiers. They all have rifles and field glasses, and they peer through the glasses alternately at us and at the *jawans*. The ridges, which are the shoulders of the pass, are so close that the Indians and the Chinese can see each other quite well with the naked eye; with field glasses, one imagines, they can see each other so well that the enemy forces must have the illusion of being within handshaking distance.

Indian troops are in Sikkim because of an Indo-Sikkimese treaty, signed in 1950, that gave India the responsibility for Sikkim's defense—along with the right, considered basic to defense, to construct and maintain communications—and also for Sikkim's external affairs. Actually, the 1950 treaty only extended the status of Sikkim as a protectorate of India, which had been defined in a treaty signed in 1890. This status presented negligible problems until 1963. In that year, Palden Thondup Namgyal, who at the time was the Crown Prince, married Hope Cooke, an American, and then, upon the death of his father, became the Maharaja of Sikkim. As a result of these two state events—which were reported in the press everywhere—certain differences between India and Sikkim crystallized. Some of these differences are ceremonial, like the form of address for the Maharaja and the Maharani; some are symbolic, like the elevation of the Maharaja's palace in Gangtok relative to the elevation of the nearby residency of the Political Officer, who is India's plenipotentiary for Sikkim and Bhutan; and some are substantive, like the provisions of the treaty.

Throughout the raj, the form of address for the maharajas of all the princely states—which enjoyed various degrees of autonomy, and included

Sikkim and Bhutan—was "Your Highness." When the princely states were merged into the Indian Union and the maharajas were divested of most of their powers and prerogatives, the Indian government granted all the maharajas the right to retain their old form of address. Sikkim and Bhutan, however, were not merged, partly because they were isolated up in the Himalayas, and partly because they were linked geographically, racially, and historically with Tibet and Nepal. When the relations between India and China soured, and Sikkim and Bhutan, among other regions of the Himalayas, were thrust into the forefront of the conflict, the Indian government, as one form of recognition of their new political importance, started addressing the Maharaja of Bhutan as "Your Majesty." Yet it continued to address the Maharaja of Sikkim as "Your Highness." From one point of view, the distinction amounted simply to a recognition of the real difference in the status of Bhutan and Sikkim—Bhutan all but sovereign, Sikkim an out-and-out protectorate. From another point of view, however, it seemed that the Maharaja of Sikkim, in being equated with the hundreds of titular maharajas, was being slighted. It is said that the present Maharaja of Sikkim would like to be on equal terms of address with the Maharaja of Bhutan, and that Hope Cooke's friends in the United States, who regard her as the first real American-born queen, would like to have her addressed as "Your Majesty." But the Indian government has had second thoughts about having granted this epithet—formerly reserved for the British Crown—to the Maharaja of Bhutan in the first place, and is reluctant to risk playing further havoc with the niceties of protocol by permitting its use in Sikkim. For the time being, the impasse has been circumvented: everyone calls Palden Thondup Namgyal "Your Highness" in his presence but refers to him in official discussions as (in addition to "the Maharaja" or "His Highness") "the Chogyal," which is Sikkimese for "the heavenly king," and thus describes the absolute secular and spiritual powers with which he is endowed in the eyes of his subjects; similarly, Hope Cooke is called "Your Highness" in her presence, and otherwise (in addition to "the Maharani" or "Her Highness") "the Gyalmo," which is Sikkimese for "the consort of deities."

Again, Gangtok, which is a modern hill station (unlike Bhutan, Sikkim has had an open-door policy for nearly a century), is strung across a ridge that connects two hills, and it happens that the palace stands on the lower hill and the residency on the higher one. This is thought to express symbolically the relationship existing between the maharaja of the protectorate and the plenipotentiary of the protector country, for the Political Officer, since the time of the first one, John Claude White, who was appointed to the office in 1888, has more or less called the tune for the reigning maharaja—or, sometimes, the maharani, if she happened to call the tune for her husband, as was the case with Thotab Namgyal, who was the Maharaja of Sikkim when White took up his duties there. How the Maharani ruled the Maharaja, and how White, as the plenipotentiary of his government, ruled the Maharani, comes across in this splendid passage from White's "Sikhim and Bhutan," the most famous book on the area. (In transliteration, there is likely to be considerable variation in the spelling of proper names; hence Sikkim or Sikhim.)

He [Thotab Namgyal] was entirely under the influence of the Maharani, his second wife.

This lady, the daughter of a Tibetan official in Lhasa, is a striking personality. Small and slight, beautifully dressed in brocades, velvets and silks, with much jewelry of rough turquoise, coral, and amber, her hair adorned with strings of seed pearls, which reached to the hem of her gown, and wearing the curious Tibetan head-dress adopted by the Maharanis of Sikhim, she was a most picturesque object, a harmony of gold and brilliant colours impossible to convey in words. . . .

She is extremely bright and intelligent and has been well educated, although she will not admit that she has knowledge of any language but Tibetan. She talks well on many subjects, which one would hardly have credited her with a knowledge of, and can write well. On the occasion of Queen Victoria's diamond jubilee, she personally composed and engrossed in beautiful Tibetan characters the address presented by the Sikhim Raj, which runs as follows:

"To the most exalted and beautiful white lotus throne of Empress Victoria —the incarnate—Sri Devi—the glorious Goddess—who has been ruling and conducting the affairs of the great Empire, being Victorious in every quarter of the globe by the dint of her accumulated virtues and merits.

THE MEMORIAL.

"Gracious Majesty,

"From the ocean of merits has sprung your glorious self, whose fame has spread all round the world like the rays of the sun. Your Majesty's reign in respect of Government, defence, of light, and in increase of prosperity has been perfect.

"It is our fervent prayer that Your Majesty's glorious reign may, with fame encompassing the world, extend to many happy years more.

"This humble vassal being extremely happy, with all his subjects, has been rejoicing at the Jubilee of Your Majesty's reign, and prays that Your Majesty shedding lustre of good, just and benign rule, shall sit on the throne for a hundred great periods of time.

"With a pure white silk scarf, to represent the sincerity of wishes."

Her disposition is a masterful one and her bearing always dignified. She has a great opinion of her own importance, and is the possessor of a sweet musical voice, into which she can, when angry, introduce a very sharp intonation. She is always interesting, whether to look at or to listen to, and had she been born within the sphere of European politics, she would most certainly have made her mark, for there is no doubt she is a born intriguer and diplomat. . . . Her common sense and clearsightedness were on many occasions of the greatest assistance to me in my task of administering and developing Sikhim, and when I laid various schemes before her she was quick to see the material advantages to be obtained and gave her support accordingly. . . .

Not long after I had taken up my new duties, Government decided that it would be to the advantage of the State to remove the Maharaja from Sikhim for a time, and Kurseong, in the Darjeeling district, was proposed as his residence. It was my unenviable task to have to convey these orders to Their Highnesses, and their reception of the news was most characteristic. The Maharaja remained silent, but the Maharani abused me roundly, called me every name she could think of, and losing her temper entirely, got up, stamped on the floor, and finally turned her back on me. . . .

With the departure of the Raja and Rani to their temporary quarters, the task of reorganising the country began in earnest.

In the present circumstances, however, any reminder that the Political Officer—now, of course, an Indian—holds the position of piper in Sikkim is presumed to be gall and wormwood to the occupant, or occupants, of the palace.

Even though Palden Thondup Namgyal, as Crown Prince, represented Sikkim in the negotiation of the 1950 treaty, he now takes exception to its external-affairs and communications provisions. And some of those American well-wishers of the Maharani would like to see Sikkim running its own external affairs, so that it could cut a figure, say, in the United Nations. Then, too, some Indian critics of their country's policy in Sikkim point to the anomaly of a democratic, anti-imperialistic India's having a little protectorate of her own. G. H. Jansen, writing in the *Statesman*, spoke for these critics when he said of the 1950 treaty, "The two countries are tied together in a hopelessly out-dated straitjacket. . . . This treaty is something of which India should be, if not ashamed, at least not very proud." He envisioned a new, ideal treaty, in which "defense would be happily left to India by Sikkim; communications, now that the main military roads have been built, could be handed over to Sikkim; external affairs could be shared, in the sense that Sikkim could be permitted, even encouraged, to take part in nonpolitical international conferences once it is understood, as it should be, that such attendance is not part of a progression towards independence," and he added, "New Delhi's doubts on this score are unfounded."

In a subsequent issue of the *Statesman*, Kazi Lhendup Dorji-Khangsarpa, who was identified as the president of a Sikkimese political party called the All Sikkim National Congress, was in print with a letter saying that a revision of the treaty was secondary, almost irrelevant, "in view of the all-important fact that Sikkim has no written constitution, that the people of Sikkim have no fundamental rights, no codified laws, a High Court without a Charter, and are ruled by 'proclamations.'" Dorji-Khangsarpa contended that in its organization Sikkim was a feudal state, administered entirely by landowners, monasteries, and the palace. And, indeed, he was supported in this view by one of those New Delhi doubters, who recently said to a visitor, "Jansen's optimism about a new treaty is a little giddy. At the time we signed it, most Sikkimese wanted to accede to the Union, merge with democratic India. Subjects of all princely states where Hindus were in the majority, as they are in Sikkim, were burning with the spirit of nationalism, and they all wanted to be Indians. But we quashed the democratic aspirations of the Sikkimese by signing a treaty, making an unholy alliance with the Chogyal, who is, after all, a relic of feudalism. That was a mistake. Now the only hope, the only permanent solution to Indo-Sikkimese relations, is a democratic Sikkim, and then there would be a point to having a new treaty."

Through bright-red-and-blue gates, ornately carved with dragons' heads, past bright Chinese-style sentry boxes, from which guards clad in bright-red felt jackets, striped kilts, and straw hats step out and salute, up a winding road affording a view of blue-green mountains with white caps, past an orchid garden, a pond, a bright multicolored chapel, up the steps and onto the veranda of a bright-yellow two-story house with a slanting red shingled roof, through a double door—and I arrive at the palace, where I've been invited to stay by the Chogyal and the Gyalmo, who show me down a hallway to my room. It is pleasantly furnished with an overstuffed raw-silk sofa and matching armchairs, a small antique English desk (a lady's desk), and a white llama-skin throw rug—presumably from the Andes—on the floor.

Suddenly, the Gyalmo swoops down and starts rolling up the rug. "Truly, truly, truly, we don't like people to step on this rug," she says, in a whispery, breathy voice.

"There is a rug like this in our bedroom, and Hope won't let me step on it with my shoes on," the Chogyal says.

"Yes, yes, yes," the Gyalmo whispers. "I have soapsies that are so pretty I won't let anyone use them. They are just kept out to be looked at."

"Here is a bell you can ring for the bearer," the Chogyal says. "If he doesn't come, just step outside the door and shout. I have three aides-de-camp. One of the A.D.C.s is always on duty, and our bedroom is right above yours."

The Chogyal and the Gyalmo conduct me into a sitting room, which contains low divans covered with rust-colored Tibetan silk and low carved tables with glass tops. A bearer appears with drinks. He has a young girl in tow. The Chogyal introduces her as the daughter of the palace driver. The Chogyal has a whiskey. The Gyalmo and the girl have Cokes. Their Highnesses make themselves comfortable on the floor, with the girl beside them.

"I feel like having a potato-salad-picnicsy-type dinner tonight," the Gyalmo says, picking up "The Ladies' Home Journal Cookbook" from a stack of cookbooks on a table. She begins leafing through the book. "I was in England a couple of Christmases ago. It seems it was ages since I was in England. In England you could have strawberries and cream. You could have strawberries and cream the whole day. Another day you could have something else, and you could have that the whole day. But here in Sikkim so many things are not available. When you get back to America, please, please, please send me some Sara Lee frozen cheesecake. If you send it on a plane that has a freezer, we'll have the cheesecake bailed out in Calcutta." She studies a page in the book. "Here's a good recipe—tomato stuffed with egg salad."

The Chogyal is showing the girl a Japanese painting pad. "Look," he says, dipping the brush in water and applying it to the pad. "You use the water, like this, to paint on the pad. See how this line is coming out black? Now you wait a few minutes and the line will disappear."

"A friend of mine gave me the pad and the brush as a present," the Gyalmo tells me. "The Japanese use it for learning quick brushstrokes. I find it very useful for practicing doing my eyebrows right."

The girl tentatively takes the pad and starts painting a picture first of the Gyalmo and then of the Chogyal, but before she can complete a likeness it disappears. She tries again and again, and always comes up with a blank page.

Presently, I speak to the Chogyal and the Gyalmo of their legendary meeting and courtship. A couple of years before coming here, I met them

when they visited the United States to show their baby, a son, to the Gyalmo's family and friends, and when I interviewed them for the "Talk of
the Town" department of *The New Yorker*.

"There was no grand design on my part to catch a king [the Gyalmo told
me then]. I just fell in love with his sad, sad eyes and sad smile and dis-
jointed and beautifully courteous manner. Truly, truly, truly. But at each
meeting he would repropose to me. I must have said yes, yes, yes six times."

"I didn't know if she meant it," the Chogyal said. "It sounded too casual.
When I did believe her, I wrote to her family. They said 'Who is this fellow?' and did some research on me. My engagement to Hope wasn't very
popular in Sikkim. It was said that I was marrying an American girl so that
I could have a foreign account. If I had wanted a foreign account, I could
have had it through the black market. No one would marry just for a foreign account. Also, the astrologers kept making us put off the wedding, because they said the year was unpropitious. But there wasn't any feeling
against the marriage on the ground that local girls were being slighted. We
often went to Tibet to get girls to marry—my late wife was Tibetan—because if one took a wife from Sikkim it would mean having Sikkimese relatives, and therefore graft and injustice, and in a king's eyes all his subjects
should be equal. It is said that dogs have no uncles and kings have no relatives."

"Even after we were married, there was feeling against me at first," the
Gyalmo said. "The Al Capone of Sikkim, a defrocked monk, said I had legs
like *tungbas*."

"*Tungbas* are sections of bamboo used for carrying beer," the Chogyal
said.

But those reminiscences of the romance that I was given in the United
States were in the nature of an outline. Now the Chogyal and the Gyalmo
graciously fill in the details for me.

Hope Cooke was born in San Francisco, in 1940. She was the only child
of John J. and Hope Noyes Cooke. When she was still a baby, her parents
were divorced, and when she was two her mother died. She became the
ward of her maternal grandparents, Mr. and Mrs. Winchester Noyes, both
of whom died when she was fourteen. She then became the ward of an
aunt and uncle, Mr. and Mrs. Selden Chapin. She studied in private
schools in the eastern United States, and also, for a time, in a school in
Iran, where Selden Chapin was posted as ambassador. She entered Sarah
Lawrence College as a freshman in the autumn of 1958. She made a brief
visit to India in the summer of 1959, and one of the places she went to was
Darjeeling. There she met Palden Thondup Namgyal, then Crown

Prince, in the bar of the Windmere Hotel, where they both happened to be staying.

Palden Thondup Namgyal, Order of the British Empire (1947), Padma Vibhushan (1954), Commandeur de l'Ordre de l'Étoile Noire (1956), who was then also an honorary lieutenant colonel of the 8th Gurkha Rifles (he is now an honorary major general of the regiment) and who was in Darjeeling visiting his command, was born in Gangtok, in 1923. He was the second son of Sir Tashi Namgyal, who ruled Sikkim from 1914 to 1963. He was educated in several boarding schools in India, and then spent three years preparing for the life of a lama. (The Sikkimese believe him to be an incarnation of a previous Chogyal, named Sidkeong Namgyal, who ruled from 1863 to 1874, and believe both of them to be successive reincarnations of the Karmapa Lama of Kham, in eastern Tibet, from which the Namgyal family migrated to Sikkim in the early fifteenth century.) When he was eighteen, his older brother died and he became heir apparent. From then on, he was actively involved in the affairs of Sikkim. In 1950, he married Sangey Deki, daughter of a Tibetan nobleman named Yapshi Samdu Phodrang, and the couple had two sons, Tenzing Kunzang Jigme and Topgyal Wangchuk Tenzing, and a daughter, Yangchen Dolma. (All three now attend public schools in England.) His first wife died in 1957.

Miss Cooke, after her meeting with the Crown Prince in Darjeeling, returned to Sarah Lawrence. They did not keep in touch during the next two years. Then, in the summer of 1961, she revisited Darjeeling. Again she stayed at the Windmere Hotel, and again she found that the Crown Prince was staying there, too. On her first evening in Darjeeling, he took her to a ball of the 8th Gurkha Rifles and proposed to her on the dance floor, and she said, "Yes, yes, yes."

Soon afterward, Miss Cooke accompanied the Crown Prince to Gangtok, where she spent a week with his family, but the idea of an American bride in the palace did not meet with favor either from his family or from the Sikkimese people generally. Miss Cooke returned to Darjeeling, and stayed on there as a guardian to Yangchen, who was then five and was in school there. Late in the autumn, Miss Cooke returned to Sarah Lawrence to resume her studies while the Crown Prince labored in Sikkim to pacify the opposition, now vociferous and organized. For instance, there was a petition presented to Sir Tashi Namgyal by the All Sikkim National Congress over the signature of, among others, Kazi Lhendup Dorji-Khangsarpa, which read, in part:

We . . . being deeply aggrieved and apprehensive, wish to bring the following facts to your immediate attention and consideration:

THAT this proposed marriage between the Maharajkumar [Crown Prince]
of Sikkim and Miss Hope Cooke is against the best traditions and customs of
Sikkim. It is not correct to say that this marriage has the approval of the
people of Sikkim. . . . The fact that the Maharajkumar states that he received permission from the Ladhi-Medhi [lamas and village elders] cannot
be accepted as "permission" per se, for they represented carefully selected
"yes-men," a fact that is known to all Sikkimese. There was, in effect, no
properly constituted body that could convey the serious objections of the
people of Sikkim on religious, economic, and security grounds, nor was that
section of the Sangha [clergy] who regard him, an incarnation, as a virtual
apostate, present. . . .

THAT . . . Sikkim's maximum revenue is between 60 and 70 lakhs
yearly. The present attitude of extravagance with reference to the Maharajkumar's proposed marriage constitutes a criminal waste of the depleted
resources of the Sikkim Government and the people.

THAT the fact that this is a second marriage of the Maharajkumar of Sikkim, and that the succession is already provided for, makes it, in the eyes of
all Sikkimese people, a matter of no great public importance. . . . Urgent
Developments Plans are being kept back for the lack of funds, many villages
are without good dispensaries, roads, schools, and clean drinking water, etc.

THAT Sikkim is a Buddhist State; the Maharajkumar is the President of
the Maha Bodhi Society, and it is repugnant to the religious feelings of the
Sikkimese masses that a considerable number of animals will be slaughtered,
and that drink will be lavishly distributed on this occasion. . . .

THAT in view of all the above-mentioned disturbing facts, it is our considered and well-thought-out opinion that, on grounds of security, Religious
feelings, Economic, and general well-being of our country as a whole, we
wish to place on record our opposition to the wasteful expenditure proposed
to be incurred in the proposed marriage.

In a princely state, opposition from politicians could be ignored, but not
opposition from astrologers, and the astrologers in Sikkim categorically
ruled out 1962 as a possible year for the royal nuptials, on the ground that
it was a disaster year. (As it happened, the year did bring the Chinese
invasion and also some natural calamities.) Finally, on March 20, 1963, a
month after Miss Cooke's graduation from Sarah Lawrence, the Chogyal
married her. "Gangtok on the day of the wedding," according to one extensive account, "presented a colorful juxtaposition of East and West, with
ten sombre-suited ambassadors rubbing elbows with red-robed lamas, maharajas, local peasants, New York débutantes, and a generous representa-
tion of the international press. Some two hundred friends and members of

the family crowded into the royal chapel, while 5,000 other guests thronged the capital city for the festivities . . . the following week of cele-bration costing some $60,000." On February 20, 1964, the marriage was blessed by the birth of a prince, who was named Palden.

Much has been written about the royal couple's life in Sikkim. At least one article was the work of the Gyalmo herself. "There is a serenity in Sikkim that gentles and fills out its countrymen," she wrote in an article in *Asia Magazine* entitled "Where Life Is Beautiful in Its Simplicity and Human Spirit Survives." "It is not a rarefied serenity of astringent and ascetic beings, rather it is a serenity born of generous natures. . . . Some-how, in the Himalayas, cradled by the beauty of Kanchenjunga and the other snow mountains, one is deeply, terribly aware of the rhythm of at-tunement between the world of spirit and of man."

The next day is the beginning of Losar, the Tibetan New Year (Sikkim observes the Tibetan calendar), and the day designated for the first durbar of the Chogyal's reign. In the palace gardens, workers are busy setting up tents decorated with colorful appliqués, in preparation for the lunch that is to follow the durbar. Nearby, the full contingent of palace guards—a com-pany and a half—is parading. Streaming into the palace compound are Sikkimese, Indian, and foreign well-wishers, who include ranking govern-ment and Army officers, high lamas, politicians, landowners, journalists, and representatives of the Rangpo Mining Corporation, the Rangpo distil-lery, the main post office, and the local girls' school—the whole of Gangtok society, about two hundred strong. They are coming to wish a happy New Year to the Chogyal and the Gyalmo, who have stationed themselves on one of many brocaded overstuffed sofas in the main drawing room. For the occasion, Her Highness is wearing a floor-length Sikkimese brocade dress, and she looks rather birdlike beside the imposing figure of His Highness, who is wearing his coronation vestments—a skirt and a tunic with long bell sleeves, all of gold brocaded with roses, the ubiquitous dragons' heads, and other good-luck symbols. In groups of two and three, the well-wishers march in through the main door of the drawing room, bow, present scarves to Their Highnesses, and, having been favored with smiles, nods, and perhaps a word, pass out through the side door. It takes two hours for Their Highnesses to greet everyone. After the guests depart (all of them are to return for the durbar and the lunch in the gardens), Their Highnesses settle down on the veranda, the Chogyal with a whiskey and the Gyalmo with a Coke, to wait for the durbar.

"Everything in the palace has a mystique," the Gyalmo says. "This morning, we had a Buddhist service for Losar in our chapel. It had a 'Golden Bough' mystique."

The conversation turns to social life in Gangtok. "Society here is very small," the Chogyal says. "You always have to invite the same people. If you don't invite the Political Officer, he feels insulted. Whether or not the Political Officer is a good dinner guest depends on who he is. One time, I invited some senior Army officers for drinks and 'Pillow Talk,' which was playing at the cinema here at the time. I didn't invite the Political Officer, since it was just an informal gathering. On the day of the party, the senior officers I'd asked happened to go to tea at the Political Officer's. These officers told the Political Officer that they were coming to the palace for drinks and then coming with me to 'Pillow Talk' that night. 'Oh, my wife and I haven't been asked,' the Political Officer said. 'We'll buy our own tickets and go there and embarrass the Chogyal.' He arrived and spoiled 'Pillow Talk' for us all."

I ask the Chogyal about his present disenchantment with the treaty that he helped to negotiate.

"There was little choice in 1950," he says. "At that time, there was quite a lot of popular agitation in Sikkim for merging with India. The Political Officer here then abetted it, but when he found out that the Indian government was not interested in integrating Sikkim, I must say his conduct was very correct; he helped to calm the agitation. Now there is no popular agitation for merging with India. Now we want to be a separate country. Indians say it's because I have done my work too well. They say that I have bought out the politicians here by giving them contracts for development work; all the money that India gives us for development work is funnelled through the palace, and there are some Indians who now regret this. They believe that the Political Officer or some independent agency should give the money. But I think the reason for the end of the political agitation is that the Sikkimese like my government. My friends in the Indian government are always telling me that monarchy is on its way out, that I have to change my government, and I'm always saying to them that people will like monarchy as long as monarchy continues to prove useful."

We are joined by an agreeable-looking Indian gentleman, who is about the same height as the Chogyal, and who, like the Chogyal, is wearing the Sikkimese skirt and tunic, but, in contrast to the Chogyal's sleeves, which fall over his hands, indicating that his hands are not meant for work, the newcomer's sleeves are rolled up. He is Mr. R. N. Haldipur, now the Principal Administrative Officer in Sikkim. During the raj, it was customary for the government of India to appoint one of its officers the dewan of a princely state. The dewan, besides serving as a sort of Prime Minister to the maharaja, was the government's eyes and ears at court. The practice was abolished along with the princely states, but in Sikkim it continues, except that now the dewan is called the Principal Administrative Officer. His position, like other aspects of Indo-Sikkimese relations today, is sensitive—even more sensitive than that of the Political Officer. To quote Jansen's article again, "The position of the . . . dewan . . . is held by an Indian officer. This is a clumsy arrangement; he is too obviously a symbol of Indian control, and his relations with the Indian Political Officer can never be easy. No official should be put in the position of having to serve two masters."

If Mr. Haldipur is under any such strain, he gives no sign of it. "Your Highness, I have made my durbar speech as much like America's State of the Union Message as I could," he says to the Gyalmo, beaming like a storybook courtier. It seems that the main item of the durbar is to be this speech of Mr. Haldipur's.

The Indian, Sikkimese, and foreign guests of the morning are all gathered in a pavilion in the palace compound, where the durbar is now in progress. The monks have finished chanting prayers. The Chogyal has just made his formal presentations and awards. There is a ripple of coughs and shuffles in the pavilion as we all wait for the next item. A Sikkimese politician sitting next to me leans over and whispers, "You've lived in America. We have an American Gyalmo. My question is this: If there is a war between Sikkim and India, will America fight on Sikkim's side? I would like your opinion."

I am taken aback. Then I remember the dreamlike setting, the Walter Mitty world of politics in a principality. I rack my brain for some sort of reply, but I am saved by Mr. Haldipur, who begins his speech.

"It is indeed my proud privilege and honor to welcome on this occasion the Chogyal and the Gyalmo, the members of the Royal Family, my colleagues, and other guests," he says, in English. "It has been an annual practice to hold the durbar on the occasion of the Losar, to review the progress and examine the shortcomings of the work done in the previous year, but this practice could not be adhered to in the last few years, due to the illness and, later on, the sad demise of the late Chogyal. Today we are happy that the circumstances have rendered it possible to hold the durbar, and it is a unique occasion insofar as it happens to be our present Chogyal's first durbar."

After talking for a time about the esteem in which the Chogyal is held by his courtiers, he continues, "The most significant and memorable event has been the Ser-Thri Nga-Sol of the Chogyal, Thondup Namgyal, who ascended the throne, by the grace of the Three Gems, as the twelfth consecrated ruler of Sikkim. The event was an occasion for universal happiness and rejoicing throughout Sikkim, and was marked by a sense of pride, belongingness, and renewed confidence that the Chogyal would continue in the footsteps of his late illustrious father. The Chogyal's intimate knowledge of his people's problems, his constant care, and keen interest in their well-being is manifest in the various activities of his government's departments. This year marks the end of the Second Five-Year Plan of Sikkim, which was financed by the generous aid from the government of India. In the initial stages, the plan suffered from a shortage of key materials, as a result of the emergency, and lack of trained personnel, which prevented it from gathering momentum, but later it gathered both speed and direction. While there will be a certain amount of shortfall in the achievement of financial targets, it is gratifying to note that the various departments have been able to complete successfully all the major projects that were included in the current Plan. . . . The orchid sanctuary at Gangtok is doing well. A committee for beautification of Sikkim was formed, and it has taken up the work of construction and maintenance of several public parks through the agency of the Forest Department. Satisfactory progress has also been reported in the field of animal husbandry. A flock of imported Rambouillet rams was recently received and distributed in north Sikkim for the purpose of crossbreeding with the local sheep so that the quality and yield of wool could be considerably improved. In addition, a sheep farm has already been opened at Dentam, in western Sikkim, where a flock of Romney Marsh sheep particularly suited to wetter areas will be supplied soon. We could not make much headway in our piggery-farm scheme at Goyzing, primarily because of lack of trained personnel and the unavoidable delay in the starting of the farm. We have since undertaken remedial measures, and the Department has already sent one of its officers for training in swine husbandry."

He mentions a few more projects, then says, "The serious threat and intrusions from across the border into our territory were matters of grave concern for us and India, but the gravity of the situation only served to strengthen the existing bonds of friendship between Sikkim and India and demonstrate conclusively the confidence in each other."

He concludes, "The task ahead is stupendous. As our Chogyal mentioned in his Speech from the Throne on the occasion of the Ser-Thri Nga-Sol, 'We shall not remain content until we have banished from Sikkim whatever traces may remain of poverty, ignorance, and disease; we shall not cease in the struggle until the light of knowledge, health, and happiness shines bright in every home of our motherland.' Let these words be the guiding star for our work. Let us hope that each day and each month brings us nearer to the goal. We are confident that under the Chogyal's wise and enlightened rule the ship of the state will move on a smooth and even keel, and let us resolve to engage ourselves honestly and purposefully to serve the people of Sikkim in order to improve their standard of living, bringing unto them greater happiness and prosperity."

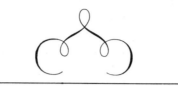

Nepal

ECONOMICALLY AND MILITARILY, the Kingdom of Nepal, which is three times the size of Bhutan and eighteen times the size of Sikkim (it has an area of about fifty-four thousand square miles and a population of about ten million), is only Bhutan and Sikkim writ large, for although it has enjoyed all the trappings of a sovereign power during the last hundred years, India sees the three Himalayan states as horses of a similar color (people in the plains sometimes call them "three pendants on India's Himalayan necklace"). India, of course, is well aware that in the last few years Nepal has been busy courting and sending forth ambassadors (Sikkim and Bhutan have so far left their foreign affairs to Indian emissaries), getting economic aid from countries all over the world, even including Israel (Sikkim and Bhutan have so far relied entirely on India for development funds), and exploiting the enmity between India and China, just as any small country situated between two huge adversaries might (Sikkim and Bhutan have so far had no political involvement with China). In fact, it is partly the recent political goings on in Nepal that have led Delhi to put a snaffle on Bhutan and a curb on Sikkim.

It is said that such difficulties as India has had with Nepal can be traced to certain anti-democratic and pro-Chinese tendencies on the part of King Mahendra Bir Bikram Shah Deva, who occupies the Nepalese throne. He has put an end to such democracy as the palace previously allowed to take hold in Nepal. He has imprisoned some of the kingdom's most important liberal leaders. He has welcomed Chinese diplomats and Chinese technicians. Above all, he has allowed the Chinese to build a highway connecting Katmandu, the capital of Nepal, with Lhasa, so that military vehicles can roll to his capital not only from Lhasa but all the way from Peking. King Mahendra maintains that his political and diplomatic activities are all directed toward the fulfillment of his nationalist dream of "opening windows on the world," and Nepal has now, at last, had an undeniable fenestration, though King Mahendra, in his wildest fancies, could not have imagined that it would take the form of an invasion so bizarre as to temporarily submerge all other considerations.

As it happens, the best of the war dispatches is from the hand of J. Anthony Lucas, for the New York *Times:*

> The world's beatniks have really gone "way out" this time—all the way to Katmandu. . . .
>
> From the United States, Canada, France, West Germany, Britain, the Netherlands, and Scandinavia, almost 200 ostentatious nonconformists have found their way to this Himalayan city, and more are pouring in every day.
>
> As they wander Katmandu's narrow alleys begging rupees from the Nepalese or lounge in dingy Tibetan restaurants smoking hashish, few of the "travelers," as they call themselves, can explain precisely what brought them here.
>
> Some say, "Well, you know, the Buddhist bit, the wisdom of the East." Others say it's hashish, which is probably cheaper, better, and more easily available here than anywhere else.
>
> Most, like Bill Digby, an American with a bushy red beard and long hair, just shrug their shoulders and say: "It's where the scene is, man! The word was out all over Europe . . . so here we are." . . .
>
> Jean-Michel Solente, a former employe of the French radio who quit to write a "150-page poem," commented: "Nobody knows how it started. Suddenly everybody was on the road headed this way." . . .
>
> "It's easy," explained an Austrian with a string of prayer beads around his neck. "You thumb your way to Istanbul. There you find a German businessman who wants you to drive his Mercedes to Teheran for him. There you pick up a Danish girl with a Vespa who gets you to Kabul. In Pakistan you sneak onto a bus without paying and in India a Sikh truck driver gives you a lift into Delhi—you've got it made."

I chance upon a member of the gentle infantry, a recruit from Pittsburgh, on the Grand Trunk Road. From head to toe he is swathed in a vetust, exotic Hudson Bay blanket, and his beard and long locks give him the look of a fuzzy bear. Staff in one hand, bowl in the other, he trudges along, clanking a cowbell that hangs from his wrist, and repeating *"Om hare, hare Krishna."*

The bearded boy says to me, "Man, I'm really going to blow my mind in Nepal. It's the Newars now. You grok?"

It seems he's freaked out on reports he has had of the matrimonial rites prevailing among the Newars, one of the main racial groups in central Nepal. Every Newar girl, as a child, is formally married to a Bengali quince. The fruit is then cast into a sacred stream, and, the immortality of the marriage having thus been secured, the Newar girl is free to marry— once she reaches puberty—again and again, provided that she takes the precaution of placing a betelnut under the pillow of the incumbent husband the night before she wishes to take a new one.

"Bengali quince! Betelnut!" he exclaims.

I head in the opposite direction.

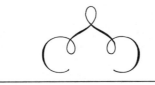

Ladakh

Some epithets for Ladakh are the Roof of the World, the Highest Desert, the Coldest Desert, Little Tibet, Little Siberia, and Snowland, and it is, from all accounts, a dead land. Although on maps the triangle that is Ladakh is given plenty of blue wash indicating rivers and lakes, what has been written about Ladakh makes it clear that the few rivers render life supportable on only a small fraction of the land (forty-one thousand acres out of a total of forty-two thousand square miles under India's control), that the lakes are either frozen over or turbulent or drying up or saline (the last are reminders that the region was once an inland salt sea), and that most of Ladakh is tableland, which, if it does not lie in the shadow of mountains, and thus in Stygian darkness, is, owing to the absence of vegetation, scorched by the sun. I obtain a place on an Air Force cargo plane, which for most of the year is the only way to get to Ladakh, and I secure Army snow gear—monkey cap, parka, special gloves with a slit for the trigger finger—and submit to an official harangue on the "do"s and "don't"s of coping with Ladakh: "Don't start peeling off your clothes if you suddenly get hot—from sun to shade the temperature can drop sixty degrees. Don't pick up anything heavy. Don't do any exercises. Don't run. Don't exert yourself at all. New arrivals often come down with attacks of pulmonary edema, which can cause death in forty-eight hours. As soon as you get there, go to your barracks, lie down, and cover yourself with as many quilts as you can stand." Then I sign this general indemnity:

To the President of India:

The consideration of the President of India (here-in-after referred to as the Government) having at my request agreed to carry me as a passenger in service transport (animal, animal-driven, motor, air, or water) belonging to the Government or hired or acquired by it . . . I undertake and agree that neither I nor my heirs, executors and administrators will make any claim against the Government or against any such servant or against any other person in the service of the Government for or in respect of any loss, damage, or injury to property or persons (including injury resulting in death) which I may suffer while boarding, alighting from, or travelling in such transport or in consequence of such travel or while or as a consequence of lodging and boarding provided by the Government or while being at, going to, or returning from work. . . . I also agree so to bind myself, my heirs, executors and administrators to indemnify and save harmless the Government and any servant of the Government or any other person in the service of the Government against any claim of demand which may be made by any third party against them or any of them arising out of act of omission or default on my part in connection with such journey's lodging, boarding and performances. The Government has agreed to bear the stamp duty on this document.

Today, I wake up in a military hut after a long rest following my arrival at brigade headquarters in Leh, the capital of Ladakh. Leh, which is at an altitude of eleven thousand five hundred feet, is in a basin with peaks of twenty-five thousand feet or more towering on three sides. I struggle free from a cenotaph of quilts and am immediately out of breath. The air is thin and dry, and my skin feels taut and rough. Standing almost against a *bukhari,* which is burning kerosene, I somehow manage to get into my clothes—layers of woollies and coats, and then the parka, the monkey cap, and the special gloves. I stagger out of the hut into still, numbing cold. I walk a few steps to the officers' transit mess, which is separated from my hut by a fence with, of all things, a kissing gate.

In the mess, a number of mournful-looking men are huddled around a *bukhari* eating a breakfast of congealed eggs and potatoes. There are no introductions, and, as if such graces belonged to another world, no one seems to expect them.

I engage one of the men—he is small and has the air of a scholar—in conversation.

"My colleagues and I have been sent here by the government to go into some of the effects of high-altitude living in Ladakh," he says. "But we have to spend several weeks acclimating ourselves. That's what the commanding officer told us, and he should know. We have to spend most of our days lying in bed until we're used to the place, but I suppose that's part of our research, too."

"You'll have plenty to research about," an officer says. "This place is a terrible hole. The Army is supposed to rotate the troops every two years, but because of the emergencies—the Indo-Chinese war and the Indo-Pakistan war—there are some *jawans* in Ladakh who have been here over three years, and some of us officers have been here as long, though we're rotated more often than the *jawans*. It is true that the regular hard routine of exercise is suspended here, and troops are expected to do only half as much as anywhere else. Even so, cases of pulmonary edema are reported all the time. There are cases of snow blindness all the time, too. And everyone goes down from here with an enlarged heart. No one seems to be able to think very clearly up here, and everyone is tired all the time. Many of the soldiers who have been here more than a year suffer from loss of memory and vagueness of mind. They all become irritable and short-tempered. Some of our soldiers say that after a year in Ladakh their hair starts to turn gray. They say you also become impotent. They say sometimes permanently so. Doctors don't know what causes it. Maybe it's psychological, maybe it's physiological—"

"Talking about the same old subject?" a voice calls out from the doorway. All rise, as if they were members of the newcomer's command. "The problems are there," an imposing-looking officer says, striding into the room. "But there is nothing to acclimation that mental posture won't take good care of. It's the mental posture that counts. One, you say to yourself, 'I'm going to like the place,' and, two, you like the place."

After breakfast, I start out in a jeep for the nearest military outpost, a battalion headquarters seventy-five miles from Leh; in this mountain desert a spare jeep is indispensable, and so an extra jeep tails me. At first, the road runs along the Indus (the Indus is called by the Tibetans the River of the Lion, because, according to their folklore, its source is in the mouth of a lion, and those who drink its waters become heroic), and there are villages in the river valley. Bands of Ladakhis in knee-length robes and high felt boots are going about on ponies that resemble Shetlands, and the houses, which have been hewn out of the mountainsides in several tiers, have, in some instances, incongruous-looking corrugated galvanized-iron roofs. There are willows and poplars, mallards and wild geese and magpies. Suddenly, the river valley and all signs of life vanish, and we are threading our way along a road of loose sand through a dry, narrow canyon. Closing in on either side of us are walls of rock and, above them, mountains, huge and oppressive. Besides the chug-chug of the jeeps, which reverberates eerily in the canyon, there is only the occasional mountain sound of falling clods of earth. As if we were travelling into a vacuum, drawing a breath becomes progressively harder. This part of the trek continues for forty-three miles, amid an endless landscape of sawtooth ridges capped with white peaks, and sandy expanses cut by narrow gorges and strewn with gigantic boulders. The terrain is as bleak as the moon's.

Finally, at the foot of a slope, the driver stops, gets out, and leads the way up to a bunker. It is the officers' mess of the battalion headquarters, and inside I find half a dozen officers gathered around a *bukhari*. One of them, a prim gentleman in an ankle-length fur coat, does all the talking. "How was the journey?" he asks me. "We don't get many visitors coming our way. Would you be so kind as to sign our visitors' book?" He gives me a huge ledger with polished brass bindings. I sign my name in an appropriately large hand. We are soon having a repast of cocoa and glucose biscuits. The discussion I heard earlier in the day is very much on my mind, and I ask the officers about the effects of service in Ladakh. There is an awkward silence, as if it were bad form to discuss the subject. Then the gentleman in the fur coat says, "In this kind of terrain, the only system of defense that is at all feasible is to set up posts as high up on the mountains as the men can survive. Sometimes these pickets are little more than bunkers with *bukharis* and flagpoles, and our men can do little more than march up to the pickets and march down again. It's impossible to stay at such heights for long. The men might camp up there for a few days, but some of the pickets are at eighteen thousand feet or above, and without frequent rotation to the bunkers below the men could not survive. Many of the men had never heard of mountains, snow, or deserts until they came up here. I myself grew up in the area of Cape Comorin." I can't help smiling at this, for Cape Comorin is the southernmost promontory on the Indian peninsula. "Shock, combined with the height and the isolation, makes for many strains," the gentleman in the fur coat continues. "So the men do think that they suffer from impotence and other things, but whether some of their diseases are real or only imagined we have not yet been able to determine by medical research. For things like pulmonary edema, however, there is a medical basis, and as soon as a *jawan* comes down with a case of pulmonary edema we evacuate him. A chap who gets it once is likely to get it a second time."

"Is it possible for me to visit one of the pickets?" I ask, and everyone laughs.

"You will have to spend some weeks acclimating yourself to Ladakh before you can go up to a picket," the gentleman in the fur coat says. "Vast

stretches of desert separate divisional headquarters from brigade headquarters, and brigade headquarters from battalion headquarters, and the
pickets may be still some days' journey from battalion headquarters. Coming up here, you must have noticed the problem we have with road communication, and the jeep roads and mule trails go up only so far. After
that, it's all on foot, and in this place you can't march very long without
collapsing."

"How do you feel about India's presence here?" I ask.

"It's a piece of real estate," he says. "And not a very good piece of real
estate. The Chinese, who have the best part of it—Aksai Chin—couldn't
even find stones there to build a road. We are here because we have to
draw the line somewhere. If we don't draw the line here, we may not be
able to draw it in the plains of India. But drawing the line in Ladakh is no
joke. The lifeline to Ladakh is an airlift from the plains of the Punjab; if
we lose our airstrips, then we lose Ladakh."

"Does anyone know whether the Chinese are making preparations for
another invasion?" I ask.

"We don't know. But from some pickets we can sight figures moving
along the horizon."

In the next day or two, I talk with a number of *jawans,* and from all I
can tell they might have stepped out into this ghostly place from the pages
of "The House of the Dead." But now I am dining with Ladakh's high
command, the dozen or so officers who have the rank to dine in the alpha
mess at Leh. We have just sat down to soup, and I find that this dinner is
part of a farewell party for an officer who is about to return to the plains
after three years' service here. The talk is overebullient. All the remarks
are directed at an officer who sits at the head of the table in the place of the
absent General Officer Commanding, and they are in the vein of the archetypal bachelor dinner: "Sir, when he gets to those fleshpots, he should
think of us, what?" and "Sir, command him not to go berserk when he
sees a sari, for, as it is said in that film, 'My Life, we'll just be Sahib and
Memsahib and go out only on Sunday.'"

The officer at the head of the table looks at his watch and says, "It's time
for the broadcast." The broadcast turns out to be an All India Radio request program for the forces. It consists of songs, mostly from old pictures,
and long lists of names of *jawans* and officers who have sent in requests.
The signal now fades out under a rush of static, now bursts into the room
strong and clear. Once, the name of an officer at the table comes through
distinctly, and everyone claps. Later, the name of another officer comes

through faintly, and the man nearest the radio shouts it out and everyone claps even harder. Dinner, which runs to many courses, is finished to the songs of the program.

As the gentleman at the outpost said, the lifeline of the military establishment in Ladakh is the air service. There are three airstrips here, at Kargil, Chushal, and Leh. The Leh airstrip, which was built in 1948, was the first, and it is still, as it was then, the *sine qua non* of India's defense of Ladakh. And the *sine qua non* of the Leh airstrip is S. Narboo, the resident engineer, who has the title of Development Commissioner. Until, thanks to him, the first plane landed in Leh, Ladakh was accessible only by mule trail. (Leh was on a historic caravan route traversing India, Tibet, and China.) Narboo was born in the Ladakh village of Skara, next to an old fort called Wazir Zorawar Singh (the fort was named after a nineteenth-century Dogra commander who conquered Ladakh for Gulab Singh, the ruler of Jammu—the southern part of what is now the state of Jammu and Kashmir—and later tried to conquer western Tibet but was defeated by the joint troops of China and Tibet), and he is one of a few local citizens who can speak a language other than the local tongue, Ladakhi; one of the even fewer who are fluent in English; and one of the still fewer than that who have crossed the seas. After elementary schooling in Leh, secondary schooling in Srinagar (fifteen days away on foot), and college in Jammu, he went to England, where he took a degree in civil engineering at Sheffield University.

I call on Narboo in his office, in a little white house that might pass for a baby secretariat. He gives me whiskey, and I down it quickly, in the vain hope of banishing the Ladakh chill, which seems, if possible, worse now than ever. The wind beats against the house as if in obedience to a supernatural order to demolish it. Narboo and I draw our chairs close to the *bukhari* and talk like two men marooned in Ultima Thule.

I ask Narboo what the circumstances surrounding the construction of the Leh airstrip were.

"When raiders came from Pakistan to try to take Kashmir in October, 1947, the government of Jammu and Kashmir realized that Ladakh was also going to be raided," he says. "At the time, there was only one garrison of state forces here in Leh and one in the subdistrict of Skardu, so, to reinforce Ladakh's defenses, the government of Jammu and Kashmir decided to build an airstrip in Leh as quickly as possible. I was in charge of the Srinagar airfield, which was the basis for Indian military operations in Kashmir. In December, Mr. D. P. Dhar, who was the Home Secretary of the government of Jammu and Kashmir, asked me if I would lead a party of Indian Army officers and soldiers to Leh and build the airstrip. It was very dangerous to go to Leh. There was a road to Leh from Srinagar, but for the most part it was just a path for pedestrians and muleteers, and it was usually closed from the middle of November until the middle of June, because of Zoji La, a pass lying at twelve thousand six hundred feet, which in the winter can be under as much as fifteen feet of snow. Zoji La has always been the main obstacle separating Srinagar and Leh. I said to Mr. Dhar, 'I'll do it.' And I did it."

I ask Narboo how, exactly, he went about the task of supplanting mules with airplanes, and before I know it he has launched into an adventure story, which persuades me that he is a pioneer, a Pathfinder in sahibs' clothing. (He is dressed in a sweater, slacks, and a jacket, and although he is short and powerfully built, he has something of the manner of a suburban type to be found almost anywhere.)

"One day," he says, "I got a telephone call from Mr. Dhar—I remember it was the fifteenth of February, 1948. He said, 'Mr. Narboo, are you still prepared to go to Leh?' I said, 'Yes.' He said, 'How long will it take you to get ready?' I said, 'It will take me two days to hand over my charge and wind up my domestic affairs.' Mr. Dhar said, 'That will do.' The advance guard of officers and soldiers who were to help me build the airstrip left on the sixteenth of February; it consisted of seventeen boys from Ladakh and two officers of the Indian Army, Lieutenant Colonel Pritijan and Lieutenant Colonel Hosajan. I left on the seventeenth of February in a big Army motor convoy of about fifty vehicles, led by Colonel Abdul Aziz. The vehicles were to take the supplies to Sonamarg, sixty miles from Srinagar, which was as far as the road was motorable; Sonamarg was eight miles from Baltal, a way station at the foot of Zoji La. We had gone only about eighteen miles from Srinagar—as far as Gandarbal—when it started snowing heavily. With great difficulty, we managed to go fifteen miles more, and then we had to stop. Colonel Aziz said, 'All my vehicles are stalled. What are you going to do now?' 'Push off on foot,' I said. 'My advance guard must be waiting for me in Gund, which is only twelve miles ahead. From the look of this snow, they can't have got any farther. I can't just abandon them there.' From villages nearby I hired a hundred and fifty porters; they unloaded the convoy and somehow hoisted all the supplies and equipment on their backs. I said goodbye to Colonel Aziz in the snow and pushed off for Gund. The advance guard was indeed waiting in Gund, and it was snowing so heavily there that the question of moving on did not even arise. In fact, to put up for the night we had to dig our way into the rest house, which was completely buried under snow—roof and everything. We were stranded in Gund for seven days and seven nights. On the eighth day, the weather cleared and we dug our way out. I got the porters together and told them, 'We march today. Let's push off for Sona-marg.' In Gund, the sun was out, but it snowed all the way to Sonamarg, which was fifteen miles away, and we didn't get there until evening. Brig-adier Faqir Singh, of the state militia, received us there and told me that we wouldn't be able to go any farther. I said, 'We have to.' He said, 'How do you propose to go a furlong in this snow?' I said, 'Our minds are made up. We shall see what we shall see.' At half past two next morning, I woke the porters up and ordered them to pack. They started crying. 'What do you want to do?' they said. 'Lead us to our death?' It was so cold that the tears froze on their cheeks. I pleaded with them and I threatened them, and by half past three we were marching. The snow was so soft and so deep that at every step we would sink in almost up to our necks. The men who led the party somehow managed to take a step, sink down, pull them-selves up with their sticks, and take another step. We pushed on. It took us almost sixteen hours to travel the eight miles from Sonamarg to Baltal. We reached Baltal about seven o'clock in the evening, and I told the por-ters that I was determined to cross Zoji La the next day. They cried, and said that they had to have six or seven days' rest for a crossing like Zoji La, and that even then they couldn't risk it without the help of a wind to blow the loose snow into the ravines. Without the rest and the wind and clear weather, they said, they would be going to certain death. I held a council of war with Lieutenant Colonel Pritijan and Lieutenant Colonel Hosajan. We granted that all the porters were Kashmiris—they were from the Gan-darbal slopes, the Gund slopes, the Kangen slopes, and the Sonamarg slopes—and knew the area well, and that they had been brought up with snow and spent all their lives in the midst of it. We granted that they carried our rations and arms and ammunition and clothes and the equip-ment for building the airstrip, and that we could not proceed without them. But we then agreed that it didn't make any sense to wait around in Baltal; there was always a chance that the weather at Zoji La would take a sudden turn for the worse. We agreed there was no alternative but to march on. I got hold of the Baltal mail-runner, whose job was to cross Zoji La when he could. He wasn't crossing it at that season, but I told him that he had to guide us over the safest trail; Zoji La is very narrow, but even so some places are safer than others. I told the porters I was determined to march on, and they cried and wailed the entire night. But we left Baltal, as we had left Sonamarg, at three-thirty in the morning. The Baltal mail-runner showed us the way. A gale came straight down at us from Zoji La. It was so strong that we could hardly breathe. It choked us and almost suffocated us. Sometimes we were forced to march with our backs to the gale—march backward. Sometimes we were forced to go down on our hands and knees and crawl up—we were afraid of being lifted bodily and blown off the trail. The whole time, we kept having to fall back before the gale, and the whole time we were afraid that the gale would shake loose avalanches to bury us. By eleven o'clock, however, we were all safely at the top of the pass. We gave out rum to the porters, and Lieutenant Colonel Pritijan and Lieutenant Colonel Hosajan and I had brandy. We drank our fill and pushed on. Now that we were over Zoji La, the trail was wider and much safer. I went ahead. I must have left the porters a couple of miles behind me when I heard a thunderous roar, as if dozens of cannons had been discharged simultaneously. I looked back. The porters were just black smudges on the white background. They had thrown down their loads and were running hither and thither. I saw why. A huge avalanche was rushing toward them. It just missed them. We didn't lose a single porter. Soon I said goodbye to the porters from the Kashmir side—Zoji La is the beginning of Ladakh—and I took a new lot from nearby villages and pushed on."

"When did you finally get to Leh?" I ask.

"On the eighth of March. I started work on the airstrip immediately. Mr. Dhar was on the wireless every day to ask me how far we had got. When I finished—it was a month-and-a-half-long job—*I* was on the wireless every day to ask Mr. Dhar when he was going to send a plane to try out the airstrip. Then Mr. Dhar told me that Air Force officers had told him that only a Viking airplane would be suitable for landing on our airstrip, and just then no Viking was available anywhere in India. But every morning when it was clear my subdivision officer and I would walk a distance of a little over a mile to the airstrip and lay a white sheet on the tarmac—the marker for landing that had been agreed upon—and scan the sky until the clouds closed up. No planes came. Every day, Pakistani raiders were advancing on Leh—as I mentioned, there was only one garrison of state forces here—and refugees were arriving ahead of them. When the raiders were only fifteen miles from Leh, I got a message from Mr. Dhar that an airplane would attempt to land that day. It was a fine morning—I remember it was the twenty-fifth of May. We walked over to the airstrip and put down the white sheet. Around eleven, I heard the drone of an engine, and within five minutes I saw the plane overhead. It overshot the airstrip, circled back, came directly over the white sheet. The plane landed, and out stepped the daredevil pilot Air Commodore Meher Singh and that popular general the late K. S. Thimayya and his A.D.C. They looked around the airstrip for about half an hour. When they were leaving, I asked Air Commodore Singh if the airstrip was all right. He said, 'Yes. With a little bit more work, it should be all right.' He said he would send in a complement of five or six airplanes the next day, and General Thimayya said that planes would fly in regularly from then on with men and equipment to build up the defenses in Ladakh. Then the three visitors flew away."

"Did the five or six planes come the next day?" I ask.

"No, they didn't come the next day or the next," he replies. "The weather was too turbulent. The complement of planes arrived on the twenty-eight of May. I remember all the pilots stepping out of the planes looking surprised, because there was a crowd of Ladakhis with baskets of grass. They were ready to feed the flying iron horses."

"How long did it take to fly in troops and supplies for the defense of Leh?" I ask.

"It wasn't until November that we had enough troops and supplies to stop the raiders and launch our counterattack," he answers. "And by then the raiders had fortified themselves so well that it wasn't easy to dislodge them. There was a fierce battle before we were able to recapture Kargil."

Sitting in my hut in Leh, pierced by shaft after shaft of bitter-cold wind, I am going over my notes, and repeatedly asking myself why a country as poor as India should fight to keep this place—for my notes read like a palimpsest on the annals of Daulat Beg Oldi, a village lying at the foot of Karakoram Pass, which has always been the Chinese gateway to Ladakh, just as Zoji La has always been the Indian gateway to Ladakh. The name of the village immortalizes a sixteenth-century invader from China named Daulat Beg, who crossed the pass from Sinkiang into Ladakh. No sooner had he and his men reached Ladakh than they were trapped by a snow-storm. They were forced to spend the night at the foot of the pass. Practically all of them perished in the night. In the morning, the two or three survivors fled back across the pass. The local inhabitants started calling the foot of the pass Daulat Beg Oldi, *"oldi"* being Yarkandi (a language of the region) for "dead and gone." However, my notes on Ladakh:

"Geography: Straddles some of the most desolate mountains in the world—the Karakoram, Ladakh, and Zaskar ranges, mostly in the Greater Himalayas—with summits like the formidable Mount Godwin Austen (height, 28,250 feet).

"Climate: Arid. The atmosphere like dry ice. In fact, so dry that the belt of permanent snow starts at eighteen thousand feet (average for Himalayas, nine thousand feet). Annual precipitation just over three inches. What little snowfall there is is swept down into narrow, sunless ravines by sandstorms and high, icy winds, which are generated by extreme temperatures, varying from 86°F. to –113°F.

"Flora and fauna: Sparse vegetation. One-crop cultivation of incredibly low yield. Such *shikars* as the markhor, the ibex, *Ovis ammon,* the red bear, the snow leopard, the wild horse, and the antelope. The Chinese now have the best pastureland. As for domestic animals, the Ladakhis keep sheep and ponies, but the monarch of all is the yak, *Bos grunniens,* or 'groaning ox'—placid, large, lumbering, and very shaggy. It is surefooted, is indifferent to cold and snow, goes without water for days, eats ice. In the Himalayas, the yak provides everything from dung for fuel to hides and hair for tents and ropes. Without yak, life insupportable. An English missionary and Himalayan traveller, George N. Patterson, lists the yak's virtues for people in these parts in the style of a litany:

> Without the yak they could have no milk; without the milk they could have no butter; without the butter they could have no tea; without the tea they could have no existence. Selah. Without the yak they could have no plough; without the plough they could have no crop; without the crop they could have no food; without the food they could have no existence. Selah. Without the yak they could have no loads; without the loads they could have no goods; without the goods they could have no barter; without the barter they could have no existence. Selah. Without the yak they could have no wool; without the wool they could have no money; without the money they could have no goods; without the goods they could have no existence. Selah.

"Life and people: Population less than one hundred thousand. Birth rate declining. Specific causes given by the government: (1) Along with Siberia, Ladakh is coldest inhabited place on the face of the earth. (2) There is a high ratio of men to women. (3) There is a tradition of dedicating at least one son or daughter to monastery, since not enough patrimony or bride money to go around, and since lamas, who are celibate, are in great demand to serve as teachers, physicians, astrologers, landlords, and, until Indian Army arrived, magistrates. (4) Though people sturdy to look at, and broad-chested, they are said to have weak hearts. In winter, retreat into houses. Form of hibernation. People are farmers and nomads. Polyandrous. Generally pacific. Merry people; e.g., renowned for endless festivals, and for singing and dancing, even in the *gompas,* or Buddhist monasteries. In matters of religion—which in most cases is Buddhism, with alle-

giance to the Dalai Lama, but in some cases is Islam—quite liberal; e.g., a
Muslim can hold office in a *gompa*. Also, one member of a family may be
a Buddhist, another a Muslim, and in such instances a common pot is used
to cook meat for both Muslim and Buddhist, perhaps with a string used to
identify meat killed under Muslim law. The worst really seems to bring
out the best in Ladakhis. The only luxuries barley beer, called *chhang,* and
tea. Salted tea, buttered tea. Yak butter. 'Without the yak . . .'

"Economics of Indian involvement: Practically everything, from kerosene to foodstuffs to buttons, has to be airlifted, and from one to four tons
of supplies are necessary to maintain one soldier here for a year. Indian
military establishment here thirty thousand strong. Plane carrying seven
tons of cargo uses up sixteen hundred gallons of aviation fuel. By the time
a jerry can of kerosene, which is burned up in a *bukhari* in a few hours,
reaches here, it costs forty rupees—a fortnight's pay for a soldier. To heat
the hundred-bed hospital here costs twelve thousand rupees a day. At minimum, everything costs eight times what it does in the plains. Entire airlift
chancy. Even on the best days, planes can fly only a few hours in the
morning, before shadows fall, and must always negotiate a maze of mountains. Some forward units completely dependent on parachute drops.
There are two semi-motorable roads to Ladakh, but neither can ever supplant air service. The better of the two roads follows the route Narboo
took, but unless snowsheds are built all along it, cost of which is unthinkable, road will remain open, as now, only during the summer months. In
addition, the road will always be subject, as now, to landslips, thus constant repairs, and will always depend on India's commitment to hold on to
the Vale of Kashmir, a commitment that is itself a drain on India's meagre
resources. Second road, though it has the advantage of circumventing the
Valley, is long, circuitous, and, if anything, more difficult to maintain.

"Rights and wrongs of Indian involvement: Voluminous arguments
from both India and China are on record in support of their separate
claims to Ladakh, or parts of it. The Chinese say that they've always enjoyed dominion over Tibet, and that Tibet has enjoyed similar dominion
over Ladakh (Ladakh has a long history of rendering to Tibet ecclesiastical fealty and tribute in the form of salt tax and such). But the Indians say
that between 1834 and 1841 Maharaja Gulab Singh, of Jammu, conquered
Ladakh and annexed it to his state. But the Chinese say that Gulab
Singh's advance in Ladakh was checked by their forces; that, according to
the peace terms, Gulab Singh agreed to pay tribute for Ladakh to Lhasa;
and that, ecclesiastically, Ladakh continued to be a vassal of Tibet. But the

Indians say that since Gulab Singh's time Ladakh has continued to be, politically, part of Jammu and Kashmir. But the Chinese say that the frontiers of Ladakh *vis-à-vis* Tibet and China have never been as they are shown on Indian maps, either during Gulab Singh's time or at any other time. To put these arguments another way, the Indians contend that the state of Jammu and Kashmir has title to Ladakh and that they have title to Jammu, so Ladakh is Indian, whereas the Chinese contend that in matters of religion and tax they've never ceased to have overlordship of Ladakh, and that, in any case, the Indian title to Kashmir is a matter of dispute today. The Indians contend that if the Ladakhis owe any religious fealty it is to the Dalai Lama, who is in India, and that the Chinese title to Tibet is a matter of dispute. Both India and China have appealed to tradition on the question of exactly what constitutes the boundaries of Ladakh, but it has been pointed out that tradition can't exist without people, and that much of Ladakh has never been inhabited. Again, both sides have appealed to place names, but it has been pointed out that places are often known by two names, one Chinese and the other Indian. Again, both sides have appealed to reports of various nineteenth-century travellers to Ladakh, but it has been pointed out that these reports conflict on matters as basic as who had rights to mine salt where. Again, both sides have appealed to the history of their administrations, but if the Indians say the village of Demchok was under their administration, as its inclusion in the 1921 census of India evidenced, the Chinese say the report of that census gives Demchok a population of only four, which is so wide of the mark that it proves India could not have had an administration there. The claims are academic, but the importance of the plateau of Aksai Chin to the Chinese is not. It links the industrial province of Sinkiang with Tibet, and if the Chinese should ever lose their hold on Sinkiang they would lose not only Tibet but Inner Mongolia. P. H. M. Jones, writing in the *Far Eastern Economic Review,* points out, 'Aksai Chin was of great importance to China. It had always been a traffic artery linking Western Tibet with Sinkiang, and the Ching dynasty had established check posts there from the middle of the 18th century. The Chinese army had entered Tibet by that route in 1950 and Chinese military and civilian workers had built the new highway along it between March, 1956, and October, 1957, which the Chinese army had since continually patrolled.' But then other authorities challenge Jones' facts and say that Jones is only repeating the Chinese case. So it goes.

"Solutions: Most seem to be on the level of the one proposed by a purveyor of drastic remedies, who says, 'Let's give this moon to the Chinese and evacuate the Ladakhis to the foothills—perhaps settle them alongside the refugees from Tibet.' "

Reading over these notes, I can't help feeling that to think about Ladakh at all—to say nothing of living here for a few years, or even a few hours— is to experience a sort of disorientation, for an air of unreality surrounds everything, from the military enterprise right down to the kissing gate.

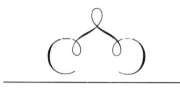

Tibet

TIBET, WHICH IS A FOUR-HUNDRED-AND-SEVENTY-THOUSAND-SQUARE-MILE PLA-
teau at an altitude varying from twelve thousand to twenty-four thousand
feet—one of the highest elevations in the world—lies between the Himalayan and Kunlun ranges, and is bounded by the People's Republic of China
on the north and east and by NEFA, Bhutan, Sikkim, Nepal, and Ladakh
on the south and west. Unlike the other Himalayan states, which only live
in fear of the Chinese, Tibet has been fully incorporated into China. In 1950
and 1951, after a series of clashes between Chinese troops and the inhabitants of the eastern marches of Tibet, the Chinese imposed on the Tibetans
a treaty known as the Seventeen-Point Agreement. Its key provisions stipulated that the Tibetans should "unite and drive out imperialist aggressive
forces from Tibet," that they should "return to the big family of the motherland—the People's Republic of China," and that their government
should "actively assist the People's Liberation Army to enter Tibet and
consolidate the national defense." Tibet had been loosely, nominally under
the dominion of China from the fourteenth century to the beginning of
the twentieth; there had been instances of Tibet's rulers' doing homage to
the emperors of China, and Chinese ambans, or representatives, had resided in Lhasa off and on. Except for this connection with China, and
some contact with Mongolia and India, Tibet had always been all but cut
off from the rest of the world. In 1904, however, the British, taking advantage of the weakness of both Tibet and China, penetrated all the way to
Lhasa. In time, they established amicable relations with Tibet, posting a

few garrisons and establishing a few trading centers, a few rest houses, and token postal, telegraph, and telephone facilities—all without reference to China. One aim of the Seventeen-Point Agreement was to restore Sino-Tibetan relations to what the Chinese believed they had been before the British penetration. In 1954, India relinquished her right, inherited from the British, to maintain the garrisons and facilities in Tibet in the Agreement for Trade and Cultural Intercourse, which gave the Chinese what amounted to carte blanche in Tibet. In 1959, soon after the Dalai Lama fled to India, the Chinese reorganized the local government in Tibet, publicized denunciations of the Dalai Lama by his ecclesiastical deputy the Panchen Lama, and put an end to whatever autonomy Tibet had enjoyed.

Altogether, about eighty thousand refugees have followed the Dalai Lama out of Tibet; though the Chinese have attempted to seal the borders, refugees continue to slip out. Their experiences dramatize the consequences of what is generally regarded as Chinese enslavement. Though numerous volunteer organizations in Europe and North America have been mobilized to help these refugees, though the Indian government has been generous in its aid to them, though the Dalai Lama's government-in-exile has supervised the work of rehabilitation, and though everyone concerned has given some thought to settling them in conditions approximating those of Tibet, transplantation has left them devastated. Having lived at high altitudes, in small settlements with sufficient food, in a cold, dry climate with few diseases, in a self-contained, static, medieval, pastoral society with a xenophobic, clannish outlook, these refugees have been plunged into the turmoil of a developing society whose languages and customs bear almost no relation to theirs. Dervla Murphy is one of many persons who have written of their hardships. Miss Murphy, who journeyed from her native Ireland to India almost entirely by bicycle, and recounted that adventure in a book entitled "Full Tilt," tells in a sequel, "Tibetan Foothold," how she took a rest from Rozinante, her bicycle, and, beginning in June, 1963, spent a few months in a refugee camp in Dharamsala—a hill station situated in the Dhauladhur spur of the Punjab Himalayas which boasts one of the best campsites, and which since 1960 has served as the seat of the Dalai Lama. Miss Murphy reports that even there, in the mountains, refugee children suffered from "bronchitis, pneumonia, T.B., whooping-cough, chicken-pox, measles, mumps, amoebic and bacillary dysentery, round-, hook-, tape-, and wireworms, scabies, septic headsores from lice, septic bed-bug bites, boils, abscesses of incredible sizes, rickets, bleeding gums, weak hearts, asthma, conjunctivitis, trachoma, and otitis media," adding, "The majority suffer from calcium and Vitamin C deficiency, and a heartbreaking number, no matter what is done for them now, will probably be partially blind or deaf, or both, in maturity."

Conditions in the camp a year later were only a little improved, as a couple of letters written to Miss Murphy by a friend named Judy Pullen indicate. (They form an appendix to "Tibetan Foothold.") Miss Pullen, a teacher, and Lois James, a nurse, had come to India in October, 1963, from the Canadian University Service Overseas, to work with the refugees. The two volunteers, who were in their early twenties, had been sent to a transit refugee camp in Kangra, a squalid town lying a couple of thousand feet below Dharamsala, and that is where Miss Murphy first met them. In 1964, the Kangra camp was moved up to Dharamsala, and both Miss Pullen and Miss James were transferred there. Miss Pullen was assigned to the Dharamsala camp's Teacher Training School, where she started imparting to about thirty lamas the rudiments of a few modern subjects, introduced into their traditional curriculum of scriptures, poetry, logic, and grammar. She wrote from Dharamsala on July 3, 1964:

> In addition to two English classes, I'm giving lectures in geography, general science, hygiene, current events, world history, etc. It all sounds very grand, but I'm just trying to give some grounding in each subject. A special translator was brought from Delhi, so I lecture in English and he translates as I go. The atmosphere became charged with excitement as they [the lamas] learned about the solar system, changes of season, etc. Late into the evening, monks could be seen clustered around the globe with flashlights and little balls trying to work out lunar and solar eclipses. . . . Zimey Rinpoche ["*rinpoche*," a title, means "blessed incarnation"], the head Lama and principal, is young, charming, and brilliant. He keeps me running to my books with his intelligent questions on satellites, soundwaves, splitting the atom, etc.

After relating some of the difficulties she had encountered at the school, Miss Pullen went on:

> Five weeks ago now, I got sick again . . . [and] began a dandy bout of jaundice and infectious hepatitis. . . . You can't imagine how frustrated and fed-up I am at losing so much precious time. . . . Three weeks ago . . . Lois [received] 120 kids, who arrived nearly dead. . . . Those kids had camped four months on the border without shelter, food, or help. They buried two of their number there and then permission came to enter India —on grounds of compassion. Seventeen were left in a nearby hospital— nearly dead—and the others came on here on a nightmare of a train ride in the most blistering heat. You wouldn't believe it unless you saw it— they're still only shells and skeletons of children. Two more have died— one in Lois' arms . . . of worm-convulsions. Lois had to cremate the body

herself. And now they're having emotional fits, hysterics, and an attempted suicide—it's so criminal I can't believe it's true.

In another letter, sent on September 4th of that year, she wrote:

Lois cracked up again about three weeks ago and spent ten days at the Mission Hospital. It was the same old liver trouble and I am quite worried, because it bothers her constantly, though she's back on the job again. It's a miracle she lasted this long, after the terrific strain she's been under since early June, when those very sick kids arrived. It was a long, hard struggle, but she lost only two of them, and even the most seriously disturbed children are now normal, healthy, and delightful Tibetan kids.

Today, I am in Dharamsala. I spend some time going around the Tibetan colony. In the yard of the Lower Nursery, small children are waiting to have their heads washed with a solution of DDT. In a classroom of the Upper Nursery, slightly older children are being taught English with the help of drawings on a blackboard. In the workshops of the Handicraft Center, Tibetan cobblers, tailors, and weavers are busy making Tibetan-style shoes, clothes, and rugs. Everywhere, there are touches of Tibet—a fluttering prayer flag here, a turning prayer wheel there, broad black strips of molding around the windows of the newly built cottages.

In a room of the Teacher Training School, making a meal of *moo-moo,* or steamed dumplings, is a fair-skinned, brown-eyed young woman dressed in a long Tibetan gown of black cotton. She is Judy Pullen. (Lois James, whose health suffered a severe breakdown, has returned to Canada, where she is now undergoing medical treatment.) Miss Pullen is still working here, still teaching her old subjects, still giving lessons in geography with the help of a globe—though now she uses copies of the *National Geographic* as well. She is not in very good health herself, but a girlish, breezy manner almost veils the fact.

I have *moo-moo* with Miss Pullen, and then she conducts me through the school. Housed in a typical tin-roofed hill-station cottage, it has, in addition to a few classrooms, some small dormitory rooms, into which double- and triple-decker beds have been fitted to make the best use of the space. She shows me her own room, which differs from most of the others only in that it contains two ordinary bedsteads, one twice as large as the other. "My room serves as a little clinic, too," she says. "This large bed is sort of a hospital bed. The sickest children in the camp on any particular day sleep here. Often there are as many as half a dozen sharing the bed. I sleep on this small bed and act as sort of a night nurse to the children. At the moment, I have five nocturnal patients. The youngest is a five-year-old girl. She was the most emotionally disturbed child you ever saw when she came here. Actually, it's amazing that these children aren't more emotionally disturbed—I mean, with all the things they've gone through. She's nearly all right now. When I leave, I'm going to make sure that she finds a good home. His Holiness the Dalai Lama has established a couple of dozen homes for Tibetan children in and around the hill station of Mussoorie, which, as you know, is about a hundred miles from here. Twenty-five children are picked to live with a foster mother and father. I'll try to get her into one of these homes—one that's just right for her."

"How did you happen to come out to India?" I ask.

"I was a student at the University of Toronto," she says. "I was doing pre-med, but I had just got engaged and I thought, Now I'll never finish medical school—I'll just get married. Then I heard Dr. Tom Dooley speak. That got me interested in working with the refugees. I asked my fiancé if I could go and work with the Tibetan refugees for a year. He said I could, just for a year. When I got to my camp, I found that I didn't think of home at all. After a year, it was clear to me that if I had really wanted to get married I wouldn't have come out here in the first place. So I decided to forget about marriage and just stay on here. First it was a year, then two, and I'm still here."

"Do you miss home now?" I ask.

"Not much," she says. "Of course, here there isn't any social life. Here you can't talk to a man without all the Tibetans looking on. If you talk to a boy in the bazaar and a Tibetan sees you, it will start a scandal among the lamas at school. Lois and I were warned about this in orientation classes, so we were prepared. Lois even gave up smoking when she came here. But my lamas are darlings. And His Holiness has a younger sister, and when she is here things get quite lively. We go on picnics, but my lamas look upon even that as very bad, so every time I go on a picnic I have a guilty conscience for six weeks. Once, I stayed out on a picnic until three in the morning. I told my lamas that I would stay out for the whole night at a cottage nearby, or they would all have been out looking for me. I confessed later to Zimey Rinpoche. I told him I was a human being—no better than anyone else."

For nearly five centuries, most Tibetans have been members of a Buddhist reform sect called Gelugpa, or "the Virtuous Order of the Yellow Hat." The order has always been led by the Dalai Lama, who has been regarded as the incarnation of Chenresi, the Buddha of Mercy (Chenresi took a vow to protect all living beings), and who has been paid homage as an absolute, divine ruler. The present Dalai Lama, the fourteenth, was born on the fifth day of the fifth month of the Wood Hog Year of the sixteenth cycle of the Tibetan calendar, or June 6, 1935. In his autobiography, which was written in English, with the help of David Howarth, and published in 1962, the Dalai Lama describes how, in 1937, he was recognized as the incarnation of the thirteenth Dalai Lama. (Being an incarnation of Chenresi, each Dalai Lama is, of course, the incarnation of his predecessor.) Tibetan notables, after the death of the thirteenth Dalai Lama, appointed a regent, who began the search for the new incarnation by interpreting certain portents. According to the Dalai Lama:

Curious cloud formations were seen in the northeast from Lhasa. . . . After the [thirteenth] Dalai Lama died, his body was placed seated on a throne . . . facing toward the south; but after a few days it was seen that the face had turned towards the east. And on a wooden pillar on the northeastern side of the shrine where the body sat, a great star-shaped fungus suddenly appeared. All this and other evidence indicated the direction where the new Dalai Lama should be sought. . . . Next, in 1935, the Tibetan Wood Hog Year, the Regent . . . saw the vision of . . . a monastery with roofs of jade green and gold and a house with turquoise tiles. A detailed description [of this vision] . . . was written down and kept a strict secret.

In the following year, high lamas and dignitaries, carrying the secrets of the visions, were sent out to all parts of Tibet to search for the place which the Regent had seen. . . .

The wise men who went to the east arrived in our region of Dokham during the winter, and they observed the green and golden roofs of the monastery of Kumbum. In the village of Taktser, they noticed at once a house with turquoise tiles. Their leader asked if the family living in the house had any children and was told that they had a boy who was nearly two years old.

On hearing this significant news, two members of the party went in the house in disguise. . . . The real leader, Lama Kewtsang Rinpoche of Sera Monastery, was dressed in poor clothes and acted as a servant. . . . There they found the baby of the family, and the moment the little boy saw the lama, he went to him and wanted to sit on his lap. The lama was disguised . . . but round his neck he was wearing a rosary which had belonged to the thirteenth Dalai Lama. The little boy seemed to recognize the rosary, and he asked to be given it. The lama promised to give it to him if he could guess who he was, and the boy replied that he was Sera-aga, which meant, in the local dialect, "a lama of Sera."

The boy's recognition of the rosary was one of many signs that convinced Lama Kewtsang Rinpoche that he was in the presence of the new incarnation. As a result, the entire search party presently converged on the house with the turquoise tiles. The Dalai Lama, remarking that small children often recall objects and people, and even passages of scripture, that they knew in their previous incarnation, continues his account:

> They offered me two drums, a very small drum which the [thirteenth] Dalai Lama had used for calling attendants, and a larger and much more ornate and attractive drum with golden straps. I chose the little drum and began to beat it in the way that drums are beaten during prayers. . . . By these tests, they were further convinced that the reincarnation had been found.

Later, the boy was taken to the holy city of Lhasa, and on October 7, 1939, he was formally initiated as Gyalpo Rinpoche, or "blessed incarnation of the glorious king." In the course of the ceremonies, he was given the names Ngawang, Lobsang, Tentsing, and Gyamtso—"the eloquent," "the wise," "the defender of the faith," and "the ocean." The designation Dalai also means "ocean," the ocean being, in Tibetan Buddhism, a symbol of infinite wisdom.

The rest of the Dalai Lama's book is a detailed record of his religious education, his assumption of responsibility for the government when he was sixteen, his efforts to reach an understanding with the Chinese, his appeals to the free world for assistance, and his flight to India. On March 17, 1959, the day before the flight, the Dalai Lama was quartered in the Norbulingka, his summer palace in Lhasa. For a week, the Norbulingka had been surrounded by thousands of Lhasans who believed that the Chinese were getting ready to kidnap the Dalai Lama, and now rumors were abroad that the Chinese were setting their artillery in position to shoot their way into the Norbulingka.

> About four o'clock that afternoon [he writes] . . . we heard the boom of two heavy mortar shells fired from a nearby Chinese camp. And we also heard the splash of the shells in a marsh outside the northern gate.
>
> At those two isolated shots, consternation and anger reached a final climax in the crowd. . . . I was not afraid of being one of the victims of the Chinese attack. . . . But I knew my people and the officials of my government could not share my feelings. To them the person of the Dalai Lama was supremely precious. . . . They were convinced that if my body perished at the hands of the Chinese, the life of Tibet would also come to an end.
>
> So when the Chinese guns sounded that warning of death, the first thought in the mind of every official within the Palace, and every humble member of the vast concourse around it, was that my life must be saved and I must leave the Palace and leave the city at once. . . . If I did escape from Lhasa, where was I to go, and how could I reach asylum? Above all, would the

Chinese destroy our holy city and massacre our people if I went—or would the people scatter from the Palace when they heard that I had gone, and so perhaps would some lives be saved? . . . Everything was uncertain, except the compelling anxiety of all my people to get me away before the orgy of Chinese destruction and massacre began. . . . I decided to go.

Twelve days later, having travelled over the high passes and through the sheer valleys of the Himalayas, the Dalai Lama arrived in Tawang, and took refuge, with a party of ninety-five officials and relatives, in the Tawang Monastery. He was granted political sanctuary in India, and he eventually settled in Dharamsala.

In the pages devoted to the Sino-Tibetan conflict, the Dalai Lama maintains that, contrary to what the Communist Chinese have said, Tibet and the Dalai Lamas were never subservient to China and her emperors but, rather, relations between the two realms were reciprocal:

> For two and a half centuries of the rule of the Dalai Lamas, until about the end of the nineteenth Christian century, there was a reciprocal personal relationship between the Dalai Lamas and the Emperors of China; a relationship of religious leadership on one side and a rather tenuous secular leadership on the other. The Emperor appointed two officials called Ambans to represent him in Lhasa. They exercised some authority, but they exercised it through the government of the Dalai Lama, and in the course of time their authority gradually declined.

He maintains, further:

> Suzerainty . . . perhaps . . . was the nearest western political term to describe the relations between Tibet and China from 1720 to 1890, but still, it was very inaccurate, and the use of it has misled whole generations of western statesmen. It did not take into account the reciprocal spiritual relationship, or recognize that the relationship was a personal matter between the Dalai Lamas and the Manchu emperors. There are many such ancient eastern relationships which cannot be described in ready-made western political terms.

The Dalai Lama sees the Communist Chinese as aggressors and invaders, and he sees them as guilty of the crime of genocide, quoting, as evidence, reports of the International Commission of Jurists—an organization made up of lawyers and judges representing some fifty non-Communist countries—which were based on testimony from the Tibetan refugees and on public statements from both sides. In attempts at rebuttal, it has been said that, regardless of how certain ritualistic and symbolic acts are interpreted or what term is employed for those ancient Eastern relationships of the Buddhist world, Tibet was always just a "region" of China, and that the Chinese did not so much invade Tibet as liberate it from feudal and ecclesiastical oppression. Edgar Snow, in his book "The Other Side of the River: Red China Today," discusses some aspects of this oppression:

> The Tibetan theocracy was an anomaly which only its inaccessibility could have preserved till now. Absolute feudalism prevailed and most people were held in serfdom. The lamas and nobility owned nearly all the land, livestock, and other wealth. Fear of devils and hell-fire for the impious combined with barbaric torture and death for fugitives from the system kept the population in subjugation, as in other feudalisms.

It may be true that the Dalai Lama's autobiography is a one-sided account of the Chinese takeover of Tibet, colored at times by his wish to justify to himself his departure from his homeland, but it may also be true that future generations will be able to glimpse Tibet as it existed during the early life of the fourteenth Dalai Lama only through the sober, poignant narrative of "My Land and My People."

One of the first persons to speak with the Dalai Lama after he started living in India was the oldest of his four brothers, Thubten Jigme Norbu. At the time of the Dalai Lama's flight, as it happened, Norbu was living in New York, but when he got news of the flight he rushed to India. Norbu has described the audience with his brother in a book he wrote with Heinrich Harrer, called "Tibet Is My Country":

> I was about to prostrate myself before him, as I had always been accustomed to do, and to present the usual *kata*, when with a gesture of the hand he indicated that I should not do so here. Wordlessly he pointed to a thanka with the picture of Sangye Chömdende Buddha; and deeply moved I laid my good-luck scarf over it. Henceforth our reverential greetings were to honour the gods alone; from now on the Dalai Lama regarded himself only as the first fugitive amongst his oppressed people.

Now, seven years later, for an audience with the Dalai Lama, I buy, at a shop in Dharamsala, a *kata*, which is a starched strip of white tulle, and go up a thousand feet—eight dizzying miles by road—above the Teacher Training School. (Miss Pullen lives in Lower Dharamsala, the Dalai Lama in Upper Dharamsala.) I then climb a steep hillside to a British-style cottage, which has been known as the Celestial Abode since the Dalai Lama took up residence in it. The Dalai Lama is on the veranda, and I approach him with my arms outstretched, the *kata* laid across my wrists in what I hope is the customary manner.

He steps forward with a strip of tulle identical to mine. I hesitate. He laughs, takes my *kata,* and presses his into my hands, saying, *"Thuji-chenja, thujichenja."*

"His Holiness thanks you," a young man says, appearing from behind the Dalai Lama. He is Tenzin Geyche, the interpreter.

"Yes, *'thujichenja'* means 'thank you,' " the Dalai Lama adds, in English. He takes both my hands in his and swings them from side to side.

The three of us are soon seated in wicker chairs around a low table. The Dalai Lama, who is wearing a lama's russet robe and rubber sandals, has a touch of the student about him—a smooth, cheerful face, close-cropped hair, and a clear, attentive gaze from behind spectacles. He begins talking animatedly in Tibetan.

"His Holiness knows a little English, but he would rather speak Tibetan, because His Holiness is not so sure about the pronunciation of English words," Tenzin Geyche says. "His Holiness says that in any event we Tibetans speak English without any expression, like the south Indians, who, His Holiness has heard, say everything in one long sentence without any expression. His Holiness says that even when we Tibetans speak Sanskrit it is not understood by Indians who know Sanskrit, because our pronunciation of Sanskrit words in Tibet is like the Japanese and Chinese people's pronunciation of English. It sounds as if we had marvels in our mouths."

"Not 'marvels'—'*marbles,*' " the Dalai Lama says, with an easy, boyish laugh.

"His Holiness is learning English because His Holiness hopes to go to America one day," Tenzin Geyche says, continuing to interpret.

"Yes, in America I would like to see a spaceship," the Dalai Lama says. "I would like to go to the moon one day. I know I can't be the first, but I don't want to be the last." He laughs.

"Has Your Holiness travelled much in India?" I ask.

"Yes, and one of the side results was to make His Holiness vegetarian," Tenzin Geyche says. "His Holiness has been a vegetarian since last year. His Holiness has become very weight-conscious. His Holiness says that he frequently goes down to the Upper Nursery and weighs himself, and that His Holiness's weight has remained exactly the same for a year—sixty-eight kilos."

"I think that's one hundred and fifty pounds," the Dalai Lama says.

"His Holiness ate meat until last year, when he started his pilgrim-ages—"

"Travels," the Dalai Lama puts in.

"—and when His Holiness had to stay in a rest house, where His Holiness was sometimes the only guest. Once, a chicken was killed specially for His Holiness's dinner in front of His Holiness. His Holiness then decided to give up meat, because of *ahimsa*. According to the Binaya Sutra, it is not wrong for a Buddhist to eat meat, provided the meat is not killed by him or killed specially for him. The meat should never be eaten if it is killed and prepared specially for him. But in the rest houses His Holiness found that the meat was being killed specially for him, so His Holiness felt that it was just as well to give up meat altogether."

"What does Your Holiness hear out of Tibet nowadays?" I ask.

"Refugees are still coming out of Tibet, and His Holiness receives reports from them. The Chinese have introduced many good reforms in Tibet. They are building roads, schools, and factories. We should have introduced some of these reforms ourselves, but we did not, because Tibet has always been very isolated and many people lived in monasteries and did not know what was going on outside them. The Chinese are doing a lot of bad things, too. Valuable ancient images have been taken from our monasteries to China. Gold and silver images have been melted down, and clay images have been broken up and mixed with manure. The Chinese have burned our scriptures in bonfires. They have used our precious manuscripts for wrapping paper; His Holiness has a page of a book that they used for wrapping paper. They have used our ancient manuscripts to blow their noses on. Many young lamas have been forced to marry. Many of them are under sentence of hard labor. In the Drebung Monastery, in Lhasa, we once had ten thousand lamas. Today, there are only three hundred, and most of them are old men. Even they are kept there for show, to impress visitors. When they are not praying for these visitors, they are forced to kill hens and pigeons and carry manure. The Chinese have harnessed the lamas to plows. They torture the lamas to death and say, 'Why don't you save yourselves with miracles?'"

"In Buddhism, you should not mind those who make you angry," the Dalai Lama says. "You should love those people who irritate you, because they are your *gurus*. In that sense, the Chinese are our *gurus*."

"What does Your Holiness think about the future of Tibet?" I ask.

"His Holiness says that there may be some changes in Tibet, owing to Communist indoctrination of the people, but that as long as Tibetans exist their loyalty to Buddhist Tibet will exist. The hope of going back is there always, but it's difficult to predict when and how. It may be that the third or fourth generation of leaders in China will be more reasonable about Tibet."

"What does Your Holiness think will be the future of the institution of the Dalai Lama?"

"His Holiness says that if the people want a Dalai Lama in the future, then there will be a Dalai Lama. But it doesn't matter whether someone is called Dalai Lama or not, because the incarnation will be there doing his work. All Dalai Lamas and other *rinpoche* lamas are blessed incarnations. But just because someone is chosen as a *rinpoche* lama or Dalai Lama doesn't necessarily mean he's always blessed. People can make mistakes, and have made them. The sixth Dalai Lama was very naughty. He drank and had many mistresses. But then he might have reached such a degree of spiritual understanding that he could do these things and still be a blessed incarnation."

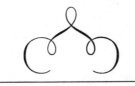

Interpretation Thereof

WHILE EVERYWHERE MULTITUDES CRIED FOR BREAD, the leaders of the nation made a great feast and praised the gods of gold, and of silver, of brass, and of iron. In the same hour came forth five fingers of a hand and wrote on the wall, and the leaders of the nation saw the part of the hand that wrote. Then their countenances were changed and their thoughts troubled them. The leaders of the nation cried aloud to bring in the astrologers and the soothsayers. Then came in all the wise men; but they could not read the writing, nor make known to the leaders of the nation the interpretation thereof.

And no one with light and understanding and excellent wisdom could be found to read the writing, and make known the interpretation and dissolve the doubts.

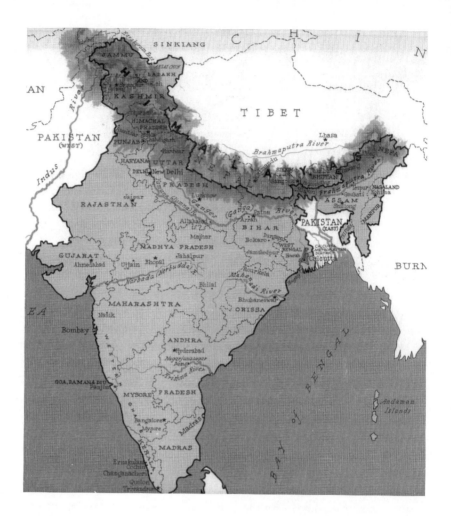

BOOK TWO

VI

Development: The Pulsating

Giant, the Aging King, and

the Strong Brown God

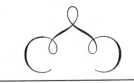

The Blast Furnace Is Alight

ONE AFTERNOON IN FEBRUARY OF 1959, several hundred administrators, engineers, designers, and laborers who had been working on the construction of a new steel plant in Bhilai, a dusty, backward village in the heart of India, gathered by the blast furnace, with their wives and children, to witness the smelting of the first iron. It was to be a trial tapping; the formal tapping would take place the following morning, when the President of India was to commission the blast furnace, and the spectators knew that if they were to face the official ceremony the next day with composure, the blast furnace would have to prove itself in rehearsal. Now, because of technical problems, the test run was repeatedly put off; it was finally fixed for seven o'clock in the evening, only to be put off again. Some of the men and their families went home for the night. Most, however, stayed on. Then, late in the evening, the molten iron flowed out of the tap of the furnace into a big vessel called a ladle. "When the blast furnace gave its first birth of liquid gold, I found Shri Dani, the Chief Civil Engineer, standing by my side," M. K. K. Nayar, who was deputy general manager of the plant at the time, writes in his reminiscences. "He was weeping like a child. I knew I was weeping, too. He ran to me and we embraced each other, and both of us wept out our excitement like children! Those few seconds I have always cherished in my memory as the most exciting moments of my life."

At the time of Independence, India was the most impoverished country in the world. Her population still lived under the shadow of epidemics and famines; ninety per cent of her people were illiterate, were engaged in subsistence farming, and dwelt in mud villages with no paved roads, no direct access to railways, no electricity, and none of the other advantages of the modern age; industrialization as yet amounted to little more than the mechanical processing of jute, cotton, and sugar; all machinery was imported; exports consisted almost entirely of shipments of jute, tea, tobacco, and hides; by and large, the economy was feudal in organization and benefited only the wealthy few who were landlords and capitalists. Even before Independence, the Indian National Congress Party, taking a leaf from the book of the Soviet Union's astounding economic growth, had drawn up Five-Year Plans and outlined development objectives for the country, and after Independence the Indian government, led by the Congress Party, entrusted the task of national planning to the Planning Commission, which, with Prime Minister Jawaharlal Nehru as chairman, functioned almost as a government within the government, controlling all economic activity, coördinating investment in the public and the private sectors, and enlisting financial and technical assistance from advanced countries. In 1951, the Commission instituted the first of four successive Five-Year Plans. The first Plan emphasized hydroelectric and irrigation projects, the second emphasized chemical and heavy industrial projects, and the third and fourth were devoted to the fulfillment of many still unrealized objectives of the two previous Plans. Taken together, the Plans revised and expanded the Soviet text into a manual for the development of India. Although this manual had many authors, from well-known politicians to anonymous technical experts, it is generally accepted that some of the most important glosses came from the hand of P. C. Mahalanobis, who has been a statistical adviser to the Union Cabinet since 1949 and a member of the government Planning Commission since 1959. (Mahalanobis was born in Bengal in 1893, was educated as a mathematician and physicist at Calcutta and Cambridge universities, and has made statistics his specialty; in 1945 he was elected a Fellow of Britain's Royal Society.) In Mahalanobis's view, as it has been expounded in public statements and in papers written over the years, countries like India have stood still economically for centuries, their standards of living and thinking are almost medieval, and now they must suddenly and rapidly enter the modern era, which began in Western Europe with the scientific and industrial revolutions—must, in fact, achieve in eighty years, or even forty, what the advanced countries of Western Europe took four hundred years to achieve. "We have been lagging far behind in the race of material progress," he has written. "We have now to run."

According to Mahalanobis, development requires increasing the supply of consumer goods, which in turn requires expanding the production of capital goods, which in turn requires training more engineers and technologists, which in turn requires increasing the facilities for and the volume of both applied and theoretical scientific research. "That the natural phenomenon is amenable to rational and unified explanation is the great breakthrough of the human intellect," he writes. "It occurred only with the emergence of science and is the characteristic mark of the modern age. . . . It is necessary for each country, however backward or small, to have as quickly as possible sufficient men with a scientific outlook who would be able increasingly to influence the thinking of the nation and of persons who have the responsibility for making policy decisions at the national level." Mahalanobis warns that because India's society has always been based on the principle of authority and on a rigid caste system, the introduction of a spirit of free inquiry—the basis of the scientific method—requires a complete departure from the past. "We used to have a great tradition of respect for the Brahman, preëminently as a teacher," he notes. "It is necessary to build up a new tradition of social appreciation of science and scientists." Mahalanobis says that the underdeveloped countries must, as they begin their scientific revolution, simultaneously prepare for their industrial revolution by building an industrial base, and that this requires concentrating on those heavy industries which can help to generate other industries. "The only permanent way of ensuring a progressively increasing production is to continuously increase our stock of tools and implements and machinery; that is, to increase what is called the capital investment," he writes. "For a single factor, the production of steel probably has the highest correlation with national income in different countries." India, however, cannot effectively increase her production of steel without substantial capital, heavy machinery, and technical skills, much of which must come from abroad. But once India has a flourishing steel industry, then, in Mahalanobis's words:

We shall be able to use our own iron ore and with our own hands produce steel; and then use the steel to produce more machinery to produce more steel and tools; and also to produce machinery to make more consumer goods. We will then not have to worry about foreign exchange every time we wish to start a new factory as we do now. Our dependence on foreign supplies will be greatly reduced. The main obstacle to rapid industrialisation being thus removed, we shall be able to increase production and employment quickly and raise the level of living.

Although India has somewhere between one-tenth and one-fifth of the world's reserves of high-grade iron ore, her production of steel at Independence was very nearly the lowest in the world; the United States, with one-third of India's reserves, had a per-capita production of steel two hundred times as great. As late as the end of the Second World War, India was producing barely a million tons of steel a year. She had only two steel plants of any consequence: the Indian Iron & Steel Co., constructed in 1918 by the British in the town of Burnpur, in what is now the state of West Bengal, and—accounting for most of the tonnage—the Tata Iron & Steel Co., constructed in 1907 by a Bombay textile merchant in a village called Sakchi, which grew into the steel town of Jamshedpur, in what is now the state of Bihar. Upon Independence, the Indian government, which aspired to a Socialist society with a limited role for private enterprise, made it clear that the existing steel plants would have to function under government controls, and that steel plants built in the future would be in the public domain.

Throughout the period of the First Five-Year Plan, the Indian government held discussions with the United States, Great Britain, and West Germany, and also with the Soviet Union, which at the time had no significant program of economic aid to India. By the time of the Second Five-Year Plan, which was drafted in 1956, and which envisaged the building of three new steel plants, the government not only had arranged for the expansion of the private plants but had reached agreements for the three new plants: one was to be built by the Krupp-Demag Combine, of West Germany, with a loan from the West German government; another by a consortium of British equipment suppliers, with a loan from the British government; and the third by the government of the Soviet Union. The agreement with the Soviet Union caused special excitement; the Indians had considerable experience in working with the British, of course, and they had some experience in working with Germans, but the Russians were strangers. Now British, West German, and Soviet engineers were all to start building new steel plants in India at about the same time, and their achievements would naturally be compared.

Since Independence, the Indian government had been conducting studies of prospective sites for new plants. All the states had been maneuvering for the industrial prizes, but fields rich in coking coal were to be found only in Bihar and West Bengal, and iron ore close to the supplies of this coal was to be found only in Bihar, West Bengal, and Orissa—three states that were sometimes referred to collectively as the Ruhr of India. It was clear that these three states were the most suitable for steel production, and, indeed, the German plant was eventually situated at Rourkela, in

Orissa, and the British plant at Durgapur, in West Bengal. But the site proposed for the Soviet plant was in Madhya Pradesh.

Madhya Pradesh was one of the poorest states in the Indian Union. Eighty-eight per cent of its population—a larger percentage than that of any other state—was rural. About twenty per cent of its population—again, a larger percentage than that of any other state—was tribal. Its per-capita annual income was lower than that of any other area—two hundred and one rupees, as against two hundred and fifty-two rupees for the country as a whole. (A rupee in the nineteen-fifties was worth about twenty cents.) "We are an undeveloped province," the Provincial Industries Committee of Madhya Pradesh noted in 1953. "Our agricultural standards are low, our educational standards are low, many of our people are underfed, diseased, and badly housed; our towns are unhealthy, our villages are unhealthier still, hardly fit to live in. The need for planning in every department is truly desperate, *but in none is it more so than in the matter of industrialization* [the italics are the committee's]." The government studies had pointed out that, of all the "non-Ruhr" states that had reserves of iron ore, Madhya Pradesh was the most suitable economically for a steel plant. It was adjacent to Bihar, and since both states were on the South Eastern Railway, one of the country's main arteries, Bihar coal could be transported to Madhya Pradesh, the cost of this haulage being offset in some measure by the saving that would result from the use of Madhya Pradesh's own sources of iron ore and also of limestone.

Within Madhya Pradesh, the area around Bhilai had been singled out by the studies as probably the best site for a steel plant. As a village, Bhilai was at this time little more than scrub, duck ponds, and paddy fields. Its contact with the modern world was confined to an occasional visit from a revenue collector or a health inspector. In fact, Bhilai was all but indistinguishable from any of hundreds of thousands of villages throughout India. The studies had pointed out, however, that the site had an abundant water supply (it was near two small rivers, the Tandulla and the Seonath); that it had—besides reserves of iron ore—deposits of manganese, limestone, and dolomite; that it was near Madhya Pradesh's own veins of coal, which, though not of the coking variety, could, it was hoped, be used as a blend; and that Bhilai was a stop on the South Eastern Railway.

The Soviet engineers, after making their own studies and tours of the several possible locations, chose Bhilai, and together the Russians and the Indians began planning for the day when Madhya Pradesh—particularly Durg, the district in which Bhilai lies, and Chhattisgarh, the division in which Durg lies—would begin to define a new India.

The *Imperial Gazetteer of India* is an incomparable survey of the sub-continent and stands as a British monument to Victorian scholarship. According to the *Gazetteer,* which was edited by Sir William Wilson Hunter and was published in 1881 and revised and reissued in 1908, "the dawn of the epoch of authentic history" over much of the area now known as Madhya Pradesh did not break until the sixteenth century; from the faint illumination cast by coins and inscriptions and by ballads and epics, however, it appears that in an earlier period the region was ruled by princes of the Rajput dynasty and minor chieftains of the Gond tribe, and that people elsewhere in India knew of the region only as Gondwana—the land of the Gonds. Gondwana, which was sandwiched between the plains of Hindustan, to the north, and those of the Deccan, to the south, was a belt of hills and plains geographically and culturally isolated from the rest of India. In fact, through the centuries the Mogul emperors were content to receive only nominal acts of homage from the princes and chieftains of Gondwana, and when the Moguls invaded the Deccan from Hindustan, they always bypassed Gondwana. In 1861, the region was brought under British administration and was given the name of the Central Provinces. (In 1956, the Central Provinces were reconstituted, with additional territory, into the present state of Madhya Pradesh.) The Central Provinces remained the most backward part of India, with a Hinduism characterized by such practices as the worship of primitive deities and spirits, which, as the *Imperial Gazetteer* lists them, included "Khermata, the goddess of the earth or the village, Marhai Devi, the goddess of cholera, Sitala Devi, the goddess of smallpox, Nagdeo, the cobra, Bhainsa Sur, the buffalo, Dulha Deo, a young bridegroom who was killed by a tiger, Hardaul, a young Rajput prince who was poisoned by his brother on suspicion of loving his [the brother's] wife, and Bhilat, a deified cowherd." In 1901, the Central Provinces had a population of almost twelve million, yet only fifty-five towns had as many as five thousand inhabitants each, and only one town had a hundred thousand inhabitants. The rest of the people lived in some forty thousand villages, which had an average of two hundred and fifty inhabitants. (Today the average is three hundred and thirty.)

Until this century, the entire Indian subcontinent was a mass of self-contained agrarian villages—as the greater part of it is today. Each village had its own weavers, potters, oil pressers, barbers, washermen, water carriers, and scavengers, and often its own carpenters for making plows, its own blacksmiths for making plowshares, and its own leather workers for skinning cattle, curing hides, and making thongs and sandals. In each village, the function of each man was determined by his caste, for the village was an ancient Hindu polity in which both duties and remunerations—often in kind—were so fixed that a man was prohibited not only from aspiring to functions reserved for other castes but even from aspiring to a function within his own caste that was different from the one to which he was born. There was no competition except between men with the same hereditary function. Even if the villagers were converted to Christianity or Mohammedanism or any other faith, the converts retained their Hindu castes and functions. The first breaches in this village tradition came with the introduction of the railway, in the middle of the nineteenth century. By the end of the century, Western articles like kerosene, mill-made cloth, and umbrellas were finding their way into the villages, and some villagers were beginning to abandon their hereditary functions. As modern education was introduced, some villagers began to leave their homes for a life in one of the handful of new urban centers. Of all the areas of the country, however, the Central Provinces proved to be the most resistant to change.

The larger villages of the Central Provinces tended to be in open, well-cultivated areas, and the smaller ones in tracts in the hills or forests. A village, large or small, was usually a cluster of mud huts, often built on high ground to avoid floods and also attacks from neighboring villages, and with a mud fort for additional defense. The farmstead was unknown, for most of the villagers were tenants at will, with no proprietary rights and no security, cultivating the land on a communal basis. At sowing time, a tenant would receive from his landlord a supply of seed grain and the use of bullocks, and after the harvest the tenant would pay back not only the original investment of seed grain but half or three-fourths of the remaining harvest as rent for the land. Trade and commerce scarcely existed, so when there was a good harvest, crops rotted where they lay, and when the crops failed, the population was decimated. (The Central Provinces lost a total of about a million people in the famines of 1897 and 1900.)

The most backward division of the Central Provinces was Chhattisgarh ("thirty-six forts"). Chhattisgarh, which comprises the upper basin of the Mahanadi River, lies in the eastern part of the Central Provinces, hemmed in by ranges of hills on the west, the south, and the north. In 1901, Chhattisgarh had a population, largely tribal, of about two and a half million, and contained fourteen out of a total of fifteen feudatory states in the area; in fact, it was to the Central Provinces what Gondwana had once been to the rest of India. The land of Chhattisgarh was for the most part a treeless expanse of small, embanked rice fields—sometimes fifty to an acre—with ridges of sandy gravel separating one field from another. The land is drenched, largely during the monsoon, with from fifty to sixty inches of rain a year. (The average annual rainfall for the Central Provinces is forty-seven inches.) In 1901, a tenant in Chhattisgarh lived in a hut valued at two or three rupees. (A rupee was then worth about twenty-five cents.) In a year, he spent for himself and his wife two or three rupees for clothes, their dress consisting of a few strips of cotton, and about fifteen rupees for food, a meal consisting of little more than a gruel of boiled rice and water. The villages in Chhattisgarh had livestock of uniformly poor quality, and were deficient even in the traditional crafts. In consequence, the villagers had as agricultural implements only a harrow to puddle and weed the fields and a heavy beam to crush the clods, the usual procedure being for one man to stand on the beam while another dragged it across the field. "The people, isolated and almost barred from intercourse with the outside world," comments the *Imperial Gazetteer,* "have developed or retained peculiarities of dress, manners, and language which distinguish them from the residents of adjoining tracts, to whom they are known as Chhattisgarhis. . . . The people are generally held to be characterized by a lack of intelligence, by backwardness in their methods of agriculture, and by a more primitive habit of life than their neighbours."

In 1906, for administrative reasons, a strip of land was detached from two existing districts of Chhattisgarh to form a new district, which was called Durg, after its main village. (The word *"durg,"* Hindi for "fortress," is probably derived from Durga, the name of the Hindu goddess of death and destruction; this goddess is the consort of Shiva and has many manifestations, one of which is Kali.) The village of Durg—Bhilai is next door—was made the headquarters of the new district, which had a population of six hundred thousand. A small fund collected for sanitation was the only civic institution in Durg, but the village was on the railway and had a local primary school, and even a local bell-metal industry.

Toward the end of June, 1955, an Indian and Soviet team consisting of about a dozen administrators, engineers, and designers, and accompanied by a skeleton staff, arrived in the village of Durg, took up residence in the Durg Circuit House, a government hostel, and began work on the Bhilai steel project. They found the red terrain infested with reptiles and insects, the climate exceptionally hot, and the villagers slow and uncomprehending. Even the most ordinary domestic animals seemed hostile. (An Indian chronicler of the period reports that a Russian, whom the writer describes as "an old veteran surveyor," hearing what he took to be the roar of a lion, "hurtled down the slope right into the arms of an Indian colleague," who, alarmed by the Russian's behavior, himself "took off from that point of the slope and sprinted even faster down to the plains." Later, it was discovered that what the Russian had heard was only the low of a cow.) Throughout the enterprise, the Indians and the Russians had to contend with differences of language and manners and working methods. Despite the aid of interpreters, Indians and Russians were apt to argue at length, only to discover that they had been making the same point. Gestures simply contributed to the confusion; for instance, a shake of the head by a south Indian signified "yes," and one by a north Indian signified "no." The chronicler, bemused, observes, "Our Soviet friends often concluded that Indians as a whole must be very diplomatic, because you hardly ever knew whether a particular attitude was negative or positive."

Meanwhile, in the Soviet Union thirty organizations and four hundred plants—at Moscow, Leningrad, Kharkov, Zaporozhye, and Zhdanov, among other places—were working, as one Soviet emissary put it, "with great fervor and care" to supply equipment for the project, and in Bhilai the team was reinforced by about thirty thousand Indians and about a thousand Russians. They were all busy surveying and clearing land, planning plant buildings and breaking ground for them, laying out an internal system of roads and railway tracks, and installing electric lines and water and gas mains. But it took nearly six months to put up the first structure in Bhilai, which provided temporary residential quarters for the team and was designated Bhilai House. This was followed by a thoroughfare, and the thoroughfare by a group of bungalows for the individual members of the team, each bungalow numbered according to the occupant's status. Of the actual plant, all that was visible after a year was the diesel powerhouse —a gray structure with asbestos sheets for roof and walls. Indeed, after two years nearly all that the general manager could see from the window of his bungalow (No. 1) was six miles of barren land, interrupted by a few huts and paddy fields; only in the distance could he make out a tower crane, in position to erect the first blast furnace. Even so, the Indians felt at each step that they were being taught the value of discipline and technical precision. "I well remember the day I went to see the laying of bricks in Blast Furnace 2," an Indian technician has written. "Everything appeared so perfect—the bricks, their arrangement, their degree of closeness—that the contractor [he was Indian] had every reason to be happy. But his happiness was short-lived, for the work was rejected by the Soviet technician. 'Too much clearance,' said he. The contractor argued with him but to no avail. *'Nyet,'* said the Russian technician, and that was all. The contractor had to redo the work."

Finally, a few months before the end of the Second Five-Year Plan, in 1961, blast and open-hearth furnaces, coke ovens, and rolling mills having all been commissioned according to schedule, the plant began putting out steel at the rate of a million tons a year. V. V. Rudakov, the Soviet deputy chief engineer, later wrote, "It took about 3.5 years to construct and commission a plant of this size on a completely new and unknown site." Looking to the future, he added, "New units of the Bhilai steel plant mean additional work for Indian people, additional employment, additional housing facilities, additional schools and hospitals, new higher levels of education and culture in India."

In 1965, in connection with the celebration of the Republic Day of India, which falls on January 26th, the Bhilai steel plant published, in English, "Ten Years of Indo-Soviet Collaboration: Bhilai As I Know [It]," a collection of reminiscences of Bhilai by Indians and Russians, which Indarjit Singh, the plant's general manager at the time, describes in a foreword as "a brochure of everlasting memories." One Indian contributor portrays the plant as "stone and steel giants rising against the blue horizon . . . unreal, incredible, wonderful," and from the contributions of other Indians it is clear that the plant inspired exaltation bordering on ecstasy. Reading the Indian accounts, which have such titles as "And We Worked with Soviet Mining Men" and "I Came to Bhilai," one cannot help feeling that the contributors, in their ingenuous amplitude of emotion, speak for all those who participated in the project, and perhaps even for all those waiting to be initiated into the industrial mysteries. Certainly the contributors seem to have regarded their Russian instructors as seers. Nowhere is this more apparent than in what the Indians record of their responses—impulsive, emotional, philosophical, adulatory—to their Russian colleagues.

Somnath Bhattacherjee, a chemist in the Research and Control Laboratory, writes, about a Russian couple with whom he had become fast friends and who had completed their tour of duty in Bhilai:

> One evening when Vanda Borovlov, my friend's wife, told me that they were going to leave us very soon, I remember, I was very much shocked and sharply I looked at her, probably to discern the similar shadows of grief on her face as well. . . . My friend and his wife came nearer, stood before me, allowed their affectionate eyes to immensely totter over my face, and then gently shook my hand, whispered GOOD BYE. In reciprocating, I could anyhow utter—Please remember. Suddenly the moment was shaken. My friend

turned his face toward the opposite direction—presumably to prevent the exposure of his pangs, but from Vanda's eyes pearly drops of tears trickled down silently as if she was separating from her own brother. . . . Those tears, dripped down from her eyes, were nothing to me but the drops of holy water of the Volga, which pervasively mingled with the stream of our Ganges, and inundated our fraternity and imperishable friendship.

Again, Sisir Chakravorti, setting down an *in memoriam* for his Russian friend Ivanovich, describes how the two met just after Chakravorti had come to Bhilai as senior chemical assistant:

I still remember the day when I found myself, during a hot summer, amidst an alien environment. I looked up with awe as a scene of unforgettable solemnity stood before me. There was the smell of the packing-box woods, the toiling labourers, the trucks and tractors racing with time, the flash of welding, the whine of various machines, the buzz of air-pumps, the rattle of riveters, the pound of hammers, and overhead slowly moved the crane with tons of load. I stood dazed for a moment, and then a frolicking summer whirlwind passed in between me and the scene, engulfing everything with its dancing dust. The scene vanished, I almost got choked with the dust. This was the first reception I got from the ruddy and dry and cruel soil of hostile nature of Bhilai scorching under the heat of a ruthless sun.

Suddenly I felt a rude push at my back and was thrown off a few feet away, the dust smearing my white clothes, and instantly a large beam fell on the spot where I was standing. It was a crane failure. I understood the benevolence of that push. Somebody had saved my life. I got up, looked— and looked straight into the eyes of a hefty Russian with a round red face where anger and sympathy struggled over the surface of a usual joviality. He regarded me for a moment in that manner. Sympathy won. And he grinned. Probably he could guess I was new. He approached me, caught hold of my arm, and asked in broken English, "You hurt?" I will never forget that tone. My oldest of acquaintances could not have shown a more genuine sympathy than was expressed in those two words uttered by an unknown giant foreigner. I smiled, clasped his hands, and said, "No. Thank you." That very moment, before we knew each other's name and background, our friendship was cemented in the warmth of his clasps through which his soul seemed to speak.

He was Ivanovich, an erection expert of Blast Furnace.

Chakravorti goes on to reflect on their subsequent friendship and the great admiration he came to have for his Russian co-worker:

Thereafter, whenever we met he always welcomed me with his usual jovial grin. Work was his passion. He worked hard and untiringly. But it was not to save his country's prestige nor that of his own. He found pleasure in it

and he felt that his toil . . . might go a long way in establishing an indus-
trially developed country. . . . In his childlike simplicity, manners, and
gossips, this was the attitude that was revealed. He was not philosophical in
his approach, nor did he bother about the theories of human relationship;
but simply believed this rule of universal fraternity to the core of his heart.

The other day, I went to visit his new working place. He was usually busy
and absorbed in his routine. Still, when he saw me from a distance, his face
lit up and the usual grin was there. A masked welder was prone over a huge
pipe with his instruments. Just then rose a hue and cry. The rope of the
crane lifting the big dome of a stove had snapped and it was coming down
straight on the welder. In a split-second, Ivan rushed to him and pushed him
with all his might. The welder rolled a few feet away. Ivan could not escape. The dome crashed on the pipe and a part of it hit Ivan, injuring him
fatally. He was rushed to the hospital, where he lay unconscious a number
of hours. Then only once he opened his eyes and muttered something in
Russian. The attending Russian nurse said "Ya" ["Da"]. His face lit up,
he grinned, and then collapsed forever. I asked the nurse about his muttering. His last inquiry was, "Is my brother saved?"

I can still feel Ivan's broad and hearty grin is pervading the atmosphere,
crossing the man-made boundaries.

Chakravorti is a natural writer. Others included in the collection are not
so gifted, and yet they manage to convey their feeling of what can only be
called regeneration as a result of working at Bhilai. There is, for example,
the testimony of K. N. Subbaraman, chief engineer from 1956 to 1959,
who, even as he exhorts the Indians to greater effort, reveals the sense of
vitality that his compatriots derived from working with the Russians:

There are many thorns to grasp, but the constant occasions teach the art
of folding them back to prevent hurt. That is the abiding reward of ex-
hausting efforts in the thrilling task of building up a mighty project. . . .
Many people . . . have revealed inexhaustible potentials for greater tasks. It
is sad these are only partly tapped. For hesitations may freeze them while
full use can redouble them by a process of catalytic regeneration.

Barriers give way before noble causes. To have a transcending purpose is
the sure way of cutting across endemic resistances and prejudices. . . . The
obstinacy of understanding melted under the convincing elucidation of the
Soviet experts; a tribute must be paid to their patience. A false picture of
inability built by the fact of inexperience was torn away by a quickness of
perception and convincing variations to set practices that intelligence poised
over gigantic opportunities could put out. Soon there was no room for any
intellectual jealousy or inferiority complex and a strong bond of coöperation
that strove to get the best out of the common thinking and experience was
established. Nothing was ever hidden from anyone who wanted to know;

and that shook off the inertia from many more, and they too strove to
learn. . . . It is strange how the old adage "When there is a will, there is a
way" gets proved again and again in all ages.

Similarly, a contribution by a man named Nayar shows the buoyant
strength of Indian morale in the face of the trials of Bhilai:

> Almost everyone started thinking in a big way. Those with small minds
> got pushed around the corner. I remember the hot summer days with mer-
> cury staying steady at 118° [and] Russians who had come from . . . the
> coldest spots in the world, standing in the hot sun and working hand in
> hand with the Indian engineers. . . . Achievements were not measured in
> terms of the pleasure of the bosses; they were measured more in terms of
> the sense of satisfaction and participation of those who performed them. . . .
> The files were dusty, but the decisions were clean and quick. In a huge
> project like Bhilai with nearly a lakh of persons at work, morale was im-
> portant. . . . I think it was the new spirit of achievement, the new spirit
> of a rising nation, that generated the morale. . . . Bhilai was a great dream
> —a national dream becoming a reality right before one's eyes.

It is, however, left to H. Bhaya, the Secretary of Hindustan Steel,
Ltd., which is the parent Indian government corporation of the Soviet,
German, and British plants (it is the largest corporation in India), to describe the sense of fulfillment experienced by those who were present at
the creation of the plant:

> The sense of awe at the magnitude of the works gave place to admira-
> tion for the grandeur and romance of steelmaking, and then it ripened to an
> abiding affection for the pulsating giant. I was initiated and had become
> part of a grand team—a team in which not only was each proud of achieving
> his own task but shared the anxieties and achievements of the others. This
> was the secret of Bhilai's success—the spontaneous loyalty Bhilai generated.
> It was the best of times; it was the worst of times. . . . It was a frenzy
> without panic, a tempo with a plan. The construction team glowed with
> pride and satisfaction at the newborn plant they had brought to life, the
> operation team was anxiously eager to nurture it to its full stature. The
> human bonds built up through such days were to last forever. All were
> wrapped up in one object. The plant was the thing. It still is and always will
> be. . . . A new faith and confidence filled me. There was a meaning and
> purpose in this vast human activity that could not but grip one's imagination.
> Each one of us were helping build the future—a future one could almost
> see, touch, and feel. . . . One also felt that the plant had now a life and
> personality of its own—quite apart from the men who worked for it—a being
> that demanded the best from us and also rewarded us with that rare feeling,
> a sense of fulfillment.

The themes of "Ten Years of Indo-Soviet Collaboration" are refined in a companion collection called "Poets of Bhilai," also published in 1965. Singh, who writes the foreword to this collection as well, notes that it is "presented to the general public as showing that apart from steelmaking, there is a wealth of other talent also available in the Bhilai Township." He recalls that the public had already viewed some of this wealth in the previous year, when the Bhilai steel plant sponsored a drama competition and an exhibition of arts and crafts. This year, he says, the Bhilai steel plant undertook a treasure hunt for music and poetry. He goes on to say that, in the search for local poetry, clubs in all sectors of what was now the prospering township of Bhilai did a preliminary screening of poems submitted in English or in any of the regional languages. A second screening followed, and now the best poems—along with their English translations, where necessary—were being offered in "Poets of Bhilai," whose contents, representing works by a total of twenty-four poets, writing in English and in nine regional languages, were, in Singh's opinion, "very high in merit and class." But, reading the poems, one feels, at least on the strength of the English translations—and, from what little I know of the regional languages, the translations seem to be faithful to the spirit of the originals, if not always to the letter—that the poetic wealth lies not so much in the craftsmanship of the poets, who are, after all, amateurs, as in the quality of their emotional response to the steel plant. (Together, the two collections serve to measure the weight of the response.) Like the Bhilai essayists, the Bhilai poets seem to be intoxicated by the possibilities of an industrial society, and—perhaps because they are standing only at its threshold—there are no poems in praise of the Luddite. Instead, the poems celebrate the factory worker and the factory town. It sometimes seems that all the invective reserved in the West today for the robots of the industrial society is here turned against the laggards of the pastoral society. To the poets with no spleen, machines operating are as romantic as sheep grazing. Ramashankar Tiwari writes (the translation, like many others in the collection, is in prose):

> Bhilai, personified, speaks of its glory and achievement not only in the field of production and its incessant efforts for the industrialisation of the nation but also of the greatest achievement, remarkable as it is, of the national and emotional integration.
> Situated in the heart of rich granary of Chhattisgarh, it is a pulsating point of India as a whole. Bhilai, synchronised with the time of machine and toil of hard labour, has become a story of success in countries beyond Ocean.

Some of the poets concentrate on the process of industrialization. For B. P. Verma, the smoke of the steel plant and all human desires are one ("The Chimneys symbolise the passion in human hearts, for growth and progress the Sky is the limit"), and they also are for S. U. Suryanarayanan ("There stand the lofty chimneys of the open-hearth furnaces. . . . If all our achievements in the country are knit into a garland, this steel plant forms its shining locket. Let this garland glitter around the neck of our mother country"). Janak U. Oza conveys the joy of Verma and Suryana-rayanan in one pithy couplet:

> Lo! the Blast Furnace is alight
> Pouring molten iron, oh WHAT delight.

Daneshwar Prasad Sharma sees the process of smelting as an almost mystical act of creation. Using the fact that the Bhilai steel plant produces rails, he writes, "Young night, running train and crowded compartment come to life when someone said 'Bhilai.'" But machines are only one aspect of the industrial process. Another aspect is human labor, and the joy of work also receives its tribute from the poets. For M. L. Chadha, work is almost a religion:

> There are some blacksheeps here! also as everywhere.
> Workshirkers petty minded, they are a slur, a shame.
> Here work is worship my Friends.

Indeed, for R. P. Agnihotri even the poet is simply one more worker:

The Nation today needs poems to raise the morale of mankind. . . . The Poet is the man of the era, creator of new age, and should divert the flow of human thoughts to the needs of progress and prosperity so that a new awak-ening rises in the world.

To other poets, it is symbolically significant that men from all over the country have been drawn to live and work in Bhilai, for this promises a strong, united India; Bhilai, says Manrakhan Lal Sahu, "is decorated, and its youth is blossomed by the cultures of all corners of the country, and the young maid speaks all the languages of India." Still other poets, however, think of the industrial and nationalistic achievement of Bhilai in terms of military prowess. Munnuwar Sherwani strikes this note when he says that his poem about Bhilai "gives the clarion call to the nation to defend our cherished freedom and our honour from the aggressor on our border." G. P. Sharma implies the identity of an enemy on the border when he gives an alarm to the nation: "Remember the fronts of NEFA and Ladakh."

Jwala Prasad Pateria, invoking historical, religious, and legendary heroes, reaches perhaps the highest pitch of patriotic expression:

Do not worry, Chacha. [Nehru was popularly called "Chacha," or "uncle."] Send us to the front and we will fight the Chinese. The Children of this steel township have hearts of steel, and they are the descendants of Shivaji, Pratap, and Rani Laxmi Bai. We have played in the plains and heights of Vindhyas, and the children of Hanuman and Bhim will burn the Dragon's land and drink his blood. Do not worry; send us to the front— the enemies will retreat—we shall guard the petals of your rose flower, the Tricolour, and every inch of Indian soil.

But Bhilai is, above all, the first step of an impoverished society on the road leading to an industrial utopia. O. N. Rao possibly had this in mind when he wrote his poem, "Dejection," almost in the form of a parable:

This is also a lyric describing the pathetic journey in the hot Sun of a person deprived of basic needs of living. He doesn't attribute directly anything to anybody for his poor plight, but in his exhortation to a fellow-pedestrian, he mentions the reasons for their long walk from birth to death, sounding some mild aspersions on human Society. . . .

Before he reaches the goal of his life, the destination, he hopes that the horizon of his dreams, neutralising the inequalities, will come true and in that aspiration for ELDORADO he continues his journey with blubbered feet. A hope sustained is a hope attained is signified in this lyric of all pathos.

The utter chaos of diction and imagery and the hyperbolic tone of Rao's poetry, like those of other contributors to the collection, help to illustrate the exaggerated response that the advent of technology can evoke in a poor country.

There is only one discordant voice in the collection. It belongs to Hillole Sen, who shows some concern about the consequences of an industrial society, almost as if he were a veteran of it rather than a tyro. But even he, by the end of his poem, has joined the chorus affirming progress. The poem reads, in its entirety:

Today it often comes to my mind that the word "Yantra" (machine) has been derived from the word "Yantrana" (pain). As a matter of fact, every pain has its jocund result.

When a conceived lady gets the pain of her child's birth she feels a sort of pleasure and anxiously waits for the moment when the child will be born and ultimately wipe off all the resultant pain. Today in the modern age, which is essentially a Machine Age (yantra-yuga), everybody feels a sort of pain of pleasure and finds the way of new creations. Amidst this the Bhilai Steel Project was born.

The land of Chhattisgarh created its place in the history of the world by a joint effort of India and Russia and people felt the pleasure of pain in the long run.

There is a curse of the machine also. It makes our minds also mechanised. The machine is good and can take the civilisation to a height, but we must avoid the mechanisation of intellect and mind, which is fatal for civilisation.

Though I came here with a fascinated mind, which was the outcome of the halo of the Bhilai Steel Project, I am still unsatisfied, and I know that dissatisfaction is the source of improvements.

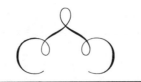

On the Banks of the Potomac

IN 1962, WORLD STEEL PRODUCTION stood at a record level of three hundred and ninety-four million tons, with Western Europe accounting for twenty-nine per cent, the Soviet Union and Eastern Europe for twenty-eight per cent, the United States for twenty-five per cent, and Japan for eight per cent. But India's annual steel production, after the first two Five-Year Plans, had risen comparatively little, going from one million to three million three hundred thousand tons. This tonnage was divided almost equally between the plants in the public sector and those in the private one, all of which were experiencing shortages; the training of skilled personnel and the mining of minerals for making steel were not keeping pace with the new plant capacity, such as it was. Some of the production difficulties at Durgapur and Rourkela, however, were attributed to the nature of their products—at Durgapur mostly wheels and axles, and at Rourkela mostly sheets and pipes, all considered by steel men to be harder to produce than rails and girders, the principal output at Bhilai, which was the plant with the best performance of all. India was spending two hundred million dollars a year importing a million tons of steel, and Bhilai, though it was more than twice the size of Durgapur or Rourkela, was designed to reach a capacity of only two and a half million tons. The Indian government was working to alleviate the shortages, and was also going ahead with a scheme for a fourth new plant. As early as 1958, an Indian engineering firm had made a favorable preliminary report on this project, which was to be situated in Bokaro, a town in Bihar lying a hundred and fifty miles northwest of Calcutta. Bokaro, as the newest project was called, would cost from nine hundred million to one and a third billion dollars to build, it was estimated, and would reach a capacity of four million tons. India once again had to search for a foreign sponsor, but neither Britain nor Germany was in a position to embark on a second plant, and India was reluctant to approach the Soviet Union, in part because so great a dependence on one country for machinery and technology was considered inadvisable, especially in the politically strategic area of steel. An approach was made to the United States, where John F. Kennedy was President. In 1958, when India had been seeking an emergency financial transfusion for the almost moribund Second Five-Year Plan, Kennedy, who was then a senator, had been co-sponsor, with Senator John Sherman Cooper, of a resolution that asked Congress to recognize "the importance of the economic development of the Republic of India to its people, to democratic values and institutions, and to peace and stability in the world." At that time, Kennedy made what Indians considered a thoughtful speech on behalf of India's economic development, touching on her specific need for steel and on the new plant at Bokaro.

We have come increasingly to doubt ourselves, to question the impact of a [foreign] policy whose substance seems so very largely military [he said, according to the *Congressional Record*]. Our sense of drift, our gnawing dissatisfaction, our seemingly hopeless predicament in reaching but the fringes of a great crisis is nowhere more evident than in our search for policies adapted effectively and concretely to the new and generally uncommitted nations which run from Casablanca to the Celebes. . . . One country in particular—India—has successfully pointed the way to progressive economic development.

He observed that India was a parliamentary democracy with universal suffrage, that she had a stable government with an efficient civil service, and that she had a mixed economy of private and public ownership. He said that India had made better use of American aid than most other recipient countries, and that by her First Five-Year Plan she herself had raised her national income by eighteen per cent. He then turned to the Second Five-Year Plan, which, he said, was in danger of collapsing, and perhaps bringing down with it democracy in India:

This plan . . . is . . . almost two and a half times as large as the first plan. It hopes to carry India across the most difficult threshold of economic growth—the establishment of capital-generative basic industries such as steel. . . . If successful, it could vigorously mobilize India's rich resources in hydropower, iron ore, manganese, coal, bauxite. The essential features of the

plan include four steel mills—one of which [Bhilai] is well advanced. . . .
Unfortunately, a serious foreign exchange crisis has forced India to pare its
plan to the core. . . . The heavy expenditures lie in the heart of the plan—
steel, transport, irrigation, power, tool plants. . . . Informed judgment tells
us that it cannot [cut more deeply into the plan], for a genuine program of
economic development is a seamless web which cannot be pulled apart or
rewoven from cheaper materials.

He went on to talk about the range of Soviet aid to India, pointing out
that although the Soviet Union had given less aid than the United States
and was a comparative latecomer in the field of economic assistance, still,
by concentrating on heavy industry, it had seized the opportunity to make
its cause one with that of India's Second Five-Year Plan, and now, in
addition to the Bhilai steel plant, was assisting with a variety of projects,
among them a heavy-machinery plant and a thermal-power plant. Stress-
ing the importance of India to the free world, he said:

India contains nearly forty per cent of all the free peoples of the uncommitted world. . . . India, the most important of all the uncommitted states,
has entered its formative period. . . . Its democratic future is delicately and
dangerously poised; it would be catastrophic if its leadership were now hu-
miliated in its quest for Western assistance when its cause is good.

Kennedy's speech, which was remembered in India for its intellectual
and emotional grasp of economic development, had, as it happened, little
effect on aid. India did not receive American aid for the plant at Bokaro,
or for any other industrial project of the Second Five-Year Plan, and the
web of economic development began to unravel. By 1962, India had received about four billion dollars from the United States, compared to only
about eight hundred million dollars from the Soviet Union, but Soviet aid,
with its dramatic industrial projects, was continuing to make the greater
impression; American economic aid not only was spread over a longer
period but was restricted—mainly as a consequence of the American aver-
sion to any Socialist pattern of state-owned industry—to agriculture and to
the military.

In 1962, however, both President Kennedy and his Ambassador to India,
John Kenneth Galbraith, were ready to abandon the shibboleth against aid
to state-owned industry, and Galbraith, like Kennedy, was a strong advocate of the Bokaro project. Since it was up to the administration to decide
how to spend the foreign-aid funds that Congress authorized, the prospects for American sponsorship of the project now seemed excellent. In the
early spring of 1962, the Agency for International Development commissioned the United States Steel Corporation to make a technical and eco-

nomic survey of the Bokaro project. The survey was completed within eight months, at a cost of $686,344, and was published in two volumes. It judged the project to be feasible, under certain conditions: that the time allotted for plant construction be extended for six years beyond the date of the completion of the Fourth Five-Year Plan, in 1971—the time limit set by the Indian government—and that the project be independent of Hindustan Steel's bureaucracy and instead be entrusted to a separate public corporation, to be managed by Americans not only during the construction period but for some years afterward. It was thought unlikely that India would balk at the conditions set forth in the survey; she had already agreed that Bokaro, which would be the most expensive single aid project ever sponsored by the United States anywhere, should take the place of all other American aid to India during the construction period. As a matter of fact, though, India was afraid that, however far she went toward meeting the demands of the survey, some of which were clearly aimed at weakening state management, the United States, when the time came for the final decision, might not be able to bring itself to further a form of Socialism abroad that it spurned at home.

In March, 1963, the Committee to Strengthen the Security of the Free World, a government body appointed by Kennedy and headed by General Lucius D. Clay, submitted to the President a rather pessimistic report on American military and economic assistance programs.

> While we realize that in aiding foreign countries we cannot insist upon the establishment of our own economic system, despite its remarkable success and progress, we should not extend aid which is inconsistent with our beliefs, democratic tradition, and knowledge of economic organization and consequences [the report noted at one point]. Moreover, the observation of countless instances of politically operated, heavily subsidized, and carefully protected insufficient state enterprises in less-developed countries makes us gravely doubt the value of such undertakings in the economic lives of these nations. . . . The only way the Congress can express its disapproval of a development loan project is through a specific prohibition in the authorization act. The committee is of the opinion that the Congress should have a strong voice in the decision as to how the United States taxpayers' money is to be spent overseas. As it is now, the executive has the sole authority for this decision.

Simultaneously, American steel and shipping interests mobilized to oppose the Bokaro project, and it was pointed out in speeches in the House and the Senate that between 1958 and 1962 American steel exports had dropped from two million eight hundred thousand tons to two million tons, causing unemployment at American docks as well as at the steel plants; that fifty per cent of the American steel exports went to Asia; that in this Asian market the United States was already being supplanted by Japan, where the working wage in a steel plant was only sixty-three cents an hour, compared to $2.29 an hour, the minimum union wage in America; and that an expanded steel industry in India might one day close the Asian market to American steel altogether. Newspapers of many political persuasions also came out against the Bokaro project. Some editorials took it as an ideological threat; for instance, the Chicago *Sun-Times* commented, "Broadly speaking, the opposite of private enterprise and individual capitalism is state ownership, state production, and state distribution. Or, if you will, Marxism. This is precisely the status of the proposed steel mill in India. . . . It would be far better to loan the necessary money to India so she could buy steel in the free world market than to endorse, with dollars, a philosophy dedicated to the overthrow of our own way of life." Other editorials regarded Bokaro as simply a bad investment; the *Wall Street Journal* commented, "Though that nation [India] has received more United States aid than any other country, its economic troubles and demands for outside assistance are not decreasing but increasing. A major reason is the bungling of India's government planners—their insistence on emphasizing industry at the expense of badly needed food output, their reliance on tangled networks of controls, their stress on socialistic projects designed more for political profit than for economic gain." And some news reports were colored by an outright hostile tone, like this one from the *U.S. News & World Report* for April 15, 1963:

> In Washington, a report on foreign aid has just been made by a special White House committee headed by Gen. Lucius Clay. This report opposed use of dollars of American aid to finance construction for socialized industries that compete with private industry in a country. . . .
>
> The first [Indian] Government mill to be completed was financed by the Russians. . . . American engineers describe the mill as extremely simple in design, but it does produce steel. Their description expresses the view that the mill is built by peasants for peasants.
>
> Russians have kept control of this whole operation, with the Indian general manager no more than a figurehead.
>
> The German experience, by comparison, had been a nightmare. . . . Trouble developed and a special commission of German technicians was appointed to find what was wrong.
>
> The commission found: Indian personnel with adequate training was extremely scarce. . . . Absenteeism had risen to 25 percent. Hindustan Steel, Ltd. . . . had 3,600 headquarters personnel, and a minor decision required

from 24 to 36 months. About 30 percent of Indians trained in Germany were given jobs for which they were not trained. . . .

British experience at India's third Government steel mill is only a little better. . . .

Private steel companies have the trained personnel, experience and means to expand to meet India's steel needs. Government stands in their way. The question is whether American taxpayers now will build new steel facilities to take the place of those that could be financed privately.

Indian officials already are wheeling out the whipsaw argument. They say that if Americans do not go ahead with the project, then the Russians will.

Many of the facts in the *U.S. News & World Report* article, like. many printed elsewhere, were disputed by both Indians and Americans. For instance, the representatives of the private steel industry in India, whose economic freedom or lack of it was one of the main points of contention in the American attack on Bokaro, were firm in their support of the project. J. R. D. Tata, chairman of Tata Enterprises, which included the Tata Iron & Steel Co., stated that it was not within the means of Indian private industry to build a steel plant on anything like the scale of Bokaro, and Bharat Ram, president of the Indian Federation of Commerce and Industry, an organization akin to the American Chamber of Commerce, wrote, in a letter to the Washington *Post:*

I want to correct an impression in some quarters in the United States that Indian private enterprise views with varying degrees of disagreeableness the Bokaro steel project. This is obviously based on an imperfect knowledge of Indian conditions and our requirements of steel. . . . Currently the per capita consumption of steel in India, taking into account domestic output and imports, is 11 kilograms; and this is one of the lowest in the world. . . . The Government of India's steel policy vis-a-vis public and private sectors of the industry is one of non-discrimination and equal treatment. This policy was recently reiterated by the India Minister for Steel and Heavy Industries. It has drawn favorable comment from the leaders of the Indian steel industry in private hands, and according to them competition between the two sectors of the Indian steel industry will not arise in view of the nationalized and controlled operation of the two sectors. So, to the Indian steel industry, Bokaro does not present any problem of disadvantageous competition. . . . I am also of the view that the lack of adequate quantities of steel is standing in the way of a more rapid development of private sector industries, including small industries where there is a marked tendency to take to metallurgical based operations, and of which steel-based are the most significant.

The American proponents of the Bokaro project also challenged the opinion that a mixed economy was identical with Socialism. They said that, even apart from the fact that in underdeveloped countries the power of rich private families was historically and emotionally associated with oppression, while state ownership was looked upon as a cornucopia of shared benefits, still, for the production of steel, many countries—including, surprisingly, Japan, the conservative business interests' favorite example of a capitalist, democratic industrial society—relied on a combination of private and public enterprise in the early stages of industrialization. Galbraith, drawing together some of the arguments in favor of the Bokaro project, wrote, also in the Washington *Post,* in August of 1963:

> The Bokaro plant has acquired a vast symbolic interest in the subcontinent. On no subject during my tour as Ambassador was I so intensively queried. . . . When the American Mount Everest team returned to New Delhi after its successful climb, it was said, jokingly, that the first question addressed to the leader at his press conference concerned his attitude on Bokaro. . . . There is agreement . . . on the favorable effect of this plant on the American economy. Our own steel industry is not expanding. As a result, firms engaged in this kind of construction and machine building have a good deal of excess capacity and idle labor force. Heavy engineering firms in western Pennsylvania, Ohio, northern Indiana, Illinois, and elsewhere would especially welcome the business and employment [from producing equipment for the Bokaro project]. . . . The experience of countries such as India with private capitalism has been different from ours. It is identified in many minds with the foreign ownership of earlier times.
>
> The Communists offer public ownership or socialism, and excoriate private ownership. If we excoriate public ownership, and insist in an equally dogmatic way on private capitalism, we leave those who believe deeply in democratic socialism no choice but to align themselves with the Communists. . . . We know from experience in Scandinavia, Great Britain, Canada, New Zealand, and even our own past that a pragmatic combination of public and private ownership is quite compatible with personal liberty. . . .
>
> The Clay Committee report . . . was greeted with unalloyed enthusiasm by the Indian left-wing press. . . . They took it as proof that the democratic socialists had no future on our side.

Although the Clay report could not be read as a clear-cut veto of projects like Bokaro (the Washington *Post* commented, "The antagonists have chosen to ignore that passage in the Clay report which declares that 'in aiding foreign countries, we cannot insist upon the establishment of our own economic system, despite its remarkable success and progress' "), one of the effects of the report's urging more congressional control of foreign-aid projects was to place the fate of the Bokaro project in the hands of Congress, and the proposal was debated there in the summer of 1963.

Senators and representatives opposing the Bokaro project said, among other things, that it was "a direct repudiation of our economic principles," that Indian planners were "inoculated with the Marxist virus," that these planners were trying to "disguise their enthusiastic bias in favor of Social-ism as logical necessity born of peculiar circumstances," and that Socialism was "merely a temporary sojourn" on the way to Communism. Frank J. Lausche, a Democratic senator from Ohio, spoke for many of them when, on the floor of the Senate, he said of growing rumors that India would, after all, ask the Soviet Union to help with the Bokaro project, "If India is saying to our government, 'Unless you give us the nine hundred million dollars promptly, we will go to Russia for aid to help establish this plant,' I would say to them, 'Go.' Red Russia will never give them the money, and if she does, it will be on terms under which India will have to sell its soul."

On August 22, 1963, the Bokaro project was debated in the House of Representatives in connection with an amendment to that year's foreign-aid bill that had been introduced by William S. Broomfield, a Republican from Michigan. The burden of the Broomfield amendment was that any single foreign-aid project in excess of a hundred million dollars must re-ceive specific approval from Congress. Silvio O. Conte, a Republican repre-sentative from Massachusetts, said in a speech in support of the amend-ment:

I want to shatter the myth of those that say the Soviet-financed mill in India is justification for our going in and building this one at this time. Their steel mill [Bhilai] was financed by a 12-year loan from the Soviets at a 2.5 percent interest, repayable in hard currency, at a total amount of $136 million. . . . Our loan, on the other hand, would amount to almost a billion dollars, a sizable chunk of the $1.8 billion expected cost of the mill. [The estimated cost of the Bokaro project rose along with the rhetoric.] This would be in the form of a 40-year development credit loan, with a 10-year grace period. Our interest will be three-fourths of 1 percent. Through long experience with these development credit loans we can be certain that we will not get too much of this money back.

In other words, we will give India about a billion dollars. The Indian gov-ernment will then form a corporation to build the mill. India will lend money to the corporation at 5¾ percent interest, not overlooking the fact that for every ton of steel made in India there is a charge of $52 a ton. *In toto,* this means that the Indian government will realize over a 20-year period, out of our $1 billion alone, about $5.5 billion.

Furthermore, we will be lucky to even receive a million dollars out of the billion that we contribute. There will also be powerful competition to sell them [the reference is to India] steel at a cheaper rate than we can sell it to India.

There is no guarantee, either, that would prevent the Indians from buying cheaper steel from the other steel-producing countries who could sell to them at a cheaper rate. That is to say, if they still have need for steel even above and beyond what Bokaro would produce.

For example, Japan could sell India a ton of steel for $102 at dockside. It would cost India $174 for a ton of steel at dockside from the United States.

Representative Conte's facts and figures might have been open to question, but it was clear that his colleagues shared his views, for the Broomfield amendment was easily carried. A few weeks later, the Indian government, concluding that the Bokaro project would fare no better in another session of Congress, debating another year's foreign-aid bill, withdrew its request. Learning of this turn of events, John H. Kyl, a Republican representative from Iowa, saluted the author of the Broomfield amendment, saying, "It is my opinion that if the gentleman from Michigan had not proceeded so diligently with his work . . . this project would have remained in the foreign-aid authorization. Mr. Broomfield thus saved this Congress and the country from making a costly mistake."

In 1964, the Soviet Union formally offered, on terms similar to those providing for the construction of Bhilai, financial and technical assistance to India in building her biggest steel plant, and in due course Indian and Soviet administrators, engineers, and designers arrived in Bokaro to take up the work.

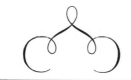

At the Confluence of the
Volga and the Ganga

AT THE TIME OF THE CENSUS OF 1951, Bhilai had an area of 28 square miles and a population of 7,116, made up of fifteen agrarian hamlets whose areas and populations varied from 482 to 2,676 acres and from 172 to 1,226 inhabitants. Ten years later, Bhilai, thanks to its new importance, had an area of 40.14 square miles and a population of 86,116. (Literate and educated persons numbered 43,179, and workers numbered 48,772, most of the latter now being engaged in such unpastoral activities as construction, mining, manufacturing, commerce, transport, and communications.) The 1961 census, in a section classifying towns with a population under five thousand as Class VI and those with over a hundred thousand as Class I, ranked Bhilai as a Class II town. In a section classifying districts according to their growth in respect to the number of new towns during this century, however, the census still ranked Durg forty-first among the forty-three districts of the state. (It contained five small towns in 1901 and eight in 1961.) Still, statistics do not add up to a community. And so to the perennial *Gazetteer*.

From the earliest times man has sought to acquire knowledge of his immediate environment, partly in order to survive but also partly because of his innate curiosity [notes the introductory volume of the *Gazetteer of India*— "Imperial" has naturally been dropped from the title—revised, edited, and launched in 1965 under the direction of Humayun Kabir, then an education adviser to the central government]. In the course of time, this led him to undertake a study of his own country and record his impressions in various tangible forms. He did not rest there. . . . Travellers' accounts [written by natives or foreigners] . . . became a recognized form of literature quite early in history. Soon, such accounts were organized in what may be called Gazetteers or Geographical Dictionaries. Today, their scope has been expanded further so as to cover the physical features and the history of a country as well as the social, political and economic life of the people inhabiting it.

In discussing present-day Bhilai, the new *Gazetteer* points out that the concept of the town, as it is understood in the West, was actually introduced to village India by the Portuguese in the sixteenth century but remained almost unknown in the country as a whole until the nineteenth century, when the British transported their little bit of England to India. Even then, the town was a hybrid affair—a cantonment of spacious bungalows and broad, straight roads, of parks and playing fields, grafted onto a village of ramshackle dwellings and congested bazaars, of narrow winding lanes with gullies leading off them. "Examples of such cultural schizophrenia are Bangalore, Poona, Ahmadabad, and Delhi," the new *Gazetteer* comments, and it goes on to say that the culturally homogeneous industrial town was nonexistent until this century, when a few industrial towns had "literally sprung up in jungles where previously tigers roamed." The account in the new *Gazetteer* continues:

> In Independent India, three new steel towns have emerged: Bhilai in Madhya Pradesh, Rourkela in Orissa, and Durgapur in West Bengal. These factories have not only brought prosperity but are altering the social landscape of the areas. Regions which were only recently backward, economically and culturally, are being pitchforked suddenly into prosperous, urban, and cosmopolitan social life. . . .
> Social life in the new industrial towns is different from social life in cities which grew around or near extant and traditional towns. In the former, the civic hierarchy shows a tendency to follow the factory hierarchy. The town is nothing more than a place where the factory workers live when they are not working. . . . As in these towns, the factory employees live in houses built by the employers, they cannot choose their neighbours. Thus . . . a Brahmin may have a Harijan ["untouchable"] or Muslim or Christian for a neighbour. . . . The lower income-levels tend, however, to overlap somewhat with the lower castes, and to this extent even the new towns tend to perpetuate traditional distances between higher and lower castes.

Being a traveller in the tradition of the earliest times, and having my share of innate curiosity, I now set out from Delhi for Bhilai to compile my notes for a future gazetteer. I am making the trip by air, but, because of turbulent weather, my plane is grounded in Bhopal, the capital of Madhya Pradesh, and late in the evening I find myself at the Madhya Pradesh Government Tourist Office as a traveller in distress. The solitary occupant of the office, which is a small one, is a slender girl with an elfin face and with straight hair down to her shoulders. She is dressed in a plain purple sari and wears no makeup. She greets me with a little Muslim salaam, introduces herself as Miss Shukla, the regional tourist officer, hears me through, and immediately sets about telephoning to arrange overnight accommodations for me. There are circles under her eyes, but her manner is patient. Eventually, she locates a room, and then she sets about telephoning to arrange for a taxi.

While we wait for the taxi, she answers a few of my questions, sitting very straight on the edge of her chair. She tells me that she has made a career of state-government service, that a woman with a career is still an oddity in India, and that her future will probably consist of a series of transfers from one place in Madhya Pradesh to another. "If the modern age ever really arrives in India, Madhya Pradesh will probably be the last to know about it," she says.

I mention Bhilai.

"I've never been there," she says. "The only industry they know here in Bhopal is rolling cigarettes and folding *pans*. They say you can always tell a Bhopali by his betel-stained lips."

It is the end of April when I reach Bhilai, and very hot, but, by courtesy of the Indian government, I am lodged in a new flat complete with air-conditioners, a refrigerator, and a hot and cold shower—conveniences scarcely known in the rest of Madhya Pradesh. Almost immediately, I go on a tour of Bhilai in a car with an Indian engineer who was trained in the United States and who has been here from the beginning of the project, as a member of its Town Planning and Architectural Section. "Bhilai is a modern temple," he says to me as he starts the car. "You will find this a clean place. There are no madding crowds here. Everything is clearly set out in sectors. The town is as advanced as the plant. Everyone is provided with a house, medical care, and education. Each child gets free primary education, two free uniforms, and free lunch. The town and the plant are two halves of the same idea, like the hammer and the sickle."

On the outskirts of the town, far from the plant, the engineer drives me past the houses of the plant directors, pointing out the residences of the general manager, the general superintendent, the assistant general superintendent, the chief engineer, the financial adviser, and the accounts officer—

all built on a grand British scale, with spacious compounds. He then drives me past two-room *pukka* dwellings with asbestos-sheet roofing, for workers earning a hundred and fifty rupees a month, and, later, past *kutcha* one-room huts, for workers earning a hundred rupees a month. Some dwellings have private bathrooms, some have semi-private bathrooms, and some have only taps with water available for between one and twelve hours a day—the comforts of the houses always corresponding to the pay of the workers. All the dwellings are carefully grouped, are numbered, and are categorized in respect to occupancy. Even those in the poorest category—shelters made out of bamboo mats—are all exactly the same size and are set out in neat rows. "This is a colony of sweepers," the engineer says when we drive past one such row. "It used to be near the houses of the State Bank employees, but they complained about its lowering the status of their sector, so the authorities made the sweepers roll up their mats and bring them over here. But you notice the orderly way we have relocated this crawling colony."

The engineer goes on to tell me in a sanguine manner that the town, which, unlike the steel plant, was designed entirely by Indians, was laid out to reproduce the social hierarchy of the plant. The idea had been to provide for each employee, at seven and a half per cent of his salary, housing that reflected his position; the better his job, the larger and the more distant from the plant his house was to be. The town that was eventually built made some compromises with the original idea, the engineer continues, but, even so, one could often tell the position of an employee by the size and construction of his dwelling, the sector in which the dwelling was situated, and, within that sector, its distance from the plant. As the engineer drives me from sector to sector along numbered roads that regularly intersect named avenues (Six Tree Avenue, Central Avenue, Forest Avenue), he points out how tidy everything is, and although I recognize that the people here, as a community, live better than people elsewhere in India, Bhilai, with its garden-city layout, recalls to my mind only architectural models and drawing boards. There are no twisting gullies and alleyways, no crowded, snarled lanes, no cows lounging in the streets, no stray dogs yelping at the heat, no litter, no stenches or acrid smells of any kind, no hawkers, no venders, no streetside stalls, no bystanders. No one seems to haggle or curse, to squat or sleep, to loaf about on the streets. Bhilai has well-organized shopping centers and the hush of the perfect suburb. I have to tell myself repeatedly that I am still in India, and that not long ago Bhilai was a Hindu village, for the town seems futuristic, unreal, dead, a forlorn first settlement on another planet—the conception of some science-fiction fantasist.

I have just been spending some time at the plant, and before I had been there very long I decided that if I were ever to give a speech about my impressions I would use for an epigraph some remarks that Nehru made in a speech he gave when he came here in 1960 to inaugurate the Rail and Structural Mill. "I have been asked to press the button or work the handle of this Rail and Structural Mill," he said. "I have followed a bit—not much, for unfortunately I have not studied engineering. I am now about to work the handle and I know not exactly what it will lead to. But of course something will happen. So should I work the handle. That is it; the goods train is to move out from the side." My own notes on the plant go, in part:

"Plant Area: 1.8 square miles, all walled in. Barbed wire on top of the wall. Observation rooms for Bhilai security guards. Clock tower. Inside wall are forty-one observation platforms for Bhilai security guards. Just beyond, huge arch, with big sign: 'Work Is Worship.' Clatter and crash of steelmaking. Hot as inferno.

"Batteries: Coke-wagon tipplers hurtling by, sounding like a dozen tramways loosed upon the world. Twenty-five to thirty tons of coal. Each battery has sixty-five cells, each cell is called an oven. Temperature in the ovens 950°. A man sweeps coal from the oven door. Coke under water shower. Crushers. Screen. Conveyor belt to blast furnace.

"Blast Furnace: Coke is used for heating iron ore, and mixed with limestone, etc., to give flow. Furnace lined with refractory bricks. One blast furnace turns out 200–220 tons of pig iron in one tapping. Molten metal collected in a ladle and kept in storage tank in hot, liquid form. Control room with diagram of blast furnace and with electric lights showing movement of material.

"Open-Hearth Furnace: Pig iron converted into steel. Chamber capacity of 250–500 tons. Process takes eight hours. Signs: 'Care Costs Nothing but Saves Rupees,' and 'More Tanks, More Trucks, More Trains, More Ships, More of Them Come Out If More Ingots Go Out.'

"Rolling Mills: Rail, merchant, billet, blooming mills. Wide central area, galleries crossing. Pulpit No. 3—a control room about eight feet from the ground, glass-enclosed. Sign: 'We Welcome Everyone Except Mr. and Mrs. Accident.'

"Workers: New-found dignity in labor in evidence everywhere. Am reminded of some other remarks by Nehru from the speech inaugurating the Rail and Structural Mill: 'A kind of atmosphere had developed in our country during the British regime, and many people used to feel that hands and feet must not be moved, only tongue should be used or pen should be used and [everyone] sit separately like a big *babu*. These times have changed or should change. Your project has many big and experienced engineers. If the big engineers only sit in the offices and act like *babus,* then they are not working properly, because I feel that every man's head and hands should move together.' A worker recites for me this pledge, taken at Nehru's death: 'We, the workers of the Bhilai steel plant, have lost in our beloved Prime Minister, late Shri Jawaharlal Nehru, the founding father of this plant, who took a keen interest in its affairs and paid several personal visits to it. He was a great statesman, a unique Indian leader of this century, and indeed a man in the traditions of peace and amity set up since Asoka. We pledge today to assume greater responsibility than before and work harder than hitherto, so that we may fulfill his dreams of economically self-sufficient India. We will consider no sacrifice great enough to achieve it. We will also follow in his footsteps in binding our people together in secular bonds rather than in dividing them, and shall not let smallness of minds crowd out our bigger responsibilities to the country.' "

At the foot of the road leading to the plant, there is a tall obelisk commemorating the friendship of the Soviet and Indian peoples. To the right is the Bhilai Technical Institute, where about eleven thousand Indian trainees are enrolled, and to the left and across the way is Ispat Bhavan ("house of steel"). This is the administration building, where I go one morning to pay my respects to Indarjit Singh, a civil servant who joined Hindustan Steel as its finance director in 1961 and came to the Bhilai steel plant as its general manager in 1963. His office is on the second floor. It is large and, unlike most Indian offices, extremely neat and comfortable. Such papers as are about are stacked in even piles on shelves behind Singh's desk, the top of which is clear; a score of chairs are arranged around the room; there is a painting of the plant and a big photograph of the President of India; the walls are panelled with teak; the blinds are drawn against the glare of the hot sun outside; and three powerful air-conditioners are blowing cool air, Singh is a tall, stout Sikh in his early fifties. He is dressed in a well-cut suit, a crisp, clean shirt, and a crisp, clean turban, and has a self-possessed manner.

I ask Singh how the expansion of the plant is going.

"We hope to reach our goal of two and a half million tons of steel per year within the next few months," he says, and he goes on to tell me that the plant reached its expected capacity of one million tons of steel per year during the Second Five-Year Plan, and its expected capacity of a million eight hundred thousand tons during the Third Five-Year Plan. "We used to produce a million tons of steel by working in three eight-hour shifts. When we start producing two and a half million tons, we will have to produce in one shift almost as much as we were first producing in a twenty-four-hour day. For this, we are increasing the number of workers on each shift and training more people for managerial jobs. It's like adding to a family, and we have the same kind of organizational problems that an American housewife has."

I ask him if the Bhilai steel plant presents any unusual difficulties.

"About sixty per cent of our products are sold to the government," he says. "Our table of prices was fixed years ago by the Tariff Commission; they were protective prices and were fixed low, so that we could export steel and compete in foreign markets and earn badly needed foreign exchange. But our wages are always rising. Like an American housewife, we must absorb all increases in cost within our strict budget."

In a manner that swings continually between the formal and the informal, Singh talks some more about his budgetary problems. He boasts that the plant has the largest blast furnace in Asia, and that Bhilai will have an ultimate capacity two and a half times that of Durgapur or Rourkela, and he guardedly mentions a current recession, which has led to a slackening in the demand for steel and a cutback in the steel production at Bhilai, in spite of the fact that foreign markets for steel have been found in Burma, Japan, and even England. "I have to confess that the plant faces one of its most frustrating periods," he says.

One of the criticisms often made of enterprises in the public sector is that they foster inefficient management. Indeed, an American economist at the Rand Corporation, William A. Johnson, in his book "The Steel Industry of India," specifically levels this charge at the new Indian plants. "The notions that a distinguished career as a civil servant qualifies a person to administer any organization and that, in any event, administrative talents necessary for managing a steel mill can be developed on the job appear to be widespread," he writes. "Both beliefs are mistaken. The successful management of a steel mill demands specialized skills derived from long experience in the industry and an administrative organization appropriate to the industry." Certainly one Indian in Bhilai who does measure up to

Johnson's criterion is a fifty-five-year-old engineer named Purtej Singh. (Singh is a common name in India.) He was a member of the original engineering team, and therefore has the status of a founding father of Bhilai, where he has been, successively, engineer-in-charge of the water works, chief civil engineer, chief engineer, and general superintendent— the position he now holds. Unlike most Indians who were not trained in the Soviet Union (Purtej Singh qualified as a sanitary engineer at Harvard), he is fluent in Russian, having learned it in Bhilai, and, unlike most Indians here, he is genuinely at ease both with Russians and with Indians. In fact, when I meet him, in his office at Ispat Bhavan, after talking with Indarjit Singh, it seems to me that he even has the proverbial unfussy, workmanlike Russian manner. He is big and burly, with gray hair and glasses, and he is dressed in a white bush shirt and white cotton trousers.

As a first question, I ask him how Russians and Indians get on together in Bhilai.

"In India, there has always been a barrier between Indians and Westerners, and there is undoubtedly a similar barrier in Bhilai between Indians and Russians," he says. "In certain economic respects, Russians in Bhilai are much better off than Indians holding the same positions; the Russians are here with better contracts, and they can afford to live better. Also, some Indians still resent being helped by foreigners. I don't think that is a very enlightened approach, though, because what alternative is there? To sink crores of rupees in a plant and then learn by mistakes? Generally speaking, I should say that the Soviet Union has given us aid on better terms than some other countries have even offered. America, for instance, wouldn't build the plant in Bokaro for us because she did not wish to build a plant to help develop a Socialist state."

I ask him how he thinks the plants at Durgapur and Rourkela compare with Bhilai.

"Since the final product in the three plants is different, the equipment in the three plants is very different and can't really be compared, but one thing that is generally accepted about Bhilai is that this is the best-designed plant," he says. "The one disadvantage here is that we have to transport our coal four hundred and fifty miles, from Bihar. The coal in Madhya Pradesh turned out to be so bad that we can't use it even as a blend. But then the iron ore here is of very good quality, and it is difficult to find a place that has both iron and coal—one or the other usually has to be brought to any steel plant."

I mention my researches into the early days of the plant.

"Even two or three years after the foundation of the plant was laid, hunters were still shooting sand grouse and duck here," he says. "At that time, there were very few of us who knew engineering, and we did a little of everything. What do you think of our new Bhilai?"

I tell him of my impressions from the drive.

"Yes, the present town is too spread out," he says. "It would have been better to build all the houses close together, and multi-storied—more on the vertical principle than on the horizontal one—and to mix all classes of people in every sector. Then Bhilai would have been more of a community; then you wouldn't have had the class distinctions based on the distance one lives from the plant. If some of us had had the knowledge and experience we have now, we would have planned the town differently."

Purtej Singh's counterpart, the Russian general superintendent, B. N. Zherebin, has returned to the Soviet Union for a gall-bladder operation, but the acting general superintendent, I. P. Zhatenko, is in a nearby office in Ispat Bhavan, and after talking with Purtej Singh I call on him to find out how things look from the Russian side of the barrier. Zhatenko, who is one of four hundred Russians living in Bhilai at present, turns out to be a handsome man in his late fifties with clear-cut features, alert blue eyes, and absolutely white hair. He is trimly dressed in a dark-green bush shirt and white trousers. In the office with him is a pleasant Russian girl whose hair is unevenly dyed with henna. She introduces herself as Lena and then adeptly sets about her job, which is interpreting.

"Conditions here must seem to you very different from those in Russia," I say to Zhatenko.

"Do not say 'Russia,'" Zhatenko admonishes me, through Lena. "It reminds me of pre-Revolutionary times. We now have the Soviet Union. As for the point you raise, I cannot make general comparisons between India and the Soviet Union. You might say that it is very hot for us in Bhilai, but then in the Soviet Union we have all types of climates—in Central Asia, there are even some corners as hot as here. There is nothing peculiar about this place."

"What area of the Soviet Union do you come from?" I ask.

"I come to Bhilai from Novokuznetsk," he says.

"Is that the Novokuznetsk in Siberia?" I ask.

"Do not say 'Siberia,' because it reminds me of pre-Revolutionary times," he says. "Now there are simply the western, eastern, northern, and southern areas of the Soviet Union."

"Had you always lived in Novokuznetsk?" I ask.

"No, I was born near Dnepropetrovsk and stayed there until 1931," he says. "Then I moved to Novokuznetsk, and stayed there for thirty-five years. I was connected with the Novokuznetsk metallurgical plant. I started as a simple worker. Then I was foreman, shop superintendent, and so on—from the back benches to the front seat. When I left Novokuznetsk, I was assistant to the general superintendent, and I am assistant to the general superintendent here. I came here, according to Indian seasons, in the middle of spring. According to our seasons, it was the middle of winter. When I flew from Novokuznetsk, the temperature was forty degrees below zero Centigrade. In Bombay, where I landed, it was forty degrees above zero Centigrade. That was just three months ago."

"How long do you expect to stay here?" I ask.

"No particular length of time," he says. "If I get used to the Indian heat, I will be here for some years, maybe. I cannot say exactly how long."

"On the whole, do you like being here?" I ask.

"I have left behind in the Soviet Union two children and two grandchildren," he says. "It is not against the rules for Soviet citizens to bring families, but the health of my wife is not very good, so she cannot leave the Soviet Union. But I like it here. We have plenty to occupy ourselves when we are not working. We read; we study English. If we have free time, we go to the cinema and see Indian, Russian, or English-language films. We go to the swimming tank at the Bhilai Club. On the occasion of the tenth anniversary of our economic collaboration here, we started an Indo-Soviet Cultural Forum, which gives us an opportunity for social intercourse, for knowing each other better and understanding each other better. So, you know, we have some friendly connections with Indians, and some Indians even know Russian—especially those who have spent two or three years training in the Soviet Union."

"Still, you must miss lots of things," I say.

"Not vodka!" he says, with a smile. "Do not think that all Soviet citizens are drunkards. Do not think that, because, according to statistics, the consumption of vodka in the Soviet Union is not as high as it is in some other parts of the world."

I ask him what types of problems the Russians have faced in running the plant in Bhilai.

"In the light of production, there can be no problems," he replies, and, without clarifying, he goes on, "The only problem we have is the lack of qualification of the Indian workers. The engineers and technicians are O.K. to work with, but their experience and skill are much less than those of the Soviet experts. The Soviet experts' aim here is to train more Indian experts and then to give them our experience. We inspect their performance in the plant every week, and, in the case of some units, every day. Indian workers can be as good as any workers. Given opportunity, everyone will work. It is only through historical conditions that one nation is more backward than another."

As I get up to leave, Zhatenko invites me to a tea party at the Indo-Soviet Cultural Forum that afternoon and also to a Russian celebration the next day, which is the eve of May Day.

I thank him and accept both invitations.

About a furlong from Ispat Bhavan is the Expansion Building, a low-slung structure that houses the offices of some of the important Soviet experts, among them E. P. Gora, who, as the chief representative of Tiaz-promexport—the state exporting agency—oversees all equipment coming into Bhilai. When I walk over that morning to meet him, by appointment, I discover that he has a group of compatriots with him. They are seated around a table, with Gora at the head, and they rise, one by one, as he introduces them to me. "Comrade Andreshenko, Comrade Roek, Comrade Vologinan, and Comrade Gormash," he says. I shake hands all around, and learn that Gormash is an interpreter, Roek and Vologinan are supply experts, and Andreshenko is a construction expert. Like Zhatenko, Gora and Andreshenko have blue eyes and pure-white hair, and they would stand out anywhere, but Roek and Vologinan might be figures in a Russian crowd. All the men except Gormash are wearing white bush shirts; he is wearing a bright plaid bush shirt. He is young, and has a crew cut and a nice smile.

When we are seated at the table, Gora invites me to address questions to him, and I ask how long he has been at the Bhilai steel plant.

"Since eight o'clock this morning," he says, with a big smile, and he adds, "Every day, I come from Bhilai House to the plant."

I remark lightly that his answer seems more philosophical than factual.

"Ah, but philosophers do not build steel plants, and we have built a first-rate steel plant here," he says. He leans back in his chair, lights a cigarette, and puffs at it energetically. His gestures, however ordinary, have a natural elegance and verve. "I first came to Bhilai in 1955, when we made decisions about the early stages of the project," he goes on. "Altogether I have spent about five years in Bhilai, and I've been here continuously for the last three years, overseeing the expansion. By now, I'm a real Indian."

Gora is soon on the subject of the weather. "Every day hot! In the Soviet Union, it is different. There is a real winter, with skiing, ice skating, and sledding. There is a real spring, with nature awakening. And you cannot describe fishing in the autumn in the Soviet Union, it is so beautiful. The water is like a mirror, the leaves are all different colors, and you sit and fish. The last autumn I was in the Soviet Union, I caught a fish that was one and six-tenths metres long and weighed sixteen kilos, and then I swam across the Dnieper River. Now I wish to catch some crocodiles. But here every day is hot."

Andreshenko, who is sitting at Gora's elbow, whispers something to him.

"*Da, da,*" Gora says, and then he says to me, "In Bhilai, we have very good air-conditioners that are helping us to stay cool and happy."

Entering into the spirit of things, I say that air-conditioning can hardly make a Soviet autumn.

"Yes, everyone is missing his motherland," he says. "But you have in India cabbage, potatoes, tomatoes, onions, garlic, meat—and we have in the Soviet Union cabbage, potatoes, tomatoes, onions, garlic, meat. Everything is the same. We can cook good Russian dishes here. My wife and daughter are here—both of them can cook—but for Soviet experts who do not have families we also have the Bhilai House canteen."

I ask Gora whether he has been to Durgapur or Rourkela.

"No, I haven't been to those plants, but Bhilai and Bokaro are the two most important of the forty technical projects in India to which the Soviet Union is rendering assistance, so we are giving our two steel plants the greatest attention. You know, the metallurgical industry here is still in its infancy, so expansion is very important. With a minimum investment, we can expand the Bhilai plant to produce three or three and a half million tons. The Bokaro steel plant will be even bigger than Bhilai. I am proud that I helped design the Bhilai steel plant." The men around the table become more attentive. Gora quickly adds, "Hundreds of Soviet experts participated in the project. It would not be correct to ascribe any special part to me. I was just in charge of the rolling mills, where we roll the steel and then cut it to definite dimensions. It is like women making macaroni —but our 'macaroni' is used for rails. So, you see, I am only a macaronist, nothing more."

I remark that transplanting the latest equipment made in the Soviet Union to a remote Indian village must have been no easy task.

"Cows," he says. "They presented the only difficulty. We did not take into account the cows. The roads in India are full of cows, and nobody moves the cows away. There are a lot of cows here. In the beginning, there was nothing in Bhilai but cows, cows, cows. I had never seen so many cows in my life. Even when we had built the plant, we couldn't operate it properly, because of the cows. I took up the matter of shooing away the cows with the general manager, and he agreed that the cows had to be moved from the territory of the plant and kept out. We agreed that cows would be allowed to enter the territory of the plant only with a special-admittance pass. But even now, after the monsoon, when it gets a little cold, all the cows in India somehow arrive at the blast furnaces in Bhilai to keep warm."

The Bhilai House canteen, where Gora has invited me to lunch with him later that day, consists of four small, stark, numbered rooms with three or four small tables to a room. At each place at each table are a single fork and a single spoon, a chunk of bread, and the daily menu, written in Russian on a little slip of white paper. I am soon seated at a table with Gora and Gormash, and we are joined by P. M. Savchenko, the Soviet chief engineer, who is a dark-haired man with the muscular build of a Russian workman.

"You can start with either *okroshka* or *sup s klyotskami,*" Gora says to me, reading off the menu. "Then you can have *vareniki tvorogom,* and then either *zrazy myasnyies lukom* or *bef Stroganov.*"

I ask him to choose for me, and he gives everybody's order to a large, good-natured-looking Russian woman, whom he introduces as "the house-keeper, cook, and waitress" of the canteen. I discover that Savchenko speaks very good English, and I ask him where he learned it.

"I did not know English when I came here, but I learned it by talking with interpreters," he says.

Gormash repeats Savchenko's remark in Russian to Gora, who listens carefully and then volunteers the information "Many Indians speak good Russian after they have visited the Soviet Union for their training."

"Do you like Bhilai?" I ask Savchenko.

"Yes, very much," he says.

Gormash repeats this to Gora, who listens carefully, as before, and observes, "We hope that in time all of India will become one great big Bhilai. That is not impossible."

It appears that protocol demands that at the canteen as well as at the Expansion Building I converse only with Gora, and I give him my attention.

"Forty years ago, Czarist Russia was as poor as India," he says. "With our social system, in a very short time we in the Soviet Union have reached the industrial level of the United States."

"But couldn't the Soviet Union have perhaps done just as well with any reasonably stable social system?" I ask. "Anyway, didn't Russia have a much smaller population and greater resources forty years ago than India has today?"

"But India is a country rich in resources, too," Gora says. "How long it will take India to become one great big Bhilai I cannot tell you, because we have no experience with the kind of social system that India is using." To illustrate the benefits conferred by the Soviet social system, Gora tells me his own story—that although his father died when Gora was four-teen, leaving his mother and a family of eight children very poor, still, thanks to the Soviet system, the entire family (except for one brother, who died in the Second World War) are now well placed, many of them as doctors and engineers. "When India is industrialized, such things will be possible here, too," he says.

As Gora talks, the waitress serves us one course after another—soup, *bef Stroganov,* watermelon, cake with ice cream, coffee—but without ever re-moving any of the used crockery, which is just pushed aside or piled up on the table without much ceremony. No one seems to mind. When we leave, the tabletop has the look of a kitchen sink.

Udayen Sen, who is in charge of the Wire Rod Mill, now in the process of being built as part of the plant's expansion, is one of thousands of young Indians who have been trained for the Bhilai project in the Soviet Union and one of scores of Indians who have returned with Russian wives. I was introduced to him during my tour of the plant, and he has invited me to visit his home and meet his wife. I go there from my lunch at the canteen with Gora. When I arrive, they are in the living room of their house, which is medium-sized and is situated some distance from the plant. Mrs. Sen—or Larissa, as she soon asks me to call her—is a shy-looking girl with dark bobbed hair ending in a neat kiss curl on each of her round cheeks. She has on sandals and a short summer dress. In a sari, she could almost pass for an Indian, especially by the side of Udayen, who is a tall, quiet Bengali. Over coffee, I ask them how they met and if they encountered any obstacles in getting married.

"For my training, I went to the steel plant at Zhdanov, a steel town," Udayen says. "It is on the coast of the Sea of Azov, in the southern Ukraine. Larissa was a worker at the plant, and we met there."

"We fell in love right away," she says, speaking English with an Indian accent. "There were no restrictions on our marriage. We applied through the normal channels for permission to get married. After a week, the registration officer summoned us, and we got married. There was no trouble."

I ask Larissa how she likes living in India.

"I first came to Calcutta, to Udayen's family, and I found everything very different," Larissa says. "My mother-in-law was so Hindu in her habits. But I had the will to adjust. I had learned to respect my father-in-law from letters he wrote to me in Zhdanov, but he died two weeks after I reached Calcutta, so I was not able to get to know him."

"Larissa has been home to the Soviet Union twice," Udayen says. "Her parents are there. We are now trying to get permission for her mother to visit us here this winter."

"My mother will find things very different here," Larissa says. "When I first came to India, I felt I had travelled back centuries. But, of course, you do not feel the backwardness in Bhilai so much—it's a modern steel town."

"Zhdanov was a small steel town, but it had a really urban atmosphere," Udayen says. "One other thing that struck me about Zhdanov was that the size of the family, not the size of the salary, was the main consideration in allotting accommodations. Then, in Russian steel towns, of all sizes, there is an excellent public-transport system—everywhere there are buses, trams, taxis. But in Bhilai there are fairly long distances to be covered within the town, only higher-ups can afford to have cars, and it wasn't until recently that we had any public transport at all."

I ask the Sens about their friends in Bhilai.

"We see as many Russians as Indians," Udayen says. "The Russians here are no different from those I knew in the Soviet Union."

Before going on to the tea party of the Indo-Soviet Cultural Forum to which Zhatenko invited me, I stop at the Bhilai Club, which has both Indian and Russian members. The clubhouse, a low, rambling structure with a card room, a billiard room, and a ping-pong room, appears to be deserted, though a large old radio is blaring Indian film music between explosions of static. Eventually, as I wander through the club, I hear other sounds. Following them outdoors, I arrive at an L-shaped swimming tank, where, under the broiling sun, Indian and Russian bathers, mostly women, are gathered. The Indian women are small and delicate, wear one-piece bathing suits with high necks, and are sitting by the edge of the pool knitting and talking. The Russian women are large and chunky, wear bikinis, and are thrashing about in the water.

Later, in the nearby Maitri Bagh (Hindi for "friendship garden")—or, rather, in its Oval, which is a sunken grassy plot in the middle of the garden—I find many of the women bathers and many of the officers and engineers I have met at Bhilai. The Indian women, who wear their hair drawn back in thick chignons at the nape, are arrayed in rich, spangled saris, with long, jingling earrings and armloads of bangles, and the Russian women, who wear their hair short, are dressed in blouses and longish full skirts of shiny materials and bright colors and thick with frills, buttons, and bows. All the women are strolling about with their friends and their husbands, who, whether Indian or Russian, wear the usual bush shirts and trousers, while a band made up of a trumpet, a cornet, a clarinet, a tenor saxophone, an alto saxophone, a euphonium, and a bass drum plays a number called "Garden in India." As I enter, a couple of attractive Indian ladies greet me warmly. They are the organizers and co-hostesses of the party—Mrs. G. D. Singh, secretary of the Forum, and Mrs. S. S. Gill, its chairman. "How do you like our band?" Mrs. Singh asks me, over the music. "It's the Bhilai Security Force Band."

"This is the first tea party we have been able to arrange all year," Mrs. Gill says. "Unfortunately, we've had only two weeks to plan the program. And many Russians had to go to some local meeting to prepare for May Day, so the attendance on the Russian side is not as good as it might be."

"The Russians are very keen to learn how to cook a curry," Mrs. Singh says. "Also how to tie a sari and how to speak Hindi. They are very keen to play us Russian music and to hear some of our music."

The band switches to "Happy Go Lucky," and, under the cajoling of Mrs. Gill and Mrs. Singh, all the Indian and Russian men move to one side of the Oval, all the women move to the other, and the two groups form two lines facing one another; in each line Indians and Russians are mixed. Mrs. Gill, with an orange in her hand, stations herself at one end of the men's line, beside an elderly Sikh with a long, scraggly beard, and Mrs. Singh, with another orange in her hand, stations herself at one end of the women's line, beside a large-eyed young girl in a green sari. Explaining that everyone is to play Pass the Orange, Mrs. Gill calls out "Rea-dy . . . stea-dy . . . go!" and starts the game off by placing her orange under the Sikh's chin, while, on the women's side, Mrs. Singh simultaneously installs her orange under the chin of her charge. With much cheering from both Mrs. Gill and Mrs. Singh ("Come on! No hands, please! Hurry up!"), and some nervous laughter from the contestants, the Sikh manfully sets about the difficult task of disengaging the orange from under his chin and fitting it under the chin of his neighbor, who is a Russian. A similar struggle is under way in the women's line, where the first two players are Indian; this creates an added complication, because both contestants have trouble keeping their shoulders covered with the ends of their saris. The object of the game is to see which side finishes passing the orange first, and though the progress of the oranges is slow, the main thing, as Mrs. Gill and Mrs. Singh say repeatedly, is that the oranges are moving down the lines. The men's side wins.

No sooner is Pass the Orange over than a rubber doll—a likeness of an Indian woman dressed in yellow and gold—materializes in Mrs. Gill's hand. The band strikes up "Over the Waves," and Mrs. Singh rushes about the Oval joining the lines to make a circle. Now the band subsides to let Mrs. Gill speak. "The game we will now play is Pass the Parcel, and it has real punishments. Whoever is caught holding the doll when the music stops will have to take the punishment," she says. There are pained cries from the guests, but as the band swells again the doll starts on her quick, bumpy course around the circle, passing from hand to hand. The music stops. A dishevelled, athletic-looking Russian woman is holding the doll. Mrs. Gill asks her to come to the center of the circle. The Russian woman comes forward with little giggles. Mrs. Gill lays a finger sandwich wrapped in waxed paper on the grass, and, following her instructions, the Russian woman kneels down, picks up the package with her teeth, unwraps it after a struggle, and somehow manages to eat the sandwich, all without once using her hands. Everyone applauds, and the band strikes up "Teri Pyari, Pyari Surat" ("Your Lovely, Lovely Face"). With giggles, shouts, and blushes, the game continues, and such additional punishments are imposed as Walk Around the Circle Backward with a Partner (a Russian woman chooses her husband and they do a retrograde turn around the circle as the band plays "Russian Waltz"), Bow to the Prettiest and Smile at the Wittiest (an Indian man bows to and smiles at his wife as the band plays "Ay Duniya Wallo," or "O People of the World"), Act Like a Hollywood Actor (an Indian man sings in a rasping voice, "Thumbelina, Thumbelina, tiny little thing . . ."), Give an Interesting Incident to Make Someone Laugh, Hop Around on Three Legs, and Fight with Your Husband in Russian.

Other games follow. In one, every man is matched with a partner who is not his wife and is made to remove one of her shoes, toss the shoe into a pile with the other shoes, scramble for the shoe, and fit it back on his partner's foot.

Later on, the guests surround a table that has been set with pots of tea, bottles of soft drinks, plates of sandwiches and biscuits, and bowls of ice cream.

The tea party concludes with Mrs. Gill standing in the center of the

Oval and dispensing a number of gaily wrapped packages. "Mrs. Vera!
. . . Mr. Gormash!" she calls out. "Mrs. Bhatia! . . . Mr. Vologinan!"
She stops suddenly. "Oh dear. We've run out of prizes. I told you everything was organized in too much of a hurry. Never mind. All of you have
been very good sports."

It is the eve of May Day. The heads of the group of Soviet experts have
asked all the Russian and Indian administrators, engineers, and designers
in Bhilai to the grounds of Bhilai House to join in the festivities, which,
according to the invitation, are to consist of speeches, a Russian variety
show, refreshments, and dancing. I am sitting beside Andreshenko, facing
a platform, and with us in the audience is practically everyone I have met
in Bhilai, each person wearing a red rosette, which was presented and
fastened on by a couple of Russian ladies stationed at the entrance. Gora
is on the stage; he is the first speaker.

"Dear Comrades, esteemed Indian guests, permit me on behalf of the
chiefs of our team to welcome you and to congratulate you on the coming
May Day—the day of international solidarity of the working people,"
Gora begins, in Russian, speaking in a clear, powerful voice, which is
amplified by loudspeakers. Gormash interprets. "May Day is a manifestation of militant forces of workers of all the countries marching
under the slogan of struggle against imperialism, for peace, democracy,
national independence, Socialism, and Communism. As far back as 1922,
V. I. Lenin wrote, 'The tomorrow in the history of the world will be
precisely the day when the peoples oppressed by imperialism will be completely roused from their sleep.' Now we are witnesses of how these prophetic words of our great leader and teacher are becoming real. People
from many countries, having unyoked themselves from foreign enslavement, are taking their place among free and independent countries." He
talks—enlivening his delivery with forceful gestures and dramatic modula-
tions of voice—as if he were in the Soviet Union, addressing Party members. The Indian guests listen with polite attention. "The celebration of
May Day in our country this year," he goes on, "is inseparably linked with
the Twenty-third Congress of the Communist Party of the Soviet Union.
An important result of the Congress is that it has determined the foreign-
policy line of our Party and the State, aimed at creating the most favorable
conditions for building up Communism, strengthening the Socialist system, and giving all-out support to the struggle of the peoples for national
and social liberation, for the consolidation of peace, for the assertion of
Leninist principles of peaceful coexistence of states with different social

systems. The Twenty-third Congress has demonstrated once more the monolithic unity of the Party—the unity which has made true a brilliant prediction by Lenin, who wrote in 1918, in the article 'The Main Task of Our Day,' that 'this is exactly what the Russian Soviet Socialist Republic needs: to stop being wretched and helpless, to become irreversibly powerful and abundant.' The Party Congress has coincided with the completion of the Seven-Year Plan, which turned out to be a paramount stage in the struggle for creating the material and technical basis of Communism. During the past Seven-Year Plan, the volume of industrial production increased by eighty-four per cent, capital construction by forty-nine per cent, and freight turnover for all kinds of transport facilities by seventy-two per cent. The gross national income increased by fifty-three per cent. The fixed capital of the people's economy increased nineteen times." Gora pauses over each statistic as if it had a bearing on the growth of India. "Our Party has gained many outstanding achievements, especially in the exploration of outer space. Still greater aims have been set forth in the present Five-Year Plan. The volume of the total social product will increase one point four times, capital-production funds more than one point five times, national income by thirty-eight to forty-one per cent, real income of the working people one point three times. In the report delivered at the Congress by Comrade A. N. Kosygin, the prospects for metallurgy were outlined as well." He turns to the subject of steel with the evident pleasure of a speaker who has enjoyed keeping his audience in suspense. "The construction of still more mighty units is being envisaged. In 1970, over one-fifth of all the steel will be produced by means of the oxygen-converter method. By the end of the Five-Year Plan, sixty million tons of hot metal and ninety million tons of steel will be produced with oxygen lancing. While strengthening the power of their motherland, the Soviet people have been honorably discharging their international commitments to the working class of other countries, and first of all to those of Socialist countries."

Gora seems now about to touch on the fortunes of India and Bhilai, but instead, in something of a non sequitur, he declares, "Our government firmly states that the further unfolding of the shameful war against the Vietnamese people will meet with mounting support to Vietnam on the part of the Soviet people, despite the deterioration of our relations with the U.S.A. on this account. The Soviet Union will also not agree to West German militarists' obtaining nuclear weapons. As Comrade L. I. Brezhnev put it in his speech at the Twenty-third Congress of the Communist Party, nearly six hundred industrial, agricultural, and other projects, and over one hundred educational and medical institutions, as well as research centers, have been or are being built in countries of Asia and Africa with Soviet assistance. This economic coöperation of the Soviet Union with young national states aims at creating important branches of national industry, strengthening their position in the world, and training their technical and scientific cadres. You and we, being in the forefront of this coöperation, may record with satisfaction that our joint work with our friends, Indian steelmakers, reached achievements of no small importance."

At last, Gora mentions Bhilai, this time availing himself of the words of a well-known Indian Communist: "The Bhilai steel plant, as Shri Shripad Amrith Dange, Chairman of the Communist Party of India, said in his speech at the Twenty-third Congress of the Communist Party, has become known to the whole of India as a symbol of Indo-Soviet friendship. Now we are to set for ourselves a new joint task, to make 1967 the year of mastering two point five million tons of steel. Dear friends, all the achievements of the Soviet Union and the fact that it can help its friends to develop their economies have become possible only owing to the victory of the Socialist system."

Gora closes by looking ahead to other occasions for celebration: "Next year, our motherland will mark the great date—the fiftieth anniversary of the Great October Socialist Revolution. In 1970, we shall celebrate the one-hundredth birthday anniversary of Lenin. May we on the occasion of these important dates wish still a greater success to our motherland! Long live the great Soviet people—builders of a new radiant future! Thank you."

Gora finishes to moderate applause, and now Indarjit Singh takes the stage. Speaking in Russian, with frequent recourse to Hindi and English words, and sounding a bit like a language student going for his first oral examination, he gives a rhetorical salute to May Day and the Soviet Union. Purtej Singh, who follows Indarjit Singh, and concludes the first part of the program, offers his thanks and felicitations in extremely polished Russian.

The variety show begins. A troupe of Russian children ranging in age from six to eleven and dressed in summer clothes crumpled by the heat file onto the stage. They are led by a lady with platinum-blond hair who is decked out in very high heels and a green satin dress glinting with metallic threads. As she conducts, the children sing, in bell-like voices, a Russian folk tune called "Young Nature Lovers," and then they sally into a new Russian song, which goes:

> "We all want to reach the moon.
> We've been there,   10
> But only in our dreams."

The younger members of the troupe file off and take their seats in the audience, and the older children, at a sign from the conductor, sing out in English, almost at a shout:

> *"Dashing* through the snow
> In a one-horse open *sleigh* . . ."

Next, another troupe, now of adults, comes onto the stage. They are led by a lady with a flushed face who continually dabs at her forehead as she explains, in precise, formal Hindi, that the words of the number they are going to sing were written by a Russian engineer at the plant. The group sings, in chorus, "Bhilai steel plant is famous for its steel, but this is not the only thing the plant is famous for. It is famous for the friendship between the Indian people and the Soviet people." For some reason, the words have been set to the tune of "It's a Long, Long Way to Tipperary."

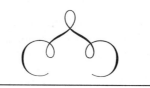

The Richest Man in India

DURING THE RAJ, THE MOST IMPORTANT PRINCELY STATE in India was Hyderabad, which lay just south of the Central Provinces and was as large as
England and Scotland put together. It was governed by a Muslim ruler,
who not only held absolute power but was reputed to be the richest man
in India, and who bore the hereditary title of Nizam—derived from the
Arabic word for "order" or "administration." The Nizam presiding at the
time of Independence was the seventh in the line of succession (the dynasty dated from the time of Asaf Jah, a Turkoman soldier who was sent
to the area in 1713 by the Mogul Emperor Aurangzeb), and he was formally addressed as the Lieutenant-General His Exalted Highness Asaf
Jah, Huzaffar-ul-Mulk-Wal-Mumilak, Nizam-ul-Mulk, Nizam-ud-daula
Nawab Mir, Sir Usman Ali Khan Bahadur, Fateh Jung, Sipha Salar,
G.C.S.I., G.B.E., Nizam of Hyderabad and Berar. (Berar, an area that had
once been part of Hyderabad, was ceded by a nineteenth-century Nizam
to the British, who then annexed it to the Central Provinces; the name
Berar nevertheless continued to be used in the title of the Nizam.) Soon
after Independence, however, the state of Hyderabad was integrated by
"police action" into India and the Nizam was divested of his prerogatives
and his estates. The Nizam, who is now eighty, lives in complete seclusion
in the city of Hyderabad, the present capital of the state of Andhra
Pradesh, into which the state of Hyderabad has been absorbed. He is still
reputed to be the richest man in India, and one of the richest men in the
world, and his most recent official biographer declares:

It is not alone the extent of his wealth which makes the Nizam's potentialities in the economic service of Hyderabad and India a substantial factor. In a setting where the country's most crying need is liquid investable capital, the Five-Year Plan has conceded a heavy deficiency in respect of such capital, and planners have had to cast their eyes right round the globe in order to try and tap sources of capital available for investment in India. The difficulty in the way of obtaining foreign capital, in view of the climate prevailing in this country, is now becoming obvious to more and more students of the subject. Indigenous capital is shy and lacks confidence. In these circumstances, the presence and goodwill of a likely investor with the resources that His Exalted Highness commands cannot but be a national asset of incalculable value.

Today, I am in the city of Hyderabad, staying in the Greenland Guest House, an elaborate old place where guests of the Nizam were once accommodated. The Guest House, which is now run as a government hostel, bears fading marks of past Muslim opulence, and is full of bearers, who are constantly stepping out of doorways and corners, salaaming, and asking in sonorous Urdu, "Would Sahib like anything?" A couple of my fellow-guests happen to be Englishmen, and at the dinner table they are reading recent but dog-eared issues of a British tabloid called *Titbits* and laughing over a series of articles called "The Amazing Nizam," with subtitles like "He's Worth Millions—but He Rules in Rags," "The Nizam Is Given Girls as Birthday Presents," "Prince Is Ordered: Sack Your Harem," and "Palace Swindlers Make a Fortune from Junk." The author of the series is Ray Asher, identified by the *Titbits* editors as "a film publicity girl."

It was a city of vast inherited fortunes and beautiful palaces [Miss Asher writes], of idle days and magic nights when money and champagne flowed side by side with the River Musi on the banks of which the city stands. . . .
One third of the state was controlled by feudal landlords known as *jaghirdars* who collected rents from the villages and blew the money in the city.
One *jaghirdar* smoked tobacco wrapped in a 100-rupee (£7) note—and he was a chain-smoker. . . .
The Nizam today is almost a recluse. He still occupies the same room in King Kothi [*kothi* is Hindi for "house," and King Kothi is one of the Nizam's five palaces] which he has had since the beginning of the century. The three windows are permanently closed. . . .
The walls are thick with cobwebs. There is dust everywhere, intermingled with hundreds of cigarette butts. . . .
On a nail in the wall hangs a *sherwani* (high collar coat) which is seldom

worn and never washed. He sleeps on an iron cot, the linen of which is rarely fresh. An adjoining bathroom is kept locked, for the Nizam bathes only once every two months.

It is obvious that Miss Asher's articles, like many similar ones in *Titbits'* sister periodicals, acquire their interest from the fact that they are the latest effusion on a celebrated personage—in this case, one of the most eccentric men in India, who is said to have a minimum retinue of eighteen hundred, made up of wives, children, grandchildren, and courtiers.

I was told in Delhi by government officers that for years now the Nizam's only connection with the world outside his palace has been through a long-standing friend, Khan Bahadur C. B. Taraporewala, who has the title of Financial Adviser to the Nizam and who spends a few hours in the Nizam's presence every day. In fact, I was told, Taraporewala functions as a sort of surrogate for the Nizam. Early one evening, I call on Taraporewala at his home—a new, solid-looking house that has a veranda fenced in with wrought iron from floor to ceiling. I am shown into a dim drawing room with a heavy, miasmatic atmosphere; there is not so much as a single electric lamp or a single fan. Taraporewala comes slowly across the room toward me. He is a tall, aging man with a sly smile and a cautious manner, and is dressed in a loose *achkan* of white sharkskin over white drill trousers.

I ask him about the nature of his service to the Nizam.

"I have been looking after the Nizam's affairs for the last thirty-five years," he says. "I can do anything the Nizam can do. I am fully empowered."

I ask him how the Nizam's wealth ranks with other great fortunes in the world.

"The question of his total wealth is a difficult one," Taraporewala says. "He is not the richest man in the world. There would be at least a couple of dozen who are richer."

"How did he accumulate his wealth?" I ask.

"As Nizam, he was god and master of his people, and he ruled like a despot from the time he came to the throne, in 1911. He also inherited a lot of wealth from previous Nizams. In the state of Hyderabad, the Nizams had a traditional form of taxation, and it was called *nazrana*. Every time a subject gazed upon the Nizam, he had to present the Nizam with a *nazrana,* or cash offering, whose amount was determined by the social status of the subject. The common people presented five silver rupees each, and the *jaghirdars* four silver rupees and a gold sovereign each. No Nizam kept any account books—all the Nizams stored their money in ordinary trunks and strongrooms. Their system of keeping money was hit or miss. The father of His Exalted Highness had a diamond that weighed a hundred and eighty-six and a half carats—the Jacob's diamond. The old Nizam bought the stone, rolled it in his handkerchief, and threw it in the drawer of a table. Years later, when a servant was dusting, he found it there. In fact, His Exalted Highness has a lot of plate and jewelry. After the 'police action' in Hyderabad, I took a full trainload of some of it to Bombay and sold it there for twenty-one crores of rupees. If I hadn't sold it then, it would have been confiscated. The government has a suspicion that a lot of the Nizam's wealth is still hidden. He had some rare coins—about forty thousand rare gold coins—and I presented them to Prime Minister Lal Bahadur Shastri. I told him each coin is worth one hundred times its face value. Shastri said 'Very good,' but not a word of thanks. The government never thanked the Nizam."

I mention Miss Asher's articles to Taraporewala, and ask him whether some of the legendary stories recirculated by *Titbits* are true.

"The Nizam is very much a legend," Taraporewala says. "He has never cared about how he looked, what he did, what he said, what the world thought of him. His world has always been within the walls of King Kothi. King Kothi belonged to a gentleman called Kamal Khan, and he had his initials, 'KK,' put on all the panels and walls, so the Nizam called it King Kothi. He has other palaces, one of them very beautiful—all of marble, and well kept up. He has a private police force of seven hundred, and he also has twenty-five hundred guards. In all, he maintains at least ten thousand people at his palaces, but he himself prefers to live in King Kothi, because he's used to it."

"Can one visit King Kothi?" I ask.

"No one is allowed there," he says. "It is completely guarded. You see, the Nizam has always been a very peculiar man, and he is getting more peculiar all the time. Because he was an autocratic ruler and no one could ever contradict him, he never learned that he could be wrong. Because he has never paid anyone with his own hands, he has never learned the value of anything; every transaction was made by his assistants, so he has never found out whether an article cost five rupees or five thousand rupees. Because he has never gone out much from the palace, he has never developed a sense of distance. Say you were going to the Hyderabad airport, and say it is ten miles from King Kothi. Naturally, it would require twenty or twenty-five minutes in a motorcar. But after two minutes His Exalted Highness will shout, 'Have we arrived?' His nerves are shattered. He's a very old man now. He repeats himself and he forgets himself."

"How does he occupy himself now?" I ask.

"His Exalted Highness usually gets up early," he says. "The first persons he usually sees are his guards and attendants. Then his Commissioner of Police, who reports on the palaces, may come. By nine o'clock, I arrive, and look after all the work in connection with his family and his property. If I have to discuss any problem with him, first I have to say, 'Sire must be right, I may be wrong,' or something like that. Then I go over the problem with him, slowly. Nine out of ten times, he says, 'No, I don't agree.' Slowly, I bring him around. Lunch is served at twelve o'clock. I am served an absolutely first-class lunch—soup, kebab, kefta, curry, and pilaf. It is properly served, on a marble-top table with a clean tablecloth. But although he has gold plates for hundreds of people, he himself eats off a tin plate, squatting on a mat in his room. All he will eat is cream and sweets. Though he's five feet three, he weighs less than ninety pounds. You see, as far back as I can remember, he has been an opium eater." (The Nizam died in 1967.)

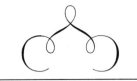

Famine and the Masonry
Across the Waters of the Krishna

BECAUSE IN 1965 THE MONSOONS FAILED TO ARRIVE, India has been suffering from the effects of a long drought, which some people are calling the worst of the century. Agriculture in the whole of India has always been ruled by her monsoons—or, rather, by the southwest monsoon, the moisture-laden wind that, rising from the Indian Ocean, brings rain to all parts of India from June through September. (The other, northeast, monsoon brings rain only to parts of Madras and Andhra Pradesh, and consequently its influence is much more limited.) The livelihood of the Indian cultivator so depends on the southwest monsoon that a delay of only a few days in the arrival of the rains can make the difference between abundance and blight. For instance, almost half the land in the country which is at present under cultivation—a hundred and forty million acres out of a total of three hundred and thirty-two million acres—is planted with rice. (The second main crop is wheat.) Sixty-four per cent of this land—almost ninety million acres—grows what is called rain-fed rice. To what extent the growth of this rice depends on the southwest monsoon has recently been explained by A. K. Dutt, an officer in the Ministry of Labour, Employment, and Rehabilitation. Discussing the four-month period of the southwest monsoon in a report, he writes:

The period available for rice cultivation may be taken to be 122 to 137 days. This period includes tillage operations to prepare the fields either for direct sowing or raising nursery [sic] for transplanting. A farmer of a 5-acre holding with a pair of bullocks and his conventional agricultural implements will generally take about a month to do all these operations. *This means that the period available for the rice crop to complete its life cycle from seed to seed within the duration of the southwest monsoon will run from 92 to 107 or at the most 110 days.* [The italics are Dutt's.]

Each day of the southwest monsoon is critical to the crop of rain-fed rice. Yet in occurrence, duration, and intensity, the southwest monsoon is so unreliable that its power is like that of a capricious god. If the monsoon rains are prolonged or fall too steadily or heavily, the rivers overflow, and there is flood and devastation; if the monsoon rains are brief or scant, the sources of water dry up, and there is drought and famine. Weirs, wells, and especially reservoirs and dams can and do provide some protection against the vagaries of the monsoon, but even if all the large irrigation projects ever proposed were built—and some of them are economically unfeasible —they might increase the harvest but they could not entirely liberate Indian agriculture from the caprices of the monsoon.

Partly because of the irregularities of the monsoon, the production of food grains since Independence has fallen far short of government expectations—some years by as much as a quarter—causing famine conditions in many states. During the First Five-Year Plan, the annual production of food grains averaged, roughly, sixty-six million tons, during the second Plan it averaged eighty-two million tons, and during the first four years of the third Plan it averaged between seventy-eight million and eighty-eight million tons; in the same period of fourteen years, to mitigate the effects of the shortages, India imported forty-eight million tons of food grains. But this reprieve was won only by mortgaging India's future and calling again and again on reserves of good will abroad, so that with each new plea the prospect of further aid appeared more bleak. In the United States, which was the main supplier of food grains on easy credit terms, warning signals had been sounded as early as 1951, when India was threatened with famine and when part of a debate in the House of Representatives over giving India a wheat loan went like this:

It is known to anyone who knows anything about India [a representative opposed to the loan had said] that they have 180,000,000 sacred cows; they have 136,000,000 sacred monkeys; they have 10,000,000 sacred or professional beggars—and all these sacred things will have a first claim on any wheat that may be procured by money lent to India. Was the gentleman [a proponent of the wheat loan] ever in India? Did he ever see a flock of sacred monkeys come in on a little grain merchant and eat him out of house and home, yet he could not punch one of them out of his grain bin? . . . They say it is religion and that, therefore, it ought not to be referred to in this debate, but it is a religion that the overburdened taxpayers of this country ought not to be compelled to support.

I fear for my Nation [a representative in favor of the loan had said] that if in connection with this bill we refuse to stand forthright and right-eously upon the premise that America will share that of which she has a superabundance with the people of the starving world, that we shall surely lose our own respect as well as destroying chances of winning and holding friends in Asia. . . . There are millions of people in India who are hungry today. . . . They are dying in their tracks on filth. America should share . . . with the starving people of India or with the starving people of any other part of the world, up to the unselfish ideal limit of our own safety. . . . I am not ashamed of the fact I believe in the American gospel which says in substance that if we "cast our bread upon the waters, it will return in due time well-buttered."

The wheat loan had been granted, but observers in India at the time had felt that, if the opponents of the loan distorted and heaped scorn on Hindu practices, its proponents looked to some hidden gains for themselves. In any event, the debate—and later ones like it—put the Indians on notice that they could not count on being given economic aid without any strings or for an indefinite length of time.

To make India economically self-reliant was the purpose of the Five-Year Plans. In the decades preceding the first Plan, India's annual rate of economic growth was about two per cent. In the course of the first three Plans, this rate of growth was nearly doubled, and the Plans, in addition to achieving some of their specific objectives, like checking inflation, increas-ing the supply of consumer goods, and resettling millions of refugees from Pakistan, prepared the way for an industrial revolution. Yet by 1966, when the government was busy drafting the fourth Plan, the whole idea of long-term planning had come under attack. The critics charged that India's meagre resources had been dissipated in gigantic industrial exhibits, like steel plants, when these resources should have been invested initially in making the country self-sufficient in food, by looking to basic require-ments for farming, like better seeds and fertilizer plants, and to food-distribution facilities, like better ports, roads, and supply stores. The gov-ernment was faulted for being unrealistically ambitious; for allowing its Plans to depend on expectations, often disappointed, of foreign assistance; and for constantly retrenching and revising the Plans, and so nullifying any advantages of long-term planning. In fact, it seemed to the critics that it was only a matter of time before such planning would be abandoned altogether in favor of *ad-hoc* economic measures. The defenders of the

Plans admitted some of these failures, but blamed them on natural disasters, like droughts; on political emergencies, like the wars with China and Pakistan; and on unforeseen setbacks in obtaining foreign exchange. One fact beyond dispute was that since Independence the population had jumped—by some estimates, as much as a hundred and fifty million—and had cancelled out some of the gains of the Five-Year Plans, including the increase in the economic growth rate. As early as 1957, Nehru had said, while visiting Bhilai, "Bhilai, Rourkela, and other great projects which are under construction are being built with the hunger of the country. . . . The agricultural production has not been encouraging. This has enhanced our burden. Uttar Pradesh, Bihar, West Bengal, and Orissa have been specially affected. . . . If sufficient food is not produced in our country, Bhilai and Rourkela will fail and also the Five-Year Plan."

V. K. Ramaswami, an economist connected with the Planning Commission, lives in New Delhi, in one of the government's best bachelor flats, built about ten or fifteen years ago for civil servants. I now wait for him in his sitting room, which is comfortably done in Indian silks; around the room are a few old miniatures, one modern painting, many books. Ramaswami bounces in. He is dressed in white tennis clothes, and, racket in hand, looks ready for a match. He is short and pudgy, and has pink cheeks, a pointed nose, and bright eyes.

After some talk about old times at Oxford, which both of us attended, for periods that overlapped, I ask him what the feeling among economists is about India's progress so far.

"Over the last year or so, at least, there has been agreement among the economists on the broad lines of planning and development," he says. "The Delhi chaps, like Sen and Raj, who differ in their political views, still broadly agree on how problems should be tackled in the next few years." Amartya Sen and K. N. Raj, who are professors at the Delhi School of Economics, are perhaps, along with Ramaswami, the best-known Indian economists. "They agree that we should continue along the lines we have been going on, complete the irrigation projects we've started. They also agree that we should have incentive prices for farmers, and that we should improve distribution methods for food grains. I remember that when we were drafting the second and third Plans, there was violent disagreement among the economists about what our line of action should be in respect to industry and agriculture—which of the two should be given priority. Today, you may have some disagreement about precisely how much money to allocate to industry and how much to agriculture, but the range of dispute is narrower than it used to be."

"In general, how do you yourself feel about India's progress so far?" I ask.

"I have always felt that our national-income statistics underestimate what has probably been achieved as a start toward the eradication of poverty," he says. "It is difficult to get statistics on the output of small industries and small businesses, and things like that. If one were to look at the quality of life in the village, one would probably detect a noticeable improvement already. Only some of this improvement, of course, would show up in certain statistics—the number of radios or bicycles now in the country, for instance—but we may have achieved more than the general statistics indicate. But the short-term economic situation has been overshadowed by the long drought that we are going through. I myself think there is a lot of truth in the complaint that in the past Five-Year Plans we rather took agricultural development for granted, and we are just beginning to recognize that we have to attend to the problems of agriculture."

"How would you rate the performance of the various Plans?" I ask.

"The first Plan was really not a Plan at all," he says. "It was just a collection of individual projects in various stages of preparation, which were grouped together to form the Plan. These projects didn't require much investment, in any case. And the years of the first Plan were fortunate for agriculture in having pretty good monsoon rains. The second Plan, however, put a severe strain on the economy, because it involved a high investment in large industrial projects. But, again, the years of the second Plan had good monsoon rains, so we didn't feel the pinch in agriculture too much. The third Plan, I agree, was quite a failure. In the draft of the fourth Plan, what is thought of as new—the emphasis on agriculture—is not new but is simply a continuation of some of the measures in the old Plans, because in many cases the fourth Plan will try to follow through in depth things that have shown promise during the previous Plans. Though it is generally agreed that we did not accomplish much with the first three Plans, we still should not ignore the fact that we did reach a good growth rate. I think that as we have gone along we have improved in our planning. We have started to think in terms of the aggregate picture, rather than in terms of individual projects. In any case, in relation to other underdeveloped countries we have not done badly. So when we call the Plans inadequate, we mean inadequate to our needs. What we really want in India is to achieve a big increase in per-capita income and to make jobs for the unemployed, so that people will have money for consumer goods. For if only a few people benefit from development, as has happened so far, and India can't break away from the status quo, then even a good growth rate is meaningless, because most of the people still don't have any money to spend. Furthermore, unless food production can be increased faster than the population expands, all development is meaningless."

C. Subramaniam, who was born in 1910 in Madras and studied law there, became prominent in the movement for Independence, and has had a long and varied political career. In the Madras state government, he served as Minister of Finance, Education, and Law, and in the central government, under Nehru, first as Minister of Steel and Heavy Industries and then as Minister of Steel, Mines, and Heavy Engineering, and, under Shastri, as Minister of Food and Agriculture. Now, under Mrs. Gandhi, he is Minister of Food, Agriculture, and Community Development. (The similarity in the titles of some of the Ministries is explained by the fact that, for reasons of politics as well as of efficiency, the various Ministries have often been reconstituted.) When I call on him, by appointment, at his office in the Minister's residence, I find him seated at a desk listening to an All India Radio news broadcast in English. He has on a white *kurta* and a white *dhoti*—both homespun—and wears eyeglasses. He gives the impression of being a large man until he stands up to greet me, and then he suddenly seems small. He offers me a chair, sits down again himself, and continues listening to the broadcast. When it is over, he tells me that he fancies himself something of a writer, and presents me with two brochures he has written. Both are Hindi translations from his native Tamil. One, entitled "My Travels About the World," has a cover like that of an atlas (it shows a map of the world and Subramaniam's face in profile); the other, entitled "Glimpses of a Few Countries I Have Seen," has a cover like that of a stamp album (it is decorated with postage stamps from England, France, Switzerland, Germany, Sweden, and Italy). I thank him for the brochures, and, turning to his political career, ask him whether it was a mere coincidence that he had moved from the Steel Ministry to the Food Ministry just about the time the emphasis of the Five-Year Plans shifted from industry to agriculture.

"I think you can defend the proposition that without an industrial base there can be no agricultural progress," he says with an air of quiet competence. "You need factories to produce chemical fertilizers, for instance. But the main thing is that now that we have learned where we went wrong in those three Plans, we must take steps to improve our performance."

I mention what some agronomists have told me—that the only way India can ever solve her chronic food shortages is to adopt the same policy for agriculture that exists for industry. They say that while in industry the government has encouraged large monopolies, for greater efficiency, and has tried to level inequities with taxation, in agriculture, because of the political and emotional appeal of land reform, the government has placed crippling, if idealistic, restrictions on the holdings of each farmer.

"No doubt we could greatly increase food production with large, mechanized farms," he says. "But the best policy is not always realistic. In the United States, which has the most widely mechanized agriculture, three per cent of the population produces eighty per cent of all the food in the country. But in our case more than eighty per cent of our population is employed on farms. If we mechanized our agriculture, we would put practically everyone out of work, and since we have so little industry, there wouldn't be many jobs for the displaced cultivators. The unemployment would create a vast social problem. In fact, we have no choice but to go on using our traditional methods of agriculture. We will always have to build our agricultural policy around manual labor and small farms with individual ownership, and give the greatest incentive to the individual cultivators. We have a precedent for this in postwar Japan and Taiwan. The holdings in these two countries were kept small, and they experienced a spurt in agriculture because of seed genetics, new chemical fertilizers, and new insecticides. Our annual yield is less than a thousand pounds of paddy per acre, but in Japan and Taiwan, because of those improvements, the yield is as much as four thousand pounds."

"Why didn't India follow the example of Japan and Taiwan earlier, then?" I ask.

"We thought at the start that we couldn't just take new strains of seeds and plant them here without extensive laboratory tests," he says. "Our climate was different, our soil was different. We held the view that these were new methods to be used only by our scientists in their laboratories. Now we are testing new methods on a large scale on the farms themselves. We hope that by the end of the fourth Plan, in 1971, there will be thirty-two million acres on which new varieties of seed grain, new chemical fertilizers, and new insecticides are in use. This does not mean that we will neglect the three hundred million acres remaining. We will try to do something for that land, too, but we can't do everything at once."

"What do you think the extent of the present food emergency is?" I ask. "Some people are already calling it a famine."

"We don't like to use the term 'famine,'" he says, "because of its associations with the British period, when the famines that occurred were always on a very large scale. In those days, there weren't even the necessary ships, ports, docks, and roads to get the food to the stricken areas, and famine meant not just deaths from starvation but also deaths from cholera and smallpox and other epidemics, which spread quickly when food and water became scarce."

I bring up a charge made by some critics that the government storage facilities are so bad that pests destroy as much as twenty per cent of the food supply.

"In storage, there is always a certain amount of loss," he says, "but it is difficult to estimate the percentage. In our case, it must be huge, and we are trying to do something about it. The most important problem, however, is raising agricultural production, but to do this we have to rely on the same administrative machinery—the civil service—that the British originally set up just to keep law and order. This administrative machinery is so cumbersome, with so many outdated procedures, that merely to get a project sanctioned can take four or five years, to say nothing of getting the project started. At the same time, the areas of economic development are becoming so technical that no civil servant is equipped to deal with them. Development requires more and more personnel with technical skills. Our need now is not for *babus* but for agronomists."

I speak to numerous people, among them Mahalanobis, Sen, and Raj, about the government's agricultural policies, and each conversation strengthens my realization that, because of the country's poverty and the government's power, it is on the validity of these men's theories that the lives of their countrymen are probably staked. The politicians, the ideologues, and the economists are, in a sense, gambling against hunger and the vagaries of the monsoon rains.

And just now the newspapers are carrying a great many articles about the heightening food emergency. Raj himself, in a series of closely reasoned articles, offers a powerful indictment of the government. He argues that although the ultimate solution to India's food problem is, of course, increasing food production, in immediate terms the food emergency is due as much to the government's failure to live up to its claim of having provided a nationally planned economy as it is to the drought. He observes that in the substandard conditions of India, the minimum daily nutrition requirement of each working adult has been put at seventeen and a half ounces of food grain, but that by making allowances for the smaller minimum requirements of women, children, and the infirm, statisticians can reduce this ration to thirteen and a half ounces of food grain per person per day, and he declares that without any increase in the present level of imports there is more than enough food grain in the country to supply this minimum ration. Yet, he says, it is all too clear that some parts of the country are without enough food grains to guarantee all their inhabitants this minimum ration, and that other parts have food grains in excess of their minimum requirements. For this disparity Raj blames the government's zonal system, which restricts the movement of food grains from some parts of the country to others under free-market conditions. The zonal system treats each of the states as an isolated, autonomous unit, and classifies them according to their claims of surpluses or deficits in food grains, for the purpose of collecting a levy from the surplus states, which the central government later distributes, along with its own, national reserves of imports, to the deficit states through a controlled market. The zonal system encourages a state that grows food grains in excess of the minimum requirement of its population to underreport its surplus, in order to evade the levy, and it also encourages a state that grows less than its minimum requirement to exaggerate its deficit, in order to increase its claim on the national reserves. Similar inducements to hide and hoard exist for individual cultivators: a cultivator in a surplus state has to pay a levy, while his counterpart in a deficit state, who as an individual may produce much more, does not. "Government policy has also vastly increased the economic power of large and medium-sized farmers, and weakened the ability of the government to get hold of their surpluses," Raj writes. "It is a measure of their strength that approximately one-eighth of all rural households own nearly three-fifths [of the rural population's] total assets." The inequities of the central government's zonal system are compounded by a secondary zonal system, which each state has imposed on its districts. In combination, the systems set state against state, district against district, and cultivator against cultivator; accelerate the artificial attrition of the central government's already undermined national reserves of food grains; exacerbate famine conditions; and force the government to divert money from long-term investments to emergency imports of more and more food grains. (Out of eighty-three million tons of food grains distributed from the national reserves in 1964–65, six million tons were imported.) Subramaniam recently said to a visitor, in defense of the zonal system, "Let me suggest the kind of thing that would happen if there were free movement of food grains. Madhya Pradesh is traditionally a surplus state, and Maharashtra a deficit one. Therefore, the price of food grains in Maharashtra is much higher. So great is the demand for food grain in a deficit state that if there were no zonal system, not only the surplus of Madhya Pradesh but also some of the remainder—the minimum requirement—would move to Maharashtra to seek higher prices. In a period of shortage, particularly of the order we have this year, what is important is to anticipate pockets of scarcity and move food grains into those areas quickly, and the zonal system enables us to do this." Raj, however, maintains in his articles that the weight of the central government's authority should support the development of a truly equitable national food policy, to guarantee people in all parts of the country the minimum requirement; this policy should mean, for the purpose of collection, a uniform levy on producers, millers, and hullers with surpluses, regardless of where they live, and, for the purpose of distribution, should involve the use of two food markets—one to provide food at competitive prices in a free market, with no restriction on the movement of food grains from zone to zone, the other to provide food at controlled prices for the stricken areas. Raj's controversial program, which also includes fiscal measures, like graduated land taxation, and social measures, like the nationalization of rice mills, has been attacked on many specific points, such as the assumption, at the center of his argument, that a minimum nutritional requirement could ever be made standard throughout the country. Nevertheless, it is generally granted that the government's present collection and distribution policy has its roots more in politics than in economics, being mainly a concession to the politicians from powerful surplus states, who form the bulwark of the Congress Party; who, in a sense, keep the politicians of the central government itself in power; and who, it is said, would not stay in office very long if they let the food grains in their states be siphoned away to the stricken areas.

The controversy over the zonal system intensifies as the drought, which has lasted for almost a year, continues with no sign of breaking. Some voices warn that this is another phase in the cycle of famine that strikes India at regular periods, much as epidemics of bubonic plague struck Europe in past centuries, and that, particularly in Orissa and Bihar, this is the beginning of another famine like the one in Bengal in 1943, when, according to some estimates, between a million and a half and three million people starved to death. The government, however, goes on denying that a threat of famine is present anywhere—or, indeed, that such famines can occur anymore. The discrepancy in the two points of view is the subject of another recent article, this one written by Kedar Ghosh and entitled "Quibbling Over Words in the Face of Famine." Ghosh points out that among Indians the failure of mendicants to obtain alms has always been a portent of famine; actually, one Hindi word for "famine" is *"durbhiksha"* —literally, "alms with tears." Late in the nineteenth century, the British, in codifying the exact limits of their responsibility toward their Indian subjects during a famine—they wanted to set guidelines for official relief procedures—defined famine conditions as existing in any part of the country where there was one death from "starvation." Under this definition, deaths caused by undernourishment or malnutrition, or by diseases related to them, were specifically ruled out as conditions constituting a "famine," because it was taken for granted that such evils were endemic in India. In practice, however, this distinction broke down, because if in an area any food, however poor, was available, at whatever price, its presence technically could, and in fact did, serve the government as a reason for not certifying the area for famine relief. After Independence, the Indians continued to live by the British famine code, but with the departure of the British the system of reporting and recording available food weakened, and in consequence an investigation for famine conditions in any given area was apt to be so slow that sometimes even before it was undertaken the famine victims had been cremated, and evidence of the cause of their death thereby destroyed. Unless deaths occurred on a large scale, about all that such investigations accomplished was to prolong the dispute over famine relief. So it is, Ghosh writes, that for months now non-official sources have been saying that Orissa and Bihar are famine-stricken, while all that time state and central authorities, like Subramaniam, have been steadfastly denying this. Ghosh goes on to describe how in Orissa parents have for some time been selling their children into slavery, hungry villagers have been crowding the cities, and petty officials have been profiting from such relief measures as have been introduced, while the government debates over the famine code, and while the cost to the nation in human life and resources mounts. To quote Ghosh's own words:

Faced with the dark prospects of famine, many asked more fortunate families "to buy" their children. It is stated that it has been common practice, even in normal times, with some . . . castes and tribal people to give away their boys on payment of a small amount per child and on condition that they will be freed from their bondage when they attain the age of 16. But this time, sellers were many and buyers few.

Meanwhile, destitutes began a weary trek to near and distant urban areas . . . in search of food and employment. Towns began to be crowded with these people and wailing cries for alms filled the air. Even when sought with tears, alms could not be had. . . . The State Government [of Orissa] . . . decided to seek guidance from Clause No. 134 of the Famine Code. Under this clause, lunatics, idiots, disabled persons, nursing mothers, and some other categories of people are entitled to gratuitous relief. . . .

Mr. Subramaniam's suggestion to the State Government to increase the number of gratuitous relief cards from 100,000 to 200,000 is a pointer to the inadequacy of such relief. . . . Cases have been reported where such cards could be obtained only for a consideration. . . .

The total relief and rehabilitation expenditure might exceed Rs. 12 crores. . . .

Work in this connexion [disbursing loans from the Contingency Fund] has been made more difficult by the local authorities' fear that if [the money were] distributed early, hungry farmers might use up the entire loans or a substantial part of them, in buying food and other immediate necessities. They seem to lose sight of the fact that farmers would not be able to work in the fields with impaired health and on empty stomachs.

Moreover, securing replacements of ploughing cattle and farm implements, which many cultivators had sold to feed themselves and their starving dependents, would take time as they have to be obtained from faraway places. . . .

The Union Food Minister would not call what exists in drought-hit areas in Orissa famine. He would describe it as "a condition of acute scarcity." What hit Bengal in 1943 was famine and it occurred under conditions of acute scarcity. The people who are being fed at free kitchens [in Orissa] . . . look the same as those who roamed the streets of Calcutta in the black days of the Bengal famine.

Another article, appearing under the byline of B. M. Bhatia, notes that what is happening now in Orissa in respect to both the administrative failure and the growing scarcity of food is repeating the history not only of the 1943 famine but also of the Bengal famine of 1865–66 (at that time, Orissa was part of Bengal), when it took a year and then an outbreak of civil violence to get the governor-general of the province to acknowledge the presence of famine and to institute relief. The history of later famines in other provinces of British India has not been very different.

Even the most liberal expenditure on relief will fail to save life once emaciation and stomach disorders due to hunger set in [Bhatia writes]. Scarcity has continued in Orissa since last year. . . . The governmental machinery for relief has not come into full operation even today. The local officials are reported to be still debating among themselves the desirability of bringing the provisions of the Famine Code into operation. This attitude might have been understandable under foreign rule, but it is simply inexcusable in a welfare state under a democratic set-up. . . .

In famine relief, time is the essence of the matter.

The drought continued until June, 1967, spreading hunger and thirst and disease, especially in Orissa and Bihar, where farmers were forced to sell what cattle and land remained in their possession to moneylenders and speculators, where volunteers tried to keep villagers occupied with work on earthen dikes against a day when there might be rain, where other volunteers staffed soup kitchens dispensing rations of three ounces of bulgur, or crushed wheat, per person every three days, and had to choose between saving a few and stretching the ration to many more and so perhaps condemning all of them to starvation, and where people began subsisting on dry grass and on the leaves and bark of trees. Reporters filed such dispatches as "All over rural Bihar today, farmers gather together in little circles and talk themselves out. Where are they going to procure seeds to farm with this year, when the monsoon finally arrives? Where are they going to raise the money with which to buy fertilizers? After two consecutive bad seasons and already in debt, who is going to extend any further credit to them?" and "Lack of ointments and jellies prevents relief from skin infections caused by the absence of washing water. Tiny children, thrusting their begging bowls under one's nose, have what little flesh remains on their faces puffed into scabs, their eyes peering through a mass of suppurating pustules constantly swarming with flies." In spite of huge shipments of food grains from abroad, the food emergency in the country worsened so rapidly that the Fourth Five-Year Plan—and, with it, many projects and hopes for the future—was abandoned without ever having been put into effect. When the 1967 monsoon came, it came in a deluge, and floods drove half a million people in Bihar alone out of their homes. By then, however, men and cattle had become so weak that they were incapable of plowing, and it was estimated that half the land in Bihar would be left unsown. Subramaniam, who in the meantime had lost his Parliamentary seat, and his Ministry with it, in a general election, suggested the dimensions of the food problem in India when, in an address to the Committee on the World Food Crisis, in Washington, he said of the protein deficiency in the Indian diet:

The most tragic aspect of protein hunger is that it strikes at the most vulnerable sector of the population—the children. On the basis of studies in my own State of Madras, where I was Minister of Education, it has been estimated that between thirty-five and forty per cent of the children of India have suffered permanent brain damage by the time they reach school age because of protein deficiency. This means that we are, in effect, producing sub-human beings at the rate of thirty-five million a year. By the time they reach school age they are unable to concentrate sufficiently to absorb and retain knowledge.

Irrigation schemes are as basic to agricultural progress as steel plants are to industrialization. At the start of the First Five-Year Plan, 23,800,000 acres were being watered by the country's main irrigation schemes, and by the end of the third Plan, 13,700,000 more acres had been brought under cultivation through the construction of new irrigation schemes, like the Bhakra-Nangal irrigation project, the Hirakud Dam project, the Beas project, the Tungabhadra project, the Damodar Valley Corporation, and the Nagarjunasagar project. The various agricultural and industrial projects have caused such a heavy drain on India's financial resources that Nagarjunasagar, which the state government of Andhra Pradesh started building on the Krishna River in 1957 with a loan from the central government that was made possible, in part, by United States aid funds, is still far from finished. When it is finished, however, the Nagarjunasagar dam will be the world's biggest masonry dam—three miles long and four hundred feet high. Its reservoir will be one of the largest man-made lakes in the world, impounding the waters of the Krishna in a hundred-and-ten-square-mile area, and having a storage capacity of 9,370,000 acre-feet. The dam will be flanked by two canals, which will be two hundred and seventy-six miles long and a hundred and forty miles long, respectively, and smaller canals, stemming from these like branches of a tree, will carry water through the surrounding land. Altogether, the Nagarjunasagar scheme is expected to irrigate 2,060,000 acres of land.

The Krishna River, which rises in the Western Ghats and, after meandering some eight hundred miles across the country, empties into the Bay of Bengal about a hundred miles below Nagarjunasagar, is held sacred by Hindus because of its association with Lord Krishna. Seven miles upstream from the site of the dam is a hill that was the home of Nagarjuna, the second-century Buddhist ascetic who founded the Madhyamika school of Mahayana Buddhism; the ascetic has given his name to both the hill, Nagarjunakonda ("*konda*" means "hill"), and to the irrigation scheme itself ("*sagar*" means "reservoir"). The early excavations for the dam—at the time they were begun, in the mid-fifties, the area was a jungle overrun by cheetahs and tigers—unearthed ruins of a two-thousand-year-old city, Vijaypura, or "City of Victory." In fact, the Archeology Department of the government of India has built a museum on Nagarjunakonda to house some of the finds, and is now in the process of reconstructing some of the public buildings of the city. An official chronicler of the scheme writes:

This [site] . . . is a rich treasure house of historic and prehistoric monuments, throwing light on a highly advanced civilization that thrived and flourished in this spot from the hoary past. Such a valley as this, treasuring a rich and glorious past, would be submerged by the formation of this reservoir.

But in order to preserve for posterity this proud cultural heritage of our glorious past, it has rightly been decided to excavate the valley before inundation and house the monuments on the top of the hill, Nagarjunakonda, that stands aloft above the waters of the Sagar overlooking majestically the huge lake below surrounding it ornamentally.

Today, I have been driving around the site of Nagarjunasagar with the chief engineer in charge of the project, A. P. Ranganathaswamy—a man in his middle years, who has a soft, round face and who wears a white *kurta* and white pajamas. The road curves around the hillsides on its way up toward the dam. Traffic consists almost entirely of huge trucks, and everywhere there are countless small shanties—merely walls built of native rock covered with thatch. The landscape is rocky and rugged and stark, its starkness being accentuated by the white glare of the sun—the hottest so far in my travels. We draw up at the site of the dam, climb a rocky slope to an observation tower called Viewpoint, and enter it through a doorway decorated with paintings of Nagarjuna and Buddha. Below us now is the huge white sloping face of the dam, with high shoulders rising on either side and the center broken by a crisscross pattern of narrow ramps swarming with men, women, and children, all weighed down by headloads of stones. Below these laborers are sheds, and trucks and jeeps piled high with stones, and above the laborers are the beams and hoisting blocks of cranes. From the observation tower, though, everything below appears small and incidental against the dam itself.

"Most big dams are made of concrete," Ranganathaswamy says. "But, for us Asians, using masonry has many advantages—it is cheaper than concrete, and in building a masonry dam we can give employment to seven or eight times as many people as we can in building a concrete dam. In a masonry dam, the actual construction is done by hand, stone by stone, with mortar—just as in building a wall. If we were using concrete, we could employ only about three or four thousand laborers. Here, even though the wages are very low, entire families can work. Laborers on a masonry dam don't have to have any special skills. Here we use the age-old method of carrying stones. Any Asian can carry a headload of stones, and we Indians are second to none in carrying loads. The work of carrying them goes on day and night—the stones have to be brought here from eight or nine miles away—but the actual construction of the dam can progress only during the day. The laborers carry stones up the face of the dam for two hundred feet, and after that cranes—the most up-to-date cranes—take over. This is the only masonry dam in the construction of which machines have been used, and this combination of carrying stones and working with cranes is very Indian. It is like our streets—the bullock carts plodding along behind late-model motorcars. We are not only building a great dam but giving our brothers employment. In a sense, the point of all economic development is to give employment."

"But is a masonry dam as solid as a concrete dam?" I ask.

"The Bureau of Reclamation in Colorado and our Central Water and Power Commission in Delhi have both made tests that have proved masonry to be as strong as concrete. But no one had tried a masonry dam this size before, because these tests were carried out only recently. We engineers say that the life of a dam depends on the silt that builds up in the reservoir. Some reservoirs start silting up rapidly, but then the silt may be washed away again. Nagarjunasagar happens to be the last dam on the Krishna River, and the other, smaller dams upstream collect most of the silt. Nagarjunasagar should last forever."

"When do you hope to finish the work?"

"We have been at it for almost ten years, though I've been here only seven years. It's not usual to change chief engineers in the middle of a project, but Mr. Jafar Ali, who was chief engineer before me, retired. We could have finished the dam a year or two ago. If we had, we could have been irrigating many more acres and feeding many more people now. The reason we haven't finished is that the central government has not been able to allocate funds. We've had to slow down all our work here. Before last year, the central government was giving us only ten crores of rupees per year, but we struggled with the central government, and last year they finally gave us twenty crores of rupees. If we keep on getting as much money as we got last year, the entire scheme should be finished by 1981."

Before coming to Nagarjunasagar, I visited the famine-stricken areas of Orissa and Bihar, which left me feeling that everything at the center of my life, and perhaps everything at the center of the lives of others, too, was beside the point. But here I am beginning to feel more myself again. My notes on the rest of the day follow: "Afternoon. Continue on Nagarjunasagar road. Rock walls on either side. Tunnel, with water gushing through, white and frothy and giddy in its speed, joining and disturbing the quiet flow of the dark-colored Krishna. 'I do not know much about gods; but I think that the river/Is a strong brown god.' Walk into 'toe gallery,' inside dam wall. Used for grouting cement if there is leakage. Over a hundred feet long, about nine feet high, five or six feet wide. Gallery floor wet and slippery, but laborers moving along with headloads of stones. Two large-eyed young girls walk past carrying stones. Marvellously saucy-looking. Outside gallery, by banks of Krishna River. Water still. Men, women, and children bathing, washing clothes, cleaning utensils. Sun hot. Eighteen cranes, red and yellow, and strong wall below. Solid wall of the dam. Unbroken lines of people moving up the scaffolding of ramps and coming down. Women wearing dirty cotton saris down to their ankles and colored glass bangles from wrist to shoulder. But vivid in red and purple and green and saffron, sometimes no more than glorious shafts of color. And tanned men, in striking white. Hard to imagine such glorious-looking laborers anywhere else in the world. Yet sadness in all this: So many thousands moving across face of dam in hot sun, loads of stones on heads. Cross river. Road rough. Farther up, half a bridge, stretching over river, then suddenly stopping short. Ranganathaswamy says bridge broken by rains and a recent flood here—the worst in a hundred years. Drought or flood. 'The brown god . . . forgotten by the dwellers in cities . . . keeping his seasons and rages.' Continue along road to other side. Ground rocky, barren, colorless. Intense sun. Clusters of laborers resting, so graceful the heat more bearable, somehow. Now 'City of Victory.' Being reconstructed, stone by stone. Ruins of ancient monastery and ancient university where once Nagarjuna instructed Buddhist monks. Auditorium of university—square. Laid out with beautiful symmetry. Walls and pillars a foot or two high. All of crumbling red stone. Beyond, museum, on low, flat-topped hill, with red *kutcha* road leading up to top. But just now museum and hill inaccessible, cut off by flood water."

City of Dreadful Night

_____

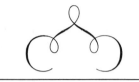

On the Banks of the Hooghly

THE CALCUTTA METROPOLITAN DISTRICT bears such a large responsibility for India's industrial effort and is such a mixture of ethnic communities and ethnic traditions that it has been seen as a perfect reflection of India as a whole and as a test case to determine whether India (or any other under-developed country) can ever succeed in building a modern, industrialized nation. Though Calcutta proper, or, technically, the Calcutta Corporation, as the largest single center in the Calcutta Metropolitan District is called, is today the official capital only of the state of West Bengal, it actually serves as the commercial and cultural capital of all of east and northeast India—an area that has a hundred and fifty million inhabitants, or a little less than a third of India's total population. (Calcutta is also, in a similar sense, the capital of Sikkim, Bhutan, and Nepal.) India's two greatest exports, tea and jute, which are grown in West Bengal and Assam, are processed in the Calcutta Metropolitan District and shipped out of the Port of Calcutta. Most of the equipment and the supplies for the steel and engineering industries in West Bengal, Bihar, and Orissa also pass through the Port of Calcutta. These three states are known for their rich deposits of iron and coal, for their concentration of heavy engineering and locomotive works, and, above all, for their production of most of India's steel. (All her ironworks except the Bhilai steel plant are in this region.) The Calcutta Metropolitan District handles—according to the latest available set of government statistics, for 1963 and 1964—forty-two per cent of India's exports and twenty-five per cent of her imports, clears thirty per cent of all bank transactions in India, contributes thirty per cent of the national revenue from income tax, and manufactures about fifteen per cent of all the goods produced in the country. Calcutta—and, by extension, the Calcutta Metropolitan District—is India's single dominant city and port.

The Calcutta Metropolitan District lies on the Hooghly, a river in the Gangetic delta of West Bengal. The Hooghly is actually an eastern channel of the Ganga, which is known by different local names in different regions, and this channel, being the only one navigable from the sea, has always been the most important commercially. About ninety miles inland from the head of the Bay of Bengal, the Hooghly, which generally runs from north to south, loops in a semicircular bend toward the west, creating a bulge of land on the eastern bank. This bulge marks the uppermost point of the river which is navigable by oceangoing ships, and it was around this point that the European traders—Portuguese, Dutch, French, and British, in that order—who sailed up the river in the sixteenth and seventeenth centuries founded their settlements. The British settlement, which was established on the bulge in 1690, by Job Charnock, of the East India Company, and was called Calcutta, grew into the capital of British India—a position it held from 1774 until 1911, when, in the reign of George V, the British built New Delhi, deeper in the interior, so that their capital might be equidistant from the three great imperial cities of Karachi, Bombay, and Calcutta. Today, the Calcutta Metropolitan District— a recent official designation for Calcutta and numerous surrounding clusters of urban communities and strings of rural villages, each with its own more or less autonomous local government—sprawls over both banks of the river and extends from the town of Budge-Budge, ten miles below the bulge, to the new township of Kalyani, forty miles above the bulge. The Calcutta Metropolitan District, where about seven and a half million people live in an area of four hundred and ninety square miles, has a population—and in a few cases an area—greater than that of any one of about eighty countries in Africa, Asia, the Americas, and Europe, among them the Congo, Ghana, Tunisia, Israel, Jordan, Lebanon, Syria, Bolivia, Chile, Cuba, the Dominican Republic, Guatemala, Denmark, Finland, Ireland, Norway, and Switzerland. Half the population of the Calcutta Metropolitan District lives in Calcutta. Across the river from Calcutta is the second-largest urban community, the Howrah Corporation. Chandernagor, the original French settlement on the Hooghly, which is now in the process of being formally incorporated, will be the third-largest urban community. And there are thirty-one smaller independent municipalities.

The majority of them date from the nineteenth century, and almost all of them came into existence with the growth of the jute industry—which was then, as it is now, the main industry in the area—its mills being established by British businessmen all along the Hooghly to take advantage of water power and water transport. Each new mill brought with it factory workers, who settled nearby in a sort of unplanned shantytown, supported and governed by the British millowners to the extent that these owners provided a modicum of municipal services. As the population and area of the original city of Calcutta expanded, this series of temporary settlements became permanent industrial slums. The mills, which, for the most part, are still in operation, and are still owned by British industrialists, are surrounded both by thick walls and by barbed wire and are protected by watch-and-ward staffs, and they are as spacious, clean, and orderly as the communities outside them are congested, insanitary, and chaotic. In addition to these thirty-one small municipalities—almost none of them have areas of more than six square miles, and some of them have areas of less than two square miles—there are thirty-two still smaller semi-municipalities and no fewer than four hundred and fifty villages. Calcutta, where the port facilities, the major river crossing, the financial markets, the fashionable residences and shops, the clubs, the official buildings and monuments, and the main university buildings are situated, is alone a city in any modern sense. Except for Calcutta and Howrah, not one of the urban or rural communities has more than six thousand ratepayers, and the rates in all of them—with the same two exceptions—are so low that the local governments have no funds for providing such services as running water, sanitation, public housing, health centers, and education, for maintaining streets and roads, or, indeed, even for adequately assessing and collecting rates. (In 1963 and 1964, the tax receipts of Howrah came to only fourteen rupees per person, and the receipts of all the other communities fell far below that, many villages collecting less than one rupee per person.) Except for Calcutta and Howrah, not one of the urban or rural communities has any borrowing capacity, any means of undertaking new projects, or any chance at all of coping with the demands of either a growing population or a changing technology. Even in Calcutta, which is responsible for most of the industrial income, funds are not always allocated to essential municipal services, because these are considered non-productive investments. Owing to the Calcutta Metropolitan District's importance to West Bengal and to India as a whole, there are hundreds of state and federal government departments and agencies and many private organizations that are all devoted to directing local affairs, and many of them have overlapping, and conflicting, jurisdictions; for instance, there are at least fifty bodies concerned with traffic and transportation. All attempts to merge the proliferating local governments have so far been frustrated by rivalries and pressure groups.

In the past, the Hooghly was the chief distributary of the Ganga, emptying into the Bay of Bengal at the westernmost point of the delta, and in the early period of Calcutta's growth it was a deep, open river, offering ideal access from the Bay of Bengal to the inland trade. Any of the oceangoing ships of the time, however deep their draft, could sail in and out of the Port of Calcutta easily at any season, for though the flow of the Ganga changed as the year advanced, diminishing in the summer months (April through June) and swelling in the monsoon months (July through September), the current of the Hooghly was so strong and constant that it swept any silt out to sea or washed it up on the riverbanks. Over the past two hundred years, however, the main flow of the Ganga has gradually shifted, and the Ganga's chief distributary has become the Padma River, which runs through East Pakistan and empties into the Bay of Bengal at the easternmost point of the delta. At the confluence of the Ganga and the Hooghly—or, rather, the Ganga and the Bhagirathi, for this is what the upper reaches of the Hooghly are called—a large sandbar has now formed, so that except during the monsoon season, when the Ganga rises over the sandbar and feeds the Hooghly, what scant water the Hooghly receives is from local drainage, and, because of the weakened current, as much as a million cubic feet of silt a year now accumulates in the riverbed. This accumulation is steadily decreasing the depth of the river, its channel being clogged by an unending series of shoals and sandbars, so that costly dredging is required to keep it open and navigable. Even when some silt is washed downstream, bore tides (these occur when the seawater trapped in the Hooghly's broad estuary is released at high tide into the channel of the river) carry it back up. At one time, the Hooghly was free of bores in the monsoon and winter months, and even in the spring months high tides came only as far as Calcutta, and whatever damage they did to the channel was offset by the strong flow of the Ganga. But now, because of the heavy deposits of silt, the Hooghly is in such a condition of deterioration that even during the monsoon, when the current is at its strongest, it does little more than check the bores ten miles below the Port. In fact, the river is so shallow and constricted that the bores, which now come almost all year round, keep gathering more momentum, rising higher over the banks, and reaching farther up the river; at present, during the powerful spring tides the bores crest as high as six feet in the area of the Port and race up as far as eighty miles north of it. Even if the river could somehow be released from the cycle of weak current, silt, bores, more silt, and weaker current, the life of the Port would still be in jeopardy, because of the sharp bends in the river. In recent years, the technology of shipbuilding and the economics of trade have led to the construction of tankers that often weigh forty thousand tons and sometimes weigh well over a hundred thousand; other heavy-cargo carriers often weigh twenty-five thousand tons. Such ships are built long and have a draft of over thirty feet. But for most of the year ships weighing more than ten thousand tons or with a draft of more than twenty-six feet cannot risk negotiating the bends to call at Calcutta. Even during the high spring tides, most big, modern ships must make their voyage in stages, sometimes discharging part of their cargo at Haldia, a subsidiary port thirty-five miles downstream from Calcutta. As for the Port of Calcutta itself, not only is it far from the open sea but its wharfing and docking facilities, which date from the nineteenth century and are concentrated in the central business area of Calcutta, are crowded, old-fashioned, and generally inadequate. Since the height of the bores and the strength of the flow in the river vary not just from season to season but from day to day, daily calculations have to be made to determine the size of the ships that can enter the port. (Heavy bore tides decrease the berthing and holding capacity by as much as twenty-five per cent.) The Calcutta Port Commissioners recently estimated that the average turn-around time for a ship calling at Calcutta was more than seventeen days—the longest and most expensive turn-around time at any major port.

The silting up of the Hooghly also threatens to choke off the supply of fresh water for much of the population along its banks. Apart from a number of large and small tube wells, the only source of fresh water for the Calcutta Metropolitan District is the Hooghly, the principal waterworks being situated at Palta, seventeen miles north of Calcutta. These waterworks were built in 1865 to provide filtered water for six hundred thousand or, at the most, a million people. At the same time, subsidiary waterworks were built to supply standpipes in the streets with unfiltered water for fighting fires, for cleaning the streets, and for washing carriages. These waterworks distribute water only to Calcutta; the other municipalities and semi-municipalities—except for Kalyani—have no municipal waterworks and only very limited access to filtered water through the tube wells, and the villages have no filtered water at all. Even in Calcutta, the amount of filtered water is so limited and its distribution so haphazard that nearly half the population now routinely uses unfiltered water from the standpipes for bathing and drinking, and in this water cholera vibrio is often found. Moreover, the equipment and the mains of the Palta water-works are so old and worn that even the filtered water is not always free from adulteration, and the mains carrying the unfiltered water are often blocked by silt. As the current in the Hooghly has continued to slacken, an undercurrent of salt water from the sea has moved farther and farther upstream, and in the summer, when this undercurrent is strongest, the salt content of the river near Palta is often ten times what is generally considered fit for human consumption. So far, engineers have managed to keep on supplying the ration of filtered water to Calcutta by pumping and storing water at Palta during the hours of each day when the salt content is lowest. But the salinity of the river is increasing so rapidly that within a few years the waterworks at Palta may be unusable for weeks or months at a time. Even moving the waterworks many miles upstream would be no more than a temporary solution. Throughout the Calcutta Metropolitan District, a full-scale water famine is an ever-present threat.

In the entire Gangetic delta, which is flat (it is uninterrupted by a single hill), the only good land is along the margins of the Hooghly. This land, which was formed over the centuries by silt deposits washed up onto the banks when the river was deep and the current strong, is nowhere more than thirty feet above sea level or more than two miles wide, for it slopes sharply away into salt lakes, brackish streams, and malarial marshes. And even these stretches of good land are subject to the ravages of an unhealthful climate; the delta is simmering hot for eight months of the year, the temperature regularly rising as high as 117°F., and it is deluged with rain for much of the remaining four months, when fifty out of a total of sixty-four inches of annual rainfall comes down in concentrated monsoon showers. Although the delta is crisscrossed by many small rivers and streams, it has always had bad drainage, and now the rivers and streams, too, are silting up and losing what little drainage capacity they once possessed. During the monsoon, when even the comparatively high ground is flooded for weeks at a time, the standing water paralyzes land transportation—and seeps into the foundations and walls of buildings—and has to be removed artificially by methods that are extremely slow and costly. Most of the Calcutta Metropolitan District is without municipally organized sewerage systems, without piped drains or sewers, and even without privately owned means of sewage disposal, like septic tanks. Most people have only the use of primitive communal latrines—low, cramped, open brick sheds with platforms above earthenware bowls on dirt floors—of which some two hundred thousand are scattered throughout the Calcutta Metropolitan District. Only Calcutta has a functioning municipal sewage-disposal system, but even in Calcutta the latrines are cleaned only erratically, and then are emptied manually into trailers, which carry the waste matter to disposal pits outside the city limits. Moreover, only about half of Calcutta's area is sewered; in the rest, sludge and ordure are carried in a maze of open gutters that run along the surface of the streets, lanes, and alleyways, and often alongside the worn water pipes, with the result that seepage is not uncommon. Stoppages and backups are so frequent that, especially during the monsoon, the contents of the gutters freely overflow into the streets. Poor drainage and poor sewerage aggravate the unhealthy conditions of life in the Calcutta Metropolitan District, where malaria, cholera, and practically all other gastro-intestinal diseases are rampant, as are smallpox and tuberculosis. Although in recent years malaria has been controlled somewhat by the constant saturation of lowlands and stagnant waters with DDT, and cholera by comprehensive inoculations, the Calcutta Metropolitan District has not been able to rid itself of either scourge. Malaria afflicts a large percentage of the population, and cholera, which is often fatal, is endemic in the entire delta, reaching its peak in the summer months of every year. The sanitation conditions, made hopeless by the water shortage and the water pollution, expose the Calcutta Metropolitan District to a permanent siege of mosquitoes, flies, and vermin—all breeding disease, carrying disease, and spreading disease.

Despite disease and an occasional but devastating famine, like that of 1943, the population of the Calcutta Metropolitan District has been growing relentlessly. The population trebled between the census of 1921 and the census of 1961, and it is expected that by 1986 the current population will nearly double. A part of this increase represents migrations from other regions of India. Indeed, thirty-nine per cent of the present population is drawn from all parts of India: merchants and financiers from Gujarat and Rajasthan; bureaucrats and office workers from Andhra Pradesh, Madras, Mysore, and Kerala; skilled laborers and entrepreneurs from the Punjab; unskilled laborers and factory workers from Bihar and Uttar Pradesh; sweepers and tanners from Orissa. The migrations began early in this century, when, because of the general increase in population throughout India and the consequent pressure on arable land, farmers were forced to leave their villages and seek work in one of the handful of urban centers. In the Calcutta area, these displaced farmers, who were often unable to bring their families with them, settled into barrackslike quarters in the *bustis* (imperfectly translated as "slums"), six or eight to a room, resigned to living under any conditions provided they could find work, save something to send home to their families, and perhaps visit them occasionally.

They generally found uncertain, temporary employment as dock coolies, rickshaw-wallahs, latrine sweepers, office peons, night watchmen, or fruit and vegetable hawkers, and they tended to live in the city as outsiders, forming enclaves, in which they kept very much to themselves, spoke only their own regional languages, followed their own religious, sectarian, or caste practices, and found jobs for new arrivals from their home villages in the trades in which they themselves had settled. Most of the minority communities entrenched themselves in the industrial areas of Calcutta and Howrah, and here they live now, as they did in the past, in little village-like *bustis,* a restless, uprooted population. (Owing to the presence of these workers, the ratio of men to women in the Calcutta Metropolitan District today is three to two.) In recent years, moreover, there has been another migration, of a different kind—an influx of destitute refugees from Pakistan. There was a lull in the exchange of refugees for some years, but they have been coming to India in increasing numbers ever since the religious disturbances in Kashmir over the theft of Mohammed's hair and the second Indo-Pakistan war. At least four million refugees from Pakistan have settled in West Bengal, where they now constitute ten per cent of the state's population, and of these at least a million have settled in the Calcutta Metropolitan District. More are still coming in search of assistance from relatives or the government. (About a quarter of a million refugees, it has been estimated, could be resettled in regions like the hills and forests of Orissa, but the government has not been able to undertake the expensive work of clearing and developing such land.) Some of the refugees have been absorbed into the labor market; others barely subsist on what they can earn from such occupations as weaving rugs, knitting sweaters, and forging bangles. They have set up makeshift colonies wherever they could find uninhabited ground—even in the swampland, though their reed-and-mud huts are regularly swept away by the monsoon rains.

Although parts of New York and parts of Tokyo have a population density comparable to that of parts of the Calcutta Metropolitan District, it, unlike the two other metropolises, has few buildings more than three stories high, and most of its people are housed in one- or two-story structures. Few of the houses are *pukka* structures, made of brick and cement. Rather, most are *kutcha* structures, made of bamboo, mud, or unbaked bricks. Except for the palatial quarters of the rich, most houses, *pukka* or *kutcha,* have no inside plumbing, and the *pukka* structures are often in disrepair. Many of these structures were originally intended only as temporary shelters for migrant workers, but they now house big families. Even so, a large number of people must sleep in and around dockyards, in factories, in offices, in shops, on construction sites, in railway stations, in hallways, and on stairways of buildings. More than half the Calcutta Metropolitan District is taken up by streams or by marshland that is unreclaimable for reasons of cost or technology; the demands on the remaining land are so intense that several hundred thousand people sleep out on the pavements and tens of thousands of people now live, as a matter of course, on low, undrained, disease-infested land bordering the salt marshes. All available public or private land is occupied by colonies of squatters. There is no place—not even the border of Calcutta's refuse dump—that is left unoccupied.

Unlike other metropolises that have grown up on the banks of rivers— such as London and Paris—the Calcutta Metropolitan District has been unable to spread out radially. Its suburbs have been forced to develop farther and farther away from the metropolitan center, crowding the margins of good land along the Hooghly. Yet every day huge numbers of people must somehow commute from these distant suburbs—many of which have no paved streets, and no room for much more than pedestrian traffic —to their jobs in Calcutta and Howrah. Even today, partly because of topography, there are only two main highways serving the Calcutta Metropolitan District—the Grand Trunk Road, on the west side of the river, and the Barrackpore Trunk Road, on the east side. Except for two major rail lines, which also run roughly parallel to the river, interurban transport is practically nonexistent, and the few public buses and trams are slow and overburdened. The two roads must therefore carry, in addition to commercial and industrial traffic, hundreds of thousands of commuting pedestrians, so at almost any time of day they are crowded with trucks, cars, bullock carts, rickshaws, bicycles, pedestrians, and pack animals. Of the two, the Grand Trunk Road, which connects the Calcutta Metropolitan District with the coal fields and steel mills of the industrial region, is by far the more important. But in the area of the Calcutta Metropolitan District even this road is narrow and in bad condition, and it passes through very congested parts of the metropolis. Until the end of the nineteenth century, Calcutta's position on the east bank of the Hooghly, separated from the land to the west, was not a serious disadvantage, for the city's raison d'être was shipping. But when land transport was developed, in the late nineteenth and early twentieth centuries, its major facilities, like the Howrah Railway Station, were necessarily built on the west side of the river, while the water-transport facilities, like the Port, remained on the east side. There is only one bridge across the Hooghly in the Calcutta-Howrah area

—the Howrah Bridge. This is Calcutta's single point of access to the rest of the country. "Indian economists ponder: What is the point of struggling to industrialize the country, of building steel mills, if one cannot adequately transport supplies, labor, and finished products?" Paul Grimes once wrote in an article on Calcutta in the New York *Times*. "What is the point of growing tea and jute, the biggest earners of foreign exchange, if one may be unable to get them to world markets? Without foreign exchange, how can the country buy generators for power plants, petroleum for trucking, tractors for farmland, aircraft for defense?"

The partition of India dislocated the entire economy of West Bengal, and particularly that of the Calcutta Metropolitan District, parts of which are only thirty miles from the Pakistani border. Not only was West Bengal deprived of important markets in East Bengal but its industry and agriculture were also severely handicapped. Before Partition, for instance, West Bengal depended heavily on East Bengal for rice, and from eighty to ninety per cent of the jute processed in the Calcutta Metropolitan District also came from East Bengal. When that supply of jute dried up, at least a million acres of land in West Bengal had to be diverted from the cultivation of rice—which is still West Bengal's biggest crop—to the cultivation of jute. The jute industry, however, has still not entirely recovered. In 1963 and 1964, industry in the Calcutta Metropolitan District absorbed, at most, a million workers—two hundred and thirty thousand in the jute industry, four hundred and thirty thousand in other organized industries, like heavy engineering, and three hundred thousand in "cottage industry," defined as any industry employing fewer than ten workers and relying on electric power, or employing as many as twenty workers but not relying on electric power. Work conditions in most of the factories are as grim as those in nineteenth-century London, and work conditions in cottage industry, which is spread throughout the *bustis,* are still worse. In the Calcutta Metropolitan District, there is chronic unemployment and chronic underemployment in all industries, in all occupations, and at all income levels. There are at least four hundred thousand adult males with no employment, and no one seems to know how they manage to stay alive. Female workers have two main occupations—domestic service and prostitution.

In recent years, the Calcutta Metropolitan District has made so little progress in extending education that a lower percentage of children attend school in its urban communities than in some of the rural areas in the state; at the time of the 1961 census, nearly half of the population over five years of age in the Calcutta Metropolitan District was illiterate and nearly half of the persons who could read and write were only semi-literate. The majority of the schools in the Calcutta Metropolitan District are run not by the government but by private charitable organizations, and, whether private or public, most of the school buildings are dismal, cramped rented or requisitioned tenements, with no facilities for playing, eating, or washing. To achieve the national aim of giving free compulsory education to all children between the ages of six and fourteen by 1986, Calcutta alone must provide at least a million three hundred thousand additional school places by that time, and at least a hundred new primary schools and a thousand new teachers every year, even if every school is used for double shifts and the city does not try to lower the high student-teacher ratio that exists now. In secondary education, the problems are equally formidable. Furthermore, the Calcutta Metropolitan District is the country's most important intellectual center, educating about thirteen per cent of all the students enrolled in colleges and universities in India, but its university, which is the largest in the world—in 1966 it had an enrollment of a hundred and thirty-five thousand regular students, along with sixty-five thousand students taking external degrees—has been in turmoil for many years, its academic life disintegrating rapidly under the pressure of its numbers.

To describe conditions even in Calcutta alone, observers have resorted to epithets like "slum of the world" and "city of death," and have strained for analogies to convey their impressions, as in this passage from the *Times* article by Grimes, which superimposes Calcutta's problems on New York:

New York is the only major port in the United States except for San Francisco (like Bombay) far to the west. There is no Boston, no Norfolk, no St. Lawrence Seaway to Chicago. The industrial complexes of Pittsburgh, Detroit, and Birmingham are all concentrated near Albany. The only highway from there to New York is the Albany Post Road. The Hudson River is so full of silt that fewer and fewer freighters can reach the West Street docks each year. . . . The municipal water supply is growing dangerously salty and unsafe to drink or use in industry. . . . Block-long lines of desperate seekers of menial jobs wait outside employment agencies. In the shadow of the Waldorf-Astoria is a shanty town where thousands of persons live in the worst imaginable squalor. Times Square swarms with beggars, many of them blind, deformed, or leprous.

When a people's will to protest against intolerable conditions—and this will is considered by some political thinkers to be as important for economic development as for political change—finds expression in the Calcutta Metropolitan District, it is likely to take the form of explosive demonstrations and pointless acts of public violence, which then suddenly subside without bringing about any improvement. Although the Calcutta

Metropolitan District has a very low rate of reported crime compared to
any Western metropolis—many *busti* areas have no record of crime at all—
public demonstrations and outbursts, some of them culminating in looting,
arson, and killing, have become commonplace in recent years. Hardly a
month goes by without a major strike over working conditions, a *hartal*
over government policy, or a riot over some minor grievance. Recently, in
Calcutta, eighty tramcars were burned in a month-long riot over a token
raise in tram fares, even though the new schedule had pegged the fares to
the distances travelled so equitably that some passengers would actually be
paying less than before; in March, 1966, during a general strike in West
Bengal that was accompanied by riots, thirty-nine people died and the
estimated loss from the work stoppage and the destruction of public and
private property was put at sixty-five million rupees, or more than half the
total revenue receipts—one hundred and ten million rupees—budgeted by
Calcutta for the fiscal year 1965–66. For many years, the Calcutta Metropolitan District's most outspoken political representatives, some of whom
belong to left-wing parties, have been elected not from the poorer con-
stituencies, which often return conservative or Congress candidates, but
from the richer ones; yet even the constituents with some money and
education, who feel that things can be changed, and are aware that they
can choose from a variety of political ideologies and candidates, seem to
ignore local issues, like water supply, housing, and education, and mobilize and demonstrate only over big national questions, like the Indian government's legislation on language or religion, or over international questions, like British policy in Rhodesia or the deployment of the United States
Seventh Fleet. The explanation most commonly advanced for the general
inertia in local matters is that the widespread poverty induces such passiv-
ity and resignation that any condition, however seemingly intolerable, is
endured. It is said that even when the poor are aroused to an act of protest
they are not capable of sustaining it, and that in the inertia of its population the Calcutta Metropolitan District is like any other poverty-stricken
community where conditions for revolution exist without the will to revolution. Bengali intellectuals, however, maintain that the demonstrations
and acts of public violence have so far served as a safety valve for pent-up
emotions but that they have only postponed the revolution that will one
day topple the established order. These intellectuals point out that Calcutta
is currently a center of Communist activity in India, the ideologies here
spanning the spectrum from conventional Marxism to the latest variety
of Maoism. (In Calcutta, the Communists publish, by one count, a daily

journal, three weeklies, and twelve monthlies, and occupy positions of power on other journals, in government, and in student, peasant, and labor organizations.) Some of these intellectuals are fond of repeating Lenin's dictum "The road to world revolution leads through Peking, Shanghai, and Calcutta."

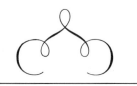

Come Again If You Leave the City

PLANE DESCENDING TO CALCUTTA. View from air: Flat, wet land. Coconut palms. Dark, muddy Hooghly. Mills strung along the river like beads. Factories. Hovels. Touch down at Dum-Dum Airport. Hot enough to fire bricks. New airport road. More hovels. Stench. Taste of grime in the mouth. Maelstrom of traffic. Roar of humanity.

🌸

The Grand, best hotel in Calcutta, on fashionable Chowringhi Road. Best neighborhood. Offices, shops, hotels, museum. Sign in the room cautions against drinking tap water.

🌸

Alongside Chowringhi, the famous Maidan—Indian Hyde Park. Two miles long, a mile wide. Green. Cosmopolitan. Girls in frocks and boys in knickers playing hopscotch, babies in prams, young men with books of Bengali verse, Europeans, athletes at gymnastics, masseurs giving rub-downs on the grass, *sadhus*. Monuments to soldiers and viceroys. Tall column to Sir David Ochterlony, a soldier in India for fifty years. At one side of Maidan, Victoria Memorial, white marble edifice with dome, sur-rounded by lakes and well-maintained gardens. Notices forbidding games or running in the gardens. At other side of Maidan, vast outline of Fort

William, then river. British Calcutta called "village of palaces," and around Maidan are grand residences, grand government buildings. Façades, mock-Gothic and colonial, now crumbling. Streets—Wellesley, Cornwallis, Amherst, Curzon. Clubs—Turf Club, Swimming Club, Calcutta Club. Two race courses, two golf courses within city limits of Calcutta.

❦

Head offices of the *Statesman*. Edited by an Englishman, A. E. Charlton. His telephone keeps ringing. "Yes, it's raining," he says into telephone. "Yes. . . . What? . . . Your ants were very right. Congratulate the ants." Then, to me: "That was my right-hand man here. He told me this morning that it would rain, because he had seen a heap of ants coming out of their hole, and he rang me up to tell me the ants were right."

❦

Howrah Bridge. People taking the evening air. Dramatic bore tide. Jetties bobbing, small boats hurrying to middle of river.

❦

Indian heirs. Harrison Road now Mahatma Gandhi Road, Lansdowne now Sarat Bose Road, Wellesley now Rafi Ahmed Kidwai Road. Old and new names used interchangeably. Even residents have two surnames, Anglicized and Bengalicized—Chatterji and Chattopadhya, Bannerji and Bandhopadhya, Mukherji and Mukhopadhya. New residential areas— Alipore, Ballygunge, Tollygunge. Restaurants—the Peiping, the Blue Fox, the Bar-B-Q, the Kwality. Fish and sweetmeats. Cinemas. Indian sahibs in raw-silk bush shirts, Indian memsahibs in saris with wide, rich borders. Women in tribal dress, complete with anklets and nose rings. Bearded Sikhs in pajamas and *kurtas*. Bengali gentlemen in *dhotis*—umbrellas in their hands. Snatches of conversation in, seemingly, every Indian tongue.

❦

Bengalis talkative, ebullient, charming people. Call themselves "the French of the East." Everywhere, emanation of Tagore, who, they say, started "India's intellectual renaissance." Shelves of books by Tagore,

about Tagore, dedicated to Tagore. Everyone constantly invoking the
Bengali contemporaries and successors of Tagore—the philosopher Sri
Aurobindo, the novelist Sarat Chandra Chatterji, the mystic Ramakrishna,
the social reformer Ram Mohan Roy, the revolutionary Subhas Chandra
Bose, and the "Nightingale of India," Sarojini Naidu. Also, the musician
Ali Akbar Khan, the dancer Uday Shankar, the painter Jamini Roy, and
the film director Satyajit Ray.

❧

Dinner at the residence of a rich Bengali. Walled compound with cast-
iron balustrades, beds of flowers, rococo fountain, marble nudes. House
with several inner courtyards, halls, chandeliers, mirrors.

❧

Unpainted buildings with rash of signs advertising businesses on all
floors. On sidewalks and streets, bamboo-and-burlap lean-tos, prostrate
bodies with bundles, sacred bulls chewing on husks of coconut. Smells—
dung, urine, sweat, incense, jasmine. Women scooping up and patting cow
dung, and other women cooking on fires of cow-dung chips. Heat at 117°.
Children washing in runnels.

❧

Roadside stalls. Signboards: "Four Annas Shave, Eight Annas Headcut,
Ten Annas Singeing Ladies' Heads." "Loafer's Delight Restaurant. Mutton Cutlis Our Specialty. Eat Them, Enjoy Them, Repeat Them." *Pan*-
wallahs folding individual scented betel leaves stuffed with lime, catechu,
betelnuts. Icemen. Sherbet-wallahs—cool blends of fruit juices, served in
gaudy glasses. Fortune-tellers and astrologers. More hawkers and venders,
with coconut meat and coconut milk, coir intoxicants and arrack, lotus
flowers. Other aromas: freshly ground pomegranate seed, coriander seed,
cumin seed, mustard seed; mint, ginger, cardamom, turmeric, cinnamon,
cloves, bay leaf; *ghi,* chilies, peppers, chutneys. Narrow, cobbled streets,
and more stalls, more kiosks, more bazaars. A bookseller and publisher, a
goldsmith, a butcher shop with goats being driven in through the door.
Everywhere: *"Baksheesh! . . . Baksheesh! . . . Baksheesh!"*

❧

Visit to a *busti* with M. S. Guha Mustaffi, assistant engineer, Calcutta Corporation. Huddles of red tile roofs crowding both sides of a paved street. Streets packed with milling, barefoot people and inquisitive, half-naked children, old cows, and stray dogs. *Pukka* houses, but moldy and decaying. Maze of spidery alleys, gullies, and footpaths leading away from the street. Ordure, rotting garbage, and mud underfoot. Overhead, wet clothes, a jumble of colors. A narrow vacant lot jammed with milch cows —the infamous *khatal,* or cattle pen. Now an agglutination of wattle-and-daub *kutcha* huts and houses, all with common walls. Near them, a tube well and, beside it, gutters and a latrine. More huts. Miserable stalls of venders. A water tap and an endless line of women waiting with buckets. "The *bustis* are on private land," Guha Mustaffi is saying, "but the Corporation tries to provide tube wells and water pumps whenever funds permit." Duck through low, narrow doorway into courtyard. Open, smoke-filled, unpaved, muddy, used communally for washing clothes and utensils and for bathing. Clustered around courtyard, a few windowless cubicles. Families of a bus-driver, a fruit seller, a taxi-driver, a tailor live in them. Go into a cubicle. Cement floor. Above, roof tiles. A single hemp *charpoy.* A few shelves holding a few utensils—iron griddle, rolling pin, pan and pot, mortar and pestle. Wife of Yusuf Mohammed, fruit seller, small and full of smiles, dressed in cotton sari printed with flowers. Brood of children. "It is very hot here in the day," she says. "Only in the evening a little breeze comes. But it is Allah's will." "Do you get enough to eat?" Mustaffi asks. "He makes only three rupees a day, and our rent is sixteen rupees a month," she says. In the doorway, a man. "You lie. The rent is only twelve rupees a month," he says. Altercation. Mustaffi explains that system is for the actual landlord to rent a house to one tenant, who sublets rooms to subtenants. The man in the doorway, Isaac, is the tenant landlord of the subtenants. Isaac complains. Collects sixty rupees monthly from subtenants, but Corporation taxes and landlord—Addy, of Addy Estates—take more than twenty rupees. Leave nothing to live on. Visit Moti Jheel ("pearl lake") Busti. Gets name from actual stagnant pond. Other *bustis,* with roofs of tile, tin, or jute sacking. Shatubabu Lane Busti, Bibi Baghan Busti, Tangra Busti, 90 and 110 Linton Street Busti, Bedford Lane Busti, Collin Street Busti, Elliot Road Busti. Southeast limits of Calcutta, and Dhapa, the city's huge refuse dump. Dhapa: open trailers piled high with refuse are pulling up and unloading on great rubbish heaps. All around, bleak, desolate encampments. A slaughterhouse. A butchered cow wheeled by. Human figures, mostly women, scavenging in the heaps. Beyond, marshland.

Look through Calcutta *Hand Book* for tourists. Come upon an appeal—in disconcerting English—some of which reads like an official apologia, some like a personal letter. Appeal opens, "Calcutta has been variously described as the city of nightmare, the city of processions, the city of filth and squalor, etc., etc.," but continues with an optimism as charming as it is pathetic:

But here live some 30 lakhs of people in about 30 sq. miles. Here you will find the multi-storied skyscrapers proudly raising their high heads to the still beyond sky, having a broad base of slum area built of mud and tiled houses. You will find here miles and miles of underground sewer through which a man can even walk erect, carrying filth and dirt to the outskirts of the city, and you will also find vast areas with service latrine where night-soil has yet got to be removed in Buckets by human agencies. Vast Concrete and Asphalted streets bordered on both sides by huge buildings will greet you on your entry to the city from the east or north whereas your entry from the west or south may possibly sicken you with sights of poor living conditions of the large number of refugees, sailors or seamen who throng the areas. . . .

You want a stroll? Go right along the Ganges [Hooghly] by Strand Road right up to the Dock areas. You feel tired in your unaccustomed long-distance walk? Just sit along the Bank of the Ganges and as our Commissioner says, throw pebbles into the water. The "Tup-Tip" sound will possibly sooth your nerves. . . .

You want a ride on the boat. In the rainy season, you are told you can have your ride on the very streets of Calcutta. . . .

Do you feel depressed for all our commissions and omissions? Why not see the night life of Calcutta and the West Bengal Government's Tourist Bureau is at your service to oblige you. . . .

Still not satisfied? Then you better go to either of the Coffee Houses. Here you will find budding politicians or scholars calmly but passionately discussing the evils of the World and you will find your problem solved in no time. . . . But if you . . . crave for majestic isolated travel—hail one of our Rickshaws—still drawn by your fellow brother who will run for Your Majesty at the risk of their lives and neither your pity nor your wrath will help them if you just do not like to avail yourself of their services. . . . The Chowringhee and Central Avenue Dalhousie area will cater to your needs, if you can pay for it. . . . A large number of Restaurants of the Park Street will be at your service with dinner, dance and whatnot. . . .

Yes—Yes—We know. You find Garbages heaped in streets, Taxi-wallas evading your calls, water supply not adequate, hazards of using a public conveyance, etc., etc.

But let us have our say. Our per capita income is Rs. 19.58 [19 rupees and 58 pices] and not Rs. 53.43 as in Bombay or elsewhere. . . . We have to look after a vast number of refugees who are yet to find their way towards a means of livelihood. You ask, why cannot we increase the per capita income if Bombay can do so? Well, well—why do we grow Jute to earn foreign exchange for India when we can grow paddy to feed our people? Why do we pay most of Income Tax, which is distributed to other provinces to meet their needs? Many such questions can be asked, but who is going to answer them?

The truncated Bengal is now Calcutta. Here come people from all other provinces, form their own communities, live in peace with Bengalees, earn for their families, and send their earnings to their native provinces. We cannot tax them. . . . You live with us and probably prefer to share our comparatively cheap living, and we prefer to live moderately so that we may yet exist as Bengalees. Cities other than Calcutta are cosmopolitan, but Calcutta still remains a city of Bengalees. . . .

Don't tell us about our failings and shortcomings. We know it all and we are being reminded of it daily. If you find anything good, tell others. Live with us in peace and come again if you leave the city. You are welcome.

This morning, I go, by prearrangement, to Rakhal Das Addy Road and to the offices of Sanat Kumar Addy, a landlord whose holdings include *busti* properties—the Shatubabu Busti and 90 and 110 Linton Street Busti among them—and also houses in other parts of Calcutta and an entire bazaar. Rakhal Das Addy Road is some distance from Chowringhi, in a poorish neighborhood. This road, like most roads in Calcutta, is narrow, but, unlike most, it is relatively quiet. The offices, a couple of rooms that occupy the ground floor of a two-story structure, are indistinguishable from those of any other traditional Indian business establishment. There is one long main room with shelves and steel cupboards along the walls, all crammed with ledgers done up in jute sacking. In the back of the room is a platform about a foot high covered with a clean white cotton cloth, on which, barefoot, a half-dozen bespectacled *babus* wearing white *kurtas* and *dhotis* sit crosslegged, poring over more ledgers. In the front of the room is a long table, around which the *seths,* or rich men, of the business, also in *kurtas* and *dhotis,* sit in chairs, conferring. A brand-new pack of cigarettes and a brand-new box of matches, which are set out on a little white tin plate in the center of the table, are the only touches of modernity in the musty office. As is the custom in such establishments, no general introductions are made, but a chair is brought up and placed for me beside Addy, who is an elderly man with a weasellike face and a circumspect air.

Behind rimless glasses, his eyes are friendly, and when he smiles he reveals a few chipped teeth.

I ask Addy how he got into the real-estate business.

"The business was started by my grandfather," he says. "The house I live in was built by my grandfather. I live there with my relatives—we all live in the same house as a joint family, and they are co-owners of the Calcutta properties. The house has seventeen or eighteen rooms. We once had a rice business, but the government has taken away our rice fields, and now our Calcutta properties are our only source of income."

I ask him if he inspects his properties in the *bustis*.

"We are handicapped," he says. "In practice, we have no status as landlords in the *bustis*. We are only *de-facto* landlords, with no power to act. Since 1937, the courts have administered our *busti* properties through a receiver. It's up to the courts to make any improvements, and even the courts can't do anything unless the tenant pays a reasonable amount of rent."

Very milky tea is now served in teacups, with a couple of biscuits on each saucer, and over the tea I learn that the receiver, Niha Ranjan Ghosh, is at the table, and that the other men around it are partners and associates of Addy.

"As a receiver, I am responsible for administration and maintenance of the property and for distribution of income to the co-owners of the property," Ghosh tells me. "We receivers are compensated by the court, but my compensation amounts to only a few thousand rupees a year. But I also have my law practice."

I ask Addy about the extent of his holdings in the *bustis*.

"We own altogether sixteen or seventeen *busti* houses and we have from three hundred to three hundred and fifty tenants," he says.

I ask him how much rent he collects from the *busti* houses.

He becomes noticeably wary. "It varies," he says. "Supposing a single family has had the lease of the same *busti* house for three or four generations—then the family may pay only eight annas per month per *kutta*, which is seven hundred and twenty square feet. The highest amount we can get per *kutta* is sixteen rupees a month. In Linton Street, I have sixty *kuttas*, and I am getting from a hundred and thirty to a hundred and forty rupees per month from them as rent, yet I hear that the land in the neighborhood of Linton Street is selling very high—from twenty to twenty-four thousand rupees per *kutta*. Then, too, the tenants who rent *busti* houses from us may sublet rooms in the houses as long as they continue to live in the houses, and we can't evict them. We must go to the court. Landlords who don't have the money to fight in the court for six, seven, or eight years can't even litigate, and so they sell their holdings for nothing, because who wants to buy property where the rents are token, where the tenants can't be disturbed, and where the *busti* houses can't be torn down? I have spent thousands and thousands of rupees litigating. I spend all my time litigating. Nothing ever comes of it, but at least it kills time."

As I am leaving, he says, "Every *busti* landlord in Calcutta would stand to multiply his income many hundredfold if all the *busti* houses were razed tomorrow. We don't want to own *bustis* any more than anyone wants to live in them. We would all like to help the poor *busti*-dweller."

From Rakhal Das Addy Road, I go to an appointment with B. Malik, the Vice-Chancellor of Calcutta University. Malik is a pleasant, thoughtful man, who looks younger than his age, which is seventy-one.

"I am at least trying to do something about the administration of the university before I leave the place," he tells me. "Let me give you an example of the kind of mess it is in. There is a very learned Sanskrit lecturer here, Bhatabi Ram Shastri. He was offered a better appointment at another university, and a proposal was made to keep him here by upgrading his post. The proposal went from one committee to another, and after two years it reached the senate, which represents faculty members, deans, and graduates. The senate agreed to upgrade him. But then someone in the senate spoke up and said that since Bhatabi Ram Shastri had been waiting for two years, the upgrading of his post should be retroactive. Someone else said that in that case Bhatabi Ram Shastri should give up his two years' salary retroactively. The post had not been advertised publicly. If it had been, Shastri might have lost out to another applicant, in which case he would not have been receiving any salary at all from the university for the last two years. Wonderful, to upgrade a man's post for his benefit, and in the process to take away his salary! I had emergency powers to make the appointment, and I immediately used them to make his upgrading retroactive. Someone else in the senate now spoke up and said, 'Sir, you took over as Vice-Chancellor a few months after his appointment came up for upgrading. Therefore, how can you retroactively upgrade him?' Our senate is full of wayside lawyers. With the help of the Ford Foundation, which has taken a special interest in Calcutta, we are now trying to streamline the administration."

I ask him what other steps are being taken to improve conditions in the university.

"We scarcely know where to begin," he says. "We are a very poor university—for seventy-five per cent of our financing we are dependent on student fees. The colleges are spread out all over the city, and there is almost no social contact between students and teachers. We don't have many residential facilities, and we don't know where or how most of our teachers and students live. We don't know what happens to the students after classes, and we don't inquire. One consequence of this is that they get involved in every major riot in the city. The university is bedevilled with strikes, and examinations and degrees are continually being put off."

Afterward, I have a drink with Samar Sen, the editor of a new intellectual English-language weekly called *Now,* and some of his friends, at his house. Every ashtray is full, and the atmosphere is a little feverish. The talk always returns to *Now,* and the best-known Bengali man of letters writing in English, Nirad Chaudhuri, and his *Now* articles, of which the following passage is fairly typical:

> . . . If I were a sphinx of granite with only the brains of man and bent on intellectual laughter, I should today burst into such a peal of guffaw as with their reverberating ha-ha would crack the vast dome of the firmament. But I am a bundle of nerves and flesh, and I suffer. I am swept off my feet at intervals by uncontrollable gusts of rage at what I see. I feel like picking up a cat-o'-nine-tails and laying about among our politicians, or want to seize a machinegun to mow down the mob or, better still, a flamethrower to cauterize the earth of a suppurating vileness. I feel like going abroad to preach a crusade like Peter the Hermit, although my efforts might turn out to be only as laughable as Don Quixote's, and the result as pitiful as the Children's Crusade. But in actual fact I can only gnash my teeth, and tear my hair.

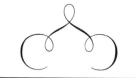

It's the Crying Baby That
Gets Picked Up

In the days I spend going around Calcutta, I constantly ask myself, "Can anyone be held accountable? Can things be changed? Where is help to come from?" I seek out political figures, government officers, some Ford Foundation planners recently arrived to attack the problems of the Calcutta Metropolitan District. Most of these men work out of the buildings in and around Chowringhi or in nearby Dalhousie Square. Some of these buildings lie so close to the Port that they seem to be right on the docks. From the inside, some of them have the feeling of old ships retired from Her Majesty's service, as if long ago they had sailed up the dark, alien river and been abandoned there by their masters.

The Central Municipal Office Building is a huge four-story structure, built in 1872. It now serves as headquarters for the municipal government of Calcutta. The Mayor, P. K. Roy Chowdhury, who governs Calcutta with the assistance of a councillor from each of its hundred wards, receives me in a large, formal-looking hall lined with impressive official portraits. At one end is an enormous conference table, and at the other are several capacious black leather sofas. The Mayor, a gentle-looking elderly Bengali, is ensconced on one of the sofas. He is dressed entirely in white, and, besides the *kurta* and the floor-length, flowing *dhoti* and the open leather sandals that Indian politicians invariably seem to wear, he has a white shawl around his shoulders. A number of Bengalis, also in *kurtas, dhotis,* and sandals, are sitting around him on the other sofas, chatting and laughing, drinking tea, and eating sweetmeats and savories. The Mayor introduces them as councillors. They all seem to be named Chatterji or Bannerji or Mukherji—the Bengali equivalents of Smith and Jones and Brown.

"I myself entered politics as a councillor, but I'm a doctor by profession," the Mayor tells me. "I became a councillor not for political reasons but for medical reasons. I wanted to do something about the health problem in the Calcutta Corporation. As a councillor, I was chairman of the Standing Health and Busti Improvement Committee for six years. I got a lot of satisfaction from doing work for t.b. control, hospital improvement, and so on."

I ask the Mayor what, specifically, is being done about the numerous problems of Calcutta.

"We have several organizations that are concurrently seeking to improve conditions in Calcutta and all its suburbs. For example, we have the Calcutta Metropolitan Planning Organization, which is getting experts and money from the Ford Foundation. It is doing the planning for the whole of the Calcutta Metropolitan District. Its work has been expedited by the West Bengal government, and I hope its plans will be carried out one day. The Calcutta Improvement Trust, which was formed in 1911, and which gets almost five per cent of the Corporation's revenue, does things like taking a plot of land from us, developing it, and returning it to our jurisdiction. The Founders' Municipal Association does good work, too. But we have not made much progress, because every problem requires money. We have twenty-five thousand municipal employees, such as clerks, police, and sweepers, and fifty per cent of the income of the Corporation goes to pay them."

I ask him what is being done about the problem of the water supply, for instance.

"We have two water mains—one sixty-two inches in diameter and the other seventy two—to carry filtered water from Palta to Calcutta, a hundred and fifty big-diameter tube wells, and fifty thousand small-diameter tube wells," he says. "We have started chlorinating our unfiltered water, and have thus brought down the incidence of cholera. Now we also have a scheme to augment the supply of filtered water by sixty million gallons per day, but it will take from a year to a year and a half to carry it out."

Next, I meet the Commissioner of the Calcutta Corporation, H. C. Mukherji, who heads the municipal civil service and supervises the work of all its officers and employees. His office, which is nearby, also has formal furnishings and an informal atmosphere, with councillors and other officials coming and going, taking refreshment, and exchanging small talk.

"My field has always been engineering, valuation, planning, and administration," the Commissioner tells me. "In the beginning, I trained as a civil engineer. After that, I qualified as a chartered surveyor in England. Except for some nominal changes in day-to-day administrative procedures, I wouldn't say that I have been able to change the administration of the Corporation in ways apparent to everyone."

A burly man stops by. The Commissioner introduces him as the chief engineer of the Corporation, and explains that he is in charge of all the municipal engineering works, plans, and estimates.

"Calcutta's worst problem is that it was never planned," the chief engineer observes. "The city has grown up without anyone's ever expecting it to have any future."

A mild-mannered gray-haired man wearing spectacles now joins us. He is the health officer of the Corporation, and his duties include supervising municipal sanitation, hospitals, laboratories, and cremation grounds, and seeing to vaccinations and inoculations. "Diseases go in cycles," he says. "In the last two years, we have been very lucky. The diseases have been on a very small scale. But this is the epidemic year in the cycle, and the epidemic might break out at any time."

"Calcutta is a bundle of problems," the Commissioner says. "I once took a couple of Ford Foundation experts from the Calcutta Metropolitan Planning Organization around the city, and I told them, 'Gentlemen, I am waiting to see how bold you are. If it were up to me, I would crash down a good part of Calcutta.' "

The Writers' Buildings, a block of red buildings built in 1880, take their name from the junior clerks of the East India Company, known as "writers," who once lived in them. They now serve as headquarters for the West Bengal government, and in them I talk with a number of Ministers of the Congress government of West Bengal. The Minister of Public Works of West Bengal, K. N. Das Gupta, receives me in his office, a large room with three air-conditioners stacked on top of each other in one window and all going at full speed. A half-drawn curtain divides the room into a sort of drawing room, which contains comfortable-looking chairs, and a sort of study, which contains a desk, a reclining chair with a well-worn cushioned footrest, and a bed with smooth, clean sheets.

"We are now beginning to construct special housing units for factory workers," the Minister tells me. "Recently, we advertised three hundred new two-room flats for such workers, and we received twenty-six thousand applications. A committee has begun screening the applicants."

He gets up, moves slowly across the room, adjusts the blinds, and absent-mindedly serves me coffee. "Because of the emergencies of the Chinese invasion and the Indo-Pakistan war, we got only two crores of rupees a year for housing during the Third Five-Year Plan," he says. "Now, for the period of the Fourth Five-Year Plan, we are asking for twice as much a year, most of it from the central government. But all this is just maneuvering. We have to ask for a lot to get anything at all."

The Minister for Local Self-Government for West Bengal, S. M. Fazlur Rahman (he is also Minister of Animal Husbandry, Veterinary Services, and Fisheries), whom I meet next, is a Muslim in his fifties, dressed in Punjabi-type pajamas and a *kurta*. "I am responsible for dispensing assistance to municipal governments in West Bengal, including any notified area authority," he informs me, putting his feet up on a footrest. "A notified area authority is an officially recognized new area that aspires to the status of a municipality."

I comment on the bewildering number of municipalities already existing in Greater Calcutta.

"You must call this 'Metropolitan Calcutta,' not 'Greater Calcutta,'" he says. "The term 'Greater Calcutta' should be reserved for the day when Calcutta is a developed city. Now, about the subject you raise, perhaps it would be a good thing to have some of the municipalities consolidated one day. But in a democracy you cannot do things without taking into account the interests of everyone concerned. Much, much legislation is required before any consolidation can take place. In my three years' tenure, I have so far been able only to consolidate two municipalities into one and to link up one municipality with the Howrah Corporation."

The Chief Minister of West Bengal, P. C. Sen, to whom I pay my last visit in the Writers' Buildings, sits behind a large semicircular desk with chairs ranged in a semicircle to his right and left. He talks to me between hearing petitioners, who enter, make their requests, and depart.

I ask him how he got into politics.

"I went into Congress politics formally in 1920, when Mahatma Gandhi gave the call," he says. "Between 1914 and 1920, I was somewhat loosely connected with the revolutionary movement of West Bengal. Part of that time, I was a student at the Scottish Church College, in Calcutta."

He orders coffee and cashew nuts, and goes on to talk about various obstacles to getting things done. "Even when we do have the resources, we can't change things quickly, because we're a democracy," he says. "We had to stop work altogether on the important new road from Dum-Dum Airport to Calcutta because a group of refugees had squatted on a piece of land it had to cross. It took us a year to gain legal possession of that land. It is a matter of people trying to assert their rights."

I ask him about the increasing public violence in Calcutta.

He gives me what I have come to recognize as the Congress line. "It is caused by political agitators who have no use for the ballot box and who are interested only in seizing power," he says. "The Maoist Communists have a cadre of saboteurs all their own, and now some of them are even talking about calling in a Chinese Army of Liberation. They say that as soon as this Army of Liberation comes, all the travail and suffering of India will be over. We have had to put some of these Communists in jail because of their connection with Communist China."

At Congress Party headquarters for West Bengal, I call on Atulya Ghosh, the Congress boss who—with two other party bosses, S. K. Patil, Union Minister of Railways, and Sanjiva Reddy, Union Minister of Transport, Aviation, Shipping, and Tourism—is considered to be all-powerful at both state and national levels; the triumvirate, which dominates the Congress Party leaders, known collectively as the "Syndicate," is said to have engineered the election of Mrs. Gandhi as Prime Minister. Ghosh turns out to be a tall, heavy-set Bengali in his early sixties, with well-groomed white hair. He is dressed in *kurta, dhoti,* and sandals, and he is wearing, incongruously, a pair of large, round-rimmed dark glasses and is smoking a cigar.

I ask him about his role as "kingmaker."

"I have no official position in the government," he says, in a big, booming voice. "I am not a Minister, I am not a mayor—how can I have any power? There can't be any position of personal power in a democratic party like the Congress. One person may become popular or strong, but by himself he can do nothing. It is all teamwork. In fact, I can't understand the interest in me. The other day, somebody wrote to me from a university in England and said he was doing a thesis on me and wanted personal details. I detest all this interest in me. I've done what I could for my country. I joined Congress as an ordinary volunteer when I was fifteen, and I have spent, all told, ten or eleven years in British jails. I have given my life to the party, and have remained a bachelor, even though I came from a very good family—my mother's side was well known for its literary activities and my father's side was well known for its money—and had many matrimonial proposals."

I ask him about the threat to continued Congress rule.

"Eighty per cent of the agitation here is by refugees for whom there is

nothing on the horizon," he says. "The remaining twenty per cent of the
agitation is by students who have no future. They are all frustrated human
beings, with no real politics to speak of."

(In subsequent elections in West Bengal, the Congress Party was all but
obliterated. The state is at present ruled by the United Front, consisting of
about a dozen parties, led by the Communist Party of India, Marxist.)

Utpal Dutt, a talented Bengali playwright, actor, and director, who is
known for his Maoist radicalism, has just been released from Calcutta's
Presidency Prison, where he was held for six months, under the Defense of
India Rules, along with many other political activists who were arrested in
Calcutta during the second Indo-Pakistan war. It was generally assumed
that the cause of his arrest was a series of vitriolic attacks he had made on
the Congress Party. He had, for instance, contributed to *Now* an article
entitled "The Indian Kulturkampf," in which he struck out against the
Congress Party and its "kept press" and traced what he regarded as a
"resurrection of fascism" and a ruthless suppression of all intellectual dis-
sent to the Congress Party's cynical exploitation of the border issue with
China.

> In October, 1962, with the Chinese invasion [he had written], a chauvin-
> ism of the most degenerate kind raised its head. . . . Vicious slogans were
> raised primarily by leaders of our ruling party. . . . It was always "the
> Dragon," "the Yellow Peril," "the Yellow Rats," "the Yellow Pirates." . . .
> There was certainly a keen competition to coin picturesque obscenities in-
> volving the snub nose, sallow complexion, and silken barbarism of the Chi-
> nese. . . . But the most devastating was his [the Union Home Minister's]
> warning to those Communists who *think* India is wrong on the border issue.
> To think is now dangerous business.

To meet Dutt, I go to the Minerva Theatre, a shabby old structure in an
impoverished area of Calcutta, where he directs his own stage company,
called the Little Theatre Group, in performances of his own plays, often
acting in them himself. Vagrants are hanging around the box office. In the
lobby, more vagrants are sitting on benches under posters and photographs
advertising "Kallol," a historical drama by Dutt about a naval mutiny in
Bombay during the last year of the raj and about the Congress Party's
compromising role in it. Upstairs is Dutt's office, a faded room with peeling walls and windows that seem never to have been washed. All over the
floor are haphazard piles of papers and junk, and in the middle of the
room are two wooden tables. At one table, two men are bent over stacks of
coins, which they are counting aloud, over and over again. At the second

table sits a dark, stocky man of medium height in a striped American T shirt. He has wavy hair and a beard and mustache, and wears glasses. This is Dutt.

I ask him how "Kallol" is being received—like everything he turns his hand to, the play is surrounded with controversy.

"Ever since we opened, more than a year ago, the Congress government of West Bengal, which is essentially a communal establishment of high-caste Hindus, has been looking for an excuse to close the play," he says. "But 'Kallol' has been such a popular success that they haven't dared to do it. The Congress Party wants to hush up its dirty toady role in the mutiny —hush up that part of history. It has seen to it that even the National Archives have only two typewritten pages with some schoolboy facts about the mutiny. We had to do research for three years to find out what really happened—how Congress betrayed the mutiny, betrayed the Indian people. The people are now realizing that there will never be enough food in the country as long as the Congress Party is in power."

I ask him what, precisely, he means.

"It is obvious that the Congress Party's power depends upon the support of the profiteers and hoarders, so the Congress Party protects them," he says. "The people haven't got anything to eat. But now they demand more than food, more than kerosene. The general strike and the riots in West Bengal last March prove this. Now the people are getting ready for a much bigger struggle. As yet, the people haven't quite realized how they should go about overthrowing this Congress government. When the people fully realize how weak the Congress government is, there will be violence. Some terrible things will have to happen before anything good can happen."

I ask him if he has a Communist revolution in mind.

"I think Communism offers a solution to India's problems," he says.

As we talk on about politics, it becomes clear that his own violence takes the form of words and art, and that in respect to specific Indian problems he is as thoroughly confounded as his chosen enemies. Yet one thing appears to set him apart, and this is that the signs of disturbance in his mind seem also to be signs of his personal torment over the problems he speaks about.

"I have had a checkered past," he tells me at one point. "My father was an agent of materialism—he was a gendarme, and the police were the backbone of the raj. Yet I was able to see through it. I had a middle-class education, but I lived in Calcutta, in the middle of these streets and *bustis*. I formed the Little Theatre Group, and we began by doing plays in English for middle-class audiences. But in recent years we have been performing in Bengali, and only in the working-class areas of the city and in poor villages. Revolutionaries are born of contradictions."

A new building on Lower Chitpur Road (the street was renamed Rabindra Sarani not long ago, but it is still called by the old name) houses the offices of the Calcutta Metropolitan Planning Organization, which since 1961 has been preparing a series of plans for the regeneration of the metropolis. The introductory volume of the series, entitled "Basic Development Plan: Calcutta Metropolitan District, 1966–1986," has just been issued. Although it is intended as a master plan for development and includes specific recommendations for immediate action, it seems to be haunted by the afflictions that paralyze the metropolis, and reads throughout more like a diagnostician's report than a prescription for a remedy. To get a first-hand impression of what the planners think, I spend some time talking with M. G. Kutty, an Indian, who is the director of the Calcutta Metropolitan Planning Organization; Dr. Colin Rosser, a British social anthropologist, who is the consultant on community facilities and services for the Ford Foundation group; and C. Preston Andrade, an American architect and urban planner, who is the director of planning for the Ford Foundation group.

Kutty, a tall, heavily built man in his forties with a chubby, boyish face and pomaded hair, sports a mustard-yellow bush shirt with a silky finish and lounges in a comfortable-looking chair like an old-fashioned bureaucrat. "Perhaps you would like to start the discussion, and summarize the history of planning in Calcutta," Kutty says, turning to Rosser.

Rosser, who is short and compactly built, and is dressed in a short-sleeved shirt, a baggy pair of trousers, and sandals, is perhaps forty, and has the appearance of someone who has spent his life burrowed deep in work. "The fact that the Calcutta Metropolitan District is the world's worst area for endemic cholera attracted the attention of the World Health Organization, and in 1959 they sent a team here to find out what could be done to reduce the incidence of all gastro-enteric diseases," he says. "The team recommended preparing a master plan for water and sanitation, and the work on the plan was begun with financial help from WHO and the U.N. Special Fund. But it was realized quite early on that the problems of the metropolis required a much broader attack. The preliminary visit of our Ford Foundation people followed, and the West Bengal government set up the C.M.P.O. and charged it with the task of preparing a comprehensive development plan. That was in July, 1961, and since then the Ford

Foundation has been helping the organization with a group of professional advisers. A succession of people have come and gone, and there are
about twenty of us here now."

"May I interject something here by way of explanation, Colin?" Andrade asks. He is tall and lean, with sharp, clean looks, and has dark-
brown eyes and light-colored hair that is turning white. "Although our
experience in most cases is with Western cities, we make a cultural adaptation quickly and have developed a considerable familiarity with the problems of the metropolis of Calcutta."

I ask Rosser and Andrade how they happened to become involved in
planning for the Calcutta Metropolitan District.

"I was with the Indian Army during the Second World War, and got
interested in India," Rosser says. "After the war, I went to Cambridge,
where I read anthropology. I came out to India again for field research. I
went to Katmandu, where I got interested in urban areas, though the
happy hunting ground of most anthropologists is the villages. When the
Ford Foundation was looking for people who had worked in Indian cities
—or, at least, were interested in Indian cities—it asked me if I would come
to Calcutta, and I came, intending to stay here two months. I've stayed
four years. It's very hard to disengage oneself from Calcutta."

"We all have our particular stories of involvement with the Calcutta
project," Andrade says.

"Until the C.M.P.O., no one seems to have taken any interest in the
city," Kutty says. "Even basic statistics and basic engineering surveys
didn't exist. In other metropolises, which already have all the statistics and
surveys, the preparation of such a master plan would have taken a decade.
We've done it from scratch in five years."

"We weren't even able to find an epigraph for the plan, though we
searched the literature," Rosser says. "Calcutta has produced so many famous men that one would have supposed it would be easy to find one
good comment on the place. Not at all. Take Tagore. There isn't one good
word about Calcutta in all his writings. He rejected the city, left it, and
founded Shantiniketan University, in Shantiniketan, a hundred miles
from Calcutta. The only comment that even came close to the kind of
thing we were looking for was something Mrs. Gandhi said the other day,
and she was speaking not about the problems of the Calcutta Metropolitan
District but about the problems of all India. She said, 'It's the crying baby
that gets picked up.' Calcutta cries from time to time—mostly in public
violence."

"The problems encountered in a metropolis of Calcutta's population, complexity, and economic significance are greater than those encountered in many sizable nations," Andrade says. "The population of the Calcutta Metropolitan District is soon expected to exceed Australia's. The planning that's going on at the C.M.P.O. now is comprehensive not only in the sense that it brings together various disciplines, like hydrology, engineering, economics, and sociology—many of the physical and social sciences—but in the sense that it considers all aspects of the needs of the community, rather than each aspect as a separate entry in the ledger of credits and debits. We don't talk about the problem of providing housing in terms of building x number of housing units. The focus of our planning is not just building x number of housing units but providing a suitable infrastructure for an integrated, comprehensively designed human city. This includes environmental services—that is, shelter, water, drainage, sewerage, refuse collection, and utilities; and social services—that is, education, welfare, health, employment, and transportation. What I'm saying is that it's easy enough to recognize the problems qualitatively, but it takes a good deal of work to analyze them quantitatively."

"We have to remember to set our sights on things we have some hope of achieving," Kutty says. "Until recently, there wasn't even such a thing as the Calcutta Metropolitan District. And the Water and Sanitation Authority, formed this year by the West Bengal government, is the first body to have jurisdiction over the entire District. Our hope is that the formation of similar metropolitan authorities for education, housing, transportation, and so on, will gradually achieve a kind of *de-facto* consolidation of municipalities. The greatest need at the moment is for a planning authority, because you can't just produce a plan and go away and leave it."

"To give you a concrete example of the kinds of problems we are up against in planning, take housing," Rosser says. "The housing emergency here requires not only the replacement of the inadequate housing of most of the present population of seven and a half million but the provision of new housing to take care of the population increase of five million expected over the next twenty years—an increase that will give us about two hundred thousand new people to house each year. If the average size of a family is five, you need roughly forty thousand new housing units a year just to cope with the population increase, and even if we could somehow build these units, that would do nothing for the people who are already here, eighty-five per cent of whom are living in housing units that do not meet the government's minimum standard of forty square feet per person. Say you wanted to do as much for the old population as for the new—you'd need at least eighty thousand new housing units a year. Now, the present annual rate of construction here is only about six thousand *pukka* housing units. To raise that figure to eighty thousand units a year, or even to forty thousand, would involve an enormous development of the construction industry, to say nothing of the development of related industries, like utilities. Even if the industries could somehow be developed, the problem of paying for the housing units would remain. Eighty thousand new housing units a year over the next twenty years would cost at least thirteen hundred crores of rupees. This is a truly astronomical figure for the budget of the entire country, let alone the budget of a single urban district. So the only thing we have been able to do in the plan is to suggest stopgap measures. Thus, we recommend building *kutcha* structures, of mud and thatch, with a life of ten or fifteen years, and perhaps building *pukka* structures later, when we have more money. The minimum cost of a *kutcha* unit is between a thousand and fifteen hundred rupees, whereas the minimum cost of a *pukka* unit is eighty-five hundred rupees."

"May I interject a comment?" Andrade says. "What we are really doing now, and what, to a very large extent, we are bound to do, is simply to build better *bustis*. The snag in the *bustis* already built is that the environmental services are either inadequate or totally nonexistent. Consequently, one of the ideas that we're working on is to see whether the sites of *bustis* can be selected in the future by planners rather than haphazardly by individual landlords, as they are now."

"The selection now is so haphazard that large areas in the center of the city of Calcutta are covered with *bustis*," Rosser says. "This is a totally uneconomic use of the land, so in the plan we recommend measures that would relate *busti* clearance from the center of the city to the development of satellite towns, where there will be some opportunity to earn a living."

"In a society initiating a really fundamental development program, the question of priorities is a very important one," Andrade says. "For instance, how high do you rate investment in housing—which is economically unproductive even though it may be of very great human importance—compared to, say, investment in education, or even in transportation? Now, in our view, the priorities that attach to public investment in housing are very low compared to, say, resuscitating the Hooghly."

"Calcutta's worst problem is simply that it is on the wrong side of the river," Rosser says. "At one stage of the plan, we actually considered moving the river to the east of the city, but that proved impractical, so other steps are being taken to resuscitate the Hooghly. The central government is building an arrangement of dams and channels—the Farraka Barrage—a hundred and sixty miles north of here, at the junction of the Ganga and the Bhagirathi, where the sandbar has formed. This should increase the flow of Ganga water into the Hooghly. Meanwhile, the Port Commission has started a program of dredging the river above and below the Port, and 'training' the river—that is, constructing barriers to guide the main flow of the water. This should increase the depth of the channel and prevent further erosion of the banks. These measures should help to push the salinity line thirty miles down. Other recommendations of the plan are building new pumping stations on the river to supplement the water supply from Palta; building more bridges, among them one in the Calcutta-Howrah area, to relieve the congestion on the Howrah Bridge, and one north of here, between Kalyani and Bansberia, to help to develop new satellite towns in that area; building new national highways and arterial roads; and developing the port at Haldia so that it can take bulk cargoes. The plan originally called for an expenditure of a thousand crores of rupees over the next twenty years, but, unfortunately, no more than a hundred crores have been allocated for the first five years, so we've had to lower our sights."

Notes and Thoughts on
Calcutta's Imperial Past

"CITIES OF INDIA," by Sir George W. Forrest (1903); "The Early Annals of the English in Bengal," edited by C. R. Wilson (1895–1911); "Old Fort William in Bengal," edited by Wilson (1906); "Bengal in 1756–1757," edited by S. C. Hill (1905); the *Imperial Gazetteer of India;* and other books to hand.

1498. Vasco da Gama opens Indian Ocean to the West.

1510. Affonso de Albuquerque takes Goa for Portugal.

1530. Portuguese vessels begin frequenting the Hooghly. Ships as far as bulge of land, small native craft to Satgaon, the commercial center nearby. Gradually build trade in Bengal silk, muslin, lac, sugar, rice. Trading posts on Hooghly.

1600. Charter of East India Company by Elizabeth.

1625. Dutch sail up Hooghly.

1639. East India Company founds Madras, first important British settlement in India.

1687. James II gives East India Company right to establish civil government in Madras. Mayor, aldermen, burgesses, guildhall, schoolhouse, jail, municipal salaries.

1688. French settlement at Chandernagor, on Hooghly.

1690. Job Charnock, of East India Company, founds British settlement, later Calcutta, at riverside village, Sutanuti. Sutanuti has already supplanted Satgaon. Charnock is said to have liked to hold court and smoke a hubble-bubble under a banyan tree in Sutanuti amid mud huts of fishermen. *Imperial Gazetteer:* "Several reasons led to the selection of this place as the headquarters of British trade in Bengal. The Hooghly River tapped the rich trade of the Ganges Valley, and Calcutta was situated at the highest point at which the river was navigable for seagoing vessels: it was protected against attack by the river on the west and by morasses on the east." Derivation of name Calcutta unknown. Perhaps from Kalikotta, a village bordering on Sutanuti, or from Kalighat ("landing place of Kali"), on the Hooghly. According to one Hindu legend, in the "age of truth" the patriarch Daksha, who was the father of Kali, the death goddess, made a sacrifice in order that he might be blessed with a son. He neglected to include Kali's husband, Shiva, in the ceremony. Kali, insulted and injured, killed herself. Shiva, grief-stricken, speared her body with a trident and carried it through creation, threatening, in madness, to destroy the world. Vishnu intervened. Saved the world by throwing a discus at the body of Kali, scattering her fragments all over the world. Wherever the fragments fell, the ground was sanctified. The most sanctified place was Kalighat, on the Hooghly, where the toes of Kali's right foot fell. (Public religious rites held for Kali every year in Calcutta.)

1696. The Nawab of Bengal, deputy of the Mogul emperor in Delhi, grants British settlers permission to build fort to protect trading interests. Called Fort William, after William of Orange.

1698. British settlers lease Sutanuti, along with Kalikotta and adjacent village, Gobindapur, from Nawab for thirteen hundred rupees a year. Expand settlement.

1707. East India Company forms the township of Calcutta, which by now has wharf, barracks, hospital, church; Bengal a separate Presidency, on par with Bombay and Madras, the company's two other Indian Presidencies.

1710. Calcutta's estimated population ten thousand.

1717. Fort William completed. East India Company leases thirty-eight more villages on banks of Hooghly.

1727. Calcutta organized into municipality, with mayor and nine aldermen, to collect ground rent and town dues for repairs of roads and drains.

1741. Fort William as altered and expanded: Large, irregular tetragon overlooking Hooghly. Brick. North side three hundred and forty feet long, south side four hundred and eighty-five feet long, east and west sides each seven hundred and ten feet long. Small, square bastions at corners, connected by curtain walls of cemented thin tile bricks—eighteen feet high, four feet thick. Inside the fort: Governor's House, magazine, military

stores, dispensary, smithy, barracks, prison, warehouses, armory, laboratory, etc. All around the outside of fort, houses of officers and employees.

1750. Calcutta's estimated population two hundred thousand.

1756. Succession of new Nawab of Bengal, Siraj-ud-daula. Differences
with the British. Nawab attacks and captures Fort William. Some British
escape to ships on Hooghly, but others are left behind. A hundred and
forty-six said to be confined on June 20th in fort's prison, the so-called
Black Hole, a room about fourteen by eighteen feet, where all but twenty-
three of them die of suffocation. The Black Hole tragedy chief event in
Calcutta's history; at least one historian says British Indian Empire its
consequence. Celebrated account of it in a letter by a survivor, J. Z. Holwell, magistrate:

> Before I conduct you into the Black Hole, it is necessary you should be
> acquainted with a few introductory Circumstances. The Suba [Nawab] and
> his troops were in possession of the fort before six in the evening. I had in all
> three interviews with him: the last in Durbar before seven when he repeated
> his assurances to me, *on the word of a soldier,* that no harm should come to
> us; and indeed I believe his orders were only general. That we should for
> the night be secured; and that what followed was the result of revenge and
> resentment in the breasts of the lower Jemmautdaars ["jemadars," or Indian
> junior officers]. . . .
>
> We were no sooner all within the barracks, than the guard advanced to
> the inner arches and parapet-wall; and with their muskets presented, or-
> dered us to go into the room at the southernmost end of the barracks,
> commonly called the Black-Hole prison; whilst others from the Court of
> Guard, with clubs and drawn scymitars, pressed upon those of us next them.
> This stroke was so sudden, so unexpected, and the throng and the pressure
> so great upon us next the door of the Black-Hole prison, there was no re-
> sisting it; but like one agitated wave impelling another, we were obliged to
> give way and enter; the rest followed like a torrent, few amongst us, the
> soldiers excepted, having the least idea of the dimensions or nature of a
> place we had never seen: for if we had, we should at all events have rushed
> upon the guard, and been, as the lesser evil, by our own choice cut to
> pieces. . . .
>
> I got possession of the window nearest the door, and took Messrs. Coles
> and Scot into the window with me, they being both wounded (the first I
> believe mortally). . . .
>
> Figure to yourself, my friend, if possible, the situation of a hundred and
> forty-six wretches, exhausted by continual fatigue and action, thus crammed
> together in a cube of about eighteen feet, in a close sultry night, in Bengal,
> shut up to the eastward and southward (the only quarters from whence air

could reach us) by dead walls, and by a wall and door to the north, open only to the westward by two windows, strongly barred with iron, from which we could receive scarce any the least circulation of fresh air. . . .

The moment I quitted the window, my breathing grew short and painful. . . .

I laid myself down on some of the dead behind me, on the platform; and recommending myself to heaven, had the comfort of thinking my sufferings could have no long duration. . . .

At this juncture the Suba, who had received an account of the havock death had made amongst us, sent one of his Jemmautdaars to inquire if the chief survived. They showed me to him; told him I had appearance of life remaining, and believed I might recover if the door was opened very soon. This answer being returned to the Suba, an order came immediately for our release, it being then near six in the morning. . . .

The little strength remaining amongst the most robust who survived, made it a difficult task to remove the dead piled up against the door; so that I believe it was more than twenty minutes before we obtained a passage out for one at a time. . . .

When I came out, I found myself in a high putrid fever, and not being able to stand, threw myself on the wet grass. . . .

The rest, who survived the fatal night, gained their liberty, except Mrs. Carey, who was too young and handsome. The dead bodies were promiscuously thrown into the ditch of our unfinished ravelin, and covered with the earth.

1757. British force under Clive and Admiral Watson, arriving in Bengal from Madras, defeats Siraj-ud-daula and French at Plassey, a village on the Bhagirathi. British given compensations, *zamindari* (proprietorship) over Calcutta, right to establish mint, etc. (In due course, British advance from Bengal to rest of India.) Clive begins work on New Fort William, near the original Fort William. *Imperial Gazetteer:* "Modern Calcutta dates from 1757."

1758. East India Company removes goods from Fort William, now used exclusively as military barracks. (Later, Holwell, having become Governor of Fort William, erects memorial obelisk at place where his fellow-sufferers were buried.)

1759. Thirty vessels call at Calcutta. Main exports opium, silk, muslin, indigo, saltpetre. Main import bullion.

1760. Area between Fort William's East Gate and Black Hole prison made into temporary church.

1764. Civil authority over much of Bengal conferred in perpetuity on

East India Company by reigning Mogul emperor, Shah Alam. Center of East India Company's power shifts from Madras to Calcutta.

1767. Fort William, with new buildings added, made into a custom-house. Wilson's "Old Fort William in Bengal": "From this time onwards its fortunes steadily declined."

1773. New Fort William completed, at cost of two million pounds, and jungle around New Fort, cleared for military reasons, becomes Maidan. Customhouse now called Old Fort William.

1774. British Parliament invests control of East India Company's Indian possessions in Governor-General and Council of Bengal. Sets up Supreme Court in Calcutta, which now officially becomes capital of British Empire in India.

1780. British Calcutta "village of palaces." But Indian Calcutta very different. William Macintosh's "Travels in Europe, Asia, and Africa" (1782):

It is a truth that, from the western extremity of California to the eastern coast of Japan, there is not a spot where judgement, taste, decency, and convenience are so grossly insulted as in that scattered and confused chaos of houses, huts, sheds, streets, lanes, alleys, windings, gullies, sinks, and tanks, which, jumbled into an undistinguished mass of filth and corruption, equally offensive to human sense and health, compose the capital of the English Company's Government in India. The very small portion of cleanliness which it enjoys is owing to the familiar intercourse of hungry jackals by night, and ravenous vultures, kites, and crows by day. In like manner it is indebted to the smoke raised on public streets, in temporary huts and sheds, for any respite it enjoys from mosquitoes, the natural productions of stagnated and putrid waters.

1818. Old Fort William demolished.

1819. Foundation stone of new customhouse laid.

1821. Holwell's obelisk, which has fallen into disrepair, pulled down.

1850. Calcutta's estimated population four hundred thousand.

1854. First jute mill in Bengal. Jute, woven on hand looms, in common use in Bengal villages in eighteenth century, but only in nineteenth introduced to England, where process of bleaching and dyeing is soon mastered. *Imperial Gazetteer:* "If it may be said that Bombay is built upon cotton, it is no less true that Calcutta is built on jute."

1858. East India Company transfers its functions in India to the British government.

1874. Opening of Howrah Bridge, giving Calcutta overland access to rest of India, where roads and railways in process of development.

1875. British get control of Suez Canal. More and more sea trade. More and more steamships—Peninsular & Oriental Steam Navigation, British India Steam Navigation, City, Clan, Harrison, and Anchor lines. Bengal gaining monopoly of many of India's exports—jute, coal, tea, hides, linseed, lac. Imports include textiles, metals, machinery.

1876. Calcutta Corporation constituted, with elected and appointed commissioners. Completes a drainage scheme, increases supply of filtered and unfiltered water, etc.

1882. Mr. R. R. Bayne, of East Indian Railway Company, while digging foundations for new Railway office building, discovers wall of Old Fort William.

1883. Bayne reports his discovery to Asiatic Society of Bengal, exciting interest of another Englishman, Dr. H. E. Busteed, who continues excavations.

1886. March. Visit of Lord and Lady Dufferin to Calcutta. Extract from "Our Viceregal Life in India," by Lady Dufferin:

This being our last day at Calcutta, we crammed a little sightseeing into it. D. and I went with Dr. Busteed to look at the site of the Black Hole. This gentleman . . . has worked away until he has discovered the exact spot where it was, besides collecting all the interesting details concerning that terrible disaster. Having found the place, which is now part of a courtyard leading to the Post Office, he has laid down a pavement the exact size of the little room called the "Black Hole," and has put up a tablet to explain this fact. Dr. Busteed gave me a little model of the place as it was, which shows that it was not a "hole" but a room. . . .

Dr. Busteed is very anxious to put up a stone to show where it [Holwell's obelisk] stood, and to place in the church a tablet with the names of the persons who died in the Black Hole, which names Holwell had been at some pains to preserve. He (Holwell) was painted by Sir Joshua Reynolds with the plan of this monument in his hand, and his descendants, who live in Canada, have the picture, and sent Dr. Busteed a photograph of it.

1886. May. Dr. Busteed writes to a Colonel Trevor:

The excavation was allowed to remain open for some short time, and attracted very numerous visitors and received much popular attention. The Government of Bengal with ready interest sympathized in the generally-felt desire that so very historical a site should be marked, and directed that what, for the present, was considered the most practicable thing under the circumstances should be done—namely, that as the roadway under which the chamber lay was essential to the Post Office traffic, the excavation should be filled in and decently paved over with granite, and that a tablet bearing this inscription should be placed on the most convenient spot near: "The stone pavement close to this marks the position and size of the prison cell in Old Fort William, known in history as the Black Hole of Calcutta."

1889. An eighteenth-century map of Calcutta and Old Fort William found in British Museum. Proves erroneous some inferences Busteed drew from his excavations and published in his work "Echoes from Old Calcutta."

1891. C. R. Wilson, with map, begins further excavations, which continue for years.

1900. Lord Curzon convenes meeting in yard of General Post Office. Considers question of another Black Hole obelisk. Assembly decides to remove massive masonry gate at one end of yard and pave with black marble the part of prison site not covered by building.

1901. Census. Calcutta's population eight hundred and forty-eight thousand. Howrah's a hundred and fifty-eight thousand. Total population of other suburbs a hundred and one thousand. Population of metropolis of Calcutta exceeded only by populations, severally, of metropolises of London, Constantinople, Paris, and Berlin. In Calcutta, fifty-seven languages— forty-one Asiatic, sixteen non-Asiatic. Greatest rate of population increase in the most crowded wards. Ratio of males to females two to one. Very high mortality rate.

1902. Lord Curzon delivers address on the occasion of unveiling marble obelisk in Calcutta to commemorate dead of Black Hole:

I daresay that the worthy citizens of Calcutta may have been a good deal puzzled on many occasions during the past four years to see me rummaging about this neighbourhood and that of the adjoining Post Office in the afternoons, poking my nose into all sorts of obscure corners, measuring, marking, and finally ordering the erection of marble memorials and slabs. This big pillar, which I am now about to unveil, and the numerous tablets on the other side of the street, are the final outcome of these labours. But let me explain how it is that they have come about and what they mean.

When I came out to India in this very month four years ago [as Viceroy of India], one of the companions of my voyage was that delightful "Echoes from Old Calcutta," by Mr. Busteed, formerly well known as an officer in the Calcutta Mint, and now living in retirement at home. There I read the full account of the tragic circumstances under which Old Fort William, which stood between the site where I am now speaking and the river, was besieged and taken by the forces of Siraj-ud-daula in 1756, and of the heroism and sufferings of the small band of survivors who were shut up for an awful summer's night in June in the tiny prison known as the Black Hole, with the shocking result that of the 146 who went in only 23 came out alive. I also read that the monument which had been erected shortly after the disaster by Mr. Holwell, one of the survivors, who wrote a detailed account of that night of horror, and who was afterwards Governor of Fort William, in order to commemorate his fellow-sufferers who had perished in the prison, had been taken down, no one quite knows why, in or about the year 1821; and Mr. Busteed went on to lament, as I think very rightly, that whereas for sixty years after their death Calcutta had preserved the memory of these unhappy victims, ever since that time, now eighty years ago, there had been no monument, not even a slab or an inscription, to record their names and their untimely fate.

It was Mr. Busteed's writings accordingly that first called my attention to this spot and that induced me to make a careful personal study of the entire question of the site and surroundings of Old Fort William. The whole thing is now so vivid in my mind's eye that I never pass this way without the Post Office and Custom House and the modern aspect of Writers' Buildings fading out of my sight, while instead of them I see the walls and bastions of the old fort exactly behind the spot where I now stand, with its eastern gate and the unfinished ravelin in front of the gate, and the ditch in front of the ravelin into which the bodies of those who had died in the Black Hole were thrown the next morning, and over which Holwell erected his monument a few years later.

Nearly twenty years ago Mr. Roskell Bayne, of the East Indian Railway, made a number of diggings and measurements that brought to light the dimensions of the old fort, now almost entirely covered with modern buildings; and I was fortunate enough when I came here to find a worthy successor to him and coadjutor to myself in the person of Mr. C. R. Wilson, of the Indian Education Department, who had carried Mr. Bayne's inquiries a good deal further, cleared up some doubtful points, corrected some errors, and fixed with accuracy the exact site of the Black Hole and other features of the fort. All of these sites I set to work to commemorate while the knowledge was still fresh in our minds. Wherever the outer or inner line of the curtain and bastions of Old Fort William had not been built over I had them traced on the ground with brass lines let into stone—you will see some of them on the main steps of the Post Office—and I caused white marble tablets to be inserted in the walls of the adjoining buildings with inscriptions stating what was the part of the old building that originally stood there. I think that there are some dozen of these tablets in all, each of which tells its own tale.

I further turned my attention to the site of the Black Hole, which was in the premises of the Post Office, and could not be seen from the street, being shut off by a great brick and plaster gateway. I had this obstruction pulled down, and an open iron gate and railings erected in its place. I had the site of the Black Hole paved with polished black marble, and surrounded with a neat iron railing, and, finally, I placed a black marble tablet with an inscription above it, explaining the memorable and historic nature of the site that lies below. I do not know if cold-weather visitors to Calcutta, or even the residents of the city itself, have yet found out the existence of these memorials. But I venture to think that they are a permanent and valuable addition to the possessions and sights of the capital of British rule in India.

At the same time I proceeded to look into the question of the almost forgotten monument of Holwell. I found a number of illustrations and descriptions of it in the writings of the period, and though these did not in every case precisely tally with each other, yet they left no doubt whatever as to the general character of the monument, which consisted of a tall pillar or obelisk rising from an octagonal pedestal, on the two main faces of which were inscriptions written by Holwell, with the names of a number of the slain. Holwell's monument was built of brick covered over with plaster, like all the monuments of the period in the old Calcutta cemeteries; and I expect that it must have been crumbling when it was taken down . . . for I have seen a print in which it was represented with a great crack running down the side, from the top to the base, as though it had been struck by lightning. I determined to reproduce this memorial with as much fidelity as possible in white marble, to re-erect it on the same site, and to present it as my personal gift to the city of Calcutta in memory of a never-to-be-forgotten episode in her history, and in honour of the brave men whose life-blood had cemented the foundations of the British Empire in India. . . . Though Holwell's record contained less than fifty names out of the 123 who had been suffocated in the Black Hole, I have, by means of careful search into the records both here and in England, recovered not only the Christian names of the whole of these persons, but also more than twenty fresh names of those who also died in the prison. So that the new monument records the names of no fewer than sixty of the victims of that terrible night.

In the course of my studies, in which I have been ably assisted by the labours of Mr. S. C. Hill, of the Record Department, who is engaged in bringing out a separate work on the subject, I have also recovered the names of more than twenty other Europeans who, though they did not actually die in the Black Hole, yet were either killed at an earlier stage of the siege, or, having come out of the Black Hole alive, afterwards succumbed to its effects. These persons seem to me equally to deserve commemoration with those who were smothered to death in the prison, and accordingly I have entered their names on the remaining panels of this monument. We, therefore, have inscribed on this memorial the names of some eighty persons who took part in those historic events which established the British dominion in Bengal nearly a century and a half ago. They were the pioneers of a great movement, the authors of a wonderful chapter in the history of mankind; and I am proud that it has fallen to my lot to preserve their simple and humble names from oblivion, and to restore them to the grateful remembrance of their country-men.

Gentlemen, in carrying out this scheme I have been pursuing one branch of a policy to which I have deliberately set myself in India, namely, that of pre-serving, in a breathless and often thoughtless age, the relics and memorials of the past. To me the past is sacred. It is often a chronicle of errors and blunders and crimes, but it also abounds in the records of virtue and heroism and valour. Anyhow, for good or evil, it is finished and written, and has become part of the history of the race, part of that which makes us what we are. Though human life is blown out as easily as the flame of a candle, yet it is something to keep alive the memory of what it has wrought and been, for the sake of those who come after; and I daresay it would solace our own despatch into the unknown, if we could feel sure that we too were likely to be remembered by our successors, and that our name was not going to vanish altogether from the earth when the last breath has fled from our lips. . . . How few of us who tread the streets of Calcutta from day to day ever turn a thought to the Calcutta past. And yet Calcutta is one great graveyard of memories. Shades of departed Governors-General hover about the marble halls and corridors of Government House, where I do my daily work. For-gotten worthies in ancient costumes haunt the precincts of this historic square. Strange figures, in guise of peace or war, pass in and out of the vanished gateways of the vanished fort. If we think only of those whose bones are mingled with the soil underneath our feet, we have but to walk a couple of furlongs from this place to the churchyard where lies the dust of Job Charnock, of Surgeon William Hamilton, and of Admiral Watson, the founder, the extender, and the saviour of the British dominion in Bengal. A short drive of two miles will take us to the most pathetic sight in Calcutta —those dismal and decaying Park Street cemeteries where generations of by-gone Englishmen and English women, who struggled and laboured on this stage of exile for a brief span, lie unnamed, unremembered, and un-known. But if among these fore-runners of our own, if among these ancient and unconscious builders of Empire, there are any who especially deserve commemoration, surely it is the martyr band whose fate I recall and whose names I resuscitate on this site; and if there be a spot that should be dear to an Englishman in India, it is that below our feet, which was stained with the blood and which closed over the remains of the victims of that night of destiny, the 20th of June, 1756. It is with these sentiments in my heart that I have erected this monument, and that I now hand it over to the citizens of Calcutta, to be kept by them in perpetual remembrance of the past.

NOTA BENE: Remember to review strange debate among Indian histo-rians about the number of Englishmen who died in the Black Hole, and even about whether the Black Hole tragedy ever really occurred. Some say, incredibly, that the Black Hole was merely a British invention to justify the conquest of Bengal, maintaining that the story is found only in British accounts, and not in contemporary Indian Muslim sources. On this point, cf. the Bengali historian A. K. Maitreya, whose work on Siraj-ud-daula represents the classic Indian attempt to find gaps in the British evidence and so refute the British with their own sources. But new information on the Black Hole based on other than British primary sources, such as the translation, by A. Hughes (published in *Bengal Past & Present* in 1958), of a newly found contemporary Persian manuscript on Siraj-ud-daula, cuts most of the ground from under the arguments of Maitreya et al. Discuss problem S. C. Hill raises: "Why the inhabitants of Bengal were absolutely apathetic to events which handed over the government of their country to a race so different from their own." Analyze differences in attitudes of British and of Indians toward history, toward the dead.

Surprisingly, Rudyard Kipling (1865–1936), who was virtually a stranger to Calcutta, is the writer most often quoted on Calcutta; he was born in India and spent his early childhood, late teens, and early twenties in the country, but the Indian cities he knew best were Lahore, where he worked for about five years on the editorial staff of the *Civil & Military Gazette,* and Allahabad, where he worked for two years on the editorial staff of the *Gazette's* sister publication the *Pioneer.* While in India, he travelled extensively, and his outlook, when not that of an imperialist, was that of a pragmatic Lahori with perhaps a trace of the spirituality of Allahabad. Certainly some of his stories and articles reveal him to be an up-country writer who spurned what he took to be the effeminate hybrid culture of Bengal and the pretensions of the British capital in favor of the rugged indigenous culture of the Punjab and the native wholesomeness of a provincial city. He wrote, in fact, very little about Calcutta, and what he did write was written between the ages of nineteen and twenty-three. Calcutta figures in one short story, three narrative poems, and a series of eight short, informal articles that first appeared in the *Pioneer* in 1889 and, in 1899, were revised and collected under the general title "City of Dreadful Night" in his book "From Sea to Sea." (Calcutta also figures in a children's story.) The short story, entitled "The Dream of Duncan Parrenness," is about a dissolute young Englishman who is a junior clerk in the service of the East India Company and who has a dream in which he confronts his future and the consequences of a wasted youth. The tale, which is a kind of moral ghost story, is forced and awkward, perhaps because it tries to re-create the idiom of the Warren Hastings period, in which it is set. In any case, although the story does contain some specific references to Calcutta ("sullen, un-English stream, the Hugli," "the foul soil north of Writers' Buildings"), the setting is incidental. Similarly, two of the poems—"What Happened" and "The Ballad of Fisher's Boarding-House," which concern the anarchic diversity of the Indian people and a brawl in a harbor boarding house, respectively—could have been set in Bombay or a number of other cities. The third poem, however, "A Tale of Two Cities"—the second city is Simla, the hill station in the Punjab that served as the British summer capital—dwells on the physical squalor and loathsome conditions of life in Calcutta, deploring the accident that brought the city into being in the first place and the avarice that sustains it. The poem, which is quoted in its entirety below, has come to be thought of almost as another curse upon Calcutta, phrases from it having become, in the English language, lasting epithets for Calcutta:

> Where the sober-coloured cultivator smiles
> On his *byles* [cattle];
> Where the cholera, the cyclone, and the crow
> Come and go;
> Where the merchant deals in indigo and tea,
> Hides and *ghi;*
> Where the Babu drops inflammatory hints
> In his prints;
> Stands a City—Charnock chose it—packed away
> Near a Bay—
> By the sewage rendered fetid, by the sewer
> Made impure,
> By the Sunderbunds unwholesome, by the swamp
> Moist and damp;
> And the City and the Viceroy, as we see,
> Don't agree.
> Once, two hundred years ago, the trader came
> Meek and tame.
> Where his timid foot first halted, there he stayed,
> Till mere trade
> Grew to Empire, and he sent his armies forth
> South and North,
> Till the country from Peshawur to Ceylon
> Was his own.
>
> Thus the midday halt of Charnock—more's the pity!—
> Grew a City.

As the fungus sprouts chaotic from its bed,
    So it spread—
Chance-directed, chance-erected, laid and built
    On the silt—
Palace, byre, hovel—poverty and pride—
    Side by side;
And, above the packed and pestilential town,
    Death looked down.

But the Rulers in that City by the Sea
    Turned to flee—
Fled, with each returning Springtide, from its ills
    To the Hills.
From the clammy fogs of morning, from the blaze
    Of the days,
From the sickness of the noontide, from the heat,
    Beat retreat;
For the country from Peshawur to Ceylon
    Was their own.
But the Merchant risked the perils of the Plain
    For his gain.

Now the resting-place of Charnock, 'neath the palms,
    Asks an alms,
And the burden of its lamentation is,
    Briefly, this:
"Because, for certain months, we boil and stew,
    "So should you.
"Cast the Viceroy and his Council, to perspire
    "In our fire!"
And for answer to the argument, in vain
    We explain
That an amateur Saint Lawrence cannot cry:—
    "*All* must fry!"
That the Merchant risks the perils of the Plains
    For his gains.
Nor can Rulers rule a house that men grow rich in,
    From its kitchen.

Let the Babu drop inflammatory hints
    In his prints;
And mature—consistent soul—his plan for stealing
    To Darjeeling:
Let the Merchant seek, who makes his silver pile,
    England's isle;

Let the City Charnock pitched on—evil day!—
Go Her way.
Though the argosies of Asia at Her doors
Heap their stores,
Though Her enterprise and energy secure
Income sure,
Though "out-station orders punctually obeyed"
Swell Her trade—
Still, for rule, administration, and the rest,
Simla's best!

By far the most substantial treatment of Calcutta is to be found in "City of Dreadful Night," which was the result of Kipling's only long visit to Calcutta. Kipling imagines the first sensations of British "backwoodsmen and barbarians" who, like him, have lived for a long time in the rustic, provincial atmosphere of the Empire, away from London and civilization, and have come to think of Calcutta as the only "real" city in India, and who travel there hoping that their heritage of civilization will be restored to them. "Let us take off our hats to Calcutta, the many-sided, the smoky, the magnificent," he writes. "We have left India behind us. . . . Why, this is London! This is the docks. This is Imperial. This is worth coming across India to see!" But in the cosmopolitan Great Eastern Hotel, where nationals of all countries are to be found, and in the splendid Maidan, whose expanse dwarfs everything except the rows of mansions of Chowringhi, and in the palaces themselves, which were built in the old times when money was plentiful, and which, like the houses in hill stations, are graced with outside winding service staircases, there is a reeking, ferocious, all-pervasive stench, worse than the worst odor of Benares, Peshawar, or Bombay. There is no escape from it, no relief except exhaustion, for it is the "Big Calcutta Stink," or, in Kipling's abbreviation, "B.C.S." "Stop to consider for a moment," he writes, "what the cramped compounds, the black soaked soil, the netted intricacies of the service-staircases, and packed stables, the seethment of human life . . . and the curious arrangement of little open drains mean, and you will call it a whited sepulchre." Thinking that any English municipal government would have solved Calcutta's most basic problem, sanitation, he blames the stench on an experiment that Calcutta was making at the time with local self-government. "In spite of that stink, they allow, even encourage, natives to look after the place!" he writes. "The damp, drainage-soaked soil is sick with the teeming life of a hundred years, and the Municipal Board list is choked with the names of natives—men of the breed born in and raised off this surfeited muckheap!"

Kipling attends a debate of the Bengal Legislative Council. The "Councillor Sahibs," as Kipling calls the Indian members, presided over by the Lieutenant-Governor of Bengal, Sir Steuart Bayley, meet in a sumptuous blue-domed octagonal chamber in a large octagonal wing of the Writers' Buildings:

There are gilt capitals to the half pillars and an Egyptian patterned lotus-stencil makes the walls gay [he writes]. . . . If the work matches the first-class furniture, the ink-pots, the carpet, and the resplendent ceilings, there will be something worth seeing. But where is the criminal who is to be hanged for the stench that runs up and down Writers' Buildings staircases; for the rubbish heaps in the Chitpore Road; for the sickly savour of Chowringhi . . . for the street full of small-pox . . . and for a hundred other things?

"This, I submit, is an artificial scheme in supersession of Nature's unit, the individual." The speaker is a slight, spare native in a flat hat-turban and a black alpaca frock-coat. . . . He talks and talks and talks in a level voice, rising occasionally half an octave when a point has to be driven home. . . . "So much for the principle. Let us now examine how far it is supported by precedent."

Western education is an exotic plant. . . . We brought it out from England exactly as we brought out the ink-bottles and the patterns for the chairs. We planted it and it grew—monstrous as a banian. Now we are choked by the roots of it spreading so thickly in this fat soil of Bengal. . . . Bit by bit we builded this dome, visible and invisible, the crown of Writers' Buildings. . . . That torrent of verbiage is Ours. We taught him what was constitutional and what was unconstitutional in the days when Calcutta smelt. Calcutta smells still, but We must listen to all that he has to say about the plurality of votes and the threshing of wind and the weaving of ropes of sand. . . .

Why do they talk and talk about owners and occupiers and burgesses in England and the growth of autonomous institutions when the city, the great city, is here crying out to be cleansed? . . .

This is the Calcutta Municipal Bill. They have been at it for several Saturdays. Last Saturday Sir Steuart Bayley pointed out that at their present rate they would be about two years in getting it through. . . .

Meantime Calcutta continues to cry out for the bucket and the broom.

Kipling continues his explorations of the city, from the banks of the Hooghly—he visits the Port Office, where efficient *babus* daily chart the channel of the Hooghly, and the Shipping Office nearby, where mercantile outcasts wait to ship out of Calcutta—to the Park Street Cemetery (that "most pathetic sight" Curzon spoke of), which contains the graves of the early English. In the course of a night, Kipling visits brothels, dance sheds, gambling houses, and opium dens, being initiated into the dark mysteries of the city as he passes from one vice-ridden, mean neighborhood to another, from the outer edge of what he regards as the inferno deeper and deeper into its center. Everywhere people are trapped and crowded together in abominable hovels resembling pigsties, and everywhere he encounters horrors that "cannot be written or hinted at" and yet are accepted as if they were the normal order of things.

Kipling borrowed the title for his Calcutta series from James Thomson's "The City of Dreadful Night":

> The City of Night, but not of Sleep;
> There sweet sleep is not for the weary brain;
> The pitiless hours like years and ages creep,
> A night seems termless hell. This dreadful strain
> Of thought and consciousness which never ceases,
> Or which some moments' stupor but increases,
> This, worse than woe, makes wretches there insane.

An age has crept past since Kipling wrote, but although his Calcutta writings are adolescent—the irony is heavy-handed and the point of view naïvely prejudiced—they continue to be remembered, because the passing of years has only preserved and multiplied the horrors of the city.

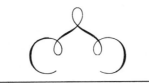

One Life, One Chance

TONIGHT, I APPROACH a large, ghostly old house in Calcutta. An elderly, bearded man wearing a Muslim skullcap is slouching at the entrance. I ask him the way to the lodgings of David McCutchion. He points vaguely toward the entrance of the house, and then shuffles away. The entrance leads into a dark and dingy hallway, where a broken-down bicycle stands next to a broken-down couch. Leading up from the hallway is a wide, unswept staircase, and I climb to the second floor. On the landing, a figure in crimson silk emerges from a doorway. The figure turns out to be a plump little girl of not more than ten, heavily made up. I ask her if she knows where McCutchion lives. She indicates that I should follow her, and silently leads me on a surrealistic walk through a series of lightless passages and into a large, untidy garret containing a narrow iron bedstead, an old cupboard, three wooden chairs, a desk, a trunk, some suitcases, and three umbrellas. To one side of the room is a typical Indian bathing area—a sloping cement floor on which stand buckets, dippers, and mugs, and a low bench. Overhead, a ceiling fan whirs sluggishly, and stretched across the room is a string from which a wet shirt is hanging. On the desk are photographs of reliefs of mythical scenes and statues of gods and goddesses from Hindu temples, and all around the room are shelves holding books on Bengal. McCutchion, who sits reading a Bengali book when I enter, is a tall, spare Englishman in his thirties. He has on big black-rimmed glasses, and is dressed like an Indian, in pajamas and a bush shirt.

McCutchion has become known in Calcutta as a Satyajit Ray film buff; in fact, in recent years he has been one of Ray's closest associates, helping him write the English subtitles for his films. After the girl in the red dress has left, I tell McCutchion of my interest in Calcutta and in Ray, who is considered the greatest film artist in Calcutta and in the country, and perhaps India's greatest living artist. "Ray loves Calcutta," McCutchion says. "All of us who live here love Calcutta, in a way. It is a nightmare of a city in terms of filth, but the people who live here make it a great city. Like all true Bengalis, Ray has a strong feeling for Bengali culture—his films draw upon every aspect of it. He is interested in everything Bengali—in Bengali literature and the Bengali language and Bengali life. When a promoter comes to him and asks him to do a film in another language—in Hindi, perhaps—he just says no. In 1964, he did a fifteen-minute segment of an hour TV show for Esso—called 'Two.' They wanted it to be in English, but he said he wouldn't do a Bengali film with English dialogue, and he did a silent film, a pantomime. He is quite critical of Bengalis who, for instance, write in English. But he's not a Bengali purist—he doesn't feel bound to use only Bengali words. In fact, he uses a great number of English words in the sound tracks of his films; he would say he uses them in the interests of authenticity. His films are notably authentic—a Bengali house in a film of his will have an oleograph over the mantelpiece. He often uses amateur actors, and will find someone to play a part who in life is like the character he plays in the film. Ray's research is very thorough. But I am always a little disappointed in his themes. A general criticism of his films, with which I agree, is that, as a rule, he does not deal with the starker aspects of Indian life. But then, as a person, he's a typical middle-class Bengali. In fact, he is striking for his ordinariness. He lives in a very simple, middle-class way. There is nothing flamboyant about him, nothing ostentatious. He knows what he wants, and he is practical in seeking it. He is completely wrapped up in his work. In some ways, he is a very lonely man. When he is not shooting, he sits in a chair in his den for seventeen or eighteen hours at a time."

I ask McCutchion how he and Ray became acquainted.

"I came to India in 1957, soon after reading modern languages at Cambridge," he says. "I first met Ray in 1960, when I was teaching English at Shantiniketan and he came there to speak to the students. He gave me his address and asked me to look him up when I was next in Calcutta. I did. At the time, he was filming 'Teen Kanya,' and I went to watch him shoot. Gradually, we got to know each other. He has introduced me to people, given me film, and in other ways been very helpful to me in my hobby, which is photographing terra-cotta art in the temples."

To meet Satyajit Ray, the director of "Pather Panchali" (Cannes Special Award), "Aparajito" (Venice Grand Prix), "Jalsaghar," "Paras Pathar," "Apur Sansar" ("Pather Panchali," "Aparajito," and "Apur Sansar" make up what is well known as the Trilogy), "Devi," "Rabindranath Tagore," "Teen Kanya," "Kanchenjunga," "Abhijan," "Mahanagar," "Charulata," and "Kapurush-O-Mahapurush," I walk along a narrow, shabby street to the house he lives in, with his wife and their only child, a son. Having passed through an unimposing entrance into an unimposing hall, and climbed a narrow and dimly lit stairway to the second floor, I reach Ray's flat. A servant lets me into a gloomy hallway, which has a couple of glass cases displaying inexpensive knickknacks, such as are often found in Indian homes. The hallway leads into a small, close, cluttered room—Ray's den. All around the walls are well-worn books, some in soft covers but most clothbound, some in Bengali but most in English. They are a jumble of titles and authors: "Persian Tales," "Myths of the Hindus and Buddhists," Pushkin, an encyclopedia (covered in brown paper but with the paper cut away to show the alphabetical contents of each volume), "The Voices of Silence," "History of India," "Cézanne," "The Dawn of Civilisation," "The Face of New York," "The Art of India," Tagore, "Classical Literary Criticism," the Upanishads, "A Passage to India," "Ancient Art of the Andes," "Great Sanskrit Plays," "Esquire Etiquette," "The Wonder That Was India." There are a couple of paintings; a piano, a tape recorder, and a gramophone; a divan piled with Indian musical instruments, spools of tape, books, magazines, typewritten sheets, and a jar of pencils; a large round table holding more books and papers; a rectangular table on which are a typewriter and a telephone; and a couple of easy chairs. Next to the rectangular table is a frayed red chair, in which Ray sits, wearing an unstarched, rumpled white *kurta,* pajamas, and leather slippers. He has a drawing board on his knees. As I enter, he puts the drawing board down and stands up to greet me. "I am working on type faces for the International Typeface Design Competition," he explains, pacing about. "I have to send my designs off to New York by the end of this week to meet the deadline. The prize is fifteen hundred dollars. If the designs are sold, I will also get royalties. I have always been interested in graphics."

Ray sits down. He is a very tall, large, rugged-looking man in his middle forties. He has thick black hair, a big nose, a wide mouth, and eyes that protrude slightly. He gives the impression of having great physical energy held perfectly under control. When he walks about, his movements are abrupt and decisive; when he is sitting, he is quite still and self-contained. His expression, unlike that of many Bengalis, is not gentle but somewhat severe and remote.

I tell Ray a little about the time I have spent in Calcutta, and mention to him that one of the things I have noticed is an intense political involvement on the part of Calcutta's artists and writers.

"Most of the interesting work in the arts here is done by left-wingers," Ray says. "I cannot think of any right-wing Bengali who has ever done anything praiseworthy. As for me, most people would probably associate me with figures who are very strongly left-wing, like Utpal Dutt. But I think politics are a mess, and, as a rule, politicians here are not men of calibre. I have not lent my name to many political causes. Recently, I did write a letter denouncing the appearance of the new National Theatre building here. I denounced the colors, the relief work, the foyer—the ugliness of the whole building. And during the general strike and riots in Bengal this March I represented the Union of Film Workers in a procession, because film people here have the reputation of not being affected by things like that, and I wanted to give the lie to this idea. I didn't stay in the procession very long, however, because I once had sunstroke and I am not supposed to be out in the sun very long."

I ask him how he feels about living in Calcutta.

"I love Calcutta," he says. "I have lived here all my life. The best of whatever is being done in the arts in India is being done here. There is great intellectual vitality here. A lot of very good Bengali writing is being done here. The Bengali theatre is very much alive here. The coffeehouses here are full of people with ideas. Only filmmaking has not attracted many intellectuals, yet from a filmmaker's point of view no city could be better, because all kinds of things happen here all the time. It is true I don't have much of a social life, but then I don't really miss it. There is no one with whom I can discuss all the things I am interested in. In fact, it is difficult for me to find time to do everything I want to do."

I ask him about some of the things he does.

"My father, Sukumar Ray, was the greatest children's writer in Bengali," he says. "I am still referred to here as 'the son of Sukumar Ray.' My grandfather wrote for children, too, though he made his living as a printer. He had many inventions to his credit, and his printing shop produced the finest printing of his day. He started and edited a children's magazine, *Sandesh,* which is the name of a sweetmeat that Bengali children love. I have revived *Sandesh* with my aunt, Leila Mazumdar. It is a monthly, and I design a new cover for it every six months. I do several illustrations for each issue, and I do other things for it, too. Recently I made a puzzle for it, a crossword in rhyme—the first crossword of its kind devised in Bengali. I have translated a lot of Edward Lear's limericks and a great deal of Lewis Carroll into Bengali for *Sandesh*. At present, I am trying to translate my father's nonsense rhymes into English, but I am having a great deal of difficulty with this."

I ask him what film he is currently working on.

"I'm just finishing 'Nayak,'" he says. (*"Nayak"* is Bengali for "hero.") "I'm also making a film adaptation of 'Gupi Gayen Bagha Bayen,' a fantasy written by my grandfather. 'Nayak' will have its world première in Calcutta in a couple of months. I wrote the scenario for 'Nayak' myself. It's my second original scenario—'Kanchenjunga' was my first. For my films, I now write my own scenarios, make sketches for the scenes, sets, and costumes, design the credits, and compose the music. Music is a strong interest of mine. Sometimes my music is in the classical Indian vein, sometimes in the light Western vein. Actually, I got interested in Western music first and came to Indian music only later. 'Nayak,' in which most of the people wear Western clothes, calls for a slightly Western score, so I use some *ragas* with hints of jazz here and there—keeping the orchestration light. The fantasy film will have lots of music and dancing, battles and demons, and so forth. I want to shoot it in a variety of locations, some of them perhaps outside India—say, the Middle East, to create an Arabian Nights atmosphere—because I would like to take my audiences here to places not familiar to them. I want to make it in color, but I am not sure I can achieve all the camera tricks that the story demands. I have to write the lyrics and tunes for a lot of songs. My grandfather's story just says 'So-and-So sings,' and I have to give him a song to sing. I also have to work on inventing a new language, because the fantasy is about a couple of boys who visit two communities. In one community, everyone has been struck dumb, but in the other community everyone speaks an unknown language. For that language I am thinking of using Bengali played backwards. When you play Bengali backwards, all sorts of funny things happen. Laughter sounds like crying. A sad song sometimes sounds like a happy song. If you play a song backwards, you get a completely new melody—it makes sense as music, but it has nothing to do with the original. I suppose the pattern could be worked out mathematically."

I ask him when he expects to begin shooting the fantasy.

"After I've finished editing 'Nayak' and it has had its première, I plan to go first to supervise a film that some of my assistants are hoping to make.

I'm going to help them with the script, the sets, the music, and the direction. Then, after I've got their film off the ground, I'll go to Darjeeling for a month to work on the script of 'Gupi Gayen Bagha Bayen.' "

I have heard that he hopes one day to film the Mahabharata, the great Hindu epic, and I ask him about it.

"I've given the idea quite a lot of thought, but I've had to drop it," he says. "I was not able to get financial backing, and when I read parts of it with a view to making a scenario, I found that I would have to deal with fourteen or fifteen main characters, and their interrelationships were too complicated for a film. It would have been a tremendous job to explain the relationships. I would still like to do a section of it one day. The film I'd most like to do now, however, is 'A Passage to India.' Of course, it would be a complete departure for me, and there are a lot of things about the novel that would present problems. When I saw the stage production of 'A Passage to India' in London, I was very much disappointed. Everything was overacted and overdone; the Indians came across as caricatures— comical and exaggerated. I think I could avoid that by using two languages in the film, so that when there are no English people present—say, when Aziz and Hamidullah are speaking together—they would speak in their own language, as they naturally would in life. I think the effect you get, even in the book, of the Indian characters' sounding comical results from the fact that they speak English."

He takes the book from a shelf, finds a page, and begins to read. " 'The young man sprang up on to the verandah. He was all animation. "Hamidullah, Hamidullah! Am I late?" he cried. "Do not apologize," said his host. "You are always late." "Kindly answer my question. Am I late? Has Mahmoud Ali eaten all the food? If so I go elsewhere. Mr. Mahmoud Ali, how are you?" "Thank you, Dr. Aziz, I am dying." "Dying before your dinner? Oh, poor Mahmoud Ali!" ' " Ray laughs explosively; he is slow to smile but quick to laugh. "In Urdu, this exchange would sound natural in a way it doesn't in English," he says.

"But surely Forster wants the effect of an Indian speaking English," I say.

"Yes, but then he can explain in the book, in a way you can't in a stage production or a film, that the dialogue is intended to show the gulf between the colonial English and the Indians. Anyway, the question is academic, because Forster won't allow the book to be made into a film."

I ask him about his own life.

"I was an only child, and I have always been more or less on my own," he says. "I was two when my father died. I hardly remember my father, and my grandfather died before I was born. After my father's death, my mother and I lived with my mother's uncle here in Calcutta. He kept moving from flat to flat, and we moved with him. I attended Calcutta University, and after that I went to Shantiniketan to study fine arts. I was at Shantiniketan for three years. There I painted a little, and I also started developing a serious interest in the cinema. I read some books on the aesthetics of the cinema—on film forms, film technique, film acting. I read books by Eisenstein, by Pudovkin, and by other great directors. I did not finish my fine-arts course, however, because the Japanese started bombing Calcutta, and I left Shantiniketan the day after the bombing started, to be with my mother, who was living here—she died in 1960. A few months after that—this was in 1943—I joined D. J. Keymer, the advertising agency, as a layout man, although I'd had no training in commercial art. After I got the advertising job, my mother and I moved to a small flat in the Ballygunge section. In 1947, my friends and I started the Calcutta Film Society, the first film-appreciation club in the city. We had something like twenty or twenty-four members. Now there are two thousand. I was married in 1949. I started shooting my first film, 'Pather Panchali,' in 1952, and finished it three years later."

I ask him how he came to make "Pather Panchali."

"When I was at Keymer, I was doing book illustrations, book covers, book design, and typography for a publisher on the side," he says. "Around 1949, the publisher asked me to do illustrations for a new edition of 'Pather Panchali,' a novel by one of the best-known Bengali writers, Bibhutibhushan Bannerji. It was first published in the early nineteen-thirties, and the author had recently died. While illustrating the book, I got the idea of turning it into a film, and I did a few rough drawings. 'Pather Panchali' is not the kind of book that most directors and producers would think of making into a film. It hasn't the dramatic structure, the single, unified episode. It has loving descriptions of rural life, of little, subtle relationships among brother, sister, parents, and an old, unwanted aunt. The old aunt dies and the daughter dies. But when I read the book I loved it, and immediately thought what a wonderful film it would make. I talked about this with Mrs. Bannerji, who knew my entire family. She had known my father and my grandfather, and knew me through the book designs I was doing. Mrs. Bannerji told me that her husband used to say, 'My books would make very good films, but no one wants them.' I showed her all the sketches for scenes I had done. There were two fat sketchbooks. She was very much impressed, and snowed faith in me by giving me the film rights. When the newspapers announced that I had been given the film rights, she started receiving letters from people who said she had no business giving the film rights of a classic to someone who had never made a film. She said to me, 'Although some of these people are close friends of mine, I have full faith and trust in you. I am sure you will do something truly remarkable.' I showed her pictures of the boy and girl I was considering for the parts in the film, and she said, 'This is exactly how I imagined the children in the book looked.' Soon after this, I went to England for six months, and in that time I saw about ninety-five films. I made a point of seeking out all the films by the big names in postwar Italy, acted mainly by non-professionals, out on the streets, without any makeup. On the boat on the way back from England, I wrote a proper scenario of 'Pather Pan-chali,' hoping to do it on the same lines as the Italians. For a year and a half after I came back to Calcutta, I went around to producers. Nobody showed any interest in filming the story, or in me as a possible director. So I took a loan of eight thousand rupees from my insurance company and started shooting. I had a cameraman new to films, Subrata Mitra. He was twenty-one or twenty-two at the time. I had Banshi Chandra Gupta as my art director. For my film editor I had Dulal Dutta, who had just started editing films. The three have been with me ever since. We were all in our twenties. I still had my job at the advertising agency, so we could shoot only on Sundays and holidays."

I recall reading a description Ray wrote of shooting the first scene:

It was an episode in the screen play where the two children of the story, brother and sister, stray from their village and chance upon a field of *kaash* flowers. The two have had a quarrel, and here in this enchanted setting they are reconciled and their long journey is rewarded by their first sight of a railway train. I chose to begin with this scene because on paper it seemed both effective and simple. I considered this important, because the whole idea behind launching the production with only 8,000 rupees in the bank was to produce quickly and cheaply a reasonable length of rough cut which we hoped would establish our *bona fides*. . . .

At the end of the first day's shooting we had eight shots. The children behaved naturally, which was a bit of luck, because I hadn't tested them. As for myself, I remember feeling a bit strung up in the beginning; but as work progressed my nerves relaxed and in the end I even felt a kind of elation. However, the scene was only half finished, and on the following Sunday we were back on the same location. But was it the same location? It was hard to believe it. What was on the previous occasion a sea of fluffy whiteness was now a mere expanse of uninspiring brownish grass. We knew *kaash* was a seasonal flower, but surely they were not that short-lived? A local peasant provided the explanation. The flowers, he said, were food to the cattle. The cows and buffaloes had come to graze the day before and had literally chewed up the scenery.

I remark now how much I like his description of this incident.

"Our idea was to shoot some footage and show it to the producers," he says. "We showed them twenty-five minutes of film, but they said they were not interested. I had a friend who had influence with some distributors, and the friend persuaded the distributors to give us some money. Now I filled all the parts and completed something like five reels of film, but when I showed them to the distributors, they said they were not interested in going on. For a year, there was no money and no work. I thought of shelving the whole thing. I told my unit and my actors that we were not going to go on. Then somebody had the idea of approaching the late Dr. B. C. Roy, who was Chief Minister of West Bengal at the time, and trying to get government financing for the film. My mother knew somebody who knew Dr. Roy, he was approached, and eventually the film was made with government money. The government gave us installments of money, for which we had to sign vouchers. We resumed working, and it took seven or eight months to complete the film. It was now the government's property, but the government did not know what to do with it. They thought of putting it out under the Community Development Department, and suggested that we change the ending. At the end of the film, the family decides to leave the village because it has been ruined by the storm. The government said that this did not fit in with the idea of community development, and that the family should try to rebuild its house. I said the author might object. The people in the government didn't know that the author was dead, and I got my way. Eventually, the film was put out under the Publicity Department of the Road Development Scheme. The film opened in a theatre in Calcutta, and was booked for six weeks. The first two weeks, the film didn't do so well. Then it picked up, and on the last day of the six weeks the house was full. But, beginning the next day, the theatre was booked for a south Indian film by S. S. Vasan, of Gemini Pictures. The theatre sent a telegram to Vasan asking him if they could postpone the première of his film so that they could run 'Pather Panchali' for a few weeks more. Vasan telegraphed back, 'Nothing doing.' Afterward, he came to Calcutta and saw 'Pather Panchali,' and on the next day he came to my house. I was very much moved by what he said. He said, 'Don't judge me by the films I make. I can appreciate good things when I see them. If I had only known how good "Pather Panchali" was!' "

I ask him what happened to the film after the first six weeks.

"We were able to find another theatre, and it ran for another six or

seven weeks. It got excellent reviews. It ran in Bombay, Delhi, and
Madras, but without subtitles. Finally, it was entered in the Cannes Film
Festival, where it was championed by the film director Lindsay Anderson.
In Cannes, it was shown after four other films, and many of the members
of the jury did not stay for it. They were too tired. A few critics stayed.
One of them—a Frenchman, André Bazin—was so impressed that he immediately arranged a second showing of the film and insisted that all the
members of the jury be present. It received a special prize as the 'Best
Human Document.' 'Pather Panchali' was followed by 'Aparajito,' the
second part of the trilogy. When I took 'Aparajito' to the Venice Film
Festival, someone asked me if I was going to make the third part. I said
yes—I don't know why—and that's how 'Pather Panchali' grew into a
trilogy. But I did two other films—'Paras Pathar' and 'Jalsaghar'—before
going on to make 'Apur Sansar,' the third part of the trilogy, in 1959. Then
I began 'Devi,' which is a particular favorite of mine. It has a very dramatic plot—the clash between old and new. It's about early-nineteenth-
century superstition—about a girl who comes to believe she is a reincarnation of Kali. A very, very grim plot, but a beautiful-looking film. 'Devi'
was based on a story written by Prabhat Mukherji. The plot was a gift to
Prabhat Mukherji from Tagore. Tagore had so many plots in his head
that he made gifts of them to promising young writers. Incidentally, I did
a documentary on Tagore for the Films Division of the government of
India, for the Tagore centenary. It was only an hour long. We had to use
still photographs and any amateur movies that we could get hold of. My
first color film was 'Kanchenjunga.' It was all shot on location—in Darjeeling, in the shadow of Mount Kanchenjunga. The thing in my mind
was to do a story unbroken in time, the action taking place in the space of
a couple of hours. I decided on an upper-middle-class story, with some
very Anglicized characters. I chose Darjeeling because it's a hill station
very popular with upper-middle-class Bengalis, and things happen in Darjeeling that could not happen in Calcutta."

A Calcutta film critic, discussing Ray's work, has written, "The Calcutta
of the burning trams, the communal riots, the refugees, the unemployment, the rising prices and the food shortage do not exist in Ray's films.
The trials of the sensitive mind trying to survive the excruciating pressure
of corruption, vulgarity, want, and total pointlessness find no echo in
him." I ask Ray now about this criticism.

"One trouble is that I have not been able to find good stories about these
subjects. I feel at home with middle-class people, but in the trilogy I dealt

with poor people. Also, ever since 'Pather Panchali' I've had to select stories that I could make into films in a few months. But if I found a good story about a *busti,* say, I would make a film of it."

I ask him what he thinks of the Indian film industry, which, measured by the number of films produced per year, was long the largest film industry in the world, though Japan has overtaken it.

"You cannot take the Indian film industry seriously," he says. "The heart of the industry is in Bombay, and although it is true that some of the films made there have some good photography, some good sound record-ing, some good acting—even the songs, though much ridiculed, sometimes have a certain quality to them—the films always collapse when it comes to the story and direction. For a good film, you need one director who has control over everything, a single guiding hand, and in Bombay the director is nobody—everything rests with the producers and distributors."

I ask him which of all film directors he admires most.

"It is not difficult to answer *whom* I admire," he says. "It's more difficult to explain why. Besides Eisenstein and Pudovkin, I admire Dreyer and Bergman very much, and Antonioni also. I got to know Jean Renoir fairly well when he was making 'The River' here in Calcutta, and I greatly admire his work—especially 'La Règle du Jeu.' I'm impressed with some of the other French directors, like Truffaut—especially his 'Jules et Jim.' I'm also impressed by the early films of De Sica—'The Bicycle Thief' and 'Umberto D.' I admire some American directors, like John Ford—particu-larly for their early work. Actually, as you may have gathered, I admire individual films more than directors. My favorites are 'The Gold Rush,' 'The General,' 'Ivan the Terrible,' 'A Night at the Opera,' 'The Seven Samurai,' and 'My Darling Clementine.' Nowadays, I am very impatient with indifferent films."

The film studios of New Theatres, Ltd., in the section of Calcutta called Tollygunge, are a group of old, dilapidated low buildings spread about a spacious compound, which also has occasional clusters of trees and, lying here and there, heaps of rubbish. I am walking toward the editing depart-ment with Ray, who at present is engaged in synchronizing the sound and film tracks of "Nayak." "Bombay studios are bigger and much better equipped," Ray tells me as we go past a forlorn-looking canteen with a counter, a few tables, and a few chairs. "But I find New Theatres adequate for my needs. People coming from abroad have been amazed by the shabby look of New Theatres. But I feel we have the essentials for making good films. I think some of my films have a great deal of polish about them, even though they were shot here. There is something exciting about producing a first-class piece of work in these surroundings."

The editing department turns out to be a few rooms along a narrow veranda. The doors are ajar, and everywhere there is a great stir—people moving around, machines clattering, odd sounds. Before going into one room, Ray takes off his slippers and leaves them outside, explaining that it's a precaution to keep dust from getting on the film. The room is hung with strips of film, and three barefoot technicians are standing there waiting for Ray, who draws up a straight-backed wooden chair and stations himself in front of a table holding tape recorders and other sound apparatus and a Moviola, or film-editing machine. As he listens to sound effects and watches frames, prompting and directing the technicians all the while, he manages to tell me that "Nayak" revolves around a film star and a crisis in his life that is slowly disclosed in the course of a train ride from Calcutta to Delhi. "I wanted to make a film about a contemporary popular hero," Ray says. "I set the story on the Calcutta-Delhi Bi-Weekly Airconditioned Express, which is the latest thing in Indian trains—it's airconditioned, and besides the usual compartments it has chair cars, like the ones in American trains. On trains, you have brief encounters that reveal a lot. Of course, there are people on trains who probably just read Agatha Christie and rest and get to their destination, but then there are the others."

There is no continuous sound track yet. Ray listens to different sounds of a jet plane and discusses putting a jet's roar into the first reel as one of the sounds of Calcutta. Now frames appear in jerks and starts on the Moviola, a rickety old machine. "These are the opening frames," Ray says. "And this is Arindam Mukherji. [Moviola: Closeup of back of man's head. Mirror. Stroke of a comb. Open suitcases with clothes, whiskey bottle.] He is the *nayak*—played by Uttam Kumar, the popular film star. Arindam is thirty-six. This is his house in Calcutta. We see him shaving with an electric razor. He is not in a very good mood. It seems that his latest film may be his first flop. Also, the morning newspapers report that he was involved in a brawl in a night club. There is a hint in the newspapers that the brawl involved a woman, but only a hint. We don't know anything more than that, but we know that any scandal could damage his career, and that he tried to suppress the story. Arindam has suddenly decided to go to Delhi to receive a national prize that he has been awarded. He says, 'I don't give a damn for the prize. I just want to get away from it all for a day.' It's too late to get a reservation on a plane, so he has to take the train. Just now, he's about to leave for the railway station. The woman with whom he has been having an affair telephones him and asks if she can come to see him at the station. He puts her off."

From the sound apparatus comes the telephone voice of a woman saying, "What is the reason? Tell me, please." Ray calls out to a technician, "There should be a pause on the sound track between 'What is the reason?' and 'Tell me, please.' She must have time to realize that he isn't going to answer the question." To extend the pause by three seconds takes nearly an hour. There is more delay, because now the click of a cigarette lighter overlaps a bit of the dialogue. "For 'Devi,' I had Ali Akbar Khan play the *sarod*," Ray says to me. "Any physicist would probably have had more sense than I had, because whenever the *sarod* sound overlapped with a consonant in the dialogue, strange things happened—sometimes 't's became 'm's. When we were mixing dialogue and music, I had to keep the volume of the *sarod* very low. Ali Akbar Khan thought I ruined his music. He hasn't spoken to me since."

New frames appear on the Moviola, and Ray resumes talking about "Nayak." "Now Arindam is at Howrah Station. [Moviola: Arindam entering train. Conductor forcibly shutting out crowds. Interior of a coupé. Old man, wrapped in a shawl, looking up disapprovingly.] Here, in the train, Arindam is first put in with this old man, who is very puritanical, the cantankerous type of reformer; he makes his hatred for drink and movies and actors known. Finally, Arindam is moved from the coupé, the best available accommodations, to a four-berth compartment. In this compartment are an industrialist, his wife, and their twelve-year-old daughter, who has a fever and is lying in an upper berth. [Moviola: Train hurtling through countryside.] Actually, the interior scenes call for two four-berth compartments, but we built only one. To distinguish the cuts back and forth, we changed things like the luggage and the seat numbers. We also changed the sound track. The train noise of Arindam's compartment is subtly different, because there is a faint rattle of glass mixed with it—like a tumbler vibrating in a rack. In trains, there are all sorts of wonderful sounds. They are almost like music. There is the sound of a platform outside, the sound in a compartment with the door shut and with the door open, the sound in the corridor. [Moviola: Arindam going into the dining car. Passengers at tables. A couple and a serious-looking girl at a corner table, drinking tea.] The girl here is Aditi. She is a journalist who writes for *Adhunika*—'Modern Woman.' She's very serious about the magazine. Arindam is pointed out to her by the couple. The wife is much excited by the glimpse of Arindam, and she suggests that Aditi go interview him for the magazine. Aditi shows no interest, because she doesn't think films are serious art, but she is eventually persuaded to talk to him. Arindam says, 'I take it you don't like films,' and she says, 'Too remote from reality. Heroes shouldn't be so godlike.' "

New frames appear on the Moviola, and Ray continues, "Arindam has returned to his compartment, and now he is having a dream. I had never done a dream before. [Moviola: Hillocks of rupees. Arindam, on a hillock, looking satisfied. Sudden darkening of the sky. Apprehension crossing his face. Skeleton arms rising from the hillocks. Arindam runs. Sinking, caught in a quicksand of rupees. Gaunt figure with outstretched hand. Arindam trying to seize the hand.] Arindam is remembering his former mentor, Shankarda, and Shankarda's warnings against leaving the stage for the commercialism of films. The sinking is to show the constant fear of 'slipping' that haunts popular stars. Arindam wakes up in a sweat. He gets out at one of the train stops and has tea in the station. He sees Aditi at the window of the dining car and holds up his cup. Aditi holds up a fork, to indicate that she's lunching. Arindam gets back on the train and sits down with her. He tells her about his dream, and she surreptitiously starts taking notes. A series of flashbacks shows that he is exposing his entire life to her. [Moviola: Image of death goddess. Excited crowds. Arindam and Shankarda lifting the image on their shoulders. Shankarda collapsing. Image falls. Arindam carrying Shankarda's body to the burning *ghat*.] At the burning *ghat*, Arindam has a crucial conversation with a friend. Arindam asks, 'Do you believe in rebirth?' The friend says, 'This is the age of Marx and Freud. No rebirth, no Providence.' Arindam says, 'I know. One life, one chance.' [Moviola: Rain, wind, cinders from the pyre.] Here is another flashback. . . ."

As it happens, I am out of Calcutta at the time of the première of "Nayak," an exuberant occasion—or so it appears from articles about it, like this one, by one of Calcutta's more influential men of letters:

"Nayak" was a fantastic blast-off. . . . A Roman arena hysteria was in evidence. . . . He [Ray] entered with a flourish. . . . Flashbulbs popped, smiles were bared. . . . Uttam Kumar . . . entered in the semi-darkness. . . . The mob howled. Mr. Kumar looked the other way. Again the howl, this time interspersed with threatening growls. . . . Mr. Kumar rose, smiled, namaskared [bowed in greeting] with Olympian sereneness from the front row of the upper balcony. The animal below whined pleasurably, and retired with soft swishings of its tail. Mr. Ray and the entire celestial front row observed the tamed beast, sitting "Like gods together, careless of mankind." A fat, blowsy flutter of middle-aged female ran from my row down the aisle, and stood agape, clutching her ten-year-old daughter's hand, before the chief god. Mr. Kumar smiled. . . . She ran . . . back to her seat, eyes and mouth still as wide-open as monsoon manholes.

It was "Nayak" come to life. It was life satirising art satirising life.

On my return to Calcutta, I visit Ray at his flat and ask him how the film is doing.

"The reaction at the première was very good," he says. "But the première was not really a good test, because the attention of even the critics in the audience was all on Uttam Kumar. So I have gone to a number of the regular showings of the film to watch the reactions of typical audiences. In Calcutta, if they don't like a film, they shout, they boo, they walk out. So far, none of this has happened. Of course one worries about a bad reaction from the public, because if the audience doesn't like a particular film, it may not be easy to find a producer to back the next one. After all, the film is made for the public, and I always hope that my films will be liked and will be discussed. I also listen to what friends and acquaintances have to say. So far, I've had about a dozen phone calls."

I ask him about the problem of financing his films.

"In Calcutta, I have a good following, and any film of mine is certain to have a good six-week run. All my films except one have made a profit, so for the producers I am probably one of the safest film investments going. I do, however, take longer than European directors. On the average, I take forty-five shooting days spread out over three months, which is not terribly fast. 'Kanchenjunga' I shot in only twenty-five days."

The telephone rings. Ray answers it, talks for a moment, hangs up, and says, "That was a friend. He telephoned to tell me that an actor I had worked with died last night. In Calcutta, actors are always dying. The actor who played the confectioner in 'Pather Panchali' died halfway through the shooting. We found a substitute and photographed him from the back. The old woman in 'Pather Panchali' was near death when I cast her for the part—she died the other day. She had been on the stage in the twenties but had been inactive ever since. She was so excited over the chance of working again that she wouldn't even discuss the question of payment. I think the film helped keep her alive."

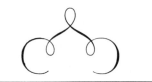

The Poorest of the Poor

"ALTHOUGH THROUGHOUT INDIA there is a general opting-out of concern about the large problems of the poor by people with any means at all," one of the Ford Foundation planners tells me, "still, all over Calcutta, in a *busti* here and a *busti* there, a ward here and a ward there, volunteers and voluntary groups are doing welfare work. We did a study of a very poor section of the city that has a population of nearly a quarter of a million, and we found there were dispensaries, family-planning clinics, hospitals, coöperatives, primary and secondary schools, reading rooms, sports clubs, all run by private welfare groups. In fact, if it weren't for this volunteer work, the city might have collapsed long ago. But each religious, ethnic, or caste group tends to concentrate exclusively on its own poor. Muslims tend to work among Muslims, Gujaratis among Gujaratis, tanners among tanners. There are, it is true, a few groups that try to cut across the divisions and work throughout the city, yet, because the problem of poverty as a whole is so vast, even they end up having their own special concerns. For instance, the Bharat Savak Samaj works among the beggars and the Bengal Ladies' Union tries to rehabilitate prostitutes. Perhaps the most dreaded work is done by the Missionaries of Charity, who devote themselves to the lowest of the low. They devote themselves to those who are rejected by the rejected and despised by the despised. They work mostly with the lepers." A Calcutta friend, commenting on this part of the work of the Missionaries of Charity, says, "They attach special importance to their work among the lepers, perhaps because to all the rich of the world, if you really come down to it, all the poor of the world are, in a sense, lepers. The rich may give to the poor, may work among the poor, but they are really afraid to live with the poor."

The Missionaries of Charity is a Catholic congregation that was founded in 1948 by an Albanian-born nun, Mother Theresa. She is still its head, and one morning I go to meet her in the congregation's convent, which is on a narrow, unpaved lane just off Lower Circular Road. It is a small building enclosed by a high wall with an iron gate. Inside the gate is a courtyard. I am shown into a room, overlooking the courtyard, that serves as a parlor. It is furnished with a round wooden table, bearing a Bible and the *Catholic Directory of India,* and a few straight-backed wooden chairs, above which hang several framed photographs of clerical personages inscribed to the Missionaries of Charity.

Mother Theresa comes in. She is tiny and slim, but imposing. Her skin is ivory-colored, as if she had not been touched by the all-scorching Indian sun. Her face is creased with wrinkles, but she does not look elderly. Her eyes are small and gray-brown, her nose is strong, her lips are thin, and, though her smile is quick, her expression is stern and purposeful. She is wearing a plain white cotton sari with blue edging and a high-necked, long-sleeved blouse. On her, the traditional Indian dress seems transformed into a practical uniform-*cum*-nun's habit. The sari has been secured to her hair with ordinary straight pins and folded so that it looks a little like a headdress, and its free end has been fastened at her shoulder with a large safety pin, from which hangs a crucifix. "It's Christ's work we are doing here in Calcutta," she says by way of greeting.

We sit down, and I ask Mother Theresa one or two general questions about herself.

"There isn't much to tell," she says. "I was born in 1910. My father was a shopkeeper, and I had a brother and a sister. I entered a Loreto convent when I was ten, and I came to Calcutta to teach in the convent here in 1929. I have been in Calcutta ever since. I feel completely Indian now. I speak Bengali very well; my Hindi is not so good. But I would prefer it if we didn't talk about me—if you've heard about one of the Missionaries of Charity, you've heard about them all. I'd rather talk about our work, which is God's work."

I ask her how the work got started.

"I found the vocation of charity here in Calcutta within the vocation of religion," she says. "Even when I was teaching in the convent, I encouraged the senior girls in the sodality to go into the *bustis* and work among the poor, but I really began this work after the Second World War, when I saw a woman dying on the street outside Campbell Hospital. I picked her up and took her to the hospital, but she was refused admission, because she was poor. She died on the street. I knew then that I must make a home for the dying—a resting place for people going to Heaven. When God wants you to do something, He has His way of letting you know it." She goes on to tell me that in 1948 the ecclesiastical authorities gave her permission to form a congregation dedicated to relief work among "the poorest of the poor." She began the work in a couple of small rooms in a house in Moti Jheel Busti, establishing a school for orphan children in one room and a Home for the Dying in the other. Soon afterward, she received her first postulant as a Missionary of Charity, and soon after that she found different quarters for the Home for the Dying, and expanded her school for orphans into the second of the original rooms. "So, in time, the congregation and its activities grew," Mother Theresa adds, and she hands me a couple of leaflets about the work of the congregation today. One leaflet, which is about the Home for the Dying, records:

Mother says, "They have lived like animals, we help them to die like angels." Here is the story of one poor unfortunate woman who was brought in from the sewer. She was a beggar who had, apparently overcome by hunger and fatigue, fallen into an open manhole. She lay there for five days barely alive and covered with maggots. As Mother put her to bed and began gently cleaning her, whole areas of skin came off in her hand. The woman, half-unconscious, murmured, "Why are you doing this for me?" Mother replied, "For the love of God." This poor waif who probably never in her life had had loving hands tend her—looking at Mother, her soul in her eyes, faith in human nature restored—gave Mother a most beautiful smile and died. That is our reward—that we should make the last moments of the fellow being beautiful.

"In Calcutta, besides the Home for the Dying, we now have a children's home, sixteen schools, twenty-three Sunday schools, eight mobile clinics for lepers, seven mobile clinics for the poor in the *bustis,* a relief center for distributing food rations, and two convents for the sisters," Mother Theresa says. "Altogether, in Calcutta, we have fifty-nine centers for our work, and two hundred and eighty-five sisters, who come from all parts of India and from many other countries, too. We also have sisters doing work in twenty other Indian cities, but most of the sisters work here in Calcutta."

According to the rules of the congregation, Mother Theresa tells me, a candidate wishing to become a professed sister must display health of body and mind, the ability to acquire knowledge, common sense in abundance, and a cheerful disposition. Then, over a three-year period, she will be admitted as, in turn, an aspirant, to learn the nature of the work of charity; a postulant, to learn the rudiments of the religious life and to test her sense of vocation; and a novice, to continue the study of the religious life, to examine the vows of poverty, chastity, and obedience, and, under supervision, to work in the *bustis* among the poor. A member of the congregation must eat the same food as the poor and wear a plain white cotton sari with open sandals and a small crucifix; a dark-blue edging on the sari serves to distinguish a professed sister from a candidate. The prescribed language of the congregation is English, and the favorite ejaculation of the members is "Immaculate Heart of Mary! Cause of our joy! Pray for us!"

A bell now begins to chime in the distance, and files of nuns in white saris move across the courtyard outside. "They are going to the chapel," Mother Theresa says. "They are going to pray for one of our sisters who died this morning of rabies. She was a trained doctor, and six months ago, when she was working in one of our leper camps, a dog bit her. She didn't take the rabies injections, because the dog was just a puppy. It must have been her time to go to God." From the distance there now comes the sound of singing—of thin, high voices raised in the words of the Lord's Prayer. "I am thankful to say she died two days after the onset of the rabies. Five of us looked after her. We will all have to take injections. People who are bitten by rabid animals take about fourteen injections. We had only indirect contact with the rabies, so we will have to take only seven—it's not so bad."

Mother Theresa now prepares to visit some of the centers of the congregation. She invites me to accompany her, and asks for the ambulance, explaining that she often travels in it, so that she can remove to the Home for the Dying anyone she may see dying on the streets or in the *bustis*.

We take our places in the ambulance, beside the driver, and are immediately surrounded by a throng of beggars—sick, emaciated, lame—all with their open palms thrust forward. "Hey, *babu!*" and "Hey, *mataji!*" and "Hey, *babu!*" they cry, in a dissonant jumble of voices.

I pass out the money in my pockets.

Mother Theresa, except for crossing herself, sits impassive. As the ambulance pulls away, the beggars retreat and fall behind.

Mother Theresa tells me that her first stop will be at the Shishu Bhavan ("children's home"), which houses nearly seventy children at present and has cared for over two thousand homeless children—orphaned, abandoned, afflicted, or disabled—since it was opened, in 1955, nursing them, teaching them, finding them foster parents, and arranging marriages for them.

The ambulance stops at a crossing, and a thin, pale man comes up to the window. "Mother, I want to find work," he says.

"I don't know of any jobs," she says. "I have already told you I can't help you."

"Please, Mother . . ."

The ambulance moves away from him.

"He has five children," Mother Theresa says, after a moment. "He has t.b., and he can't do heavy manual work. People who can't do such work are the hardest to find jobs for. We are treating him at our t.b. clinic. We can do nothing more."

At the next crossing, a small boy with a sad, wasted face appears at the open window and extends his hands in appeal to her. She crosses herself, opens the door, picks him up, and takes him into the ambulance. "He needs food," she tells me, "and at the Shishu Bhavan we distribute relief rations."

The Shishu Bhavan, like the convent, has a high wall with an iron gate leading to a courtyard. But here, pressing against the gate, is a crowd of anxious-looking women, some of them old but most of them young, and all of them dressed in faded cotton saris, carrying cotton bags, and holding folded yellow cards.

Pulling the boy by the hand, Mother Theresa goes into the crowd of women, shouting, in Bengali, "Form a line! Form a line! Everyone will get her ration, but you have to form a line first."

The women do not budge, so Mother Theresa, coaxing and prodding them, lines them up herself. They begin moving into the courtyard, past a model of a grotto, and onto a veranda, where several sisters are working around a barrel of grain, a barrel of powdered milk, some large gunny-sacks filled with more grain, and a stack of cartons marked "Non-Fat Dry Milk—Donated by the People of the United States of America." As the line of women moves along, one sister scoops up portions of grain with a measure and transfers them to the women's cotton bags, another sister measures portions of powdered milk into polyethylene bags and hands them out, and other sisters replenish the stores of grain and milk in the barrels from the gunnysacks and cartons, and check and punch the ration cards. A girl of about ten stares, unsmiling and without comprehension, at the face of her ration card, on which is printed:

Catholic Relief Services
NCWC
Food for Peace
A Free Gift from the People of America
Distributed by the Missionaries of Charity

Mother Theresa, after she has seen the boy from the ambulance receive his ration, strides into a little room off the veranda, where about twenty babies lie on small pallets and in basketlike wicker cribs. A plain-looking Indian nun, who wears glasses and has the cheerful manner of a primary-school teacher, is occupied in tending the babies. She is Sister Lourdes.

"Oh, Karuna, you are crying," Sister Lourdes says, bending over a baby. "You always cry whenever there are visitors and my back is turned. Oh, your diaper is wet." Sister Lourdes changes Karuna's diaper and then makes the rounds of the room, checking the diapers of the other babies.

Mother Theresa, kneeling on the floor and clapping her hands, calls, *"Shiggri, shiggri, shiggri"* (*"shiggri"* is Bengali for "quickly"), and two little boys about eighteen months old toddle up to her. "Say good morning," she says to them.

They burble.

"Oh, here is a bright fellow with a big grin," she says, picking up a third little boy, who looks about three and is dressed only in shorts. "Naughty, naughty, naughty William. He smiles the whole time, does nothing else." Turning to me, she says, "A few months ago, no one thought William would live, but now he has been adopted by the Belgian Consul. That means he has a monthly stipend of twenty-five rupees, and he'll be able to go to an English-speaking boarding school." She straightens an overturned chair and sits William down on it. "There! Now, William, you look like a sahib in your chair."

Mother Theresa goes over to a crib, lifts the arm of a baby, and admires a gold bangle on the arm, saying, almost to herself, "What a nice present from a visitor!" She moves across to another crib. "Here is a little foundling who was left in the compound of a church in Howrah," she says, chucking him under the chin. She goes from crib to crib. "This is Helen. This is Angeline. This is Josephine. This is Patricia. This is Agnes. This is another Agnes. This is Krishna." She turns to me suddenly and says, "I must talk to the sisters here about the funeral of the sister who died, but we will meet in a few minutes." She leaves, telling Sister Lourdes to take me through the rest of the Shishu Bhavan.

Sister Lourdes calls another sister to take charge of the nursery, and leads me back to the veranda, which is now occupied by children just finishing their lunch. "Besides the nice little nursery room, we have here a nice dormitory room for the young children and a nice big dormitory room for the big girls," Sister Lourdes says. "The big boys we send to a little Boys' Town that the Catholic Church runs in Gangarampur. We use this veranda for meals because we are short of space."

Moving around among the children, she shoos them all into a room crowded with beds for their afternoon rest, but the children all stretch out on the bare floor—some under the beds, some in a small open area at the far end of the room.

"They like the floor because it's cooler," Sister Lourdes says, and she conducts me into the dormitory for older girls. Some of the girls are in their teens, and others seem to be in their late twenties or early thirties. Many of them are obviously pregnant.

A girl in a printed sari, who has a round, expressionless face and paralyzed legs, drags herself across the floor. "This is Philu," Sister Lourdes says. "She has been with us for six years. She lost the use of her legs after a bad case of typhoid."

Back in the ambulance, Mother Theresa tells me that she is now going to the house in Moti Jheel Busti where she first started her work, and where she still has the original school, to take measurements for a new blackboard. "Ordinarily, we don't have special buildings for schools now," she says. "During the good season, we hold our classes under the trees, and during the monsoon we meet wherever we can find shelter."

At Moti Jheel Busti, the ambulance stops at the stagnant pond, and immediately a crowd of children collects and starts following Mother Theresa, calling "Hey, Sister!" or "Hey, Mother!" or "Hey, *mataji!*" A few grownups join the train, shouting *"Jesu pranam!"* (Bengali for "Praise be to Jesus!").

A fair-skinned man intercepts Mother Theresa. "We Anglo-Indians are scattered all over this *busti,*" he says in a stutter, wheezing and coughing. "We would all like to live together, Mother."

"Your old nonsense again," she says, and adds firmly, "Go to the sister at the mobile clinic across the way and ask her for cortisone for your asthma. Go along."

The man shuffles away, muttering to himself.

With children still following us, we go down a narrow street to a small brick building, pass through a wooden gate with a cross on it, walk across a courtyard, and enter a sad-looking old house. The school consists of two dark rooms, which have peeling walls, rows of low wooden benches, two crèches, and a few nursery pictures. As Mother Theresa is taking the measurements for the blackboard, an old man, extremely drunk and wearing only a *dhoti,* appears from somewhere, kneels down, and clutches her legs. "Please forgive me for drinking, Mother," the old man says.

"Stop drinking," Mother Theresa says, without interrupting her work.

"I can't."

"Then I can't forgive you."

Back in the ambulance, Mother Theresa tells me that we are now going to the Home for the Dying, which is near the Kali Temple. "When we wanted to move the Home for the Dying out of Moti Jheel Busti, we made a request to the Calcutta Corporation for new quarters," she says. "They gave us a *dharamshala* [a shelter for travellers] that used to serve as the overnight hostel for pilgrims to the Kali Temple, and we moved there in 1954. The *dharamshala* had two halls, and we made one of them into a dormitory for dying male street cases and the other into a dormitory for dying female street cases. Some street cases are brought to the Home for the Dying when they are nearly dead, and we can't do anything about them—many are dead within a few minutes. Some street cases are too old, too crippled, or too far gone with t.b. ever to leave the Home for the Dying, and we go on nursing them until they die. But some street cases can be helped to recover, with calcium and vitamin injections. In fact, out of eighteen thousand five hundred street cases we've admitted to the Home for the Dying so far, about ten thousand have got well enough to leave."

"Do you follow these up after they leave you?" I ask.

"We try to keep an eye on them if they are not well when they leave," she says. "Because many of them would rather live in the streets and beg than stay in the Home for the Dying, they go as soon as they can get up. But many of them come back to the Home for the Dying to die."

The Home for the Dying is a one-story yellow house off a typical Indian crossroads crowded with shops and pavement stalls. Two Indian sisters come out to greet Mother Theresa. One is short and plump, with a round face, and is dressed in the sari with blue edging. She is Sister Barbara. The other is thin, dark, and small, and is dressed in the plain white sari. She is Sister Lillian. "Our sisters always work in pairs," Mother Theresa says to me. "In emergencies, two heads and four hands are better than one head and two hands."

The entrance to the yellow house is marked by a signboard reading, "Corporation of Calcutta Nirmal Hriday Home for Dying Destitutes," and by an elaborate framed scroll headed "Holy Father's Message to Mother Theresa." Inside is a large, austere hall with an overpowering rancid smell. On each side of a long central aisle is a low platform extending the entire length of the hall. On the platforms and in the aisle are low beds, set so close together that there is very little space to move among them. They have no bedclothes, and consist of narrow metal frames with mattresses sheathed in polyethylene. Stretched out on the mattresses are men of all ages, and boys as well, some of them disfigured, all of them wrinkled and thin and motionless, their bodies mere forms, their eyes fixed in expressionless stares.

Sister Barbara, Sister Lillian, and Mother Theresa walk through the hall, stopping at one bed or another to take a pulse or to straighten a head or a limb and place it in a more restful position. Mother Theresa moves around quickly and is methodical. Sister Barbara always has something cheerful to say, and she talks fast. Sister Lillian follows shyly, seldom speaking, but smiling continuously. None of the men in the beds, however, seem to take notice or register recognition, except for one man, who soundlessly sits up as they approach. He seems to be in his thirties, with a strong-looking body, but he has the same expressionless eyes. He soon falls back on the mattress.

"The Corporation ambulances bring in people who collapse on the street —street cases so hopeless that hospitals won't take them," Sister Barbara tells me. "At present, we have sixty-eight male street cases and seventy-four female street cases here. They have no known relatives, no shelter, no food. Most are cases of starvation; for the last six years things have been very bad. No one has died so far today, but you can never tell—someone may die at any moment. We try to make them as comfortable as possible. We make the beds very low, so that they can't hurt themselves if they fall out. They are so helpless."

We have reached the end of the hall, where there is a passageway, with more beds in it, holding more men. This leads into another hall, which is crowded with women, most of them almost naked. Their bodies are gaunt and their eyes wild and demented. Some of the women are sitting upright on their beds; others are lying down, crying and moaning. One woman, who is completely naked, begins to scream, and Mother Theresa rushes over and covers her with a towel.

"Once they get this sick, they have no strength even to move, yet they can scream," Mother Theresa says.

Back in the ambulance, as we are driving to one of the congregation's leper camps, at Dhapa, Mother Theresa talks about criticisms that are occasionally made of the work done by the Missionaries of Charity. It is said that their staff is medically untrained, though the major part of their work is with the sick; that their efforts are often restricted to the most extreme and dramatic cases, though they might do more to alleviate suffering if they helped care for people with more hope of living; and, in particular, that their work at the Home for the Dying does little more than prolong misery, for even when the people admitted there are nursed back to health, they are turned out to the streets to face the old problems of starvation and filth. Of these criticisms, Mother Theresa says that although the Missionaries of Charity may not have extensive medical training, their work gives relief to those who would otherwise have no relief; that although their work at the moment may be restricted, they are always trying to widen its scope; and that although their work at the Home for the Dying may be concentrated on medical attention, they do try, whenever they can, to effect rehabilitation of the street cases who get better. "We minister to all those with whom we come in contact," she says. "We turn away no one—we always try to make room for one more person in our homes and camps. For when we feed a hungry person, we feed Christ, and when we clothe a naked baby, we clothe Christ, and when we give a home to the homeless, we are giving shelter to Christ. When we know the poor, we love them, and when we love them, we serve them. There are more people here in Calcutta now who care about the poor and serve them than there were when we started. Our work would be impossible without these people. We say in the morning, 'Today we have no food for relief,' and that day someone will bring us food. It's wonderful how it comes. Just yesterday, a Brahman gentleman died. He loved mangoes, and his daughter brought us crates of beautiful mangoes, and every child in the Shishu Bhavan had a mango. Two weeks ago, a few Hindu ladies got together and cooked rice and curry, which they took to a leper camp and fed to the lepers. We need warm hearts that will love and loving hands that will work."

We reach Dhapa. Large vultures with long, thin legs glide overhead. From the refuse dump, a rough, untarred road goes alongside a slaughterhouse, where emaciated buffaloes are now being herded through a gate. A few yards beyond the slaughterhouse is a dirty river, which seems to have no flow at all. We cross the river over a small bridge, get out of the ambulance, and pick our way among puddles and stones on the slimy, uneven bank.

"The lepers have to live wherever they can," Mother Theresa says. "In the marshes, under the trees—wherever they can find a place. So far, we have not had the means to build a colony for them, but we have a mobile clinic where they can come for medicine and treatment, and at least once a week we call at different places. We began our work for the lepers because, like the dying, they couldn't get help anywhere. Everyone shrank from them."

Leprosy, which is caused by *Mycobacterium leprae,* and which takes cutaneous, tubercular, and neural forms, has such manifestations as depigmentation, lesions, ulceration, nodules, thickening of tissue, mutilation, loss of sensation, loss of sight, and impairment of speech. It disfigures the face and hands especially, and through the ages has therefore been associated with so-called "leonine" faces and "claw" hands. It is not known exactly how the disease is contracted, how it is transmitted, why only human beings seem to be susceptible to it, or whether there is any cure for it— though it can sometimes be arrested through hygiene, isolation, and medication. What is known is that the disease is fostered by malnutrition, filth, and squalor. In recent years, thanks to improved standards of sanitation, leprosy has practically disappeared from the richer countries of the West, but in poorer countries, especially in areas of Africa and Asia, it is chronic for as much as ten per cent of the population. In fact, leprosy is now associated almost exclusively with dark-skinned, poor people living in tropical climates.

I ask Mother Theresa how many lepers there are in the Calcutta area.

"No one knows," she replies. "But some say two or three hundred thousand."

Ahead is the camp. It consists of rows of huts of stone or clay built wall to wall and with low red tile roofs, like the houses in the *bustis.* Between the rows of huts are muddy lanes. Cows, dogs, and chickens are everywhere. The place swarms with flies, and overhead are the vultures. Scores of men, women, and children are out in the open—standing outside doorways, lying on *charpoys* in front of the huts, or squatting on the ground in the shade of a few trees. Most of the people are missing fingers or toes; some have lesions at the mouth and no noses.

"Everything takes shelter here," Mother Theresa says to me. "We get rid of the dogs one day, and more come the next."

"Salaam!" and *"Jesu pranam!"* the people call out to Mother Theresa as she moves around among them. She goes from hut to hut, greeting them by name and asking questions, listening, giving advice about medicine, about diet, about keeping cows tethered. "So the medicine has brought your fever down, Das," she says to a man who has lost all his fingers. "That's good. I see your children are doing well, too. That's good."

She tells me as we walk toward a hut, "One trouble with these camps is that very sick cases are mixed with not-so-sick cases, and so we rented this hut to isolate the very, very sick."

"What about all of you who work here?" I ask. "Isn't it dangerous for you?"

"Up to now, thank God, nothing," she says. "But we have to be ready."

We go into the hut, which is a few feet square. A line, on which wet cloths hang, is strung across the room. On the floor are two *charpoys* and a mattress sheathed in polyethylene, with three badly mutilated men lying on them.

The man on the mattress is sobbing. "No amount of medicine helps!" he cries out, in a heavy, constricted voice.

"The pain will go away," Mother Theresa says, bending over him and feeling his forehead. She helps a sister give him a morphine injection.

When we are outside again, she says to me, "In the early stages, the disease is not so painful, but people at his stage are in terrible pain."

When she has gone around to all the huts and has started back to the ambulance, those who can walk follow her, entreating, pleading, and crying for more medicine and more food. Mother Theresa, as she walks on, keeps talking to them, saying "Yes," and "Tomorrow," and "I will try." She crosses herself continually.

Leaden Echo, Golden Echo

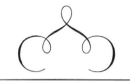

Reflections: "Gaze of Lazarus"

As I THINK ABOUT THE FEW WEEKS I have just spent here in Calcutta, I can find no words to describe its filth, its disease, and its misery. At first, I felt that I could accept Calcutta, that it wasn't as bad as I had thought it would be. But now I know I cannot accept Calcutta. I dwell on the names of the Britons celebrated by the monuments in Calcutta's streets—deaths endowed with purpose by later generations—but then I think of the countless deaths of the unnoticed Indians on those streets, forgotten in death as in life. I remember the time I spent with Satyajit Ray—a man of great talent who survives in the midst of Calcutta's chaos and suffering—but though "Nayak," the film he has just finished, deals with modern, prosperous, middle-class Indians, it is soon seen to be also about death, and about how these modern Indians have lost even their parents' sustaining faith in reincarnation. The perception that Calcutta forces upon me is not of the fact of death—which perhaps I can accept—but of the process of dying, possibly the dying of an entire population, for Calcutta's spreading poverty, like the slow strangulation of the Hooghly River, foreshadows something more frightening than personal death: it foreshadows racial extinction. I fear Calcutta. I reject Calcutta. But how can I prevent Calcutta from obsessing me? Feeling near hysteria, I ask myself how the species could have reached such a point of degradation and yet have adapted itself to that degradation, for the adaptation seems to show only how the will to survive bends us downward. In my head, images of Calcutta surface like suppressed nightmares rising to haunt the conscious mind. A leprous beggar drags himself through a crowded Calcutta bazaar; his face is ulcerated, his hands are mutilated, and his lungs and vocal cords are so damaged that his plea for alms is little more than a croaking sob; the people, themselves thin and sickly-looking, shrink back to make way for him, their faces showing the dread of contagion. If there were any consolation in the belief commonly held among the well-off that since Calcutta's poor live like animals their pain is less than human, the crying leper destroys that belief and leaves me with no consolation whatever.

I recall that in earlier times in Europe a poor, diseased person, especially a leper, was called a "lazar," that "lazar" came from the name of Lazarus, and that Lazarus is mentioned in the Bible in two connections: in a parable of Jesus in Luke, and in an account of a miracle of Jesus in John. In Luke, Lazarus was a leprous beggar who had collapsed at the gate of a rich man's house, where he begged for scraps from the rich man's table. When Lazarus died, he went to Heaven and was comforted by Abraham, but when the rich man died, he went to Hell and was tormented by flames. The rich man looked up from Hell and saw Lazarus with Abraham, and begged Abraham to send Lazarus to him with a few drops of water. Abraham answered, "Between us and you there is a great gulf fixed: so that they which would pass from hence to you cannot; neither can they pass to us, that would come from thence." The rich man asked Abraham, then, to raise Lazarus from the dead, so that he might testify to the living members of the rich man's family about the torments of Hell. Abraham answered that if the rich man's family would not heed Moses and the prophets, they would not heed someone raised from the dead. In John, a sick man named Lazarus of Bethany died and was buried for four days in a cave sealed by a stone. Jesus went to the cave with the sisters of Lazarus, ordered the stone removed, and cried out, "Lazarus, come forth!" The account continues, "And he that was dead came forth, bound hand and foot with graveclothes; and his face was bound about with a napkin. Jesus saith unto them, 'Loose him, and let him go.'"

Although there are other references to the resurrected Lazarus in the Bible, almost nothing is said about what happened to him in his second life, but I remember once reading a weird, haunting psychological meditation on the life of the resurrected Lazarus. It was a fable entitled "Lazarus," by the Russian writer Leonid Andreyev (1871–1919). "When Lazarus rose from . . . the mysterious thralldom of death, and returned alive to his home," the fable opened, "it was a long time before anyone noticed the evil peculiarities in him that were later to make his very name terrible." People noticed, however, that his body was bloated, his skin cracked and slimy, his color livid, and his look solemn and incommunicative, and that he had about him the stench of death. During the festivities at which his relatives and friends celebrated his resurrection, one of the merrymakers asked him, "Why don't you tell us, Lazarus, what was There?" Lazarus said nothing, but the merrymakers saw that he was "looking straight at them, embracing all with one glance, heavy and terrible." From then on, all who happened to meet his eyes were permanently seized by an incomprehensible lassitude and dread; his relatives and friends came to fear and avoid him. All day long, Lazarus would sit in front of his house in Judaea, alone and motionless, and stare into the sun. "The thought suggested itself to people that the cold of the . . . grave had been so intense, its darkness so deep, that there was not in all the earth enough heat or light to warm Lazarus and lighten the gloom of his eyes," Andreyev wrote. At the end of the day, Lazarus would follow the sun into the desert, and anyone who saw him there, walking always toward the sun, found it impossible to forget the sight of his black silhouette against the huge red disc of the sun. People who heard about the "evil peculiarities" of Lazarus scoffed at the reports of his power and came from far away to see him for themselves.

Those who felt any desire to speak, after they had been stricken by the gaze of Lazarus [Andreyev wrote], described the change that had come over them somewhat like this:

All objects seen by the eye and palpable to the hand became empty, light, and transparent, as though they were light shadows in the darkness. . . . [The darkness] was dispelled neither by the sun, nor by the moon, nor by the stars. . . .

The vast emptiness which surrounds the universe . . . stretched boundless, penetrating everywhere, disuniting everything, body from body, particle from particle. . . . There was no more a sense of time; the beginning of all things and their end merged into one. . . . A man was just born, and funeral candles were already lighted at his head, and then were extinguished; and soon there was emptiness where before had been the man and the candles.

One day, Andreyev continued, a famous sculptor decided to go from Rome, where he lived, to Judaea to see Lazarus. Although the sculptor was renowned throughout the empire for the beauty of his work, he felt that his sculpture lacked "life," "soul," and "radiance," and he hoped to be inspired by the sight of a man miraculously raised from the dead. He saw Lazarus and, like all the others who had come to see him, was transformed by the experience. The sculptor returned to Rome and afterward created only one sculpture, "a thing monstrous, possessing none of the forms familiar to the eye, yet not devoid of a hint of some new unknown form." Someone happened to notice, however, that under one of the monstrous projections of this sculpture was a beautifully carved butterfly, "trembling as though with a weak longing to fly." Although the sculptor felt that this work was the truest thing he had done and that what everyone else considered beautiful was "a lie," his friends were shocked and revolted by the sculpture, and one of them destroyed it with a hammer, sparing only the butterfly.

The Emperor Augustus felt that he was invincible to the curse of Lazarus, and summoned Lazarus to Rome in order to confront him. At the encounter that followed, Augustus said to Lazarus, "My empire is the land of the living; my people are a people of the living and not of the dead. . . . I do not know what you have seen There, but if you lie, I hate your lies, and if you tell the truth, I hate your truth. In my heart I feel the pulse of life; in my hands I feel power, and my proud thoughts, like eagles, fly through space. Behind my back, under the protection of my authority, under the shadow of the laws I have created, men live and labor and rejoice." Augustus, who had previously commanded Lazarus to sit with his face averted, now boldly looked into his eyes, to see Rome and the empire, all the cities, kingdoms, and civilizations throughout time "swallowed up in the black maw of the Infinite." Augustus felt stricken by the knowledge of death, but then he thought with tenderness of his subjects, "fragile vessels with life-agitated blood and hearts that knew both sorrow and great joy." He gradually regained his hold on life, and he ordered Lazarus' eyes to be put out with hot irons. Lazarus died in the desert of Judaea, shunned and alone, a spiritual leper.

The Russian fable is nineteenth-century rhetoric at its morbid extreme, but its central idea—the power that the knowledge of death can have over the living—modulates in my mind, here in India, like a sombre musical theme; the theme of "Lazarus" shifts to E. M. Forster's "A Passage to India," and I think of the elderly Englishwoman whose hold on the value of life was undermined by her experience in one of the many, identical Marabar caves, a dark, circular, tomblike chamber that responded to all distinct human sounds—the squeak of a boot or the blowing of a nose, a fragment of spoken poetry or an outburst of profanity—with a single, reverberating echo, which, insofar as it could be expressed by the human tongue, was "boum" or "bou-oum," or "ou-boum." For her, afterward, religious faith, devotion to truth, appreciation of beauty, generosity of spirit, strength of purpose, subtlety of mind, fineness of feeling, eloquence of expression, nobility of action, all human accomplishment—indeed, all human effort, experience, and understanding—existed but had no value.

She had come to that state [Forster wrote] where the horror of the universe and its smallness are both visible at the same time—the twilight of the double vision. . . . If this world is not to our taste, well, at all events there is Heaven, Hell, Annihilation—one or other of those large things, that huge scenic background of stars, fires, blue or black air. All heroic endeavor, and all that is known as art, assumes that there is such a background, just as all practical endeavor, when the world is to our taste, assumes that the world is all. But in the twilight of the double vision, a spiritual muddledom is set up for which no high-sounding words can be found; we can neither act nor refrain from action, we can neither ignore nor respect Infinity. . . . What had spoken to her in that scoured-out cavity of the granite? What dwelt in the first of the caves? Something very old and very small. Before time, it was before space also. Something snub-nosed, incapable of generosity —the undying worm itself. . . . The abyss also may be petty, the serpent of eternity made of maggots. . . .

But even what spoke to her in the cave was lost in the twilight of the double vision:

As she drove through the huge city [Bombay] which the West has built and abandoned with a gesture of despair, she longed to stop . . . and disentangle the hundred Indias that passed each other in its streets. The feet of the horses moved her on, and presently the boat sailed and thousands of coconut palms appeared all round the anchorage and climbed the hills to wave her farewell. "So you thought an echo was India; you took the Marabar caves as final?" they laughed. "What have we in common with them? . . . Good-bye!"

So, at the close of the journey, India, in her vastness, mocked what the Englishwoman thought she had seen there—the abyss she had taken as final. In a different way, what had spoken to me in Calcutta—through, for instance, the crying leper—seemed to me, for a time, final, too. It was as though in Calcutta I had confronted the Lazarus of Andreyev.

But, gradually, I somehow managed to resume travelling and working. While knowing that I could never again be free of Calcutta, in time I came to realize that the leper was one India in "the hundred Indias" that I passed in the streets, one theme in the many that my journey introduced and developed in my mind. Now, as I continue my explorations, old refrains, figures, and phrases return, and are picked up and restated, in a dissonant crescendo of leaden tones against golden tones.

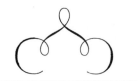

Enclave: "Few Ways of Life Can Equal the Goan in Merriment and Mad Abandon"

GOA, THE FIRST WESTERN FOOTHOLD on the Indian subcontinent and the last of the colonial possessions here to be relinquished, is a triangle of land nearly sixty-five miles long and about thirty-seven miles across at its widest point. It lies some two hundred miles south of the city of Bombay, along the coast of the Arabian Sea, on the slopes of the Western Ghats. It is wedged between the states of Maharashtra and Mysore. With Daman and Diu, two tiny Portuguese settlements north of Bombay, Goa formed the Portuguese empire in India from 1510, when the Portuguese soldier Affonso de Albuquerque took it for the Portuguese crown, until 1961, when the Indian Army marched into Goa and "liberated" it. A year later, Goa, Daman, and Diu together were designated a self-governing Union territory. Now Goa, which has a population of about six hundred and fifty thousand, is considered to be more "European" than any other part of India; one out of every three Goans is Christian, one out of every three speaks Portuguese—the mother tongue of Goa is Konkani—and educated Goans pride themselves on being as fluent in English as Indians anywhere. I decide to indulge myself in a little European holiday in India, and look through some travel literature on Goa. The brochures describe the place as "a land of rolling green hills and paddy fields, palm-fringed lakes and waterfalls," "a veritable garden of exotic fruits and plants and flowers rivalled in colour only by the vivid dress of the friendly people," "a rippling playground of water." One booklet claims that Goa is "as picturesque as the rugged Aegean Islands of Greece and the Dalmatian Coast of Yugo-slavia, the ancient villages of England, the enchanting Channel Islands off France, and the magnificent Costa Brava in Spain." "Impenitent individuals though the Goans are, they like to gang together and have their fun," says a foreword to a book of humorous drawings entitled "Goa with Love," by Mario Miranda, a *Times of India* caricaturist (he signs his drawings Mario). The foreword goes on, "More than anything, they seem to want to be amused; indeed does not the whole of Goan life seem to be one whirl of excitement? . . . And few ways of life can equal the Goan in merriment and mad abandon."

Today, in Panjim, Goa's capital, which is a resortlike city on the River Mandovi, I am dining at the Hotel Mandovi with a colleague of Mario's, Chinu Panchal, who covers Goa for the same paper. The menu:

ASPARAGUS SOUP

= ! =

FISH À CAPRICE

OR

PRAWN BALACHAO

= ! =

CHICKEN MASSALA TANDURI
POTATOES—VEGETABLES

OR

ROAST WILD DEER
ROAST POTATOES
VEGETABLES

= ! =

MILLES FEUILLES

OR

FRESH PINEAPPLE

= !! =

COFFEE

Wine, contraband through much of India, is readily available here, and Chinu and I are soon dining on venison and drinking a Bordeaux.

"Panjim is a dead place," Chinu says, with exaggerated solemnity. "It is scarcely alive in the daytime. By eight in the evening, it's as dead as if there were man-eating tigers on the streets. In the three months I've been here, you might say I've been carrying on an investigation of why this is so. I've reached a conclusion: The Portuguese rulers felt that if they allowed their Goan subjects to go out after dark, they would have bad thoughts."

I think of the famous beaches in and around Panjim—Donha Paula, Gaspar Dias, Calangute, Vegator, and Caisua—and remark to Chinu that I'd like to go swimming in the Arabian Sea.

"You won't find many people here going into the water," he says. "People here are not much interested in getting wet. A Goan goes to the beach as if he were going to a party—in a suit and tie, a felt hat, and his best Bata-made shoes. What Goans like about the beach is the idea of going there and seeing one another. Goans love to dress up, and people in Goan high society give formal buffets with music—practically every Goan plays the violin—as if they were living in nineteenth-century Vienna. The young Goan socialites will go to a dance with their parents, and during the dancing a boy and girl may flirt a little. The following Saturday night, the boy will go serenading under the girl's window, and perhaps sing a *fado*. You see, Goans think they are very Latin."

The summer house of Marcelino da Lima Leitao, where I am drinking Coca-Cola this morning with a couple of Goan political chiefs, is on a hilltop covered with black rock and swept by sea breezes. My host is tall and dark, with a thin mustache, and his wife is small and slim, with a pointed face. She is dressed in a frock, like a European woman, and has her hair pulled back with a ribbon. My fellow-guest is Dr. Jack de Sequeira, a large man, dressed all in white, with black hair and a bushy white beard, which he playfully fondles, now and again covering his mouth with it.

"Nothing can be done here until we settle the main issue in Goan politics, the question of Goa's status in the Indian Union," Mr. Leitao is saying energetically. "For administrative convenience, some Indians want to merge Goa with Maharashtra. The Maharashtrawadi Gomantak Party, which has a majority in our Legislative Assembly, leans toward this idiotic policy. But we United Goans, as the opposition party, stand for a separate and enlarged, Konkani-speaking state of Goa, which would take in parts of Maharashtra and Mysore."

"Mr. Leitao founded the United Goans and is still its moving spirit," Dr. Sequeira tells me. "He didn't stand for election to the Legislative Assembly, because, like Gandhi, he wants to stay above party politics."

"My wife stood instead, and won," Mr. Leitao says. "I intend to continue as a kingmaker in Goa's next election—especially south of the River Zuari, where we United Goans are a force to reckon with."

I ask why it is so important for Goa to be a separate state.

"We Goans are very, very different from Indians," Mrs. Leitao says passionately. "Our music, our folk dances, our dress, our food are all different. We are not accustomed to living on one chapatti and a few chilies a day. We want a full plate of rice and curry at lunch and another one at dinner. Our behavior is more sophisticated and more Westernized. If we were merged with Maharashtra, we would lose our individuality. Maharashtrians are very aggressive people. They have expansionist ideas, and they think that Maharashtra is a law unto itself."

"We want to preserve our distinctive, romantic, easygoing Goan character," Mr. Leitao says.

Dr. Sequeira suddenly brushes a mosquito from his beard. " 'Down with the mosquitoes!' has been my fighting cry at the Legislative Assembly," he says. "The government sprays with DDT, but it does no good. Our drains are defective, our water pipes are defective, septic tanks are few and far between. What we are going to have in Goa is a mosquito raj."

One evening, Chinu and I drive to the nearby village of Mardao to have a drink at Signor Marques's bar, a favorite haunt of the Goan cognoscenti. Marques's bar is a small room dimly lit by oil lamps. It has a low ceiling with wooden rafters, and green walls, which are hung with religious pictures and family photographs. There are a couple of marble-topped tables and about a dozen wooden chairs. At one side of the room, a narrow, open staircase, its steps littered with empty bottles, leads to an upper story. On the floor, there are crates of Coca-Cola and, around them, cigarette stubs, ashes, bits of paper, cockroaches. In one corner, under a mirror and a couple of shelves of medicine, is a high, square table crowded with bottles of spirits and wines. Stationed by this table is a tall, plump man with a shock of uncombed gray hair, a stubble of some days, narrow eyes, and a big grin, which shows that many of his teeth are missing. An amulet hangs from a chain around his neck. Now and again, he mixes drinks for the few people who are in the room or pulls banknotes out of his pockets and riffles through them. He is Signor Marques.

We order a round of drinks. As we are sipping them, a small, elegant man whom Chinu introduces as Pythagoras, a wine merchant, joins us. "Before the Indian Army marched in and 'liberated' us, there was no limit to the wines and spirits I could import," Pythagoras says, with the soft "d"s and "t"s that I have come to associate with Goans speaking English. "Now wines and spirits have been taxed out of the market, and it's difficult to get a license to import them."

"In the good old days," Marques says, entering the conversation from his corner, "House of Lords, House of Peers, very cheap. Queen Anne, Old

Smuggler, only nine rupees. For eleven rupees, Johnnie Walker, Haig & Haig, White Horse. First-class beer: Beck's, from Germany; St. Pauli, from Switzerland; Amstel, from Holland; Gloucester, from England, and Guinness stout, from Ireland; Asahi, from Japan. In the old days, so many wines—Portuguese wine, Fererina wine, port wine Numbers One, Two, Three, Four, Five. And W Special, best imported brand. And VV, the best in its company's line. Now duty on a bottle of table wine is twelve rupees. In the old days, wine *tinto, vino blanco,* Lagoste, champagne. Brandy— Castolan, Remy Martin, Hennessy. Now India making Beehive brandy, trying to ape the foreigners."

"That's the price of freedom and progress," Chinu says.

Pythagoras throws out his neat hands and shakes his head.

"Marques still runs a very good bar," says a young man, joining us. He is pleasant-looking and has a trimmed black beard. He turns out to be Mario Miranda himself. "You'll still find swingers flying down from pro-hibition-cursed Bombay just to wet their whiskers here."

Mario enters into conversation with a lean, animated man at the next table, and *he* turns out to be Hugh de Souza, the editor of *A Vida,* which, with three thousand readers, is the main Portuguese-language paper in Goa.

We have another round.

"Goans still have special importing privileges for some items, and they exploit them fully," Chinu says. "The number of Seven O'Clock razor blades imported from England each year is enough to shave all the Goans for the next century."

More rounds follow. Everyone in the bar joins in the conversation, and the connection between remarks becomes more and more obscure.

"The colonizers thought it was their mission to eat, drink, and be merry, and at one time Goans offered them their women as a matter of course. Now there are so many half-breeds."

"When the Portuguese first got here, the Goans who resisted conversion to Christianity had their hands cut off or were roasted alive."

"But what is 'liberation'? Indian majors came and pounced on our transistors. The Indians abolished our fortnightly lotteries and our system of compulsory night duty for taxis."

"Nowadays, a junior clerk requires a dowry of at least three thousand rupees and a doctor or lawyer thirty thousand and upward, which means that the girls here are going unmarried."

"My favorite Goan club is Casco. It rhymes with 'Moscow.' "

"All the dancing girls are gone from our temples, but does that mean our temples are any more holy?"

The lamps sputter and start going out.

"In the old days, we having the best German lamps in Goa," Marques says. "Nowadays, only local lamps. No good. So many brands, but none of them giving satisfaction. These local lamps not got even one moment's life. Hopeless. Always giving much trouble. Wick burning down, we having to light it again, but we having to wait to get the glass cold, so the customer having to wait in the dark for half an hour. When we lighting it—*phudk,* they falling off the wall like melons. That time no light, this time no light."

I wake from an afternoon nap in my room at the newly constructed Tourist Hostel in Panjim. It is suffocatingly hot, and the room is full of the whine of mosquitoes. I find that the fan overhead has gone dead. I try the radio beside my cot. Nothing happens. I turn on the tap in the washbasin. There is only a whoosh of air. I call for a bearer. No one comes. I go down to the little office of the hostel. There is no sign of the clerk. The few guests at the hostel are standing around talking excitedly. I learn that the clerk, the cook, the bearers, and the sweepers have all gone home, that there is no water, no electricity, no ferry or taxi service, and that newspapers, hospitals, workshops, post offices, and hotels have all shut down. Everything has come to an abrupt standstill, for there is a general strike on in Goa.

According to the guests, the government and the strike leaders are busy passing out handbills and trading insults. The government has declared the strike illegal and has set in motion the machinery to restore essential services in Goa by calling in the Army; the strike leaders have excoriated the government for reneging on promised wage increases; the government has said that the country's economy is in recession and everyone must bear with a period of hardship; the strike leaders have said that the workers are in no mood to go back to their jobs and that the general strike is an omen of things to come in all of India.

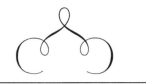

City: "Only Four Annas on the Mat"

"WE WERE ANCHORED IN THE HARBOUR of beautiful, sun-girt Bombay," begins a Victorian description by Sir George W. Forrest of the most famous city on the Arabian Sea. "The fishing boats, with their large brown lateen sails, were gliding away. . . . Steamers and brigs, and Arab dhows, with their broad, raised poops . . . are anchored before us; and not far from the dhows are two turret ships of ugly but imposing presence, meant to protect the gate of our Indian Empire. In the far distance rises into sight a well-wooded hill, and between it and a long spit of land lies the city of Bombay, whose towers and domes soar clear in the serene and transparent air." Today, the Taj Mahal, a grand, air-conditioned hotel on the harbor of this forked peninsula, stands as a typical Indian monument to the splendor of the Empire: the British architect who designed the hotel intended it to face the harbor, but, by a queer accident, the Indian workers who executed his design transposed the plans, so that the hotel, though it is on the water, faces the street. At the Taj Mahal, I have found refuge from another Bombay, whose decaying tenements and mud hovels lie huddled and choked in the chaos of the modern commercial city that serves as the capital of the state of Maharashtra.

A correct elderly man enters my room at the hotel. "Salaam, Sahib, I am your winebearer," he says. He has a serviette over one arm and carries a silver tray on which are arrayed a bucket of ice, a wineglass, a corkscrew-*cum*-bottle opener, and, incongruously, a bottle of beer. Putting down the tray, he swishes the bottle around in the ice and, as if he were serving wine, wraps it in the serviette, opens it, and pours a few foaming drops into the wineglass for me to taste. "There is prohibition here in Maharashtra," he says, "but a calling is a calling, and no one can take it away. Imported black-market wine is hard to get, so I serve the guest-sahibs imported black-market beer."

I taste the beer and thank him, and he withdraws.

Wherever I go in Bombay, the question of prohibition comes up in one form or another, as if it were the main concern here. Though the Indian Constitution directs all the states to "endeavor to bring about prohibition of the consumption except for medicinal purposes of intoxicating drinks," each state has its own intricate laws on drinking, and Maharashtra is one of just three states that have legislated total prohibition. The only way anyone in the state can obtain a drink legally is by appearing before a medical board and satisfying it that he cannot live without intoxicants. He is then certified as an alcoholic and issued a permit that allows him to buy from licensed shops for alcoholics twelve bottles of beer or one bottle of spirituous liquor a week. Although this procedure has recently been liberalized—with a testimonial from a family doctor, anyone over forty can receive a permit—and the weekly quota has been raised by fifty per cent, the only escape from prohibition for most poor people is still cheap liquor produced by illicit distillers and sold at black-market shops and speakeasies. These places have proliferated in dry areas throughout the country, and especially in Bombay, which is the center of the illicit-liquor trade, as I discover for myself one evening when a friend who is a Bombay *bon vivant* meets me at the Taj Mahal and takes me on a tour of illicit night spots.

The first speakeasy we visit is a clean, well-lighted place nearby. The proprietor is an Afrikaner from Capetown. "My booze is the best in Bombay," he says, serving my friend. "The very best. I get it from good distillers, and good distillers know their fermentation. They let nature take its course." My friend samples the Afrikaner's distillate and pronounces it "soda water."

Our next stop is a little loft over a tenement. It is called Auntie's, and it has tables and benches, a tub, and a kerosene stove, on which a pot simmers. In one corner, there is a crib, in which a baby is crying, and, beside it, a crèche bearing the inscription *"Gloria in Excelsis Deo."* The proprietor, who is a woman trailed by three or four children, throws a towel over the crib to muffle the cries of the baby, washes a glass in the tub, and brings the glass over to us, along with a jar of chalky liquid.

My friend pours himself a drink and tosses it down. "Almost, but not quite. No fire," he says.

We go through a spiderweb of streets and alleyways to the back of another tenement. My friend approaches a dark, barred window, taps out a signal, and thrusts a rupee note through the bars. A few moments later, the neck of a brown milk bottle appears between the bars. My friend kneels quickly under the window and opens his mouth. There is a jerk of the bottle, and a thick brown liquid splashes into his mouth. "This is it!" my friend exclaims contentedly. "This is the real stuff!"

The subject of the production and consumption of alcoholic beverages is one of the most divisive political issues in the country, mostly because of a campaign for national prohibition that has long been waged by Gandhians, who are found in all parts of India, and who are an important force in Indian politics and in the ruling National Congress Party. In Gandhi's mind, the achievement of national prohibition was bound up with the realization of his lifelong dream—freedom for the so-called untouchables from the religious, social, and economic taboos that had always kept them at the bottom of Hindu society. Drinking was most widespread among the untouchables, and Gandhi felt that it was one more hindrance to their advancement. He often expressed himself strongly on the question of prohibition, saying, "The drunkard forgets the distinction between wife, mother, and sister," and "I would rather have India reduced to a state of pauperism than have thousands of drunkards in our midst. I would rather have India without education if that is the price to be paid for making it dry," and "If I was appointed dictator for one hour for all of India, the first thing I would do would be to close without compensation all the liquor shops . . . compel factory owners to produce humane conditions for their workmen and open refreshment and recreation rooms where these workmen would get innocent drinks and equally innocent amusements," and "I hold drink to be more damnable than thieving and perhaps even prostitution. Is it not often the parent of both?" And so on.

I spend some time talking with state Ministers, prohibitionists, and social workers.

My first encounter is with Dr. Rafiq Zakaria, Maharashtra's Minister of Urban Development. He lives in a fashionable area of Bombay, in a large, light bungalow decorated in modern style, with bold colors. I am sitting with him on a spacious upstairs veranda, which is cooled by a mild wind from the sea. Zakaria, who is having a breakfast of cornflakes, French toast, and mangoes, has a square face, with a dimple in each cheek, and wears glasses with heavy frames. Three children, all young and well-behaved, are playing on the floor of the veranda, supervised by Mrs. Zakaria, who is a little chubby, and who has a pretty, young-looking face, with round eyes and a charming smile, and long black hair that swings down to her hips in a plait. "By and large, the members of the Cabinet believe in liberalizing prohibition," he tells me when the subject comes up in our conversation. "If prohibition were lifted today throughout India, we could realize from twenty to forty crores of rupees in liquor revenues in Maharashtra alone within a year, and from two hundred to four hundred crores in the country as a whole. But there is still a powerful section of the Congress Party that favors prohibition, because of Gandhi and the history of drinking among the untouchables and the other backward classes."

My second encounter is with Maharashtra's Minister of Prohibition, who is himself a Gandhian and comes from a backward class, and who receives me in a large, dingy office. He tells me, "If we ever abolish prohibition in Maharashtra, we'll become like the corrupt Westerners—drink, wear promiscuous cowboy pantaloons, become the slaves of the drunken Americans."

My third encounter is with a social worker from the Prohibition Department—a middle-aged woman named Maltee Tendulkar, who has published a prize-winning essay, "Drink, the Devil." It opens with this epigraph, which is fairly typical of the tone of the piece:

First Sip is last leap from Death Cliff,
Such is alcohol the curse on humanity,
Invites sorrow, misery, and untold grief,
Enters blood and disrupts the gravity . . .
Billions are dead and millions dying,
Battles are lost and Empires vacated,
While regiments of addicts denying
Sobriety for Victory but get craving placated.

She explains how the social workers in her department go about the task of lifting "the curse on humanity" from Maharashtra. "We in the Prohibition Department go from town to town, village to village, and find out which homes are worst hit by drink," she tells me. "In the daytime, we seek out the women and talk with them about their troubles. We ask them why their husbands don't bring home all their earnings, why they aren't saving money, why their husbands beat them. Finally, we confront them with the fact that their husbands are drunkards. At first, the women deny it. But after a while they admit the truth. In the evening, we attack the men themselves. Ninety per cent of them usually feel guilty about drinking anyway, and we begin with the guilt. We lecture them on how drink is the source of all evil, how it destroys the body, the mind, and the home. We tell them drink raises the blood pressure, addles the brain, and makes people go insane and die. We tell them it gives people cancer of the throat, cancer of the lungs, cancer of the liver. We teach them Marathi songs." Suddenly, in a high-pitched, cracking voice, she sings:

"Drink is the seductress
That breaks up the marriage.
Drink is the locust
That eats up the harvest.
Drink is the fire
That cremates the father.
Drink is the plague
That swallows up the home."

I am riding toward Bombay in a suburban train. A well-dressed man sitting next to me takes a flask and a brass cup from an attaché case and pours himself out a peg of Scotch whiskey. I express surprise. He introduces himself, and I learn that he is a highly placed politician.

"The public is against prohibition," he tells me, over the din of the train. "The law just can't be enforced, even though most of our policemen spend most of their time pursuing the offenders. After a man has spent a long day at work under our terrible conditions, he is going to drink. But under prohibition he has to drink poison, and the moonshiners and bootleggers who make it and sell it ride around in big cars. True, prohibition was Gandhi's dream. Great men have great dreams, but we lesser mortals have to ask the practical question of whether the dream lends itself to administration. Anyone who looks at the government's Report on Prohibition will know what I mean."

The Report, which is very much in the news just now, is the result of several years of travel, inspection, and collection of oral and written testimony by a team that the central government appointed in 1963 to review the administration of prohibition throughout the country. The team noted, among other things, that from ancient times Indians had produced and consumed a variety of liquors, fermented from rice, barley, millet, sugar, and cashew; that there had always been a native toddy industry, toddy being a drink made from the sap of palm trees—palmyra, coconut, date, and sago—which grow all over India; and that, in fact, there had always been a caste of toddy-tappers, whose occupation had consisted of drawing sap from the palm trees, fermenting it, and selling it in toddy shops. The team reported that in dry areas people were now drinking such forms of intoxicants as colognes, after-shave lotions, nose drops, and paint thinners, and concoctions prepared with such adulterants as spirits of ammonia, tincture of opium, and chloroform, and that in all the slums of these dry areas illicit stills had been set up. (In one slum area, four hundred and eighty-seven illicit stills were operating within a one-mile radius.) The operators of these stills were preparing their mash from such ingredients as rotten fruit and nuts, and to speed up the process of fermentation they were using, in place of yeast, such chemicals as sulphuric acid, ammonium chloride, and copper or ammonium sulphate, or such other substitutes as rancid meat and fish, frogs, lizards, and cockroaches. The distillers, to avoid detection, often hid vessels of fermenting mash in manholes and cesspools, or under the slaughtering platforms of tanneries; they boiled the fermented mash in a cheap and easily assembled contraption consisting of, at the least, a couple of earthenware jars connected by a bamboo section, or, at the most, kettles, copper tubing, and storage drums; and they collected the condensed vapor and fusel oil. Although the first draught of this distillation might be drinkable, subsequent draughts increasingly acquired the impurities, sometimes lethal, of the original mash. The distillate was then poured into bicycle or automobile inner tubes or football bladders and given to carriers. These carriers were likely to be either women, who wore the inner tubes and bladders under their clothes, simulating pregnancy, or lepers, who travelled with impunity because they were so feared that even the police left them alone. The distillate was taken to black-market shops and speakeasies, where it was sold to customers as "snake juice." The illicit-liquor trade had become a huge business, because, with an investment of a few rupees, the moonshiners and bootleggers could gather hundreds of rupees in profits, and, meanwhile, in the words of the Report, "the consumer neither bargains nor bothers to know whether the liquor he has been purchasing has been for days concealed under layers of excrement . . . or has been made from a wash [mash] to which have been added poisonous and putrid substances." Even though all the evidence in the Report seemed to point to the need for repeal of prohibition everywhere, the Report, in its conclusion, called for total national prohibition, partly on historical grounds; it attributed all the great disasters of history —including the premature death of Alexander the Great and the fall of his empire, the collapse of the Maginot Line, and the American defeat at Pearl Harbor—to the effects of alcohol.

"Prohibition is another of those lost causes to which the Indian government is always dedicating itself," a Bombay journalist says to me in the course of an evening walk. "Instead of tilting at windmills, the government ought to spend a little time on the streets chasing the true criminals." He leads me into a narrow street. On either side are rows upon rows of sleeping figures, who belong to Bombay's homeless poor. Some are on rattan mats and are covered, others on bare ground and all but naked. We pass someone covered from head to toe with a white sheet, like a corpse, then two thin children sleeping in each other's arms, then a young couple taking shelter in a doorway. The woman draws back into the doorway, crying. The man crouches passively. The street is lined with little tenement houses, all of which have curtained windows, and from each tenement comes the sound of a voluptuous *raga* or, jarringly, Western mood music interrupted by announcements from the Voice of America or the B.B.C. Barkers move up and down the street, calling after passersby or catching at their sleeves. They shout, "House Number Two! *Nautch* and *ragas!*" "Number Ten! Best Anglo-Indians!" "Number Fourteen! Japanese, Burmese, Ceylonese!" Ahead is an open, curtainless window, which reveals a brightly lit square parlor. A number of girls dressed in blouses and petticoats are seated on benches along the walls. A fat woman in her early forties with a bunch of keys tucked into the waist of her sari sits at a desk by the window. "Come in! Come in!" she calls out to us. "Our house has a good name for fun all over Bombay. This is a first-class house. All my girls have studied in convents. My girls are blessed."

We walk through more streets—passing tenements checkered with yellow light, stalls crowded with tins of *ghi* and baskets of sweetmeats, areas along the roadside where venders cook and sell food—assaulted by the sounds and smells of the close, sleepless Indian night.

"A Congress politician owns all the tenements in the street we just left," the journalist says. "He owns all the girls who live in them, too. He has an agent who manages the business and pays protection money to the police. The agent is in league with a gang that roams the streets, covers the railway stations and bus depots, and makes forays into the villages in search of fresh supplies of good-looking girls. Sometimes the girls are no more than nine or ten, and the gang will buy them from their parents for a small sum. If the girls are older, the gang will lure them with promises of jobs as nurses or maids. Once they get the girls, they hand them over to the agent, who installs them in the tenements, which are managed like forced-labor camps. Every day, the girls are made to work for as many hours as they can physically endure it. Every night, a couple of men in the pay of the agent come with nightsticks and take away most of what they earn. The girls are made to live four to a room, to cook for themselves, to make and wash their own clothes, and to buy whatever they need within the confines of the street, where the politician owns a few shops that sell all the necessities—everything from saris to *ghi* and tobacco. The girls can never escape. The agent, the police, and the gang see to that. Once, some of these girls joined with others in the city to try to form a union of prostitutes to protect themselves from the profiteers. They sent a petition to the Prime Minister in Delhi, who forwarded it to the Home Minister, who forwarded it to some Congress politicians in Bombay. These politicians happened to be the very profiteers from whom the prostitutes were trying to protect themselves. Naturally, nothing came of the petition. Whether one goes to a house where a fair-skinned young girl charges fifty rupees for a night and receives her customer in a bedroom or whether one goes to a street where a dark-skinned old woman sells her body for a few annas and receives her customer in a stall, one is swelling the income of one profiteer or another."

We turn into a long, narrow, noisy, crowded street. Set back on either hand, alongside open drains, are stalls—or cages, as they are called—with tall, hinged grilles giving on the street. In the front part of each cage are a primus stove, some tin water buckets, enamelled washbasins, earthenware water jars, and a few brass pots and pans; on the floor is a rattan mat, and on the walls hang a few little mirrors, or pictures of Hindu gods and goddesses or of Gandhi and Nehru. In the back part of the cage are a couple of cots, half concealed by dirty gauze curtains, and a cubicle, often with a warped door, that serves as a lavatory. Inside the cages are Punjabi, Madrasi, Bengali, and Maharashtrian women, who press against the grilles, posing, boasting, cajoling, begging, insulting, cursing, hissing, coughing, and spitting. Occasionally, there is a young girl, with ribbons plaited into her oiled hair, and dressed in new, gaudy clothes covered with glittering sequins and spangles, but most of the women in the cages wear faded clothes and have dark or sallow pockmarked faces stained with betelnut juice and painted with kohl and rouge.

"Didn't your mother teach you any manners?" one of them calls out. "Come here! Only six annas on the cot! Only four annas on the mat—special rate!"

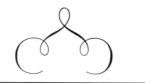

Arts: "'Om' on the Infant's Tongue"

SINCE POPULAR, COMMERCIAL FILMS distributed throughout the country are viewed by more people than films shown anywhere else, Indian film stars exert a greater influence over the lives of more people than any other entertainers in the world. The films are usually romantic or religious melodramas, and the Indian fan magazines tend to present their subjects as gods in human form, glamorous beings whose incarnations are governed by the special fate of poignant struggle and magical success, and whose existence is pervaded by an atmosphere of sex and mysticism. Here, for example, is Sunil Dutt, one of the most ardently worshipped of the stars, telling his life story in an issue of *Filmfare*:

> Long, long ago, my parents were married. Time passed. On a hot day when the sun was at its zenith, when anxiety, hope, and expectations of the household had reached the pitch, a child was born. It was my parents' first-born and they called him Balraj. The grandmother, a woman of great faith, dipped a knitting needle in honey and inscribed the word *"Om"* on the infant's tongue. Her hope was that the child should taste the sweetness of success throughout his life. . . . Balraj went through a hard period of struggle, suffered privations, tasted the bitterness of ambitions being thwarted. At last there came a thaw in the cold frustration and aimlessness. Balraj shed his frustrated self to become Sunil Dutt. The end of Balraj's struggles saw the birth of Sunil Dutt.

A tableau comes to mind from a visit I once made to a film studio in Madras: Half a dozen small, dark men who are dressed in nineteenth-century British Army costumes lounge around outside a studio building. A couple of other men are carrying a painted backdrop through the doors of the building. Inside, in a room with bright-blue walls on which hang cheap commercial calendars, sticks of incense burn in front of a statue of Lakshmi, goddess of money. This is the office of the general manager of the studio. He is a thin, dark man with a long red mark painted from his hairline to the bridge of his nose, and he is haggling about the price of processing film with another dark man, who is boiling water with an immersion coil. In another room, with bright-pink walls, one man is sitting at a dressing table with strong lights, another on a broken-down plastic-covered sofa. The man at the dressing table has thick, wavy black hair, a narrow mustache, and a dimpled chin. He wears a very tight, bright shirt, tight, bright trousers, scarlet socks, and pointed Teddy-boy shoes. The top buttons of his shirt are open, to expose his chest. He is M. G. Ramachandran, one of the great heroes of the southern screen. The man on the sofa is also in tight, bright clothes; he has his hair combed up in a pompadour. He is known simply as Nagesh, and is the greatest comedian of the southern screen. They are talking about their fees. Inside and outside the studio buildings, small, dark, thin men are making elaborate patterns on the floor or the ground with white powder—an ancient religious custom among orthodox Hindus in the south. That was some time back, in Madras, the center of the film industry in the south, but tonight I am in Bombay, the undisputed capital of the entire Indian film industry, at a dinner party given by R. K. Nayar, a young director who is the current sensation of Bombay cinema. Besides Sunil Dutt, several other ascendant stars are here. Sadhana Shivdasani is here. I. S. Johar is here. Sonia Sahni is here. Everyone is turned out in opulent clothes and dazzling jewels. We are all in the living room before dinner, sitting around an artificial fountain and drinking spiked lemonade. There is the smell of incense in the air. I am sitting between Johar, a stocky but good-looking comic actor, and Sonia Sahni, a beautiful Kashmiri ingénue, and Sonia is telling me how she and Johar first met.

"I was a coed at the university in Srinagar," she says. "One day, my girl friends and I heard that I. S. Johar was shooting a picture in Srinagar, and we went to watch."

"I saw Sonia looking on," Johar says. "She took my fancy right away."

"There was a shortcut to my house, but it involved climbing a four-foot wall," Sonia goes on. "I was used to that wall, and on my way home that day I climbed right over it. I happened to look around. There was Johar. I'll never forget the expression on his face. He was struggling to get his big stomach over the wall. I fell in love with him then and there, head over heels. Without even giving a thought to my B.A. finals, I followed Joharji to Bombay. But when I got here, I felt like such a hick. I started reading magazines on how to put on makeup, how to do one's hair, how to dress—how to look smart. I didn't even know how to make conversation, so I engaged a lady teacher to give me a course in conversational topics. Then Joharji got me into the films."

"Our film 'Goa' has made more money than practically any other Indian film," Johar says.

"Our film industry is the cruelest in the world," Sadhana says, joining us. She is a pretty, light-skinned Sindhi girl with large dark-brown eyes. "A while ago, word got out that I had a thyroid condition. Within two days, another actress was approached for my part. Maybe it is true what they say—that the only protection stars have is their black."

"Black is black money," one of the guests nearby explains. "You cannot bank black, because the whole point is to escape the taxes by not having any record of these earnings."

"The whole economy of Bombay would collapse without black," Johar says. "People have to spend it fast and spread it around, so they won't get caught with it. Many women turn black into diamonds and emeralds and wear them at secret 'black parties.' "

"Don't people get caught?" I ask.

"When someone does get caught, there's always a way out," Johar says. "Our society is built on bribes. Recently, the government found lakhs of rupees in an actress's house. It was in a false ceiling in her bathroom. But the case became such a legal tangle that the government and the actress just decided to split the bathroom black."

"The way to make the greatest amount of money is to produce one-man films—have one's own studio, be one's own writer, producer, director, and actor," Dutt says. "I produced a one-man film and it made a tremendous amount of money. But then I am a very popular actor in India."

"My last three films all had silver jubilees," Sadhana says. She goes on to explain to me, "A twenty-five-week run is a silver jubilee, a fifty-week run is a golden jubilee, a seventy-five-week run is a diamond jubilee, and a hundred-week run is a platinum jubilee."

India teems with languages. There are fourteen officially recognized regional languages, two hundred and fifty major dialects, and thousands of minor languages and dialects—some from the Indo-European language family, some from the Dravidian, some from the Sino-Tibetan, and some from the Austric, and many, therefore, completely unrelated to one another. English, which was the official language during the raj, has never been understood by more than three per cent of the population. The closest thing to a national language is Hindi, yet it is understood by only forty per cent—or, at most, fifty per cent—of the population. Most Indians can understand only one language—that of the place in which they were born.

Since Independence, the regional linguistic communities have become conscious of their separate languages. Each takes pride in its separate identity, and each is interested in studying its own language and developing its own literature. The few Indian writers who themselves write in English but can read the work of regional writers maintain that nearly all regional literature is the product of provincial jingoism, nurtured by propagandists and isolationists who consistently confuse literary adulation with critical evaluation. The many regional writers who write in their mother tongues but can read the work of those who write in English maintain that literature written by Indians in English is the product of a colonial outlook, nurtured by Anglophiles and neo-imperialists who give themselves airs. R. K. Narayan, an Indian writer from the state of Mysore who writes in English but reads Kannada, the language of his region, has said of the Indian writer K. V. Puttappa, also from Mysore, who writes in Kannada, and who is perhaps the best-known of the regional writers, "Puttappa's work may be as good as he thinks, or it may be quite ordinary. The regional languages as yet have no tradition of criticism in a modern sense, and someone whose work is confined to a regional language has no chance of measuring himself against standards of world literature."

Puttappa lives in the city of Mysore, the capital of the state, and I call on him at his home. He has a square face with a pointed chin and a wide smile, a white mustache, and white hair, which is parted in the middle and waves flat to the sides. He is dressed in a white *kurta* and white pajamas. The living room of his house, where he receives me, is quite bare, except for window curtains embroidered in variegated patterns, some with butterflies and others with flowers, and a pair of bookcases, one holding books in Kannada, the other books in English. Tiny, noiseless mango flies hover in the air.

I ask Puttappa what he thinks the future of the English language is in India.

He screws up his eyes. "The toadies say that English is a highly developed language," he says querulously. "But my sources inform me that it's no more so than Chinese, Russian, or our Sanskrit. If an Indian knows just a few words of English, he struts around in a suit and tie, like the

decadent Westerners." Puttappa gets up and strides around the room waving his arms, and suddenly seems transformed into a capricious, fairy-tale
tyrant. "I was Vice-Chancellor of Mysore University, and I know what a
dead weight English is in our universities," he says, sitting down again.
"Hardly anyone here really *knows* English anymore, yet it's retained as the
compulsory language of instruction in the Indian universities. There are
rolls and rolls of students who have failed simply because they didn't understand the language of instruction. When I succeeded in introducing
Kannada as a language of instruction for undergraduate work at Mysore
University, everyone laughed at me. But all the students who were taught
in Kannada passed, and seventy per cent of the students who were taught
in English failed. To make multitudes of students fail because they don't
know English—that is a crime against the Himalayas! We should all
study in our regional mother tongues."

"But if Indians cut themselves off from the English language, won't
they be cutting themselves off from a great deal of modern scientific
knowledge?" I ask.

"You obviously have the conception that our regional mother tongues
are inferior," he says, shaking a finger at me. "Maybe some of the regional
mother tongues are a little deficient at the research level. But not so at the
literary level. In fact, the truth is that English classics are improved by
being rendered into Kannada. I have electrified lakhs of Kannada readers
with my translations of 'The Pied Piper of Hamelin' and 'The Hound of
Heaven.' But Kannada classics can never be translated into English, because English can never convey their electricity."

I ask if the regional languages actually have a significant body of literature.

"It is true that some of the regional mother tongues had no classics until
a few years ago," he says. "But since then they have produced classics as
great as Dante or Milton, Wordsworth or Longfellow. I have studied Milton and Dante and Longfellow, and my poetry is superior to theirs, because my moral vision is Indian. The Indian moral vision has always been
greater than that of all other peoples, because we stand on the peaks of the
Himalayas, while the rest of the people in the world stand only on the tops
of houses. It will take the rest of the world five hundred years to achieve
the moral vision of our *rishis*. Ten Miltons together, drawing on an
English language with ten times its present vocabulary, could not have
produced even a few lines of my 'Ramayana Darshanam.' If I make this
statement to anyone who doesn't know Kannada, he guffaws. He guffaws
because he is ignorant."

I ask him if there are many contemporary Kannada writers.

"Yes, there are," he says. "One is in the field of novels, another in the field of social plays. I am in the blank-verse field."

I ask him how he first came to write in Kannada.

"When I entered college, in my nineteenth year, I had contempt for Kannada," he says. "The professors who taught in English came to the classroom wearing suits and neckties, but the *pandits* who taught in Kannada came in *dhotis* and *kurtas*. I had contempt for them. I became a great admirer of Wordsworth and Longfellow—I learned Longfellow's 'A Psalm of Life' by heart. I started writing poetry in English, but I changed over to Kannada when, as a student, I met the Irish poet James H. Cousins, who was visiting our university. I showed my poems to him, and he asked me why I didn't write my poems in my own mother tongue. I told him that English was the key to literary success. He said, 'You should not look down upon your own language. Tagore wrote in his own language, and look what great work he did.' I started studying Kannada with *pandits* in *dhotis* and *kurtas*. I have written about three thousand blank-verse lyrics in Kannada. I have written about fifty books. I have written one novel, which three Kannada critics have called the greatest novel ever written. 'Anna Karenina' is a little like it."

Puttappa goes on to recite, in an English translation by a translator known simply as Shyama, what Puttappa considers one of his best-loved satirical poems, "The Cuckoo and Soviet Russia," published under his nom de plume, Kuvempu. In this poem, the poet dreams that he has left Mysore far behind and is touring the Soviet Union. He finds that the entire country is one huge, perfect Socialist factory, where all living creatures are working with ideal efficiency. His attention is arrested by a wailing sound he hears in the utopia, and, looking around, he discovers that it is the cry of a cuckoo bird. He lends his ear to the bird, who complains that in the Soviet Union cuckoos must sit on their own eggs, because laying them in the nests of other birds would be parasitic, and also that they must keep their nests on the ground, because living in treetops would violate the utopian principle of equality and arouse the envy of all those below. The bird begs him to smuggle one egg out of the country and take it to Mysore, where cuckoos can still be their parasitic, lofty selves, with their own eccentric songs and ways. The poet obligingly slips one of the bird's eggs into his pocket and carries it back to Mysore. But in Mysore, as he is examining the egg, it mysteriously leaps out of his hand and breaks open on the ground. "'What did the egg produce?'" Puttappa finishes the recitation in a loud singsong. "'Not a cuckoo chick! No, not at all!/There popped out a Soviet spy and caught me!/What propaganda even in the cuckoo egg!'" Puttappa laughs heartily at his own poem. "Thousands upon thousands of Kannada readers have laughed and laughed over my 'Cuckoo,'" he says. "But a Russian who is compiling a Kannada-Russian dictionary wrote me a letter and said my 'Cuckoo' was a personal insult to him and to the Soviet Union. I wrote him back and told him I'd written a good few poems in praise of Lenin."

As I am leaving, Puttappa says, "My epic 'Ramayana Darshanam' is written in a totally new form, and no foreigner will be able to appreciate it for five thousand years. Foreigners do not have the Himalayan vision."

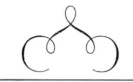

Religion: "We Don't Agree"

FROM A MAKESHIFT STAGE under a *shamiana* at Palam Airport, in New Delhi, a Sikh serving as master of ceremonies, who is dressed in yellow robes and a blue turban and wears a long, neatly groomed beard, calls out through a microphone in Punjabi, "Khalsa, shout with me! *'Vah guru ji ka Khalsa! Vah guru ji ki fateh!'* ["The pure are the chosen of God! Victory be to our God!"]" With him on the stage are Indian politicians and dignitaries, and all around the stage are *sirdars* and *sirdarnis* (Sikh men and women)—thousands, tens of thousands of them, a sea of beards and turbans, chignons and veils.

"*Vah guru ji ka Khalsa! Vah guru ji ki fateh!*" roars the crowd.

"In the name of the Prime Minister of India, in the name of the Home Minister of India, in the name of the Governor of the Punjab, shout with me, Khalsa, in greeting! *'Sat Sri Akal!'* ["True Timeless One!"]."

"*Sat Sri Akal!*" responds the crowd.

"Khalsa, it's after twelve. The airplane is due. Get ready to shout your greeting! Shout your greeting to the relics. Khalsa, be ready to shout *'Sat Sri Akal!'* so loudly that our voices will be louder than the engine of the plane and will reach the ears of the pilot. Be ready to shout off his ears!"

The airplane is bringing home the relics of Guru Gobind Singh (1666–1708), who was the last in a succession of ten Sikh *gurus,* and the crush here today is only a small part of a crowd that lines the route from the airport all the way to the center of the city. The arrangements for the welcoming reception about to get under way are set forth in an official program, in English:

12:20 P.M.

1. The relics will arrive at Palam Airport.

12:25 P.M.

2. They will be brought down from the plane by . . . officials in uniform.

12:25 P.M.

3. They will be received near the plane by the Prime Minister of India.

12:30 P.M.

4. They will be handed over by the Prime Minister to the Governor of Punjab at the same place.

12:35 P.M.

5. They will be carried by selected Panj Piaras ["five loved ones," who represent Guru Gobind Singh's first five disciples] to the *shamiana* in the airport grounds where V.I.P.s are generally received.

12:35 P.M.

6. Ninety Sikhs in uniform will provide a guard of honor for the relics.

12:40 P.M.

7. In the *shamiana* the relics will be placed on a platform.

12:40 P.M. to 1:15 P.M.

8. The Prime Minister, the Governor, and the Chief Minister of Punjab will make brief speeches, if they so desire.

9. The relics will then be in the charge of the Government of Punjab. That Government has arranged to carry them from the Palam Airport in a procession to the Rakabganj Gurdwara.

10. A military band will be in attendance at the airport and play suitable tunes at appropriate times.

11. An aircraft will shower petals on the relics while they are taken out of the plane and taken to the *shamiana*. (If the Delhi Flying Club, which has been requested, agrees to do so.)

The story of the return of these relics, according to notes in the back of the program, began in 1964, when Tara Singh, the greatest modern leader of the Sikhs, pressed the Indian government to undertake a search for Guru Gobind Singh's *kalgi tora*—a plume studded with semiprecious stones which was used as a turban ornament by princes. (Tara Singh's quest was part of a recent resurgence of interest among most of India's religious and ethnic communities in the mementos and records of their past.) For two years, the government searched the British Museum and the Victoria and Albert Museum for some trace of the Guru's plume, but wasn't able to locate it. The researchers discovered, however, that a number of weapons thought to have once belonged to the Guru—and therefore considered relics of the faith—had in 1849 fallen into the hands of James Andrew Broun Ramsay, the First Marquess of Dalhousie and Governor-General of India, when, after the Anglo-Sikh wars (1845-46 and 1848-49), he annexed to the territories of the East India Company most of the Punjab, then under the dominion of the Sikhs. The Marquess had subsequently written about the booty, in a letter to the East India Company's board of directors in London:

> It would not be politic . . . to permit any Sikh institution to obtain possession, either by way of gift (for the intrinsic value of them is insignificant) or by means of sale, of these sacred and warlike symbols of a warlike faith. If your Hon'ble Court should desire to have these arms for your collection, they shall be transmitted; but if your Hon'ble Court are not solicitous regarding them, I shall feel gratified by receiving your permission to purchase them . . . for myself. They have naturally much interest in my eyes; and would form a memorial which would hereafter be highly prized as well by myself as by those who may follow me.

The Marquess of Dalhousie had eventually been permitted to keep all the relics except one sword, which was placed in the Museum of the East India Company, in Madras, and in 1966 the Indian government, upon making inquiries, learned that some of these relics—two spears, two shields, a scimitar, and a golden quoit—were now in England, in the possession of a descendant of Dalhousie, Lady Edith Broun Lindsay. She agreed to restore them to the Sikhs.

Sikhism, which was founded by a Hindu reformer, Guru Nanak, in the fifteenth century—a period of strife, anarchy, and forced conversions of Hindus to Islam—has a long history of warlike traditions, especially since the time of Guru Gobind, who organized the Sikhs into a militant theocracy. The Guru initiated five of his disciples, the original Panj Piaras, into a casteless, martial fraternity, which he called the Khalsa ("the pure"). They were from different castes, but he made them all drink *amrit,* or nectar—stirred with a double-edged dagger—out of one bowl, and gave them the new Khalsa surname, Singh, which means "lion." He made each of them vow always to wear *kesh* (unshorn hair and unshorn beard), a *kanga* (comb), a *kara* (steel bracelet), a *kirpan* (sabre), and *kachha* (knee-length drawers), and laid down four rules of conduct for the Khalsa: never to cut or shave the hair anywhere on the body; never to use alcohol or tobacco; never to eat meat from animals slaughtered according to Muslim law; and never to take revenge on Muslims by raping their women. The Guru, proclaiming all Sikhs equal, asked to be received into the Khalsa himself, and after this had been done, he declared that

the succession of *gurus* was at an end and that the Granth, a compen-
dium of teachings, sayings, and hymns from the first five and the ninth of
the Sikh *gurus* (and from Hindu and Muslim saints as well), was the
personal, immortal *guru* of every Sikh. He hailed the Khalsa with the
words "*Vah guru ji ka Khalsa. Vah guru ji ki fateh.*" Within a few days,
eighty thousand followers and disciples had joined the Khalsa. (The word
"Sikh" is probably derived from the Pali *"sikha"* or the Sanskrit *"shishya,"*
either of which means "disciple.") Today, most Sikhs are members of the
Khalsa; those who are not follow Nanakpanthi, or Nanak's Way, concentrating on the peaceful teachings of Guru Nanak. The Sikhs, who at present number eight or nine million, have no official priesthood, all adults
being free to officiate at religious rites. Most of the Sikhs, men and women,
wear the five emblems—or the Five Ks, as they have come to be called
—and observe the rules of conduct of the Khalsa. Although Sikh theologians are still debating the precise significance of the emblems and the
rules, there is general agreement that Guru Gobind Singh intended the
Khalsa to be an army of soldier-saints to fight for righteous causes, that
some of the emblems may have been adapted from Hindu customs (Hindu
holy men wore long hair and beards, and Hindu soldiers wore a thread or
amulet around the wrist as a talisman in battle and knee-length drawers as
a basic uniform), and that the four injunctions were probably meant as a
rudimentary code for the soldier's way of life. Indeed, Sikhs refer to themselves in their writings as the Fawj, or army, and all men have the surname Singh (although not all Indians named Singh are Sikhs). All Sikhs
think and speak of the Granth as though it were a living spiritual instruc-
tor, popularly referring to the book as Guru Granth Sahib, or Sacha Pad-
shah ("true emperor"), taking the book out in processions, and venerating
it in a temple, which they call a *gurdwara* ("house of the *guru*"). In the
gurdwara, the Granth is exhibited daily with great ceremony; every morning it is wrapped in silks and placed on a divan under a canopy. Throughout the day, worshippers bring offerings of cash or kind, make their obei-
sances, and hear readings and chants from the Granth—readings that, on
occasion, continue for days or weeks.

Now, at the Palam Airport, the master of ceremonies is shouting again
and again, with mounting intensity, "*Sat Sri Akal! Vah guru ji ka Khalsa!
Vah guru ji ki fateh! Sat Sri Akal!*" The plane carrying the relics is about
to land, and lined up near the runway are elephants, camels, horses, and a
truck equipped with a revolving display case and a copy of the Granth—
all this being the regalia for the procession to the Rakabganj Gurdwara.

"Khalsaji, calm yourselves—sit down," the master of ceremonies is saying. "Don't be restless. Why don't you sit down, Khalsaji?"

A *sirdarni* in rich-looking *salwar* and *kameez* (Punjabi-style trousers and shirt) who is standing next to me moans, "But where is the Guruji's *kalgi tora?* The British have robbed our religion of the sacred *kalgi tora!*"

"The Prime Minister of India will soon be speaking to you," the master of ceremonies continues.

"What does the Prime Minister care about our relics?" the *sirdarni* cries. "The Prime Minister is here only to deceive the Khalsa. But no one is going to rob us of Punjabi Suba."

Suddenly the plane lands, and the crowd gives a deafening roar. *"Sat Sri Akal!"* everybody shouts as the plane taxis in.

Ever since the time of Guru Gobind Singh, the daily prayer of the Sikhs has included the chant *"Raj karey ga Khalsa"* ("The Sikhs shall rule"). For a while, after the decline of the Mogul Empire in the eighteenth century, the Sikhs did rule the Punjab, which they consider their homeland, but the British won it from them in the Anglo-Sikh wars. Thereafter, under the raj, the Sikhs, the Hindus, and a good many Muslims were united in the national struggle for independence, but when the Punjab was divided, in 1947, with East Punjab going to India and West Punjab to Pakistan, and widespread riots and religious massacres followed, the Sikhs, who, partly as a matter of self-protection, had all along opposed the formation of a Muslim nation, now demanded that part of East Punjab be made into a separate, Punjabi-speaking state, which they referred to as Punjabi Suba ("the province of Punjab"). Some of the more extremist Sikhs spoke of Punjabi Suba as a religious state that would be ruled by Sikhs, would have Punjabi as its official tongue, and, though formed as a state in the Indian Union, would function as an autonomous unit. More moderate Sikhs spoke of Punjabi Suba merely as a linguistic state that would be ruled by Punjabis—both Hindus and Sikhs. All Sikhs soon became fiery partisans of Punjabi Suba in one form or the other, but the Indian government tried to suppress the movement; some of the government officers contended that Punjabi Suba, whether based on religion or language, would mean a division of East Punjab into a Hindi-speaking Hindu state and a Punjabi-speaking Sikh state, and that this Sikh state might one day try to proclaim itself the separate nation of Sikhistan. They contended that East Punjab, with an area of about thirty-seven thousand square miles and a population of about twelve million, was a viable administrative unit just as it was, and that, in any case, the Punjabi-speaking people were not a distinct unilingual community, being also fluent in Hindi. The idea of another partition—this time forced by the Sikhs—with more riots, more massacres, and more refugees, was insupportable. In 1956, the Indian government, in response to agitation from other regional linguistic communities, divided and reorganized many of the old British provinces and princely states to reflect more accurately the distribution of these communities throughout the country and to give nearly every major linguistic community a state in which it enjoyed a majority or a preponderance. Thus, Telegu became the language of Andhra Pradesh; Assamese of Assam; Hindi and Bihari of Bihar; Gujarati of Gujarat; Kashmiri of Jammu and Kashmir; Malayalam of Kerala; Hindi of Madhya Pradesh; Marathi of Maharashtra; Kannada of Mysore; Oriya of Orissa; Rajasthani of Rajasthan; Hindi of Uttar Pradesh; Bengali of West Bengal. However, in order to preserve peace in East Punjab, the Indian government left it much as it was: a bilingual state, using both Hindi and Punjabi. The Sikhs felt that the Indian government had employed one standard for East Punjab and another for the rest of the country, and that discrimination against the language of the Sikhs was discrimination against the Sikhs themselves. They felt that the Indian government was in danger of being overrun by Hindu chauvinists intent on instituting a Hindu raj, in which the Sikhs would be converted to Hinduism and absorbed into an all-Hindu India. The Sikhs, as a small minority, would be in no position to put up resistance for long.

The idea of a Sikh-ruled Punjabi Suba had its strongest champion in Tara Singh, who was born of Hindu parents in 1885 and was converted to Sikhism in his teens. He started fighting for Sikh causes in the early nineteen-twenties, when he joined a Sikh movement to change the system of management of the Golden Temple, the most important temple of the Sikhs, which stands in Amritsar, the holy city of the Sikhs, in East Punjab, a few miles from the border of West Punjab. At that time, the temple was under the hereditary care of a group of devotees who had acquired the reputation of being in the power of local British administrators; indeed, in 1921 the resident British administrator had actually taken possession of the keys to the treasury of the temple, setting off a fierce Sikh struggle—first for the return of the keys and later for complete control of the management of all Sikh temples. The British, after battling the Sikhs for three years, had been compelled to pass the Sikh Gurdwaras Act in 1925. This act placed the management of all Sikh temples under an elected body of Sikhs called the Shiromani Gurdwara Prabandhak (Central Temple Management) Committee. Over the years, this committee grew into a kind of Sikh parliament, collecting tithes, and even maintaining a semi-military corps of volunteers, called Akali Dal, or Army of Immortals. Within the committee, Tara Singh from the very beginning led a faction that wanted to coöperate with the Indian National Congress Party for independence; another faction in the committee was interested only in the advancement of the Sikh community. Tara Singh's faction won control of the committee, and Tara Singh served off and on as its president, taking part in the civil-disobedience movement and occasionally going to jail. At the time of the Second World War, however, he began to drift away from the Congress Party, because he felt that it was being too indulgent to the Muslims and was neglecting the Sikhs. To the day of Partition, he resisted the formation of Pakistan. In fact, it was charged that the worst period of riots over Pakistan had been prompted by one of his speeches, in which he challenged the Muslims to a holy war, saying, "O Hindus and Sikhs! Be ready for self-destruction, like the Japanese and the Nazis. Our motherland is calling for blood, and we shall satiate the thirst of our mother with blood. We shall trample Pakistan. If we can snatch the government from the British, no one can stop us from snatching the government from the Muslims. We have in our grasp the limbs of the Muslim League, and we shall break them. Spread from now on the solemn affirmation that we shall not allow the League to exist. The world has always been ruled by minorities. The Muslims [Moguls and earlier Muslim conquerors] snatched the kingdom from the Hindus, and the Sikhs seized it from the hands of the Muslims, and the Sikhs ruled over the Muslims with their might, and the Sikhs shall even now rule over them. We shall rule over them and shall get the government by fighting. I have sounded the bugle."

After Partition, Tara Singh took up the cause of a Sikh-ruled Punjabi Suba. In a stream of tracts and speeches, he attacked the government for falsely professing secular ideals and for failing to protect the Sikh minority. In one typical compilation of grievances, he listed a number of recent Hindu insults to his religion:

1. In the last week of July, 1957, several cigarette cases were thrown into the sacred tank of the Golden Temple, Amritsar.

2. On the 31st of July, 1957, the sacred *keshas* of Ajit Singh, a boy of twelve years of age, were cut off while he was asleep, by one Baldev Raj, who was arrested, tried, and let off by the Magistrate on furnishing a security of good behavior for one year. . . .

4. Two cigarettes were sent to one Gurcharan Singh, Prop.: Kuldeep Cloth Store, Patiala, by post on 1st August, 1957. . . .

9. On 26.9.57, one Hindu, Nandi by name, put a burning cigarette on the head of a Sikh, Rawel Singh, at Kartarpur, District Jullundur.

And so on. In other tracts, Tara Singh listed such economic grievances as the difficulties that Sikh refugees who had gone to West Bengal in search of jobs as drivers encountered in obtaining government transport licenses.

In 1961, on the fourteenth anniversary of Independence, Tara Singh took a vow to "fast unto death" within the precinct of the Golden Temple unless the government granted a Sikh-ruled Punjabi Suba. Public fasts were the ultimate weapon of civil disobedience, and in the past the threat of such martyrdom had been used against the government, British or Indian, so successfully that the fasts had acquired what amounted to a fixed pattern: the statement of a political issue with great emotional content; the identification of the issue with an important leader; a well-publicized period of negotiations; the announcement of the date and place of the fast; the commencement of the fast, with growing crowds keeping vigil around the leader; and daily—sometimes hourly—bulletins on his health. Before matters reached a crisis, the government usually offered some sort of concession, on the theory that if the leader perished, the hostility of his followers would be such that order could be preserved only by totalitarian means. Tara Singh's fast followed the usual pattern, but the government did not capitulate, and after forty-three days Tara Singh, physically and spiritually worn down, gave up his fast. He was arraigned in the Golden Temple by the Shiromani Gurdwara Prabandhak Committee for breaking his vow and thus betraying the tradition of Sikh martyrdom, and was sentenced to clean the shoes of all the Khalsa who came to worship at the temple during a five-day period. He did his penance, but he was never quite able to regain his old authority over the Sikhs.

The offices and powers once reserved for Tara Singh were gradually assumed by his deputy—and later his adversary—Fateh Singh. Fateh Singh, who was born in 1910 or 1911 (no one seems to know exactly when) of Muslim parents, and, like Tara Singh, was converted to Sikhism in his teens, spent most of his life in relative obscurity, though he managed to make a small reputation by reciting hymns from the Granth and by helping in the construction of new temples. Fateh Singh emphasized the linguistic rather than the religious aspect of Punjabi Suba, and though the government maintained that his linguistic state was merely another version of Tara Singh's more extremist religious state, still, Fateh Singh's demand, because it appeared more reasonable, was harder to ignore. On the seventh and eighth of August, 1965, Fateh Singh discussed

Punjabi Suba with Prime Minister Shastri at a conference in New Delhi also attended by the Union Home Minister and other leading government officials. Arjan Singh Budhiraja, who accompanied Fateh Singh in the capacity of secretary, kept a record of the talks and subsequently published it. It is highly colored—Fateh Singh scores all the debating points, while Shastri and his companions sit wide-eyed and silent, registering surprise—but, all the same, the record, which reads like a playlet, captures an atmosphere quite typical of Indian political confrontations. One section goes:

Santji ["saint," meaning Fateh Singh]: When in other parts of India states have been formed on the basis of language, then what are the obstacles that stand in the way of Punjabi Suba? Our religion is not at all safe in free India. Do you not know that in the Punjab, at several places, the Holy Granth has been burnt? . . . There have also been instances of sacrilege at the Sarovar (Holy Tank) of the Golden Temple in which several packets of forbidden cigarettes were thrown. . . . Even Dr. Sushila Nayyar, the Health Minister of your Central Government, has outraged our religious sentiments.

Shastriji (*hurriedly*): What is that? Just tell me what she has done.

Santji: Dear Sir, please listen patiently. She said here in Delhi that in the days of the Sikh Gurus there were no barbers but now there was no dearth of them. . . . (*Stroking his beard*) Sushila Nayyar had looked down upon the Sikhs who grow beards and uncut hair. . . . She went even beyond this as she later said that Shri Guru Amar Das [the third *guru*] . . . was utterly negligent of his body and concluded that the Sikhs were a dirty lot. . . . Even Vinoba Bhave [a renowned disciple of Gandhi], whom you regard a saint and friend of all, has injured Sikh sentiments while speaking at Gurdwara Jagat Sudhar at Calcutta. He suggested the letter "n" be deleted from the word *"kirpan"* to make it *"kirpa"* (grace). Although he later on apologized for it through a letter, yet why should such malicious suggestions be made at all? What business have your leaders to meddle with our religion? This (*holding his* kirpan) is our religious symbol. . . .

Shastriji: We never heard of all this before. (*He kept looking at Santji in astonishment.*) . . . We could be willing to remove all your grievances to your satisfaction. . . .

Santji: Nothing but Punjabi Suba can delight my soul.

Punjabi Suba was not granted, however, and on August 29, 1965, Fateh Singh wrote, "I have determined my program. Publicly I will burn myself alive. . . . Let all the Sikhs pray for me by reciting the text of the Scriptures: 'O vacillating mind, be firm to resolve; the first step toward the fire has been taken. Now there is no release except through self-immolation.' "

Today I am in Amritsar to meet Tara Singh and Fateh Singh. "It's not very difficult to meet Master Tara Singh or Sant Fateh Singh," a friend says. (Tara Singh once taught in a Sikh school and has ever since been known as Master Tara Singh, and Fateh Singh has been known as Sant Fateh Singh ever since he gained a reputation as a Sikh divine.) The friend goes on, "There's no point in trying to reach Master Tara Singh on the telephone. He has a telephone, but he can't hear well enough to use it; he's eighty-one years old. But anyone can see him by going to his house. He sits and suns himself in his garden most of the day. Sant Fateh Singh has not yet announced the date on which he will burn himself for Punjabi Suba. He has taken sanctuary in the Golden Temple. If he comes out, he'll be arrested for causing political disturbances with his threats of self-immolation. There is only one way to see him. You have to telephone Arjan Singh Budhiraja at Kwality Papermart, the unofficial headquarters of high Sikh politics. Don't say anything to him about Master Tara Singh, because Master Tara Singh and Sant Fateh Singh have been at it hammer and tongs over their Punjabi Subas for years now."

I go to the house of Tara Singh, which is in a run-down part of the city, and find him sitting in a wicker chair by a smoky cooking fire in his garden. He looks very old and weather-beaten, but his beard is feathery and full, reaching down to his chest. "When the water for my bath is boiled, put out the fire!" he calls out in Punjabi to a servant. "And bring two glasses of tea—a plain one for my guest, and one with aniseed and licorice for me. And bring some glucose biscuits, too."

I ask him about his running feud with Fateh Singh.

"Sant Fateh Singh has become the stooge of the central government," he says. "He has betrayed the Sikh cause of a Sikh-ruled Punjabi Suba, even though the Sikhs are in danger of being seduced by Hinduism and losing their religious identity. For a Sikh, conversion to Hinduism has always been easy. All he needs to do is shave his beard and cut his hair. During the British times, there was no great temptation for a Sikh to become a Hindu, because we Sikhs enjoyed special privileges granted to minorities and were protected as a community. After Independence, the government did away with these special privileges, on the ground that the British system only perpetuated social divisions and that in a secular country there was no need for any special protection of minorities. Since then, there has been a rebirth of Hindu chauvinism, and now a Sikh is tempted to pass as a Hindu in order to find employment and get ahead. We must protect the Sikh, put a stop to the temptation to defile his religion. The only way we can do this is to form a Sikh-ruled Punjabi Suba, with the right of secession, in which the virile Sikhs can multiply and pull our community up, leaving the soft-fleshed Hindus to trail behind."

"What would happen to Hindus living in a Sikh-ruled Punjabi Suba?" I ask.

"Sikhs living in cities like Calcutta will just have to come to our cities, like Amritsar, and take over the property of these Hindus, and the Hindus living in our cities, like Amritsar, will have to move out," he says. "But creating the Sikh-ruled Punjabi Suba won't lead to a religious war, because we will exercise our right of secession only if we continue to be ill-treated by the Hindus."

"Santji has said everything that he feels needs to be said about his Punjabi Suba," Arjan Singh Budhiraja tells me when I telephone him. "But if you want to have a *darshana,* you can come to the Golden Temple, and I'll see what I can do."

I leave my shoes at an entrance to the precinct of the Golden Temple and walk across the cold marble courtyard. Straight ahead is the temple itself. It is made of carved marble, its domes and pinnacles covered with gold leaf, and it is surrounded by an artificial lake—the Sarovar—in which some of the Khalsa are bathing, with their *salwars* and *kameezes* and *kachhas* billowing around them in the water. To one side is a building called Akal Takht ("throne of the immortal One"), which houses relics of the *gurus* and serves as a meeting place for the Shiromani Gurdwara Prabandhak Committee. It looks like a small fortress. Budhiraja silently leads me through a pair of steel doors in one corner of the Akal Takht, up a spiral staircase, and into a little room, where Fateh Singh, who has a wavy white beard streaked with black, sits on a cot, wrapped in a blanket. Around him are several dishevelled, conspiratorial-looking followers with long *kirpans* hanging at their sides. At his right hand, however, stands a follower in a gray business suit.

"Be seated," Fateh Singh tells me, indicating an armchair opposite him. Fateh Singh looks rather heavy and pale. I ask after his health.

"I am living on *prasad,*" he says, in a mild voice. "If the government does not meet all my demands for Punjabi Suba, I will set fire to myself, as I have already declared."

I ask him if the Sikhs would be content to live permanently in India once a Punjabi Suba was formed. Would they feel protected as a religious minority?

"I want Punjabi Suba."

I put the question to him again.

The man in gray intervenes. "A foolish man asks a hundred questions and gets no answer, but a wise man asks one question and then waits and gets all the answers," he says.

My spirits drooping, I ask Fateh Singh what his self-imprisonment in the sanctuary is like.

"I wake up at three o'clock in the morning. I say some prayers. I have tea. I go back to sleep. I wake up again. I say some prayers. I have tea. I go back to sleep. I wake up again. I have tea. I talk to the Khalsa. I say more prayers. I go back to sleep. I wake up again. I write a bit. Then I go back to sleep."

Fateh Singh calls for some tea. From an adjacent room comes the monotonous sound of a hand pump being worked, and in due course tea is served to us in tall brass glasses. Fateh Singh drinks his tea, then lies back on his cot.

Khushwant Singh, the Sikh writer, whose recently published "A History of the Sikhs" is the most authoritative work on the subject since Captain Joseph Davey Cunningham's "History of the Sikhs," written more than a hundred years ago, argues that in India "the only chance of survival of the Sikhs as a separate community is to create a state in which they form a compact group, where the teaching of . . . the Sikh religion is compulsory, and where there is an atmosphere of respect for the traditions of their Khalsa forefathers." The second Indo-Pakistan war and the resulting tensions on the border between East and West Punjab made it urgent that India have the complete allegiance of the Sikhs, and in 1966 (soon after my encounters with Tara Singh and Fateh Singh) the Congress Party leaders conceded, in principle, a linguistic Punjabi Suba. They made it known that the area of East Punjab in which the Sikhs had a majority would become the new state of Punjab, and most of the area of East Punjab in which Hindus had a majority would become the new state of Haryana. (The remaining part of East Punjab in which Hindus had a majority would be annexed, chiefly for geographical reasons, to the Union territory of Himachal Pradesh.) This decision appeased the Sikhs but angered the Hindus throughout East Punjab. The Hindus living in the area now allocated to Haryana felt that the richest part of East Punjab would go to the Sikhs and that Haryana would be reduced to the role of poor relation, and the Hindus living in the area now allocated to the new Punjab felt that it would actually be a religious state, in which Hindus would be treated as second-class citizens. Religious riots followed. In one town in East Punjab, a Hindu mob trapped three Congress Party leaders in a local shop and burned them alive. Other acts of brutality followed, but late in 1966, in spite of the protests, the government went ahead and divided up East Punjab. The Hindu politicians of Haryana and the Sikh politicians of Punjab continued to battle, however—now over the city of Chandigarh, the capital of the former state of East Punjab. When the Punjab was originally divided between India and Pakistan, Lahore, its old capital, had gone to Pakistan, and Nehru's government had commissioned Le Corbusier, the French architect, to build a new capital—Chandigarh—for East Punjab. Le Corbusier, just before his death, in 1965, had been able to design the city (in collaboration with another French architect, Pierre Jeanneret, and two British architects, Maxwell Fry and Jane Drew) and to complete the main buildings—the Legislative Assembly, the High Court, and the Secretariat—and these public buildings were regarded by Hindus and Sikhs alike as symbols of new power, so now Haryana and Punjab both claimed Chandigarh as their capital. Yet the public buildings of Chandigarh could not be successfully partitioned or adapted to house two new governments, and the cost of building a second new capital was unthinkable. (Recently, I spent some time in Chandigarh, which was still under construction, with Philip Johnson, the American architect, and although, like others before us, we talked about the city in such terms as "artificial," "eccentric," "alien," and "unsuited to Indian conditions and needs," we still found ourselves admiring its monumental aspiration. Nehru had said when the city was first conceived, "Let this be a new town, symbolic of the freedom of India, unfettered by the traditions of the past.")

About a month and a half after the new states were formed, Fateh Singh, in order to secure Chandigarh—and also the recently built Bhakra-Nangal irrigation project nearby—for Punjab, began a "fast unto death" as a prelude to his threatened self-immolation. (Yogiraj Suryadev, a Hindu leader in Haryana, began a counter-fast to secure Chandigarh and the irrigation project for Haryana.) When Fateh Singh had fasted for nine days, seven of his disciples, who had been keeping watch over him, appeared on the balcony of the Golden Temple in saffron robes, ready to immolate themselves in sympathy with the self-immolation of Fateh Singh, set for the next day. Crowded around the Sarovar, the Khalsa were keeping vigil, brandishing *kirpans* and spears, and calling out *"Sat Sri Akal!"* Over a public-address system, a voice proclaimed, "The time is nigh. Pray to God, for only He can save our Khalsa brothers and our leader." On the roof of the Golden Temple, attendants were preparing ceremonial fires of scented woods and incense. Inside the temple, other attendants were preparing the fire in which the self-immolations were to take place. But a few minutes before the announced time of the self-immolation of the disciples an emissary from the Indian government, himself a Sikh dignitary, raced through the crowds, across the marble floor of the courtyard, and up the steps of the Akal Takht, and was admitted to the presence of Fateh Singh. The time set for the self-immolation of the disciples came and went. The attendants led the Khalsa in prayers, which continued until dusk. Finally, Arjan Singh Budhiraja appeared on the balcony, accompanied by the government emissary, and announced to the Khalsa that a compromise had been reached: Mrs. Gandhi would personally arbitrate the issue of Chandigarh—and also of the Bhakra-Nangal irrigation project—and she would appoint a commission to arbitrate all other disputes between Punjab and Haryana. This compromise, however, was only a restatement of assurances she had given all along, and the crowd shouted, "We don't agree! We don't agree! We want Chandigarh!" Fateh Singh silenced the shouts by appearing on the balcony and breaking his fast with two glasses of orange juice—one drink as a courtesy to photographers.

Tara Singh denounced the agreement between Fateh Singh and Mrs. Gandhi, and called for a Sikh-ruled Punjabi Suba with the right of secession, and a government officer commented, with some exasperation, "Tara Singh himself was born of Hindu parents, and Fateh Singh, as far as anyone can discover, of Muslim parents, but our people have a way of forgetting these things. Guru Nanak set out to found a religion that would bring Hindus and Muslims together under one roof. Now some of these Sikhs want to partition the country to make Sikhistan. They're already trying to partition buildings in the name of religion, and tomorrow they'll be partitioning rooms."

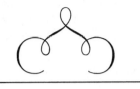

State: "A Palanquin, a Parasol, a Drum"

BEFORE INDEPENDENCE, INDIAN NATIONALISTS like Tara Singh (he died in 1967) were, by and large, united by the cause of liberating their country from British colonial rule. But since Independence the nationalists have split up into religious and regional factions, with the result that Balkanization has become the greatest political threat to the survival of India as a national entity. Kerala, which the government formed as a linguistic state in 1956 by combining the old Malayalam-speaking princely states of Travancore and Cochin with the Malayalam-speaking section of the old Presidency of Madras, and which has an area of about fifteen thousand square miles, has sometimes been chosen as a model by political scientists studying the effects of Balkanization. It has also been chosen as a model of what may be in store for India twenty years from now. Kerala is fast becoming an agricultural slum; its population has been rising even more rapidly than that of the rest of India, and the amount of arable land is limited, so that more and more people are being forced to rely on less and less land for subsistence. Kerala has one of the highest rates of unemployment in India, partly because more and more people are being displaced from jobs in agriculture and there are no new jobs opening up in industry. Kerala also has the highest rate of literacy in India, and a great deal of political and social unrest; the power of the state government has frequently been eroded to the point of anarchy and mob rule. As a state, Kerala held its first elections in 1957 and elected a Communist government—the first time that Communists had come to power through free popular ballot in a major election in India or anywhere else in the world.

Today, I begin a leisurely tour of Kerala in a hired car with a stiff, elderly driver who wears a starched uniform of dark-blue broadcloth and keeps his only worldly possessions, a change of clothes, wrapped up in a newspaper parcel next to him on the seat. The state occupies a narrow strip between the Western Ghats and the Arabian Sea, on south India's Malabar Coast; it has extremely lush lowlands along the sea and heavily forested highlands along the mountain range. On the coast, unspoiled white beaches are washed by a gentle surf, and the entire countryside, being watered by rivers that flow down from the mountains, is laced with canals and lakes. Everywhere, there are groves of palm trees, tall and cool-looking, and so numerous and dense that for miles they cover the land like a canopy. We drive past plantations of tea, coffee, and rubber, gardens of pepper vines, orchards of fruit and nut trees, and fields of sugarcane, paddy, cassava, beans, peas, and lentils. Along the roads are palm-thatched huts, coconut and toddy shops, and cluster after cluster of small home-steads, one cluster scarcely thinning out before another begins. In fact, the countryside is so thickly populated that the state looks like one continuous tropical village.

I break my journey at Trivandrum, the capital of Kerala, and put up at the state Guest House, a white colonial building with well-tended lawns and flower beds, wide verandas, and large, high-ceilinged rooms containing such old-fashioned furniture as carved and fluted side tables and glass-fronted china cupboards. In the dining room, above a sideboard, there hangs in a carved oval frame a black-and-white print showing a woman at the seashore, her long hair swept up on her head and her hand daintily lifting her long skirts as she stoops to pick up something—perhaps a sea shell. Lining the wall all the way from the bottom of the staircase in the foyer to the door of my room upstairs are rococo-framed reproductions of Hogarth's engravings "Marriage à la Mode." Between the last two Ho-garths is another romantic-looking woman, this time in color—blue eyes, rosy lips, flaxen hair in ringlets and kiss curls—set in another carved oval frame, whorled and lacy.

In ancient times, it is said, Phoenician, Israelite, Greek, Roman, and Arab traders all visited or settled on the Malabar Coast, and in more recent times Portuguese, Dutch, French, and English merchants successively es-tablished colonies in the Malabar area. The descendants of many of the early settlers still live in their own distinct—and often antagonistic—communities in Kerala. To a large degree, Keralan politics, which are known for their turbulence, are dominated by the clashing of caste and communal pressure groups.

The state has a population of twenty million, about sixty per cent of the people being Hindu, about twenty-one per cent Christian, and about eighteen per cent Muslim. Among the Hindus, there are some four hundred and twenty castes and subcastes, with Brahmans, by religious tradition, the highest, and Pulayas, who are aboriginal tribesmen, the lowest, but more than half of the Keralan Hindus belong to one of two castes: the Nairs, who are in general the wealthiest and most influential, and who number two million four hundred thousand, and the Ezhavas, who are in general the poorest and most depressed, and who number three million seven hundred thousand. The Nairs are known for their martial and authoritarian traditions and for their matriarchal feudalism. Until recently, a few Nair families controlled vast estates, which were cultivated by lower-caste, serflike tenants. The Ezhavas include plantation workers, tenant farmers, landless laborers, and fishermen, but most of them are toddy-tappers—a traditional occupation of the lower castes in south India. Until recently, the Ezhavas were not admitted into the presence of high-caste Hindus—were not allowed to enter the houses of high-caste Hindus, come near Hindu temples, attend public schools, or even use public roads, because, in the social system of the region, the Ezhavas were considered "untouchables," and a high-caste Hindu thought any contact with an untouchable defiling. Although technically the Ezhavas are no longer classified among India's "scheduled castes and tribes" (a euphemism for "untouchables," derived from a list of groups that are guaranteed special protection by the Constitution), in actuality they are still part of this outcast population, which, in India, numbers over a hundred million. Among the Christians, again, there are many sects and denominations, but more than half of the Keralan Christians are Catholics and belong to one of two sects: the Syro-Malabar Christians, who are in general the wealthiest and most influential as a sect, and who number a million four hundred thousand, and the Malabar Latin Christians, who are in general the poorest and most depressed as a sect, and who number a million. The Syro-Malabar Christians are considered to be descendants of the first high-caste Hindu converts to Catholicism, and have a social and economic status parallel to that of the Nairs; the Malabar Latin Christians are considered to be descendants of more recent, lower-caste Hindu converts to Catholicism, and have a social and economic status parallel to that of the Ezhavas. The Muslims, who are descendants either of Arab traders believed to have come to the

Malabar Coast in the ninth century (these descendants are called Mop-
lahs) or of Hindu converts, are, like the Christians, divided into various groups that mirror in some ways the caste distinctions of Hindu
society.

The political history of the state really began in 1957, with the Communist government. The Communists came to power mainly through the
support of the Ezhavas and the scheduled castes, who had grown to respect the Party volunteers for their dedicated work on behalf of the poor in
the villages. Two years later, the Communists lost power, mainly because
of a violent protest movement led by Christians and Nairs, whose hostility was aroused by the Communist government's sponsorship of comprehensive bills for state control of education and for land reform; the
Christians favored land reform but opposed any state interference in their
schools, and the Nairs favored state education but opposed any government redistribution of their estates. Together, the Christians and the Nairs
dominated the state Congress Party, which charged the Communist government with reducing Kerala to anarchy. The Communists, in turn,
charged the Congress Party with engineering disturbances in order to have
a pretext for deposing the Communist government before it had had a
chance to prove itself in office. In 1959, the Congress government in Delhi
dismissed the Communist government in Kerala and proclaimed President's Rule. Elections were held in the state in 1960, but the factionalism
now cut so deep that no party was able to win a clear majority. The Congress Party, however, did achieve a plurality and was able to form a shaky
anti-Communist coalition government. There was dissension in the coalition, and it was dissolved within two years, but Congress managed to continue in power for another two years. Then it was brought down by
the defection of a predominantly Christian wing. Elections were held
again in 1965, and again no single party won a clear majority. Most
of the candidates nominated by the Communists were in jail, having been
put there under the Defense of India Rules, yet the Communists managed
to win a plurality. The elected candidates were not released from jail,
however, and so were prevented from forming a government. Instead, Kerala was once more placed under President's Rule. (In subsequent years,
the Communists returned to power in Kerala, and also made gains in
other states.)

R. Sankar is an Ezhava who emerged as a Congress leader in Kerala
during the anti-Communist protest movement and went on to become
Deputy Chief Minister and then Chief Minister of the anti-Communist

coalition government. He lives about two hours' drive from Trivandrum, in the town of Quilon, where I go to meet him. His living room is furnished a little like a theatre-in-the-round. Against the walls there are wooden sofas with bright cushions, and in the center of the room there is a round table with four chairs. Sankar is sitting at the table. He is a big, jovial-looking man with a full face and thick, wavy gray hair, which is brushed straight back.

I ask him about the circumstances of the fall of the coalition government.

"The Nairs and Christians could not abide the fact that an Ezhava was the leader of their state government," he says. "The Communists naturally hated my government, but then they are agents of foreign powers and have no use for our Indian democratic setup except as a way of coming to power."

I ask him about the political instability in Kerala.

"We may never have a stable government," he says. "Three-quarters of our people can read now. Because of the enlightened education policies of the old princely governments of Travancore and Cochin, we are ahead of the rest of the country. Among the people who work in, say, a little cigarette factory, you'll find that nine laborers out of ten have clubbed together and hired the tenth to read them the newspapers while they work. But a great many of our people can't find any work. The population increase here—about twenty-five per cent between the census of 1951 and the census of 1961—has far outstripped the number of jobs created by new industries. Everywhere, we have a lot of educated people who can't find jobs and who spend their time reading newspapers and getting grandiose ideas about their political rights."

I ask him about the possibilities of developing industry in Kerala.

"Before Independence, all we had here was one glass factory, one ceramics factory, one titanium factory, and a fertilizer plant," he says. "After Independence, in the First Five-Year Plan, we were awarded a DDT factory, which was built. In the second Plan, we were awarded a shipbuilding plant, a heavy-electrical-goods factory, and a photochemical factory. Negotiations for the first plant are still going on. The second plant was reallocated to another state. The third plant was dropped altogether, in favor of an oil refinery, which, fortunately, we have been able to build. In the Third Five-Year Plan, however, we got nothing, though I tried my best with the Planning Commission in Delhi. The country's resources were too limited."

Since 1964, there have been two Communist parties in India—the Right Communists, who are formally known as the Communist Party of India, and the Left Communists, who are formally known as the Communist Party of India, Marxist. Each claims to be the true Communist Party, but as a rule the Right Communists follow the Soviet line and the Left Communists the Chinese line. In Kerala, the leader of the Right Communists is Achuta Menon, who at present happens to be in the Soviet Union. Unni Raja, a prominent Keralan Right Communist and the editor of a small Right Communist political weekly published in Màlayalam and called *Navayugam* ("new age"), is in Trivandrum, at the headquarters of the Right Communists, a two-story building with a large blazing-red signboard by its entrance, over which flies a red flag. I have come here to meet him. The rooms are large and empty, and look unused. There are no carpets, no curtains—just a few cane-bottomed chairs. In one of the rooms I find Unni Raja, a tall, thin, gray-haired man with a long chin, a wide mouth, and a small gray toothbrush mustache and heavy gray eyebrows. He is wearing a white bush shirt and a white ankle-length south Indian garment called a *mundu*.

I ask Unni Raja about the ideological differences between the Right Communists and the Left Communists.

"We accept the Soviet position that the world Communist revolution can come about through peaceful means," he says. "We think that there is general discontent in India and that the popular democratic forces are turning against Congress. We feel that if we are hasty in taking up arms the people won't support us. But the Left Communists, like the Chinese, believe that world revolution can come about only through violence. The Left Communists deny that they have connections with the Chinese, but we think that they, like the Albanian Communists, are hand in glove with them. Conditions in India today, however, are very different from the conditions in China at the time of her revolution."

I ask him if violent revolution was not one of the original tenets of Marxism.

"Marxism is a proposition, but different conditions require different applications of the proposition," he says. "Dialectical materialism can never change. The fact that the sun rises in the east cannot change. The fact can't get dated. Only the application of the fact to particular conditions—particular countries—changes."

I ask him if he has ever had any doubts about applying the Marxist proposition to Indian conditions.

"Doubts there will always be, no question about it," he says. "Naturally, when we are faced with new problems and a new situation, we have our doubts. In the early days, it was not easy for me to accept such acrobatics of the Party as the denunciation of Stalin or our Party's abandonment of the Calcutta Thesis in 1951. The Calcutta Thesis assumed that India was ready for violent revolution, and advocated the use of subversion and terrorism—tactics that Mao Tse-tung had used to win control of China. From head to foot, I still bear the bodily scars of my fight for the Calcutta Thesis, for which I had gone to prison, for which I had been whipped. When you have lived your life by certain ideas, it's difficult to make adjustments to changes."

I ask him how he became a Communist.

"I broke with the Congress Party when Gandhi persuaded a leader of the untouchables to call off a hunger strike he had undertaken to gain admission to Hindu temples for his people. That was the beginning of my disillusionment. I became an active political worker in the Communist Party. Now the time is past for using civil-disobedience tactics to win admission to the temple. Now, in a figurative sense, the temple has to be burned down."

One of the most eminent Keralan Brahman communities—the Brahmans of the Brahmans, as it were—is the subcaste of the Namboodiris, who stand at the apex of the caste pyramid, and who, for the most part, still live in feudal isolation as intellectual aristocrats. One of the most eminent Namboodiri families—the Namboodiris of the Namboodiris—is the family of Elamkulam Manakal Sankaran Namboodiripad, the General Secretary of the Communist Party of India, Marxist, and he is one of the two most important Communist leaders in India (the other being S. A. Dange, the Chairman of the Communist Party of India). He was the first Communist in India to hold high office; he served as Chief Minister of the first Communist government in Kerala. (In 1967, he won this office back.) The Indian journalist D. R. Mankekar, in his book "The Red Riddle of Kerala," discusses Namboodiripad:

> Even his bitterest adversaries concede that E. M. S. Namboodiripad is the ablest political operator in Kerala. A person of highest integrity, against whose name there is not a breath of scandal, with a long record of selfless service . . . E. M. S. is adored by the people. . . .
>
> He is an excellent organizer, an outstanding propagandist, and a top party theoretician. He has vision and an imagination in a land where the average run of politicians are small men with petty politics and a narrow communal outlook.
>
> Above all, E. M. S. is human, simple, and natural . . . but ruthless and

inexorable in political warfare. . . . There is about him the glamour of a high-class Brahman who sacrificed his wealth and dedicated himself to the services of the people and the Party.

Namboodiripad, like Unni Raja, has his office in Trivandrum—in the headquarters of the Left Communists, a building almost indistinguishable on the outside from the headquarters building of the Right Communists, except that the signboard does not have a red flag over it. I call on Namboodiripad in his office—a cubbyhole barely large enough for a desk and a couple of chairs. He is short and heavy, with gray hair and a smooth, quiet face, which, at a closer look, reveals an underlying tension. He wears glasses, and has on a worn blue bush shirt and a white *mundu*.

I remark that the Right Communists say the split between the two parties is essentially a reflection of the Sino-Soviet split.

"That is their malicious propaganda," he tells me, struggling with a bad stammer. "They say it because their position on the issue of Congress rule, on which we broke with them in 1964, is thoroughly unjustifiable. So they allege that we are for violent revolution, which we are not, and that we are foreign agents—the stock charge of all anti-Communists." As he speaks, he fans himself with a newspaper.

I ask him what he thinks are the real differences between the Left and the Right Communists.

"The Right Communists feel that the Congress government in Delhi is—though not fully, at least to a certain extent—pursuing progressive Socialistic policies, that its foreign policy of non-alignment can lead to peace, that its land reform, as far as it goes, is having some success," he says. "We don't think so. We believe that the Congress government is just another monopolistic, bourgeois government, and most Indian Communists agree with us. We now have a card-carrying membership of a hundred and ten thousand—three out of four Indian Communists. But there is not a direct connection between Party membership and popular support. We had a card-carrying membership of just twenty thousand in the election of 1965 in Kerala, yet we polled more than a million votes. Our tactic is to join forces with the Right Communists and other parties to form popular fronts, and so take over the state legislatures. But the question is whether we will be allowed to win by fair means. The Congress Party is a past-master at employing political detention and ruthless suppression."

I ask him what the Communists would do if they should come to national power.

"It would depend upon the stage of the economy when we came to power, but we would almost certainly extend the public sector, redistribute the land, and remove all kinds of burdens—debts, rents, taxes—from the backs of the cultivators. We would nationalize industry, nationalize the financial institutions. We would do away with the use of private capital."

I ask him what kind of policy a Communist government in India would have toward religious, communal, and caste groups.

"We would observe a complete separation of the government and religion as long as religious leaders did not try to interfere with the government."

I ask him how he became a Communist.

"I had a traditional Namboodiri upbringing—strict and austere," he says. "I had a traditional Namboodiri education—private tutoring in Malayalam literature and Sanskrit scriptures. I was made to learn the Rig-Veda by heart. After that, the Namboodiri tradition called for me to settle down to a life of devotional prayers and rack-renting. But instead I was sent to a Western-type college, which I abandoned for the nationalist movement for independence. I reached Leninism through Gandhiism. As I look back, it seems to me that Gandhi was a bourgeois leader and Gandhiism simply a stage in the history of Indian capitalism. I left the Congress Party to found the Communist Party in this region. We remained underground until after Britain and the Soviet Union became allies in the Second World War. Then the Communist Party was legalized. I sold my patrimony to raise money to start a Communist newspaper."

V. K. Sukumaran Nayar, who took his doctorate at Yale University, and who is now chairman of the Department of Political Science of the University of Kerala, in Trivandrum, observes Keralan politics with a degree of detachment that the politicians themselves could not be expected to show. Nayar invites me to tea, and we sit in a small drawing room in his house and talk about Kerala.

"India may have the largest democracy in the world, but most of the voters are illiterate," he tells me, speaking rapidly and with ease. "Maybe they know nothing more of a political party than its symbol—yoked bullocks for Congress, corn and sickle for the Right Communists, hammer, sickle, and star for the Left Communists, and so on. Most of the parties in Kerala claim to have Socialist goals of one kind or another." He gets up, walks across the room, and leans against a large glass-fronted cupboard crammed with children's toys—the main piece of furniture in the room. "The differences between the parties I've mentioned, and the other parties in Kerala as well—the Praja Socialists, the Revolutionary Socialists, the Samyukta Socialists, the Kerala Socialists, the Jana Sangh, the Swatantra, the Muslim League, the Kerala Congress—are almost entirely in leadership, in organization, and in the interest groups that support them and have split them into factions. In Kerala, the Congress Party failed to absorb these interest groups and emerge as the dominant political party, and so gave the Communists a chance to fill the political vacuum, but the Communists have also failed to absorb these interest groups into a common ideology. Religious, caste, and communal interest groups have their own organizations, and most of them are headed by very strong men, with whom the government must perpetually bargain. Every Keralan continues to think of himself as Nair, Ezhava, Namboodiri, Syro-Malabar Christian, Malabar Latin Christian, or Moplah, with fierce loyalty to his family and his home."

In 1914, Mannatha Padmanabhan, a Nair, founded the Nair Service Society, with the aim of reforming his caste's matriarchal system, and the system, which had concentrated land holdings in the hands of a few families, was, in effect, abolished in 1925. Today, the Nair Service Society, to which most Nairs belong, runs coöperatives, medical centers, colleges, secondary schools, and printing presses of its own, and has a thousand constituent units in the villages of Kerala. Padmanabhan, who served as head of the organization for forty years, lives not far from Trivandrum, in the village of Changanacheri, and this is where the organization has its headquarters and many of its more important institutional centers. The organization's buildings in Changanacheri, I discover when I go to meet Padmanabhan, are new and garish; they stand out like a new village within the village.

"You can find Padmanabhan sitting under a tree in front of the N.S.S. headquarters," a passerby tells me. "He always sits there." Indeed, Padmanabhan is there, sitting in a wicker chair on a patch of lawn. He is a very old man dressed in a white *mundu,* a white *kurta,* and brown leather sandals, with a white shawl folded neatly over his shoulders. He has thin white hair and only a few teeth. His hands are very wrinkled. Slowly, with the aid of a walking stick, he gets to his feet, and then he calls to a man who is sitting at some distance, in another wicker chair, and this man comes over and introduces himself as a Malayalam-English interpreter.

When we are all seated, I ask Padmanabhan, through the interpreter, about the social aims of the Nair Service Society.

"The purpose of the N.S.S. has always been to make all the subcastes of Nairs feel that they belong to one happy Nair family and to work for the social uplift of all Nairs," he says.

I ask him if it wouldn't be better to work for the social uplift of all the people, whatever their castes.

"We have built all kinds of Nair institutions," he says, haltingly. "If we abolished the N.S.S., to whom could we transfer their ownership? I have been trying to get the N.S.S. to drop 'Nair' from its name, but it's very difficult to get the other Nairs to agree. During my years of work for the Nairs, I have travelled five thousand miles in India, touring and giving speeches, in an effort to eradicate distinctions among the many Nair sub-castes and also among other castes and subcastes. Our work has indirectly helped other castes. There are even marriages between Nairs and Ezhavas now. If there had been such a marriage twenty-five years ago, there would have been a murder in the family. We are making strides, and although other castes have worked together for such progress, the N.S.S. deserves special good marks."

I ask him whether he thinks India will ever be able to rid itself of caste barriers.

"The caste system has been here as long as Hindus have, and the Nairs can't end the caste system all by themselves," he says. "It will take a long time to end it. In the meantime, we must work within it. The nature of the world is such that you can't do anything quickly. I believe all mankind is one, but it is not easy to put that belief into practice."

In 1902, an Ezhava who was an ascetic and who came to be known as Shri Narayana Guru founded an Ezhava welfare organization, the Shri Narayana Dharma Paripalana Yogam, or Society for the Protection of the Moral Law of the Venerable Narayana, which is second only to the Nair Service Society as the most powerful caste organization in Kerala and now has *its* own schools, training colleges, and constituent units in the villages. The work of Shri Narayana Guru, who died some years ago, is being carried on by several leading members of the organization, one of whom is M. K. Raghavan. I call on him in Cochin—an old, crowded town on the Arabian Sea, which is, after Bombay, the busiest port on India's west coast —where he lives in a single-story house set in a lush Keralan garden. He receives me in a small sitting room dominated by a picture of Shri Narayana Guru, with pictures of Buddha and Christ on either side. Raghavan, who is dressed in a bush shirt and a *mundu,* is a striking-looking man in his middle years. He has a narrow strip of mustache, and eyebrows that stick out over the tops of big glasses.

I ask him about the purpose of the Shri Narayana Dharma Paripalana Yogam.

"Most of us Ezhavas have always had the same occupation—tapping
and processing toddy from palm trees, especially coconut palms. There are
toddy-tappers all over south India. Elsewhere, our caste is known as Bil-
lavas or Nadars. There are a lot of us here in Kerala because there are a lot
of coconuts here. From the time the Aryan invaders came to India, three
or four thousand years ago, and introduced the caste system and made
slaves of our people, we had no rights. We even had to keep sixty-four feet
away from any Hindu temple. We had to keep thirty-six feet away from
Brahmans and sixteen feet away from Nairs—and untouchables had to
keep twelve feet away from Ezhavas. From ancient times, our Ezhava
women were forbidden to wear any clothing above the waist in the presence of Brahmans and Nairs. But Shri Narayana Guru taught that there
was one universal caste, one religion, one god, and he led a movement
against untouchability. He founded the S.N.D.P.Y. because he felt that
unless all caste distinctions were abolished, unless there was some kind of
equality between man and man, there could be no social justice—we
Ezhavas would always be slaves. He inspired the Ezhavas and, through
them, all the other untouchables, even before Gandhi. Now untouchability has been abolished by law, but in practice it persists. Untouchables are
beaten when they refuse to perform their traditional functions in the villages, like serving as scavengers and disposing of dirty leaves after people
have eaten from them. We have to continue to fight to abolish untouchability from the souls of high-caste Hindus."

Indian Christianity is said by many Indian Christians to go back to the
time of St. Thomas the Apostle, who is supposed to have reached the
Malabar Coast in 52 A.D., eight or nine years before St. Paul arrived in
Rome, and to this day there is a greater concentration of Indian Christians
in this area than anywhere else in India (four million out of the total of
ten million Christians in India). The Malabar Christians are divided
into a number of sects, distinguished by affiliations with different foreign
or heretical Christian communities, and therefore by different rites and
doctrines. The original Malabar Christians accepted communion with the
Roman Catholic Church, but, probably because of commercial contact
with Persia, they used a Syro-Chaldaic form of the liturgy of the Eastern
Church, and so have come to be known as Syro-Malabar Christians. After
the arrival of Portuguese missionaries in the sixteenth and seventeenth
centuries, some of them abandoned the Syro-Chaldaic liturgy and adopted
instead the Latin liturgy of the Roman Catholic Church, and so have
come to be known as Malabar Latin Christians. Other Syro-Malabar

Christians in the meantime severed their connection with the Roman Catholic Church altogether and established relations with the Jacobite Church in Syria, and so have come to be known as Malabar Jacobite Christians. Some of these Malabar Jacobite Christians later returned to the communion of the Roman Catholic Church but retained some of the Jacobite liturgy, and so have come to be known as Syro-Malankarese Christians. Other Malabar Jacobite Christians established relations with the Protestant denominations, and so have come to be known as Marthomite, or Reformed Jacobite, Christians. There are other small sects and denominations of Christians as well. Beyond liturgical and doctrinal distinctions, many Keralan Christians still observe the hereditary castes of their Hindu forefathers.

Both the Malabar Latin Christians and the Syro-Malabar Christians have their archdiocesan headquarters in Ernakulam, a modern-looking town of temples and churches that is a suburb of Cochin. In the area of Ernakulam, the Malabar Latin Christians far outnumber the Syro-Malabar Christians, and the presence of the two archdiocesan headquarters in the same town has been a source of contention for years.

The head of the Malabar Latin Christians is His Grace the Archbishop of Verapoly, Dr. Joseph Attipetty, and I arrange to meet him at his house in Ernakulam. The house has a rather Mediterranean atmosphere. It overlooks the sea, it is entered by a silver-painted iron gate, and it is built around a courtyard that is planted with bushes and a palm tree and is dominated by a silver-painted statue of Jesus. Dr. Attipetty receives me in a room illuminated by stained-glass windows, where he sits at the head of a large conference table surrounded by empty chairs. He has a plump, merry face, and is wearing a crimson cap—under which tufts of gray hair stick out—and a white cassock that is quite tight around his middle.

I ask him about the relations between the Malabar Latin Christians and the Syro-Malabar Christians.

"Both the Syrian Christians and the Latin Christians believe that they alone are true to the original Christianity of St. Thomas," he says, whistling his "s"s a little. "The Syrian Christians think that they are the truest because they are the oldest; we think that we are the truest because we believe that the Syro-Chaldaic liturgy led the Indian Christians into heretical practices that were corrected only when the Portuguese missionaries came, in the sixteenth century. The sacraments of the Latin Christians and the Syrian Christians have always been very similar. Sometimes we've even attended one another's services. The main difference between us has always been in the details of the two liturgies, especially the languages of the two Masses. The Syrian Christians, with the consent of the Church in Rome, said their Mass from the very outset in Syro-Chaldaic, which is like Aramaic, the language Jesus spoke. But we, from the very outset, said our Mass in Latin. Since the Second Vatican Council has sanctioned the use of the vernacular for the Mass, even that difference between them and us may eventually disappear, for Malayalam may become our common liturgical language."

"Is there a chance, then, that you and the Syro-Malabar Christians may one day unite?" I ask.

"No, none at all—mainly because of the caste system among the Indian Christians here," he says. "During the episcopate of my predecessor, the Latin Church won a lot of new converts. Most of them were Ezhavas who were trying to escape from the oppression of the Hindu caste system. But some of the established Latin Christians were descendants of high-caste Hindus, and they objected to the new Ezhava converts' sitting or standing next to them in the churches. So we had to build separate churches for the Ezhava Latin Christians. Nowadays, some of these Ezhava Latin Christians are being admitted to the churches of the high-caste Latin Christians. But the Syrian Christians don't want anything to do with the Ezhava Latin Christians, so they now consider all Latin Christians untouchable. There are some Syrian Christians who won't have anything to do with me, even though I am a high-caste Latin Christian and my family has been Christian since the time of St. Thomas the Apostle. When an Ezhava came to my family's house, he had to stand outside and speak to us from there. These things are rooted very deeply in the past, and though we are constantly having dialogues and meetings, we can't change such things in a day."

The head of the Syro-Malabar Christians is His Grace the Archbishop of Ernakulam, Dr. Joseph Parecattil. (In 1969, he was made a cardinal and became one of two Indian Princes of the Church, the other being His Eminence Valerian Cardinal Gracias.) His residence, I discover when I go to meet him, resembles that of the other archbishop very closely, and the room in which he receives me is decorated in almost the same way. Dr. Parecattil, who wears a white cassock and a gold cross on a gold chain, has dark skin, white eyebrows, and short, fluffy white hair. There is an air of tranquillity and contentment about him.

I ask him about the relations between the Syro-Malabar Christians and the Malabar Latin Christians.

"We are both under the Pope," he says. "But socially we will always be divided by caste, for the Latin Christians as a community belong to the low castes—they are so listed in the official census. Also, our church is by far the older. I know that some people doubt whether St. Thomas the Apostle came here and founded our church, but if he didn't come here, where did he go?"

I remark on the strangeness of carrying the Hindu caste system over to Christianity, and ask how a Christian knows what Hindu caste he is descended from.

"The world has always been full of social distinctions, and the Church is no exception," he says. "There has always been a kind of public understanding about caste among the Indian Christians. Indian Christians have always observed Hindu caste, and even Hindu customs, like consulting horoscopes, in order to preserve their position in Hindu society. We don't delve deeply into these questions, because to do so would only make trouble. Actually, within our church we have even further social distinctions, based on one's relationship to the original Indian converts of St. Thomas. The families of Sanoorikal, Pakalomattam, Kalli, and Kaliankayu claim to be direct descendants. There are many claims like that. My own family claims to go back to the time of St. Thomas, too."

Returning to Trivandrum, I go to pay my respects to His Grace the Archbishop of Trivandrum, Benedict Mar Gregorios. He is head of the Malabar Syro-Malankarese Christians, who number a hundred and sixty thousand. The Archbishop's office is in a two-story house in the compound of the Mar Theophilos Training College. The college grounds are extensive, and they are lush with banana trees and coconut palms. All around the house in which the Archbishop has his office are dark young men in long white robes. One of them, who is carrying a breviary under his arm, shows me upstairs to the office, which is hung with religious pictures and dark-blue draperies. The Archbishop, who is sitting behind a desk, is a gray-bearded, bright-eyed, friendly-looking man dressed in a long fawn-colored robe with a sash of bright-pink satin. Around his neck is a heavy gold chain from which hangs a gold cross studded with stones of the same bright pink, and on his head is an unusual headdress embroidered with a geometrical design in white, yellow, and gold on a black background. He speaks in an easy way about the confusing diversity of the Indian Christian communities—playing with his gold chain while he talks—and concludes his remarks with a quotation from the Bible: " 'Vanity of vanities, saith the Preacher, vanity of vanities; all is vanity.' "

There are at present fifteen thousand Jews in India, and, according to one Indian-Jewish tradition, the first Israelites to come here settled in a port not far from Cochin that was called Shingly. There are several theories about the arrival of these first Jewish settlers: that they came from Israel in the tenth century B.C., during King Solomon's reign; that they came from Judaea in the first century A.D., after the destruction of King Herod's temple; that they came from Majorca in the fourth century; that they came from Persia in the fifth century. Whenever it was that they came, by the time the Portuguese arrived on the Malabar Coast, in the sixteenth century, a Jewish settlement was flourishing in Shingly—or Cranganore, as it was then called. The Portuguese destroyed the settlement and dispersed the Jews, who eventually found a patron and protector in the Hindu Maharaja of Cochin. He gave them land on which to build a synagogue in Cochin. The synagogue was built in 1568 and rebuilt in 1664, and stands today—the oldest in India, serving the oldest congregation of Indian Jews. These and the other Jews of Malabar, who do not marry outside their own community, are themselves divided into three distinct groups—White Jews, Black Jews, and Slave Jews—who, in turn, do not marry outside their own groups. The distinction between the White Jews and the Black Jews is supposedly based on the lighter complexion of the White Jews, but, confusingly, some of the White Jews have dark complexions. Although the White Jews enjoy a higher social status than the Black Jews, the Black Jews are generally thought to be the original settlers, and the White Jews to have come as refugees from the Spanish Inquisition. The Slave Jews are regarded as outcasts by both the Black Jews and the White Jews. This form of ostracism seems to be based on the Hindu idea of untouchability, and until recently, just as the untouchables were excluded from Hindu temples, the Slave Jews were excluded from the synagogues of the other Jews. Although there is now more contact among the three groups, the old distinctions of social status persist.

The acknowledged leader of the Jews of Malabar is a White Jew, S. S. Koder, who is a merchant in Cochin and is the wealthiest Jew in Kerala. He lives in a flat next door to his business—a general store that consists of one long hall containing display shelves and steel cupboards. I call on Koder at his flat, where he receives me in a large, cluttered living room that has a ponderous atmosphere. The furniture, which is of heavy teakwood carved with flowers, birds, and animals, is in what might be called Indo-Portuguese style. Seated on a camelback sofa is Koder, a big, heavy-jowled man dressed in a long-sleeved white bush shirt and white trousers.

"The furniture in this room was originally in the palace of the Maharaja of Cochin," Koder tells me, speaking English with a thick accent that sounds Middle Eastern. "It will be the nucleus of an exhibition of Malabar Jewish arts that we are going to mount for the celebration of the four-hundredth anniversary of our synagogue, which is in Jew Town, where practically all the Jews in Cochin live. I am trying to get some of the Jews in New York to come over for the celebration."

I ask him how long his family has been in Malabar.

"Since the time of my great-grandfather, who came to India from Baghdad," he says. "But, unfortunately, neither my great-grandfather nor my grandfather had any interest in family history, so we have no family records."

Koder is an amateur historian of the Indian Jews, and I ask him to tell me something about their history.

"We were persecuted by the Portuguese, but we prospered under the Dutch and, later, under the British," he says. "Now, though, we have begun to worry about our economic future in this country. At Independence, there were twenty-four thousand Jews in India; nine thousand have since left. Some of them have gone to America, Canada, England, or Australia, but most have gone to Israel, where there is land in plenty, and cows and chickens. Take the case of the Sassoons of Bombay, who are known to everyone as the Rothschilds of the East. They owned mills in Bombay, which used to be worked by Jewish laborers. They sold their mills to the Hindus and packed up and went to Israel. The new Hindu millowners find that they can get Hindu laborers who are much better trained for the jobs. The Jews are worried about competition. They're afraid they may not be able to keep up even their old standard of living, meagre though that is. In Cochin, there are only a hundred of us Jews left, and even this community may be dying out. Our sons and daughters can't find marriage partners in India. A marriageable son of a White Jew these days has no more than half a dozen girls in all India to choose a wife from."

Jew Town, where Koder takes me to visit the synagogue, turns out to consist of one narrow, rather European-looking dead-end street, on which there are, first, small shops, then whitewashed houses—often with a gable facing the street and occasionally with a Star of David on the door—and then, at the end of the street, the courtyard of the synagogue. The synagogue, which is also white, has only two rooms. One is a vestibule, in which a prominent brass plaque commemorates Koder's father as a benefactor. The other is a beautiful hall hung with old chandeliers and decorated with old blue-and-white Chinese tiles. At one end of the hall are a few marble steps leading to a little raised area, where, behind a half-open silken curtain, there is a carved wooden box painted red and gold, a golden crown, and three copper plates.

"This is our Ark of the Covenant," Koder says, going up to the box. "It is all Dutch work on teakwood. It contains our scrolls. This crown was given to us by the Maharaja of Travancore. These copper plates are the oldest records of Indian Jewry. They record certain privileges that were reserved for princes but were extended to the first Jewish settlers. Although some scholars disagree, my view is that the settlers mentioned in the copper plates came here in the fourth century A.D. and founded their settlement in Shingly, and that this settlement lasted a thousand years." He tells me that although the copper plates are inscribed in the old Tamil alphabet, he knows the English translation of the inscription by heart, and he goes on to recite most of it: " 'Hail, and Prosperity! The following gift was graciously made by him who had assumed the title of King of Kings, His Majesty the King Sri Parkaran Iravi Vanmar, whose ancestors have been wielding the sceptre for many hundred thousand years.' " He pauses to explain that the gifts were granted to a Jew named Joseph Rabban, of the village of Anjuvannam, and consisted of "tolls on boats and carts, the revenue and the title of Anjuvannam, the lamp of the day, a cloth spread in front to walk on, a palanquin, a parasol, a drum, a trumpet, a gateway, a garland." He continues the recitation: " 'To Joseph Rabban the Prince of Anjuvannam and to his descendants, sons and daughters, and to his nephews, and to the sons-in-law who married his daughters in natural succession. So long as the world and moon exist, Anjuvannam shall be his hereditary possession.' "

Before leaving Kerala, I pay a courtesy call on its governor, Bhagwan Sahay, in Trivandrum. His residence, the Raj Bhavan, is built on a rise and overlooks the green slopes of the Kerala countryside, which here is dotted with the red roofs of bungalows. The Governor receives me in a garden, where he is having elevenses with Mrs. Sahay and a pretty daughter-in-law, Pamela, who is here on a visit. The three are seated on wicker chairs and are chatting with one another. All about are elegant little high tables painted with pastoral scenes. Each table supports a silver tray, a silver teapot, and a silver jug. Uniformed bearers are circling around serving tea and coconut milk, pastries and nuts. The Governor, a tall, broad-shouldered man in his fifties, smiles happily as Pamela, under the stern gaze of her mother-in-law, keeps playfully adjusting the end of her sari to cover her head. (Well-brought-up Indian girls, especially brides, are taught to keep their heads covered in the presence of their elders.)

A man introduced as Colonel Raja, the brother-in-law of the former Maharaja of Travancore and an old friend of the family, arrives to drive Pamela to Kovalam, a beach a few miles away. They invite me to join them, and I accept.

"They ought to build lots of hotels and a drive all along this beach," Pamela says as we are driving down the coast.

"A very well-known American travel agency has just written to me to say that they want to build this place up as a resort for honeymooners from all around the world," Colonel Raja says. "A big American airline is prepared to land a Boeing in Trivandrum once a week. But our airport can't even receive Viscounts. And there are no air-conditioned hotels."

The beach, which is sheltered by palms, extends indefinitely, and there isn't a soul in sight. The sea is calm and blue. At Kovalam, we pull up in front of a bathhouse, which is near the unoccupied palace of the former Maharaja, and go inside to change.

When we come out, Pamela has put on an old sari for bathing. She walks slowly into the water.

Colonel Raja takes a couple of planks and bamboo poles and lashes them together to make a raft, which he paddles out into the sea. Pamela climbs onto the raft and lies down. With one hand, she shades her eyes from the sun. The raft moves farther and farther away from the shore.

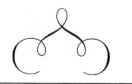

Politics: "My Father's House"

After the British transferred the capital of India from Calcutta to Delhi, in 1911, the British, over a period of twenty years, built a completely new city, New Delhi, just to the south of the old city. Although many modern office buildings have since gone up in the center of New Delhi, and its contours have expanded to take in many growing suburban colonies, the main features of the British city remain intact, so the capital continues to wear an expression of colonial grandeur: wide, tree-lined avenues bordered by stately white colonial residences, which have large, high-ceilinged rooms, colonnaded verandas, spacious gardens, and long red gravel driveways. But the high-ranking politicians and government officers who now live in these houses are all Indians. One such house at present serves as the official residence of Mrs. Indira Priyadarshini Gandhi, who in 1966 became the third Prime Minister of India. The first Prime Minister was her father, Jawaharlal Nehru, who held office from 1947 to 1964, and the second was Lal Bahadur Shastri, who held office from 1964 to 1966. It was generally agreed that her strongest suit in bidding for the office was the fact that she was a Nehru.

The Nehru family name appeared sometime after 1716. In that year, an ancestor named Raj Kaul, who belonged to a small, proud Kashmiri Brahman community in the Vale of Kashmir, moved to Delhi, where he became a petty official at the court of the Mogul Emperor Farrukh Siyar, who thereupon settled on Raj Kaul a small estate in Delhi situated by the side of a *nahar* (Urdu for "canal"). Raj Kaul and his descendants became known as Kaul-Nahars, and in time "Kaul" was dropped and "Nahar" was corrupted to "Nehru." The family was relatively obscure until the time of Motilal Nehru, who was born in 1861, in Allahabad, where the Nehrus had settled. In due course, Motilal became one of the most successful barristers in Allahabad. His only son, Jawaharlal, was born in 1889 (there were also two daughters), and, as was customary for the sons of rich Indians, was sent to England for his education. Jawaharlal studied at Harrow, at Cambridge, and at the Inner Temple, and then returned to India and settled down in his father's house in Allahabad to practice law. He married a tall, slim Kashmiri Brahman girl, Kamala, and their only child, Indira Priyadarshini, was born in 1917. Soon after the child's birth, it was discovered that her mother had tuberculosis; Kamala died of the disease when Indira was nineteen. Indira, herself a frail child, was brought up in a house that became a center of political activity in the early twenties, when both her father and her grandfather were prominent figures in the movement for independence. Indira's formal education was frequently interrupted—her father was in and out of jail— and she never completed her university education; she attended Oxford for a short period, and there met a childhood friend, the late Feroze Gandhi (no relation to Mohandas K. Gandhi), who at the time was a student at the London School of Economics. They were married in 1942— despite some resistance by her family, because he was neither a Brahman nor a Hindu nor a Kashmiri but a Parsi. She had two sons by Feroze Gandhi—Rajiv, born in 1944, and Sanjay, born in 1946—but after some years she and her husband lived, for the most part, separately. She resided with her father in the Prime Minister's house in New Delhi, where she served as his hostess and confidante, entertaining diplomats and political dignitaries. She also undertook missions abroad, and, for a time, directed the affairs of the Congress Party.

Today, I go to call on Mrs. Gandhi. On the way, I pass the house where she lived with her father, which has been turned into the Nehru Museum. Her present official residence, which is opposite the tennis courts of the Delhi Gymkhana Club, is very much like other New Delhi colonial houses, except that a tent is pitched outside the gate for security guards, and inside the gate, in the garden, there is a red, blue, and yellow *shamiana* under which are arranged a table and matching chairs. As I am crossing the driveway, Mrs. Gandhi arrives in a chauffeur-driven white Impala, preceded by a guard on a motorcycle and trailed by half a dozen government officers in a large, rather old-looking black sedan. She gets out of the car, followed closely by a courtly, elegant gentleman, and comes over and greets me. She is a tall, handsome woman with a confident, intelligent face, and she is wearing a white homespun cotton sari with cinnamon-colored edging and a necklace of brown wooden beads. She introduces the elegant gentleman as Feliks Topolski, remarking that he is her houseguest and also that he is the artist whose large mural of the coronation of Queen Elizabeth II is on view in Buckingham Palace. She leads the way to the veranda and into the house—first into a room that is like a typical middle-class Indian drawing room, except that it contains a television set, and then into her own parlor, which is simple, cool, restful, and, by Indian stand-ards, modern. The dominant color in the room is blue. There are many books and pictures around, including a portrait of her father.

Mrs. Gandhi sits down on a sofa, holding herself very straight. Topolski picks up a drawing pad and a crayon from a table, takes a chair opposite her, and begins sketching, his crayon scratching rapidly across the drawing pad.

"I am living here only temporarily," Mrs. Gandhi tells me. "The Prime Minister has to do a lot of office work, meet a lot of people, and do a lot of entertaining. There's plenty of space for the office work here, but there just isn't enough space for all the other things I have to do. I'd like to move, but it's such a bother. I suppose one day I may move back into the house where my father lived as Prime Minister. It should have been kept as an official residence for the Prime Minister. It would have been, except for Shastri. Because of his reverence for my father's memory, when he suc-ceeded my father he didn't want to move into my father's house. At the time, he was living in a government house—the house of a Minister With-out Portfolio. He solved his space problem by expanding into the govern-ment house next door, which happened to be available. This particular house is the one I had as Minister of Information and Broadcasting. When I became Prime Minister, I stayed on here because I didn't know what else to do."

When Mrs. Gandhi became Prime Minister, Nehru's younger sister, Vijaya Lakshmi Pandit, touched off a controversy in the press by raising doubts as to whether her niece's health would stand up under the pressure of the office. I ask Mrs. Gandhi about her health now.

"In India, food is a measure of one's wealth and health," she replies. "Here, if you don't look well fed, people think you are ill. A little while ago, I put on some extra weight, and, with great effort, I lost it again. Everyone said, 'Indu, you look ill. What's the matter?' I am very fit. I keep fit by holding to a daily routine. The first thing in the morning, at five o'clock, I do my yoga exercises for fifteen or twenty minutes. Not those contortions of the body that require holding certain positions for a fixed period of time—I don't have the patience for that kind of thing—but my own forty-eight versions of the ancient yoga exercises. I begin with the exercise for the forehead, then the eyes, then the nose—all the way down to the toes. Even so, I don't have the patience to do all forty-eight every day."

I ask her about her schedule for the rest of the day.

"After the exercises, I like to do the flowers for the house, though I've been able to do them less and less often since I became Prime Minister," she says. "After that, I look through the newspapers, and then work at the desk in my bedroom for an hour or so, depending on how many urgent telegrams have arrived in the night. Then I do my ablutions and have my breakfast. Around seven, I look at my urgent correspondence, and at seven-thirty or eight I begin receiving callers. I finish with them by nine or nine-thirty and leave the house. I spend the rest of the day in Parliament, if it is in session, or, if it is not in session, I stay in my office in the Parliament building or attend meetings or functions, and then I come home for a late lunch and an afternoon nap."

Topolski now moves to her left and asks her to look in his direction.

"I think I am too deep a person to be sentimental about holding this office," she says, gazing past Topolski's head at a vase of sweet peas and jasmine. "I don't think public office is anything to be sentimental about. For me the Prime Ministership is just another job. I have always lived in the public eye. Even when I was a student in England, I was treated as if I were somebody, and in India I have been somebody all my life. But I wouldn't want you to think that I come from a courtly tradition, because our family has always been closely bound up with the life of the people, and I have been friends with people from all walks of life since I was a child. Just this morning, I received a group from a polytechnic college and talked agriculture with them. Later on, one of them, a girl of about nineteen, knelt at my feet." She adds, as an afterthought, "Just overcome with respect, I suppose."

I ask her if press reports were true when they said that Nehru wanted her to succeed him as Prime Minister and that she could easily have done so.

"I was numbed by my father's death, and at the time I didn't want to think about holding any office," she says. "But I thought if I helped Shastri to become Prime Minister, then, when he got the office, he would consult with me, and in that way I would still have some influence on the future of our country. Shastri insisted that he needed to have me in his Cabinet, so I consented to become Minister of Information and Broadcasting. I did many things for Shastri, but once he got himself established as Prime Minister he didn't consult me on any of the major issues."

I ask her opinion of Shastri as Prime Minister.

"Basically, he just didn't have a modern mind," she says. "He was an orthodox Hindu and full of superstitions. You can't lead the country out of poverty with superstition. You need a modern, scientific outlook for that. The orthodox say that we Indians are rich in our cultural heritage. Nowadays that just won't do—you must have a modern mind. But Shastri's dead, and it serves no purpose to dwell on our differences."

I ask her about one of the criticisms commonly made of her leadership— that there is not much difference between her policies and those of Shastri, since, for one thing, most of the politicians who served in Shastri's government are now serving in hers.

"As much as you might want to, you can't change Ministers, because they represent strong power blocs," she says, with a sigh. "But I try to be my own mistress as much as I can. I rely on several advisers outside the government, though I try to play no favorites. Each of these advisers can brief me on a particular angle of a problem. I have to see all the angles."

According to press reports, the Congress Party chose Mrs. Gandhi as Prime Minister over other contenders for the office because she had received the support of Atulya Ghosh, S. K. Patil, and Sanjiva Reddy. I ask her whether she had had to battle for the support of the triumvirate.

"Quite honestly, I was the only natural choice for the job," she says. "I got elected because of my public standing. Even while my father was alive, I was the only Indian who could draw crowds as large as his, both in the north and in the south."

Topolski hovers around her, studying her nose.

I ask her about some of her recent pronouncements in which certain politicians saw a rejection of the Socialist principles of her father.

"Sometimes I get carried away when I'm giving speeches," she says. "But, quite honestly, could anyone know my father's principles and policies better than I do? I first started going with him to sessions of the Congress Party when I was two, and throughout his years as Prime Minister I was his closest associate. The reason many of these politicians take exception to my statements is that some of them speak from the left and some from the right. Take defense. When there is a threat to the integrity of the territory of your country, you can't just sit still. In fact, there is a relationship between political influence and military power. Yet if I accept military aid or other forms of economic aid from America, I am attacked by the left for leaning to the right. If I accept aid from the Soviet Union, I am attacked by the right for leaning to the left. It is true that the minute you are indebted to someone he will try to put pressure on you. But there is no doubt that if we had not accepted wheat and other foodstuffs from America since Independence there would have been real famine. Isn't it silly to worry about entanglements and pressures when you are faced with such fundamental things?"

Topolski moves and sketches her from a three-quarters angle.

"Sometimes I feel there are no solutions to the huge problems our country faces," she goes on. "A solution to a problem only seems to create more problems. I am not afraid to say that the Congress Party has become moribund. It has scarcely a single leader with a modern mind. When I was president of the Congress Party—in 1959—I introduced a scheme for revitalizing it. My idea was to train a cadre of workers who would then function as a political élite and direct the affairs of the party at the state and national levels. These party workers were to be trained in the particular problems of their regions and to brush up on their knowledge of our goals and policies. The party had to be rebuilt from the grass roots up, and I felt that training a new élite was the way to do it. The scheme was launched in the south, and by the time I left the presidency we had trained a cadre of a hundred. But the party president who followed me thought it was a waste of time, and killed the whole scheme with a mere stroke of the pen. So our party workers remain as backward and ignorant as ever. They don't know how the voters in their districts feel on even one issue. How often have I been told by a party worker in a district, 'Don't discuss this, don't discuss that—it's too controversial. The people here won't like it.' When I go ahead and say what I like anyway, I often discover that people will change their minds if I give them the right information. The trouble is that Congress has never succeeded in evolving into a modern political party. Sometimes I feel that even our parliamentary system is moribund. Everything is debated and debated and nothing gets done. Everything that can be exploited for political purposes is exploited. On top of all this, the inertia of our civil service is incredible. In the civil service, everyone gets promoted according to seniority, so you may get a very good young man but he has to wait twenty or thirty years to acquire the influence to do anything significant, and by that time he's probably so worn down by the bureaucracy, and his ideas are probably so out of date, that he's dead wood —we have a system of dead wood replacing dead wood. You can't change this system of promotion, because everything in a civil servant's life is based on it—the size of his salary, the size of his office, the size of the accommodations provided by the government, the quality of his children's education. It's difficult to take such things away once someone has got used to having them. Sometimes I wish we had had a real revolution—like France or Russia—at the time of Independence."

As Mrs. Gandhi said, Congress—which was founded in 1885 as a nebulous national congress for discussing Indian problems, and which became the main force behind the movement for independence—has never succeeded in transforming itself into a national political party with a coherent national program; almost from its very beginning, it has represented a conglomeration of interest groups and a diversity of political ideologies. At present, one of its bitterest critics is Chakravarti Rajagopalacharya—India's greatest living elder statesman—who joined the Congress Party in 1906. He was a close associate of Gandhi and Nehru, and in independent India he served first as the Governor-General of India (this office was abolished in 1950, when India became a republic) and later as Chief Minister of his native state of Madras. In the middle fifties, however, he left the Congress Party, charging that it was destroying the country with a new form of tyranny—that through the central planning of Socialism it was building up a class of people who were dependent on the party and supported it out of self-interest, and who therefore threatened the survival of Indian democracy. In 1959, with the backing of conservative business interests, he founded the Swatantra ("freedom") Party, which advocates a free-enterprise system with minimal government interference in the economy. Although Congress has always been the governing party and is still the only party with significant strength in every state, in recent years the Swatantra Party, the Communist Party, and some smaller opposition parties have put aside their ideological differences and together fought Congress in elections, dislodging Congress from power and forming united-front governments.

Today, I am in Madras, a city that serves officially as the capital of the state of Madras and unofficially as capital of all of south India, to meet Rajagopalacharya—or Rajaji, as he is popularly known. I call on Rajaji in a little cottage he uses for an office on the property of T. Sadasivam, whose thirty-two-page weekly, *Swarajya* (another word for "freedom"), is regarded as Rajaji's mouthpiece. The cottage has brick walls painted cream and a sloping bamboo roof, and looks new and fresh, and so does the room in which Rajaji receives me. On the floor is light straw matting; there are a few wicker chairs, painted green, with cushions on them, and a divan bed with a pale-green and white chenille bedspread. A painting of Gandhi hangs on one wall and a sketch of him on another. Rajaji, who is eighty-eight years old, is sitting in a wicker chair. He is a slight, frail man, with a little thin white hair on the sides and back of his head. He has on glasses with pale tortoise-shell frames. He is wearing a white homespun tunic with buttons down the front. The tunic is open and reveals a V-necked homespun shirt, also with buttons down the front, and a white homespun *dhoti*. On his feet are sandals.

"I am not so good in my ears," he tells me. "And my eyes are also bad—I had cataracts and I still have severe myopia." He removes his tortoise-shell glasses and substitutes for these a larger pair, rimmed in black, which make his thin face look all glasses. "My sense of smell is good and my sense of touch is very good. But my digestion is very bad. I am an old man, and sometimes my health is not good, but I am a happy man. According to my own lights, my mind is good, but the Congress government in power in Delhi does not seem to think I am very clearheaded. All my life, I have been engrossed in some kind of work. I have never required the usual tonic of recreation. Most of my work now is for *Swarajya*. Every week, there is the front-page article to write, and my personal notes to the reader—the 'Dear Reader' column—and sometimes there are other opinions and observations I want to write down for *Swarajya* readers, and so I contribute a third article. *Swarajya* has a circulation of between fifteen and eighteen thousand, but it deserves to have a circulation of a hundred and fifty thousand. I have been writing for a long time, mostly in Tamil. I have written books, articles, stories, and fables. But on the whole I am not a man of letters—that you may take as a correct statement. I have written mostly for specific causes I was working for—propaganda for the abolition of untouchability, for instance. But when I reread my own writing, I like it."

He goes on to tell me a little bit about himself. "I came from a very poor Brahman family. We were fairly orthodox, but not too orthodox. My father had a little bit of land and was a revenue collector for the village. He earned five rupees a month. I vividly remember rupees being counted and placed in heaps. In those days, it was all good silver rupees—now it is only paper. My father was not educated, but he believed in educating his children. He made my elder brother sit for his matriculation examination twelve times, and my elder brother failed twelve times. My next-oldest brother passed his matriculation on his seventh or eighth attack. My brothers were educational flops, but I got my B.A. and LL.B. with flying colors. I was married when I was about to sit for my LL.B. examination. In time, my wife and I had five children—three sons, two daughters. I was left a widower when the children were young, and bringing them up was quite difficult, especially because I was in the economic limbo of the non-coöperation movement. One of my daughters married one of Gandhi's sons, even though in those days mixed-caste marriages were unknown here. My other daughter lost her husband at quite an early age. One of my sons died. Another, who works on a newspaper here, is now very ill. My third son, who never got married, sits in Parliament in Delhi. He's in Congress. He refuses to join the Swatantra Party."

I ask Rajaji what he thinks of Mrs. Gandhi.

"Mrs. Gandhi has come into the picture because she is the daughter of Nehru," he says. "Like most women, she makes quick decisions, but she does not know the machinery of government. I don't wish her bad luck, but the capacity for keeping a large government under control cannot be assumed in her case."

I ask him about his relationship with the Congress Party over the years.

"I began to take an interest in politics in 1901 or 1902, as soon as I qualified as a lawyer. When I became a Congress man, there were two main ideological positions in Congress. The moderates were for dominion status under the British, the radicals for complete independence. I joined the radicals. In 1907, the Congress ranks split—the moderates broke with the radicals and seized positions of control in the movement. We radicals remained in the wilderness until 1916, when the two groups reached a compromise. In 1919, Gandhiji came into Congress, and after that I was a Congress man heart and soul. We in Congress had only one aim—to win freedom by noncoöperation. In 1935, the British Parliament passed the Government of India Act, which gave us dominion status. Then followed a long period of suspension of the noncoöperation movement. In 1939, when the Second World War broke out, Congress opposed the war; we couldn't get the British to agree to give us independence after the war, and so we didn't want to help them fight the war—though later we supported the war effort."

I ask about his break with the Congress Party.

"Like Barry Goldwater, I believe that Socialism kills individual effort, and that without individual effort there can be no progress," he says. "India has so many good, clever businessmen, and it is businessmen who are responsible for progress everywhere. The pace of what industrialization there has been under Congress has been too hasty, and it has been achieved by inflicting on India a crippling national debt and crippling taxation. This policy has been almost fatal for the country. But there is still hope for progress, if our five hundred million people will make up their minds to work. The rich would get richer, but the poor would get richer, too."

Village: "Revolution in the Heart and Revolution in the World"

GANDHI OFTEN DISCUSSED WITH HIS DISCIPLES his dream of a new social order, which he hoped the Indian government would adopt once India was free, and which he believed would eventually supplant other social orders—capitalism, Socialism, Communism—throughout the world. The new social order was to be based entirely on the principles of love, brotherhood, and nonviolence, and was to be free of the evils of exploitation, coercive government, and a centralized economy. The new order would liberate the five hundred thousand Indian villages from the oppressions of poverty, ignorance, and the caste system, and provide a moral alternative to revolutionary violence. He called this new order *sarvodaya* (Hindi for "uplift of all"). Under *sarvodaya,* each village was to govern itself and to have its own self-sufficient, non-industrial economy, its families either buying necessities from coöperatives or manufacturing them at home. Gandhi's celebrated spinning wheel, or *charkha,* on which a family could spin its own yarn for cloth, became a popular symbol of *sarvodaya.*

In 1951, four years after India's independence and three years after Gandhi's death, Acharya Vinoba Bhave (*"acharya,"* an honorific title, is another word for *"guru"*), a Maharashtrian Brahman, then fifty-six, who was one of Gandhi's earliest disciples, discovered what he thought was a way of attaining *sarvodaya.* In that year, he travelled from Wardha, a small town in Maharashtra, where he was living in Sevagram (an *ashram* founded by Gandhi), to a district in south India called Telengana, to preach the message of nonviolence to villagers there who were helping Indian Communists wage guerrilla warfare. One evening, Vinoba, as he is generally known, was conducting a meeting in the village of Pochempelli, in Telengana. According to one of many now legendary versions of what happened there, while he was sitting on a dais with a few landowners, and the many landless poor, most of them untouchables, were sitting on the floor below, an old man stood up and asked how impoverished untouchables like him could ever hope to get land if not by violence. Vinoba asked the old man how much land he thought the untouchables of Pochempelli needed. After consulting the other untouchables, the old man said eighty acres. Vinoba turned to the landowners, each of whom owned hundreds of acres of land, and asked, "Do you think all that land is yours? Is it not God's creation? Have not the children of God an equal share in it?" (Gandhi's term for untouchables was "Harijans," or "children of God.") To his surprise, one landowner stood up and announced that he would donate a hundred acres to the poor people of the village. Vinoba believed that this spontaneous act of charity had revealed to him the way to attain *sarvodaya*—through voluntary land reform. For the next thirteen years, Vinoba journeyed throughout the country, walking eight or ten miles a day, from village to village, and urging landowners to share their land with the poor. Each morning, while it was still dark, he would set out, with a storm lantern in hand, followed by a crowd of men, women, and children. Some of them were *sarvodaya* volunteers who had pledged their lives to the movement, and others were villagers who had dropped whatever they were doing to walk for a time—from a few hours to a few weeks —with Vinoba. The *sarvodaya* workers marched with all their worldly possessions, which usually amounted to just a bundle of clothes and a spinning wheel, and they rested and took food and shelter in the villages along the way. Some of the villagers brought their entire families, young and old, and carried their provisions with them. Villagers and *sarvodaya* volunteers would sing hymns while marching, and then, as they entered the town or village where they expected to put up, they would chant such slogans as:

> "In our village, without land
> No one shall be, no one shall be.
> In our village, poor and needy
> No one shall be, no one shall be.
> Victory to India! Victory to Gandhi! Victory to Vinoba!"

Along the way, Vinoba would stop and address meetings, soliciting gifts of land.

Although by *bhudan* ("gift of earth;" *bhu* is Hindi for "earth" and *dan* is Hindi for "gift"), as the campaign was called, Vinoba won four million acres for *sarvodaya,* it was found that much of this land was barren or rocky or in such odd parcels that it could not be cultivated. In any case, in 1965 he abandoned *bhudan,* and turned his full energies toward another Gandhian movement already under way, called *gramadan* ("gift of village"—to the villagers). Under *gramadan*—in intention a legalistic contrivance but in practice another visionary scheme—landowners in each village were asked to transfer the title to all their holdings to a village assembly, which was to represent all the families in the village and was to manage the affairs of the village in the interests of all. One-twentieth of this land was to be distributed by the village assembly among the landless poor. The rest of the land was actually to remain in the possession of the landowners in perpetuity, for their private use, but the landowners were to contribute at least one-fortieth of the produce from this land to the village, and they were not allowed to sell or mortgage their land without the consent of the village assembly. The landless villagers—the cultivators, the traders, and the workers—were, for their part, to contribute at least one-thirtieth of their earnings in labor, cash, or kind to the village. The theory behind *gramadan* was that land reform was to be brought about by voluntary action, for it was hoped that once the principle of sharing was accepted, the landowners would see the wisdom of collective ownership and would distribute all their land equally among the villagers through the village assembly. As the campaign got under way, the principle of sharing land was extended to include sharing skills and services, and the ideological vocabulary of *gramadan* was enlarged to include terms like *jivandan* ("gift of life service"), *sadhandan* ("gift of tools"), *sampattidan* ("gift of wealth"), *buddhidan* ("gift of intelligence"), *shramdan* ("gift of social service"), and *premdan* ("gift of love"), and the movement became associated with or gave rise to several institutions, like Shanti Sena (the Peace Army), Sarva Seva Sangh (the Service of All Society), and the Gandhi Ashram, the largest homespun-cloth and village-industries organization. Vinoba chose the extremely poor, caste-ridden, overpopulated, backward state of Bihar as the first battlefield for his revolution, and issued a pronouncement to the nation calling for Gramadan-Toofan (*"toofan"* is Hindi for "storm"):

> Gramadan-Toofan is a movement for the liberation of the village. In this we have no conflict with anybody nor do we have to wait for government legislation. Just one day, as soon as possible, all the village people—masters, wealthy persons, labourers—together decide and change the management of

their village. The village land should provide food for every villager; *charkha* would provide cloth for everyone. The elders would resolve conflicts and the youth would defend the village. Neither police nor courts, neither coercion nor force. Everything to be done with brotherliness. This is possible, and what other way have we?

The followers of Gandhi and Vinoba began dreaming of a day when there would be enough *gramadan* village-assembly representatives in a state legislature to take control of it and so bring about *pradeshdan* ("gift of state") and in due course enough *pradeshdan* state representatives in Parliament to take control of it and so bring about *deshdan* ("gift of country").

Vinoba, who is in his seventies, has now mostly discontinued his walks and his public appearances. The major part of his work has been taken up by Jayaprakash Narayan, one of Vinoba's earliest adherents. The ideas of Vinoba and Narayan have often been derided by political commentators, politicians, and government officers as "impractical," "unrealistic," and "utopian." Narayan's reply has always been, "There are only two ways—Vinoba's and Mao Tse-tung's."

Jayaprakash Narayan has his home in Baburbani, a constituent hamlet of the village of Kodar-ha Naubarar, in the Ballia district, which lies between the Ganga and the Gogra Rivers in Uttar Pradesh. The villagers in this region are cultivators; although they may be served by a railway line, their commonest means of transport is a bullock cart or an elephant. At present, Baburbani has five hundred inhabitants, or fifty-five families, who live in forty mud huts, who together own twenty-six spinning wheels, and who have three small *pukka* public buildings—a temple, a veterinary station, and a meeting place called Gandhi Bhavan (Gandhi House). Baburbani has about a hundred acres of arable land, all of which was originally owned in equal shares by the only two living members of Narayan's family—Jayaprakash and his brother, Rajeshwar Prasad. In 1954, Rajeshwar Prasad, who was settled in a business in Bombay, sold his share to other landowners, and Jayaprakash Narayan gave more than half of his share to landless village cultivators at a *sarvodaya mela,* which he had organized for the purpose of *bhudan.* (Almost all the rest of the land is still in his possession and is farmed by hired cultivators.) Since then, Baburbani has held a *sarvodaya mela* every year to rededicate itself to the principles of the movement. This year's *sarvodaya mela* has special significance: Baburbani has decided to adopt *gramadan.*

Narayan and his wife, Prabhavati, are going to the village to attend the *mela,* and the day before the *mela* I fly with them, in the early afternoon, from Delhi, where he has been lecturing on *sarvodaya,* to Patna, the capital of Bihar, on the first leg of the complicated journey to Baburbani, for which careful arrangements have been made. J. P., as Narayan is affectionately called, is about six feet tall, with a strong, square face, thoughtful gray eyes, and a shy smile. He is sixty-four, and in appearance he has aged considerably since I first met him, eight or nine years ago. His gestures have become slow and deliberate, his speech quiet and unassertive, and he has the simple manner of an ascetic. He is dressed in a spotless homespun *dhoti* and *kurta,* and, in the plane, sits passively under the watchful maternal eye of Prabhavati Bahen (*sarvodaya* workers often drop their surnames and instead address one another as *"bhai"* and *"bahen,"* or "brother" and "sister"). Prabhavati Bahen wears a plain white homespun sari, the free end of which she uses occasionally to blot her forehead. She is silent and looks serious. Once or twice, J. P. tries to doze, his long legs stretched out before him, his long hands resting on his knees, but the flight is very bumpy and he is jolted awake.

At Patna, a jeep and a driver are waiting for us, and we drive due west on a dusty road for about forty miles to Arrah, a small rural town with a marketplace and a few grain shops. We get out of the jeep, stop at a tea stall and are served strong tea in earthenware cups, and proceed on foot along an oozy mud track to the bank of the Ganga, where a boat and a boatman are waiting for us. We get into the boat and move into the current. It is twilight now, and a gentle breeze is rising from the river. There is only the sound of the oars dipping in the water and the loud throb of crickets on the banks. It takes us about a quarter of an hour to cross the Ganga, and we reach the opposite bank in the dark. Here a bullock cart and a couple of villagers are waiting. We climb into the bullock cart and start out across dark unplowed fields, an old man walking ahead of us with a staff in one hand and a lighted lantern in the other, to show the bullocks the way. The wheels of the bullock cart are loose on the axles, and the bullocks constantly stumble, so the cart sways and rocks with a sickening slowness. It takes us an hour and a half to cover the three miles to Baburbani. After passing a row of lightless huts, we reach a small, square, thatch-roofed mud house, which shows up reddish-yellow in the glow of hurricane lamps that are hanging on the outer walls over a terrace; it is J. P.'s house, which he occasionally uses as a retreat when he is not travelling through the country for the cause of *sarvodaya.* A number of people are waiting outside the house to greet J. P. and Prabhavati Bahen. In addition to a caretaker, they include a party of men who have arrived in advance to make arrangements for the *mela:* a couple of servants; a stenographer; Dhirendra Majumdar, chairman of the Sarva Seva Sangh; Kapil Bhai, a leader of the Gandhi Ashram; and several other *sarvodaya* leaders.

We all go inside. The house is built around an open packed-earth court-yard lined by a veranda, off which are simple whitewashed cubicles with packed-earth floors. The cubicles contain plain, benchlike cots, kero-sene lamps, and earthenware pitchers. We all sit down on straw mats spread out on the veranda floor near the kitchen, and Prabhavati Bahen and the servants pass us brass plates heaped with lentils, green vegetables, potatoes, chapatties dripping with *ghi,* and guavas.

It is the day of the *sarvodaya mela.* "The village is full of sparrows," J. P. says, washing his hands and face and drying them with a towel from an old-fashioned washstand, which is next to a drum of water at one end of the veranda. "They've been coming and pecking at their reflections in that mirror for years," he goes on, looking at a very dirty mirror on the wash-stand. "They've got so used to pecking there that even when I put some newspaper over the mirror, they go right on pecking at the same place."

Outside J. P.'s house, a crowd of villagers from Baburbani and neigh-boring hamlets and villages has gathered. J. P. goes out, and they immedi-ately surround him, pleading for food, medicine, jobs. J. P. tries to talk to each one individually.

"I have nothing to eat," one of the villagers says. "My family has noth-ing to eat. I can't find work."

"Do you have any relatives who can help you?" J. P. asks him over the hubbub.

"No, none," he says.

"Where are you from?" J. P. asks.

"Sitabdiara," he says.

"What is your name?" J. P. asks.

"Ram Lal," he says.

"If I hear of anything, I'll be thinking of you," J. P. says.

J. P. starts walking away from the house. The villagers follow him, still pleading. "Wherever you go in India, there is always a crowd of suppli-ants," J. P. says to me.

We are walking along a mud lane. On one side are the mud huts of Baburbani; on the other side are an orchard of apple, guava, and mango trees, and a small chicken coop with a flock of white leghorns. Ahead is the temple—a brick and cement structure, bare except for a lingam and a statue of Shiva—and then a large bamboo shed in which rows of straw pallets have been put down for the *sarvodaya* volunteers. Across from this is Gandhi Bhavan, its door open and a *shamiana* set up across its front for the *mela*. Inside Gandhi Bhavan, which consists of one large hall and four small rooms, about twenty *sarvodaya* volunteers, dressed in homespun *dhotis* and *kurtas,* are seated on a mat on the floor. We enter, and the villagers following J. P. sit down wherever they can find a place—inside the hall or under the *shamiana*. There is no furniture of any kind, but pasted all over the walls are quotations in Hindi, from, among others, J. P., Dhirendra Majumdar, Vinoba, Gandhi, Buddha, Confucius, Jesus, Mohammed, Marx, Shaw, and Norman Thomas, extolling, variously, self-reliance, work, village industry, and the spinning wheel, and invoking God, the Ganga, and the President of India. ("'If rich people are unwilling to give us voluntarily their wealth and the power arising out of that wealth so that we may use it in everybody's interests in coöperation, it is definite that our country will have bloody and violent revolution.' —Mahatma Gandhi.")

J. P. takes a seat among the other leaders at the far end of the hall, facing the gathering. Each *sarvodaya* volunteer rises in turn, gives his name and his village, and talks about the progress he has made in enlisting villagers in *gramadan*.

"I and two of my companion *sarvodaya* volunteers arrived in a village," a large, round man is saying, in Hindi. "At the first hut where we stopped, the cultivator who lived there asked us what we wanted. We tried to explain the meaning of *sarvodaya* to him. He asked, 'What can I do about it?' I said, 'We would like to stay with you and talk further.' He said, 'This is my time to eat.' I said, 'We know it is time to eat, because we, too, are hungry.' He said, 'My rice is getting cold.' I repeated, 'We are hungry, too.' He said, 'Do you want to eat up my rice?' I said, 'I wouldn't have put it that way.' He said, 'I am going to eat. There is no rice for strangers here. There is not enough rice even for my children.' I explained to him our *sarvodaya* practice of the touring party dividing up and quartering singly, one to a hut—"

"Get on to what happened about *gramadan!*" Majumdar calls out.

"Did you ever get any food?" J. P. asks.

"I said to the cultivator, 'At least help us find some other villagers who will take us in.' He said, 'Why should I do that?' I said, 'Why not?' After a few hours of talking and searching about the village, we got fed, but no sooner had we finished our meal than the villagers turned us out."

The reports from the *sarvodaya* volunteers continue for some time. People in the audience keep shuffling and coughing, and now and again someone starts to snore.

A man with an uncomprehending but reverent expression gets to his feet and makes his way to Acharya Ramamurti, a *sarvodaya* worker who is sitting next to J. P. and is presiding over the meeting. He gives Ramamurti a stack of papers and returns to his place on the floor.

Ramamurti, having informed the assemblage that these are formal documents offering Baburbani to the *gramadan* movement and that one of them changes the name of the village from Baburbani to Jayaprakash Nagar (*"nagar"* means "town"), launches into a harangue. "What is written on these papers? What for these signatures? What is this *gramadan?"* he asks. "It is liberation of the heart. Gandhiji said that the change in the life of the poorest and weakest man in the village is the measure of the economic development of the country. But if we measure our present development schemes with that yardstick, we have to admit that the poorest, weakest man is falling farther and farther behind and the richest, strongest man is pulling farther and farther ahead." Ramamurti tells about visiting a village in which the government, as part of a development scheme, had recently built a motorable road. There he met a villager who wanted to dig up the road. The villager explained that since the construction of the road government officers had been bringing a stream of dignitaries to the village to see the road, and the villagers had been burdened with the problem of providing food for these visitors. "The villager's logic was no road, no officers, no extra mouths to feed," Ramamurti continues. "Since ancestral times, the villagers had walked in the mud, amid thorns. They preferred it. What was the use of development? If they didn't want development, why should you think they would want *sarvodaya?* One of the simplest demands of *sarvodaya* is that the people wear cloth made from yarn they spin themselves, yet many villagers would rather buy mill-made cloth than spin their own yarn. Today, in all the huts of Baburbani, is there one person who thinks about the village? We merely reside in the village. Our heart does not accept that this village is ours, that our sufferings are common." He discusses this theme at length and concludes, "Though it is a pity, the bigwigs in the country are busy with small, petty things. Therefore, brothers and sisters, busy yourselves with the big task in your small village."

Now it is J. P.'s turn to talk. Like the speakers who have preceded him, he has no prepared text, no notes, and no sense of time; his speech is in the tradition of Indian leaders who know that the people in their audiences have come not to study their words but to have a *darshana*. He talks on for a couple of hours, touching at random on many subjects, including population and war. "Although I am a supporter of family planning, Vinobaji and I think that the problem of the population explosion may have been exaggerated," he says at one point. "Vinobaji says, 'God has designed us so we can take care of ourselves. Every new baby means a new mouth and a new stomach to feed, but it also means two new hands and two new feet.' But everywhere there is inflation and scarcity. We spend all our money on defense while our people are hungry and go naked. If Pakistan and China want to invade us, we should try to fight them not with tanks and mortars and airplanes and bombs but with Gandhiji's methods of complete nonviolence and noncoöperation. We should be prepared to suffer the consequences of our enemies' violence until we shame them with their own evil-doing and they pull back."

He finally turns to *gramadan*. "My picture of the Indian village is that it remained more or less the same for hundreds of years, in spite of India's succession of conquerors," he says. "But when the British came, they established an all-powerful bureaucracy. Its influence reached into every village. Everything was done for us by the government. The British taught us to think of the government as mother and father, which was a form of slavery. Our masters have departed, but we continue to have the outlook of dependence. What we still have in India is a form of statism, with everything imposed from above, rather than true democratic Socialism or grassroots democracy, with everything done by the people themselves. Ours is a rural country, and most of our people live in villages. Yet the country continues to be run from a few big cities. Vinobaji and I feel that if our country is ever to be great again, every village must be encouraged to participate in the government. Our villagers must stop thinking like children or slaves. They must assume adult responsibilities. This is the point of *gramadan*." He goes on to clarify some details of the *gramadan* system. "Once your village constitutes itself into the village assembly, composed of an adult representative from each of your families, the village assembly will manage all the affairs of the village. But no village can be accepted into the *gramadan* movement unless at least seventy-five per cent of its people agree to these conditions. We started the *gramadan* movement in Bihar. So far, several thousand villages in the state have joined the movement, but some of these are only constituent hamlets of villages, and in any case there are, all together, seventy-two thousand villages in Bihar. Yet we don't have even a hundred full-time *sarvodaya* volunteers in Bihar, and many of them won't stay with the work.

Critics of *gramadan* say that we're doing nothing more than collecting a lot of empty pledges. But we say our revolution is not merely a matter of changing the legal relationship of the village to its land—it's a matter of changing men's hearts so that they begin to wonder why they have always done things in a certain way and how things can be done better. Change must take place in the heart and mind and radiate outward. This is what Gandhiji meant by the double revolution—revolution in the heart and revolution in the world. The aims of *gramadan* could be accomplished by legislation and force. If we didn't care about the cost in human terms, perhaps that might be the best way to do it. But we do care about the cost in human terms. The critics of *gramadan* say we're impractical and utopian, and it is true that there are five or six hundred thousand villages in our country and it may take many, many years to enlist them all in *gramadan*." J. P. finishes by saying, "But in the history of the world many years is not a long period."

At the end of the meeting, everyone joins in singing a hymn celebrating *gramadan*.

Jayaprakash Narayan was born in 1902 in Sitabdiara, in the Chapra district of Bihar, near Baburbani. His father was a junior officer in the Irrigation Department. Jayaprakash went to school in his village and then, when he was seventeen, to the British government college in Patna, on a government scholarship, to study science. In his second year, he took part in a student noncoöperation movement and left college. Soon after that, he married Prabhavati Prasad, the daughter of a distinguished lawyer who was one of the leaders of the Congress movement in Bihar. In 1922, his father-in-law made arrangements for Prabhavati to live with Gandhi and his wife, Kasturba, in Gandhi's *ashram* while Narayan, with financial help from his father and his father-in-law, went to the United States to continue his education. For seven years, he studied, off and on, at the state universities of California, Iowa, Wisconsin, and Ohio, supporting himself in whatever way he could—by waiting on table or picking fruit. While he was in the United States, he came under the influence of some fervent Communist students and became a Communist himself, and after receiving an M.A. in sociology from Ohio State University he returned to India. He did not, however, join the Communist Party of India, because on instructions from the Comintern it was keeping aloof from the movement for independence and he thought of himself as a nationalist. Instead, he joined the Congress Party, becoming a close ally of Nehru and serving as the leader of its Socialist wing. In the thirties, partly in reaction against the Stalinist purges, he abandoned Communism for what he called Democratic Socialism, and began advocating a combination of Marxist ideology and Western democracy. Like the other Congress leaders, he was frequently imprisoned. One of the main episodes in his political life occurred in 1942, when he escaped from a jail by climbing down the prison wall on a rope made of *dhotis*. Subsequently, he organized a band of saboteurs who derailed trains and cut telephone wires, and in time he acquired the reputation of a romantic revolutionary hero. After Independence, Narayan and some other Socialists left the Congress Party to found a separate Socialist party, but it was routed in elections and was eventually supplanted by several other Socialist parties. In 1952, in the course of a twenty-one-day fast that Narayan undertook for purposes of introspection and self-purification, he realized, according to a pamphlet he wrote entitled "From Socialism to Sarvodaya," that "materialism as a philosophical outlook could not provide any basis for ethical conduct." Elaborating on this thought, he wrote in an essay entitled "Social and Human Reconstruction" (his thoughts are diffused and repeated through a medley of speeches, pamphlets, and essays):

The individual asks . . . why he should be good. There is no God, no soul, no morality, no life hereafter. . . . He is merely an organization of matter . . . destined soon to dissolve into the infinite ocean of matter. He sees all around him evil succeed—corruption, profiteering, lying, deception, cruelty, power politics, violence. He asks, naturally, why he should be virtuous. Our social norms of today and the materialist philosophy which rules the affairs of men answer back: He need not. The cleverer he is, and the more gifted, the more courageously he practices the new amorality.

Narayan now felt that the only hope of creating a new moral order, in which men would work for one another's good, in which there would be no corruption or exploitation, and in which the well-being of all would take precedence over the self-interest of individuals, was to follow the path Gandhi had shown. In 1954, therefore, he renounced party politics and Socialism, and plunged into the new politics of what he called "the *bhudan* Ganga." To quote "From Socialism to Sarvodaya" again, "*Sarvodaya* also has its politics. But it is politics of a different kind: politics of the people, as I have called it, as distinct from the politics of party and power. . . . Rather, its aim will be to see that all centres of power are abolished. The more this new politics grows, the more the old politics shrinks. A real withering away of the state!"

One evening, as Narayan and I sit talking on the veranda of his house, I ask him to elaborate on his early life.

"My memory is not as good as it used to be," he says. "I am getting on in years. Anyway, I have always lived in the present and have never taken much interest in the past. I once picked up a Hindi biography of me that someone had written, and read the first few pages. They told about how I was born between two sacred rivers, how holy I was—things like that. I said to myself, 'This is not a biography, it's a hymn,' and I put it down and never looked at it again."

I bring up some criticisms that have been made of the *sarvodaya* movement, particularly the point that the moral ideals of *sarvodaya* only cloud the real economic issue of land reform.

"There will always be criticism of anyone who tries to do any good in the world or tries to teach human beings to be good and to work for one another's good," J. P. says. He goes on, "For many years, the government was investing mainly in big, showy industrial projects, like steel plants, but I think the money would have been better spent in teaching our people to solve some of their own most basic, ancient problems. One of the basic problems in our country is that of the disposal of waste—rubbish and human excrement. Go to any of our railway stations and you'll find them befouled—the public latrines, the platforms, the tracks, sometimes even the train compartments. Drive along any road when it's dark, and the headlights will pick out the forms of crouching people. Go into any village: the only people who have private latrines are the landowners; the other villagers dump all their waste outside their doors, so the lanes are filthy. The villagers will keep their own huts and yards clean, but they have no concern about taking care of the public places. Our people have no community sense."

He observes that among the Hindus all work considered unclean was traditionally performed by the untouchables. But now some of the untouchables, as a result of Gandhi's crusade, were able to find other kinds of employment, and even Hindus who paid lip service to Gandhi's ideals continued to regard work like the disposal of waste matter as unclean. Standards of sanitation, therefore, were even lower than they had been in Gandhi's lifetime. Gandhi taught that each man should dispose of his own waste, and he practiced this himself. He recommended that each villager should, for instance, bury his own excrement; he said it would require, at most, the use of a spade. But Gandhi's teaching had little or no effect. In recent years, the government had begun small-scale experiments in the villages with a series of methods of waste disposal, such as boring deep holes in the fields for the villagers to use. This method required only that each villager throw a little dirt into a hole after using it. But the villagers either failed to use the holes or, if they did use them, did not take the trouble to throw in the dirt. Then the government tried a slightly more expensive method—septic tanks, which had the advantage of requiring no more attention on the part of the villagers than being cleaned every few years. But the villagers did not train themselves to use the septic tanks, any more than they had trained themselves to use the holes.

"The irony is that human waste could be an important natural resource," J. P. says. "It could be used not only as an organic fertilizer but also as fuel. I myself have a well-known device that turns waste into fuel—I have it right in this house. Waste is deposited in it and the device is then sealed; the waste ferments and builds up a gas that can be burned in the device for cooking. All the food served at my house is cooked by my wife with that gas."

Later, in the calm of the evening, when the only sounds in the village are the sputtering of hurricane lamps and the occasional lowing of cows as they are being tethered for the night, I reflect that perhaps the time has come for me to leave India and to start another journey, in order to discover, in study and in writing, my experience in India. I recall that in the many months I have spent in India I have travelled from the Himalayas to Cape Comorin, from the Bay of Bengal to the Arabian Sea, going by airplane and helicopter, by steamship, scow, and gondola, by train, lorry, car, jeep, and bicycle, by bullock cart and sled, by elephant, horse, mule, and yak, and on foot; that I have followed the peninsular coastline, traced the courses of rivers, traversed the mountains and plains, and penetrated into the interior; that I have visited old kingdoms and old villages, new districts and new townships, talking with tourists, guides, musicians, dancers, actors, painters, writers, poets, students, critics, filmmakers, philosophers, prophets, saints, priests, missionaries, mendicants, farmers, laborers, tribesmen, headhunters, maharajas, courtiers, soldiers, doctors, pioneers, engineers, machinists, economists, planners, administrators, politicians—inhabitants of a country where today one-sixth of the world's people and one-half of the world's democratic people live. I think of the thousands and thousands of miles I have travelled, the thousands and thousands of pages of notes I have taken, and the hundreds and hundreds of books, papers, and pamphlets I have gathered to read, and then my thoughts go back to the first day of my Indian journey. *Arrival. Immediate sense of vividness and space. Everything seems vast. Sky very open and high. On*

*the streets, people's faces full of expressions, reactions. And, however ragged
the clothes, there is an extraordinary feeling for color. But poverty everywhere, and soon sense of vividness gives way to a morbid excitement, a
sort of hysteria. Too much to take in—exhaustion. Everything begins to
seem the same—indifference. But a continuing disturbance in the subconscious, an apocalyptic state of mind. India unlike other parts of the world
in that poverty is constant, inescapable, assails one at every turn. The
poverty here is harder to live with than the poverty of the West, where
the poor at least have some recognizable clothing to wear and some recognizable shelter to protect them, and live out of sight, perhaps out of mind,
in slums. But the poor here are in rags or almost naked. No protection
from sun, wind, or rain, no place to rest. Bodies thin as lines. Children have
the faces of the old; the old the faces of children. How do the more fortunate manage to live amid such unending scenes of wretchedness? They
live in fear of poverty themselves, regarding it as a personal threat. If not,
why this defensiveness? Also, why the curious fatalism that creeps into
their words whenever they discuss the subject? They teach themselves to
see only what they want to see, yet the scenes must stay in the subconscious,
suppressed but not forgotten, to emerge in half-remembered dreams. Poverty is another form of death. It diminishes every aspect of life: the way
people think, talk, dress, work, deal with one another, grow old—it is all
childlike. This is the Indian childhood. It also diminishes the way they
die. A dead woman in a gutter. Vultures flying overhead. Death is in the
air. "Any man's death diminishes me."*

It is the dawn of the day of my departure from Baburbani and the
beginning of the end of my stay in India. A mahout comes with an elephant to take me to the bank of the Ganga. The mahout sits on the elephant's head, with one leg draped over the elephant's ear, and he carries a
long stick with a hook at one end. The elephant has no howdah, but
stretched across its back, on either side of a sort of rail made out of a
couple of logs tied together, are layers of mud-brown burlap sacks. The
mahout guides the animal to where I am standing, on a rise of a few feet
next to the house. He touches the elephant's back with the hook, and the
elephant kneels down. I mount the elephant's back and sit sidewise on the
burlap sacks, holding on to the rail. The mahout pulls one of the elephant's ears and says, in Hindi, "Go!" Slowly the elephant rises and
lurches forward.

"Active, Active," the mahout says, addressing the animal, "anyone
would think you were the Queen of India. You need a manservant just to

wash and massage you, another just to bring you branches to eat, another just to exercise you. But I have to wait on you all by myself. Active, Active, where are the weddings and *melas* to earn your livelihood?" He continues, talking almost to himself, "When they are wild they run, but when they are tame they won't move. If you don't handle an elephant the right way, it will kill you."

There is no protection from the branches of trees overhead, and the animal's gait is a dizzying roll and jolt. She seems to take forever to lift her feet. We spend two hours making the three-mile journey back to the river.

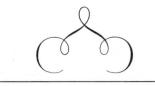

GLOSSARY

IN RECENT YEARS, MANY INDIAN WORDS *have come into the English language and are included as a matter of course in English dictionaries, but I have italicized—and often translated in the simplest terms—nearly all the Indian words in this text, because in the English-speaking world the understanding and use of them are still quite haphazard; for instance, most people are now familiar with the word* guru *(spiritual teacher) but not necessarily with its correlative* chela *(a guru's disciple). The few Indian words, like* sari *and* maharaja, *that I have not italicized are so firmly established in English usage that italics could have been mistakenly read as indicating special emphasis. Perhaps I should add that there is no one accepted orthography for all the Indian languages. I have tried to spell the Indian words phonetically whenever possible and have listed them in this glossary in the grammatical form in which they appear in the text.*

aap: you (formal)

acharya: spiritual teacher

achkan: man's tuniclike coat

aftab: sun

ahimsa: doctrine of refraining from the taking of life (Buddhist)

Akal: the One (Sikh)

akhara: secular organization of holy men (Hindu)

amban: Chinese representative

amir: title of nobility (Muslim)

amrit: nectar

ananda: joy

anna: monetary unit—one-sixteenth of a rupee

apong: rice beer

aryan: noble

ashram: hermitage

Atman: universal soul (Hindu)

ayah: nursemaid

baba: old man

babu: clerk; English-educated gentleman

bagh: garden

bahen: sister

bakkhu: loose robe

baksheesh: alms; tip

bango: cluster of villages

basha: bamboo hut

begum: queen, princess, or lady of
high rank (Muslim)

bhai: brother

bhang: hemp intoxicant

bhavan: house; home

bhavasaghara: ocean of existence

bhudan: gift of earth

bodi: tuft of hair on back of shaven
head (Hindu)

Bon: a form of animism

buddhidan: gift of intelligence

bukhari: stove

bulgur: parched crushed wheat

busti: slum

chacha: uncle

chapatti: unleavened pancake-shaped
bread

charas: hemp intoxicant

charkha: spinning wheel

charpoy: light bedframe strung with
tape or light rope

chela: spiritual disciple; pupil

chhang: barley beer

chogyal: heavenly king

choli: woman's short-sleeved blouse

crore: ten million—one hundred lakhs

dada: grandfather; elder brother

dakshina: south

dan: gift

dana: almsgiving

darshana: holy audience

deedar: exhibition

deshdan: gift of country

dewan: administrative officer at
prince's court

dha: gonorrhea

dharamshala: shelter for travellers

dhoti: loincloth of varying length

dupatta: veil

durbar: prince's court

durbhiksha: alms with tears; famine

dzong: fortress

ekka: one-horse vehicle

fakir: mendicant; devotee

fawj: army

gaddi: cushion

gam: village headman

ganja: hemp intoxicant

gerua: religious robe (Hindu)

ghat: bathing or landing place at riverside

ghi: clarified butter

gompa: monastery (Buddhist)

gram: chick-pea

gramadan: gift of village

gumnaam: nameless

gunamaya: goodness

gurdwara: shrine (Sikh)

guru: spiritual teacher; master

gyalmo: consort of deities

hadj: pilgrimage to Mecca (Muslim)

hamdard: sympathizer

hammam: bath

hartal: general strike

havan: sacrificial fire

havildar: army sergeant

hawaghar: air house

hookah: water-cooled smoking pipe;
hubble-bubble

howdah: seat, usually with canopy, on
elephant's back

hujra-e-khas: special chamber
jadu: magic
jagadguru: universal teacher
jaggery: coarse brown sugar made
    from palm sap
jaghirdar: landlord; rent collector
jawan: army recruit
jemadar: junior officer in Indian Army
-ji: suffix denoting affection and respect
jivandan: gift of life service
kachha: knee-length drawers
kalgi tora: ornamental plume for tur-
    ban
kameez: shirt
kanga: comb
kangri: pot of hot coals carried for
    warmth
kara: steel bracelet
kata: ceremonial scarf
kebang: meeting
kesh: unshorn hair and beard
khalsa: pure
khatal: cattle pen
kirpan: sabre; dagger
kirtana: chanted hymns
kohl: antimony used for darkening
    edges of eyelids
konda: hill
kothi: house
kumbha: pitcher
kurta: shirt
kutcha: temporary
kutta: 720 square feet of land
la: mountain pass
lakh: one hundred thousand
lama: priest (Buddhist)
lathi: bamboo stick bound with iron
lingam: phallus, especially a symbol
    of Shiva
maharaja: king (Hindu)

maharajkumar: crown prince (Hindu)
maharani: queen (Hindu)
maharishi: great seer (Hindu)
mahout: elephant driver
mantra: Vedic hymn or prayer
mata: mother
maulana: scholar (Muslim)
maulvi: learned religious leader (Mus-
    lim)
maya: illusion
mela: festival; generic musical scale
    pattern
mithun: *Bos frontalis,* straight-horned
    bison
moksha: salvation
moo-moo: steamed dumplings
morung: men's dormitory
mridangam: barrel-shaped drum
mullah: learned religious teacher
    (Muslim)
mundu: man's ankle-length garment
naga: naked; naked holy man
    (Hindu)
nagar: town
nahar: canal
namaskar: greeting (Hindu)
namaz: worship (Muslim)
natya: art of dance
navayugam: new age
nawab: prince (Muslim)
nazrana: tax
nirasa: freedom from emotional at-
    tachments
pan: betel-leaf masticatory
pandit: learned religious teacher
    (Hindu)
pice: monetary unit—a hundredth of
    a rupee
pita: father
ponung: tribal dance

pradeshdan: gift of state
pralaya: end of the world (Hindu)
prasad: blessed food
premdan: gift of love
puja: worship (Hindu)
pujari: worshipper (Hindu)
pukka: permanent
punya: merit (Buddhist)
puranas: Sanskrit sacred poems
puri: light fried wheat cake
purna: perfect; full
qahwa: tea
raga: melodic scale pattern
raj: rule, especially British rule
rehnuma: leader
rinpoche: blessed incarnation (Buddhist)
rishi: seer (Hindu)
rong: district
rupee: basic monetary unit; current value approximately fourteen cents
sadhandan: gift of tools
sadhu: holy man (Hindu)
sagar: reservoir
sahib: honorific title equivalent to "sir"
salaam: greeting (Muslim)
salwar: trousers
samadhi: trance
sampattidan: gift of wealth
sangam: union; confluence
sangha: congregation; association
sant: saint
sarangi: bowed stringed instrument
sari: woman's draped garment
sarod: plucked stringed instrument
sarvodaya: uplift of all
sati: custom of self-immolation of widows (Hindu)

satya: truth
sayid: religious or inherited title (Muslim)
sepoy: sentry
seth: businessman; rich merchant
shagird: pupil
shahnai: wind instrument
shakti: creative energy; female essence
shamiana: cloth canopy
shastri: religious title (Hindu)
sherwani: man's knee-length coat
shiggri: quickly
shikar: game animal; hunting expedition
shikara: gondolalike boat
shloka: Sanskrit sacred verse
shramdan: gift of social service
shri: venerable
silsillah: genealogy
sirdar: honorific title; Sikh man
sirdarni: honorific title; Sikh woman
sitar: plucked stringed instrument
snana: bathing
sri: same as shri
stupa: shrine (Buddhist)
suba: province; ruler
swarajya: freedom; self-rule
swatantra: freedom
tabla: hand drum
takht: throne
tala: rhythmic musical cycle
tamasha: spectacle
tapasya: meditation
tiffin: light meal
tirtha: passage; ford
tonga: one-horse vehicle
toofan: storm
triveni: triple-braided
tulsi: holy basil
tum: you (familiar)

ustad: master
uttarayana: northward
vina: plucked stringed instrument
visada: freedom from ignorance
vizier: high official (Muslim)
-wallah: person or thing employed
about or concerned with
something
yajna: sacrifice
yantra: machine

yantrana: pain
yantrayuga: machine age
yoga: effort; union with God; religious system (Hindu)
yogi: adherent or practitioner of the religious system of yoga
zamindari: land proprietor; proprietorship
zeenat: decoration

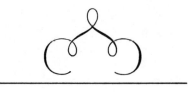

INDEX

WHAT IN ENGLISH may pass for the given name, surname, or middle name of an Indian simply by virtue of the fact that it is placed first, last, or midway in a series of names may not actually be part of the person's name at all. Instead, depending on his religion, his community, his place of birth, or his mere preference, a name may designate caste, subcaste, village, patronymic, honorific or religious title (sometimes self-bestowed), or something similar. For the purpose of this index, however, I have followed, as far as is practicable, the accepted English usage, and otherwise I have alphabetized the names of the Indians by what would be understood locally as the most important name, and have made cross-references wherever it seemed necessary.

Anjuvannam, 494
Ansari, 158
Arackal, Father Thomas, 231
Arail, 100
Aranyakas, 113
Army: in Chinese conflict, 171-83; in
    Goa, 445, 446, 447; in Kashmir,
    132; in NEFA, 219-21, 222, 224,
    225-26
Arrah, 510
Aryans, 112-13, 169, 488
Ashawari, Khwaja Nuruddin, 135-38
Asher, Ray, 333-34
Asia Magazine, 245
Asiatic Society of Bengal, 396
Assam, 179, 185, 186
astrology, 8, 87-88, 101, 114
Atharva Veda, 60
Attipetty, Dr. Joseph, 489-90
Aurangzeb, Emperor, 12, 136-37, 332
Aurobindo, 372
Avadhutas, 94
A Vida, 446
Azad Kashmir, 127, 148
Aziz, Colonel Abdul, 259

Baba. *See* Khan, Alauddin
Baburbani, 509-15, 517-19
Badarinath, 168
Bagra, 187-94, 198
Bahadur Shah, Emperor, 12
Bakar Id, 128
Balasaraswati, 61, 62-64
Balkanization, 476, 477
"Ballad of Fisher's Boarding-House,
    The," 402
Balsara, Dinshaw, 67, 68
Baltistan, 177
Bande, Abdul Rahim, 129, 135, 137,
    148, 152, 154, 156-57
Bande, Khwaja Balagi, 137
Bande, Khwaja Nuruddin, 149, 154,
    157-58
Bandipore, 131
Bangalore, 312
Bannerji, Bibhutibhusan, 413
Barahoti, 170, 171
Baramula, 131
Barrackpore Trunk Road, 365
Bashiruddin, Mufti, 131
Bayley, Sir Steuart, 405

Bayne, Roskell R., 396, 398
Bazin, André, 416
Beas irrigation project, 350
Beas River, 112
Beg, Hazrat Mirza Qalandar, 136
Benares, 78
Bengal: famine of 1865-66 in, 348;
    famine of 1943 in, 346; Nawab of,
    392; Presidency of, 392. *See also*
    East Bengal; West Bengal
Bengali language, 408, 410, 411, 468
"Bengal in 1756-1757," 391
Bengalis, 408, 410
Bengal Ladies' Union, 422
Bengal Past & Present, 401
Berar, 332
Betts, 200
Bhagavad-Gita, 78
Bhagavan, 114
Bhagirathi, 394
Bhainsa Sur, 290
"Bhairavi," 55
Bhakra-Nangal irrigation project, 350,
    475, 476
Bharat Savak Samaj, 422
Bharata, 60, 63
Bharatanatyam, 61, 63, 64
Bhatia, B. M., 348
Bhatt, Khwaja Ghulam Hassan, 128
Bhattacharya, Mohadev Chandra, 49
Bhattacherjee, Somnath, 294-95
Bhave, Vinoba, 506-8
Bhaya, H., 297
Bhilai, 289, 340; growth of, 311, 312;
    May Day in, 328-31; social life in,
    312, 314, 325-31; steel project in,
    292-301, 302, 315-22, 330; town
    planning in, 312, 313-15, 319. *See
    also* Bokaro project; steel production
Bhilai House, 293
Bhilai Technical Institute, 316
Bhilat, 290
Bhopal, 313
Bhutan, 169, 170, 173, 177, 182, 227-
    33, 237, 250, 357
Bhutto, Zulfikar Ali, 145
Bihar, 78, 289; agriculture in, 340;
    drought in, 349; land reform in,
    508-9; language, 468
Binaya Sutra, 277
birth control, 14-18